PAOLO GUENZI & SUSI GEIGER

SALES MANAGEMENT

A MULTINATIONAL PERSPECTIVE

palgrave
macmillan

First published 2011 by
PALGRAVE MACMILLAN

Palgrave Macmillan in the UK is an imprint of Macmillan Publishers Limited,
registered in England, company number 785998, of Houndmills, Basingstoke,
Hampshire RG21 6XS.

Palgrave Macmillan in the US is a division of St Martin's Press LLC,
175 Fifth Avenue, New York, NY 10010.

Palgrave Macmillan is the global academic imprint of the above companies
and has companies and representatives throughout the world.

Palgrave® and Macmillan® are registered trademarks in the United States,
the United Kingdom, Europe and other countries.

ISBN 978–0–230–24595–2

This book is printed on paper suitable for recycling and made from fully
managed and sustained forest sources. Logging, pulping and manufacturing
processes are expected to conform to the environmental regulations of the
country of origin.

A catalogue record for this book is available from the British Library.

A catalog record for this book is available from the Library of Congress.

10   9   8   7   6   5   4   3   2   1
20   19   18   17   16   15   14   13   12   11

Printed and bound in China

Contents overview

Contents

Part six   Evaluation of the sales force

18 Sales organization performance and evaluation   465
Paolo Guenzi and Susi Geiger

List of figures

List of tables

Preface and acknowledgements

Paolo Guenzi and Susi Geiger

This book has come about as a result of our engagement in taking current sales research issues into the classroom. We believe that what we learn in our activities as academic researchers is both valuable to and valued by postgraduate, MBA and executive students. This book therefore marks an attempt to break down the research/teaching divide in the sales arena by presenting students with the fundamental and most pertinent concepts in sales management education alongside up-to-date reviews of research and original research that shows students how such concepts are arrived at and how they evolve. We have endeavoured to be sensitive to the different cultural and business contexts in which readers of this book may find themselves; we hope that using data and cases from a broad range of countries will bring some of the issues raised quite literally 'closer to home' for our readers.

Engaging in these tasks would not have been possible for the editors of this book on their own. We are lucky enough to have found enthusiastic and generous contributors in some of the best sales researchers and educators in Europe and beyond. This book lives through their contributions and knowledge, and we are forever grateful for their willingness to work with us in turning this book into a reality. While in many business schools, sales management and education is still considered of somewhat lesser importance than more 'traditional' marketing management topics such as brand management, consumer behaviour or marketing communication, we are convinced that this book demonstrates the sales research community to be a vibrant and multi-faceted one that can greatly contribute to sustained business performance. We also wish to thank the managers who helped us in the writing of the case histories. A special thank you goes to Adriano Costantini who co-authored the Bearzot case history in Chapter 18.

We would like to thank Palgrave Macmillan, and especially Mark Cooper and Martin Drewe, for their trust in the concept of this book and for their support throughout its genesis. We would also like to acknowledge the support we received from our respective institutions in writing and editing this book. We are grateful to the Global Science Sales Institute for providing a long overdue home for the global sales research community, and to many of its members for participating in this project either as contributors or as reviewers. Finally, and most importantly, we would like to thank our families for their patience and moral support throughout this project.

List of contributors

George J. Avlonitis

George J. Avlonitis is Professor and Chairman of Marketing at the Department of Marketing and Communication at the Athens University of Economics and Business. He is also Director of both the Athens Laboratory for Research in Marketing and the Executive Postgraduate Program 'Marketing and Communication with New Technologies' of the same department. He was President of the European Marketing Academy (EMAC) 2008–10. His research, teaching and consulting activities are in the areas of product policy, sales management, industrial marketing, technological innovation and strategic marketing. He has published more than 160 articles in international conference proceedings and the most prestigious international journals in marketing including *Journal of Marketing, Journal of the Academy of Marketing Science, International Journal of Research in Marketing* and *Journal of Product Innovation Management*. Professor Avlonitis is on the editorial board of eleven international journals including the *Journal of Business Research, European Journal of Marketing and Industrial Marketing Management* and has been honoured several times with the Best Paper Award. He is Fellow of the Chartered Institute of Marketing and one of the founders of the Greek Marketing Academy, of which he is also President.

René Y. Darmon

René Darmon is an Emeritus Professor at the ESSEC Business School, France. He is also currently affiliated with Laval University, Canada. He holds a PhD from the Wharton School, University of Pennsylvania. He served in the Marketing Department at McGill University, Montreal, from 1975 to 1990, before joining the ESSEC Business School where he held successively the positions of Dean of Research and Dean of the Faculty. He is a former President of the French Marketing Association. His research focuses on sales force management, marketing research and marketing decision models. He has published numerous articles in international conference proceedings and more than 30 articles in international journals such as *Industrial Marketing Management, Journal of Business Research, Journal of Personal Selling and Sales Management, Journal of the Academy of Marketing Science, Journal of Marketing Research, European Journal of Operational Research* and *Journal of Marketing*. He has contributed to 14 books. He has been on the editorial boards of many international journals and won numerous awards for his research work. He has been a consultant in a range of companies and organizations in many countries.

Christophe Fournier

Christophe Fournier is Professor of Marketing at the Institute of Management and Enterprise Science at Montpellier University, France. His research interests are the evolution of selling, sales contests, burnout, ethical climate and turnover. He has published in international journals such as *Journal of Business Research, Journal of Personal Selling and Sales Management, Journal of Business and Industrial Selling* and in French journals such as *Revue Française de Marketing, Décisions Marketing* and *Recherche et Applications en Marketing*. He is supervising a Master in Negotiation and Sales Team Management.

Susi Geiger

Susi Geiger is a Senior Lecturer at University College Dublin, Ireland. Her research interests lie in the areas of market interactions, both in consumer contexts and in the business-to-business arena, with an emphasis on buyer-seller interactions. She participates in a number of international interdisciplinary research groups studying market practices and sales phenomena, and in 2006 was a Visiting Researcher at the University of Auckland Business School. Her work has won several awards and appeared in a wide range of international journals such as *Journal of Personal Selling and Sales Management, European Journal of Marketing, Marketing Theory, Journal of Marketing Management, Industrial Marketing Management, Consumption, Markets and Culture* and many others. Dr Geiger is on the editorial board of *Industrial Marketing Management* and acts as a regular reviewer for a range of international marketing journals. Together with Paolo Guenzi, she has recently edited a *European Journal of Marketing* special issue, 'Sales Management in the 21st Century'. Her teaching areas are sales management, marketing management and consumer and buyer behaviour, which she teaches to undergraduates, postgraduates, MBA students and executives.

Paolo Guenzi

Paolo Guenzi is an Associate Professor at Università Commerciale Luigi Bocconi, Milan, Italy. His principal teaching areas are sales and key account management and marketing management, both to undergraduate and graduate students and to executives. He is the coordinator and teacher of many courses on sales management and personal selling at SDA Bocconi School of Management. He also teaches on the Executive MBA, on the Executive Masters in Marketing & Sales and on the PhD in Management of Università Commerciale Luigi Bocconi. He has published many articles in international journals, including *Journal of Business Research, Industrial Marketing Management, European Journal of Marketing, Journal of Marketing Management* and the *International Journal of Service Industry Management*. He is on the editorial boards of some international journals and a reviewer for others. He is the Track Chair of the Personal Selling and Sales Management Track of the European Marketing Academy Conference.

Ann-Kristin Hansen

In 2006, Ann-Kristin graduated from the University of Münster, Germany, with a Master of Science and Business Administration. After working for two and a half years as research assistant and doctoral candidate at the Institute of Marketing in Münster, Ann-Kristin gained a PhD in Economics from the Westphalian Wilhelms-University of Münster. In 2009, she joined Johnson & Johnson (EES) as Market Analyst.

Manfred Krafft

Professor Krafft is Head of the Institute of Marketing at the Marketing Center, Münster. He gained his PhD from the University of Kiel. In 1999, he was hired by WHU – Otto Beisheim School of Management where until late 2002 he was the Otto Beisheim Endowed Chair of Marketing, Head of the Marketing Department, and Director of the Center for Market-oriented Management. That year, he accepted a position in charge of the Institute of Marketing at Münster. He has published articles in the *Journal of Marketing*, *Journal of Marketing Research*, *Marketing Science*, *Interfaces* and *International Journal of Research in Marketing* and in reviewed German academic journals. He is also a reviewer for several German and international journals, (such as *Marketing Science*, *International Journal of Research in Marketing*, *Interfaces*, *Zeitschrift für Betriebswirtschaft* and *Zeitschrift für betriebswirtschaftliche Forschung*). He is the author of two books, on *Sales Force Compensation* and *Customer Retention and Customer Equity* (both in German). His research focuses on customer relationship management issues, direct marketing and sales management. Professor Krafft is winner of the first ISMS Practice Price for his extraordinary transfer of scientific concepts into corporate practice. In 2002, he spent a sabbatical at INSEAD, Fontainebleau, and Northwestern University, Evanston, US.

Piotr Kwiatek

Piotr Kwiatek is Assistant Professor of Marketing in the Department of Marketing Strategy at Poznan University of Economics, Poland. He is a co-founder of B2B Centrum for Sales and Marketing on Professional Markets in Poland and the author of a bestselling book on loyalty programmes in Poland. Professor Kwiatek is affiliated with the Global Sales Science Institute, an organization of academics and practitioners representing a network for the exchange of knowledge on sales in research, education and practice. With particular experience in the banking industry, where he developed strategies and plans for loyalty programmes directed at banks' cardholders, he has also worked as a consultant for companies in other industries.

Vincent Onyemah

Vincent Onyemah is a Professor at Babson College, USA. Dr Onyemah gained his PhD and MSc in Management from INSEAD, Fontainebleau, France. He also holds a

MBA degree from IESE Business School, University of Navarra, Spain and a BSc in Civil Engineering from the University of Ibadan, Nigeria. His principal areas of teaching and research are personal selling and sales force management. His articles have appeared in the *Harvard Business Review*, *Journal of International Business Studies*, *Journal of Personal Selling & Sales Management*, *International Journal of Human Resource Management*, *Marketing Letters*, and *European Journal of Marketing*. Dr Onyemah is also a consultant on professional selling and sales force management for the International Finance Corporation - World Bank.

Nikolaos G. Panagopoulos

Dr Panagopoulos is a Lecturer of Marketing at the Athens University of Economics and Business. Prior to entering academia he worked for seven years as a consultant for many major local and multinational companies operating in Greece. His research, teaching, and consulting interests revolve around customer relationship management, sales and sales management, and advanced data analysis. He has published articles in international scientific journals such as *International Journal of Research in Marketing, Industrial Marketing Management, Journal of Personal Selling & Sales Management, Journal of Business Research, European Journal of Marketing* and the *Journal of Selling & Major Account Management*. His work has been presented at many international scientific conferences both in the EU and the US. Dr Panagopoulos was a founding member of the Global Sales Science Institute and serves as an editorial board member for *Industrial Marketing Management, European Journal of Marketing* and the *Journal of Selling & Major Account Management*.

Juliet F. Poujol

Juliet F. Poujol has a PhD in Marketing from Montpellier University, a MBA from Birmingham University (UK) and a degree in International Business from Bologna University (Italy). She is an Associate Professor at the Institute of Management and Enterprise Science and the Research Center in Management and Markets of Montpellier University, France. She previously worked in sales roles and as an Export Manager. Her research on sales force management and customer relationships has been published in journals specializing in those fields, such as *Journal of Business Research, Journal of Personal Selling and Sales Management, Journal of Service Management, International Journal of Services, Economics and Management* and *Journal of Business and Industrial Marketing*.

Sergio Román

Dr Román is an Associate Professor of Marketing at the University of Murcia, Spain. He teaches many courses in the field of marketing. In 2002 he was Visiting Researcher at the University of Arizona. His research interests focus on personal selling and sales management, business ethics and e-commerce, and his work has been presented at several international conferences. In 2005 and 2006 he received the Best Paper Award in the American Marketing Association Conference. His articles have appeared in the *Journal of the Academy of Marketing Science, Industrial Marketing Management, Journal of Business Research, International Marketing Review, Journal of Business Ethics, Journal of Business & Psychology, International Journal of Market Research, European Journal of Marketing, Journal of Marketing Management* and the *British Journal of Educational Psychology*, among others.

Dominique Rouziès

Dominique Rouziès received her PhD from the Faculty of Management at McGill University, Canada and joined HEC-Paris, where she was Chair of the Marketing Department (2005–6). She is currently the Academic Director of the Executive Master in Marketing and Business Development and the Master in Marketing Intelligence. She was a Visiting Scholar at the University of Florida, Gainesville, US, in 1998. She has published in the *Journal of Marketing, International Journal of Research in Marketing, International Journal of Human Resource Management, Journal of Personal Selling & Sales Management, Journal of the Operational Research Society, Journal of the Academy of Marketing Science, Journal of Business Research, European Management Journal, Journal of Euromarketing, Marketing Letters* and some French academic journals, and also serves as a reviewer for several international and French academic journals. She has also published in the business press (among them, the *Financial Times* and French newspapers) and has contributed chapters to several books.

Laszlo Sajtos

Dr Laszlo Sajtos is a Senior Lecturer in the Department of Marketing at the University of Auckland Business School. He was awarded a PhD in Marketing from the Corvinus University of Budapest in 2006. His research interests are focused on the area of service branding and relationship marketing, including issues related to service recovery and customers' forgiveness in service failures, and investigating the effects of market-based assets on customers' risk perception and value creation. His articles have appeared in leading international journals, including the *Journal of Service Research, Journal of Advertising Research, Industrial Marketing Management, Australasian Journal of Marketing* and *Acta Oeconomica*.

Antonis C. Simintiras

Professor Antonis Simintiras holds the Chair of Marketing at the School of Business and Economics, Swansea University. He has had many years experience in industry and has held managerial positions in both Hellenic and American companies. He has held visiting professorial appointments in France, Spain, Austria, Greece, Finland, the US and China. He acts as a consultant for various companies and government organizations. His research interests are in the areas of sales negotiation and sales management, consumer behaviour and cross-cultural research methodology. He has published over 50 refereed articles and his work has appeared in the *Journal of International Business Studies*, *Journal of Business Research*, *Industrial Marketing Management*, *Management Decision*, *Journal of Marketing Management*, *Journal of Managerial Psychology*, *European Journal of Marketing*, *International Marketing Review*, *International Journal of Consumer Marketing*, *Quality Management Journal*, *Productivity*. Author of a book on global sales management, he has also edited books and several national and international conference proceedings.

Marco Aurelio Sisti

Marco Aurelio Sisti is a Senior Lecturer in the Department of Marketing of SDA Bocconi School of Management, where he is the Head of Marketing Community and of the international Channel & Retail Management Academy and coordinator of many Open Enrolment and Custom Programs on sales management topics. He is also Contract Professor of Marketing at LUM Jean Monnet University, Casamassima, Italy. He teaches sales and key account management on the specialized international Master's and on the global MBA. Formerly he was Head of Custom Programs in the SDA Bocconi's Marketing Department. His research interests and publications are mainly in the fields of sales key account and retail management.

Gabriele Troilo

Gabriele Troilo is an Associate Professor at Università Commerciale Luigi Bocconi, Milan, Italy, where he mainly teaches marketing management. He is the coordinator and teacher of many courses on marketing management at SDA Bocconi School of Management. He also teaches on the Executive MBA and the PhD in Management of Università Commerciale Luigi Bocconi. He has published several articles in international journals including the *Journal of Business Research* and *Industrial Marketing Management*. He has published many chapters in international books and is the author of *Marketing Knowledge Management: Managing Knowledge in Market-oriented Companies* (Edward Elgar). He is on the Executive Committee of the European Marketing Academy, where he is the Vice-President for Conferences.

John Wilkinson

Associate Professor John Wilkinson is currently Associate Head of School and Offshore Program Director, School of Marketing at University of South Australia, based in Adelaide, Australia. His research and teaching interests, including PhD supervision, mainly relate to personal selling and sales management, although he also has a strong interest in business-to-business marketing. He is a Fellow of the Australian Marketing Institute and a Council member of its South Australian branch. He also is a Chartered Member of the UK-based Chartered Institute of Marketing. Professor Wilkinson joined the University of South Australia after working in the corporate world with organizations such as Unilever South Africa (initially in product development, then in business-to-business marketing), Kodak Australasia (mainly as Manager, Marketing Information and Analysis) and Alcoa of Australia (as Product Manager – Foil and then National Market Manager – Ingot).

Introduction: sales management in the twenty-first century

Paolo Guenzi and Susi Geiger

Contents

Ultradent in Europe: changing sales models and distribution approaches

Dr Dan Fischer, dentist, researcher and university professor, founded Ultradent Products Inc. in 1979 in Salt Lake City with the aim of improving the techniques and products used by dentists and enable them quickly to resolve their patients' problems with minimally invasive methods. Dr Fischer invented more than 500 highly innovative items that led the company to become one of the most important in the world in the healthcare/dental industry, with over 1,000 employees and exports to over 100 countries. The remarkable growth of Ultradent in the past ten years caused the President and the management to rethink the company's sales strategy and the distribution of its products in international markets, which in the past was handled by only one exclusive distributor/importer in each individual country. The goal of this change in business strategy was to increase market coverage and the availability of products for dentists.

The first experiment of transition from exclusive to multi-dealer distribution took place in 2003 in Germany, where new agreements were developed with local distributors replacing the previous one. Lars Svalin, Ultradent's European Business Manager, managed the change with excellent results. A few major distributors, organized in reseller chains that cover 99 per cent of the market, characterize the German market. Each distributor centrally manages its purchases and this helps to simplify the business relationship with Ultradent. The German dentist is not inclined to purchases brokered by the classical figure of the 'seller' or 'promoter' and is thus more oriented to order from retailers through call centres or during meeting opportunities that are frequently organized by dealers in open house events. These peculiarities of the German context prompted Ultradent to implement a developmental strategy in this market focusing on its relationship on the one hand with the distributors' headquarters, providing ongoing support to optimize inbound logistics, and on the other with individual retailer chains, widely spread throughout the country, mainly based on providing continuing education.

Considering the success achieved in Germany, in 2005 Ultradent decided to undertake the same change in Italy, under the leadership of Aurelio Gisco. The positive experience in the German market was a useful starting point, but the implementation of the strategy in the Italian market, which was characterized by profound differences with the German one, imposed the need for numerous adaptations. Aurelio decided to maintain the incumbent importer, Riccardo Ilic', using its knowledge and transferring its experience to four new dealers located in different geographic areas. He invested mainly in training the sales force of the new dealers and in the means of communication and marketing needed to make the company's products known by downstream customers. For this reason, in Italy Ultradent carried out campaigns aimed not only at the dentist, but also at the final user of his services, the patient. To give an example, Ultradent created its own magazine aimed specifically at dental surgery waiting-rooms. In this magazine, instead of presenting its products, the company informs patients about treatments and innovative therapies for their health. The result has been excellent: in addition to showing the work done by Ultradent sales specialists in the field, the magazine encourages patients to ask their dentist about additional services that, in turn, generate new business and have a positive impact on retailers. After three years of immediate success Aurelio decided to strengthen the relationship with customers further by increasing the number of dealers and creating a Customer Relationship Management (CRM) system designed to consolidate the relationship with the distributor and its sales force on the one hand and the dentist on the other. The study of the needs of these customers allowed Ultradent to adapt to the changing market by offering customers numerous value-added services, rather than just the simple sale of goods.

In 2008, the business structure in the Balkans was changed, and while the existing distributors have been kept active, new dealers have joined it. As in the Italian case, this has placed a considerable challenge in integration of distributors, but it has led to a swift increase in market penetration. Given the specific nature of the area, the Balkan countries required a dedicated corporate figure (a Regional Manager) to ensure constant and direct local support, but the size of the market is not likely to justify establishing a sales branch to offer products directly.

Thanks to the excellent outcome of choices made from 2003 onwards, in 2009 Ultradent began a three-year strategic business development plan in the key markets of southern Europe. It aims to implement the multi-dealer strategy so far successfully implemented in Germany, Italy and the Balkans. The responsibility for this commercial development strategy has been entrusted to Aurelio because of his deep knowledge of the distribution structures and business processes that characterize the countries involved: France, Spain, Portugal and Turkey. In all these markets, the strategic choice is to expand the number of distributors, while maintaining the relationship with the Ultradent dealer already working in the country for many years because of the valuable experience and relationships they have, which are deemed necessary to achieve the growth targets. Another strategic choice was to manage change without opening other direct subsidiaries, but with the support of an Ultradent European structure. This structure must be able to offer all the tools dealers need: training, organization of lectures with international speakers, tools used in communication, events, etc. The goal is to further strengthen the Ultradent brand, consistent with the targets transmitted from the American parent company, and to reduce the identification of the brand with the exclusive local distributor. The challenge presented to Aurelio is to exploit the growth potential in the various markets, addressing local circumstances and the current period of economic stagnation.

The French market stands out from the others because of the higher price level than average that it has adopted, its 'catalogue' sales mode and, consequently, the limited influence of the sales representative or promoter. In this case, an understanding of the decision-making process and of the possibly greater involvement of the dentist with the brand plays an important role. The Spanish market is characterized by very strong economic constraints, marked price competition and fragmented distribution. Portugal is similar to Spain and relative to the size of the market has an excessive number of competitors. Finally, the Turkish market is complex because it is divided into regions of very different cultures, ethnic groups and purchase processes.

Sales management in the twenty-first century

It is hardly an overstatement to say that there is a palpable sense of transformation in the sales management arena. In sales practice, many commentators have observed rapid changes in the way selling is done and managed in the twenty-first century. Some of the catalysts of change have been external to sales organizations, such as the internationalization of competition in a virtually borderless Europe and an increasingly globalized world economy, as exemplified by the case company above. The sudden end to years of economic growth in many developed economies in Europe and elsewhere in 2008 has contributed to increasingly heated competition among many sales organizations. Rapid technological developments have also been an important catalyst of change, with the replacement or supplementation of personal selling by internet sales channels in many industries. Other changes have been customer-driven, such as heightened customers' price sensitivity, an increased emphasis on value and the desire for co-creation of value.

As a consequence of these external developments, sales organizations themselves have had to undergo at times dramatic changes. Observers have noted, for instance, a move towards relationship and solution selling and a need for more customer-centric sales cultures; greater interest in interfunctional cooperation; increased emphasis on sales productivity; and a heightened awareness of ethical issues concerning sales practitioners (Geiger and Guenzi 2009). This introductory chapter will briefly explore some of these challenges and developments and, against this backdrop, outline how the remainder of this book will introduce students, managers and other interested readers to sales management issues in a fast-changing, highly challenging, multicultural environment.

Sales management as a strategic endeavour

In line with many other contemporary sales researchers and authors (for instance Piercy and Lane 2009), the editors and contributors of this book see the Sales function firmly as a boardroom topic. In many of today's business-to-business firms, the Sales function holds the key to one of the most valuable long-term assets a firm possesses: their customer relationships. The days when the Sales department could be seen as an operational function that would simply execute what Marketing and other corporate functions told them to are long gone. Traditionally, many firms held a product perspective, where Research and Development departments were tasked with developing innovative product ideas, Manufacturing was focused on producing goods of high quality and Marketing was supposed to stimulate demand for them. From this perspective, salespeople had only to take the orders from the customers and, perhaps, make sure that the goods were subsequently delivered to them. Today, however, we are faced with a very different business environment, one where products are often interchangeable from one supplier to the next, often subject to low margins and intense competitive pressures, and where many companies outsource their manufacturing altogether; an environment where the main value-creating activities are those associated with services writ large. In this environment, goods are seen merely as 'distribution mechanisms for service provision' (Vargo and Lusch 2004, p. 3); knowledge is the fundamental source of competitive advantage, value creation is a joint endeavour between the selling firm and the customer, and the long-term financial wealth of a firm is determined by its capacity to adopt an outside-in, customer-driven perspective (Rust et al. 2010). In this new world where value creation does not happen in factories but at the customer site, salespeople have evolved from order-takers to customer managers who are tasked with establishing and managing customer relationships, pursuing consultative and other value-adding selling activities, overseeing customer service delivery and satisfaction and monitoring the profitability of the relationship. For this role, salespeople often need to draw on knowledge that is widely distributed in the selling firm: for instance, held by Marketing (unique selling features, value in use, competitive advantage, segmentation, branding), Operations (product issues, production scheduling, quality control, R&D, delivery timeliness and reliability) or Finance (profit and loss information) (Storbacka et al. 2009). Salespeople thus become not only externally-faced customer consultants, but also internal orchestrators for customer value creation.

If we take seriously this idea of salespeople as orchestrating internal functions on behalf of the customer, with a view to increasing customer value, then, rather than taking orders from other functions, salespeople need to be placed in a central and empowered position within their own organizations. Especially in recessionary times, the consistent alignment of Sales with corporate strategy and the organizational empowerment of the customer management function can lead to important productivity improvements and greater customer satisfaction (Zoltners et al. 2008) and increase value both for the customer *and* for the selling organization. While we may not quite go as far as Piercy and Lane in suggesting that 'sales is the new marketing' (2009, p. 4) – after all, most contributors and both editors of this book work in a Marketing department – we fully concur with these two authors in placing two central issues at the heart of a rethinking of the Sales function: one, that the traditional executional role of Sales, twinned with the often lofty inside-out view of the traditional corporate Marketing function, is an insufficient dichotomy for today's powerful purchasers who often have complex demands. And second, that once power shifts to the buyer and, with it, responsibility to the field, traditional ways of managing the sales force need to be revisited. As in our case study, developing and manufacturing high-quality products almost becomes the easiest part of the corporate process; the important decisions that can make or break a firm's success are often related to its sales model and go-to-market strategy.

Sales management 2.0

To react to these two important shifts described above – increasing environmental turbulence and complexity, and an increasing awareness of the value that lies in the Sales function – many firms have at times radically altered their sales operations. In this context, some business commentators have heralded the advent of 'sales 2.0'. Sales 2.0 has been described by two of its early proponents, Seley and Holloway, as 'the proper alignment of Sales and Marketing as well as sales resources and customer opportunities to create a leveraged approach to sales force deployment and territory coverage', including segmenting sales process steps, customers and opportunities and matching these segments with the most profitable sales channels available, depending on customer preferences (Seley and Holloway 2009, p. xiv). While estimates are that less than 1 per cent of US firms currently practice sales 2.0 consistently ((Seley and Holloway 2009), it may also be that some insightful sales organizations have already implemented a sales 2.0 strategy without even realizing it! Because, regardless of whether one likes the label and its appropriation of the 'web 2.0' moniker, sales management 2.0 captures many aspects of how sales organizations across the globe have tried to respond to the catalysts of change described above. These companies, just like Ultradent in our introductory case history, have tried to increase sales force productivity while at the same time getting closer to their customers through implementing a more scientific approach to sales management, where hunches and instinct are substituted by business analyses, where precious and costly sales resources are allocated to the most valuable and high-potential customers, where a diverse range of direct and indirect channels are managed for optimal market coverage, and where technological in addition to more traditional marketing tools – the internet, social media, mobile phones – are used to service some customer segments and to support the sales cycle.

What it interesting in this alleged move from a 'sales 1.0' to a 'sales 2.0' universe is not necessarily only the technological associations that may go along with the label – for instance, extensive use of social media for customer reference management, lead generation or qualification – but that this move advocates viewing Sales as the central value-creating function of the firm. If sales companies are more and more reliant on the Sales function for long-term survival, then that function needs a scientific, analytical approach that can ensure sharing of best practices, scalability of processes, a steady stream of income and high responsiveness to individual customer preferences. From this perspective, sales management 2.0 means:

- 'closing the loop' between Marketing and Sales and indeed other functions in the firm, so as to ensure effective and consistent lead generation, qualification and customer communication;
- restructuring the Sales function to integrate different communication channels and customer touchpoints, which all work together to deliver a consistent customer experience;
- rethinking the motivation and incentive package for salespeople in order to move away from a 'lone wolf' model and towards a team mentality;
- utilizing Customer Relationship Management and other advanced technologies to enhance customer engagement and salesperson effectiveness;
- tracking productivity through leading rather than lagged measures (such as financial turnover) and managing the demand pipeline through an early warning system; and
- leading the sales force with a vision.

Many of these issues will be covered in detail throughout this book.

It may need to be noted that the so-called 'web 2 and 3' technologies also play their part in this new strategy. Social networking sites such as Facebook or Twitter allow many salespeople to customize their customer communications to the requirements of the customer and for the customer to access company, salesperson and product information whenever it is convenient for them to do so. These 'social selling' technologies also allow salespeople enhance their personal brand and value through, for instance, blogs or podcasts. Customer reference management and lead generation especially are now heavily influenced by the existence of social media sites. But even these cutting edge technological developments can be brought back to the same fundamental issue at the heart of the entire sales 2.0 movement: that today companies have to be able to deliver a consistent, high quality and value-adding customer experience across multiple channels and in very diverse cultural contexts – and the Sales function is an important contributor in achieving this goal.

Overall, changes that allow for such a culturally sensitive and consistently high quality customer experience should help a firm to make the Sales function not only more productive, but also more responsive and adaptable to evolving customer needs and market dynamics, and lead to what Palmer and Bennett (2009) call a 'scalable sales organization' – where neither the Sales function is hostage to the firm (or rather the Marketing department's often fanciful promotional ideas) nor the firm hostage to an unpredictable Sales function that is run and executed on intuition rather than proven best practices. Our preliminary case vignette gives an example of a firm that has implemented changes to its sales model on a highly analytical and incremental basis and where best practices from one market were carefully adopted in the next. Whether Sales Managers or academic commentators adopt the '2.0' label for their efforts to think through sales operations more carefully, strategically and scientifically does not matter very much. In all likelihood, this label will be substituted by another management term *du jour* soon enough. What matters is that senior managers and Sales Managers alike are cognizant of the potential contributions the Sales function can make, as well as the responsibilities it may shoulder in today's fast-changing, highly competitive, customer-dominant markets. We hope that this book contributes to helping present and future managers navigate their way through those sales management challenges.

Aim of the book

This book aims to lead reflective managers, executive students and postgraduates through the many challenging issues affecting sales organizations in the twenty-first century. It does so with a broad multi-country perspective. We believe that this perspective is especially important in today's selling environment: as more and more companies decide to operate on a global scale, they are increasingly forced to deal with issues relating to a diverse workforce, different environments and sales management challenges that have not been encountered before. As seen in the case that opens this introductory chapter, especially in culturally highly diverse regions such as Europe and the Pacific Rim, marketeers and Sales Managers need to understand what issues are similar across countries and what issues may be unique to certain cultures and environments. While academic research in the area of professional selling and sales management has become more open to perspectives from across the globe in recent years, very few student-focused texts have presented perspectives from a range of different countries. This book is designed to deliver to its readers a broad range of contributions from academics working in 11 different countries, based on their experiences in teaching and consulting for sales organizations in vastly different cultural and geographic contexts.

Using this multinational and multi-perspective approach, this book covers the main topics of sales management such as leadership, training, recruitment, compensation, control systems and performance evaluation, as well as important current topics that are often overlooked in other textbooks. Examples of such topics are the impact on selling and sales management of Customer Relationship Management technologies, sales team issues, the integration and coordination of strategies, processes and resources between Marketing and Sales and the issue of price delegation to salespeople. We believe it is important to introduce students to the breadth of topics that are affecting the world of selling and sales management and to investigate them across multiple cultural and industry contexts.

The distinctive characteristics of this book are:

1. *A focus on selling and sales management in a diverse range of countries*: selling and sales management are necessarily rooted in local markets, because customer contact programmes mostly have to be managed locally. It is our experience as educators of students and executives in Europe and elsewhere that they frequently question the applicability of cases and frameworks which take the perspective of big multinationals from remote headquarters only. Managers need to feel that a sales management textbook's authors speak their own language, know what their situation is and cite examples that sound more familiar to them. We hope that this book does this, and that students will be able to recognize at least some of the contexts in which our chapters have been written.

2. *A solution-oriented approach paired with up-to-date academic knowledge.* Almost every chapter (with the exception of Chapter 14, which presents original research in the area of sales force control systems) starts with a short case scenario introducing the reader to a managerial problem. The rest of the chapter focuses on how that problem can or should be dealt with by executives, through the introduction of the most recent theoretical models and frameworks. The final part of the chapter tries to give readers some answers on how the problem was (or could have been) managed by the company, as well as tools like check-lists or managerial audits. In this way, the reader will be introduced to up-to-date academic knowledge of the sales arena, but always with a view to utilizing this knowledge in practice.

3. *The inclusion of current topics that are not typically found in sales management textbooks.* The coordination of Marketing and Sales departments, price delegation to salespeople, leadership of sales teams and managing change in the sales force are examples of issues that more and more Sales Managers are forced to grapple with, but that traditional textbooks or popular business literature do not systematically cover, but that this book does.

4. *A user-friendly approach for postgraduate and executive students.* Executive students especially face a dramatic lack of time. This book introduces them to what is truly useful for their specific needs in the area of sales management, and simultaneously allows the educator to pick and choose from a range of topics those that are most relevant to their teaching and learning requirements. We do not include chapters which focus on basic concepts like the buying process and the marketing mix in general, as such issues are widely covered elsewhere. Within the individual chapters, readers will have access to a concise but complete overview of the key models, concepts and empirical evidence on each topic.

5. *An in-depth analysis of case histories.* As well as using many short illustrative cases, we include some longer cases which allow readers to gain a more in-depth understanding of the problem and of the potential and actual solutions.

6. *A more diverse style, combining theory with empirical evidence.* To complement theory, methods and models, we use multiple types of empirical evidence: short case histories, long case histories, panel data and original research findings.

Pedagogical structure

In order to bring out the book's main objective of being solution-oriented *and* academically strong, the typical chapter will present the reader with the following structure:

Learning objectives and chapter outline: the chapter begins by listing its chief learning components and outlining the structure of the chapter and the principal components of the topic under review.

Introductory case problem: most chapters start with a typical real-world example of a company facing a particular situation. The situation is reflective of the topics that are covered in the chapter and is set in a particular cultural context.

The topic: all chapters present the most relevant conceptual models and/or empirical findings on the topic, including examples wherever possible. In covering the topics, authors typically try to answer the following questions: What is the topic about (e.g. What is sales force training?)? What do we know about it? What should managers do to better manage it?

Case problem revisited: most chapters present one 'in-depth' case study, highlighting the issues faced by an organization on the topics that had been covered. In some chapters multiple short case studies or original empirical research are presented.

Summary: A brief summary of the chapter's contents, drawing attention to the principal lessons to be learnt, is given.

Key points: all chapters end with a synthesis of relevant points for managers: for instance, what should managers do to manage the sales training processes successfully?

Check-list or audit: at the end of the chapter, authors typically propose practitioner-oriented models, tools, check-lists, audits, etc.

References and further reading: complete references for all articles and books mentioned in the main text of each chapter are listed as well as suggestions for further reading, to help readers towards more in-depth, specialized contributions on the topic.

Content of the book

The framework in Figure I.1 shows the guiding framework of the book's structure. As explained above, we see sales strategy as directly related to a firm's overall corporate strategy. The Sales function represents a core value-creating activity and therefore has to be aligned with the firm's overall strategy. Some of the main decisions that have

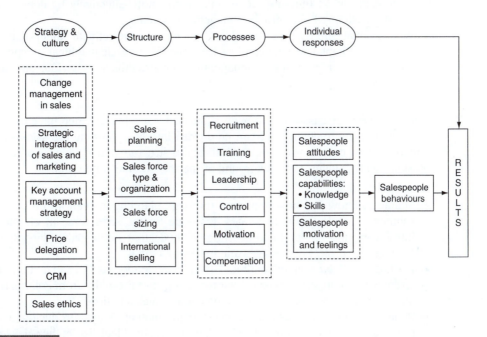

Figure I.1　A sales management framework

to be made in relation to the strategic direction of the sales force are covered in the following chapters:

- How can we adapt the sales force to changes in the environment? This issue is covered in Chapter 1 by Paolo Guenzi, where he emphasizes the importance of a sales force that is open to change and illustrates how such change may be managed through the case of the Italian arm of a large European automobile spare parts manufacturer.
- How can we coordinate the two main customer-facing functions of Sales and Marketing? As Gabriele Troilo points out in Chapter 2, it is vital for any customer-facing firm to have the two main customer touch-points strategically aligned and working together in order to maximize customer knowledge and intimacy.
- If we place the main strategic emphasis on customer relationships, how can these be managed effectively and efficiently by the Sales resources? Chapter 3 gives answers to this question; in it, Marco Aurelio Sisti explains what Key Account Management strategy options a company has at its disposal and how it can best decide where to focus resources.
- If we take the tenet of salespeople as strategic value creators seriously, how much latitude do we need to give them? This is a topic that is rarely discussed in traditional sales management textbooks, but it is taken up by Manfred Krafft and Ann-Kristin Hansen in Chapter 4, who work through the specific issue of price delegation to the sales force both theoretically and through the case study of a large multinational chemicals company.
- What is the role of customer-facing technologies in Sales? In Chapter 5, Nikolaos Panagopoulos describes how information technology can be used to get closer to customers and at the same time serve them more effectively by deploying and sharing Customer Relationship Management systems.
- What guidance do we give our salespeople from a firm's ethical standpoint? Sergio Román, in Chapter 6, explains just how significant a clear ethical perspective is for the sales force and how managers can ensure ethical behaviour among their employees.

Once these strategic issues have been addressed, sales leaders then have to plan the sales effort in more detail. This can be divided into first planning the sales structure and then laying out the processes that utilize this structure and a given set of resources most efficiently, against the background of specific external conditions.

- Managers know just how important thorough planning is even in turbulent environments. Laszlo Sajtos illustrates this issue for the sales force in Chapter 7 by introducing the reader to forecasting methods that allow Sales and Marketing Managers to project future sales and market potential.
- In Chapter 8, Piotr Kwiatek outlines the main advantages and disadvantages of different ways of organizing the sales force, using case examples from Poland. He also discusses the possibility of outsourcing certain sales functions.
- René Darmon continues this discussion in Chapter 9 by introducing a novel, practical yet sophisticated method of determining the ideal size of the sales force.

- A significant structural decision for a sales organization is the issue of exploring new markets abroad. In Chapter 10, John Wilkinson introduces the reader to the fundamental challenges and decisions to be considered when thinking about 'going global' with a firm's sales operations. He illustrates his arguments with two Australian companies who have built up sales operations in south-east Asia.

These structural decisions are vital for many companies as they will have far-reaching consequences. At a more operational level, and therefore also somewhat more flexible, are the sales management processes that are covered in the third and fourth sections of this book. These processes represent the traditional remit of Sales Managers and Sales Directors; while they are typically covered in standard sales management textbooks, the chapters in this section offer new theoretical and empirical material to the reader.

- Chapters 11 and 12 explore processes by which competencies can be fostered in the sales force by considering the recruitment and training of salespeople respectively. Christophe Fournier and Juliet Poujol (Chapter 11) highlight the importance of the recruitment decision and talk the reader through ways of engaging in recruitment processes. In Chapter 12, George Avlonitis uses the example of a Greek pharmaceutical wholesaler to emphasize the value of sales training.
- Once competencies have been created in the sales force, a Sales Manager's task is to nurture and direct it. In Chapter 13, Paolo Guenzi offers a novel take on leadership issues by drawing parallels between leading sales teams and sports team coaching and presents the case of an Italian truck manufacturer.
- Forecasting is the basis of a continuous directing and evaluating of the sales effort, a topic that Vincent Onyemah explores with a multi-country data set in Chapter 14. He shows that in many sales organizations control systems are unaligned with strategic intent, and therefore sub-optimal in directing sales efforts. Suggestions for improvement of such situations are given.
- Still on the topic of directing sales effort and closely related to control, Antonis Siminitiras (Chapter 15) explores different motivational theories that may help Sales Managers extract greater effort from their sales forces. Following on from his chapter, Dominique Rouziès discusses the various compensation options Sales Managers have at their disposal in Chapter 16.

Once all strategic decisions on sales force structures and processes have been made, Sales Managers have to monitor how their implementation affects those working 'at the coal face', in relation to salespeople's attitudes, motivations, knowledge, emotions and behaviours. These issues are explored in Chapter 17 by Susi Geiger, who extols managers to be mindful of the often intense pressures many sales individuals find themselves under in their profession, and who proposes a range of self- and team-management tools for a healthy and productive work environment.

The final chapter, Chapter 18, revisits many of the issues raised in the previous chapters in its exploration of the question of what makes a sales organization successful. While Paolo Guenzi and Susi Geiger do not claim to be able to deliver a definitive answer to this central question of the chapter, they broaden the reader's horizons to various aspects of 'success' in the sales force both theoretically and by working through a case example from the Italian branch of a multinational firm.

Taken in the round, the chapters and Figure I.1 present the reader with a comprehensive and novel way of connecting the many different tasks and concerns of sales
management. We wish the reader an enjoyable and informative time exploring these
many issues with the contributors of this book.

References

Geiger, S. and Guenzi, P. (2009) 'The Sales Function in the Twenty-first Century: Where
are we and Where do we Go from Here?', *European Journal of Marketing*, 43 (7/8):
873–87.

Palmer, M. and Bennet, M. (2009) *Sales Management 2.0: Managing in the Sales 2.0
Environment*. Santa Barbara, CA: Sales Insights Inc. .

Piercy, N.F. and Lane, N. (2009) *Strategic Customer Management: Strategizing the Sales
Organization*. Oxford: Oxford University Press.

Rust, R.T., Moorman, C. and Bhalla, G. (2010) 'Rethinking Marketing', *Harvard Business
Review*, 88 (1/2): 94–101.

Seley, A. and Holloway, B. (2009) *Sales 2.0: Improve Business Results Using Innovative
Sales Practices and Technology*. Hoboken, NJ: Wiley.

Storbacka, K., Ryals, L., Davies, I.A. and Nenonen, S. (2009) 'The Changing Role of
Sales: Viewing Sales as a Strategic, Cross-functional Process', *European Journal of
Marketing*, 43 (7/8):. 890–906.

Vargo, S.L. and Lusch, R.F. (2004) 'Evolving to a New Dominant Logic for Marketing',
Journal of Marketing, 68 (1): 1–17.

Zoltners, A.A., Sinha, P. and Lorimer, S.E. (2008) 'Sales Force Effectiveness: A Framework for Researchers and Practitioners', *Journal of Personal Selling and Sales
Management*, 28 (2): 115–31.

Part one

Formulation of the sales programme: defining sales strategies and sales force culture

1

Managing change in the sales force

Paolo Guenzi

Contents

Learning objectives

After reading this chapter, you should be able to:

- Recognize the critical importance of managing change in the sales force today.
- Understand how to apply change management models in a sales force context.
- Understand critical barriers to change.
- Know the key factors needed to implement change management initiatives successfully in the sales force.

Chapter outline

Sales managers are often in charge of implementing strategic change in the field at the level of the salesperson-customer interface. This task is usually very challenging for a number of reasons and these will be discussed in this chapter. With the intention of enabling sales executives to gain useful insights into the issue of change management in the Sales function, this chapter is structured as follows. First, to stimulate readers' attention, a case problem is presented. Second, the concept of change management and the different types of organizational change are introduced. Third, the most relevant models regarding change management are reviewed. Fourth, the specific aspects and key success factors in managing change in the sales force are examined. Then, the case presented at the beginning of the chapter is discussed in detail. Finally, several key points in managing change are offered.

Bosch Automotive Aftermarket (BAA), Italy

In 1886, Robert Bosch founded the Workshop for Precision Mechanics and Electrical Engineering in Stuttgart. Today, the Bosch Group is a global supplier of technology and technological services. The Bosch Group comprises Robert Bosch GmbH and its more than 300 subsidiaries and regional companies in over 60 countries. If its sales and service partners are included, then Bosch is represented in roughly 150 countries. Each year, Bosch spends more than €3.5 billion (8 per cent of its sales revenue) on research and development, and applies for over 3,000 patents worldwide.

In the areas of automotive and industrial technology, consumer goods and building technology, some 280,000 associates generated sales of €45.1 billion in 2008.

The automotive market is Bosch's core business and consists of three interrelated markets. The first is Original Equipment, in which Bosch is a worldwide leader in gasoline systems, diesel fuel injection systems, chassis systems brakes and chassis systems control, energy and body systems, radio navigation systems and car radios, and automotive electronics. The second is the spare parts market provided to car manufacturers and sold with their brand. The third is the independent Automotive Aftermarket, where all products are sold under the Bosch brand to end-users (i.e. car drivers) through car repair shops, spare parts retailers, etc.

The Automotive Aftermarket division supplies spare parts and information for Bosch products and systems, sells workshop and car accessories and provides after-sales service for Bosch products. Within the Automotive Technology business unit, the Automotive Aftermarket division is responsible for the supply, sales and logistics of automotive parts for after-sales service, as well as diagnostics and workshop equipment (e.g. testers), technical information, training and consulting for car repair shops. Moreover, it is responsible for the Bosch Car Service concept and global technical after-sales service for automotive products and systems from Bosch. The global team comprises some 3,700 people worldwide, working in the division, in the regional subsidiaries and in the agencies located in 132 countries.

The Italian Bosch Automotive Aftermarket (BAA) division is characterized by a complex distribution system, whose main players are:

- wholesalers (first-level customers);
- spare parts retailers (5,000 outlets in Italy), which are considered second-level customers;
- car repair shops (about 40,000 in Italy), considered third-level customers.

This structure has resulted in difficulties in coordinating what is increasingly a multi-product, multi-client market. As a consequence, the company wanted to increase coordination and cross-functional integration, with the specific goals of increasing flexibility, reducing response time and improving customer service.

The Italian BAA Division sells a broad range of automotive spare parts (windscreen wipers, fuel, oil and air filters, batteries, spark and glow plugs, ignition coils and cables, drive belts, etc.) and diagnostics equipment for repair shops (such as engine system testing, emissions analysis, brake testing, chassis geometry testing, power measurement, etc.). It also offers a number of services: one example is ESI (Electronic Service Information), that is a broad range of CD-Roms with a huge amount of information and technical data on the automotive industry and products. ESI help the owners of repair shops to access all the information required to do their job. These CDs provide information on Bosch products, working times, suggestions and tips for planning activities and how to optimize the use of diagnostics software. The Italian BAA Division is also involved in many special projects; for example Bosch Car Service, which is a sort of franchising network of specialized repair shops certified by the Bosch brand.

The strategic change

Historically, BAA sold to first-level wholesalers as well as second-level spare parts retailers and third-level repair shops. In 2001, it radically changed its distribution strategy, and decided to focus exclusively on 150 big and well-structured first-level wholesalers. These customers, which were chosen as those with the highest competencies and resources, were divided into different categories.

1. Bosch Dealer: medium-size companies with their own inventories and a well-structured organization, usually with multiple branches across Italy. They have their own sales force and technical assistance personnel to servicing their downstream customers. They sell almost exclusively Bosch branded products.
2. Bosch Partner: smaller firms with a narrower assortment of Bosch products, and with lower-level technical, commercial and financial resources and requirements.
3. Bosch Distributor: multi-brand wholesalers, whose offer consists of products manufactured by different suppliers.
4. Special Channels (e.g. oil producers, local public transportation companies, etc.).

In short, BAA decided to focus on a relatively small number of first-level customers only, and to delegate the management of all relationships with second- and third-level spare part retailers and repair shops to these wholesalers. This implied for BAA salespeople a radical switch from a sell-in to a sell-out approach.

The Italian BAA Division had four departments:

1. Sales: The Chief Sales Manager was the head of 15 employed salespeople ('Area Managers') and about 100 independent sales reps. Their main responsibilities were: supporting the growth of customers; supporting the launch of new products in the market; broadening and deepening the range of BAA products supplied to customers at all levels in the distribution channel; applying discounts and differentiating commercial conditions (such as payment terms, financial support, etc.) for individual customers.
2. Marketing: One Marketing Manager headed about 15 people. They were mainly Product Managers, Trade Marketing Managers and Communication Managers. Their main responsibilities were: product management (positioning, pricing, advertising, etc.), driving through development of specific marketing plans for different product lines; market research, sales forecasts, customer satisfaction analysis; supporting the sales force through the provision of technical information on all products, reports on market and financial performance of different products, making support calls to customers, etc.; designing and producing all promotional literature (e.g. catalogues, leaflets, point-of-sale materials); launching new products in the market.
3. Sales Administration: One manager and ten people were in charge of the administration of all payments, invoices, order processing and customer service. Among other things, they had to check the orders (e.g. adequacy of financial conditions, promotional prices), provide all first-level customers with information on price lists, discounts, stock availability and order processing, manage returns and delivery errors, manage claims, which in most cases have to do with logistics and delivery time, call on first-level customers to install software and systems for data processing and order fulfilment, as well as provide information on procedures for data processing, order processing, stock-keeping and logistics.
4. Technical Support: This department was very important for BAA. Technicians in the department focused on the provision of technical services to first-level customers. Their main responsibilities were: managing technical training for all customers; providing continuous telephone support to all technicians of customers; contributing to creating, organizing and training all those in the 500 repair shops involved in the Bosch Car Service project; managing all aspects of guarantees.

The radical change in BAA distribution strategy implied switching from the traditional selling approach to a Partnership approach based on the identification and implementation of win-win strategies with customers. As a consequence, Area Managers had to become Relationship Managers adopting a consultative approach with first-level customers, developing specific business plans and creating added value for the customers.

Traditionally, the Marketing function mainly targeted end-users (car drivers) and focused on brand management and communication strategies, while the Sales department focused on distributors. Moreover, the Marketing function tried to implement strictly the standard guidelines provided by the German headquarters, while the Sales department called for local adaptation to the characteristics and needs of the Italian market.

As a consequence, conflicts and problems of poor coordination were quite frequent. A change management project was needed to properly implement the new Partnership approach. This implied designing a set of interconnected activities, as well as identifying and overcoming a number of potential barriers to change.

Introduction: what is change management?

The pace of change has never been greater than in the current business environment, where change comes in all shapes, forms and sizes.

Change management has been defined as 'the process of continually renewing an organization's direction, structure, and capabilities to serve the ever-changing needs of external and internal customers' (Moran and Brightman 2001, p. 111).

Balogun and Hope Hailey (2004) report a failure rate of around 70 per cent of all change programmes initiated. This poor success rate indicates the fundamental lack of a valid framework of how to implement and manage organizational change, as what is currently available to academics and practitioners is a wide range of contradictory and confusing theories and approaches (Burnes 2004).

First of all, managers should recognize that there are different types of change, requiring different approaches. According to By (2005), three categories of change can be identified, characterized by the rate of occurrence, by how it comes about and by scale (see Figure 1.1).

In terms of rate of occurrence, a typical distinction is between continuous (or incremental) and discontinuous (or radical) change. Discontinuous change is change which is marked by rapid shifts in either strategy, structure or culture, or in all three (Grundy 1993). Contrastingly, continuous (or incremental) change can be defined as the ability to change continuously in a fundamental manner so as to keep up with the fast-moving pace of change (Burnes 2004). Advocates of this type of change argue that change is best implemented through successive, limited, and negotiated shifts.

As for how change comes about, a distinction is made between planned change and emergent change. The planned approach model of change is mainly top-down driven, and is rooted in the managers' belief that the company needs to discard old behaviours, structures, processes and culture before successfully adopting new approaches (Bamford and Forrester 2003). Such directive approaches may work well in situations of crisis, where major and rapid changes are required and there is no scope for widespread consultation or involvement.

In contrast with this, the emergent approach tends to see change driven from the bottom up (Bamford and Forrester 2003; Burnes 2004). In this perspective, change is

		Type of Change	
		Incremental	Radical
Entities involved	Whole organization	INCREMENTAL ADJUSTMENT	CORPORATE TRANSFORMATION
	Department	FINE-TUNING (CONVERGENT CHANGE)	MODULAR TRANSFORMATION

Figure 1.1 A taxonomy of scale of change
Source: adapted from By (2005).

also interpreted as a process of learning, whereby strategy development and change emerge from the way a company as a whole acquires, interprets and processes information about the environment in which it operates (Dunphy and Stace 1993). The approach stresses the promotion of 'extensive and in-depth understanding of strategy, structure, systems, people, style and culture, and how these can function either as sources of inertia that can block change, or alternatively, as levers to encourage an effective change process' (Burnes 1996, p. 14). Therefore, the emergent approach to change suggests that managers should focus their attention on building change readiness and facilitating for change, rather than providing specific pre-planned steps for each change project and initiative.

Finally, different types of change can be identified depending on scale, that is a combination of the number of entities involved (e.g. a single department or the whole organization) and the type of change (incremental versus radical). Based on this, the BAA case represents a situation of corporate transformation, where change is clearly radical and involves the whole organization. In this perspective, sales managers' decisions affect and are affected by decisions made by the top management and by other departments' managers: in the light of such interdependence, integration and coordination of choices and efforts is crucial.

Models to manage change successfully

Models of change management can be divided into two categories: some models identify key success factors, whereas others take a process perspective and typically identify a sequence of steps that should be followed.

Models based on key success factors

A popular framework for managing change in organizations is McKinsey's 7S model, which is a way of thinking about development or remodelling of companies. Its name comes from the seven factors that McKinsey found essential in the context of organization development: strategy, skills, shared values, structure, systems, staff and style.

Normally, when a company sets out to change its organization, the seven Ss are dealt with in a given sequence. In the first phase the strategy is usually determined. The next step is to define what the organization must be especially good at in order to be able to implement its strategy, in other words, what skills it must develop or otherwise acquire. The final step is to determine what changes are needed in the other five factors to make the change a successful one.

Strategy tells a company how it must adapt itself to its environment and use its organizational potential, whereas the analysis of skills answers the question of how the strategy ought to be implemented. These skills define the changes that need to be made in the other five Ss: structure, systems, staff, style and shared values.

A company's *structure* refers to the way business areas, divisions and units are grouped in relation to each other. This is perhaps the most visible factor in the organization, and that is why it is often tempting to begin by changing the structure.

Systems can be defined as the procedures or processes which exist in a company and which involve many people for the purpose of identifying important issues, getting things done or making decisions. Systems provide management with powerful tools for making changes in the organization.

The *staff* factor is concerned with the question of what kind of people the company needs. It refers to the total know-how possessed by the people in the organization.

Style consists of the leaders' personal symbolic actions. Leadership and management style is not necessarily a matter of personal style but of what the executives in the organization do, how they use their personal signalling system.

Shared values, finally, refer to one or more guiding themes of the organization's culture, things that everybody is aware of as being specially important and crucial to the survival and success of the organization.

According to Beer et al. (1990), three interrelated critical factors to manage change successfully are:

1. coordination: teamwork must be stimulated by properly redesigning structures and processes;
2. commitment: people must be motivated to change, especially through rewards and incentives;
3. competencies: new skills and capabilities should be developed, especially by investing in training and coaching.

By successfully leveraging these factors, managers should effect three types of responses of personnel:

1. cognitive responses: people should know why the change is needed, what has to be changed and how, who is responsible for change, etc.;
2. affective responses: people should accept the change and feel motivated to change; this implies agreeing upon the why, what and how specified above;
3. behavioural responses: the ultimate goal of change processes is to modify what people do and how they do it.

However, Laabs (1996) reported that 20 per cent of people in an organization are change-friendly, 50 per cent are 'fence sitters' and 30 per cent resist or even deliberately try to make the initiative fail.

Therefore, change leaders should recognize that it is important to proactively manage the meanings their organization's members attach to change. Such meanings can be interpreted in terms of shared mental models, that is, common perceptions, beliefs and priorities that may help successful change implementation. Since change implies uncertainty and ambiguity, the input of management into the beliefs their workforces hold is especially important when companies undergo radical changes. In doing this, change leaders should carefully avoid their efforts being perceived as brainwashing or manipulative mind control. Rather, ideally, they should use open and clear communication based on facts and data.

In short, leaders should manage meanings in order to:

• create shared perceptions and interpretations so that members' actions are guided by a common definition of the situation;
• justify their actions and the changes they introduce to the organization;
• recruit followers and motivate members of the organization to support their actions.

The management of meanings by strategic leaders primarily involves shaping organization members' perceptions and interpretations about: (1) the environment; (2) the state of the organization and its performance; (3) the organization's vision and goals; (4) the appropriateness of various means, decisions, and actions employed by the organization to achieve its goals; and (5) the ability of the organization to make progress toward meaningful goals.

Neal and Tromley (1995) suggest that a sales organization considering any change initiative should consider three factors:

1. Culture: when radical changes are expected, culture change is needed. Culture consists of the set of values, beliefs and assumptions underlying the behaviour of individuals.
2. Social systems: to change the behaviour of personnel, companies can invest in recruiting, training and reward systems. Recruiting new hires and selecting the adequate 'survivors' in downsizing initiatives is especially important for change leaders, whose leadership style should fit the new culture of the organization.
3. Technology and work design: technology change can strongly support organizational change, which mainly implies redesigning structures and processes, e.g. by introducing teams.

Sirkin, Keenan and Jackson (2005) suggested the duration, integrity, commitment, effort (DICE) model, which identifies the four 'hard' variables representing the key success factors in more than 1,000 change management initiatives monitored by the Boston Consulting Group worldwide. These four variables are:

1. Duration: the authors argue that it is essential to formally review the transformation project frequently (at least bimonthly) by scheduling milestones and assessing whether the target has been reached. Carefully monitoring the change project's progress implies providing reports, determining whether achieving the milestones has had the desired impact on the company, discussing the problems, determining improvements, etc.

2. Performance Integrity: members of the change management project teams should possess adequate skills and traits. This is usually difficult to obtain since in most companies senior executives are reluctant to allow star performers to join the team. In addition to this, the team should be cohesive and well led. This requires defining clear roles and responsibilities, as well as finding the right team leaders: ideally they should tolerate ambiguity, possess good problem-solving skills, be results oriented, methodical, organizational savvy and willing to accept responsibility.

3. Commitment of both senior executives and the staff members most affected by change. Managerial support mainly consists in communication processes: the authors recommend, as a rule of thumb, that top executives should be talking up a change initiative at least three times more than they think they need.

4. Effort: companies should carefully consider the additional workload required of employees to cope with the change process. Employees are usually busy with their day-to-day activities and if their workload increases too much the change project will probably fail. The authors suggest that since no one's workload should increase by more than 10 per cent, the company could decide to take away some of the regular work, especially for those employees playing a key role in the transformation process.

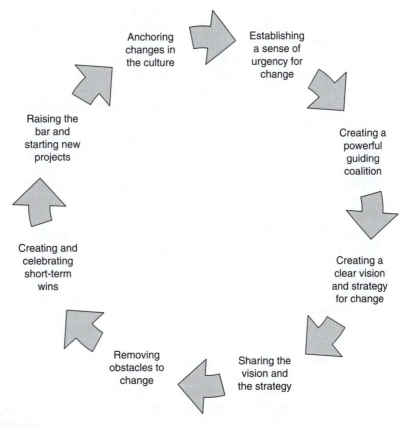

Figure 1.2   Steps of successful change management processes
Source: adapted from Kotter (1995).

Process models

Kotter (1995) suggested that successful change management processes are the result of a series of eight sequential and interrelated phases (see Figure 1.2):

1. establishing a great sense of urgency, in such a way that most people in the organization see the current situation as more dangerous that launching into the unknown. This goal can sometimes be accomplished by deliberately creating situations of crisis. As a rule of thumb, Kotter states that about 75 per cent of a company's management should honestly be convinced that business as usual is completely unacceptable;

2. creating a powerful guiding coalition to achieve the critical mass needed to win over the opposition. Power of the coalition should not be interpreted in terms of the hierarchical level of its members. Rather, power is typically a combination of titles, information, expertise, reputation and relationships, because the coalition should always include members that are not part of senior management;

3. creating a vision clarifying the direction in which the organization needs to move and, ideally, the strategy developed for achieving the vision. The vision should be simple, easy to understand and communicate and capable of creating interest. Without this vision, priorities are not clear and plans, directives and projects may be confusing and perceived as incompatible: the vision should be the unifying focus of all programmes;

4. communicating the vision and eventually the strategy to achieve it. Every possible communication channel should be used to make employees perceive that the change is useful and possible. Two-way exchange of information is sometimes extremely important in allowing the collection of feedback from personnel before it is too late. It is also important that change leaders teach by example and behave consistently with the undergoing change: by walking the talk they should try to become a living symbol of the new values, attitudes and behaviours that are requested from employees;

5. removing obstacles to the new vision, such as inadequate organizational structures or reward systems that create conflict between the new vision and employees' self-interest;

6. orchestrating and creating short-term wins. Meeting and celebrating short-term goals helps boost the credibility of the renewal process, keeping the urgency level high and forcing detailed analytical thinking that can clarify or revise the vision. Since big transformations take time, without some short-term success many people are at risk of giving up and losing faith in the change process. Therefore, change leaders should deliberately plan for visible and measurable performance improvements, create these improvements and recognize and reward employees involved in them;

7. avoiding declaring victory too soon. Rather, successful change leaders typically use the credibility gained through short-term wins to raise the bar further and start renewal projects that are even bigger in scope than the initial ones;

8. anchoring changes in the corporate culture to make them last as long as possible. New behaviours should be rooted in shared values and norms of conduct so that they are not subject to early degradation. To institutionalize change, companies

should continuously and deliberately show people how their own, individual new behaviours and attitudes have helped the company improve performance. Furthermore, organizations should manage the succession to the next generation of top management by promoting change champions.

Claret, Mauger and Roegner (2006) developed a model which emphasizes four critical processes to implement change projects successfully:

1. managing communications to clarify the reasons for change and the expectations about the individual goals, tasks and behaviours.Special attention should be given to the provision of customized, innovative and two-way information exchange. People affected by change should know what they need to change and why;
2. giving role models to all people affected by change: top managers' actions are particularly relevant here because followers should see their leaders and peers walk the talk;
3. developing new skills and competencies in those affected by change in such a way that they feel they are ready and well prepared to deal with the challenges of the new context;
4. reinforcing change by creating the supporting conditions needed to modify processes and individual behaviours. Examples of such conditions are incentives, rewards and information systems.

In addition to this, all members of the organization should develop a personal insight in order to identify their individual fears standing in the way of change.

Managing change in the sales force

Hurley (1998) suggests a number of reasons why managing change in sales organizations is 'special'.

First, since salespeople are boundary spanners and the Sales department as a whole manages direct interactions with accounts, customers may be alienated by the disruption associated with change and take away their business. Hence, changes in sales organizations can be extremely risky, and properly communicating the change to customers is a critical success factor.

Second, salespeople typically spend most of their time in the field in different territories. Therefore, compared to change involving other departments, the existence of many different people, locations and levels creates more challenges in establishing momentum for change among a critical mass of the sales organization.

Third, since salespeople's remuneration is typically largely related to market performance, change directly threatens the level or variability of sales force income. As a consequence, compared to other personnel, salespersons may be more reluctant to change, because unlike other employees in the organization they have to take upon themselves the risk of losing money.

Finally, salespeople are, generally speaking, very practical and tactically oriented: hence they may feel discomfort with the abstractness and uncertainty that radical change entails.

Starting from these considerations, Hurley (1998) proposes some general rules for managing change in sales organizations:

1. the vision of the future relationship with customers should be clear and grounded in good market analysis;
2. expectations about earnings during the change process should be carefully managed;
3. complex and abstracts ideas in the vision should be translated as much as possible into concrete behaviours and actionable programmes;
4. the vision and the rationale for change should be communicated clearly and completely across all levels and locations;
5. salespeople's resistance to change should be reduced by involving them in the process;
6. change progress should be measured and monitored continuously;
7. specific change management structures should be created (e.g. task forces);
8. change leaders should be empowered at all levels/locations;
9. multiple parts/processes of the systems should be changed in an integrated and consistent manner.

Managing change in a sales force typically implies modifying the organization, execution and evaluation of the selling effort.

Change management programmes in the sales force have frequently been driven by Total Quality Management (TQM) and Re-engineering projects, that is, by situations of corporate transformation where revolutionary change is linked to a guiding overall vision. Many TQM and Re-engineering efforts have been failures. Among the key success factors for such initiatives, the most frequently cited ones are adequate leadership, commitment from the top, a supportive structure, employees' involvement, communications management, education and training, the use of measurement and analytical techniques for redesigning critical processes and the adoption of adequate reward and recognition systems.

According to a survey on sales organization reinvention change initiatives reported in Colletti and Chonko (1997), the most frequently cited objectives of sales force reinvention are improving sales productivity, improving sales coverage to current customers and growing overall sales. The expected results are not only to grow revenues, but also to improve customer satisfaction and increase profit margins. To do this, companies mainly change the field organization structure, customer segmentation, sales jobs, training and performance measurement systems. They typically do not change recruitment policies, sales channels and compensation packages. Interestingly, the most difficult aspects to manage have to do with change implementation at the level of processes and people.

Colletti and Chonko (1997) recommend that companies follow a five-step process to implement sales change programmes successfully (see Figure 1.3):

1. assessment of the current external situation (e.g. changes occurring in customers, competitors, macro-environment) and internal context (e.g. changes in strategy, available resources, etc.);
2. redesign of sales leadership, strategy, tasks, structures and processes, which implies articulating and disseminating a clear vision of the desired new situation;

3. modification of measurement systems: companies should change what to measure and how to measure. A typical example is the effort made to calculate customer profitability to see if the company is focusing on the right accounts, as well as to estimate the return on time invested, in order to make sure that salespeople are spending their time on the right activities. Measurement is extremely important in change initiatives for several reasons. First, accurate measurement procedures can help justify why the change is needed by providing measurable goals to be accomplished. Second, if the impact of change on results can be measured, empirical testing can reveal what works well or not in the change, thus facilitating learning and continuous improvement. Third, having measurable measures of success provides opportunities for energizing the improvement process: in fact people feel motivated by reaching quantifiable measures of performance, and demonstrating the capacity to succeed reinforces employees' perceptions of their ability to succeed in the future;

4. development of sales support programmes, such as training, rewards, customer relationship management, supervision and coaching, Marketing and Sales integration, etc.

5. change implementation: the time needed largely depends on size and complexity of the sales organization, time pressure, type of change, etc. Generally speaking, since actual implementation mainly occurs at the individual level, it is critical that the sales force 'buys in' to the change management programme from its earliest stages and is continuously motivated and reinforced to accept change.

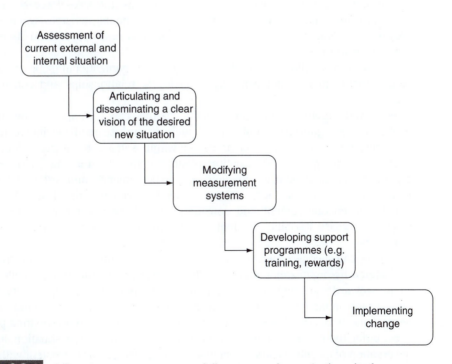

Figure 1.3   A five-step process to successfully manage change in the sales force
Source: adapted from Colletti and Chonko (1997).

At the level of individual salespeople, Chonko et al. (2002) suggested that two requisite conditions for change are sales force perceptions of the organization's readiness for change and the learning orientation of the sales force.

Perceived organizational readiness for change is the cognitive precursor of either behavioural resistance to or support for change. Such perception embodies the individual salesperson's belief that the change is useful and that the organization possesses the ability to implement the change successfully.

Individual learning orientation of salespeople is reflected in their attitude towards questioning extant knowledge, challenging preconceived ideas and assumptions and actively seeking information.

Chonko et al. (2002) posited that in times of change both perceptions of organizational readiness for change and individual learning orientation positively affect individual performance and overall corporate outcomes. According to the authors, perceptions of organizational readiness for change and individual learning orientation can be positively affected by the company's culture, organization climate and policies.

As for corporate culture, it is argued that perceived readiness for change is higher in companies whose main values are market orientation and entrepreneurship. Market orientation is characterized by a continuous effort to create customer value, to collect and disseminate customer and competitor information, and by organization-wide responsiveness to customer needs. Entrepreneurship is characterized by risk tolerance, support for proactivity, receptivity to innovation and resistance to bureaucracy. Market orientation and entrepreneurship can also affect salespeople's model of learning: in companies where the former prevails, the sales force should mainly use exploitation (i.e. focus on incremental improvements), whereas where the latter prevails, situation exploration (i.e. focus on radically new approaches) should be the preferred learning style.

Organizational climate reflects the level of organizational support, openness of the organization, supervisory style, quality of relationships and conflict among members.

Perceived organizational readiness for change can be improved by many elements of the organizational structure, such as the use of a facilitative leadership style seeking to inculcate a clear vision within sales subordinates, decentralized strategic planning and the adoption of an organic structure, i.e. a decentralized organizational architecture with fluid job responsibilities and strong lateral communications. In fact all these elements, together with informal leadership support, that is the encouragement and consideration salespeople receive from their colleagues, increase flexibility, facilitate communication flow and stimulate emergent processes.

Finally, salespeople's perceptions about organizational readiness for change can be fostered by organizational policies like investment in training and willingness to change reward and compensation systems when the posited change affects the salesperson's job. In fact, the individual salesperson's ability and motivation to modify their behaviours so as to implement change successfully largely depends on their possibility of acquiring the new competencies and skills required in the new situation, as well on the creation of incentives and compensation schemes seen as consistent with the new requirements.

CASE PROBLEM REVISITED

BAA Italy: what happened?

In the following the case is used as an illustrative example of how McKinsey's 7S framework can be applied to the managing of change in organizations.

Strategy

Radical changes entail substantial modifications of corporate strategies and goals. New strategies should be clear and easy to communicate, and new goals should be easy to justify, quantify and measure. These key success factors are apparent in the words of Paolo Colabucci, Sales Manager at BAA Italy at that time.

> *From a strategic standpoint, change was driven by two main goals.*

> *The first one was to cut costs by reducing managerial complexity. For example, from the adminis-·trative standpoint, Bosch had to manage thousands of invoices every month and had a huge list of insolvent customers.*

> *The second goal was to increase revenues by targeting big dealers which could sell and provide service support for the whole set of Bosch products, especially technical goods, which could not be either purchased or distributed by small–medium sized distributors, due to the lack of qualified technical staff or the pretty big warehouse and financial requirements.*

> *In the process of change it was crucial to share our vision and to clearly communicate our goals to customers and employees alike. You might discuss methods, timing and tactics, but the vision must be definitely shared. In addition to this, it was of fundamental importance to root our vision of the future and our goals into hard data and objective facts. We had to support our view concretely by showing research, figures and trend analysis to justify why we thought we had to go that way.*

Skills needed to successfully redesign and manage key processes

Generally speaking, in change management initiatives companies should analyse and redesign critical processes when needed, especially so as to identify the critical skills needed to implement the change successfully. Such processes may be both back-office activities and customer interaction management on the front line. For example, BAA Italy mapped and redesigned some critical processes, in order to clarify roles and responsibilities, the goal being to reduce ambiguity and conflicts. Therefore, after identifying key processes the company developed for each of them the responsibility, approval, support, information and control (RASIC) matrix, which clearly indicated, for each phase of the process under investigation, the people involved in terms of Responsibility, Approval, Support, Information and Control.

In line with the literature on change management, the BAA Italy case also supports the critical role played by *communication processes* both with internal (subordinates, colleagues from other departments, etc.) and external counterparts (e.g. customers). As pointed out by Colabucci:

> *We let everybody – including customers – know about our real sales and product targets. We also wanted to inform everybody about the results of the change process. So, for instance, we immediately bought a maxi-LCD screen (which cost €10.000 at the time ... it took me three*

months to have such investment approved!) placed right there at the entrance of our building, so that everyday everybody could see at once what the target for each channel and line of products was, together with sales progress made daily. So everyone could know exactly what was happening. We also developed an intranet connecting all members of the sales force so that anyone could see their colleagues' results. Of course, they all remained anonymous. This was not meant to create jealousy or the like, but to let anyone have benchmarks and a clear picture of the situation. The same was true for customers who could see how they were growing compared to others: again, this was done anonymously. This gave rise to a virtuous cycle simply by letting information until then reserved circulate. Everyone knew exactly what they had to do and by when and also what the others were expected to do and the progress the others were making.

This was an important achievement in a context where traditionally such type of transparency was not accepted. That was a really hard struggle . . . but it really turned out to be a key factor.

In some cases, changes in processes were only short term, tactically-oriented. For example, pricing and discount policies were made very flexible at the beginning of the change initiative. This decision was taken so as to support the change process by orchestrating some early wins when needed. In fact, the company wanted to keep performance high in the short term to reinforce employees' and customers' commitment.

Shared values and culture

When the change management process started, Bosch was changing its priorities in terms of key corporate values. Moral integrity had always been a top priority, together with securing their employees' work but now value number one had become an entrepreneurial spirit and a spirit of initiative: the company wanted personal contribution from its employees. This called for, among other things, an empowering leadership style, a reduction of bureaucracy in many business processes and higher job mobility coupled with more meritocratic career advancement opportunities. Also, the strategic change at BAA Italy called for a stronger market-oriented culture.

To change the corporate culture, one should start from the top: it is of fundamental importance that top managers accept, witness and spread across the whole company the key values of the new culture. To do this, members of the board needed to demonstrate and embody such values by showing consistent actions, i.e. by modifying their everyday decisions and behaviours. This is not easy to accomplish. This was how Paolo Colabucci, Sales Manager at BAA Italy, stimulated in the CEO the shift from a product-oriented culture to a customer-oriented culture, which was a necessary precondition to successfully implement the change:

I repeatedly said that we were a product-oriented company rather than a customer-oriented one. This made the CEO criticize me. He said 'How do you dare make such an accusation?', to which I replied: 'I just have a question for you: how many customers do we have, and how many product codes do we deal with?' Well, he knew about product codes but had no idea about customers. So I told him: 'That's the way it is, I know how many customers we have, while you don't. Yet, you know how many product codes we deal with. This means that you focus on logistics and products while you don't care about customers so much. Well . . . I guess you should!'. Since he was a smart person he realized I was right: we were not truly customer-oriented. So he started being sort of obsessed with it. He started going around asking everybody, 'How many customers do we have?'! He had changed his mindset completely, and this is how some changes in mentality were introduced. In turn, this gave rise to radical changes in many key processes. For example, we completely redesigned information systems to calculate each customer's profitability. Before the change, we had no information about it, since sales statistics were organized only by product.

This statement clearly points out that major modifications in the company culture must be accompanied by substantial modifications in support systems (e.g. information systems), otherwise it is extremely difficult to implement change in practice.

Furthermore, an important way to modify the corporate culture is to change some *rituals*. For example, to stimulate employees' entrepreneurship, Colabucci decided to change the way meetings were managed. This is how he describes this change:

> *Traditionally, the company used to have meetings where some people said nothing at all. So I told them: 'Just don't come next time if you have nothing to say. Even if it is rubbish you have to say it anyway.' I used to say: 'Let's do some brainstorming because from someone's rubbish there may stem someone else's good idea.'*

> *Yet, it was not so easy to encourage brainstorming in a company with a strong hierarchical culture, where everybody tended to be reluctant. So I even decided to play games like: 'If you say nothing, you have to leave the room,' Thus, using a little bit of 'violence' we could arouse creativity and people who had always kept silent until then, when forced to speak, would often contribute the best ideas.*

Another example of change in rituals refers to the challenge of stimulating a culture of interdepartmental interaction and cooperation. In Colabucci's words:

> *Once there were separate dinners out for salespeople and members of the Marketing department. We started to have inter-functional meetings and dinners where they all had a chance to get to know each other.*

> *We did the same with the colleagues from information systems, who could decree success or failure of our projects, because they could dramatically facilitate the circulation of information and the possibility to have concrete data to refer to. Therefore, for example, I often invited them to our dinner meetings where we celebrated our department's accomplishments. I wanted to let them feel part of the team.*

In addition to this, the company also started to take some people from the Sales department and move them to Marketing and vice versa.

Corporate culture can also be changed by modifying some aspects such as, for example, the company *language* (Homburg and Pflesser, 2000). An example of this is provided by Colabucci:

> *I have abolished the word 'manage' from my own vocabulary, because when you are busy managing something you have already lost ground in comparison with those who are developing their business. Therefore, one should only 'develop'. We had people in charge of 'coordinating' something. Well, a person who coordinates rarely has responsibilities . . . so we have renamed many of them 'business development managers' or 'channel leaders', which sounds more dynamic.*

Even changing the dress code was a way to try to modify culture, attitudes, and behaviours. As stated by Colabucci:

> *We began not to wear ties because we wanted to have people feel they were part of a team where they were expected to work hard and face a change instead of feeling like managers supposed to manage business as usual. We impoverished the formal aspect in a sense while enriching the substantial one.*

Style: leadership

Change leaders must be credible, and their leadership style should incorporate personal values and personality traits which are consistent with the values of the corporate culture. For example, as stated above, a major modification of Bosch's corporate culture was the emphasis now placed on the employees' entrepreneurial attitudes and capabilities. This calls for a leader who stimulates and supports *empowerment and risk-taking*. This was clearly a characteristic of Colabucci, as demonstrated by the following statement:

> I used to say: 'maybe at the beginning you do ten things, eight are wrong and two are right. Yet later it may go the other way round: you do eight right things and two wrong ones. If you stand still you might make no mistakes, but you don't contribute to any achievement either.' This is why I kept saying: 'Just do it, just try, we'll surely learn from our mistakes.'

Similarly, a *participative leadership style* was needed to foster followers' entrepreneurial spirit. Again, this was part of Colabucci's style, as demonstrated by the following quote:

> I remember that at first everybody said 'Yes, Sir', and at the end many would say 'No, I disagree', which helped me grow as well.

Radical changes usually require a radical *discontinuity* in the management team. Hence, hiring leaders from outside can be a wise choice, as witnessed by Colabucci:

> For many customers it was important to interact with a new Sales Manager. I told them: 'I have nothing to do with what has been done so far. I only know that I am here to do something else.' I was credible because, while being very competent about the products and the market, I had not contributed to building up the situation as it was. Many customers understood that Bosch really wanted to change things by introducing some new managers coming from outside. They saw me as a living proof of Bosch's willingness to change.

On the other hand, hiring a new leader from another company may create some problems internally, because the newcomer may lack *credibility*. To gain credibility, the leader should be perceived as competent, honest and powerful. The company and the leaders can and should do whatever they can to improve such perceptions. In Colabucci's words:

> At the beginning some people thought: 'this guy is too young and doesn't know the Bosch world...soon he won't be around anymore.' In Bosch, people who started a change process were rarely granted credibility as employees were generally not in favour of it and were bound to tradition. In fact, one of the main values for Bosch is 'We have always done so successfully since 1890'. So it's truly difficult to say, 'Starting tomorrow we'll do it another way'. I had to give the impression of being given a strategic mission instead of being seen as a person who, as a latecomer coming from outside, wanted to put in hand all that had been discussed previously before introducing change processes which perhaps were not welcome and not even shared from a strategic viewpoint. I was successful especially because I was given special power on many decisions, which was highly unusual and demonstrated that I was backed by a strong commitment from the top management.

> People trust you if they see that you have concrete ideas and possess the necessary competence. Fortunately, I had technical and market competence. This helped me a lot.

> Another key success factor was that I was very clear to people. If they are not aware of what is both positive and negative about the change process, they feel confused, overpowered by ambiguity and they stand still, they just don't move. You've got to be very outspoken.

The leader's communication style is especially important in change management initiatives, since it has a strong impact on the cognitive, affective and behavioural responses of individuals affected by change. A communication style characterized by clarity and openness is usually a relevant trait of successful change leaders.

Structure

In terms of organization structure, two major modifications were made at BAA Italy. The first has to do with reduction in the sales force size. In fact, since BAA Italy would no longer manage 4,000 customers but 150, the company needed to downsize its sales force. Therefore, BAA Italy decided to relocate to dealers many members of its sales force, which reduced from 100 agents to 30. Only ten salespeople did not accept this proposal. A key variable in the successful implementation of this process was proving that everyone would earn more in their new roles. For BAA Italy, the main advantages were that agents helped convey the culture of Bosch to dealers, and that salespeople (and their customers) did not move to competitors. Agents did not lose their jobs and continued working with their customer base. Often they also had new career advancement opportunities in the dealers' organizations. Finally, they put their portfolio of downstream customers at the disposal of dealers, who broadened their customer base and hired experienced salespeople.

The second relevant change was that the company created formal teams, thus giving rise to a matrix organization structure. In fact, Area Managers became leaders of Selling Teams, each one incorporating a couple of agents and one member from each of the other three departments: Marketing, Sales Administration and Technical Assistance.

Staff

Bosch realized that most of its employees did not possess the set of skills and competencies needed in the new scenario. At the same time, the company understood that investing in training was a necessary step to motivate people to change. In fact, many employees felt a lack of self-confidence. Empowerment also required an increase in employees' capabilities. Therefore, most members of the organization from all four key departments were involved in inter-functional coaching, training in team-building and training to develop management skills and competencies.

In short, the training process at BAA Italy consisted of the following steps:

1. definition of the 'ideal profile' of Area Managers in terms of skills and competencies required by the new approach;
2. self-evaluation of Area Managers in such skills and competencies;
3. comparison of the ideal and actual profiles, leading to the identification of individual gaps in skills and competencies and areas for improvement;
4. aggregation of individual gaps and improvement priorities to identify group-level priorities (e.g. managerial competencies versus relational soft skills);
5. application of the same process to all other members of sales teams.

Systems

In addition to the above cited interventions two other modifications were important to support and successfully implement change at BAA Italy. The first involved *planning*: all salespeople were provided with an information-based customer planning tool aimed at setting goals, developing projects, tracking progress, monitoring problems and creating benchmarks for every single customer.

Secondly, the company completely revised the *incentive system*. The challenge here was to change employees' priorities from monetary rewards to career development opportunities and professional growth. To do this, for example, the company strongly invested in cross-functional training and interdepartmental coaching, stimulated cross-functional mobility and redesigned job advancement paths.

Summary

Figure 1.4 summarizes in a model the key concepts of the 7S framework applied to change management in the sales force. It illustrates the most important success factors Sales Managers should focus their attention on.

The change management audit proposed at the end of this chapter explains the key questions managers should answer when strategically planning and executing a structured approach for managing change in the sales force.

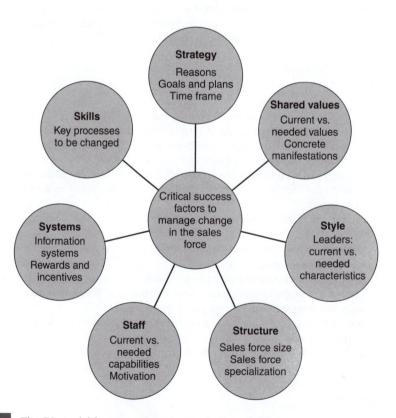

Figure 1.4   The 7S model for managing change in the sales force

Key Points

1. In the world of selling, companies increasingly have to deal with change.
2. Sales Managers should recognize that there are different types of change, requiring different approaches. Depending on the rate of occurrence, how change comes about and the scale of change, different priorities should be set.
3. Successful change management implies focusing on coordination, commitment and competencies. The ultimate goal is to effect cognitive, affective and behavioural responses of personnel. To do this, change leaders should proactively manage the meanings their organization's members attach to change.
4. Many different models have been proposed to manage change successfully. Among the most important ones, it is worth mentioning the seven-step model suggested by Kotter (1995), the DICE model and McKinsey's 7S model.
5. The key message of these models is that a structured, integrated and consistent set of interrelated changes are needed at different levels of the organization.
6. Managing change in the sales force is 'special' for a number of reasons. Therefore, sales managers should follow some specific 'rules' such as the ones suggested by Hurley (1998) and adopt a structured approach like the one suggested by Colletti and Chonko (1997).
7. The BAA Italy case is an example of the application of McKinsey's 7S models to successful change management in the sales force.

Running a change management programme audit in your company

The following audit is intended to help Sales Managers diagnose problems in change management programmes

Strategy	What are the goals of change? What are the most important courses of action needed to accomplish such goals? What are the reasons behind these new goals? What is the role of time in strategy implementation? What are the most important goals in the short run, and which other ones are of fundamental relevance in the long term?
Skills	Which key processes will be affected by the undergoing change? How should they be modified?
Shared values (culture)	Which values characterize the corporate culture now? Of the current values, which ones support change, and which ones are obstacles to change? Which new values are needed in the new scenario? How can such new values be spread across the organization?
Style (leadership)	Who will be the relevant change agents in the organization? What leadership style should they possess? Which characteristics should they possess? How can the company support them?
Structure	Should the organization of the sales force be modified? Why? How? Should the rest of the organization structure be changed? Why and how?

| Staff | What skills and competencies are needed in the new scenario? How can they best be developed? How can salespeople and other relevant employees be motivated to change? Should the company hire new salespeople or keep the current ones, trying to modify them through training, coaching, etc.? |
| Systems | Which systems should be modified to support change? How? For example, should information systems and incentive systems be modified? If yes, how? |

References

Balogun, J. and Hope Hailey V. (2004) *Exploring Strategic Change*, London: Prentice Hall.

Bamford, D.R. and Forrester, P.L. (2003) 'Managing Planned and Emergent Change within an Operations Management Environment', *International Journal of Operations and Production Management*, 23 (5): 546–64.

Beer, M., Eisenstat, R.A. and Spector, B. (1990) 'Why Change Programs Don't Produce Change', *Harvard Business Review*, 68 (6): 158–66.

Burnes, B. (1996), 'No Such Thing as...a "One Best Way" to Manage Organizational Change', *Management Decision*, 34 (10), 11–18.

Burnes, B. (2004) *Managing Change: A Strategic Approach to Organisational Dynamics*. Harlow: Prentice Hall.

By, R.T. (2005) 'Organisational Change Management: A Critical Review', *Journal of Change Management*, 5 (4): 369–80.

Chonko, L.B., Jones, E., Roberts, J.A. and Dubinsky, A.J. (2002) 'The Role of Environmental Turbulence, Readiness for Change, and Salesperson Learning in the Success of Sales Force Change', *Journal of Personal Selling and Sales Management*, 22 (4): 227–45.

Claret, J., Mauger, P and Roegner, E.V. (2006) 'Managing a Marketing and Sales Transformation: Profiting from Proliferation', *The McKinsey Quarterly*, 76: 111–21.

Colletti, J.A. and Chonko, L.B. (1997) 'Change Management Initiatives: Moving Sales Organizations from Obsolescence to High Performance', *Journal of Personal Selling and Sales Management*, 17 (2): 1–30.

Dunphy, D. and Stace, D. (1993) 'The Strategic Management of Corporate Change', *Human Relations*, 46: 905–20.

Grundy, T. (1993) *Managing Strategic Change*. London: Kogan Page.

Homburg, C. and Pflesser, C. (2000) 'A Multiple-Layer Model of Market-Oriented Organizational Culture: Measurement Issues and Performance Outcomes', *Journal of Marketing Research*, 37 (4): 449–62.

Hurley, R.F. (1998) 'Managing Change: an Ethnographic Approach to Developing Research Propositions and Understanding Change in Sales Organizations', *Journal of Personal Selling and Sales Management*, 18 (3): 57–71.

Kotter, J.P. (1995) 'Leading Change. Why Transformational Efforts Fail', *Harvard Business Review*,73 (2), 59–67.

Laabs, J.J. (1996) 'Expert Advice on How to Move Forward with Change', *Personnel Journal*, 75 (7): 54–62.

Moran, J.W. and Brightman, B.K. (2001) 'Leading Organizational Change', *Career Development International*, 6 (2/3): 111–21.

Neal, J.A. and Tromley, C.L. (1995) 'From Incremental Change to Retrofit: Creating High-performance Work Systems', *Academy of Management Executives*, 9 (1), 42–53.

Sirkin, H.L., Keenan, P. and Jackson, A. (2005) 'The Hard Side of Change Management', *Harvard Business Review*, 83 (10): 108–18.

Further reading

Chonko, L.B., Roberts, J.A. and Jones, E. (2006) 'Diagnosing Sales Force Change Resistance: What We Can Learn from the Addiction Literature', *Marketing Management Journal*, 16 (1): 44–71.

Jones, E., Roberts, J.A. and Chonko, L.B. (2000) 'Motivating Sales Entrepreneurs to Change: a Conceptual Framework of Factors Leading to Successful Change Management Initiatives in Sales Organizations', *Journal of Marketing Theory and Practice*, 8 (2): 37–49.

Piercy, N.F. and Lane, N. (2005) 'Strategic Imperatives for Transformation in the Conventional Sales Organization', *Journal of Change Management*, 5 (3): 249–66.

Smollan, R.K. (2006) 'Minds, Hearts and Deeds: Cognitive, Affective and Behavioural Responses to Change', *Journal of Change Management*, 6 (2): 143–58.

Weeks, W.A., Roberts, J.A., Chonko, L.B. and Jones, E. (2004) 'Organizational Readiness for Change, Individual Fear for Change, and Sales Manager Performance: an Empirical Investigation', *Journal of Personal Selling and Sales Management*, 24 (1): 7–17.

2
Integrating sales and marketing

Gabriele Troilo

Contents

Learning objectives

After reading this chapter you should be able to:

- Understand the benefits and risks of Sales–Marketing integration.
- Identify the market and organizational conditions your company is facing, in order to understand how much integration is needed.
- Decide at which level your company needs to create Sales–Marketing integration.
- Identify the current barriers to integration your company is facing.
- Select the most appropriate set of integration mechanisms, given the integration levels your company wants to achieve.
- Benchmark the characteristics of Sales–Marketing integration mechanisms adopted by your company with those used by a sample of European companies, and the outcomes of this adoption.

Chapter outline

The objective of this chapter is to disentangle the complex issue of managing the integration of Sales and Marketing units. Although several companies strive for an effective coordination of these two units, achieving an appropriate level of integration is all but a simple task. The chapter starts with a review of market and organizational conditions that make Sales–Marketing integration a necessity for many companies. Then, attention will be paid to the different levels at which integration can be achieved and to the cultural, organizational and infrastructural barriers that make it difficult to gain effective integration at the different levels. The heart of the chapter consists of a review of the integration mechanisms a company can use in order to achieve that objective. Specifically, the focus will be on managerial systems and changes in the organizational structure allowing the company to improve the level of Sales–Marketing integration. A final section of the chapter reports on the results of a survey conducted on a pan-European sample of companies regarding the level of Sales–Marketing integration achieved and the integration mechanisms mostly used to gain this result. The audit tool provides a simple way of helping the reader to assess the level of integration reached by their company and the usage of integration mechanisms.

CASE PROBLEM

Italian Bubbles

In July 2008, A.Z., CEO of Italian Bubbles,[1] the leader in the Italian sparkling white wine market, was going into his office after a meeting with the Sales Director and the Brand and Communication Director (responsible for all marketing activities). As usual at the end of these meetings, his only thought was, something needed to change! Italian Bubbles had operated very profitably in its market leader position for a long time because of the high quality of its products and its strong value for money positioning. However, it was evident to everyone in the management team that the efficiency and effectiveness of its marketing-related activities were far from satisfactory and competition was becoming a real issue, especially in some areas of the country. In this last meeting, he learned that the Sales unit had already decided upon – and communicated to the sales force – an aggressive price discount campaign for distributors in order to tackle the strongest competitors, while the Brand & Communication unit had just approved a new, very costly communication campaign aiming at repositioning the company brand in the upper part of the market. For this reason the Brand & Communication Director had asked for an extra budget for her unit, provoking a tough reaction from the Sales Director. In fact, he started complaining that Sales was trying to reduce its expenses as much as possible and these resource-saving efforts would be swept away by marketing expenditures completely out of control. As usual, the meeting ended in nothing but reciprocal accusations of poor knowledge of the market, ineffective managerial actions and the wish to increase personal power. A.Z. knew the situation very well. The real problem was that Sales and Marketing were characterized by mutual distrust, resulting in poor collaboration. Further, it was not very clear just who was responsible for what, and this usually led to people not taking responsibility for necessary decisions and activities. Something should be changed, and quickly!

The situation described is far from uncommon. It in fact describes a typical Sales–Marketing conflict, leading to waste of resources, inefficient allocation of marketing effort, and ineffective marketing actions. The remainder of this chapter aims at providing a framework to understand the reasons why Sales and Marketing units are often not aligned and to describe some tools to improve their integration.

The need for Sales–Marketing integration: market conditions and organizational contingencies

Interdepartmental integration consists in the coordination of activities, decisions and strategic and operative processes across different departments within the organization. A widely accepted managerial tenet is that the need for integration of different organizational units grows in parallel to the increased specialization of those units. In other words, when different organizational units are specialized in order to deal with particular tasks, activities, processes or sections of the external environment, then a need appears to integrate those units so that their efforts can be unified and directed to the achievement of superordinate organization goals.

---

[1] The name of the company is fictitious for privacy reasons, but it does exist and the situation has been directly experienced by the author as consultant of the company.

A widespread belief is that since Sales and Marketing are separate departments or units within a company, there is a need to integrate their efforts. In fact, it is said, the more integrated they are the more efficient and effective a company's market activities will be (Guenzi and Troilo 2006, 2007). This is all the more true in contemporary market environments, whose characteristics push companies towards the search for higher levels of efficiency and effectiveness of their decisions (Cespedes 1993; Kotler et al. 2006; Matthyssens and Johnston 2006). In fact, a general condition of most modern markets is increased uncertainty, due to:

- the evolution of technology, which continuously moves forward the frontier of manufacturing, distribution and communication possibilities;
- the increasing demands of customers, which undermines long-held competitive positions;
- the systematic reshaping of competitive landscapes, caused by the emergence of new market actors and the innovations used to acquire stronger market positions;
- the new regulatory constraints regarding environmental sustainability, consumer protection and social responsibility which stimulate an increased pace of innovations.

The consequence of this environmental uncertainty is an increase in the need for companies to achieve, process and use high quality information efficiently and effectively, and this in turn creates the need for tighter coordination and unity among organizational sub-units (Gupta et al. 1986; Ruekert and Walker 1987). As for the specific integration between Sales and Marketing, some market conditions make this integration all the more necessary (Figure 2.1).

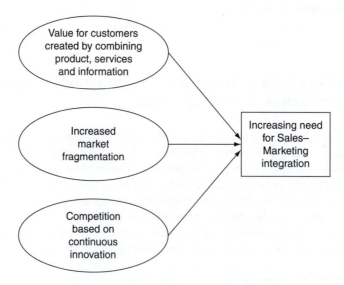

Figure 2.1 Market conditions fostering the need for Sales-Marketing integration

Market conditions fostering the need for Sales–Marketing integration

First, in most markets today, *value for customers is created through a combination of product features, customer service and information*. Customers – both business and consumer, both trade and end-user – have access to a much wider set of information and can use it to clearly define their expectations and select the right product to meet their needs. Moreover, customers require support along the whole buying and usage process, with pre- and post-sale services and information to enable them to gain the most out of their purchases. Hence, a need for Sales and Marketing integration arises. In fact, people in Sales and Marketing units usually have different perspectives and views of the market (Rouziès et al. 2005; Homburg and Jensen 2007). Salespeople have great knowledge of individual customers and territories, built on day to day relationships with their clients. Marketing people tend to have a wider picture of the market and the actors operating in it, built on systematic market analysis and marketing research. Since salespeople have daily contact with the market, they can provide the company with fresh and updated insights about market changes, whereas marketing people can combine those inputs with others gained from other sources and design consistent offerings and activities. Finally, marketing people have the responsibility for designing product offerings which are consistent with target market expectations, whereas salespeople have to adapt offers to specific customer requirements in terms of service and information. Given all this, integrating Sales' and Marketing's efforts allows a company to design and deliver value propositions that are more effective in meeting and satisfying customers' expectations, which, in turn, leads to sustainable competitive advantage.

Secondly, most markets in the last few years have witnessed a *continuous process of fragmentation*. Market fragmentation is mostly due to the revolutionary change caused by information and communication technologies which allow companies to obtain and retain more precise intelligence about smaller segments of the market. In fact, more powerful databases and data-mining abilities increase the possibility that companies may have to challenge long-held segmentation strategies and that new segments will emerge. Micro-marketing activities can be implemented and companies can design customized offerings for smaller segments right down to individual customers. The possibilities the internet offers to establish personalized relationships with customers increases dramatically companies' ability to interpret the evolution of customer preferences. On the demand side, customers are asked to participate in the design of the offering and can thereby obtain products and services whose features are tailored to their specific and individual requests. Hence again, a need for Sales and Marketing integration arises. In fact, salespeople's and marketing people's orientation is usually focused on different elements of the market (Rouziès et al. 2005; Homburg and Jensen 2007). Marketing people's brand and product orientation allows them to identify which target segments are more suited to buy the offering and to receive sales efforts. Contrastingly, salespeople's customer orientation and fostering of relationships can help them to identify differential customer response to promotional tools and to design customer-specific programmes. Moreover, the field experience of salespeople can contribute to the selection of segmentation criteria which not only take into account differences in sought benefits or brand attachment, but also behavioural and relational specificities of customers. That said, integrating Sales' and Marketing's efforts allows the company to grab the opportunities offered by market fragmentation by focusing promotional and distribution efforts and making superior returns on marketing investments.

Thirdly, *competition in many of today's markets is shaped by innovation*. Many companies build their differentiation strategies on their innovativeness and innovative capabilities, bringing a systematic launch of incremental or radical new products. Continuous innovation requires a strong control on the pace of innovation with planned obsolescence of products and services. As a consequence, the life cycle of most products and services shortens dramatically, and to make this strategy financially sustainable payback periods should shorten accordingly. Thus, companies are required to be very efficient in the allocation of resources in order to keep costs under control, and to be very effective in servicing the right market segments in order to generate immediately a consistent flow of revenues. Hence, again, a need for Sales and Marketing integration arises. In fact, the Sales unit and the Marketing unit have different time orientations, mainly due to their specific reward and compensation systems (Rouziès et al. 2005; Homburg and Jensen 2007). Where marketing people's long-term focus leads a company's innovation strategy towards latent customer needs and future markets, salespeople's focus on actual customer needs help transform such innovation strategies into customer education activities that bring customers closer to new products and services. Further, salespeople's focus on short-term results helps drive promotional and distribution strategies, so that commercial efforts are addressed to those customers who are more sensitive to a new product's features enabling it to rapidly achieve a wide distribution. Hence, integrating Sales' and Marketing's efforts allows the company to design marketing programmes in support of new products and services which mean it will not suffer from having insufficient resources or fall short of market and financial performance.

Organizational contingencies fostering the need for Sales-Marketing integration

The market conditions described above create an external context where companies that integrate Sales' and Marketing's efforts are better prepared to respond to the evolution of the market and gain a stronger competitive position. However, this does not mean that Sales–Marketing integration should be sought at any cost.

There are two issues that have to be taken into account. The first is that the assumption behind the need for integrating Sales and Marketing is that the two functions are separated in different organizational units. The second is that the need for integration is contingent upon certain organizational factors (Gupta et al. 1986; Ruekert and Walker 1987; Dewsnap and Jobber 2000) (Figure 2.2).

As regards the first issue, in many European countries, whose industrial systems include many small and medium-size enterprises, there are still many companies that do not have any formal Marketing unit, whereas a specialized Sales unit is much more common. Research on this topic is very limited: it is interesting to note that in research carried out in the UK on 284 firms with more 100 employees, Piercy (1986) reported that 55 per cent of them had no Marketing department, and that research carried out in the UK and Australia twenty years later by Dawes and Massey (2006) showed that a pretty high number of companies still stated that they did not employ anybody with

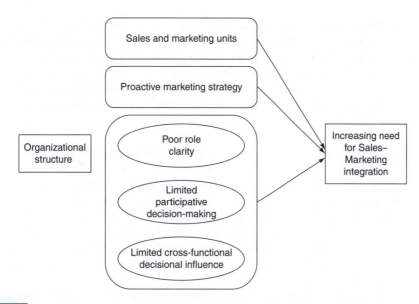

Figure 2.2 Organizational contingencies fostering the need for Sales–Marketing integration

the term Marketing in their title. This being so, it can be said that the need for integration between Sales and Marketing depends on the *structural location of the Sales and Marketing units*. In those companies, usually small and with a strong product or technological orientation, where there is no formal Marketing unit, the need for integration is simply non-existent, and the coordination of those activities which traditionally fall under the name 'marketing' (communication, pricing, customer service etc.) is not an issue because they are under the responsibility of the same person, typically the owner or a person directly reporting to him/her.

A different situation occurs when there is a Marketing unit, but it reports to the Head of Sales or a Commercial Director (e.g. Homburg, Jensen and Krohmer 2008). This is quite typical in many European companies where the Marketing unit's responsibility is limited to communication and promotional activities (catalogue design, website management, trade exhibition participation, contact with specialized communication agencies, etc.). In these cases Marketing is a staff unit reporting to Sales, and integration is not a critical issue because it is achieved by keeping most tasks within the same domain of responsibility.

The need for integration becomes a real managerial issue when Sales and Marketing are two separate organizational units, each with specialized tasks and a manager in charge of the unit. In their empirical research carried out in Germany and the US, Workman, Homburg and Gruner (1998) document four different types of reporting relationships between Sales and Marketing units:

- Sales and Marketing in functionally organized autonomous business units, each one in charge of the typical sales and marketing specialized tasks, and reporting directly to the business unit manager or to a Vice President of Sales and Marketing;
- Sales and Marketing in functionally organized business units with a corporate Marketing group, in charge of the coordination of marketing activities and planning across the different business units;

- Marketing in a business unit that shares a sales force with other business units, with the Head of the Marketing department reporting to the business unit manager and the Head of Sales reporting to the CEO or Managing Director;
- Sales and Marketing in corporate groups shared by multiple business units, where the business unit manager has no direct control over marketing and sales activities, and the Heads of the Sales and Marketing corporate groups report to the CEO or Managing Director.

In all four reporting relationships, sales and marketing specialized tasks are allocated to separate organizational units, each of them having a manager in charge. All these cases call for the integration of Sales and Marketing, because, in the absence of that, the activities of the two units may achieve suboptimal results due to the repetition of tasks and overlap of activities, which in turn yield redundancy and inefficiencies.

The separation of Sales and Marketing in different organizational units is a necessary but not sufficient condition to call for the need for integration. In fact, the need for integration increases according to certain organizational characteristics regarding organizational strategy and structure.

Regarding organizational strategy, more integration is needed when a company pursues a *proactive marketing strategy*. Basically, this means that the company does not consider the served market as the ultimate competitive arena but it continuously acts to expand the scope of its activities: by introducing product innovations to drive customer preferences, by venturing into new technological domains to augment the value of its offering, by creating new markets or new market segments to challenge the actual market structure. Since a company like this continuously ventures into new domains, the ability to collect market information rapidly and transform this information into marketing knowledge and capabilities requires strong coordination between Sales and Marketing. Contrastingly, a company characterized by a reactive marketing strategy competes in well established competitive arenas, and relies on historic views of the market and on consolidated marketing capabilities. Such a company can act with a more limited degree of integration because both Sales and Marketing can manage their specialized tasks according to managerial models that have become common wisdom, thereby reducing the need for information sharing and processing.

As for organizational structure, more integration is needed when a company has a *poor functional role clarity*, a *limited degree of employee participation in decision-making*, a *limited cross-functional relative influence over decisions* (Dewsnap and Jobber 2000; Troilo et al. 2009). The functional role clarity of the company as a whole will impact upon the extent to which it clearly defines the specific roles, goals and responsibilities of Sales and Marketing. When clarity is poor, tasks are not allocated to the two units according to precise criteria, there is confusion over who is responsible for what and repetition of tasks is very likely as well as their late execution or even non-execution. Thus, when the organization is characterized by poor functional role clarity, integrating Sales' and Marketing's efforts is all the more needed, because if no attention is put on integration many market activities will be inefficiently and ineffectively designed and executed.

In the case of very centralized decision-making processes, employees are not much involved in the decision-making process. As a matter of fact, they are less inclined to share information and to commit to the execution of market activities. People from both units are less stimulated to provide feedback and insights, their feeling of ownership of projects is poor, and the use of information coming from the other unit is diminished. Hence, a centralized decision-making authority has to be balanced with processes and mechanisms apt to foster integration between the two units.

Finally, an organization is characterized by limited cross-functional relative influence over decisions when every organizational unit has full control over its decisional domain and very limited power on the decisional domain of other units. This situation prevents the organization from gathering to the full the information on which decisions might be based and does not permit the exploitation of the full range of competences and perspectives available within the organization from different organizational units. To favour the exchange of information, perspectives and competences across different units, a company like this has to design and implement appropriate integration mechanisms between Sales and Marketing.

Different levels of integration

In the previous section it has been stated that today's markets are characterized by features which push companies toward the increased integration of the Sales and Marketing units. However, it has also been said that certain strategic and structural factors make the need for a higher degree of integration more urgent. Further, that interdepartmental integration consists of the coordination of activities, decisions and processes, and that a company can set and achieve integration objectives at each and all levels of its organization.

All that said, a question arises: what are the different levels at which integration between Sales and Marketing can be pursued and achieved?

Integration has two components: interaction and collaboration (Kahn 1996; Kahn and Mentzer 1998; Kahn 2001). *Interaction* refers to the systematic information and communication flows between the two units. When two departments are integrated personnel of the two meet regularly, participate in joint decisional committees and working teams, exchange information by several devices (phone, email, etc.). These flows of information and communication are done according to formal procedures and yield material artefacts such as reports and memoranda.

Collaboration, in contrast, refers to shared objectives, resources and activities, to mutual understanding and trust, to common goals and vision. Thus, personnel of two integrated departments develop a common vision of the future, put themselves in the shoes of each other in order to acquire a different perspective on issues and tasks, share portions of resources and put energy in the achievement of joint goals. In short, interaction has to do with exchange of information, whereas collaboration has to do with a positive attitude toward the other organizational unit that translates into cooperative behaviours.

Interaction and collaboration are complementary components. Interaction represents the structural side of integration, collaboration represents the affective side, which leverages the involvement of people of one unit on the issues, tasks and responsibilities of the other unit. A real integration between Sales and Marketing is there when both interaction and collaboration between the two units are in place. However, the two can be pursued and achieved separately, through the use of different

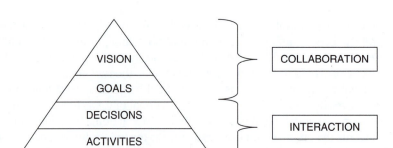

Figure 2.3   Different levels of integration

mechanisms. Interaction is the basic level of integration, on which collaboration can be built; collaboration is the higher level of integration, whose achievement requires more sophisticated mechanisms and more time. Hence, the different levels of integration between Sales and Marketing can be represented with a pyramid, with basic levels staying at the bottom and more sophisticated ones being added on top (Figure 2.3).

Integration of activities occurs when Sales and Marketing coordinate their own activities on which they have autonomy and full control, through exchange of information about plans, schedules and responsibilities. For example, when Marketing has decided to extend a line of products, meetings are organized with salespeople in order to design and execute trade promotion campaigns and to obtain the support of distributors to the product line extension in terms of shelf space and in-store communication. On the other hand, when Sales decides to go for trade marketing activities with a national retailer in order to strengthen the relationship with it, meetings are organized with marketing people to assess the impact of this on the positioning of the company's brands.

Integration of decisions occurs when Sales and Marketing jointly take decisions on matters regarding market activities. For example, both sales and marketing personnel take part in a team in charge of brand health assessment with responsibility for advancing proposals for next year's marketing plan. Or, people from the two units set up a committee in charge of assessing market opportunities for new products and services.

Integration of goals occurs when Sales and Marketing have joint goals to be reached. This is the case when the two units have joint responsibility for the achievement of market results, they are jointly rewarded for this achievement, and they jointly decide the metrics to be used to measure those results.

Integration of vision occurs when Sales and Marketing share the same vision of the market in terms of mindsets to interpret market evolution and development, the future needs of customers, market threats and opportunities and the strengths and weaknesses of competitors.

Integrating activities basically requires the appropriate planning and execution of each unit's actions. Thus, it can be achieved by way of frequent communication between the two units and the sharing of high quality and relevant information. Integrating decisions requires the design of organizational processes, systems and roles which support the joint decision-making process. Integrating goals has to do with the more strategic process of goal-setting, based on a structured and formal process of resource-sharing and usage. Hence, it requires the design of organizational processes and systems for assessment and reward, the definition of marketing and sales metrics, and the clear identification of roles and responsibilities for the joint achievement of market results. Integrating visions is a cultural issue. It requires people from the two units to develop a shared view of the market, composed of the different perspectives characterizing the individual units, through joint learning processes and knowledge development.

Thus, the different levels of integration impact differently upon organizational culture, structure, processes and systems. For this reason, they have to deal with different barriers and require the use of different integration mechanisms.

Barriers to integration

Many obstacles can reduce the effectiveness of, make it difficult, or impede Sales–Marketing integration within a company. A proper identification and management of these barriers is a prerequisite to gain the benefits of integration.

Barriers to integration can be divided into three main categories (Griffin and Hauser 1996; Fisher et al. 1997; Maltz 1997; Dewsnap and Jobber 2000; 2002): cultural, organizational and infrastructural (Figure 2.4).

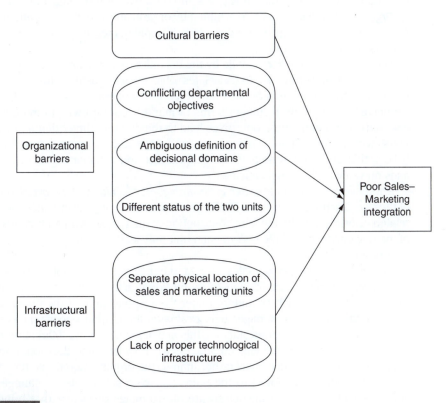

Figure 2.4   Barriers to Sales-Marketing integration

Cultural barriers are determined by the processes through which the two organizational units create their own specific sense of community. In fact, in many companies there is still a widespread conviction that a Marketing Manager should possess strong analytical skills to support strategic thinking, whereas Sales Managers should possess solid field experience and operational abilities to support relational capabilities. In short, thinking versus acting.

This conviction quite often leads to the creation of an in-group identity built on contraposition to the other group. Indeed, inter-group relations are often affected by reciprocal stereotypes ('marketing people live closed in their offices and do not really know customers', 'marketing people do not have a real sense of the market since they only interpret it through market research reports', 'salespeople have a very narrow view of the market since they are focused on their area and their clients', 'salespeople's only goal is to sell immediately and at any cost', etc.); each unit develops an idiosyncratic language that is quite often not clearly comprehensible to the other unit; a functional identity is often developed to the detriment of company identity, whereby people feel they belong to the functional unit more than to the company as a whole.

All these factors lead to the creation of two separate communities, which find it difficult or costly – psychologically or operationally – to invest time and energy to increase both interdepartmental interaction and collaboration. As a consequence, the quality and frequency of communication, the willingness to share resources, to understand each other and to go for the same goals and objectives are strongly reduced.

Organizational barriers are determined by organizational structures and managerial systems which are not properly designed or implemented to favour cross-functional interaction and collaboration.

The most typical barrier is made by the definition of *conflicting or difficult to complement departmental objectives*. In fact, Sales' objectives are usually linked to short-term results in terms of revenue or customer retention, whereas Marketing's objectives are connected to long-term results in terms of market share growth, brand development and market creation. These objectives lead to the different time orientation of the two units, which affects how decisions are made and tasks executed, and makes them believe that allocating time and effort to interact and collaborate with the other unit adds no value to their own activities.

Another organizational barrier is an *ambiguous definition of the decisional domains* of the two functions, which can lead to interdepartmental conflict. Since most market-related decisions require the joint contribution of the two units an ambiguous definition of the responsibility and the task of each unit may lead to inefficiency and inefficacy in the execution of activities.

An unclear definition of Sales and Marketing personnel's job descriptions (e.g. who is responsible for the design of promotional activities?), a tendency informally to take over tasks which should be under the responsibility of the other unit (e.g. a long-experienced Sales Manager who evaluates the market opportunities for a new product although the responsibility for this activity is that of the Marketing Manager), managerial turnover which leads managers to consider some decisional domains as related personally to themselves rather than to the organizational role they have (e.g. a Marketing Manager moved to the Sales unit who still wants to manage the relationships with advertising agencies), are all examples of factors that bring the two units to overlap, invade the other's domain, act more on the base of their perceived own decisional domain than the formal one. All these factors lead to conflict between personnel of the two departments, thereby diminishing the returns on market-related decisions.

The last important organizational barrier is a *difference in status between the two departments*. If one of the two units traditionally gains more consideration within the company, if top managers come regularly from one of the two units and not from the other, if compensation levels of personnel are quite different between the two, it is very likely that the organizational climate between the two departments will not be favourable to integration, but, on the contrary, will lead to opposition, mutual distrust, and conflict.

In conclusion, conflicting functional objectives, ambiguous decisional domains, and status difference between Sales and Marketing make communication processes difficult and inefficient, and nurture mutual distrust and unwillingness to understand each other, to share goals and resources and to cooperate in joint objectives.

Infrastructural barriers are a third category of obstacles. Physical and technological infrastructures should be designed to favour the efficiency and effectiveness of organizational processes. However, a lack or an inappropriate availability of those infrastructures can be an impediment to Sales–Marketing integration.

The first type of infrastructural barrier is *physical location*, that is, the allocation of office space to the two units. Quite often Sales' and Marketing's offices are located in different buildings: usually salespeople spend most of their time off the company premises executing their selling tasks; especially in big multinational corporations, the Marketing unit is often centralized at headquarters, whereas regional branches have a local Sales unit. Thus, physical distance impedes face to face communication, and limits informal information-sharing processes – that is, hall talks, informal meetings etc. – as well as the development of social relations based on strong affective bonds, that make a fundamental pillar of a collaborative climate.

A second type is *technological infrastructure*. A lack of proper information systems connecting personnel of the two departments and allowing them to share information rapidly has a negative impact on the mutual availability of data and information necessary to taking effective market-related decisions and executing efficient market actions. As a consequence, interaction between Sales and Marketing is negatively affected. Collaboration may be negatively impacted, too. In fact, if each unit relies only on its own proprietary set of information to take market-related decisions and act accordingly, the other unit will appear more and more distant in terms of routines to accomplish tasks and mindsets used to make sense of market phenomena. Hence, mutual understanding and sharing of goals and vision are more difficult to achieve.

The negative effects of cultural, organizational and infrastructural barriers to Sales–Marketing integration can be overcome by implementing various integrating mechanisms, each different in nature and differentially apt, to foster interaction or collaboration.

Integration mechanisms

Once a company has a clear view of environmental and internal factors which can increase the need for Sales–Marketing integration, and of the barriers which are actually impeding or limiting it, it can design and implement integration mechanisms to produce integration at different levels (Figure 2.3): activities, decisions, goals, visions.

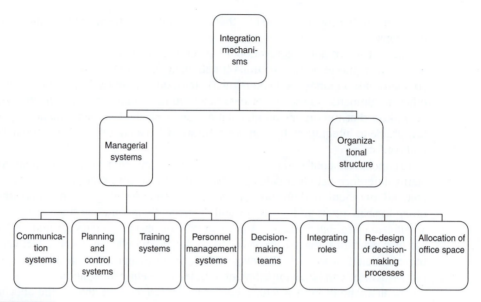

Figure 2.5 Integration mechanisms

There are two main categories of integration mechanisms (Dawes and Massey, 2005; Dewsnap and Jobber, 2000; Leenders and Wierenga 2002; Rouziès et al. 2005): *managerial systems* and *organizational structure* (Figure 2.5).

Both categories are able to effect interaction and collaboration, because they can improve information-sharing and cooperative behaviours within the organization. However, specific mechanisms within each category are more apt to impact one of the two types of integration.

Among managerial systems, a fundamental role is played by *communication systems*. The design of formal communication procedures that govern information flows between the two departments can increase the level of interaction and lead to the enhanced integration of activities of the two units. For example, the frequent exchange of sales or market research reports to build a common repository of market knowledge; the design of a shared customer database where both units can add or draw information; the schedule of regular meetings between personnel of the units to comment and build a shared interpretation of market phenomena; the participation of personnel of one unit in formal meetings of the other unit in order to bring a different perspective on market phenomena. Further, communication systems can also affect the level of collaboration by enhancing mutual understanding and reciprocal trust (Salazar 2008). For example, if marketing people participate in customer calls alongside sales people, if sales people participate in the design of market research or in a brief to a communication agency, personnel of the two units can achieve a deeper understanding of each other's working routines, tasks, and decision-making procedures, and develop a more encompassing view of the 'thought worlds' of their colleagues (Homburg and Jensen 2007), thereby increasing the level of mutual respect and trust. In short, communication mechanisms are able to overcome both organizational barriers regarding separated and non-coordinated decision-making processes and cultural barriers related to the existence of departmental fiefs which function through self-reflective functional stereotypes and idiosyncratic languages.

Planning and control systems are another set of critical managerial mechanisms which allow the company to coordinate, assess and improve the decision-making processes of different organizational units. An example of how such systems can impact upon the integration of decision-making and goals between the two departments is the design of planning and control systems that identify a set of metrics to assess the company's market performance which combine measures of Sales' and Marketing's activities, that give joint responsibility to the two units for the sales and marketing budget and plans and that make the two units share the responsibility for the merchandizing and promotional plans. Here, the planning and control systems allow the two units to align their own objectives and plans, to rely on the competence and knowledge of the other unit in order to sharpen their own actions and to gain a deeper understanding of each other's processes and activities. In short, planning and control systems can enhance both interaction and collaboration by overcoming organizational barriers related to different and separate functional objectives, as well as cultural barriers created through limited knowledge of each other's domains of action.

One more important managerial system a company can use to favour Sales–Marketing integration is *training systems*. Having Sales and Marketing people participating in joint training programmes, having personnel of one unit participating in the training programmes of the other, focusing training programmes on team building and team working, are good examples of the way the two departments can share knowledge and develop common cognitive schemes to interpret market phenomena and guide market actions (Troilo 2006). The company training system can be designed in such a way that the two units not only learn managerial models and methods but also develop a positive attitude towards team working and an organizational climate supportive of mutual respect and trust. By so doing, Sales and Marketing can develop an integrated vision of the future market and align efforts and activities to this common view. In other words, training systems can help personnel of the two units to overcome cultural barriers and differences in thought structures and knowledge.

There are also important managerial systems governing the *evaluation, compensation, career, incentives and rewards of personnel*. All these systems are able to guide individual and group behaviours towards specific short-term and long-term objectives, and create commitment of personnel toward the achievement of those objectives. Hence, a company can use them to direct attention and commitment towards the objective of increased interaction and collaboration between the two departments. Examples of this are the design of joint incentives for the two units; the design of career paths where job rotation across the two units allows people to become familiar with and learn the working routines and processes of each other; the definition of compensation levels and career paths which are homogenous across units so as to not raise any perception of inequity in terms of salary, access to top organizational positions and career opportunities. These systems are able to overcome cultural barriers related to the perception of differential departmental status and unequal consideration that can impede the creation of a collaborative environment between the two units.

The second category of integrating mechanisms consists of those related to organizational structures. There are several structural devices that can be used. The first is the creation of *decision-making teams* composed of members of the two functions. These teams can be made responsible for market performance objectives, market-related decisions and market activities. Another option is to create temporary cross-functional teams responsible for specific projects, for example the development of a new product or service, the design of a programme to increase customer satisfaction and loyalty, the creation or enrichment of the customer database. Both permanent and temporary cross-functional teams are apt to create integrated goals for the two units and a sense of ownership in the decisions the teams are responsible for.

The second structural mechanism is the creation of specific *integrating roles*. Trade Marketing Managers, Category Managers, Demand Managers, Key Account Managers are typical roles that can be created with the clear objective of integrating Sales and Marketing decisions and activities. The main task of these roles is to sharpen Sales' and Marketing's abilities to increase the efficiency and effectiveness of market-related decisions. For example, Category Managers in a consumer goods company can use the product knowledge of marketing people and the customer knowledge of sales people to design a development plan for the product category that can be proposed to distributors as a win-win strategy. Further, a Key Account Manager in an industrial company can build on customer information collected by sales people and recommend to marketing people some strategic guidelines for the development of new products tailored to the specific needs of that account. Integrating roles thus enables an increase in the level of interaction and collaboration between Sales and Marketing by overcoming organizational barriers related to conflicting functional objectives.

Another structural mechanism a company can use to increase the level of Sales–Marketing integration is to *redesign market-related decision-making processes* in order to increase their level of involvement in the decisions themselves. Both academic literature and effective managerial practices have shown that decentralized decision-making structures allow the company to have more involved and committed employees. Moreover, recent empirical literature on Sales–Marketing interface (Krohmer et al. 2002; Troilo et al. 2009) has suggested that an increased cross-influence of two departments on each other's decisions improves the effectiveness of decision-making processes and increases the interaction and collaboration between the two units. Combining the evidence of the two, it can be suggested that decentralizing the decision-making power and increasing mutual influence can enhance integration between the two units. This means that, for example, decision-making power over trade promotions (a typical Sales decision) can be assigned to a middle-level Marketing Manager, or, on the other hand, power over launching a new service to enter a new market segment (a typical Marketing decision) can be assigned to a Sales Marketing Manager. Redesigning market-related decision-making processes can help the company enhance both interaction and collaboration between the two units by increasing the communication flow between them and creating a sense of joint ownership of the results of the decision taken.

The last structural mechanism regards the *allocation of office space* to the two units. Since physical proximity helps informal communication, unplanned meetings and quicker exchange of information, location of the two organizational units near each other is able to enhance interaction as well as collaboration and to overcome infrastructural barriers which reduce information flow and cultural barriers through limited knowledge of each department's people, working routines and practices.

The dark side of integration

The previous sections have been devoted to highlighting the market and organizational conditions which make integration between Sales and Marketing departments necessary for a company, and the different mechanisms that can help achieve this objective. However, it cannot be said that integration has only potential benefits for the company and no costs.

The whole presentation of this chapter might induce the reader believe that the relationship between Sales–Marketing integration (SMI) and organizational performance (OP) is always positive and linear (Figure 2.6a). However, it can be the case that this relationship is non-linear and assumes a U-shape (Figure 2.6b) or an inverted U-shape (Figure 2.6c).

The U-shape relationship shows that a high organizational performance might be achieved only if the level of Sales- Marketing integration is either extremely low or very high.[2] Where this is not the case and there is a mid-range level of integration, this can be detrimental for the company and lead to poor organizational performance. The inverted U-shape, indeed, shows that a very high performance can be achieved only at mid-range level of integration, whereas both a very low and a very high integration may be conducive to a poor performance.

The explanation for these relationships can be traced back to the costs that both interaction and collaboration may induce. In fact, interaction implies a notable information exchange and communication flow between the two departments. But such interaction requires a lot of time to be invested by the personnel of the two units in order to meet the other unit's personnel, to exchange and make sense of more information, to participate in joint training sessions – that is, a lot of time that takes them

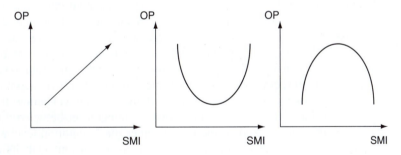

Figure 2.6   The relationship between Sales–Marketing integration (SMI) and organizational performance (OP)

---

[2] Since organizational performance has many determinants, it can be assumed that a high performance can also be achieved when Sales–Marketing integration is limited. Examples of this can be a very large company that gains strong bargaining power over its distributors, or a company whose competitive position is due to technological know-how protected by patents, or a company that gains a monopolistic position in the markets where it operates. Although it can be assumed that limited Sales–Marketing integration reduces the efficiency and effectiveness of such companies, the favourable conditions they are able to earn may allow them to achieve a very high performance.

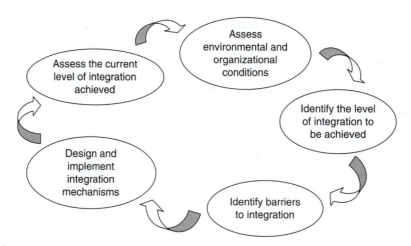

Figure 2.7   The Sales–Marketing integration process

away from other activities. Equally, collaboration is based on mutual understanding, respect and trust and the development of these attitudes requires a lot of time and cognitive and affective effort. Moreover, a negative side effect of excessive collaboration might be the reduction of diversity and the development of homogenous, less varied perspectives to make sense of market phenomena. The subsequent reduction in creativity and innovation capabilities may then have a negative impact on organizational performance.

In short, although interaction and collaboration have positive effects in terms of efficiency and effectiveness, they can also have negative effects on the same outcomes, because of the time and cognitive investment they require and the excessive homogeneity they may yield. As a consequence, the achievement of the benefits of Sales–Marketing integration requires an investment whose benefit can be experienced only after the company working routines become efficient and yield to rapid exchange of information and communication flows, and if the collaborative working environment is kept lively enough to stimulate divergent thinking and novel perspectives.

In conclusion, there is no optimal level of integration between Sales and Marketing. Every company should monitor whether the integration level achieved leads to gains in terms of efficiency and effectiveness, consistent with its culture, organizational structure and managerial systems and with external market conditions. Figure 2.7 presents the different steps of the Sales–Marketing integration process. In the Appendix, two simple tools for the assessment of the level of integration achieved and the corresponding integration mechanisms used are presented.

Empirical evidence from a pan-European sample

In order to give empirical evidence to some of the considerations presented in this chapter a survey has been carried out on a sample of 326 European companies. The survey consisted of a structured questionnaire sent to Sales or Marketing Managers of companies in five countries: France (67 companies), Germany (67), Italy (72), the Netherlands (60), and the UK (60). The sample was made up of companies operating in several industries (both consumer and industrial markets, both goods and service ones), that have more than 50 employees, with the Marketing unit separate from the Sales one. The average number of employees in the Marketing unit is 78, whereas the average for the Sales unit is 110.

The objective of the research was to answer the following questions:

1. What is the level of achieved integration between Sales and Marketing?
2. What are the most used integration mechanisms?
3. What are the effects of those mechanisms on different levels of company performance?

The level of achieved integration between Sales and Marketing

In the second section, it was stated that integration can be achieved at different levels: activities, decisions, goals and vision, the first two through the interaction component of integration, the second two through collaboration. It has also been said that different levels of integration require different mechanisms, and it can also be assumed that collaboration relies on interaction, that is, collaboration can be developed only after an effective level of interaction has been put in place.

Managers were asked to rate their own company or strategic business unit (where the company had more than one)[3] in respect of 11 items representing an encompassing view of achieved integration:

1. Common goals
2. Team spirit
3. Same vision
4. Mutual understanding
5. Mutual respect
6. Mutual trust
7. Share information
8. Share resources
9. Friendly relationships
10. Good formal communication flows
11. Good informal communication flows

Table 2.1 shows the results obtained.

Results show that companies declare a pretty high integration, although interesting differences can be noted for the different levels. As for the interaction component of integration, it appears that Sales and Marketing share information in a noticeable way, although this seems mostly due to informal processes rather than formal ones.

---

[3] All ratings are based on a 1–7 scale, where 1 is limited and 7 high.

| **Table 2.1** | Different levels of integration achieved |

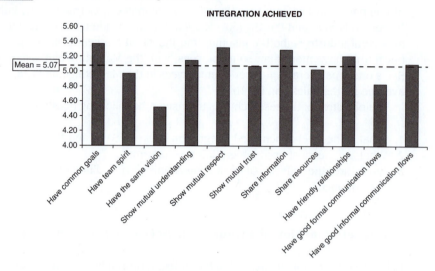

Thus, this result suggests that communication systems seem to rely more on informal, personal communication flows, rather than formalized structured ones.

This result seems also confirmed by the fact that there is a high level of collaboration achieved in terms of goal-sharing, and mutual respect, trust and understanding. Hence, the cooperative component behind integration seems very well developed, and this may lead to more informal exchange processes. Interestingly, but not surprisingly, the dimension which gets the lowest score is shared vision. The development of a shared vision requires the creation of a collective mindset encompassing the future of the market and the position of the company in it, and this is the hardest part of integration to create and nurture. Moreover, this result may also indicate that in many companies, the vision is only held by top management or the entrepreneur, so depriving the rest of the organization of a powerful common attitude to guide it towards the future.

The use of integration mechanisms

The research investigated the use of different integration mechanisms. Managers were asked to rate the frequency of their own company or strategic business unit (SBU)'s use of 14 integrating mechanisms. The list was selected with the aim of covering the majority of the managerial processes and structural devices a company may use to foster innovation:

1. Formal meetings between Marketing and Sales personnel
2. Customer visits made jointly by Marketing and Sales personnel
3. Marketing personnel attending Sales department meetings
4. Sales personnel attending Marketing department meetings
5. Marketing and Sales personnel jointly attending executive education courses
6. Marketing and Sales personnel jointly attending team-building training
7. Job rotation between Marketing and Sales departments

8. Transferring of personnel from Marketing to Sales departments (or vice versa) during their career progression
9. Cross-functional teams (CFTs), including Marketing and Sales personnel, responsible for market-related decisions
10. Reward systems for Marketing and Sales personnel based on common objectives
11. Information-sharing between Marketing and Sales departments
12. Integrating roles (e.g. Trade Marketing Managers, Key Account Managers)
13. Physical proximity of Marketing and Sales offices
14. Use of ICT to communicate and exchange information (email, video conferencing, databases, internet)

Table 2.2 displays the results obtained.

For managerial systems, the results show that communication mechanisms are the most used. Face to face communication through formal meetings, the participation of personnel of one unit in meetings of the other unit, the use of ICT and the use of other devices of informal sharing enhance the exchange of information between Sales and Marketing departments. Further, reward systems based on common objectives appear to be very much used, whereas job rotation and transfer of personnel across the two units do not seem to encounter much favour. As for structural mechanisms, integrating roles, physical proximity as well as the use of cross-functional decision-making teams appear to be quite common in the companies investigated.

The effects of integrating mechanisms

The last question the research was designed to answer was how effective is the use of different integrating mechanisms. Since effectiveness can be evaluated at

Table 2.2 Use of Integration mechanisms

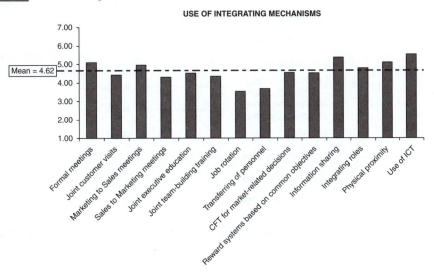

different levels, four different measures have been chosen to give evidence for this factor. Two are strictly related to the integration issue: integration achieved (as a combination of the different levels presented previously) and perceived effectiveness of integration. Perceived effectiveness measures the level of satisfaction regarding Sales–Marketing integration, considered as the perception of benefits compared to effort. It plays an important role because empowerment and commitment have a perceptual, subjective foundation. Hence, more than the actual integration achieved what drives individual behaviours is a comparison of the effort to be invested in relation to the benefits that may be gained. Then a couple of organizational performance measures have been selected, in order to give evidence for the broader impact interdepartmental integration can have on the results of the company. Superior customer value represents a combination of the capacity of the company to be responsive to customer needs, to develop creative solutions for customers' needs, to be quick in its market actions, and to innovate. Market performance is a combination of typical market performance indicators: sales growth, market share, customer retention, customer satisfaction and profitability. Managers have been asked to rate their company/SBU in comparison with its major competitors in the last three years.

To measure the effect of each single mechanism with the performance measures selected, a linear regression analysis has been run. Results are shown in the following Figures (2.8, 2.9, 2.10 and 2.11). Dotted lines represent non significant relationships: it

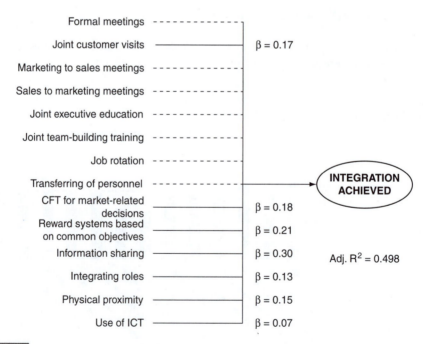

Figure 2.8 The effects of integration mechanisms on integration achieved

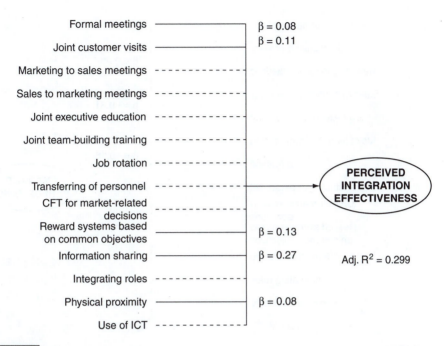

Figure 2.9   The effects of integration mechanisms on perceived integration effectiveness

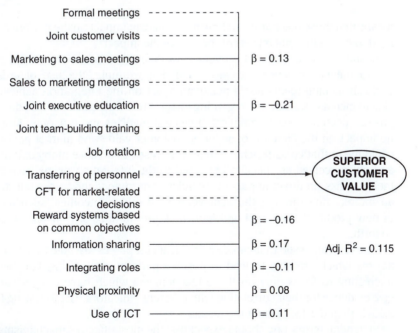

Figure 2.10   The effects of integration mechanisms on the creation of superior customer value

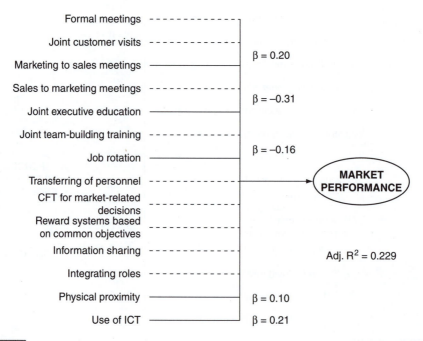

Figure 2.11 The effects of integration mechanisms on the creation of market performance

means that those mechanisms show no significant impact on the performance indicator used. Beta coefficients represent the size of the impact.

Results show that the effectiveness of different mechanisms varies a lot according to the performance indicator used. For example, the use of cross-functional decision-making teams has a positive impact on the integration achieved but is not able to increase satisfaction regarding integration, maybe because the decision-making process becomes more complicated since it involves more people. Moreover, it has no impact on the creation of superior customer value and market performance. This could mean that cross-functional teams are used to achieve many different objectives and not perceived as specifically related to the integration of the two units. Further, their use has no direct impact on broader performance indicators but they may have an indirect one through the achievement of other outcomes, such as the number of new products developed and launched, the number of new accounts served and so forth.

One relevant issue that can be raised is if companies are able to select those mechanisms which are able to lead to positive performance effects. For this reason it is interesting to focus only on those mechanisms which have a significant effect and give evidence for their correlation with different indicators. The following Figures (2.12, 2.13, 2.14 and 2.15) present the results.

In general terms, one should expect that the most effective mechanisms are also the most used (that is, one could expect those mechanisms to be positioned close to the diagonal in the graphs).

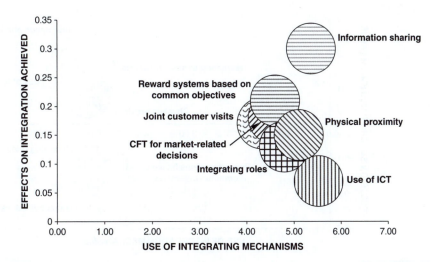

Figure 2.12 The relationship between use of mechanisms and impact on integration achieved

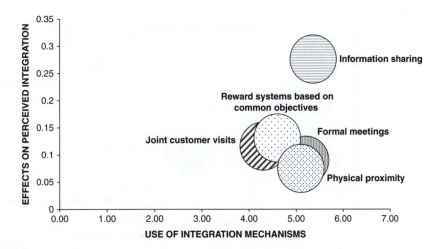

Figure 2.13 The relationship between use of mechanisms and impact on perceived effectiveness of integration

As for integration indicators, results show that companies are well able to select those mechanisms which have a positive impact on integration, although some do not affect the perceived effectiveness of integration.

As for broader performance indicators, it is interesting to note that some of the mechanisms used have a negative impact on the creation of superior customer value and market performance.

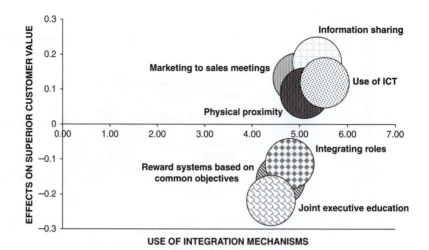

Figure 2.14 The relationship between use of mechanisms and impact on superior customer value

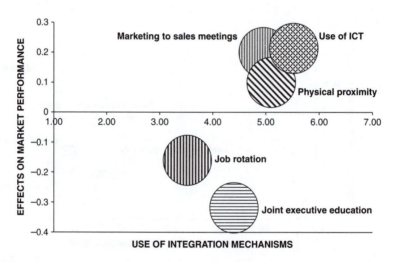

Figure 2.15 The relationship between use of mechanisms and impact on market performance

In conclusion, the results of the research confirm that:

1. Integration mechanisms are able to lead to enhanced integration between Sales and marketing but not all mechanisms perform the same way. Hence, companies should carefully choose a combination of mechanisms that are consistent with the levels of integration that they expect to reach;

2. The use of integration mechanisms can have both positive and negative effects, because the benefits and the efforts connected to the use of each of them are different. Hence, companies should select those mechanisms which are most consistent with their culture, organizational structure and managerial systems;

3. Given the differential nature of mechanisms and the impact of different performance indicators, companies should monitor regularly the level of integration achieved and that still needed, in order to design a combination of mechanisms which is able to close the gap.

Summary

The integration between Sales and Marketing is a hot topic for many companies today. Although the benefits of an effective coordination of these two units are easy to imagine, the achievement of this objective is quite an arduous task. In fact, there are several barriers that make Sales–Marketing integration difficult to achieve, given that Sales and Marketing people often do not share the same cultural background and organizations do not necessarily have structures and processes in place that support effective integration. This chapter has focused on the description of the levels at which integration can be pursued and the different integration mechanisms companies can use, in order to achieve the benefits stemming from highly integrated units. Specifically, managerial systems and changes in the organizational structure are the two categories of mechanisms that seem to promise the best results. In order to support theory with good practice, the results of a survey conducted on a pan-European sample of companies report on the level of Sales–Marketing integration achieved and the integration mechanisms mostly used to gain this result.

Key points

1. In today's modern markets integration between Sales and Marketing can provide the company with many different benefits, although it is not without risks.

2. According to several market and organizational factors a certain amount of integration is beneficial, but this does not necessarily mean following the 'the more the better' rule.

3. Sales–Marketing integration can be achieved at different levels: activities, decisions, goals, vision.

4. Cultural, organizational and infrastructural barriers can limit or impede the integration between the two organizational units.

5. The identification of the specific level of integration to be achieved is a prerequisite to choosing the appropriate set of integration mechanisms.

6. The results of a Pan-European research provide a good overview of the set of integration mechanisms currently used by a number of European companies, and highlights the ones that are more impactful in terms of integration achieved, superior customer value created and market performance.

A sales-marketing integration audit tool

A tool for assessing the state of Sales–Marketing integration of your business unit/company and the type of integration mechanisms that can foster integration

In my business unit/company, Sales and Marketing departments:

	Strongly disagree						Strongly agree
Have common goals	1	2	3	4	5	6	7
Have team spirit	1	2	3	4	5	6	7
Have the same vision	1	2	3	4	5	6	7
Show mutual understanding	1	2	3	4	5	6	7
Show mutual respect	1	2	3	4	5	6	7
Show mutual trust	1	2	3	4	5	6	7
Share information	1	2	3	4	5	6	7
Share resources	1	2	3	4	5	6	7
Have friendly relationships	1	2	3	4	5	6	7
Have good formal communication flows	1	2	3	4	5	6	7
Have good informal communication flows	1	2	3	4	5	6	7

To what extent are the following mechanisms used in your business unit/company to achieve integration between Sales and Marketing departments:

	Never used						Very often used
Formal meetings between Marketing and Sales personnel	1	2	3	4	5	6	7
Marketing and Sales personnel make joint customer visits	1	2	3	4	5	6	7
Marketing personnel attend Sales department meetings	1	2	3	4	5	6	7
Sales personnel attend Marketing department meetings	1	2	3	4	5	6	7
Marketing and Sales personnel jointly attend executive education courses	1	2	3	4	5	6	7

Marketing and Sales personnel jointly attend team-building training activities	1	2	3	4	5	6	7
Job rotation between Marketing and Sales departments	1	2	3	4	5	6	7
Transferring of personnel from Marketing to Sales departments (or vice versa) during their career progression	1	2	3	4	5	6	7
Cross-functional teams, including Marketing and Sales personnel, are responsible for market-related decisions	1	2	3	4	5	6	7
Reward systems for Marketing and Sales personnel are based on common objectives	1	2	3	4	5	6	7
Information-sharing between Marketing and Sales departments	1	2	3	4	5	6	7
Managers whose role in the organization is to bridge between Marketing and Sales departments (e.g., Trade Marketing Managers, Key Account Managers)	1	2	3	4	5	6	7
Marketing and Sales offices are in close physical proximity to each other	1	2	3	4	5	6	7
Marketing and Sales personnel use ICT to communicate and exchange information (email, video conferencing, databases, internet)	1	2	3	4	5	6	7

References

Cespedes, F.V. (1993) 'Coordinating Sales and Marketing in Consumer Goods Firms', *Journal of Consumer Marketing*, 10 (2): 37–55.

Dawes, P.L. and Massey, G.R. (2005) 'Antecedents of Conflict in Marketing's Cross-functional Relationship with Sales', *European Journal of Marketing*, 39 (11/12): 1327–44.

Dawes, P.L. and Massey, G.R. (2006) 'A Study of Relationship Effectiveness between Marketing and Sales Managers in Business Markets', *Journal of Business and Industrial Marketing*, 21 (6): 346–60.

Dewsnap, B. and Jobber D. (2002) 'A Social Psychological Model of Relations between Marketing and Sales', *European Journal of Marketing*, 36 (7/8): 874–94.

Dewsnap, B. and Jobber D. (2000) 'The Sales–Marketing Interface in Consumer Packaged-goods Companies: A Conceptual Framework', *Journal of Personal Selling and Sales Management*, 20 (2): 109–19.

Fisher, R.J., Maltz, E. and Jaworski, B.J. (1997) 'Enhancing Communication between Marketing and Engineering: The Moderating Role of Relative Functional Identification', *Journal of Marketing*, 61 (July): 54–70.

Griffin, A. and Hauser, J.R. (1996) 'Integrating R&D and Marketing: A Review and Analysis of the Literature', *Journal of Product Innovation Management*, 13 (3): 191–215.

Guenzi, P. and Troilo, G. (2006) 'Developing Marketing Capabilities for Customer Value Creation through Marketing-Sales Integration', *Industrial Marketing Management*, 35 (8): 974–88.

Guenzi, P. and Troilo, G. (2007) 'The Joint Contribution of Marketing and Sales to the Creation of Superior Customer Value', *Journal of Business Research*, 60 (2): 98–107.

Gupta, A., Raj, S.P. and Wilemon D. (1986) 'A Model for Studying R&D–Marketing Interface in the Product Innovation Process', *Journal of Marketing*, 50 (April): 7–17.

Homburg, C. and Jensen, O. (2007) 'The Thought Worlds of Marketing and Sales: Which Differences Make a Difference?', *Journal of Marketing*, 71 (July): 124–42.

Homburg, C., Jensen, O. and Krohmer, H. (2008) 'Configurations of Marketing and Sales: A Taxonomy', *Journal of Marketing*, 72 (March): 133–54.

Kahn, K.B. (1996) 'Interdepartmental Integration: A Definition with Implications for Product Development Performance', *Journal of Product Innovation Management*, 13 (2): 137–51.

Kahn, K.B. (2001) 'Market orientation, interdepartmental integration, and product development performance', *Journal of Product Innovation Management*, 18 (5): 314–23.

Kahn, K.B. and Mentzer, J.T. (1998) 'Marketing's Integration with Other Departments', *Journal of Business Research*, 41 (1): 53–62.

Kotler, P., Rackham, N. and Krishnaswamy, S. (2006) 'Ending the War between Sales & Marketing', *Harvard Business Review*, 84 (7/8)): 68–78.

Krohmer, H., Homburg, C. and Workman, J.P. (2002) 'Should Marketing be Cross-functional? Conceptual Development and International Empirical Evidence', *Journal of Business Research*, 55 (6): 451–65.

Leenders, M.A.A.M. and Wierenga, B. (2002) 'The Effectiveness of Different Mechanisms for Integrating Marketing and R&D', *Journal of Product Innovation Management*, 19 (4): 305–17.

Matthyssens, P. and Johnston, W.J. (2006) 'Marketing and Sales: Optimization of a Neglected Relationship', *Journal of Business and Industrial Marketing*, 21 (6): 338–45.

Maltz, E. (1997), An Enhanced Framework for Improving Cooperation between Marketing and Other Functions: The Differential Role of Integrating Mechanisms, *Journal of Market Focused Management* 2, 83–98.

Piercy, N. (1986) 'The Role and Function of the Chief Marketing Executive and the Marketing Department. A Study of Medium-Sized Companies in the UK', *Journal of Marketing Management*, 1 (3): 265–89.

Rouziès, D., Anderson, E., Kohli, A.K., Michaels, R.E., Weitz, B.A. and Zoltners, A.A. (2005) 'Sales and Marketing Integration: A Proposed Framework', *Journal of Personal Selling and Sales Management*, 25 (2): 113–22.

Ruekert, Robert W. and Walker, Orville C. Jr. (1987) 'Marketing's Interaction with Other Functional Units: A Conceptual Framework and Empirical Evidence', *Journal of Marketing* 51 (1), 1–19.

Salazar, J. (2008) 'Look at Each Others' Eyes, Smile, and Be Happy', *Journal of Happiness Studies*, 8 (2): 26–39.

Troilo, G. (2006) *Marketing Knowledge Management: Managing Knowledge in Market Oriented Companies*. Cheltenham: Edward Elgar.

Troilo, G. De Luca, L. and Guenzi P. (2009) 'Dispersion of Influence between Marketing and Sales. Its Effects on Superior Customer Value and Market Performance', *Industrial Marketing Management*, 38 (8): 872–882.

Workman, J.P. Jr., Homburg, C. and Gruner, K. (1998) 'Marketing Organization: An Integrative Framework of Dimensions and Determinants', *Journal of Marketing*, 62 (July): 21–41.

Further reading

Beverland, M., Steel, M. and Dapiran, G.P. (2006) 'Cultural Frames that Drive Sales and Marketing Apart: An Exploratory Study', *Journal of Business and Industrial Marketing*, 21 (6): 386–94.

Evans, K.R. and Schlacter, J.L. (1985) 'The Role of Sales Managers and Salespeople in a Marketing Information System', *Journal of Personal Selling and Sales Management*, 5 (2): 49–58.

Homburg, C., Workman J.P. Jr. and Jensen, O. (2000) 'Fundamental Changes in Marketing Organization: The Movement toward a Customer-Focused Organizational Structure', *Journal of the Academy of Marketing Science*, 28 (4): 459–78.

Matthyssens, P. and Johnston, W.J. (2006) 'Marketing and sales: Optimization of a Neglected Relationship' *Journal of Business and Industrial Marketing*, 21 (6): 338–45.

Strahle, W.M., Spiro, R.L. and Acito F. (1996) 'Marketing and Sales: Strategic Alignment and Functional Implementation', *Journal of Personal Selling and Sales Management*, 16 (1): 1–17.

3

Designing and implementing a Key Account Management strategy

Marco Aurelio Sisti

Contents

Learning objectives

After reading this chapter, you should be able to understand the fundamentals of Key Account Management (KAM) programme development:

- The rationale of a KAM programme and its complexity.

- How a key account relationship may evolve over time.

- The typical opportunities and risks associated with a KAM programme.

- How to segment the customer portfolio with KAM logic.

- What a Key Account Plan is and how it can be organized.

- Some critical organizational issues for KAM implementation.

Chapter outline

Managers and companies have long been intrigued by and involved in the development of new competitive selling approaches. In the last two decades, the fast rise of KAM programmes has caught the attention of both academics and executives. But often the business community seems to underestimate the real impact of KAM on the market and on sales organizations. This chapter aims to provide executives with some ideas, models and practical tools to enable them to learn, or to enhance their knowledge, about this fashionable relationship selling approach. To introduce this topic, we start by presenting a case history to stimulate your attention on the development of a brand new KAM programme. Then we go through some managerial issues (based on a literature review and case histories) before ending with some key points.

Rossi Motoriduttori Group[1]

Rossi Motoriduttori Group Spa (RMG) is an Italian firm based in Modena, in northern Italy. It is a subsidiary of Habasit AG, market leader in the production and sales of industrial conveyors. RMG is one of Europe's largest industrial companies for the production and sales of gear reducers and motors, electrical brake motors and similar products. In the past it has supplied Original Equipment Manufacturers (OEMs) and, marginally, final industrial customers. The sales organization consists of direct sales people and dealers, located worldwide.

For decades products have been the company's priority in value creation. But since innovations started to slow down several years ago, service has become an important part of the value package. Recently, searching for new competitive advantages, RMG's Board realized that a static product-centric selling approach could potentially weaken its leadership position. Customers (both OEM and end-users), especially the more dynamic and competitive ones, clearly demonstrated they were more demanding, sophisticated and looking for higher value based on solutions rather than just the supply of products. Selling integrated *customer-centric value propositions*, projected to meet more sophisticated needs is seen as a key success factor at RMG. The new deal has become 'to sell more and better' by developing profitable and long lasting 'selected' relationships, even if this means opening themselves up to major risks. With a customer base of thousands of units, and a sales force composed of typical 'traditional' geographically focused sales people, trying to achieve these goals by developing a KAM programme was a big gamble for the whole company. RMG started to take on the KAM philosophy, developing a strategic selling approach for the first time in its history. The decision to explore this option was originally 'propelled' by Habasit AG. Around 2004, the Swiss company controlling RMG started with a deep rethink of its marketing strategy, aiming to face new challenging international competitors. It developed an international KAM programme designed to manage the corporate accounts centrally (with local support from the subsidiaries) and the national ones locally. The experience gleaned during the programme convinced the top managers to share it with subsidiary controlled companies like RMG. So in 2007 the Italian company launched a brand new programme, which is still being developed and implemented, to confront both internal and external challenges and difficulties.

Figure 3.1 RMG's motors and gear reducers

[1] *Special thanks to Rossi Motoriduttori and Habasit AG's management, and to Andrea Lazzari for his precious support while writing this case history.*

Opportunities in RMG

Despite its longstanding market leadership founded on product excellence, in the last few years the customer need for value has been changing, mismatching the traditional selling approaches. With more demanding markets and competitors who were still product-oriented, RMG has seen a great opportunity in building or consolidating more solid and long lasting relationships. Fuel for the new approach has been and still is the numerous potential mutual benefits: for example, deeper reciprocal knowledge and privileged information access (technical and commercial); superior value proposition and customization thanks to specific technical and commercial support (for both products and services); priority access to product and market innovations; selective benefits from sharing reciprocal business networks. For RMG this has meant working on relationships to win new business, increasing the share of whole customer spending and benefitting from positive referrals.

Key account identification

The company has traditionally served many industries, principally focusing sales on the OEMs. To develop a well targeted KAM programme, RMG first resegmented and ranked the strategic markets in order to prioritize them (e.g. plastics and mechanical handling). Inclusion of a customer in a strategic market has been the critical factor in identifying it as one of the key accounts. Customers (current and potential ones) have been ranked using economic and competitive data (i.e. turnover and potential purchases of products and services, customer share). The analytical tools used to segment the portfolio have been *ABC Analysis* on turnover and an *Attractivity Index*. The final segmentation divided the portfolio into three tiers: strategic key accounts (high performance – high potential); potential key accounts (high potential – low performance); maintenance and/or marginal accounts (low potential – low performance). The first two tiers have been redistributed among the sales force by putting them under the responsibility of the Key Account Managers. The remaining accounts have been shifted to a different sales structure, including a distributor. Formal Key Account Plans have not yet been developed and implemented. They are still a work in progress.

Key account organization and incentive management

The move towards a true KAM programme has been progressive. The first big change in 'key accountization' of the firm had to do with customer portfolio management. Recently, the sales force has, in fact, been managing thousands of accounts. Now, following the first strategic segmentation, the targeted portfolio was reduced by about 75 per cent. Only 25 per cent of the whole portfolio is considered truly strategic, but the company has decided to approach the KAM logic progressively, avoiding implementing too many deep changes too quickly into the sales organization. The first change has been the move from a geographic to a market specialization. The new sales force has been required to focus not only on specific strategic industries, but also on the key accounts. This will be increasingly possible in the future following the development of an effective customer database. The sales force's job has been reviewed in depth and adapted to the new relational selling approaches. *Training* on KAM logic has been projected to facilitate the adoption of the new sales role of developing wider and deeper business relationships in the key accounts. In the past, a real point of weakness for RMG, was its limited capacity to network with the key roles in the customer's purchasing centre. This was the result of a closed selling culture and a wide array of existing and potential customers in the portfolio. Too many customers and too much spread proved too time consuming for the sales force.

KAM: an ongoing process

RMG in 2010 is still in a developmental stage: a formal key account budget (for expenses, as well as other costs) has not yet been fully activated. The company is designing and fine-tuning new internal dedicated processes to help and to support the Key Account Managers in their 'new' jobs. A Key Account Manager is progressively evolving from a barely coordinator role, to a real managerial one, fully in charge of the company's key accounts. This is a critical factor whose importance for the programme's success is well known at RMG. Nowadays, team working is considered a common activity, but it is still too limited on specific projects, and is not based on widely shared cross-functional and formal processes. There is a growing need to move from informal teams to semi-formal ones. Dedicated teams at this developmental stage are still considered premature. The company has started systematically to involve more and more people in the key accounts' life and management. Finally, some significant changes have been made in the compensation plan. KAM-based incentives have been introduced to motivate people to develop the business strongly in the existing key accounts and in potential new ones. Since most Key Account Managers are part of the direct sales force, the current pay mix is made up of a continuing fixed part and a small variable portion. Incentives are linked to the achievement of both quantitative and qualitative goals, which at present are set only for each individual Key Account Manager. Generally speaking, 'key accountization' of the sales unit and of the company as a whole is an ongoing process.

Introduction: what is Key Account Management?

Key Account Management (KAM) can be likened to a managerial philosophy (Ojasalo 2001) and to a complex managerial approach that considers it possible and advisable to provide special treatment for individual customers as well as customized solutions. In other words, KAM aims to capture and to deliver a superior value, 'from' and 'to' the best customers. How? By managing them with clear priorities and showing a higher level of internal and external coordination so as to build long lasting, remunerative relationships (McDonald et al. 1997). Unlike other approaches, KAM strives to pool some of the most important resources of both the seller and the buyer. For the first, the approach sets in motion a small internal organizational revolution by asking some sales people to move from traditional selling approaches to modern and more relational ones. For the buyer, in order to achieve real coherence, the approach requires progressively higher investment in the financial and non-financial relationship. KAM programmes, at *local* or *global/international level*, distinguish themselves from other selling approaches because of their systematic aims to manage the strategic accounts with clear priorities and a superior level of customization for products and/or services; to provide mutual seller-buyer interaction, cooperation and coordination of reciprocal resources; and to have seller-buyer team coordination and integration (either cross-functional or functional). All KAM programmes should be designed to achieve consistent relational, competitive and economic benefits. Their concrete implementation may depend a great deal on the level of the strategic relationship developed (or developable) with the key accounts. In fact, understanding how a relationship may evolve strategically over time, is a necessary preliminary condition before developing or fine-tuning a formal KAM programme.

According to the size of the key accounts, their international nature (multinational, international or national) and the degree of procurement centralization, the company may develop the strategic programme at global and/or local level. In the first case, worldwide customer leadership is assigned to a dedicated account manager responsible for planning, organization and coordination of global key account strategy. He or she is leader of an international team and manager of the response to diversities in the local market. At this level, international coordination is a critical issue and the development of sophisticated virtual working platforms for many companies is a necessary precondition to guarantee fast managerial processes. On the other hand, only a purely national/local organization is required when local key accounts show a limited degree of internationalization or simply highly decentralized governance.

What are the stages of a KAM relationship?

Selling relationships are dynamic and difficult to classify since their status usually depends on many environmental and internal factors. Several studies (Wotruba 1991; Millman and Wilson 1995; McDonald, Rogers and Woodburn 2000; Wagner and Johnson 2004) conducted in the past have sought to isolate and make a deep analysis of the different possible stages of the buyer-seller relationship. The model presented in Figure 3.2 helps do this by clustering selling relationships into five possible stages. They are plotted along the diagonal, starting from 'very poor' (bottom left) to 'very close' (top right) relationships. Each customer position on the diagonal is a function of the buyer's and the seller's common strategic intents and investments in a strategic relationship. These can be the result of several factors, for example, customer share; reciprocal involvement in innovative activities and joint profitable projects; the quality and quantity of shared strategic information; the length and stability of purchases; the type and size of supply agreements; the level of integration achieved by the organizations. Sales managers must weigh these factors coherently within the specific business context in

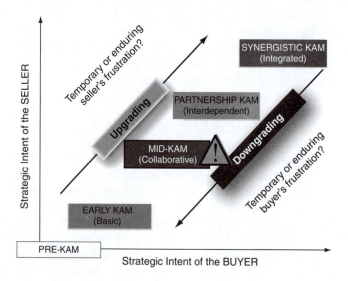

Figure 3.2   Stages of KAM relationships
Source: adapted from Millman and Wilson 1995; McDonald et al. 2000.

order to position each account in the model. In doing so, they should remember that this is a dynamic model: some accounts may in fact move through higher or lower stages. Assessing each customer's actual stage is thus a critical exercise, necessary to predict future stages and in turn to allocate profitably the company's strategic resources. This needs to be done while keeping clearly in mind that not all potential key accounts (typically those positioned in the lower stages) may be interested in upgrading their current relationship to higher stages. To enable you to apply the model to your actual management context, we will now explore the features of the different relationship stages in detail.

Pre-KAM

The seller and the buyer are in the pre-trading phase. The buying company is considered as having high potential to develop a solid, long lasting business relationship. Exchange of data and information are prior to the decision to engage in transactions. The mutual strategic intent is minimal and trust is mainly based on reputation. Negotiation is mainly if not exclusively price-based; the selling and buying behaviour is essentially transactional.

Early-KAM

This is the very beginning, often temporary stage of a strategic relationship. The potential key account formally enters the company's portfolio. The customer share is usually very small. The selling approach is still almost always price-driven and very transactional. Much emphasis is placed on the search for efficiency, especially by the buyer. The relationship is far from showing long lasting mutual investments, trust or deep sharing of sensitive pieces of information. The seller is like one vendor among several, constantly being tested. The buyer and the salesperson are the key players in the relationship. Long lasting permanence of the account at this early stage would suggest that the sales manager reconsider the account's actual status for the company (from potential key account to normal or marginal account) or review and update ineffective sales strategies.

Mid-KAM

Here the real mutual cooperation begins on the basis of higher customer openness and the supplier's perceived credibility. The customer share starts to be consistent, positioning the seller as a preferred supplier (McDonald, Millman and Rogers 1997). Contact between the two parties is multifunctional, often under the formal coordination of a Key Account Manager. Access to sensitive data and information is higher. In negotiations, price is still a critically important factor, but no longer the main one. The buyer should be, in general, more open and available to evaluate the entire value proposition. A company with a very high percentage of key accounts in this stage is at high risk. Exit barriers for key accounts are in fact still low: exit is, unfortunately, easy even though supplier investments are considerable and profits not yet very high.

The relationship may remain at this stage for a long time without necessarily moving to a partnership. Deeper analysis and formal Key Account Plans are introduced for some accounts, but the level of formal coordination and integration with the account is still low.

Partnership-KAM

This is the real strategic stage where the two parties start to be interdependent in several ways. Maturity shows a common acknowledgement of reciprocal importance, a high level of investments in mutual innovations, preponderance of the seller in the customer's purchasing and a very intensive cooperation and interaction. Selling is truly relational and often supported by a consistent integrated team selling approach. The Key Account Manager prepares a formal Key Account Plan for most or for every account. He/she is meant to share part of this entire plan with the customer team. Long lasting relationships are planned (even formally) well in advance, with great attention to balancing investments and return on investment. Information exchange, including of sensitive data, starts to be continuous and widely accepted by both the organizations. Entry barriers at this level may discourage potential competitors from investing in and fighting for these accounts. Exit and entrance barriers start to be very high; to withdraw from the relationship might be difficult and very expensive.

Synergistic-KAM

At this stage, interaction achieves the highest possible level of intensity and development. The two organizations start systematically to create joint value in the market place, rather than as two separate entities. The seller and the buyer are fully integrated, even formally. Vertical channel integration is a common option.

Frustration or Transit-KAM

What happens if a key account ends up in the top left or in the bottom right area of Figure 3.2? These cases must be carefully considered when managing the dynamics of key account relationships. They show an asymmetric level of mutual investment and strategic intent between the buyer and the seller. In the top left area, the risk for the seller of losing time and money is very high. The Key Account Manager should assess how feasible and affordable it is to plan additional and innovative selling efforts in order to move the relationship up to the diagonal. In the case of endurance failure, there might be no other alternative than to reduce the selling effort. Experience tells us that it is not uncommon unfortunately to find potential key accounts with little or no interest in upgrading their current relationship. Ultimately, the bottom right area is also very critical, albeit not easy to assess. There, a key account tends to perceive the relationship as asymmetrically disadvantageous. Usually it requires careful and timely KAM intervention in order to manage the account's expectations or to improve the seller's investment so as to move the relationship up to the planned stage.

Main benefits and pitfalls of running a KAM programme

The growing complexity and dynamics of industrial markets constantly push a selection of buyers and sellers to pay more attention to building more profitable and successful long-term relationships based on quality, mutual trust and business partnerships. Along the supply chain, enhancing production, delivery and adding differential value have become critical for both parties. Sellers who have decided to do this, have started to introduce changes in both their local and global go-to-market strategies by updating (or dramatically redesigning) their sales channels and sales force organizations. Not surprisingly, a recent survey has shown that about 76 per cent of the companies interviewed introduced important changes in their sales structures.[2] About 80 per cent of them did this with the clear purpose of refocusing on their key accounts. Why have so many companies become highly sensitive to KAM practices? Reasons may vary widely depending on industries and market specifics; nonetheless some common factors can be brought to light. There is growing sensitivity to the effects of globalization (including the speed of market changes), to lean production systems, and to cost savings but on condition of retaining high quality products and services. For sellers, the response time, the capability of adding and delivering value faster than costs, has become a clear 'key success factor', albeit at the price of consistent business risks (McDonald et al. 2000). At the same time, buyers have usually become more powerful, demanding and aware of marketing dynamics and they are looking for highly reliable suppliers at global and/or local level.

So, investing strategic, often scarce, resources in long term relationships is a serious task. Too many companies have discovered how difficult it is, and how much commitment and patience are needed to make it work successfully. Many sales and marketing managers are not yet convinced of the positive effects associated with KAM either at local or global level. This, in some cases, may depend on their being only in the early stage of their programme development: a young programme needs more time to be effective and productive. Sometimes negative perceptions may also depend on the lack of commitment internally, from senior managers or sales people. Externally, on the customer side, we might consider the possibility of low interest in developing real collaborative relationships.

Before running a KAM programme and before demanding in turn that customers invest in a long term relationship, senior managers should carefully analyse the potential benefits and risks, and to what degree the strategic goals of buyers and sellers match. Let us analyse some of them.

Benefits associated with the development of a local and global KAM relationship for the seller may vary widely depending on the company's marketing strategies and goals. For simplicity's sake, they can be grouped in three main benefit categories: relational, competitive and economic. The first are usually necessary to gain a competitive advantage and fundamental to achieve economic gains (Figure 3.3). In the following lists some typical examples of benefits are presented.

---

[2] McKinsey, *Customer and Channel Management Survey.*

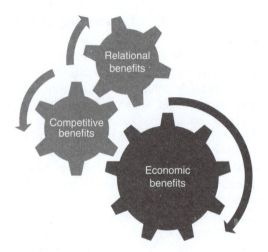

Figure 3.3   The wheels of KAM benefits

Relational benefits

- **Knowledge**. Deeper and wider customer knowledge.
- **Network**. Opportunity to develop and consolidate a long term relational network inside the customer's purchasing centre. In the external marketplace, the seller can take advantage of a potentially higher level of positive referrals. Finally, the seller may also exploit the buyer's sales and after-sales channels to provide a higher level of service that takes advantage of an existing local network provided by the buyer.
- **Image**. Positive impact when the key account's image is strong.
- **Exit Barriers**. Opportunity to build exit barriers for the key account. Tightening the relationship, the supplier can make it difficult to withdraw from the relationship because of high estimated switching costs.
- **Processes**. The challenging relationship can push the supplier to improve its internal processes making them faster and more effective. The company may also have the opportunity of learning a great deal about how to improve directly from its experiences with the key account.
- **Planning**. Due to a stronger relationship and mutual trust, the company can secure in advance an increasing number of orders, with a positive impact for both production and sales planning processes.

Competitive benefits

- **Market share**. Possible improvements of both customer share (penetration) and cross-selling in the key accounts.
- **Value**. Stronger capability to offer superior competitive value, as a result of deeper customer knowledge.

- **Entry Barriers**. Opportunity to build entry barriers for dangerous competitors. Based on the stronger relationship and wider access to customer information, the Key Account Manager should be able to make a competitor's life more difficult. Basically, he/she should be able to anticipate competitors' moves.
- **Business Development**. At the Partnership- or Synergistic-KAM stages, there is the opportunity to join the customer's business network at local and/or international level. This may prove useful for entering new markets and for strengthening the company's presence in existing competitive and attractive markets (Möller and Halinen 1999).
- **Innovation**. Chance to develop joint incremental or radical product innovations.

Economic benefits

- **Sales**. Improved sales as a result of the higher trust, customer knowledge and perceived value.
- **Behaviour**. Possible reduction of customer's sensitivity to price leverage. This is a common consequence of closer relationships based on trust.
- **Savings**. Costs savings result from economies of experience and more effective coordination with the key account's units. The lean philosophy can be very helpful and economical for both players.
- **Pricing**. Opportunity to improve the coordination of pricing strategies for the customer at international level. This may happen if the company develops an international KAM programme designed to centralize customer management.

For the buyer, benefits may vary widely depending on its strategies, business needs and organization. Benefits can also be influenced by the type of product categories handled by the seller, their financial impact on the buyer's profits and the associated supply risks (Kraljic 1983; Van Weele 2000). Generally speaking, most of the benefits listed above can reasonably be adapted to the buyer's standpoint.

Main pitfalls

Doubts about the real effectiveness of KAM are often linked to the appearance of dangerous side effects. Some of these are related to the seller's organization and internal processes. Others simply refer to unforeseen and undesired customer behaviours. An excessive rise in customer expectations and demand is always around the corner, pushing the seller to face unplanned additional selling costs. This is the case in relationships that have moved for too long to the top left corner of the model illustrated in Figure 3.2. Negative effects may also impact the buyer's organization. Where there is a lack of senior manager commitment, unclear procedures and weak internal support devoted to KAM, managers may feel isolated within the company. They may be sucked into the middle of a matrix structure that easily fuels deep and frequent cross-unit and cross-function battles. Conflict may arise due to ill will among the other sales people or, even worse, from area managers who may not be willing to provide local help to account management. If not adequately motivated and involved in KAM implementation, area managers may in fact consider it as simply a way in which they will lose business power and control over the company's best customers.

Recently, a leading international company in the automotive aftermarket business developed a strategic programme focused on its dealers. After an initial strategic segmentation to assign the key accounts' status, the company redesigned its entire sales force organization, formally introducing the new role of Key Account Manager. As their job title suggests, the aim was for these managers to become immediately fully responsible for the best dealers and to report directly to the national sales director. But local territorial support was still a critical factor and the company was concerned that an internal silent 'war' could ensue, led by area managers. So it decided to develop an integrated incentive system, which guaranteed higher involvement and cross cooperation. More examples relating to KAM risks can be easily found. The point is, however, to remember that potential side effects can be foreseen and managed if there is solid commitment and sponsorship by the company's senior management. It is a matter of regular monitoring so that timely recoveries and adjustments can be made.

How to develop an effective KAM programme: a managerial process

The development and the implementation of a KAM programme can be seen as a circular managerial process, as depicted in Figure 3.4. It ideally begins by assessing the mutual benefits and risks for the seller and the buyer (Step 1). Executives, as described earlier in the chapter, must evaluate the strategic fit of these benefits with their business

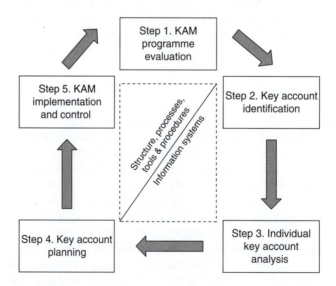

Figure 3.4 The KAM process

goals. For companies which have already initiated a similar programme, this means running a periodical programme review to confirm, adjust or even discontinue it. For those who have not run the programme previously, KAM requires the adoption of a new managerial philosophy, the design of a specialized key account-centric structure, processes and procedures, and of course adequate support.

The following step (Step 2) answers a crucial question: 'Which of our current and potential accounts are the best for us?' Their identification and selection is a necessary precondition to setting up the selling processes and the sales force management strategies. This step means continually assessing all the information gathered from a comprehensive and effective customer relationship management system (customer database and marketing information systems).

Key account identification must be followed by a deeper analysis (Step 3). The evaluation of the stage of relationship, the business characteristics and goals, as well as customer needs, operating processes and performances are necessary for the entire planning process (Ojasalo 2001). The preparation of a Key Account Plan (KAP) (Step 4) is the formal step intended to provide an analytical picture of what is going on in the key account, what the seller strategically aims to achieve in it and how. Pricing strategies, level of customization and the quality of selling efforts are a typical part of key account strategies. To make them feasible and actionable, the company must also ensure some organizational minimum conditions (Step 5) relating to the decisions to be made regarding the redesign and the adaptation of the:

- sales force structure and selling processes;
- customer management procedures;
- analytical CRM;
- individual and team control and incentive system to keep the salespeople, as well as the managers involved, highly motivated (Sengupta et al 1997).

Setting up a key account strategy is best implemented by senior management making periodical check-ups of the programme and, if necessary, fine-tuning it and introducing adjustments in one or more of the five steps described.

Which are the company's key accounts?

A question that always worries senior managers is: 'Are we investing our strategic resources into our real strategic accounts?' Commercial frustration is, in fact, always around the corner and the risk of spending too much time and precious scarce resources on the wrong customers is terribly high. Regular assessments of which are the actual or the potential best accounts is a critical success factor in KAM logic. Wrong decisions at this level may 'sink' the entire programme by leading it to dramatic unsatisfactory performance. To avoid such an outcome, an effective *Customer Portfolio Analysis* (CPA) is needed. Its objective is to assess a number of different accounts according to their past performances and their potential contribution to the company's goals (McDonald, Rogers and Woodburn 2000). Periodical analysis can help executives fine-tune customer segmentation, consequently making their commercial

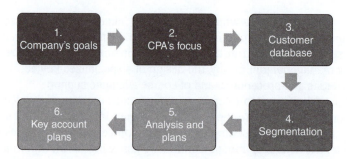

Figure 3.5   The key account identification and planning process

strategies more effective. CPA can be seen as a six-step process, as shown in Figure 3.5.

It starts with a deep understanding of the company's sales and marketing goals in relation to the KAM programme (Step 1). The company must decide if the analysis should refer to all types of customers, products, geographic markets or only to specific ones (Step 2). The fact that not all customer types and markets should be targeted by a KAM programme is not surprising. Better focus could increase the probability of its success (Napolitano 1997). CPA proceeds with the selection of the qualitative and quantitative data needed to segment customers according to their relative importance for the company's strategies (Step 3). Data can be listed, chosen and weighted according to how relevant, and reliable, they are for the company's objectives. The selection of tools is the next logical step (Step 4). Some examples are provided in this chapter in the following sections. Their adoption should lead to final segmentation and assignment of strategic status to a selection of accounts (Step 5). The CPA ends with the definition of strategic guidelines for each customer segment, key accounts included (Step 6). This provides a necessary managerial base for the preparation of Key Account Plans.

The role played by the customer database

The engine of CPA and KAM is the marketing information system and, in greater detail, the customer database (see Chapter 7). Unfortunately many companies base their key account selection analysis only on very limited databases. A poor data set can completely undermine the entire segmentation effectiveness and, consequently, KAM performance. Companies which have not yet done so, should seriously consider rapidly investing in building an information system, since this process takes time, requires strong senior management commitment and deep sales forces involvement. Full availability of data and information is a necessary precondition, albeit an insufficient one, for effective key account identification. A solid and reliable database should always include a selection of bi-dimensional data such as those listed for example in Table 3.1 regarding:

1. The *Customer profile*, useful to assess its potential to meet the company's business goals. These data are generally more difficult to collect since in most cases they are

based on subjective evaluations and provided principally by often reluctant sales people.

2. *Historical performances*, useful to assess the customer's historic and current economic, competitive and relational contribution to the company's goals. These data are supplied by the administration and/or by periodical field surveys.

Data fields can be grouped, for example, by financial (i.e. sales, profits), competitive (i.e. customer share, market standing of the customer), relational (i.e. image of the customer, satisfaction and loyalty) or structural (size and organizational) aspects.

Table 3.1   Examples of data from a customer database

Customer Profile	Historical performances
Turnover	Sales (i.e. turnover and volume)
Size and organization	Customer profitability
Image	Customer satisfaction and loyalty, including cross-selling parameters
Spending (volume and value) for the selected product categories	Sales conditions (applied and fulfillment of sales conditions)
Financial stability and reliability	Share of the customer (market share)
Quality of customer organization and people	Age of relationship (new, consolidated, declining)
Sensitivity to price, technical and commercial innovations	Current stage of KAM relationship
Ease of access (geography, openness)	Sales effort in a given period
Other	Other

Examples of tools to identify the key accounts

Several methodologies and tools can be used to assign key account status. One of the most widely adopted and easy to use is undoubtedly *ABC Concentration Analysis*. It is used to assess how many economic values such as turnover, volumes or profit are concentrated in the hands of a few customers. With this type of analysis the status of key account is assigned when a minority group of customers is verified as contributing to the majority of the economic value analysed. High business concentration means in fact higher commercial risks if there are commercial relationships that are not well managed or secured. Despite ABC's wide adoption, its main methodological limit lies in its nature: it analyses only past economic performance and not the customer profile or potential fit with the company's goals. Two examples of ABC implementation are now described. The first one (ABC Pyramid) simply tiers existing customers by processing one economic variable at a time. The second one (ABC Matrix) assigns key account status by evaluating two variables at the same time. Let us see how they work.

The *ABC Pyramids* helps the sales manager to assess the degree of concentration of the company's customer portfolio. It applies when a few customers prove to contribute to the largest portion of the supplier's economic performance (such as turnover, volume or profitability). As depicted in Figure 3.6, ABC methodology groups the customers into three separate tiers, each of different importance.

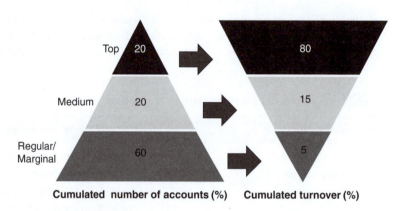

Figure 3.6 An example of ABC pyramidal segmentation

- **Tier A – 'Top accounts'**. These are the most important customers, representing about the top 20 per cent (sorted from the biggest to the smallest contributor), making up about 70–80 per cent of the total portfolio value (i.e. turnover).
- **Tier B – 'Medium accounts'**. This intermediate group consists of the next 10–15 per cent of customers and makes up about the next 10–15 per cent of the total portfolio turnover.
- **Tier C – 'Normal and marginal accounts'**. These are the remaining 60–65 per cent, which accounts for the final 5–10 per cent of the portfolio's turnover.

The example in Table 3.2 shows strategic concentration in a 20-customer portfolio. Only four top accounts (about 20 per cent of the base) together account for about 80 per cent of total turnover.

The ABC Matrix is a useful tool to segment the customer portfolio by running and crossing two ABC Analyses in parallel.

In the example shown in Figure 3.7, the first ABC Analysis tiers the customers using overall turnover as a segmentation base; the second one tiers the portfolio with respect to turnover made with a specific and strategic product line. If both the ABCs are relevant, showing high levels of economic concentration, then the results can be integrated into a unique matrix. So each account is labelled twice according to the status assigned by each segmentation. In the ABC Matrix, those accounts labelled AA, AB or BA lie in the top right quadrant. Companies adopting only these historic and economic criteria to identify their strategic accounts usually consider them as *Key Accounts*. *Regular* and *Marginal Accounts* stand, on the contrary, in the opposite lower left quadrant. *Development Key Accounts* lie along the diagonal, from the top left to the bottom right corner.

Table 3.2   ABC Analysis

Customers	Turnover (000 €)	Cumulated Turnover (000 €)	Cumulated number of customers	Cumulated number of customers (%)	Cumulated Revenues (%)	
Customer_1	1,800	1,800	1	5%	30.2%	
Customer_2	1,200	3,000	2	10%	50.3%	A
Customer_3	900	3,900	3	15%	65.3%	
Customer_4	850	4,750	4	**20%**	**79.6%**	
Customer_5	300	5,050	5	25%	84.6%	
Customer_6	189	5,239	6	30%	87.8%	B
Customer_7	150	5,389	7	35%	90.3%	
Customer_8	100	5,489	8	**40%**	**92.0%**	
Customer_9	68	5,557	9	45%	93.1%	
Customer_10	56	5,613	10	50%	94.0%	
Customer_11	53	5,666	11	55%	94.9%	
Customer_12	51	5,717	12	60%	95.8%	
Customer_13	47	5,764	13	65%	96.6%	
Customer_14	46	5,810	14	70%	97.3%	C
Customer_15	40	5,850	15	75%	98.0%	
Customer_16	36	5,886	16	80%	98.6%	
Customer_17	33	5,919	17	85%	99.2%	
Customer_18	22	5,941	18	90%	99.5%	
Customer_19	18	5,959	19	95%	99.8%	
Customer_20	10	5,969	20	100%	100.0%	
Total	**5,969**					

Noticeably, the ABC Matrix shows the same major limitation already seen with the other ABC methodology: it does not tier key accounts on the basis of their potential contribution to the company's strategic goals. Many accounts, especially those in an early relationship stage, do not yet provide significant business performance. But they might have great potential to provide superior business performances in the future (see Figure 3.2). The same reasoning, but with opposite results, can be easily applied to a selection of customers who, despite their good historical results, report low future potential or declining performances.

The last tool to be described in this chapter is the *KAM Matrix*, which segments the customer portfolio by crossing two variables: potential attractiveness of the customer and its historical contribution to the company's goals. Compared to other tools this matrix seems to be more complete and capable of fulfilling the strategic need for key account segmentation. The example in Figure 3.8 comes from an Italian industrial company selling control machineries. Its sales manager segmented the customer portfolio with KAM logic to achieve a solid durable growth in both sales and

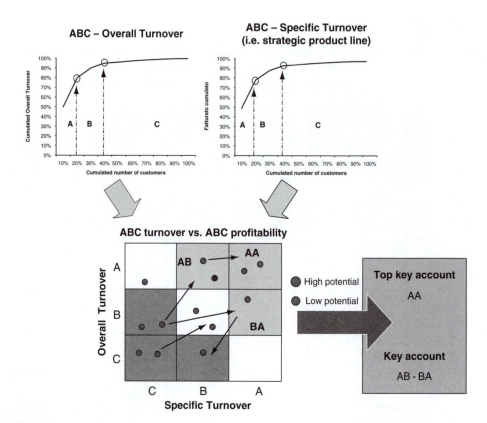

Figure 3.7 The ABC Matrix

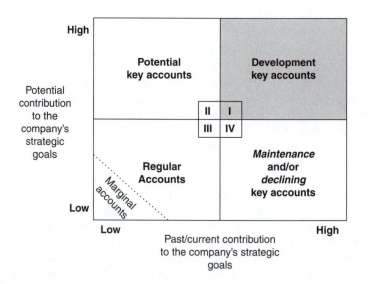

Figure 3.8 The KAM Matrix

competitive position. The Y axis shows the Customer Attractiveness Index (potential contribution) calculated on the basis of:

1. size of customer business;
2. annual average spending for the targeted products;
3. customer's competitive position into its markets;
4. customer's sensitivity to technical innovations.

The X axis describes the Performance Index (past/current contribution) calculated on the basis of:

1. turnover (overall and strategic products);
2. profitability;
3. customer share;
4. degree of mutual cooperation.

Finally the company's portfolio was segmented into five main groups of accounts. Quadrant I is made up of the company's Development Key Accounts which have good to excellent past/current performances. These accounts still have a high potential contribution for the future. In Quadrant II there are the Potential Key Accounts whose performances are not yet really noticeable, but are expected to be very attractive in the future. It is not uncommon to find some "C" accounts here, especially those recently opened and where the company should really invest more resources to develop the relationship and the business. Quadrant III is composed of some Regular and Marginal Accounts usually showing medium to low performance and attractiveness. Traditional salespeople and solely maintenance selling activities are more reasonable for managing these accounts. Finally, the bottom right Quadrant IV is where the Maintenance and/or Declining Accounts are positioned. This is a very complicated and difficult selling area and additional deeper analysis is often needed. Maintenance accounts are usually those already saturated but still providing good business. They are not the best accounts, but still important ones to be consolidated and defended from competitors' attacks. The opposite is true of those accounts still providing good past/current performance but unfortunately showing a clear declining trend in business. For these, consolidation or a progressive downgrade of the relationship are the only possible selling scenarios.

Key Account Planning

The goal of planning is to contribute to business success by following a logical sequence of analytical activities that should lead to targeted goals, and some actionable strategies. Key Account Planning represents the last level in an ideal planning hierarchy made up of corporate, marketing and, in some cases, segment plans. Key Account Planning is widely considered a necessary part of an outstanding world class KAM programme, and is very helpful for the systematic identification of emerging opportunities and threats, for facing changes, for improving cross-functional relationships and better

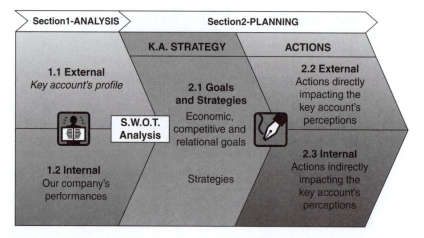

Figure 3.9   The Key Account Plan flow

allocating scarce financial and non-financial resources (McDonald 2007). More specifically, the Key Account Plan (KAP) is a managerial tool designed to improve key knowledge, vision and everything related to goal-setting and strategy planning. It is a sort of 'main customer file', also very useful for supporting internal business communications. For example, when other units are deeply involved in the account management processes, then a good Key Account Plan can make all the difference. The KAP can be local or global depending on the geographic level of strategic account management. It is typically edited by a Key Account Manager only for a selection of Development, Potential and even Maintenance Key Accounts. Figure 3.9 shows an example of a typical KAP structure, and is followed by a detailed description of its contents. Usually a plan starts from the company's goals and from the strategic cluster.

Section 1: Key Account Analysis

This section is entirely dedicated to data collection and analysis. The Key Account Manager should spend time in depth examining all the data and information in order to identify key opportunities and major threats in managed strategic accounts. Analysis is also critical so that the Key Account Manager knows the company's real strengths and its ability to handle key accounts.

The key account profiling part is dedicated to the investigation, organization and analysis of all the suitable data and information regarding the 'Key Account profile'. Usually it begins with an overall introduction to the key account's businesses, history and strategies. Then it proceeds with an analysis of the company's macro and micro environment, highlighting the most relevant and critical forces at work which may influence the current and future key account performance. Additional analysis can focus on the customer's business positioning, image and economic performance. Careful attention must also be paid to the customer value model and buying process and organization.[3] The key roles and players involved in purchasing and usage must be clearly identified and analysed, also highlighting how much and how well they are covered by the current sales network. Finally, this section should enable the KAM to identify and understand which are the major opportunities to be exploited are and which are the risks to be minimized (Ryals and McDonald 2008) in his/her key account.

To assess the company's competitive strengths and potential weaknesses, a great deal of historical performance data must be reported and analysed: sales, volumes, profitability, product portfolio performances, value delivered, sales conditions, quality of credits, competitive position and more. The manager should also evaluate the selling and communication efforts, the development of past special activities and projects in the key account. Finally, a comprehensive evaluation of the quality of the relationship is required.

The outcomes of the two sections (1.1 and 1.2) can be synthesized into a common SWOT Analysis (see Figure 3.10), an analytical tool helpful for setting up the future business goals, the strategies for the key account and an effective action plan.

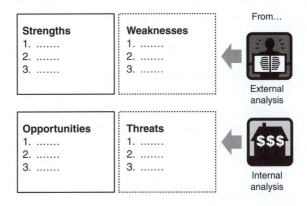

Figure 3.10   SWOT Analysis

Section 2: planning goals, strategies and actions

The best KAPs are those that actually deliver actionable strategies and feasible goals. The clearer the link between the SWOT Analysis and the subsequent goals (2.1) to be achieved in the key account, the better. The goals can be economic, competitive, relational or a mix of all of these. The strategies are made up of general actions or guidelines explaining broadly how to achieve the goals. For example, strategies could refer to the price and sales conditions; to the value to be offered (including post-sales services and logistics), to the type of promotion (i.e. branding, brand image, promotions, advertising), etc.

---

[3] The buying centre includes all members of the customer organization who play any sort of critical role in the purchase decision process: initiators, users, influencers, deciders, approvers, buyers and gatekeepers. Innovators and promoters can also be included.

The KAP should also include everything related to team management both at local and, if applicable, at global level. The team can be seen internally (i.e. Key Account Manager, other sales people, colleagues from other functions involved in the KAM processes) or externally (i.e. inside the customer's decision-making unit). The KAP is complete when the detailed actions (2.2) and required resources are set up. In other words, everybody must be clear on the following:

- What the Key Account Manager plans to do: actions can be external, and so visible to the client. Others could be internal only, within the seller's organization and not directly visible to those outside the company.
- Who has to be involved in the seller's and buyer's organizations while implementing the plan.
- What financial and non-financial resources are needed.

A final time schedule (including goals, strategies and actions) is required, to be accompanied by an estimate of the KAM costs and a managerial evaluation of the difficulties forecasted during the plan's implementation.

How is the KAM process to be organized?

When developing a KAM programme, in deciding how to implement it and organize and manage the company's strategic efforts, common doubts arise: 'Should the company radically change the sales force structure and its selling processes? Are the salespeople suitable for managing customers with KAM logic? How should the other functions be involved in the KAM processes?'

A recent study suggests that building long-term trust in the market and developing relationship selling approaches requires greater control over Key Account Managers' actions (Guenzi, Georges and Pardo 2009). Strategic customer management, superior value delivery, higher coordination and integration between the supplier and the buyer all call for radical changes. Deep innovation, beginning with the seller's organization, roles and internal processes, is strongly advised. Sales forces are, in fact, typically organized by geographic area, product lines, market segments and channels (see Chapter 8). KAM, for its strategic focus, requires the highest level of *customer-centric specialization*. Sales leaders must be able to manage the key accounts as a whole, and not as just as separate parts. The most important accounts should be assigned to the best sales managers, selected ad hoc, trained and supported internally to perform, individually and possibly in teams, their challenging job. All these decisions might be strongly influenced by the overall stage of the KAM relationship and by the buyer's business and organizational complexity.[4]

---

[4] Key account complexity is the result of its size, complexity of the centre of purchase and purchasing process, number of sub-market units, degree of internationality, competitive dynamics etc. Supplier firm complexity depends on its offering (number and variety of product lines, items and services sold), distribution channels, processes organization, degree of internal coordination, etc.

Matrix organization versus traditional organization

How integrated should the KAM processes and responsibilities be? What organizational model should be adopted? These are some of the biggest worries for senior managers while developing or fine-tuning a strategic account management programme. Many organizational models are proposed with the aim of finding the optimal solution since a wrong choice here may determine the failure of credibility for the entire KAM programme. Modern advanced solutions opt for matrix organization, where a Key Account Manager is fully responsible for the key account and for all the associated business processes. These organizational solutions are suggested especially if the key accounts are very complex in terms of needs, organization and internal processes. To deal with these accounts, unquestionably deeper and stronger cross-unit coordination and participation becomes a clear key factor for success. Contrastingly, if the key account complexity is moderate to low, the seller may develop self-contained key account units (Capon 2001). There, most of the activities can be broadly managed by the Key Account Manager with external, but limited, support from other company departments. Basic solutions like this last one are often only the starting platform for a KAM programme. If the key account portfolio should then evolve to more sophisticated and complex relationships, the company should be strongly encouraged to shift to a customer-focused matrix organization.

Key account teams

Due to the nature of KAM, teams are a necessary part of the strategic programme. They usually cross the company's units, divisions or geographic areas (Verra 1994), contributing a wide array of competencies and supports to the value proposition.

Table 3.3	Different types of Key Account Teams
Informal teams	The traditional sales person, or the Key Account Manager, is responsible for sales and for the business relationship. Interactions with other units are not explicit and not codified. Usually no incentives are planned for the people providing their support.
Semi-formal teams	KAT members meet often, if possible on a regular basis, to share goals, strategies and tactics, also to solve problems. There is no real formal hierarchical dependence on the Key Account Manager. Team incentives can be adopted to keep people motivated to create superior value and work for the team. The manager may spend some time dealing with the heads of different units. The purpose of the team is to ensure commitment and to facilitate internal processes.
Dedicated Teams	Some people with different functional competencies become formally part of one or more KATs dedicated to the management and support of a selection of key accounts. Depending on company and business specificity, team members can be hierarchically subordinated to the KAM structure while maintaining a formal relationship with the unit. Team incentives are provided.

As mentioned above, Key Account Teams (KAT) may have different degrees of formalization depending on the customer's and supplier's business and organizational complexity. Table 3.3 describes some typical examples of KATs.

Typical competencies of Key Account Managers

Key account managers play a very special role, often focused on just one or a few very important accounts and with the mission of maintaining the business as well as finding new opportunities (Zoltners, Sinha and Lorimer 2004). The responsibilities, attitudes and skills required to play this role successfully may vary widely, depending on the type and number of accounts in the strategic portfolio and the stage of the KAM relationship but also on the number and quality of the internal supports provided by the seller's organization.

Unless several companies have implemented only aesthetic changes, a real Key Account Manager no longer plays the role of a traditional salesperson. In fact, the role involves an organizational quantum leap in terms of managerial responsibility and competencies required. He/she is definitely more exposed while weaving the net outside with the account and also within his/her own organization. Typically, some distinctive competencies emerge:

- strong commitment in creating superior value for the customer;
- high analytical capability so as to be able to assess customer needs, understand the customer's marketing environment, business model, financials and organization complexity and to discover unexploited sales opportunities;
- solid marketing and long-term planning competencies;
- solid problem-finding and solving capabilities;
- solid cross-functional knowledge and competencies;
- refined negotiation and personal communication skills.

A Key Account Manager must also prove to be a real team manager, leader and motivator, able to negotiate and consistently obtain other people's commitment in terms of both support and cooperation.

Summary

Key Account Management is a widely used selling approach. Companies adopt it for several reasons, essentially to improve their ability to create and obtain the highest possible mutual benefits from their best customers and prospects. How? By building and securing long lasting, profitable mutual relationships. Key account relationships show several evolutionary stages, varying in terms of intensity, level of integration, common shared values and strategies. Not all the key accounts are, in fact, equally important and real partners for the supplier. Key accounts' identification, in depth analysis and Key Account Planning are only part of the KAM programme's complexity. For its execution the company should set up ad hoc account management procedures and develop a matrix selling organization. As a result the sales force must be specialized in accordance with the customer's status, thus influencing salespeople's recruiting and training processes, compensation and evaluation systems. The role played by a Key Account Manager is tough and challenging and, finally, KAM is probably the greatest and most difficult field in which to develop and execute a real local and/or global relationship selling strategy.

Key points

1. Developing a KAM programme for some companies is just an evolutionary step but for most, it is more of a revolution, offering great business opportunities but also involving higher risks and potential additional costs (monetary and non-monetary).
2. The lack of strong senior management commitment, along with the lack of formal organizational structures and processes, are probably the most common reasons why KAM programmes fail. Senior managers should continuously build and provide KAM with a favourable environment in which to operate and stimulate the whole organization to think horizontally (across units) and not just vertically, as most people are accustomed to doing.
3. The adoption of the five-step KAM process described in this chapter may be very helpful for companies. It can lead them to organize their strategic resources better, to set the right goals and to plan effective micro-marketing strategies.
4. Key accounts' identification can be supported by several analytical tools, useful in setting strategic priorities and for developing effective strategic action plans. The use of a customer database is one of the key success factors in a KAM programme.
5. KAM strongly requires cross-functional and team-based selling approaches. According to the company's and market's complexity, Key Account Team may be informal, semi formal and formal ones.
6. A Key Account Manager plays a crucial role in promoting the adoption of KAM, responsible for the whole key account and so for the key account team. He/she has to be a team leader and an external and internal integrator.
7. RMG is an interesting example of a company that has married the KAM philosophy, progressively developing a challenging KAM programme into an international environment.

References

Capon, N. (2001) *Key Account Management and Planning: The Comprehensive Handbook for Managing your Company's Most Important Strategic Asset* New York: The Free Press.

Guenzi, P., Georges, L. and Pardo, C. (2009) 'The Impact of Strategic Account Managers' Behaviors on Relational Outcomes: An Empirical Study', *Industrial Marketing Management*, 38 (6): 300–311.

Kraljic, P. (1983) 'Purchasing Must Become Supply Management', *Harvard Business Review*, 61 (5): 109–17.

McDonald, M., Millman, T. and Rogers, B. (1997) 'Key Account Management: Theory, Practice and Challenges', *Journal of Marketing Management* , 13 (8): 737–57.

McDonald, M., Rogers, B. and Woodburn, D. (2000) *Key Customers: How to Manage Them Profitably*. Burlington: Elsevier Butterworth-Heinemann.

Millman, T. and Wilson, K. (1995) 'From Key Account Selling to Key Account Management', *Journal of Marketing Practice*, 1 (1): 9–21.

Möller, K. K. and Halinen, A. (1999) 'Business Relationships and Networks: Managerial Challenge of Network Era', *Industrial Marketing Management*, 28 (5): 413–27.

Napolitano, L. (1997) 'Customer-supplier Partnering, a Strategy Whose Time Has Come', *Journal of Personal Selling and Sales Management* , 17 (4): 1–8.

Ojasalo, J. (2001) 'Key Account Management at Company and Individual Levels in Business to Business Relatiosnhips', *Journal of Business and Industrial Marketing*, 16 (3): 199–218.

Ryals, L. and McDonald, M. (2008) *Key Account Plans: The Practitioners' Guide to Profitable Planning*. Oxford: Butterworth-Heinemann.

Sengupta, S. E., Krapfel, M. A. and Pusateri, M. A. (1997) 'The Strategic Sales Force: Workload, Compensation and Technology all Affect the Key Account Management', *Industrial Marketing Management* , 6 (2): 28–34.

Van Weele, A. J. (2000) *Purchasing Management: Analysis, Planning and Practice*. London: Chapman & Hall.

Verra, G. (1994) *International Account Management: An Organizational Dilemma*. Rotterdam: Erasmus University.

Wagner, S. M., & Johnson, J. l. (2004). 'Configuring and Managing Strategic Supplier Portfolios'. Industrial Marketing Management.

Wotruba, T. R. (1991) 'The evolution of personal selling', *Journal of Personal Selling and Sale*s Management, 11 (3): 1–12.

Zoltners, A., Sinha, P. and Lorimer, S. E. (2004) *Sales Force Design for Strategic Advantage*. New York: Palgrave Macmillan.

Further reading

Bacon, T. R. (1999) *Selling to Major Accounts: Tools, Techniques, and Practical Solutions for the Sales Manager*. New York: AMACOM.

Capon, N., Senn, C. (2010) 'Global Customer Management Programmes: How To Make Them Really Work', *California Management Review*, 52 (2), 32–55

Cheverton, P. (2008) *Key Account Management*, 3rd edition. London: Kogan Page Limited.

Ryals, L.J., Rogers, B. and Rogers, B., (2006) 'Holding Up the Mirror: The Impact of Strategic Procurement Practices on Account Management', *Business Horizons*, 49 (1), 41–50.

Weitz, B.A., Castleberry, S.B. and Tanner Jr., J. F. (2008) *Selling Building Partnerships*, 7th edn. New York: McGraw-Hill International.

4

Delegation of pricing authority to salespeople

Manfred Krafft and Ann-Kristin Hansen

Contents

Learning objectives

After reading this chapter, you should be able to:

• Recognize the critical importance of delegating pricing authority to the sales force.

• Weigh up the advantages and disadvantages of delegating pricing authority.

• Understand critical factors that drive pricing authority delegation.

• Identify the conditions under which pricing authority is positively related to business performance.

Chapter outline

This chapter deals with the question of what factors drive pricing authority delegation to salespeople and under what conditions price delegation may be beneficial for the company. With the objective of helping sales managers in their decision as to whether pricing authority should be delegated to the sales force or not, the chapter is structured as follows. After the introduction, a real case history is presented to demonstrate the relevance of the pricing authority issue. Subsequently, the pros and cons of delegating pricing authority are discussed, before important drivers of price delegation are presented. Afterwards, we return to the real case history to show how pricing delegation can be efficiently implemented in an organization. The chapter concludes by returning to the case history and presenting the management implications derived from it and agency-theoretic research in economics and marketing science.

Dow Chemical Company

The Dow Chemical Company was founded in Midland, Michigan in 1897 by the Canadian-born chemist Herbert Henry Dow and remains headquartered in the same town more than 110 years later. Today, Dow Chemical Company is one of the largest chemical companies in the world. With annual sales of $54 billion and 46,000 employees worldwide Dow is a leading science and technology company that provides a broad range of innovative chemical, plastic, and agricultural products and services to customers in more than 160 countries. Dow operates in six segments: Performance Plastics, Performance Chemicals, Agricultural Sciences, Basic Plastics, Basic Chemicals, and Hydrocarbons and Energy. Dow's $28 billion Performance portfolio (covering the three segments Performance Plastics, Performance Chemicals and Agricultural Sciences) serves customers in markets around the world with an extensive range of differentiated plastic, chemical and agricultural solutions. The portfolio's innovations improve lifestyles in many ways – making cars safer, buildings more energy-efficient, food healthier, water cleaner, computers faster, electronics more durable...and more. By accelerating innovation and growth, while increasing market and customer focus, the Performance portfolio is creating businesses and brands that deliver higher margins and consistent profitability for the company. Dow's Basics portfolio of leading basic plastics and chemicals generates annual revenues of $26 billion. It spans the three segments Basic Plastics, Basic Chemicals and Hydrocarbons and Energy and serves more than 6,000 customers worldwide. The Basics portfolio is an integrated source of raw materials for Dow's Performance portfolio and meets the changing needs of a myriad of industries – from packaging, personal care, toys, pipes and tools to adhesives, de-icers, pharmaceuticals, paper and construction. The Basics portfolio is growing primarily through joint ventures that enable Dow to reduce capital intensity, expand globally and obtain access to advantaged feedstock and energy. Dow's various products help bring thousands of consumer goods and industrial supplies to market – from toys, tools and textiles to pharmaceuticals, personal care products and water purification technologies. Nearly everyone in the Western world uses Dow's products without even knowing that they do so. Some of Dow's product highlights are listed below:

- Paper coating polymers from Dow are used in the paper and board industry to improve strength, brightness, opacity and readability for brochures, graphics and books.
- Ion exchange resins from Dow are used to purify water around the world for drinking water, power plants, waste water treatment and pharmaceuticals.
- Polyurethane material from Dow offers automobile part manufacturers better cushioning for seats and reduction in noise, vibration and harshness in interior parts.
- Innovative thermoplastic resins from Dow eliminate the need for paint in consumer products such as TVs, reducing volatile organic compound emissions and improving the recyclability of TV cabinets.

The key to Dow's success lies in aligning technologies and capabilities with customers' specific needs – and backing that with outstanding customer support. Therefore, Dow decided at the beginning of the twenty-first century to change its global sales organization from a product-centric to a customer-centric one in order to emphasize the value of customer information in the organizational structure. While this restructuring helped to increase the efficiency and effectiveness of its global sales organization, it also resulted in the negotiating units of the company – especially the account managers – facing the challenge of how to manage the negotiations for the diversified range of products with the buying firms. In the product-centric organization, each account manager was a specialist for a limited range of products and sold them to several customers. The reorganization necessitated them being in control of negotiations for nearly the whole product portfolio – except the highly specialized products – with a handful of customers. Whereas product expertise can be achieved by intensive training and experience, price calculation is a major challenge in the chemical industry because of the risks connected with the high dependency on oil, gas and energy. Since these non-substitutable raw materials are scarce resources, their prices vary a lot over a period. Consequently the problem arises, how can the company prepare its sales staff for tomorrow's price negotiations if a major cost component of the product is unknown today? The fact that the customer-centric approach demands account managers negotiate a broad range of products especially means that price negotiations have to be carefully prepared. In particular, the question has to be addressed: what pricing latitude should be given to the account managers? Does it make sense to give them full authority regarding the negotiation of prices? Or should this freedom be limited because they cannot oversee the impact of price reductions for all of the products? Dow found an innovative solution to deal with these issues. Its organization of price negotiations and the design of the account manager's pricing authority is described at the end of the chapter.

Introduction: the relevance of delegating pricing authority

The decision of delegating pricing authority to the sales force is a major concern of sales managers (Mishra and Prasad 2004). Pricing authority can be defined as the degree to which a sales force employee is empowered to negotiate and undertake reductions of a product's or service's list price without consultation of the sales manager. A current survey of 188 firms in the industrial machinery and electrical engineering industry in Germany indicates that firms vary widely in this regard; 15 per cent of the companies have little to no price delegation, while 64 per cent give medium and 21 per cent high to even unlimited pricing authority. Given these differences in the degree of delegating pricing authority, it is hardly surprising that the issue of (de-)centralized pricing has been examined in several publications before (Bhardwaj 2001; Dolan and Simon 1996; Joseph 2001; Lal 1986; Mishra and Prasad 2004, 2005; Stephenson, Cron and Frazier, 1979; Weinberg 1975, 1978). While the existing sales management literature discusses the advantages and disadvantages of conceding pricing authority to the sales force and, hence, whether or not to delegate pricing authority, the objective of this chapter is not only to provide evaluation tools to help in the deliberations about the price delegation decision, but also to deduce the managerial implications for those market situations where pricing flexibility is inevitable. In particular, based on the Dow Chemical case study, this chapter aims to develop recommendations for sales managers regarding the organization of the sales force if pricing latitudes are required.

Advantages and disadvantages of delegating pricing authority

To deepen the understanding of the relationship between the sales force employee and the sales manager (or – if sales negotiations are conducted by account managers – between the account manager and the next higher-level authority), a theoretical framework, namely agency theory, can be used. Agency theory is focused on the analysis and optimal design of contracts between a principal (e.g. the sales manager) and an agent (e.g. the sales force employee) to whom the principal delegates decision-making authority (in our scenario, pricing authority; Krafft 1999). In general, agency theory assumes uncertain sales environments and information costs that make it difficult to monitor the agent's behaviour perfectly (Krafft 1999). In the setting of price negotiations between a sales force employee and a customer, the effort of the sales force employee (agent) to sell a product cannot be observed by the sales manager (principal) (Lal 1986). This situation means that, for instance, there is the risk of the sub-optimal agent substituting selling effort by price discounting if his/her goals differ from the principal's (Joseph 2001). To avoid this and related problems, compensation schemes and control systems that realign the incentives of both parties have to be designed so that they aim at the same outcome (incentive compatibility; John and Weitz 1989). These issues are discussed in more detail in Chapters 16 (Compensation) and 14 (Control Systems). However, before problems such as organizational requirements are addressed, the general decision of whether and how much pricing authority should be delegated has to be made. Because pricing decisions are major elements of the company's marketing strategy and therefore of substantial corporate importance, the exercise of price-setting authority within the organization has to be well balanced. Although there is no broad general solution, the following lists of pros and cons should help you to gain a broader understanding of the scope and impact of the price delegation decision. The lists are based on comparative statistics stemming from agency theory and similar models.

Reasons for the delegation of pricing authority (Dolan and Simon 1996):

* Quicker reaction to changing market, competition and customer conditions (higher flexibility);
* informational advantage of the salesperson;
* personal relationship between the sales force employee and the customer;
* motivation of the sales force employee;
* better assessment of customer's reservation value during the sales call (optimal customization of prices);
* lower coordination costs;
* decrease in the workload of the sales manager (the sales manager can concentrate on strategic challenges).

Reasons against the delegation of pricing authority (Dolan and Simon 1996):

* Sales employee may fail to see the consequences of his/her price reductions;
* risk of sub-optimal substitution of selling effort by price discounting;
* risk of inconsistencies across customers, segments or countries;

- high levels of autonomy and personal responsibility may lead to mentally over-loaded salespeople and an increase in control costs;
- higher qualification of sales force employee required (increase in labour costs).

Although the number of advantages exceeds the number of disadvantages, the reasons *against* the delegation of pricing authority outweigh the reasons *for* the delegation of pricing authority. Thus, sales management literature predominantly recommends restricting pricing latitude in the sales force (Dolan and Simon 1996; Stephenson, Cron and Frazier 1979). Some authors even found negative correlations between the degree of pricing authority and company performance and therefore strictly advise against delegation of pricing authority (e.g. Stephenson, Cron and Frazier 1979). However, in many market situations there may be a need for a pricing strategy that enables the sales employee to make at least limited price adjustments.

Delegating pricing authority or not? A managerial guideline

The question of whether pricing authority should be delegated to salespeople is not a simple yes or no decision. The answer depends on several market and organizational determinants. Below, the different variables that may influence a manager's decision to delegate pricing latitude are introduced, which should help them decide if this is an appropriate action or not. Broadly, these influencing variables can be categorized into environmental factors, organizational determinants and behavioural determinants.

Environmental factors

The environmental context of a business unit is likely to influence its organizational structure. Hence, environmental conditions can likewise affect the necessity to decentralize decisions – and also whether or not to delegate pricing authority to the sales force. When deciding about the degree to which pricing authority should be delegated, two environmental characteristics should be considered in particular, namely *market turbulence* and *competitive intensity*. Market turbulence describes the rate of change in the composition of customers and their preferences (Jaworski and Kohli 1993). Companies operating in more turbulent markets are likely to have to customize prices in order to cater to customers' changing preferences, whereas in stable markets customer preferences do not change a great deal (Lal 1986). For instance, if it becomes evident during a negotiation that a customer prefers a modified version of the product that the salesperson is trying to sell, the salesperson has to react quickly. To avoid a situation in which the customer does not buy any units of the old version of the product, resulting in high stockholdings or, even worse, disposal costs, the sales force employee has to be able to offer price reductions in order to close the sale. Thus, companies operating in more turbulent markets have a greater need to adjust prices quickly because otherwise customers might switch to another supplier.

The second environmental factor that influences the decision of delegating pricing authority is competitive intensity. In the absence of competition, the sales unit may perform well with centrally determined prices because the buying firm is bound to the organization's products or services (Weinberg 1975). Due to the buyer's dependence, price assessments are not required to close the sale. By contrast, under conditions of high competition, the buying firm has many alternative options to satisfy its needs. If the salesperson is not able to respond to the price expectations of the purchaser quickly, the company is likely to lose such a customer to competitors (Dolan and Simon 1996). When it is evident that a purchaser would switch supplier if the price is not reduced, it is complicating the negotiation process unnecessarily if numerous consultations with the sales force manager or even top executives are then required. Therefore, the higher the competitive intensity in an industry, the more pricing authority should be delegated to the sales force.

Organizational determinants

Compensation

A company likes the salesperson to exert the maximum selling effort and generate sales for the whole organization. However, the salesperson, for whom effort is costly, will make this effort only if he/she is adequately compensated (Joseph 2001). As is pointed out in Chapter 16, compensation is the most important reward used to motivate salespeople (Basu et al. 1985). Ideally, compensation should be tied to the salesperson's selling effort, but since management cannot observe the sales agent's effort, the two parties have to contract on observable variables such as realized profits and the prices charged. The objective of management should be to set up a compensation plan that motivates the salesperson to negotiate prices that maximize his/her own utility and the company's expected profit (Nagar 2002). To avoid the risk of sub-optimal substitution of selling effort by price discounting, commission rates have to be set as a percentage of the realized gross margin rather than total sales, as the following example from Hansen, Joseph, and Krafft (2008) illustrates.

> Consider a product with a list price of €100 and marginal cost of €80. If the salesperson is compensated on sales with a commission rate of 5 per cent, a sale at list price yields €5 in income. Reducing the price to €90 leads to a commission-based income of €4.50, a decrease of only 50 cents. On the other hand, if the salesperson is compensated on realized gross margins, with a commission rate of 25 per cent a sale at list price yields €5 in income. Discounting the product to €90 leads to commission income of €2.50, a decrease of 50 per cent.

Evidently, commission rates based on realized gross margins can substantially reduce the motivation to lower price and should therefore be preferred over incentives based on revenue if pricing authority is delegated and marginal costs are high. However, care is required if salespeople sell products with different gross margins. The salesperson will allocate his/ her time such that the amount of time devoted to the most profitable product is largest (Weinberg 1975). Products with lower gross margins might be neglected in negotiations or, at worst, not even be offered to the customer. Therefore, the commission plan should include special incentives for selling low margin products or product bundles if the firm's product portfolio requires this.

To summarize, incentives based on realized gross margins definitely reduce the risk of sub-optimal substitution of selling effort by price discounting because price reductions negatively affect the compensation and, hence, the utility of the salesperson. If an organization is only able to compensate the sales force based on sales quantity or revenue, delegation of pricing authority might lead to sub-optimal results and therefore should be avoided or reduced to a minimum. This might be the case if cost structures are too risky to be revealed to sales staff or if variable costs are rather negligible compared to fixed costs and, hence, realistic gross margins for products cannot be calculated easily.

Sales Force Automation

Another determinant that might impact the pricing delegation decision is the company's use of technology. Especially dedicated Sales Force Automation (SFA) applications have offered technological support to sales representatives and sales managers since the 1980s. SFA can be defined as the application of information technology to support personal selling activities and the sales function (Rivers and Dart 1999). Information technology comprises both hardware (desktop computer, laptop, etc.) and software. SFA software applications offer a broad range of functionality and make it possible to collect, store, analyse and distribute customer-related data to the salespeople and manager (Schillewaert and Ahearne 2001). A number of benefits may result from SFA implementation, including improved customer relationships, intensive reporting, higher cash flows, improved salesperson productivity, greater transparency of all sales processes and better quality management reports (Buttle, Ang and Iriana 2006). According to Buttle, Ang and Iriana (2006), the following advantages of SFA appeal to different stakeholders:

- Salespeople: shorter sales cycles, more closing opportunities, higher win rates.
- Sales managers: improved salesperson productivity, improved customer relations, more accurate reporting, reduced cost-of-sales.
- Senior management: accelerated cash flow, increased sales revenue, market share growth, improved profitability.

Since SFA enables the sales manager and the upper management to gain more insight into all sales-related processes, the use of SFA will invariably make delegation of pricing authority easier for the firm (Ramaswami, Srinivasan, and Gorton 1997). SFA helps to minimize the possibilities of misuse of pricing authority by salespeople due to its capacity for all-embracing control and reporting. In other words, SFA enables sales managers to utilize to the full the advantages of delegating pricing authority to salespersons. Therefore, companies using SFA have good grounds for leaving price responsibility with the sales force.

Control system

To further support the price delegation decision, the design of the sales organization's control system has to be investigated (see also Chapter 14). While using incentives based on gross margins can be seen as a self-regulating control mechanism because this performance metric guarantees that price reductions affect the salesperson's compensation, additional control instruments are needed to ensure that salespeople do not misuse pricing authority in other ways than arbitrary price discounting. Two contrasting sales management philosophies for controlling the sales agent are behaviour- and outcome-based control (Anderson and Oliver 1987). An outcome-oriented control system is characterized by little monitoring and managerial direction but objective measures of outcomes (Krafft 1999). Behaviour-based management systems represent an opposing philosophy, with considerable monitoring, high levels of managerial direction, and subjective and complex methods of evaluating salespeople (Krafft 1999). The former approach emphasizes the output of the salesperson as the basis for his/her performance evaluation, while the latter emphasizes the effort of the sales agent in judging his achievements (Anderson and Oliver 1987). Since measurement of the salesperson's effort, behaviour and capabilities is very difficult, behaviour-oriented control systems require comprehensive monitoring of the sales staff by their supervising managers and an extensive reporting system which is used by all employees throughout the company. From a measurement point of view, controlling the sales force on an outcome-oriented basis is easier because only the achieved results, such as the number of new customers acquired, the number of sales calls or achieved contribution margin, are evaluated. Considering the question of delegating pricing authority or not, companies with a focus on outcome-based control systems seem to have a better basis for controlling the negotiated price and hence better grounds for conceding pricing latitude. However, companies with a good behaviour-oriented control system may also be able to delegate pricing authority successfully. If all actions of a salesperson are monitored extensively, his/her output is more likely to result in outcomes that benefit the organization. Therefore, although there is a higher tendency in companies with outcome-based control systems to delegate pricing authority (because in general, those companies' sales agents have greater freedom in designing workflows) compared with companies using behaviour-based control systems, the premise for delegating pricing delegation is not so much a question of the control system but rather of the intensity of monitoring that the control system offers. As will be seen in the second part of the Dow Chemical Company case a behaviour-oriented control system is definitely combinable with successful delegation of pricing latitude to salespersons. To conclude, the general recommendation is that a high intensity of monitoring increases the prospects of successfully delegating pricing authority – independent of the use of output- or input-based control systems. Indicators of high intensity monitoring are the number of meetings between sales manager and sales agents or the number of salespersons supervised by a sales manager (i.e. span of control).

Information asymmetry

It has been shown that a high level of information asymmetry between a salesperson and a sales manager can provide a strong reason for delegating pricing authority (e.g. Lal 1986). In the area of sales management and sales negotiations, information asymmetry implies that the sales agent and the sales manager do not have identical information about the selling environment. Due to the division of labour between sales managers and salespeople, a certain degree of information asymmetry always exists between these two parties. It is intuitively plausible that the sales agent has better local sales knowledge emerging from established relationships and interactions with customers compared with his/her supervising manager. Although a salesperson may not know the exact conditions that are likely to occur in his/her sales territory at the beginning of every sales period, it is possible for the sales agent to collect this information by investing some effort (see here and below, Lal 1986). The sales manager is not able to gather this information about the changing sales environment as fast as the salesperson due to his/her distance from the sales territory. Hence, the degree of information asymmetry depends on the speed of changes in the local conditions of the sales environment. If the selling environment is relatively stable, the sales manager is able to analyse the market situation nearly as well as the sales representative because information is constant over time and the need to consider new developments in the market immediately does not arise. On the other hand, information asymmetry can be a problem when the organization's customer base is extremely heterogeneous with respect to individual customer sales response functions. The management may be aware of the distribution of the average customer response function, but in the case of a heterogeneous customer base, the average response function is only a rough approximation of the actual selling environment reality. Customers' response functions can vary a lot across the whole customer base. Precise information is needed to decide what price should be charged to each customer. And knowledge about the customers' individual response functions can only be improved through personal contact with the customer, and this investment of sales effort is the sales agent's task. This leads to the conclusion that the more heterogeneous the customer base, the greater the level of information asymmetry between salespeople and sales managers. In a nutshell, the greater the level of information asymmetry between sales agents and sales managers, the higher the required degree of pricing authority delegation: the salesperson's superior knowledge about customer preferences and reservation values will make price delegation profitable for the firm. However, it is important to mention that where there is information asymmetry, control instruments and incentives must be put properly in place to mitigate the misuse of advanced information and pricing latitude. Thus, pricing authority should only be delegated in combination with control instruments.

Behavioural determinants

While the *formal* control systems described above can be considered as essential requirements for the pricing authority decision, the role of *informal* control systems is often underestimated in both managerial practice and sales research. However, informal elements of control, such as corporate culture, institutional values and interpersonal trust in an organization, are also crucial for the successful decentralization of decisions. Informal elements of control serve to complement and support formal efforts such as procedures, reporting methods or performance measures in preventing the misuse of pricing authority in an organization (see here and below Christ et al. 2008). Thus, managers have to understand how the interplay of formal and informal control impacts the overall effectiveness of decentralizing pricing decisions. The costs of formal control systems in particular should not be neglected. Intensive reporting requirements may, for instance, lead to inefficient use of labour time and hence labour

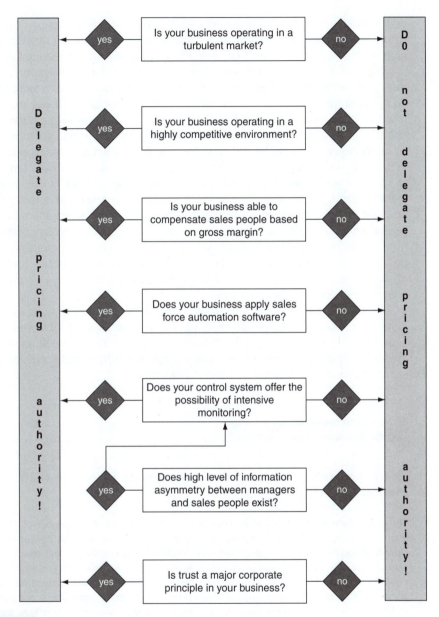

Figure 4.1   Guidelines for the delegation of pricing authority

costs. In such cases, it might be beneficial to replace some elements of formal control systems by some kind of informal control. Also, the psychological cost of formal control must be considered when designing the overall control environment in an organization. Sales force employees might perceive formal control as a signal of mistrust in their competence and integrity. They may also regard certain control mechanisms as an encroachment on their privacy. These potential perceptions decrease the sales representative's motivation and might lead to the corrosion of trust throughout the whole organization. Since trust can be seen as a key determinant of successful cooperative behavior, cooperation becomes difficult to ensure *despite* strong formal control mechanisms if formal rules become 'the bullet to bite' for the sales force. It is commonly known that trust is reciprocal, i.e. that if people do not feel trusted they in turn do not trust the other party. As the controlled person feels mistrusted, reciprocity will lead to a cycle of mistrust, which increases the hazard of non-cooperation – the direct opposite of the outcome planned by the implementation of formal control mechanisms. Thus, management should focus on enhancing distinct values such as trust and belief in and reliance on individuals in the corporate culture. A very simple tangible action is a flexible work time programme. It allows employees to work flexible hours in execution of their job and demonstrates that management trusts them to complete their tasks on time regardless of when they are executed. In the sales unit, allowing salespeople some pricing authority (e.g. in the chemical industry, 3 to 5 per cent variation from the list price) instead of zero pricing latitude might be a step in this direction. For the pricing authority decision, a combination of formal and informal control mechanisms seems to be a proper base for successful delegation. Figure 4.1 summarizes the recommendations in this section.

The second part of the case history below of Dow Chemical Company illustrates that informal control mechanisms may serve as a motivational tool as well as an organizational guideline for respectful behaviour within an organization. Dow's principle 'freedom to act' represents a very trustful corporate culture and serves as a basis for successful pricing delegation and overall performance.

CASE PROBLEM REVISITED

The organization of the Sales unit and its interplay with Marketing

The value chain in the chemical industry is characterized by a high number of multi-level elements with refineries, power and gas plants at its beginning and the consumer at its end. Dow is squeezed in the value chain between feedstock and customers. The company is located very close to the raw material production. As a chemical company, it processes feedstock in order to sell the resulting products to companies downstream in the value chain such as consumer product manufacturers, pharmaceutical manufacturers or agricultural companies, which in turn sell their processed products to distributors, the retail market or directly to the customer. According to Dow's customer-centric organization of the sales unit, each account manager negotiates the sale of the company's products with a selected number of complex industrial users. On average, the turnover by account manager lies between €15 million and €100 million per year.

As outlined in the first part of the case history, Dow's business is cyclical with a limited window for long-term planning. In particular, salespeople have to justify Dow's need for short-term pricing to their counterparts in sales negotiations due to the high price volatility of the raw materials which make up a major cost component of the company's products. This raises difficulties as the buying firm has a strategic interest in long-term pricing so that it can better plan its own product cost calculations. Therefore, the products' price calculations have to be designed carefully and should be based on an intensive analysis of the feedstock market and the competitive environment. At Dow, this is mainly the task of the Marketing department. Based on the assumption that the buying firm also conducts a lot of market research and is therefore aware of current feedstock indices, Dow has to adjust its product prices according to the movement of the raw material prices. Otherwise the buying firm might switch to another supplier. To avoid miscalculations, the Marketing department favours short-term pricing because the shorter they set prices, the better they can anticipate price trends in the feedstock market. However, this short-term pricing approach hinders the account managers in establishing long-term relationships with their customers, who are interested in long-term contracts with fixed prices over different time periods. To deal with this conflict between Marketing's wish for short-term pricing and Sales' demand for long-term contracts, Dow implemented a matrix organization for the Marketing and Sales unit. This organizational approach challenges Marketing and Sales to come to a compromise in the decisions that impact upon both departments. In terms of price calculations, this means that they have to agree upon a special pricing strategy. Hence, once the Marketing department has developed a tactical pricing policy for a specific product it has to obtain feedback from the account managers, who are better informed about customers' reservation prices because of their interaction with the buying firms. In this context, Marketing and Sales also have to discuss over what time period they can set prices. As a result of this mandatory coordination process, the company overcomes the problem of potential conflict between daily customer realities and the Marketing vision because market performance grows best in an environment that maintains a certain level of both perspectives: while, on the one hand, Marketing as advocate of short-term planning takes care to avoid losses from unforeseeable price increases at the feedstock market, on the other hand, the Sales department as the advocate and voice of the customer emphasizes the need for long-term considerations.[1]

The design of pricing authority

Compared to other chemical companies, Dow allows its account managers a high degree of pricing authority in sales negotiations. Especially in the Basics chemical segments, in the highly competitive environment of the basic chemical industry, price is a crucial parameter. In the Performance portfolio segments, which cover chemical products that are more specialized, price is rather a secondary factor since the buying firm has difficulty in purchasing those products from another supplier. Therefore, the pricing authority of account managers differs across these two product lines, because of the relative influence of the competitive environment, as explained previously. While the account managers are allowed to deviate a little from the list prices developed by the Marketing department in the highly competitive Basics segments, tolerance in the specialty segments is lower and can even be zero.

Several organizational factors as well as emphasis on distinct values in corporate behaviour determine the success of the comparably high degree of price delegation to the account managers. First of all, Dow's management has a high level of confidence in all its employees, something reflected in the corporate principle 'freedom to act'. With this approach, management signals its reliance on employees' decisions and belief in their competence. In the organizational structure, this is also mirrored in flat hierarchies. In the Sales unit, although there are supervising

---

[1] This characterization of Dow's Marketing and Sales units is contrary to the common belief that Sales is always rather short-term oriented, while the Marketing department is mostly distinguished as comparatively long-term oriented. However, due to the specifics of the chemical industry, Marketing's ability to make long-term plans are limited. Likewise, Dow's Sales unit has to ensure that the establishment of long-term customer relationships is not neglected.

sales managers who should be consulted if necessary, management relies on the decision-making competence of the account managers regarding all customer requirements because they are considered to know most about their customers' needs. Instead of being frightened that the account managers might misuse their informational advantage, Dow's management relies on the fact that the salespeople's superior knowledge about customers' preferences and reservation values will make price delegation profitable for the firm. Hence, control through strict hierarchies is not Dow's way of business. Furthermore, Dow does not utilize intensive formal reporting. According to the account managers' statements, the delegation of responsibilities motivates them to act in a way that benefits the organization. An extensive performance review at the end of each year serves as the only formal control instrument.

The importance of trust is also reflected in the interplay between Marketing and Sales required by the matrix organization. As outlined above, the feedback of the account managers is of great importance in developing the pricing strategies for Dow's different products. Consideration of the Sales unit's opinion leads to a general acceptance of the Marketing unit's pricing strategies in the sales force and enhances two-way trust in the organization: the account managers perceive the fact that their assessment regarding prices has been taken into account as a signal of trust in their skills and integrity. After pricing strategies for the product portfolio have been determined, it is the task of the account managers to defend them in sales negotiations with buying firms. From that time on, the Marketing department has to trust the account managers not to deviate too much from the desired prices without good reason. Since the account managers do not want to lose Marketing's trust in their customer knowledge and hence lose their voice in the price calculations, they try hard to achieve the desired prices in order to avoid disappointing the Marketing department. This reciprocal reliance on the other department's competences is an essential determinant for Dow's successful delegation of pricing authority. Only when the account manager accepts the pricing strategy designed by the Marketing department, will he/she try everything they can to adhere to it. On the other hand, Marketing has to trust the account manager only to endorse reasonable price reductions, based on the superior information that the account manager obtains in the course of the negotiation and which was not available in the run-up to the meeting with the buying firm. However, although Dow offers its account managers comparably high pricing latitude, it is still limited. If a customer requires large price reductions, the account manager has to confer with the Marketing department. In a team decision, Marketing and Sales employees can better evaluate the arguments of the buying firm and hence improve the quality of their decision-making regarding potential price cuts. The necessity to consult the Marketing department for high level price reductions helps avoid wrong assessments of the purchaser as a result of the account manager's personal relationship with the buyer or the like. Hence, within a limited range of price cuts, trust is used as an informal control element to manage the account managers' behaviour. When it comes to decisions that require larger price reductions, team discussions with those at the same hierarchical level serve as a more formal requirement to ensure the correct decision is made.

While many companies compensate their sales employees based on their achieved revenue or margin, Dow's compensation plan is rather complex. Of course, financial goals play a role in the evaluation process of the account managers, but much more important is the achievement of qualitative goals as well as 360° feedback. For instance, objectives such as achieving new product listings or sales of slow-selling goods resulting from joint production are also considered in the evaluation process. In the sales context, the dissemination of customer-specific knowledge obtained in sales calls is part of the performance review. The significance of knowledge transfer in the performance evaluation process serves as a formal control instrument that helps avoid potential misuse of informational advantage. To control dissemination of customer information, the account managers' colleagues from the Marketing department are especially consulted to assess whether the account manager circulates all the information that is necessary to develop customer-specific marketing programmes and to design pricing strategies.

To summarize, flat hierarchies, reliance and trust as corporate principles and the salespeople's voice in the products' price calculations allow Dow to delegate pricing succcessfully to the account managers. These organizational and behavioural factors are supported by a formal performance assessment process that each employee is subjected to once a year. Hence, Dow focuses on an informal control system via the emphasis of values such as belief in each individual's performance and reliance on an employee's competences, and supplements this with the more formal control instrument of annual performance reviews that emphasize behavioural goals.

Summary

The question of whether a firm should delegate pricing authority to its salespeople can be considered as one of the major issues in decentralized sales force control. Since final prices directly and strongly affect a company's bottom line, the decision as to whether and to what degree salespeople are allowed to negotiate prices and the consequent design of pricing authority delegation control is of crucial importance to the firm. In this chapter, we have attempted to identify those situations where it is appropriate to delegate pricing authority to salespersons or not. Agency theory served as a fruitful theoretical foundation for identifying major drivers in the decision-making for this managerial issue. Recommendations from sales management literature complemented these factors that either supported or weighed against delegating pricing authority to salespeople.

Our example from Dow Chemical Company shows that environmental conditions, organizational characteristics (such as compensation or sales force control system design) and behavioural aspects (e.g. corporate culture, values or trust) play a role in the optimal design of a sales force's pricing authority system and the degree to which this is delegated. It has been shown that exogenous market factors, e.g. volatility of feedstock prices and/or competitive intensity, pushed Dow to allow its salespeople to negotiate prices to a large degree. Transferring such authority to salespersons and, in general, providing Dow's salespeople with a substantial 'freedom to act', evidently strengthens its employees' bond to the company. The Dow case is also an interesting example of how pricing authority affects the quality of and need for collaboration between Marketing and Sales units. As Chapter 2 on the Sales– Marketing interface has explained in more detail, these two parts of the company have to work hand in hand to optimally trade off price, volume and gross margin effects. Despite recent research efforts (e.g. Frenzen et al. 2010), we still lack sufficient understanding of the complex domain of optimally delegating pricing authority. However, we hope that this discussion of the relevant academic literature, with additional insights from sales management practice and the Dow case, have shed some light into how the complex issue of adequately delegating pricing authority to salespeople can be addressed.

Key points

1. Pricing authority can be defined as the degree to which a sales force employee is empowered to negotiate and undertake reductions of a product's or service's list price without consultation of the sales manager.

2. Reasons for the delegation of pricing authority are, for instance, the ability to react more quickly to a changing market, competition and customer conditions, the ability to take advantage of the salesperson's informational advantage and their personal relationship with the customer, and reduction in coordination and management costs.
3. Reasons against the delegation of pricing authority include the inability of sales employees to see the consequences of their price reductions, the risk of substituting their selling effort by price discounting, the risk of inconsistencies across customers, segments or countries and the potential overloading of salespeople if they are not properly qualified to deal with the added responsibility.
4. Delegating pricing authority cannot be treated as a decision independent from other elements of the sales force control system. It is affected quite substantially by other factors such as organizational structure, corporate culture, design of sales force control systems, etc.
5. In general, it is recommended to delegate pricing authority to salespeople if the firm

   a) operates in turbulent environments;
   b) struggles with a high degree of competitive intensity;
   c) is able to compensate salespersons by gross margins;
   d) applies Sales Force Automation solutions;
   e) observes a substantial degree of information asymmetry;
   f) runs a sales force control system allowing for intensive monitoring; and
   g) is characterized by trust as a major corporate principle.

References

Anderson, E. and Oliver, R.L. (1987) 'Perspectives on Behavior-based Versus Outcome-based Sales Force Control Systems', *Journal of Marketing*, 51 (4): 76–88.
Basu, A.K., Lal, R., Srinivasan, V. and Staelin, R. (1985) 'Salesforce Compensation Plans: An Agency Theoretic Perspective', *Marketing Science*, 4 (4): 267–91.
Bhardwaj, P. (2001) 'Delegating Pricing Decisions', *Marketing Science*, 20 (2), 143–69.
Buttle, F., Ang, L., and Iriana, R. (2006) 'Sales Force Automation: Review, Critique, Research Agenda', *International Journal of Marketing Reviews*, 8 (4), 213–31.
Christ, M.H., Sedatole, K.L., Towry, K.L. and Thomas, M.A. (2008) 'When Formal Controls Undermine Trust and Cooperation', *Strategic Finance*, 89 (7), 39–44.
Dolan, R.J. and Simon, H. (1996) *Power Pricing – How Managing Price Transforms the Bottom Line*. New York: The Free Press.
Frenzen, H., Hansen, A., Krafft, M., Mantrala, M. and Schmidt, S. (2010) 'Delegation of Pricing Authority to the Sales Force: An Agency-theoretic Perspective of its Determinants and Impact on Performance', *International Journal of Marketing Research*, 27 (1): 58–68.
Hansen, A., Joseph, K. and Krafft, M. (2008) 'Price Delegation in Sales Organizations', *Business Research*, 1 (1): 94–104.
Jaworski, B.J. and Kohli, A.K. (1993) 'Market Orientation: Antecedents and Consequences', *Journal of Marketing*, 57 (3): 53–70.
John, G. and Weitz, B. (1989) 'Salesforce Compensation: An Empirical Investigation of Factors Related to Use of Salary Versus Incentive Compensation', *Journal of Marketing Research*, 26 (1): 1–14.

Joseph, K. (2001) 'On the Optimality of Delegating Pricing Authority to the Sales Force', *Journal of Marketing*, 65 (1): 62–70.

Krafft, M. (1999) 'An Empirical Investigation of the Antecedents of Salesforce Control Systems', *Journal of Marketing*, 63 (3): 120–34.

Lal, R. (1986) 'Delegating Pricing Responsibility to the Salesforce', *Marketing Science*, 5 (2): 159–68.

Mishra, B.K. and Prasad, A. (2004) 'Centralized Pricing Versus Delegating Pricing to the Salesforce Under Information Asymmetry', *Marketing Science*, 23 (1): 21–7.

Mishra, B.K. and Prasad, A. (2005) 'Delegating Pricing Decisions in Competitive Markets with Symmetric and Asymmetric Information', *Marketing Science*, 24 (3): 490–7.

Nagar, V. (2002) 'Delegation and Incentive Compensation', *Accounting Review*, 77 (2): 379–95.

Ramaswami, S. N., Srinivasan, S. S., and Gorton, S. A. (1997), 'Information Asymmetry Between Salesperson and Supervisor: Postulates from Agency and Social Exchange Theories', *Journal of Personal Selling and Sales Management*, 17 (3): 29–50.

Rivers, M.L. and Dart, J. (1999) 'The Acquisition and Use of Sales Force Automation by Mid-Sized Manufacturers', *Journal of Personal Selling and Sales Management*, 19 (2): 59–73.

Schillewaert, N. and Ahearne, M. (2001) 'The Effect of Information Technology on Salesperson Performance', in *ISBM Report*, 5. Location: Pennsylvania State University Press.

Stephenson, P.R., Cron, W.L. and Frazier, L. (1979) 'Delegating Pricing Authority to the Sales Force: The Effects on Sales and Profit Performance', *Journal of Marketing*, 43 (2): 21–8.

Weinberg, C.B. (1978), 'Jointly Optimal Sales Commissions for Nonincome Maximizing Sales Forces', *Management Science*, 24 (12): 1252–8.

Weinberg, C.B. (1975), 'An Optimal Commission Plan for Salesmen's Control Over Price', *Management Science*, 21 (8):.937–43.

Further reading

Evans, K. R. and Beltramini, R.F. (1987) 'A Theoretical Model of Consumer Negotiated Pricing: An Orientation Perspective', *Journal of sarketing*, 51 (2): 58–73.

Larkin, I. (2006) 'The Cost of High-powered Incentives: Salesperson Gaming in Enterprise Software', *Harvard Business School Working Paper*, Boston, MA: Harvard Business School.

Ganesan, S. (1993) 'Negotiation Strategies and the Nature of Channel Relationships', *Journal of Marketing Research*, 30 (2): 183–203.

Wilken, R., Cornelissen, M., Backhaus, K. and Schmitz, C. (2009) 'Steering Sales Reps Through Cost Information: An Investigation into the Black Box of Cognitive References and Negotiation Behaviour', *International Journal of Research in Marketing*, 27 (1):. 69–82.

5

Customer Relationship Management (CRM) system implementation in sales organizations

Nikolaos G. Panagopoulos

Contents

Learning objectives

After reading this chapter, you should be able to:

* Recognize the critical importance of CRM systems today.

* Understand critical barriers to CRM systems acceptance and usage.

* Know the key factors needed for the successful adoption of CRM systems in the context of sales force management.

* Understand how CRM systems impact on sales performance.

Chapter outline

This chapter deals with one of the most difficult challenges modern sales organizations face: the successful implementation of a Customer Relationship Management (CRM) system. With the aim of helping sales executives to manage the implementation process (from system design to roll-out and sales force acceptance), the chapter is structured in four parts. The first part (Problem) presents a problem in a real case history to stimulate readers' attention regarding CRM system implementation. The second part reviews the relevant literature on CRM systems with the aim to synthesize this literature into managerial concepts such as a process for successfully implementing a CRM system and a model for assessing the return on CRM investment. We then return to the case history presented in the first part and examine how CRM was adopted by the company. The chapter concludes with a process for running a CRM audit as well as a list of key points for sales executives.

Pharmatron Hellas

In April 2001 George Zisis, Sales Director at Pharmatron Hellas (PH), entered the meeting room in the company's affiliate in Athens. He had been asked to come up with a plan for how the company could effectively implement a CRM system into its sales organization. Jim Papadopoulos (CEO) and the members of the board of directors had decided to implement a CRM system in the company's affiliate in Greece with the aim of increasing sales and profits and to enable them to gain a clearer picture of the affiliate's performance. George had spent the last six months reviewing business and sales processes and evaluating alternative CRM system vendors. He was very nervous about the meeting, as this was the first time that either he or the company would implement a CRM system. George had been charged with the task of selecting a CRM vendor and implementing it. He had selected an international vendor on the basis of price and competitive practices. Indeed, this vendor had supplied most of Pharmatron's competitors. Prior to CRM implementation, the company was using written reports from salespeople to collect data about customers and competitors and to forecast sales. However, salespeople were not systematically filling in the reports, since time was always sparse. In addition, George had realized that much of the information collected through the salespeople's reports was never actually used by management. Today, George had to defend his choice and propose a plan to get the sales force to buy-in to it.

What is a CRM system?

Defining CRM is not an easy task. This is because different stakeholders (i.e. software and hardware vendors, consultants and application service providers) use their own definitions of CRM (Plouffe et al. 2004). In addition, earlier studies as well as vendors of CRM systems coined the term Sales Force Automation (SFA) to 'refer to the use of computer hardware, software and telecommunications devices by salespeople in their selling and/or administrative activities' (Morgan and Inks 2001). Although related to SFA, however, CRM is a much broader concept, which includes not only the automation of sales processes (as SFA does) but also the development of customer strategies. To aid our discussion, we employ a recent classification (Tanner et al. 2005), according to which CRM comprises three interrelated aspects: *strategic*, *analytical* and *operational*. Although both strategic and analytical aspects of CRM are very important, our focus is on the operational aspect of CRM. Operational CRM consists of business processes and technologies facilitating the implementation and automation of CRM strategies and models developed at the strategic and analytical level. From a sales force standpoint, therefore, a CRM system involves the automation of customer-related processes such as lead management, opportunity management, scheduling, sales planning, route planning, territory management, making sales presentations, documenting buyer objections, retrieving product information, configuring product specifications, customer contact management and sales forecasting (Hunter and Perreault 2007; Tanner et al. 2005).

A recent study reveals that worldwide CRM software revenue totalled $7 billion in 2006 (Sims 2007). This clearly shows that companies continue to spend an immense amount of money on sales technology. Data on CRM system spending in the European Union (EU), however, suggests a different picture, since EU companies are spending less than their US counterparts (*Datamonitor* 2006). In particular, a Gartner study suggests that the market for CRM software in the EU totalled $1.9 billion in 2005 (Brown 2006). According to this study, growth in countries such as Italy and Germany remains lower than the rest of the world, while market growth in countries such as the UK, Sweden, Norway and Denmark has been more consistent with that in the US, for instance. Finally, the same Gartner study shows that 12.1 per cent of the total CRM software market is related to SFA software.

Despite high investments and advances in information technology (IT), however, CRM system failure rates constitute a paradox. Indeed, research reports indicate that between 55 per cent and 75 per cent of CRM projects fail because salespeople reject the technologies (Speier and Venkatesh 2002). Unfortunately, according to a global survey, which showed that less than 40 per cent of firms implementing CRM systems have end-user adoption rates above 90 per cent (Dickie 2006), this trend has remained unchanged. The reasons for CRM system failure are many and complex and it is these reasons to which we will turn our attention next. However, before we proceed with discussing how to implement a CRM system effectively, it is important to make a distinction between two seemingly related though different concepts: CRM system *acceptance* and CRM system *usage*.

The distinction between CRM system acceptance and usage

CRM system acceptance (adoption) refers to the initial attitudes and reactions of salespeople towards the CRM system. It is at this stage that an individual salesperson

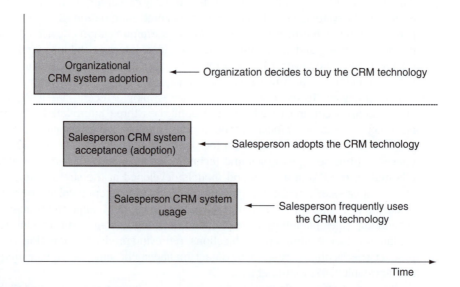

Figure 5.1   The distinction between CRM system acceptance and usage

will decide to accept the new technology or not. CRM system usage, however, refers to the extent or frequency with which a salesperson uses a CRM system, after the system has been introduced and adopted by the sales force (Sundaram et al. 2007). Importantly, frequent CRM system usage is an important prerequisite for maximizing the potential of the CRM system (Sundaram et al. 2007).

Figure 5.1 also shows us that organizations base their decision to accept CRM technology on different factors than individuals (salespeople) do. Recognition of this has important ramifications for our understanding of how CRM systems are accepted by salespeople. In particular, the adoption of a CRM system is a two-stage process (Frambach and Schillewaert 2002; Parthasarathy and Sohi 1997). Initially, organizations decide to adopt a CRM system, and then, subsequently, individual salespeople adopt it. Thus, the process of CRM implementation by the sales force starts only after the organization has decided to buy a CRM system.

Key success factors of CRM implementation

Salespeople are often forced to adopt the CRM system because their organization has decided to adopt it. However, not all salespeople will buy in at the same time; some will immediately embrace it while others will be reluctant and resist it. While there is a myriad of factors inhibiting CRM acceptance by the sales force, many authors agree that two important reasons for their not accepting a CRM system is that it is not viewed by salespeople as a sales enablement tool or that it is considered as an onerous imposition that they are required to use. Notwithstanding the difficulties associated with successful CRM implementation, the relevant literature offers many guidelines to sales executives charged with the task of gaining salespeople's buy-in. In what follows, we provide a synthesis of the relevant literature by outlining the most prominent factors of CRM implementation success and elaborate on those factors' managerial implications. To aid our discussion we follow the literature (e.g. Schillewaert et al. 2005) and group these factors in three categories: CRM system factors, organizational factors, and salespeople's factors (see Figure 5.2).

This categorization is a useful guide for managers since it includes most of the factors that can play an active role in the effective implementation of a CRM system.

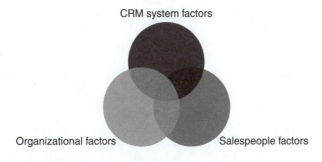

Figure 5.2   Understanding what drives successful CRM implementation

Two points are worth mentioning, however: first, none of these factors is more important than the others in the overall implementation process, and, secondly, there are important interplays among the three groups of factors. Thus, management should simultaneously consider all categories during system implementation. In addition, managers should bear in mind that all three categories of factors are under their control; it is their task to design the implementation process carefully, taking each factor into account.

CRM system factors

This category of factors is related to the characteristics of the CRM system per se. Table 5.1 displays the four factors that fall into this category.

System ease-of-use

This refers to the degree to which the prospective user expects the technology to be free of effort (Robinson et al. 2005). Thus, sales executives aiming at increasing the acceptance rate among members of the sales force should work towards making tasks easy and purchasing CRM systems that are user-friendly.

System usefulness

This is defined as the prospective user's subjective opinion that using a specific technology will probably increase his/her job performance (Robinson et al. 2005).

Table 5.1   CRM system factors related to effective implementation

Factors	Implications
System ease-of-use	• User-friendly interface • Easily understood • No severe changes in daily workflow
System usefulness	• Helps daily workflow • Saves time • Allows for more things to be done • Allows things to be done better • Provides up-to-date information • Provides accurate information
Compatibility with existing systems	• Compatibility with all aspects of work • Fits into work style • Fits with the way salespeople like to work
Professional fit	• Increases the level of challenge in salespeople's careers • Increases the amount of variety in salespeople's careers • Increases the opportunity for more meaningful work

System usefulness has been found to be an important factor of CRM acceptance in several studies (e.g. Avlonitis and Panagopoulos 2005). Ironically, however, many organizations neither built CRM systems around sales force needs nor do they communicate CRM systems' benefits. Even more important is the fact that sales management may have a more optimistic picture regarding CRM benefits than the sales force. In particular, the sales force may believe that the system is providing less adequate or accurate information compared with management (Gohmann et al. 2005). Thus, sales executives should strive to assess what benefits their salespeople seek from a CRM system and then try to match these needs to specific CRM features. This could be done by conducting a series of interviews or by surveying salespeople on what they regard as important in their tasks.

Compatibility with existing systems

This is the degree to which the CRM system fits with the salesperson's existing values, previous experiences and current needs (Speier and Venkatesh, 2002). Thus, management should work towards demonstrating how the CRM system fits into previous processes, thereby facilitating the smooth implementation of the system.

Professional fit between the salesperson and the technology

When the CRM is perceived by salespeople as having a negative impact and/or disrupts the sales process to the point that the system does not play to their strengths as salespeople, the system will not be accepted (Speier and Venkatesh 2002).

Organizational factors

The second category of factors displayed in Figure 5.2 is concerned with the characteristics of the organization and managerial activities (see Table 5.2).

Planning CRM implementation

Quite often CRM implementation is a convulsive reaction to competitive and industry forces and not a planned process. But how should managers plan CRM implementation? Although planning can be a cumbersome process, the following steps can guide managers in their endeavour (Honeycutt et al. 2005).

First, managers should set specific and measurable goals and articulate a clearly communicated purpose for CRM implementation. The two most important goals related to CRM implementation are to increase salesperson efficiency and effectiveness. However, companies need to be very specific in what they expect from CRM usage. Although setting the right goals appears to be easy, in practice most companies either set too many goals or they set the wrong ones (Honeycutt et al. 2005). Consider, for instance, the case of a company that has set the objective of reducing time spent on administrative tasks and increasing sales. The major problem with these objectives, however, is that in reality they are not easily measurable: how and whether a company evaluates time spent on administrative activities may also be subject to a lot of criticism. Thus, managers need to set realistic, specific, relevant and measurable

Table 5.2   Organizational factors related to effective implementation

Factors	Implications
Planning CRM implementation	• Design a proactive planned process • Define specific and measurable goals • Define a clear purpose for CRM • Involve a cross-functional team • Foster intra-organizational trust • Foster a climate of information-sharing • Seek feedback from the sales force
Communicating CRM objectives and benefits	• Communicate objectives and expected outcomes • Gain consensus • Allow for two-way communication • Set accurate expectations
Setting appropriate metrics	• Develop appropriate metrics and key performance indicators to monitor overall process • Outline sales tasks and activities that are impacted by CRM
Training	• Before CRM introduction • During CRM introduction • Establish regular training courses on CRM usage
Technical support	• Create a help desk • Answer questions • Resolve problems related to mobile connectivity • Collaborate with the vendor
Organizational culture	• Entrepreneurial values • Customer-centricity • Learning orientation
Change programmes	• Outline how the new technology can enhance the salesperson's value within the firm • Outline how it can help salespeople increase their productivity
Management behaviours	• Facilitative leadership • Encouragement of system use • Top management commitment
Reward schemes	• Carefully tie usage to bonuses

objectives for CRM usage and plan for any supporting mechanisms that will aid them in the evaluation process.

Secondly, managers should employ a cross-functional team in CRM planning, vendor selection, purchasing and the implementation processes (Honeycutt et al. 2005).

Implementing a CRM system in the organization should not be department-specific but an interdepartmental endeavour. Although the CRM system is for the Sales function, one should bear in mind that customers are in contact not only with the sales force but also with other functions of the company (i.e. service and technical personnel, customer support employees, Marketing employees, accounts executives etc.). A truly customer-centric CRM system should be designed to capture all customer contacts and all relevant information that stems from these contacts. Building a cross-functional CRM system, however, is not an easy task. Management should foster a climate of information-sharing between Sales and other functions. This can be accomplished by increasing intra-organizational trust, which refers to the willingness of employees to rely on other organizational members in whom they have confidence (Pullig et al. 2002). The effective functioning of a CRM system relies largely on sensitive customer information, which salespersons should be willing to share with the rest of the company through an increased feeling of trust. In a climate of information-sharing and trust, salespeople will be more willing to work towards CRM system implementation (Pullig et al. 2002). In addition, CRM planning should involve employees outside the Sales function. This might be accomplished through cross-functional meetings on a regular basis. One great problem with cross-functional teams, however, is that employees from different departments have different goals, priorities and working plans and that this undermines cross-functional collaboration. A plausible solution to this problem is for top management to be involved in the formation, functioning and evaluation of cross-functional teams.

Thirdly, managers should actively seek feedback from the sales force (Honeycutt et al. 2005). Feedback can be obtained by running a survey or conducting a series of interviews with salespeople to identify what tasks they would like to be automated or not and what should be the desired functionalities of a CRM system. Unfortunately, many managers do not realize that the salesperson is the 'internal customer' whose needs have to be satisfied during system implementation (Avlonitis and Panagopoulos 2005). In addition, early involvement in the planning process creates feelings of inclusion, fairness and ownership and, thus, it softens resistance to change related to the introduction of a CRM system (Morgan and Inks 2001).

Communicating CRM objectives and benefits

Before a CRM system is introduced, management needs to communicate the objectives and the expected outcomes from CRM usage throughout the entire organization until consensus is reached (Honeycutt et al. 2005). Successful communication implies that management facilitates two-way communication and sets up accurate expectations for users regarding CRM's return on investment and usage.

Setting appropriate metrics

Effective CRM implementation needs to be accompanied by the development of appropriate metrics that will ensure the effective monitoring of its implementation and usage throughout the entire lifetime of the project (Honeycutt et al. 2005). Unfortunately, many companies do not invest in developing the right metrics and key performance indicators (KPIs) to track CRM usage and outcomes. This is because it is difficult to link

sales outcomes with intangible benefits derived from CRM usage, such as better territory planning or time utilization. Regardless of the difficulty associated with measuring
the effectiveness of a CRM system, however, managers need to develop metrics to
guide the successful implementation of the overall project. Of course, the development
of metrics will be influenced by the idiosyncrasies of the industry and the company
itself.

Training

CRM system implementation changes the way salespeople do their jobs and introduces new requirements (Dickie 2006). Thus, it is imperative that managers develop
formalized sales force training programmes on system usage. Training will also help
salespeople understand the benefits obtained from using the system. Training can
take two forms: general computing skills and CRM system competence. Training programmes should be planned prior to CRM implementation to introduce the sales force
to the new requirements. However, training must be ongoing during the roll-out and
implementation process so as to facilitate the smooth introduction of the CRM system.
Remember: the CRM implementation process is an ongoing endeavour; it does not
end with system introduction, but rather it has to be managed throughout the entire
lifetime of the project. Therefore, training must also be an ongoing process, as new
requirements emerge and new salespeople are recruited.

Technical support

Companies also need to provide technical support to salespeople regarding CRM system usage. Adequate technical support enhances salespeople's understanding and
reduces the required effort needed to use the CRM system. Usually, technical support
is formally provided by the CRM vendor; however, companies need to involve their
IT department in the provision of technical support.

Organizational culture

Companies implementing a CRM system do not give much attention to 'soft' issues
surrounding implementation. One such issue is organizational culture, which is the set
of underlying assumptions, beliefs, norms and behaviours that characterize the functioning of an organization. Although there are several dimensions of an organizational
culture, our focus is on those with the maximum impact on CRM implementation. The
first of these refers to 'entrepreneurial values', that is, the shared beliefs that promote
tolerance for risk within the organization, the encouragement of proactive behaviour,
receptiveness to innovation and resistance to bureaucracy (Pulling et al. 2002).

The second cultural dimension is customer-centricity, which involves those shared
values, norms, artefacts and behaviours that focus on satisfying customers' needs
and creating long-term profitable customer relationships (Pulling et al. 2002). Under
a customer-centric culture, the CRM system will be viewed as a primary mechanism
through which information on customer needs is collected, stored and analysed to
facilitate organization-wide customer-focus.

The third dimension of organizational culture is learning orientation, which refers
to an organization's desire and willingness continually to understand its environment,

learn new skills and information and use new knowledge (Raman et al. 2006). As such, it would be reasonable to expect that learning organizations will be more prone to adopt a CRM system due to their increased desire and capacity for learning more about customers.

Change programmes

Most salespeople do not have the ability to foresee how CRM systems can aid them in the selling process. In addition, salespeople fear the new technology as they view it suspiciously as a threat to their own jobs. Thus, sales executives should make all necessary efforts to develop change programmes that will outline how the new technology can enhance the salesperson's value within the firm and how it can help them increase their productivity. A change programme should aim to facilitate the smooth transition from the old to the new technology, thus reducing resistance to CRM-related change.

Management behaviours

Sales Managers and Field Sales Supervisors play an important role in stimulating salespeople to accept the CRM system (Avlonitis and Panagopoulos 2005). In particular, supervisors who support the CRM system by explicitly encouraging its use can induce salespeople to adopt the system. This is because supervisors are in close, frequent and direct contact with the salespeople whom they supervise, thereby fostering a climate of trust. There is some evidence in the literature that when a salesperson perceives his/her supervisor to be 'pressing' them towards usage, then he/she will eventually use the CRM system (e.g., Schillewaert et al. 2005). In addition, salespeople may view supervisors as 'mentors' to whom they can direct all of their questions regarding system usage. Managers at higher layers of the sales organization can also play an important role in accelerating CRM acceptance; there is evidence showing that facilitative leadership, which focuses on people development and developing a learning climate, creates an environment where CRM systems are fully utilized by the sales force (Pullig et al. 2002). Finally, the successful implementation of a CRM system presupposes that Sales Managers are committed to the new system. With the assumption that salespeople trust management, a strong commitment from managers signals the importance of the project and reduces salespeople's resistance.

Reward schemes

Salespeople view time as a precious resource that they carefully allocate across various activities. This might be more pertinent in situations where a relatively large portion of their compensation is directly tied to their performance (e.g. incentive payment). Thus, it is not unreasonable to expect that salespeople will view CRM usage as another onerous imposition that increases their workload or takes up time otherwise spent with customers, on making sales and thus earning them more money. Consequently, it has been suggested that CRM usage must be an integral part of salespeople's compensation scheme in order for them to use it. However, as noted by Ahearne et al. (2004), one needs to bear in mind that tying usage to performance runs the risk of salespeople monitoring and manipulating usage in order to gain their bonuses.

Salespeople factors

Managers need to take into account the characteristics of salespeople before rolling out the CRM technology. Salespeople can differ in many respects, such as demographic characteristics (age, educational level), attitudes toward change, predispositions, ambitions, goals, etc. Consequently, it is reasonable to expect that the introduction of new technology will not be accepted in the same manner by all salespeople. Among the various individual differences that can possibly affect CRM implementation, the most prominent are those displayed in Table 5.3.

Salesperson age, educational level and previous IT knowledge

Many salespeople, primarily older ones, have been working for years without any technology at all. Thus it is likely that they will resist the new technology, largely due to a lack of knowledge and technological fear (technophobia). Younger salespeople and college graduates, on the other hand, have been recently exposed to the usage of new technologies during formal education and thus they are more likely to accept the CRM system.

Sales experience

In general, less experienced salespeople have a more positive attitude towards CRM systems, are more receptive to using them, feel less threatened by them and believe that CRM systems can make them more productive (Keillor et al. 1997). The logic behind this assertion is that experienced salespeople, who are usually more productive and effective than less experienced salespeople, have developed rigid working structures and follow their own practices, which they are less prone to abandon for

Table 5.3   Salespeople factors related to effective implementation

Factors	Implications
Age, educational level, previous IT knowledge	• Resistance by older, less educated, less IT-experienced salespeople • Manage technophobia
Sales experience	• Manage the more experienced salespeople
Predispositions, perceptions and attitudes towards the CRM system	• Manage risk-aversion • Manage stress related to introduction of CRM • Minimize information overload
Effort	• Ensure that adequate effort is exerted
Fears related to CRM introduction	• Fear of monitoring • Fear of losing power • Fear of losing job

the sake of the new technology. Therefore, managers need to address questions raised by experienced salespersons, such as 'why change something that worked well for years?'.

Predispositions, perceptions and attitudes toward the CRM system

Salespeople develop perceptions and attitudes towards the new system that can greatly inhibit the process of implementation and acceptance. Risk-aversion, for instance, is a negative predisposition against new things such as a new technological tool. Salespeople who are risk-averse will be less wiling to adopt the CRM system. In contrast, there is evidence suggesting that salespeople with an innovative predisposition, attitude and action tendencies towards adopting new information technologies will be more willing to accept the CRM system. Moreover, the introduction of a CRM system into the sales organization may increase role ambiguity and role conflict experienced by salespeople. Role ambiguity (i.e. a stress situation in which a salesperson lacks clear direction about the expectations of his/her role in the job or organization) and role conflict (i.e. the degree to which the work expectations and work requirements of two or more people are incompatible) can have a dramatic and negative impact on salespeople's performance. Thus, sales executives should strive to monitor the extent to which salespeople feel either uncertain about using the CRM technology or that the CRM technology is in conflict with other sales activities and demands (Rangarajan et al. 2005). Finally, if salespeople perceive that the amount of information provided by the system exceeds their capacity to handle, process and utilize it effectively (information overload), then it is highly possible that they will resist the system or underutilize it. Clearly, one should not overestimate the power of information; more is not always better when it comes to CRM implementation. It is always better to rely on a few selected bytes of information rather than to overwhelm the sales force with an inordinate amount of data that they simply cannot handle.

Effort

Effort is the amount of energy expended by salespeople on both the physical and cognitive demands of performing the task of integrating CRM technology into their daily activities. Hence, sales executives should make sure that salespeople are expending the necessary amount of effort to integrate the CRM system into their jobs. However, it should be mentioned that many salespeople will perceive that the adoption of the CRM system necessitates substantial and perhaps disproportionate time and effort be expended for its proper utilization. One way to reduce their reluctance to spend time on CRM is to provide salespersons with technical support (24/7 online support) and training classes.

Fears related to CRM introduction

Fear is a negative emotion which unfortunately exists whenever organizations are trying to innovate and change current work practices. Like any other innovative work practice, the CRM system can create fears among the sales force with deleterious effects for its performance. These fears can take three forms. The first type of fear is of increased level of monitoring by management (fear of 'big brother'). Secondly, salespeople may fear loss of power. Prior to CRM implementation, salespeople were literally the owner of customer relationships and information about them. That gave them a relatively higher degree of power over other employee groups in the organization. With the advent of CRM systems, however, the salesperson is increasingly being asked to share with the company his/her knowledge about the customer. This, in turn, may lead to an increase in fear of losing his/her power. Finally, some salespeople may fear losing their jobs due to the introduction of CRM. If these fears are not controlled, it is possible that salespeople will resist the CRM system or even try to sabotage its acceptance.

Is there an optimal level of CRM system usage?

Organizations make significant investments and devote a lot of effort in their attempt to gain salespeople's buy-in. But what happens after, say, all salespeople have accepted the CRM system as an integral part of their daily workflow? Should management now make all necessary efforts to maximize usage among salespeople? The answer to this question is definitely not. Salespeople, and their companies, are primarily interested in building relationships with their customers and in maximizing sales results. These goals, however, can only be achieved through face-to-face interactions with their customers. Therefore, if a salesperson increases his/her time spent on CRM usage, this will decrease time spent in the field, thereby hurting his/her sales performance. Time is not an unlimited resource and it has to be optimally allocated across the various tasks, with differing effects on their performance. For instance, Ahearne et al. (2004) found that CRM usage has a positive effect on sales performance up until a specific point; beyond that, CRM usage has diminishing returns and actually lowers performance. This study has several important implications for managers. For instance, if CRM usage and performance are related, then it is natural to expect that managers should monitor, track and fix under- or over-utilization. However, managers need to strike a balance between their need to track usage and the privacy rights of salespersons. Even if the company has implemented an open policy of tracking usage, the salesperson could manipulate the use of technology to align his/her usage levels with company directives (Ahearne et al. 2004). Importantly, an open policy of tracking could signal that management is closely monitoring their behaviour, thereby decreasing trust between managers and salespeople. In the end, it is management that has to decide whether to publicly or privately track CRM usage and what to do with over- and under-users (Ahearne et al. 2004).

Other less apparent negative consequences of increased CRM usage may be related to the capabilities of modern wireless CRM devices. Consider, for instance, a salesperson spending his/her day making calls to customers. In the past, the salesperson would go back to company headquarters and upload customer and competitive data into the server manually. However, with the availability of wireless devices (utilizing 3G networks and VoIP technologies) the salesperson does not have to return to the office. He/she simply has to upload the data using the wireless device, regardless of whether he/she is on the road or in his/her own house. One would question whether this is a problem or an opportunity, as technology saves time travelling back to the office.

Although for some salespeople this would be considered as an opportunity, for many others this could be a threat. This is because they may feel that time spent in the office is beneficial for several reasons: they can discuss with their supervisor problems that they faced in the field, they can ask for any necessary support, and, most importantly, they can interact with others in the company. Interaction is vital for keeping employees up to date with company developments and to increasing feelings of team coherence and organizational commitment. Thus, although advances in sales technology make jobs easier it is important to remember that personal interaction is also a vital component of the sales job.

A process for successful CRM implementation and usage

As previously discussed, there are many reasons for CRM systems' failure to be accepted by salespeople. Hence, sales executives need a concrete process upon which to base their implementation efforts. This section therefore outlines one such process that can facilitate the smooth implementation of a CRM system. The process involves a series of interrelated steps, which are shown in Figure 5.3 and subsequently explained.

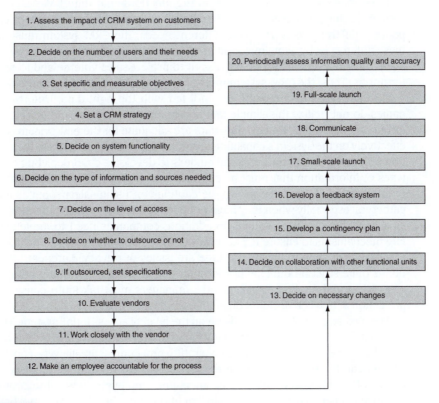

Figure 5.3   A managerial process for effectively implementing a CRM system

The first step involves an assessment of the impact of the CRM system on customer relationships, especially where the system will be visible to customers. This can be accomplished by surveying customers on their feelings regarding the CRM system. A relevant issue is to assess whether the CRM system offers any benefits to customers.

The next step involves a decision on the number of users and their needs. Caution should be taken regarding the fact that users holding different positions within the organizational hierarchy (salespeople, field sales supervisors and sales executives) will have different needs. Thus, management must carefully study the various needs and develop a blueprint to guide later stages of CRM development. Then, management should move forward by setting specific and measurable objectives for CRM implementation. Critical questions that beg an answer are: What exactly is expected from system usage? What gains are to be expected from system usage? How will the CRM system facilitate CRM processes? Note that different companies and industries may need to develop their own goals. Related to the setting of objectives is the development of a rigid CRM strategy that will tie CRM usage to CRM objectives. The essential elements of a CRM strategy at the level of the Sales function are to outline the processes of acquiring new customers, retaining and growing existing customers, recapturing lost customers and ending non-profitable customer relationships. Thus, management has to define the specific tasks and activities that account for each of these four CRM processes as well as the linkage of each with CRM usage.

Next, management must decide on the functions that the CRM system must possess for each type of user identified in the second step. Since different groups of users perform different tasks and have different needs, the CRM system must account for these differences by allowing for different uses and functions. For instance, Sales Managers often use spreadsheets (e.g. Excel) to project sales volume and to analyse sales territories. Thus, the CRM system must allow managers to perform these tasks.

No CRM system is perfect if it is not fed with the right data. Unfortunately, companies do not realize this simple fact and many CRM failures are a direct outcome of erroneously assuming that existing data are adequate for the new system. To capitalize effectively on the system's capabilities, companies need to reorganize their data collection processes. To this end, a useful guide is to develop a chart depicting the necessary types of information that must be collected and who is going to contribute each type of information. A note of concern: be cautious on using salespeople as information-gatherers, especially when they have not been selected, trained, motivated and treated as a valued information source. In addition, companies need to implement controlling mechanisms to ensure the accuracy of information being entered into the system. Finally, equally important at this stage are issues of privacy. European Union legislation is quite strict on the type of customer and employee information that companies can collect and analyse. Consequently, managers must take into consideration data protection acts when deciding on sources and types of data used in a CRM system.

The next step involves the decision on the level of access to the system. The renewed capabilities of accessing and using information that are generated by CRM introduction must be in line with organizational operating procedures. Specifically, companies must be very careful when deciding on the level of access to information, especially when this involves information about customers and employees. It is not uncommon for an employee either to abuse or poach information when he/she leaves the organization. Unethical behaviour of salespeople in regard to CRM use is not a rare phenomenon.

Salespeople may manipulate, spy or use information for personal advancement. Thus, management must carefully decide which users will have what kind of access to what types of information.

An important decision that has to be made at the eighth stage is whether to outsource CRM system development or whether to develop it internally (out-house versus. in-house development). Few organizations possess the necessary skills and capabilities for developing a CRM solution. Importantly, one needs to consider not only a company's ability to build the system but also to maintain, support and feed it with relevant data. If an outside vendor is chosen, then management has to set the specifications that will enable vendor evaluation and selection. Among the many criteria that a company can use to evaluate CRM vendors, competence and responsiveness are two of the most prominent dimensions. Of course, industry experience and costs associated with the choice of a particular vendor are also important dimensions. Once a vendor has been selected, management has to work closely with the vendor to specify the various functions of the CRM system that were identified in the fifth step.

It is also very important to make an employee accountable for the CRM implementation process. There is no clear-cut solution for all companies regarding the functional area from which this employee should come from. The decision depends on the nature, objectives and structure of the organization. In some instances companies may have to create a new position for handling the CRM implementation process. Alternatively, they may need to set up a cross-functional team.

Next, those charged with CRM implementation should outline any necessary changes that must be implemented to facilitate the smooth introduction and usage of the CRM system. These changes might revolve around the transformation of sales and CRM processes, organizational structure, culture and human resource systems (i.e. selection, training, evaluation and reward schemes). Related to this, an important decision that has to be made is concerned with the way that the sales organization will collaborate with other functional units (such as Marketing and IT). This is important, since in many instances CRM implementation fails due to alienation among a company's functional units. For example, early involvement of the IT department in the implementation process can ensure that the company can handle the software and hardware requirements implied by the introduction of a CRM system.

The next step is to develop a contingency plan that will enable management to confront the various technical problems associated with CRM implementation. Such problems may revolve around incompatibility with previously used IT systems and databases or connectivity problems, especially when the CRM system employs a wireless service provider to upload and download data.

Another important activity is to develop a feedback system that will enable the organization to assess the attainment of CRM objectives (system acceptance and usage, system return on investment (ROI). Importantly, the feedback system must be in line with the objectives set at the third stage of the implementation process.

Once all previous steps have been executed, it is time to launch the CRM system. It may be better initially to launch the system to a small sample of salespeople in order to gain insight into its actual operation. At this initial step, management should target innovative, risk-happy, young and well-educated salespeople who will play the role of project champions among their colleagues. Gaining Field Sales Managers' buy-in is also very important. Management should strive to gain salespeople's feedback and make any necessary changes or handle any objections. They should also provide training and move cautiously, as users gain experience.

With the assumption that reactions to the small-scale launch are positive and encouraging, management needs to communicate to the entire sales force the benefits and the expected outcomes as well as the types of data that must be collected and uploaded onto the system. The task is to manage salespeople's expectations and overcome their objections by selling them the benefits that will accrue from the CRM implementation process. The goal is to cultivate a culture of anticipation, excitement and positive thinking about the new CRM system.

It is then time to launch the CRM system full-scale. A fruitful way to do this is during a sales organization meeting, which gives the launch an official yet festive air. Management should be very careful at this all-critical stage. It should provide additional training and technical support to everyone in the Sales unit. The goal should be to get salespeople to use the system often, since frequency of usage can lead to the system becoming integral to the salesperson's job.

Finally, the last stage is to set up a monitoring mechanism that will periodically check information quality and accuracy and ensure proper functioning of the system. It should be noted that it is one thing to get the sales force to accept the system initially and quite another to keep them using it over the course of time. Remember: the continued and effective use of the CRM system by the sales force is an ongoing process which should be carefully monitored and managed.

Assessing CRM performance

Companies implement CRM systems with the aim of increasing sales (effectiveness) and profits (efficiency). In addition, they are seeking to streamline their sales process in order to enhance salesperson performance, improve customer satisfaction and leverage customer relationships. Among other things, such gains are largely an outcome of an increase in salespeople's knowledge of customer needs, greater ability to communicate with customers, better allocation of sales resources and selling time and faster access to relevant and timely information. Whereas anecdotal evidence suggests positive returns from CRM investment, academic research is somewhat inconclusive (Hunter and Perreault 2007; Sundaram et al. 2007). Nevertheless, companies implementing a CRM system in their sales organization should strive to develop appropriate metrics and KPIs on the basis of which they can assess the effectiveness and efficiency gains from it (Honeycutt et al. 2005). These metrics can be grouped in three major categories (see Table 5.4).

One should bear in mind, however, that quantifying the impact of CRM investment on the sales organization is always a challenging process, simply because many of the accrued benefits from CRM implementation are intangible (e.g. improving customer segmentation processes, improving decision-making). Nevertheless, management should strive to assess the outcomes of the CRM initiative for at least some of the metrics mentioned.

Sales Managers are also charged with the difficult task of justifying the return on CRM investment (ROCRMI). Although there are various ways to evaluate an investment

Table 5.4   Examples of metrics for evaluating CRM system performance

Company-related metrics	Customer-related metrics
• Revenue/sales growth • Profits growth • ROI • Customer service expenses • Competitive intelligence processes • Decision-making processes • Customer segmentation processes • Sales resource allocation processes • Alignment between sales and other functions • Faster access to information	• Customer retention • Customer acquisition • Customer referral processes • Customer satisfaction • Customer lifetime value • Customer share-of-wallet • Customer size-of-wallet • Customer cross/up selling efforts

Sales force-related metrics

• CRM usage
• Improved attitudes towards CRM
• Decreased information overload
• Reduced sales force turnover
• Sales performance
• Market and competition knowledge
• Customer targeting
• Territory and call planning
• Time management
• Presentation skills
• Reduced time spent on administrative tasks
• Increased time spent in the field
• Reduced errors associated with manual processing
• Enhanced ability to practise adaptive selling

like a CRM system, our focus here is on its ROI. Our approach draws on basic economic and investment evaluation theories. ROCRMI can be calculated as in the model shown in Figure 5.4:

This model for assessing ROCRMI requires a breakdown of revenues and costs into smaller measurable elements and a metric to assess each of them. Although different companies and industries have different approaches to calculating CRM-related revenues and costs, a general framework is shown in Table 5.5.

$$\text{ROCRMI} = \frac{\text{Revenues attributed to CRM usage}}{\text{Costs (initial + maintenance costs)}} \times 100$$

Figure 5.4   A model for calculating ROCRMI

Table 5.5   Framework for calculating revenues and costs associated with the implementation of a CRM system

COSTS

Initial costs

- Software and hardware
- System customization
- Project management costs
- Consultant costs
- Other costs

Maintenance costs

- CRM software upgrade fees
- Supporting software upgrade fees
- Syndicated data fees
- Mobile service provider fees
- Hardware upgrade
- Ongoing training
- Project management costs

REVENUES[1]

Estimating the impact of the CRM system on revenues (i.e. the monetary amount of sales) and the degree to which differences in revenue can be attributed to CRM usage can be a daunting task. One relatively simple process for doing this is to:

1. Identify all relevant sales force activities that are affected by CRM usage (e.g. call planning, customer targeting, etc.).
2. Estimate the extent to which salespeople perform each of these activities by using the CRM system. Estimation can be based on archival data (e.g. recorded usage) or by surveying salespeople.
3. Estimate the percentage of revenues which can be attributed to CRM system usage. One way to do this is to use a multiple regression model with salesperson performance as the dependent variable and sales force activities as independent variables. The r-squared (per cent) generated by the regression equation is the targeted estimation of the percentage of revenues attributed to CRM system usage.
4. Calculate the difference in the average monetary amount of sales between top- and low-performing salespeople. Do this by sorting salespeople by their sales performance. Top-performing salespeople are those who stand one or more standard deviations above mean performance; low-performing salespeople are those who stand one or more standard deviations below mean performance.
5. Multiply the r-squared (per cent) calculated in step 3 by the difference in the monetary amount of sales calculated in step 4. This is the monetary amount of sales attributed to the usage of CRM per salesperson.
6. Multiply the outcome of step 5 by the number of salespeople in the company. The result is the monetary amount of sales attributed to CRM usage for the entire sales force.

---

[1] Estimation of revenues attributed to CRM usage is based on the work of Engle and Barnes (2000). Readers wishing to delve into the details of this method are advised to read the original work.

Company background

Pharmatron Hellas (PH) is the Greek subsidiary of Pharmatron, a pharmaceutical company that is globally ranked tenth in terms of market share. PH is ranked tenth in terms of market share and first in terms of sales growth in the Greek market. It markets its products to a wide variety of stakeholders, such as physicians, pharmacists, pharmaceutical warehouses, patients and various opinion leaders (e.g. hospital managers, public insurance managers). Its leading brands are in several therapeutic categories (cancer treatment, rheumatoid arthritis and asthma, infectious diseases, cardiovascular and metabolic diseases, diseases of the central nervous system and treatments in women's health including osteoporosis and vasomotor symptoms of the menopause). Three of its brands account for 25 per cent of its total sales volume. The company employs 200 people, with 80 per cent of these working in marketing and sales positions across its four business units.

Sales process

As in most other European countries, the selling process in Greece involves a series of calls made to physicians' offices, clinics, hospitals, and health management organizations (HMO) with the aim of increasing awareness of the company's products, detailing product characteristics and benefits, promoting their prescription over competitors' drugs, and building relationships with physicians. Salespeople are heavily engaged in planning their daily routes, setting objectives for each call and prioritizing customers according to a number of different criteria. Previous research had shown that salesperson activities (customer analysis, meetings, presentations, planning and territory management, administration and external information exchange and learning/training for new products) amounted to approximately 18 per cent of the annual sales volume across countries. In addition, Greek physicians' offices are small (one to three physicians), while the government heavily regulates sales efforts directed at physicians. Finally, Sales Managers are involved in monitoring and evaluating sales calls and in preparing forecasts and sales reports.

CRM implementation objectives

Management set several objectives for CRM implementation. In particular, system implementation was aimed at:

- Automating sales and business processes. Prior to CRM implementation, Sales and Marketing employees were spending an immense amount of time manually analysing market and competition data.
- Enhancing information integration and management through use of common processes and a company-wide platform.
- Facilitating the process of planning Marketing and Sales activities, such as segmentation, targeting and positioning.
- Facilitating reporting and budgeting processes.
- Enabling better resource allocation.

- Optimizing customer management through better targeting and database marketing (email and mobile phone lists) in both Sales and Marketing.
- Developing a company-wide database for all customer and stakeholder groups.

CRM implementation process

Back in 2000, management faced the decision of selecting and implementing a CRM system. Although a few European affiliates had already implemented their own in-house CRM system, management decided to purchase a commercial CRM system. Immediately following management's decision to buy and implement a CRM system, George Zisis was appointed the project leader. It was quickly understood that George had to monitor and record the milestones of successful CRM implementation in other subsidiaries of Pharmatron operating in Europe. With the initial assessment of these efforts came the realization that the Italian subsidiary was very similar to the Greek one in terms of culture and market conditions. As a consequence, George travelled to Italy, where he recorded the processes of successful CRM implementation. Upon his return to Greece, he was asked to develop a business plan outlining the CRM objectives and the processes and specifications that were required for its effective implementation, such as functionalities, data availability and price. On the basis of the business plan, management determined the processes for selecting a CRM vendor. In a subsequent step, management started a series of conversations with Pharmatron's headquarters in Europe with the aim of persuading the board of directors of the necessity of purchasing a CRM system and setting out its specifications, which were included in the business plan. Having gained the board of directors' approval, management proceeded with the selection of the CRM vendor. After carefully screening three competing vendors on the basis of various specifications (e.g. system functionality, ease-of-use, database quality, service quality and price), management decided to purchase the Avanet[2] CRM system, which had been developed by a France-based multinational vendor of CRM systems. It must be stressed that the vendor's role was critical for the successful implementation of the CRM system. The importance of the vendor is reflected in its provision of training, technical service and consulting services regarding organizational and implementation issues. However, according to one Pharmatron executive,

> ... despite [the] vendor's importance in facilitating system implementation, the most critical role was played by our people, our own organizational culture and our own mindset. Even if the vendor had not been as good as it turned out to be, a strong culture towards CRM would have ensured that the implementation is effective.

Avanet was eventually launched in 2001. System implementation lasted approximately ten months, from purchase to full operation. System implementation involved several stages. It should be noted that the effective execution of each stage is a factor of success in the CRM implementation process. As one executive put it 'One needs to be very cautious with the system implementation process, especially when this is done for the very first time. He/she needs to move step-by-step to ensure that everybody agrees with the outcomes of each stage'. The various stages of the CRM implementation process are described in what follows.

First, a project committee was created, composed of four employees from Sales and Marketing. The committee's primary role was to specify the needs of each department, to initiate system

---

[2] The name of the CRM system has been changed to comply with the company's request to preserve anonymity.

customization (parameterization) and to specify the type of data that had to be fed into the system. The role of Marketing and Sales was central to the implementation process. According to one PH executive,

> *early involvement of both Sales and Marketing employees was deemed to be an essential factor of CRM implementation success, because Sales and Marketing often have diversified and even opposing needs with regard to information assimilation and usage. Thus, bringing in both viewpoints sets the stage for creating a climate of consensus and, subsequently, for effective implementation.*

Notwithstanding the important role of Marketing and Sales, the company considers that the role of other departments (i.e. accounting and IT) was also important, albeit to a lesser extent. This is because prior to system implementation most of the information-gathering and analysis was conducted within the Sales and Marketing units. Second, key contact employees from both vendor and buyer organizations worked together to develop parameters for and customize the various system functions to the needs of the company. This process resulted in the customization of the Avanet system to the specific needs of the Marketing and Sales departments. Third, salespeople were trained to use the system by the vendor. Fourth, Avanet was pilot-tested for a short period of time in each of PH's four business units with the objective of identifying any problems associated with its usage and suggesting any areas for improvement. The project leaders' team was also charged with the difficult task of gaining acceptance from Sales and Marketing employees; specifically, the team worked hard to present the benefits of the system and to overcome objections. The project leaders' team also worked intensely to ensure that the system would be embedded within the company's day-to-day operations. Importantly, the committee asked for salespeople's feedback in order actively to involve them in the implementation process. Fifth, sales management asked sales reps to provide a list of email addresses and mobile phone numbers for all of the physicians whom they were calling upon. This information was subsequently entered into the CRM system, with the aim of using it for ustomer management across all available distribution and communication channels. One should note, however, that customers were not aware of the CRM system and strategy that the company was pursuing. As one executive put it, 'Even if some of the customers are aware of our efforts, I do not feel that there is a problem; or at least we are not aware of any problem.' Today, Avanet is used by 95 medical reps and 55 managers in various positions across the Sales and Marketing hierarchy.

Barriers or problems with CRM implementation

Needless to say, the CRM implementation process was not an easy way out. Management faced several barriers throughout the entire process. However, ten barriers were the most prominent, all of which related to organizational and business processes. First, and perhaps foremost, the predominant culture inhibited the effective implementation of the CRM system. As one executive mentioned,

> *Issues like lack of training, technical problems or information inadequacies are not the greatest problems. The most difficult part of a system implementation is related to people and their mindsets, especially when these people are high in the organizational hierarchy. You have to gain people's commitment and to lead by example.*

Second, people were resistant to accepting guidelines from their colleagues. As one executive said, 'People react better to evaluation when this is done by executives from the parent

company'. Third, older (over 50 years old) salespeople expressed fears about the new technology. Their technophobia was largely due to a lack of previous knowledge and experience
with technology, especially since this was the first time that the company was implementing a
CRM solution. Fourth – given that the system was designed to track sales calls, activities and
performance – many salespeople viewed the system as a micromanagement tool that could
potentially limit their autonomy. Importantly, salespeople also felt that their power was diminishing as they had to share their market knowledge throughout the company. Fifth, there was a
complete lack of accountability. No person was really in charge of the implementation process
and, consequently, no unit or individual was held accountable for the success of the process.
Sixth, salespeople viewed the CRM system as an additional activity that would add time to
their already heavy workload. This problem was further amplified by the fact that some Sales
Managers were asking salespeople to upload more and more data onto the system. As a consequence, the system became a foe instead of a friend. Seventh, Marketing employees were not
fully exploiting the capabilities of the system. Eighth, the Sales and Marketing functions were
not actively involved in the process of developing the system's parameters. Ninth, informational
needs between the Sales and the Marketing departments varied greatly. Tenth, no employee
from the IT department was accountable for the CRM system. As one executive mentioned,
'Knowing that someone from IT is appointed to the system increases feelings of psychological support, the feeling that someone is there for me, who will support me, in case I need
him/her.'

Faced with these barriers, management felt that it had to do something. Although, as mentioned by one executive, some of the problems are time-resistant and will never disappear, the
following actions took place:

- All necessary efforts were made to involve salespeople in implementation of the system as
  early in the process as possible. Early involvement was considered an important strategy for
  increasing salespeople's buy-in.
- Similarly, since field Sales Managers hold a key role in gaining salespeople's buy-in,
  management strived to involve them in the implementation process.
- A series of customized ad-hoc training classes were initiated to decrease feelings of technophobia among members of the sales force.
- Monthly quotas were set for every salesperson in order to assess what can be gained from
  system usage.
- The data that was fed into the system was directly tied to specific decision needs. Thus, no
  information would be collected and entered into the system unless it was absolutely necessary.
- A report addressing usage for every individual was developed which was not publicized,
  but rather was individually communicated through face-to-face meetings with Field Sales
  Managers. A major goal of this process was to reposition salespeople from demand creators
  to 'territory managers' for whom the CRM system was an indispensable tool.

Changes related to CRM implementation

CRM implementation did not drive significant changes within the company. The most important change due to CRM introduction was that some people were appointed to lead the whole
process. In addition, there were some other changes:

- *Hiring procedures.* Once a new salesperson was hired, he/she was immediately assigned to a
  specific territory and was given a notebook.

- *Training.* Newly hired salespersons were trained in CRM usage by the vendor.
- *Performance evaluation.* Territory coverage was taken into account based on statistics generated by the CRM system. Prior to system implementation, salespeople were evaluated solely on the basis of sales volume; after system implementation, however, the company started to link sales volume to sales call productivity as well as to investments made to retain customers.

CRM effectiveness

Although assessing CRM effectiveness is a cumbersome and equivocal process, management believes that the CRM goals were to a great extent attained. As one executive put it, 'The CRM system changed our company's operations'. However, salespeople have not yet fully accepted the CRM system. Particularly with regard to connectivity, management believes that there is a lot of space for improvement, as salespeople do not connect to the system as often as is desired. Moreover, although there is 50–60 per cent system usage, the company considers that this is still low. Specifically, salespeople are not getting the most out of the system in terms of territory management, knowledge management and data analysis. As one executive put it:

> To gain the most out of the CRM system, we need to have an employee in every business unit who will be charged with overall supervision of the CRM system. He/she needs to set usage objectives, develop the appropriate metrics and be accountable for CRM usage; as yet, this is not the case.

Conclusion

The case addressed a number of issues related to CRM system implementation in PH's sales organization. Although the case is industry-specific, one can draw a number of general conclusions relevant to other companies and industries as well:

- Successfully implementing a CRM system for the first time is a challenging process, which has to be carefully planned and managed.
- The best way to start the implementation process is to outline all sales tasks and activities that will be affected by the CRM system. In particular, one needs to answer the question 'How does the CRM system affect sales processes, such as territory planning, customer targeting, customer analysis and customer strategies?.
- Next, specific, realistic and measurable objectives should be set.
- Every company has its own idiosyncrasies, needs and strategies; accordingly, the process of implementation can vary significantly from company to company.
- Choose a CRM vendor and treat it as a partner.
- Before launching the system, changes should be made to human resource systems and company culture. People issues are often the most important factor in CRM failure.
- Move slowly, as users gain experience. Manage their expectations and perceptions, which will drive usage and outcomes.
- Get employees from various functions involved and gain their feedback.
- Manage resistance by offering incentives, setting expectations and fostering a climate of consensus.

Summary

This chapter highlighted some of the most important aspects regarding the CRM implementation process with the intention of providing managerial insights and guidelines. Here, we summarize our previous discussion by presenting an overall process for CRM implementation that can guide managerial decision-making (see Figure 5.5). According to this process, companies base their decision to adopt (or buy) a CRM system on several things, such as the company's business and customer strategy or competitive and industry forces.

Once the company has adopted the CRM system, Sales Managers are charged with the task of implementing the system into the sales organization. The first challenge that they face is to get salespeople to adopt (accept) the system, since the introduction of a CRM system quite often calls for abandoning old working practices and changing daily workflow. There are several barriers to the acceptance of the new system, all of which are controllable by sales management. These barriers can be grouped into three categories: CRM system factors, organizational factors, and salespeople factors. On the assumption that managers have effectively dealt with these barriers, salespeople will accept the system and start using it more frequently, until the system becomes an integral part of their jobs. Only then can the system impact on individual salespeople's performances, which, in turn, will affect overall company performance by either increasing revenues or decreasing costs. In conclusion, CRM implementation

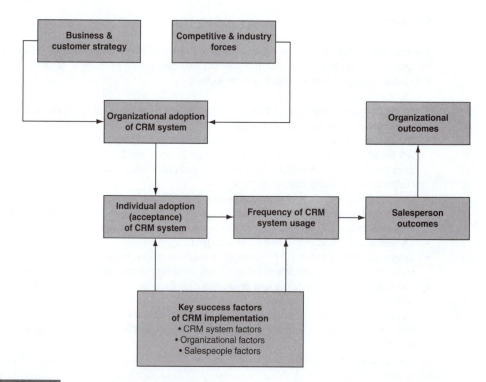

Figure 5.5   A process for understanding and managing CRM system implementation

is just like any other company investment: it needs time, resources and managerial intervention to generate returns.

Key points

Sales Managers interested in managing a CRM initiative in their organizations should bear in mind the following:

1. Cultural and people issues – not technological ones – are often the most important reasons behind CRM failure.
2. Automating sales processes cannot enhance performance by itself; automation needs to be connected to the fundamental customer strategy that the organization pursues.
3. A deep understanding of how the system impacts on customer strategy is necessary for effective implementation.
4. Managers need to outline the impact of the CRM system on sales- and customer-related processes; they also need to look into the consequences of the system for the entire Sales function.
5. The Sales Manager can have a dramatic effect on the success of the CRM project through appropriately planning and managing the entire process.
6. Developing metrics and KPIs are very important for securing successful implementation.
7. Salespeople are those who are in closest contact with your most valuable resource: customers. Thus, efforts should be made to satisfy salespeople's needs and overcome their fears and negative feelings regarding CRM.

Running a CRM audit in your company

The audit presented in Table 5.6 is intended to help sales managers diagnose problems during CRM system implementation. Ideally, managers should anonymously submit the audit to their salespeople *prior* to CRM system implementation. Responses should then be analysed with the aim of identifying any problem areas. Specifically, a large number of 'No' responses to the questions included in the audit suggests that the sales force is not ready to accept a CRM system and interventions should be initiated (e.g. training, communication). In addition, managers can identify urgent issues that need to be addressed to secure the effective implementation of the CRM system.

After the CRM system has been introduced to a small number of salespeople, Sales Managers can use the audit presented in Table 5.7 to evaluate sales force reactions towards the CRM system *before* it is implemented full-scale. As with the previous audit, this audit of salespeople who have been experimenting with the new system should be submitted anonymously. Then, responses should be analysed with the aim of identifying any problem areas. Specifically, a large number of 'No' responses indicates that the sales force faces problems with the CRM system; managers then need to address each issue in order to ensure that the CRM system will be accepted when the system is launched full-scale.

Table 5.6 An audit for diagnosing problems prior to CRM system implementation

Question	Response
Salespeople-related issues	
Using technology in my job is a good idea	YES
	NO
I intend to use technology in my job when it becomes available	YES
	NO
Among my peers, I am usually the first to try out new technologies	YES
	NO
My analytical skills explain most of my success as a salesperson	YES
	NO
I am very keen to try new things in my job	YES
	NO
Learning new things for my job is a priority for me	YES
	NO
I like to take risks	YES
	NO
I can easily handle information that is needed to perform my job effectively	YES
	NO
Management-related issues	
The top management of my firm has a positive attitude towards change	YES
	NO
My customers would want me to use new technologies	YES
	NO
There is a climate of trust in our company	YES
	NO
I have actively participated in every big decision that this company has made	YES
	NO
Management sets accurate expectations regarding what it expects from me	YES
	NO
I am well aware of the duties that will be required of me	YES
	NO
I do not face conflicting demands in my job	YES
	NO
The top management of my firm has a positive attitude towards risk	YES
	NO
Management encourages proactive behavior	YES
	NO
The top management of my firm has a positive attitude towards innovative work practices	YES
	NO
Management encourages learning new skills and new information	YES
	NO
In our company customers are our top priority	YES
	NO
Management focuses on people development	YES
	NO

Table 5.7   An audit for diagnosing problems during the CRM system launch

Question	Response
CRM system issues	
The system decreases the time needed to do my activities	YES
	NO
The system can help me increase my performance	YES
	NO
The system is helpful for my job	YES
	NO
The system provides up-to-date information	YES
	NO
The system provides the information I need on time	YES
	NO
Data provided by the system is quickly updated	YES
	NO
I can easily find the information I need	YES
	NO
The information provided by the system is clear	YES
	NO
I do not have any connection problems when using the system	YES
	NO
I can easily plan my sales activities by using the system	YES
	NO
Interacting with the system does not require a lot of mental effort	YES
	NO
I find the system user-friendly	YES
	NO
Using the system increases the level of challenge in my career	YES
	NO
Using the system increases the opportunity for more meaningful work	YES
	NO
Using the system increases job security	YES
	NO
Using the system allows me to use more discretion in my job	YES
	NO
Using the system enhances my relative power in the company	YES
	NO
Using the system will be compatible with all aspects of my work	YES
	NO
I find the task of integrating the system into my job fairly easy	YES
	NO
I intend to make regular use of the system for my work when it becomes available	YES
	NO

Table 5.7	(Continued)

Question	Response
Management-related issues	
My company has trained me extensively in using the CRM system	YES
	NO
I have actively participated in the system buying decision process	YES
	NO
I know exactly what management expects from me regarding system usage	YES
	NO
My company provides adequate technical support for the system	YES
	NO
I have access to the resources I will need to use the system in my job	YES
	NO
My customers would want me to use the system	YES
	NO
I feel certain about how I am expected to handle my activities using the new system	YES
	NO
The demands of my job and the demands due to the system are in line	YES
	NO

References

Ahearne, M., Srinivasan, N. and Weinstein, L. (2004) 'Effect of Technology on Sales Performance: Progressing from Technology Acceptance to Technology Usage and Consequence', *Journal of Personal Selling and Sales Management*, 24 (Fall): 297–310.

Avlonitis, G.J. and Panagopoulos, N.G. (2005) 'Antecedents and Consequences of CRM Technology Acceptance in the Sales Force', *Industrial Marketing Management*, 34 (May): 355–68.

Brown, J. (2006) 'Europe increases its CRM investments', *Computing*, 26 JULY 2006, http://www.computing.co.uk/computing/news/2161123/europe-buys-crm, accessed 10 October 2007.

Datamonitor (2006) 'European CRM Growth Lagging Behind Rest of World', 28 July 2006, http://www.computerwire.com/industries/research/?pid=630B0618-2F9B-450B-ABE6-7FD4EB993AC2, accessed 10 October 2007.

Dickie, J. (2006) 'Demystifying CRM Adoption Rates', *Customer Relationship Management (CRM) Magazine*, 10 (7): 14.

Engle, R.L. and Barnes, M.L. (2000) 'Sales Force Automation Usage, Effectiveness, and Cost-Benefit in Germany, England and the United States', *Journal of Business and Industrial Marketing*, 15 (4): 216–42.

Frambach, R.T. and Schillewaert, N. (2002) 'Organizational Innovation Adoption: A Multi-level Framework of Determinants and Opportunities for Future Research', *Journal of Business Research*, 55 (2): 163–76.

Gohmann, S. F., Guan, J., Barker, R. M. and Faulds, D. J. (2005) 'Perceptions of Sales Force Automation: Differences between Sales Force and Management', *Industrial Marketing Management*, 34 (4), 337–343.

Honeycutt, E.D. Jr, Thelen, T., Thelen, S.T. and Hodge, S.K. (2005), 'Impediments to Sales Force Automation', *Industrial Marketing Management*, 34 (May): 313–22.

Hunter, G.K. and Perreault, W.D. Jr (2007), 'Making Sales Technology Effective', *Journal of Marketing*, 71 (January): 16–34.

Keillor, B.D., Bashaw, E.R. and Pettijohn, C.E. (1997) 'Salesforce Automation Issues Prior to Implementation: The Relationship between Attitudes toward Technology, Experience and Productivity', *Journal of Business and Industrial Marketing*, 12 (3/4): 209–19.

Morgan, A.J. and Inks, S.A. (2001) 'Technology and the Sales Force – Increasing the Acceptance of Sales Force Automation', *Industrial Marketing Management*, 30 (5): 463–72.

Parthasarathy, M. and Sohi, R.S. (1997) 'Salesforce Automation and the Adoption of Technological Innovations by Salespeople: Theory and Implications', *Journal of Business and Industrial Marketing*, 12 (3/4): 196–208.

Plouffe, C.R., Williams, B.C. and Leigh, T.W. (2004) 'Who's on First? Stakeholder Differences in Customer Relationship Management and the Elusive Notion of "Shared Understanding"', *Journal of Personal Selling and Sales Management*, 24 (Fall): 323–38.

Pullig, C., Maxham, J.G. III and Hair, J.F. Jr (2002) 'Salesforce Automation Systems: An Exploratory Examination of Organizational Factors Associated with Effective Implementation and Salesforce Productivity', *Journal of Business Research*, 55 (5): 401–15.

Raman, P., Wittmann, M. and Rauseo, N. (2006) 'Leveraging CRM for Sales: the Role of Organizational Capabilities in Successful CRM Implementation', *Journal of Personal Selling and Sales Management*, 26 (1): 39–53.

Rangarajan, D., Jones, E. and Chin, W. (2005) 'Impact of Sales Force Automation on Technology-Related Stress, Effort, and Technology Usage among Salespeople', *Industrial Marketing Management*, 34 (May): 345–54.

Robinson, L., Marshall, G.W. and Stamps, M.B. (2005) 'Sales Force Use of Technology: Antecedents to Technology Acceptance', *Industrial Marketing Management*, 34 (May): 407–15.

Schillewaert, N., Ahearne, M.J., Frambach, R.T. and Moenaert, R.K. (2005) 'The Adoption of Information Technology in the Sales Force', *Industrial Marketing Management*, 34 (4): 323–36.

Sims, D. (2007) 'CRM a $7 Billion Industry in 2006', *Customer Inter@ction Solutions*, 25 (March): 6–16.

Speier, C. and Venkatesh, V. (2002) 'The Hidden Minefields in the Adoption of Sales Force Automation Technologies', *Journal of Marketing*, 66 (July): 98–111.

Sundaram, S., Schwarz, A., Jones, E. and Chin, W.W. (2007) 'Technology Use on the Front Line: How Information Technology Enhances Individual Performance', *Journal of the Academy of Marketing Science*, 35 (1): 101–12.

Tanner, J.F. Jr, Ahearne, M., Leigh, T.W., Mason, C.H. and Moncrief, W.C. (2005) 'CRM in Sales-intensive Organizations: A Review and Future Directions', *Journal of Personal Selling and Sales Management*, 25 (Spring): 169–80.

Further reading

Agnihotri, R. and Rapp, A.A. (2010) *Effective Sales Force Automation and Customer Relationship Management: A Focus on Selection and Implementation*. New York: Business Expert Press.

Ahearne, M., Jones, E., Rapp, A. and Mathieu, J. (2008) 'High Touch Through High Tech: The Impact of Salesperson Technology Usage on Sales Performance via Mediating Mechanisms', *Management Science*, 54 (4): 671–85.

Avlonitis, G.J. and Panagopoulos, N.G. (2010) 'Effective Implementation of Sales-based CRM Systems: Theoretical and Practical Issues', *International Journal of Customer Relationship Marketing and Management*, 1 (1): 1–15.

Buttle, Francis (2008) *Customer Relationship Management: Concepts and Technologies*, 2nd edn. Burlington, MA: Butterworth-Heinemann.

Panagopoulos, N.G. (2010) *Sales Technology: Making the Most of your Investment*. New York: Business Expert Press.

6

Ethics in personal selling and sales management

Sergio Román

Contents

Learning objectives

After reading this chapter, you should be able to:

- Recognize the critical importance of ethical selling behaviour today.
- Distinguish ethical from unethical selling behaviour.
- Understand the ethical decision-making process.
- Understand the factors that can affect a salesperson's ethical behaviour.
- Explain how management can promote ethical selling behaviour.
- Know what to do when unethical selling practices have taken place.

Chapter outline

Ethical issues are faced by people in almost every function in business life including accountants, financial managers, purchasing people and market research employees. As salespeople generally work across departmental boundaries and therefore without close supervision and since they are most of the time under intense pressure to meet sales quotas, they are susceptible to behave in unethical ways. This chapter deals with the key topic of ethics in personal selling and sales management. The chapter is structured as follows. First, the importance of ethics in the field of personal selling and sales management is explained. Second, a typology of unethical sales behaviour is presented. Third, the un/ethical decision-making process is described. Then sales management actions to prevent unethical behaviour along with several rules for sales managers to react to unethical sales behaviour within their sales team are given. Finally, a case history where an un/ethical situation was experienced is presented.

An unethical scenario?

In 1992 Hollywood released a film *Glengarry Glen Ross*, the story of a failing real estate office in which four real estate agents are warned by management that two of them (the 'losers') will be fired if major property sales are not immediately made. On the other hand, the top seller is promised a Cadillac 'El Dorado'. Over the next 24 hours, one salesman decides to hatch a scheme to burgle the office, steal the leads and sell them to a rival. Another experiences an emotional breakdown. And the perennially confident top performer of the team forces a sale on a particularly vulnerable client.

Not long ago, the author of this chapter was in his office when a financial services salesperson arrived. She offered him a credit card. He already had two so he said no, thank you very much. She did not listen and told him she had to meet a sales quota each week or her company would fire her. She continued by telling him that her father was dead, her mother had cancer, and as the only daughter she was in charge of paying the bills. After all that, he changed his mind and got the credit card. He never used it, and after a year he finished the contract and decided not to use any of this bank's services any more. Moreover, he told this story to all his friends and relatives.

Introduction: sales force ethics – are they really that important?

The depiction of salespeople as deceitful charlatans concerned only with closing sales and earning commissions does little to enhance the professional image the career and the majority of its practitioners deserve. Think about it. When was the last time you saw a salesperson depicted in a positive light on television or in the movies? Unfortunately, we have all had regrettable experiences with salespeople such as those described in the opening vignettes. The historically negative stereotype of salespeople is however changing as many people begin to understand the key role that salespeople play in the economy. Yet, many companies still discourage the term 'salesperson' from being printed on the business cards of their sales staff, preferring labels such as 'client advisor', 'marketing representative' or 'business consultant' to describe the sales function.

Salespeople, it seems, are especially vulnerable to moral corruption because they are subject to many temptations. In particular:

- Because of the interpersonal nature of their work, they are exposed to greater ethical pressures than individuals in many other jobs.
- They work in relatively unsupervised settings.
- They are primarily responsible for generating the firm's revenues, which at times can be very stressful.
- They are often evaluated on the basis of short-term objectives.

Sales Managers therefore have to exercise care regarding potential ethical issues in their sales force. Unethical behaviour can even generate liability problems for salespeople's organizations through both intentional and inadvertent statements. For example, in 1998 ethical violations at Prudential Insurance became so pervasive that the company's management eventually estimated its liability from a pending class action lawsuit at $2 billion (O'Brian 1999). Among the voluminous courtroom testimony in the case was this nugget: 'Your judgment gets clouded out in the field when you are pressured to sell, sell, sell.' There is also a consensual view across business disciplines that ethical sales behaviour plays a significant role in determining financial performance, long-term viability and customer retention (e.g. Román and Munuera 2005; Román and Ruiz 2005; Grisaffe and Jaramillo 2007).

A typology of unethical sales behaviour

This section explores the ethical issues salespeople deal with when interacting with their customers or their employers. Previous studies have shown that salespeople regard ethical transgressions against customers as being less unethical than any controversial actions against their employer or competitors. Accordingly, special attention is paid to discussing ethical issues concerning customers.

How to define ethical sales behaviour

Ethical selling behaviour is a highly elusive construct and is often situation-specific. Ethics reflect the moral principles and standards of a community. Exaggerated sales claims may be acceptable in one part of the world, yet they may be viewed as an unethical practice elsewhere. Nevertheless, it can be argued that ethics requires an individual to behave according to the rules of a moral philosophy with an emphasis on the determination of right and wrong. More specifically, ethical sales behaviour is related to widely 'recognized' societal norms such as fair play, honesty and full disclosure. Recently, Román and Ruiz (2005) provided a more general definition of ethical sales behaviour: 'Fair and honest actions that enable the salesperson to foster long-term relationships with customers based on customer satisfaction and trust'.

The US National Association of Sales Professionals' (NASP) Standards of Professional Conduct is a good starting point for understanding ethics in the world of personal selling. As shown in the excerpt below, these standards place special emphasis on having in mind customers' best interests.

NASP Standards of Professional Conduct

As a member of NASP, I pledge to conduct business in the best interests of my customers, my employer, the public and the sales profession. I will strive to act in accordance with the following standards:

Ethics and Professionalism: I will act with the highest degree of professionalism, ethics and integrity.
Representation of Facts: I will fairly represent the benefits of my products and services.

Confidentiality: I will keep information about my customers confidential.

Conflicts of Interest: I will disclose potential conflicts of interest to all relevant parties and, whenever possible, resolve conflicts before they become a problem.

Responsibility to Clients: I will act in the best interest of my clients, striving to present products and services that satisfy my customers' needs.

Responsibility to Employer: I will represent my employer in a professional manner and respect my employers' proprietary information.

Responsibility to NASP members: I will share my lessons of experience with fellow NASP members and promote the interests of NASP.

Responsibility to the Community: I will serve as a model of good citizenship and be vigilant to the effects of my products and services on my community.

Continuing Education: I will maintain an ongoing program of professional development.

Laws: I will observe and obey all laws that affect my products, services and profession.

Source: http://www.nasp.com/

Customer-related ethical issues

Table 6.1 summarizes the most common un/ethical issues salespeople encounter when interacting with their potential buyers or current customers.

The behaviours presented in Table 6.1 are clearly unethical. Some of them may lead to closing the sale in the short term (e.g. exaggerating the characteristics of the product or applying high-pressure selling techniques). Yet, these behaviours will damage the relationship with the customer in the long run because they do not lead to the satisfaction of customer needs. Moreover, in some cases unethical actions do not mean closing the sale in the short term. This happens, for example, when the customer realizes that the salesperson is actually not telling the truth about the benefits of the product. The most important unethical actions shown in Table 6.1 are discussed below.

Dishonesty

As part of their job, salespeople are expected to present their products to customers with lots of enthusiasm. Nevertheless, there is a difference between enthusiasm and fraud. In other words, it is clearly unethical to be dishonest and provide false or deliberately inaccurate information about the characteristics of the product or other information related to the product/services offered. In addition, criticizing the competition always 'cheapens' the salesperson in the eyes of the customer. This is especially true when the information given about competitors cannot be objectively verified.

While lying to a customer about a product or service benefit is clearly unethical, salespeople will find themselves many times in more ambiguous ethical situations. For instance, if the customer asks for some relevant information about the product and the salesperson is not sure of the answer, should the salesperson tell the customer that he/she does not know? Or what if the salesperson does not tell the customer about a certain feature the product does not have, is that lying? What are the consequences of

Table 6.1	Examples of customer-related unethical practices

- Exaggerate or lie about the characteristics of the product (e.g. value, utility, quality, price, benefits, post-sales service) or about competing products.
- Implement high-pressure or manipulative selling techniques.
- Focus on closing the sale without considering the satisfaction of customer needs at all and/or:

  o Sell a product that the customer clearly does not need.
  o Sell the customer a more expensive product when a cheaper one would do the job.
  o Sell the customer a higher number of items than needed.

- Promise something to the customer that the salesperson knows his/her company will not support.
- Offer bribes to the customer and/or 'special' entertainment.
- Intentionally overcharge a customer.
- Pass the blame for something the salesperson did wrong onto the employer.
- Tell the customer that his/her complaints have already been notified to the selling company when this is not true.
- Present a sales promotion as unique and specifically tailored to the customer when it is the same for all the customers.
- Increase the quantity of an order to make the sales quota without the customer's permission.
- Pretend to be a market researcher when actually doing phone sales or pretend to be returning a message when making a cold call.
- Give confidential information about one customer to other customers who happen to be their competitors.
- Say to customers that something is beyond the salesperson's control when it is not.
- Offer special pricing or better terms to a particular customer beyond what is reasonably expected and without the approval of the selling company.
- When the salesperson is assigned to a new sales territory, put pressure on former customers so that they do not buy from the new salesperson (from the same selling company).

Source: Author.

telling half-truths? Unfortunately, salespeople very often face these ethical dilemmas. When customers become aware of such 'half-truths', the long-term damage to the relationship can be far worse than any short-term loss (i.e. not making the sale) produced by being honest. The bottom line is that salespeople who choose to provide complete information, even when it presents the company in a less than favourable light, can give themselves a high degree of credibility with the customer. In addition, dishonesty not only harms the customer, but can lead to legal action and financial liabilities fpr the company, as shown in the example earlier in this chapter.

Deception, manipulation and high-pressure selling tactics

The issue of deception is closely related to dishonesty. Selling a product to a customer that he/she does not need through high-pressure selling techniques or implementing deceptive or misleading influence tactics can become serious ethical issues. In such cases, the salesperson leaves the customer with an impression or belief different from what could be expected of a customer with reasonable knowledge, and that belief or impression is factually untrue or potentially misleading. High-pressure and manipulative selling tactics are only acceptable from an ethical perspective when the salesperson uses them to persuade a reluctant customer to purchase a product the salesperson is completely sure would be beneficial for them. This is likely to happen when the salesperson is dealing with an inexperienced customer with little information about the product.

It is also necessary to point out that from a strict ethical perspective, salespeople should be able to help their customers make purchase decisions that will satisfy their needs and long-term satisfaction. But what if the salesperson cannot identify customer needs because the prospect has not given him/her all the relevant information? Or what if even with this information the salesperson does not have the skills and expertise to identify those needs? Is he/she behaving unethically? In the first case the salesperson is not acting unethically. In the second case, it can be argued that the salesperson is behaving in a less than professional manner, but he is not unethical either. To complicate the issue, let us imagine that the salesperson has successfully identified customer needs, but unfortunately his/her company does not have the resources or product range to tailor the offering to that particular customer. The salesperson offers the product of his/her company that best meets those needs, but it is not the 'perfect' solution for the customer's problem. In such a case, is the salesperson behaving unethically? Again, this is a tough question to answer. If we are to apply business ethics rigorously, the salesperson should sacrifice a short-term sale (because he/she does not have the product that best meets the customer's needs) to build a good and honest reputation and increase the probability of future sales.

Entertainment, bribes and gifts

Providing entertainment for potential or current customers is a common practice in the field of personal selling. In some industries entertainment is seen as part of the approach used to get new customers. This is particularly the case when competing products are very similar. A good example is the pharmaceutical industry. Meeting a customer for lunch is an accepted business custom in this industry in most places, and certainly it is the case in Spain. It is a good way to build a more personal relationship with the customer and get the job done at the same time. The issue is often 'How much is too much?' That is to say, the ethical problem arises when customers are taken out for very expensive meals or customers are taken to nightclubs. For instance, a survey carried out in the US revealed that 49 per cent of male salespeople and 5 per cent of female salespeople had taken customers to topless bars (Zeiger 1995).

In a similar fashion, gifts can also be common in certain industries. Yet, it is very important to differentiate between a gift and a bribe. The bribe is wrong from an ethical perspective and, usually, from a legal perspective as well. It is not very clear how to distinguish between a gift and a bribe. But a token of insignificant value, such as a pen imprinted with the company logo or a desk calendar, raises no real ethical concerns. A bribe, on the other hand, is clearly an attempt to persuade the prospect/customer receiving the gift. A gift can be considered a bribe when it is considerably expensive (e.g. a LCD TV). A financial 'present' (no matter the quantity) is always a bribe. The problem is that 'special' gifts can have an influence on whether or not the order is given and the size of the order. For example, nowadays some companies selling to hypermarket chains offer purchasing managers a discount on the price of a LCD TV for their personal use. This may be quite 'effective', but it can be considered a bribe.

Even if the salesperson wants to behave ethically, some customers request 'special treatment' (special gifts or entertainment) in order to close the sale. To deal with these difficult ethical situations, many companies and/or industries on both sides of the buyer-seller dyad have established policies for handling entertainment and gifts. On the part of the buyer, these rules prohibit them from accepting any meals, gifts or favours that might compromise their integrity (see for example AXA's Code of Ethics, p. 161 below).

On the part of the seller, a good example is the Spanish Code of Practice for the Promotion of Medicines (http://www.farmaindustria.es/). This code establishes that gifts offered to health care professionals cannot exceed a value of €30. Article 11.1 of the Code also stipulates that:

> 11.1. *Entertainment expenses at professional and scientific events should be reasonable at all times, and their cost cannot exceed what recipients would normally be prepared to pay for themselves in the same circumstances. The concept of entertainment expenses includes the payment of actual travel, registration and subsistence expenses by the company, which must be reasonable and not out of proportion, and be limited to the days on which the scientific meeting is planned to be held. Entertainment expenses cannot be extended beyond a reasonable period after the event.*
>
> Source: http://www.farmaindustria.es/

However, although rules may attempt to solve the ethical problems described above, they are hard to enforce and sometimes they simply do not exist. Accordingly, Sales Managers and salespeople must judge what is a reasonable gift and adequate entertainment in their industry.

Employer-related ethical issues

Unfortunately, salespeople may behave unethically in their relationship with their employers too. Salespeople work, most of the time, away from their employer. That is, they usually work in unsupervised settings. Therefore, the Sales Manager has to rely on their honesty and integrity when reporting on things such as the number of sales calls made or how sales calls were made (by phone or face to face). For instance, if a salesperson is evaluated on the number of sales calls made each month but has not made the target number, the salesperson may be tempted to list a sales call with a customer for the current month that he or she intends to contact the following month. Likewise, Sales Managers have to be very careful so that salespeople do not misuse company resources. Among these are transportation (cars, air travel) and technology (mobile phones, computers, PDAs). Sometimes, salespeople feel their compensation is not enough or company policies do not allow a sufficient budget to cover business expenses. In those circumstances, they may use their mobile phones for personal calls or pass off a meal with friends as a business-related expense. A survey carried out in the US revealed that 60 per cent of Sales Managers said that they had caught one of their salespeople cheating in an expense report (Strout 2001). Table 6.2 summarizes

Table 6.2	Examples of employer-related unethical practices

- Put non-business-related expenses on the expense account.
- Cheat on a sales report in terms of the number of calls made or the duration of the sales calls or the type of call (face to face v telephone).
- Report selling more items than actually sold.
- Misuse company resources (e.g. use a mobile phone for personal use when this is not allowed by the company).
- Give information about the selling company or the market to the competition.
- Give friends and relatives company gifts meant for customers.
- Do not tell the company about customer complaints regarding the salesperson's behaviour.
- Exaggerate a customer's complaint to obtain additional discount from the employer for the customer.
- Present fictitious orders from customers to meet the sales quota, then once the quota has been met say that the customer does not want the product.
- Receive payment in cash for a sale made and delay giving it to the company.
- Delay a customer's orders to the next month in order to meet the sales quota for that month.
- Promote the selling of products of other competing companies when this is not allowed by the employer.

Source: Author.

the most common unethical practices related to the salesperson's employer. In order to avoid these things happening, it is very important for companies to have a policy on the personal use of business resources and that salespeople become familiar with that policy. Also, the Sales Manager, as a key role model to follow, needs to provide a good example with appropriate use of company resources.

The unethical decision-making process: determinants and consequences

The ethical decision-making process is shown in Figure 6.1. To start, the salesperson faces an ethical situation. The salesperson will have the intention to behave ethically or not. This intention is then translated into action (i.e. decision/behaviour). Both intention and action are influenced by personal factors (characteristics of the salesperson) and external/situational factors (e.g. company policies, competitors). For example, a young and inexperienced salesperson with a strong need to succeed may intend to behave unethically when meeting a potential customer (e.g. exaggerating product benefits to close the sale). Yet, the salesperson is aware that his/her company will eventually contact the customer to check his/her purchase satisfaction and whether they intend to purchase again from them in the future. Therefore, the salesperson decides not to exaggerate product benefits. The result of this decision can be twofold. The customer does not buy the product, since its characteristics were not very 'convincing'. Or the buyer takes the product and is satisfied with its performance (because expectations as a result of a true description of the product are met). Below, each of the components of the ethical decision-making framework is explored.

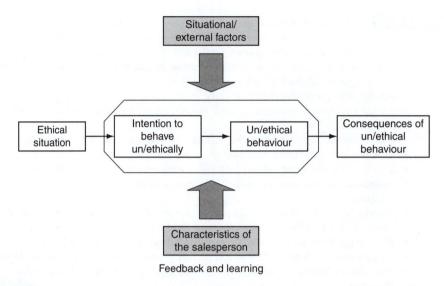

Figure 6.1   A model for ethical decision-making
Source: Author.

Ethical situation

Each ethical situation has some degree of moral intensity. Moral intensity is the extent to which a salesperson believes an issue (lying about competitors' offerings) has a moral component. Therefore, moral intensity varies from one salesperson and situation to the next. A salesperson facing an ethical situation will recognize that: his/her final decision will affect others (e.g. the customer, his/he employer, his/her family's welfare) and that several alternative actions are available (behaving ethically or not).

Intention to behave un/ethically

This component involves the intention to behave un/ethically as the result of an assessment of the ethical situation in the light of one's priority structure of values and one's stage of moral development (Wotruba 1990). People have a wide assortment of values besides moral values, and sometimes conflicts arise among them. For instance, economic and political value orientations can be negatively related to ethical value orientations. Thus, a salesperson might identify the morally correct alternative but because of the higher priority of their other values the salesperson's final behaviour does not reflect the moral ideal. A salesperson's stage of moral development is also relevant at this stage. In particular, it has been stated that an individual progresses through an irreversible sequence of six moral judgment stages, grouped into three levels: *Preconventional*, *Conventional* and *Principled* (Wotruba 1990). As one proceeds through this hierarchy, there is increasing consideration for the welfare of others and for what is fair and right in terms of a universal sense of justice.

Un/ethical behaviour

This component implies the translation of intention to action. As shown at the beginning of this section, there are many potential blocks to converting intention to action. For instance, the pressure to reach a short-term sales goal might create substantial moral dissonance within a salesperson, inducing a temporary ethical 'compromise' believed necessary to achieve the goal. In this case, short-term behaviour is not consonant with long-term ethical standards and intentions. Similarly, when making an ethical decision, conflict between personal values and the values held by the organization may give rise to ethical conflict (i.e. ethical value incongruence), in which case job-related outcomes may be negatively affected (e.g. job satisfaction or performance).

Characteristics of the salesperson

Several characteristics of salespeople have been found to affect their ethical decision-making. The following describes the most important ones.

Age, experience and education

Prior research has found that older, more experienced and better educated salespeople are more ethical in their behaviour than younger and less experienced salespeople (Román and Munuera 2005). A plausible explanation for this is that they display more conservative and strict ethical tendencies and hold less compromising interpretations of what can be judged ethical. In addition, older and more experienced salespeople have been exposed longer to ethical dilemmas, both in business and non-business contexts, and they are therefore more willing to accept and conform to ethical standards and behave accordingly. Also, it can be argued that the educational process is designed to foster critical thinking and the ability to view situations from multiple perspectives.

Gender

Saleswomen have been reported to be more 'sensitive' in selling situations than salesmen and have been found to be more ethical in their decisions (Singhapakdi et al. 1999).

Moral philosophies

Empirical evidence reveals that salespeople with different moral philosophies differ in their moral judgments about some ethically questionable actions (Tansey et al. 1994). In particular, *absolutist* salespeople (also known as deontologist) tend to follow a universal moral code, express a high concern for the welfare of others, stress social justice and avoid making gains from violating salient moral norms. *Subjectivist* salespeople (also known as ethical egoist), on the contrary, tend to maximize the personal gains to be made from violating salient moral norms.

Ego strength

This characteristic refers to the overall psychological inner strength that an individual brings to his or her interactions with others and with the social environment. This cannot be assessed independently of the nature of the person's needs and the conditions of the surrounding sales environment. Salespeople with high ego strength tend to be more resistant to impulsive, high-pressure selling tactics; however, they can also become immune to seeing things from others' perspectives. Therefore, a moderate level of ego strength is better when it comes to ethics.

Machiavellianism

Machiavellianism has been used as a term for a personality trait or as a way in which to describe a particular class of person. The core of this personality type can be explained in terms of manipulative, persuasive behaviour to accomplish personal objectives. A machiavellian may also, if necessary, employ aggressive, exploiting and devious behaviour to achieve personal and organizational goals.

Situational/external factors

Within these factors, we can distinguish legislation, the influence of significant others and corporate culture and policies. Due to its importance, the latter will be discussed in the next section of the chapter.

Legislation

Legislation causes ethical decisions to be adjusted or at least reconsidered according to changing regulatory frameworks. Law is usually the lowest common denominator of ethical behaviour, and several salespeople believe they are ethical if they do not violate the law. But even for such people, ethical issues can occur when dealing in multinational markets or competing with suppliers from other countries having other cultural and legal norms. In the US, the Uniform Commercial Code (UCC), cited in the excerpts below, is the most significant set of laws affecting selling. It sets out the rules and procedures for almost all business practices. Selling is particularly addressed in Article 2.[1] For example, section 2–313 addresses regulations regarding express warranties and product descriptions made by the salesperson:

> Uniform Commercial Code. 2–313. Express Warranties by Affirmation, Promise, Description, Sample.
>
> 1. In this section, 'immediate buyer' means a buyer that enters into a contract with the seller.
> 2. Express warranties by the seller to the immediate buyer are created as follows:
>
>   a) Any affirmation of fact or promise made by the seller which relates to the goods and becomes part of the basis of the bargain creates an express warranty that the goods shall conform to the affirmation or promise.

---

[1] For a complete discussion of the UCC, visit the website at http://www.law.cornell.edu/ucc/.

b) Any description of the goods which is made part of the basis of the bargain creates an express warranty that the goods shall conform to the description.

c) Any sample or model that is made part of the basis of the bargain creates an express warranty that the whole of the goods shall conform to the sample or model.

3. It is not necessary to the creation of an express warranty that the seller use formal words such as 'warrant' or 'guarantee' or that the seller have a specific intention to make a warranty, but an affirmation merely of the value of the goods or a statement purporting to be merely the seller's opinion or commendation of the goods does not create a warranty.

4. Any remedial promise made by the seller to the immediate buyer creates an obligation that the promise will be performed upon the happening of the specified event.

Source: http://www.law.cornell.edu/ucc/

Significant others

This term refers to individuals (peers, supervisors, competitors, family, friends and so on) who are in a position to influence the (un/ethical) actions of salespeople. For example, superiors have a strong impact on the ethics of their subordinates. This influence can vary considerably from one company to another, and can be either positive or negative, depending on the signals sent by the top executives. The extent of the impact depends on factors such as the organizational distance (number of organizational boundaries or levels that separate the superior from their subordinates) and the amount of legitimate authority of the superior. Competitors' actions can also affect ethical decision-making since questionable behaviour may be considered more necessary under intense competition, or when such behaviour is regularly employed by competitors.

Consequences of un/ethical behaviour

Outcomes of un/ethical actions can involve negative consequences to be avoided in the future (higher levels of job stress, customer dissatisfaction, etc.) as well as positive consequences to pursue (e.g. customer loyalty as a consequence of ethical actions). These consequences are learning experiences which can modify future behaviour of the salesperson when dealing with an ethical situation. For instance, let us consider the following example:

A retail salesperson has exaggerated mobile phone benefits to an inexperienced consumer. This consumer eventually purchases the phone. A couple of days later, the consumer goes back to the store to complain about the the product since it has not performed as expected – and as indicated by the salesperson. The salesperson is punished by his/her immediate sales supervisor (his/her commission has to be returned and the sales manager warns him/her not to act that way again). This negative experience will be in the mind of the salesperson the next time he/she is dealing with an inexperienced buyer.

Sales management actions to prevent unethical sales behaviour

This section discusses the main policies Sales Managers can implement to foster ethical sales behaviour and prevent unethical behaviour. When a climate is created where ethical values and behaviours are fostered and supported, more ethical behaviour is expected to exist. These policies are summarized in Figure 6.2.

Code of ethics

Ethics codes can be particularly relevant to those who work in Sales. The presence and enforcement of codes of ethics are very important for reinforcing ethical behaviour (Ingram et al. 2007). Those in Sales need to perceive that ethical behaviour is expected of them by their organizations, that unethical behaviour will not be rewarded and that it is possible for them to succeed while behaving ethically. The existence of ethics codes that formalize organizations' ethical values positively influences sales professionals' perceptions of their organizations' ethical values. For example, the financial group AXA claims that its values are team spirit, integrity, innovation, pragmatism and professionalism. The excerpt below provides more information about AXA's professional code of ethics.

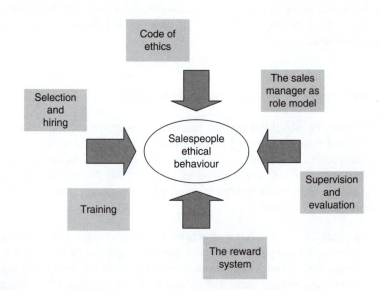

Figure 6.2 Management's policies to foster ethical sales behaviour
Source: Author.

AXA's Professional Code of Ethics

Most of AXA's companies adhere to the professional code of conduct in force in the country where they operate. In order to harmonize the ethical practices governing AXA's client relationships around the world, a professional code of ethics has been drawn up at Group level.

In addition to the national and international regulations that AXA subsidiaries are subject to, AXA's professional code of ethics is based on the following fundamental principles for their customer relations: quality advice, transparency, non-disclosure of confidential client information, fair competition, and fighting fraud and money laundering. The code of ethics also contains a policy statement on how to handle staff complaints.

Source: http://www.axa.com/

Unfortunately, some firms have used such codes as public relations statements and the information provided is too vague, general and void of sanctions to be meaningful. During group meetings or through the use of videos or podcasts, top management of the company should make clear their personal commitment to business ethics. When developing the code, the sales team should have some voice because they are more likely to support policies that they have helped develop. Communicating the code to the sales team is extremely important. All employees should be provided with a written copy of the code of ethics and given an opportunity to read it. Ideally, the immediate supervisor (i.e. Sales Manager) should go through the code with each individual salesperson allowing him/her an opportunity to ask questions. At the conclusion of this meeting the employee should sign an agreement that he/she has read and understands the code of ethics. It is critical that explicit actions are then taken to see that the code is policed and enforced. The sales team needs to know that management is taking serious action to ensure that the code is followed. When a violation arises, the sales team should be quickly informed of punitive actions taken against the 'violator'. If violations are routinely ignored, the code of ethics' effectiveness soon diminishes.

Finally, it is recommended that annual sales force audits be conducted regarding ethical behaviour in the sales force. This audit should indicate what ethical dilemmas the sales force is faced with in their daily tasks. Also, the audit should determine salespeople's perceptions regarding corporate guidance for dealing with these situations. The audit will also provide an opportunity for management to gain a better understanding regarding the sales force's perception of management's overall commitment to conducting business ethically.

Selection, hiring and training

Selection implies bringing into the organization the 'right kind' of individuals – those who have values and beliefs consistent with the organization or who can be taught the organization's values. Sales Managers must be cognizant of this when recruiting and hiring and attempt to assess the ethical values of job candidates. This is particularly relevant since ethical conflict stemming from value incongruence is associated with lower organizational commitment and greater turnover. In addition, certain personality traits such as machiavellianism, ego strength and locus of control can also be considered in the selection process.

Training can be used to reinforce salespeople's positive attitudes towards ethical values and prepare salespeople to behave ethically. Training should also provide salespeople with the necessary knowledge to enable them to distinguish ethical from unethical practices. For example, the Sales Manager can present salespeople with several different ethical scenarios and ask how they would respond to each. Then the Sales Manager can discuss with salespeople how the organization wishes such a situation to be handled. Although not all possible situations can be covered, at least salespeople will begin to understand how a range of typical situations should be dealt with.

The reward system, supervision and evaluation

The reward system comprises a set of processes through which behaviours are directed and motivated to achieve individual and organizational goals. Compensation plans emphasizing salary are recommended when firms want their salespeople to adopt an ethical long-term orientation and invest time servicing accounts to realize future sales. Under this system the company assumes most of the risk of lost sales and the salesperson little, so he/she feels less pressure to win immediate sales, thereby reducing the chance of unethical practices being used. In contrast, plans emphasizing incentive pay are advocated when firms want their salespeople to achieve immediate sales. In short, Sales Managers developing an ethical sales team should not reward them on a 100 per cent commission basis related to sales made, but compensate their various activities, not just the outcomes achieved (sales volume).

Apart from the above, there has to be a commitment from management that the satisfaction of long-term customer needs is a priority in the company. A behaviour control system allows for non-sales goals, such as account maintenance and service (see Anderson and Oliver (1987) and Chapter 14 for a more complete discussion of this topic). A longer perspective can be assumed because immediate results can be balanced against long-term sales relationships and outcomes. In contrast, in an outcome control system sales techniques may be compromised as short-term goals are pursued. In a behaviour-based control system managers are directive with their salespeople (they specify desired conduct rather than settling for outputs, however achieved) and are well informed about their activities (i.e. inputs). Consequently, the risk of detection and punishment of unethical actions is much higher in such systems. That is, the opportunities for unethical behaviour decrease in a behaviour-based control system and, hence, the salesperson is more likely to suffer any 'cost' associated with behaving unethically.

Supervision is likewise very important for fostering ethical behaviour. Sales Managers may send confusing messages to salespeople when questionable behaviour is ignored or even encouraged through non-verbal messages (i.e. looking the other way). Regardless of the presence of a business code of ethics, questionable behaviour must be curbed through proper supervisory feedback. The supervisory action of the immediate supervisor has a major role in influencing ethical conduct.

The Sales Manager as a role model

Managers play a critical role in setting the ethical climate in their organizations (Mulki et al. 2009). They should understand the importance of their own ethical behaviour, so that they set an appropriate standard to follow, since supervisors serve as role models for ethical behaviour within organizations. In other words, Sales Managers influence the ethical behaviour of salespeople by virtue of what they say and what they do. For example, the Sales Manager who urges subordinates to behave ethically, yet who regularly overstates products' capabilities when accompanying salespeople, is sending an ambiguous message to his/her subordinates.

Management's reaction to unethical selling behaviour: a checklist

Unfortunately, the policies described in the above section do not ensure ethical selling practices. That is to say, it is possible that some salespeople may behave unethically, despite the above policies. This penultimate section of the chapter provides a checklist to help managers in case unethical behaviour has taken place within his/her sales team (see Figure 6.3).

First, the Sales Manager has to *assemble all the relevant information* related to the unethical behaviour. It is extremely important for the Sales Manager to gather as much information as possible from different sources (e.g. other members of the sales force, customers, competitors, the salesperson under consideration). Any solution should deal with all the facts. If some key information is not considered, the Sales Manager is unlikely to find the best way to resolve the ethical problem.

Then, the sales manager needs to *analyse all the information gathered*. In particular, he/she must answer the questions shown in Figure 6.3 relating to the legality, ethics and morality of the salesperson under investigation's behaviour.

Once the information has been evaluated, the Sales Manager has to *make a decision*. Basically, this means either punishing the salesperson or not. It is extremely important that whatever the final decision is, it is taken into consideration on any future instances when the Sales Manager has to deal with unethical behaviour in his/her sales team (this feedback effect is indicated by the arrow returning to the first part of the model). That is to say, management's policy in dealing with unethical behaviour must be consistent over time in order to send a clear message to the sales team.

Previous research has found that when punishing unethical behaviour, Sales Managers are more likely to use a more severe form of disciplinary action when poor performers are involved (Bellizzi and Hite 1989). This is in fact more likely to happen when Sales Managers are rewarded on the basis of short-term sales outcomes, as Sales Managers generally do not actually sell, but succeed when their salespeople succeed. As a result, a Sales Manager may be willing to ignore ethics violations, particularly those in which top sales performers are involved and those associated with no apparent negative consequence. But, importantly, by basing their response on an assessment of the consequence, a Sales Manager may overlook unethical behaviour

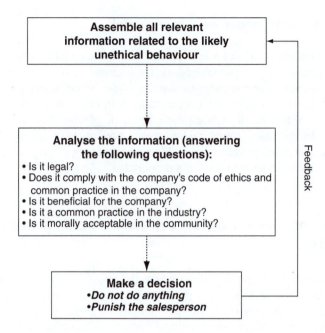

Figure 6.3 A checklist for management's decisions on ethical issues
Source: Author.

until it is too late to correct it and something serious happens (e.g. significant lawsuit, negative publicity).

When Sales Managers punish a top sales performer, they run the risk of losing a valuable member of the sales team. Of course, this hurts them because their rewards (pay and promotion) are influenced by the sales performance of the salespeople they supervise. On the contrary, when a poor performer is involved, a Sales Manager may seize the opportunity to punish an ethical violation severely. In that case, the Sales Manager has little to lose and perhaps something to gain. Salespeople observing the disciplinary reaction may heed the message and losing a poor performer may be only a modest loss or even a desired outcome. However, when top performers are treated differently, the double-standard message becomes the operating rule and top performers recognize that their questionable behaviour is not subject to firm disciplinary action. The bottom line is that if unethical selling behaviour is to be curbed, first-line Sales Managers (immediate supervisors of salespeople) must somehow be rewarded for using discipline when ethics violations are detected and punished accordingly when such violations are ignored.

In the rest of this section, we are going to apply the checklist to a real example that happened when the author of this chapter bought a new car not long ago.

Having gone to two dealerships in the same city asking for quotes on identical cars, it turned out that the final price of the car was the same in both dealerships. Surprisingly, the way the salespeople reached the final price was different. The salesperson of the first dealership (salesperson A) offered a higher discount (11 per cent) as opposed to the 10 per cent offered in the second dealership (dealership B). Yet, the initial price (the manufacturer's recommended price) in dealership A was higher than in dealership B. Faced with this situation, the manufacturer's web page was consulted and it was soon discovered that the recommended price had been 'inflated' in dealership A (this allowed them to offer a 'special' discount). The car was therefore purchased from dealership B.

The Sales Manager in dealership A could have found out about the unethical behaviour of his salesperson by asking him why the prospective customer had not bought the car despite the 'special' discount offered. In this way, he/she could have seen the details of the offer submitted to the customer and spotted that the initial price did not correspond to the manufacturer's recommended price. The next step would have been to answer the following questions:

• Was this a legal practice? Dealerships and manufacturers in this industry operate independently. Dealerships can establish the initial price they want to set since the manufacturer's initial price is only a guide. Therefore salesperson A's tactics can be considered legal.
• Does it comply with the company's code of ethics and common practice? The Sales Manager should be familiar with this issue in his dealership. Providing the dealership has a code of ethics, it is very unlikely that this practice would be considered ethical; yet it is highly likely to be a common practice in the dealership.
• Is it beneficial to the company? In the short run, this practice can be beneficial because it can translate into a sale as a consequence of the 'higher' discount. Yet in the long run the customer might realize that the discount was not 'high' and might not purchase again from the same dealership. Furthermore, it is possible (as actually occurred) that the prospective purchaser sees through the deceptive selling tactic and therefore does not buy the car and spreads negative word of mouth about the dealership.
• Is it common practice in the industry? Years ago, when the Internet did not exist, it used to be common practice. Consumers did not have complete information about manufacturers' prices, and dealerships would habitually quote higher initial prices than nowadays.
• Is it morally acceptable in the community? This is the toughest question to answer. In this case, it was wrong because the salesperson actually said that the initial price was the manufacturer's recommended price, which was not true. In other cases the issue is not so easy to evaluate since dealerships charge additional costs on top of the initial price of the car such as transportation, cleaning and so forth.

As a result of the above, the Sales Manager could speak with salesperson A and indicate his concerns about his behaviour. However, management does have a problem if his behaviour, while it contravenes the ethical code of the company, is common practice among salespeople. In such a case, management should explain that this action is in direct detriment to the long-term benefit of the company and its reputation and that punitive measures would be taken if such tactics were employed again in the future. If, on the other hand, this were a case confined to a single salesperson's unethical behaviour, and not common practice, the Sales Manager could directly warn, punish or threaten to dismiss the salesperson if this were to happen again.

Pharma Plus[2]

The company, the sales team and sales management activities

Pharma Plus is a French pharmaceutical company, focusing on the discovery and development of novel peptide-based drugs. The company produces medicines in France, but sells them throughout Europe. Pharma Plus's management is made up of individuals equipped with unique skills and international experience in their respective fields. Together, they form a dynamic and dedicated team of professionals under whose leadership Pharma Plus has earned its reputation as an innovative, growth-orientated company.

The company's subsidiary in Spain currently employs a Sales Manager and 35 salespeople. Their territories are divided according to geographic size, keeping salespeople's travel time to a minimum. Yet the sales team has recently been reduced to 27. This action was taken after the Sales Manager, Antonio Martínez, realized that the sales force was underutilized. Each territory was studied to determine the optimum number of calls per day from a well-planned itinerary. Similarly, each current account was analysed to determine how many calls per year were required to offer the desired amount of service and selling time. This analysis produced the current territory design and an increase in the number of calls per week. Nevertheless, the Sales Manager pointed out to the French Vice-president of the company that despite the reduction in the number of salespeople, the sales team needed two sales supervisors to help him manage and control the sales force more efficiently.

Salespeople in Spain work independently and do not normally need day-to-day supervision or contact with their Sales Manager. The evaluation process for the time being is numbers-driven. In fact, the Sales Manager conducts a formal performance review with each salesperson at the end of the year only if their sales quota has not been met. Only objective performance information (mainly sales made) is considered in the evaluation. Salespeople are paid a straight salary of €18,000 annually plus commission of 0.25 per cent on sales paid monthly. In addition to earnings, the salespeople receive all the normal fringe benefits, plus a company car. They are reimbursed for all 'allowable and reasonable' business expenses after submitting a monthly expense report. However, reimbursement under this plan is contingent on the salesperson submitting receipts or detailed records justifying their expenses. Evidently, the processing and evaluation of these claims demanded much time that sometimes the Sales Manager simply did not have. Accordingly, the Sales Manager did not put too much emphasis on controlling the expenses of the most experienced salespeople (those working for the company more than 15 years), as long as their quota was met.

The company has no formal written code of ethics. However, in the past the President has emphasized the importance of following industry regulations, especially concerning gifts and entertainment.

Roberto Soto's way of doing business

Roberto, one of the top performers of the Spanish sales force, earned €40,000 in commission on product sales in the previous year. He has no university education, yet he has more than 30 years of experience as a pharmaceutical salesperson. Not only does he always make his quota, but he

---

[2] The situations described in the following case are based on real stories. The names of the companies and the people are fictitious.

is also well liked by everyone. Antonio is happy with Roberto. He is making a lot of money for the company, and he has not heard any formal complaint about his way of selling. Yet Antonio is aware that Roberto's customers are the grateful recipients of cards for every occasion, tickets to sporting and entertainment events and other 'special' gifts. Every time Roberto sees the perfect gift for one of his customers – whether it is a wallet or a tennis racquet – Roberto buys it and presents it personally. For many years Roberto has squeezed part of the cost of these gifts into his travel and expense budget. In fact, Roberto is the salesperson with the highest expenses of the entire sales team.

Roberto has just had a nice, healthy breakfast. It is 9.30 in the morning and he is calling Juan, one of his old friends, who recently took early retirement at the age of 55:

ROBERTO: 'Hi, Juan. How's it going? Have you seen what a nice day it is today! What about playing a tennis match in a couple of hours?'

JUAN: 'That sounds pretty good to me. But shouldn't you be calling on customers at that time?'

ROBERTO: 'Well Juan, I'm going to be calling upon a couple of them this morning. They are very important customers for my company but it should not take me more than an hour. As for the others, I was supposed to pay them a visit today, but I took them to a nice restaurant last Friday, so I guess that's enough....'

JUAN: 'But what about your boss? Won't he care?'

ROBERTO: 'I guess he will; I'll do a little paperwork this afternoon and I'll report that I've seen six customers this morning, as I was supposed to. Fortunately, it's not easy for my boss to keep track of where I've been and know how many customers I've called on each day.'

JUAN: 'Well, I guess it's up to you. See you on court then!'

A different way of doing business: Elvira Pinada

Elvira has a degree in pharmacy and a Master of Business Administration. She is also one of the top performers of the Spanish sales team, despite the fact that she has been working for the company for only three years. Last year she even made 'salesperson of the year'. Elvira attributes her success to dedication and the desire to 'give the company a full day's work for a full day's pay'.

Elvira believes that her role is to educate clients about drug benefits and drawbacks. She also thinks that any form of entertainment is inappropriate because her goal, as a technically trained sales representative, is to have a meaningful conversation about her company's products. When Elvira takes her customers for lunch, the meals never cost more than the prevailing local standard for a reasonable meal. Furthermore, she is not very keen on giving gifts. If she does offer a gift to a customer, she makes sure it is a gift that will benefit the medical practice (e.g. a scientific book).

It is 14.45 p.m. and Elvira is still waiting to see her last call of the day. She is in a hospital located 60 km from her house. She has to call her husband to tell him that she will not be able to pick the children up from school. She knows he is not going to like it. It is not the first time she has been too late for the children and it will not be the last.

While waiting in the doctor's office, Elvira bumps into Julian Alcatraz, a newly hired sales-man from one of the competing pharmaceuticals companies. Elvira met Julian five years ago at university, when she was in her last year of pharmacy and he was in his first.

ELVIRA: 'Hi Julian, how is it going with your new job? Do you like it?'

JULIAN: 'Well, I'm kind of disappointed. Some doctors do not seem to be very interested in the product. Yet they ask me for "things" that are very difficult for me to get.'

ELVIRA: 'What kind of things are you talking about?'

JULIAN: 'Well, you know. For example, some of them want me to treat them and their families to flashy vacations.'

ELVIRA: 'Oh boy! You need to be very careful. Let me give you a piece of advice.'

JULIAN: 'I'd really appreciate it.'

ELVIRA: 'At this point, you may have realized that doctors are getting increasingly fed up with the number of salespeople waiting to see them. Sometimes there are more sales-people in the waiting-room than patients! As a highly qualified salesperson, you need to become a partner with the doctor –establish a trusting, credible relationship based on what you know and what you can offer. Also, you need to give them 24/7 access to infor-mation about the medications you sell. You can do that in person, by phone or via the internet.'

JULIAN: 'So are you saying that it's my product knowledge and objective medical knowledge that will win trust?'

ELVIRA: 'You got it. The best way to capture market share, boring as this may sound, is to present compelling clinical data that proves your drug is superior to another. You will stand out if you're organized, can answer the physicians' questions promptly and offer creative ways to educate doctors. Yet, sometimes you also need to give them something "special". We've all been there!'

JULIAN: 'OK, Elvira, many thanks for your help.'

ELVIRA: 'No problem. Hope it helps!'

Summary

A salesperson's unethical behaviour is a complex construct that can have devas-tating consequences for the selling company (e.g. lost customers, negative word of mouth, liability issues). On the other hand, ethical sales actions promote customer relationship-building. In today's highly competitive environment, companies that value the critical importance of long-term relationships with their customers should establish a business environment where the potential for unethical behaviour is at a minimum. This chapter has provided several guidelines for managers to foster their sales force's ethical behaviour.

Key points

1. A salesperson's ethical behaviour can play a critical role in the formation and maintenance of long-term buyer-seller relationships. Unethical behaviour, both intentional and inadvertent, can even generate liability problems for salespeople's organizations

2. Ethical selling behaviour is a highly elusive construct and is often situation-specific. Ethics requires an individual to behave according to the rules of a moral philosophy with an emphasis on the determination of right and wrong.
3. Ethical sales behaviour can be defined as fair and honest actions that enable the salesperson to foster long-term relationships with customers based on customer satisfaction and trust.
4. Dishonesty, deception, manipulation, high-pressure selling techniques and bribes are typical examples of unethical selling behaviours when interacting with customers.
5. Salespeople may behave unethically in their relationship with their employers. Typical examples are misuse of company resources and cheating on sales reports.
6. Ethical decision-making is influenced by personal factors (characteristics of the salesperson) and situational/external factors (e.g. company policies, competitors).
7. Sales Managers can implement several policies to foster ethical selling behaviour. These policies include development and enforcement of a code of ethics, selection and hiring, rewarding, supervising and evaluating and leading by example.
8. Management's response to unethical selling behaviour depends on the extent to which the action is legal, complies with the company's code of ethics and common practice in the company, is beneficial for the company, is a common practice in the industry and is morally acceptable in the community.

References

Anderson, E. and Oliver, R.L. (1987) 'Perspectives on Behavior-Based Versus Outcome-Based Salesforce Control Systems', *Journal of Marketing*, 51: 76–88.

Bellizzi, J.A. and Hite, R.E. (1989) 'Supervising Unethical Salesforce Behavior', *Journal of Marketing*, 53: 36–48.

Grisaffe, D.B. and Jaramillo, F. (2007) 'Toward Higher Levels of Ethics: Preliminary Evidence of Positive Outcomes', *Journal of Personal Selling and Sales Management*, 27: 355–71.

Ingram, T.N., LaForge, R.W. and C. H. Schwepker Jr (2007) 'Salesperson Ethical Decision Making: the Impact of Sales Leadership and Sales Management Control Strategy', *Journal of Personal Selling and Sales Management*, 27: 301–15.

Mulki, J.P., Jaramillo, F. and Locander, W.B. (2009) 'Critical Role of Leadership on Ethical Climate and Salesperson Behaviors', *Journal of Business Ethics*, 86 (2): 125–41.

O'Brian, B. (1999) 'Prudential fined $20 million by NASD over its sales of variable life insurance', *Wall Street Journal*, 9 July: c1, c11.

Román, S. and Munuera, J.L. (2005) 'Determinants and Consequences of Ethical Behavior: an Empirical Study of Salespeople', *European Journal of Marketing*, 39 (5/6): 473–95.

Román, S. and Ruiz, S. (2005) 'Relationship Outcomes of Perceived Ethical Sales Behaviour: The Customer's Perspective', *Journal of Business Research*, 58 (4): 439–45.

Singhapakdi, A., Vitell, S.J. and Franke, G.R. (1999) 'Antecedents, Consequences, and Mediating Effects of Perceived Moral Intensity and Personal Moral Philosophies', *Journal of the Academy of Marketing Science*, 27 (1): 19–36.

Strout, E. (2001) 'Are your Salespeople Ripping You Off?', *Sales and Marketing Management*, February: 56–62.

Tansey, R., Brown, G., Hyman, M.R. and Dawson, L.E. Jr (1994) 'Personal Moral Philoso-phies and the Moral Judgements of Salespeople', *Journal of Personal Selling and Sales Management*, 14: 59–75.

Wotruba, T. (1990) 'A Comprehensive Framework for the Analysis of Ethical Behav-ior, with a Focus on Sales Organisations', *Journal of Personal Selling and Sales Management*, 10: 29–42.

Zeiger, R. (1995) 'Sex, sales & stereotypes', *Sales and Marketing Management*, July: 46–56.

Further reading

Ferrell, O.C. and Gresham, L.G. (1985) 'A Contingency Framework for Understanding Ethical Decision Making in Marketing', *Journal of Marketing*, 49 (3): 87–96.

Gundlach, G.T. and Murphy, P.E. (1993) 'Ethical and Legal Foundations of Relational Marketing Exchanges', *Journal of Marketing*, 57: 35–46.

Hunt, S.D. and Vitell, S.J. (1986) 'A General Theory of Marketing Ethics', *Journal of Macromarketing*, 6 (Spring): 5–16.

Lagace, R.R., Dahlstrom, R. and Gassenheimer, J.B. (1991) 'The Relevance of Ethical Salesperson Behavior on Relationship Quality: The Pharmaceutical Industry', *Journal of Personal Selling and Sales Management*, 11: 39–47.

Singhapakdi, A. and Vitell, S.J. (1991) 'Analysing the Ethical Decision Making of Sales Professionals', *Journal of Personal Selling and Sales Management*, 11 (4): 1–12.

Part two

Formulation of the sales programme: defining sales force investment and structure

7

Sales planning and forecasting

Laszlo Sajtos[1]

Contents

---

[1] I would like to thank two companies for their contribution: Heinz Wattie's and Frucor. In particular, I would like to express my appreciation to Phil Webb (Supply Chain Manager at Frucor), Stuart Sheng (Demand Planner at Frucor) and Kurt Allen (Financial Planning Manager at Heinz Wattie's) who made themselves available for interviews and provided valuable information for the completion of this chapter. I would also like to thank Geoff Whitcher (Commercial Director of the University of Auckland Developments) for organizing the interviews with Frucor. Last, but not least, I would like to thank Roderick J. Brodie (Professor of the Department of Marketing, University of Auckland Business School) and Henning Kreis (Junior Professor of the Free University, Berlin) for their helpful comments on previous versions of this chapter, and Helga Arlington for her copy-editing services.

Learning objectives

After reading this chapter, you should be able to:

- Discuss the critical role of forecasting in the firm and understand its link with planning.
- List the key steps of the forecasting process.
- List the types of forecasting methods and understand how to choose between them.
- Discuss the challenges and the complexities of forecasting.

Chapter outline

Forecasting surrounds us in our everyday lives and it is more embedded in our activities than we might expect. It is there when we prepare for a three-day camping trip, deciding how much food and drink we need to take without either carrying too much weight or running short, and it is also there when we try to estimate how much electricity we will use in a month, in order to choose the right plan for our household without getting penalized by the electricity company. Forecasting is very common in a number of business domains; for instance, in Finance, Economics, Sales, Marketing, Production and New Product Development. It is primarily economists who prepare forecasts of gross domestic product (GDP), unemployment and inflation, which serve as the basis for macroeconomic policy-making. Marketing and Sales forecasts aim to predict demand for an existing or a new product or product category, after which the Production department is able to plan the raw material requirements, production and storage capacity required. In this chapter, forecasting will be introduced through examples from the fast moving consumer goods (FMCG) industry, based on interviews with experts in the areas of sales, demand planning, supply chain and finance. Nevertheless, the chapter aims to underline that forecasting is a universal activity; it requires coordinated input from all departments in the organization and has strategic implications for the entire company. We demonstrate this point through an extended case study of a New Zealand-based consumer goods company.

CASE PROBLEM

Case history of new product forecasting.
Frucor Beverages – 'Failure in sales forecasting, success in the market'

Frucor Beverages Ltd was established as an arm of the New Zealand Apple and Pear Marketing Board. Initially Frucor sold apple juice on behalf of the Board, but in 1962 the company entered the market with its first juice brand, 'Fresh Up'. Between 1981 and 1992 Frucor introduced three more juice brands into New Zealand. One of these, 'Just Juice', rates alongside Coca-Cola as the best known beverage brand name in New Zealand. During the 1990s Frucor diversified into various areas such as chilled juice, carbonated soft drinks and bottled water. This diversification strategy, along with first-class production facilities and a strong, countrywide distribution network assured the company's number two position in the New Zealand beverage market.

For the last five years Frucor has introduced new products every year and has outperformed all other beverage manufacturers combined. Figure 7.1 shows Frucor's strong new product sales within the Total Ready To Drink Beverages in the Service Station Organized market in relation to other suppliers in 2008/9 (52 weeks to 14 June 2009). Frucor has introduced several New Zealand 'firsts' including a sparkling fruit mineral water, jelly and yoghurt drinks, flavoured still water, chilled coffee, and its major success, the *V* energy drink. Over the last 15 years the company has established a reputation for innovation, which provides the company with a source of sustainable competitive advantage.

As in many other countries, Red Bull was the first energy drink brand in the New Zealand market. The energy drink market was still considered very young when Frucor decided in 1997, six months after the arrival of Red Bull in the New Zealand market, to take up the challenge with Red Bull, the global market leader, and launch its new product under the name *V* there.

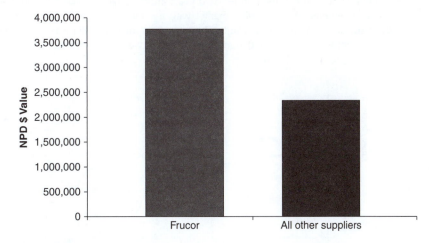

Figure 7.1   Comparison of annual new product sales (in dollars): Frucor v other manufacturers

(Period: Year to 14 June 2009; Products: New products within Total Ready To Drink Beverages (excluding alcohol); Market: Service Station Organized (including BP Organized, Mobil Organized, Caltex Organized, but excluding Shell).

Source: Frucor.

Although Frucor had already had numerous successful product launches, the short history of the energy drink as a product category created a challenge for sales forecasting. In order to estimate the potential sales of *V*, Frucor analysed Red Bull's overseas performance, especially in markets with similar conditions to New Zealand's.

As well as its examination of market trends and characteristics, Frucor also sought to understand how its main competitor (Red Bull) had positioned its product. Red Bull had been positioned as a party drink and hence was primarily sold in bars and pubs. Frucor's marketing team – rather than positioning *V* as a party drink and thus a strong competing brand to Red Bull – instead developed a unique, occasion-based positioning with a strong focus on distribution channels such as supermarkets, petrol stations and convenience stores. Frucor understood that the lives of today's consumers are jam-packed, with longer working hours and increasing time spent on leisure activities. Stress levels are forever on the rise and people search for more energy to complete their daily tasks. Consumers turn to beverages, such as coffee, cola and sugary foods for increased levels of concentration and productivity. They want a shift from energy deficit to normal or enhanced energy levels to deal with challenges which can be physical, mental, emotional or social. Frucor realized that consumers need energy during the daytime, for instance while studying, working, driving, socializing or playing sports (see Figure 7.2), and hence *V* was positioned as a *daytime* energy drink; a new and unique slot in the emerging energy drink market. This strategy proved a resounding success. However, since the beverage market is constantly evolving, Frucor had nonetheless constantly to monitor the positioning of not only the energy drinks, but also other products, such as colas, sport drinks and waters.

Based on the fairly limited data that Frucor was able to gather on the international trends and on Red Bull's performance, its initial sales forecast was 1 million products for the first year. The forecast sales (for the first 12 months) and the production plan were, however, further challenged by issues with the packaging. Despite Frucor's success in identifying a gap in the energy drink market, its team's forecast became pessimistic when Frucor had sold all its stock a month after the product launch because the cans were being sourced from Canada with a lead time of 8 to 12 weeks. Despite the initial hurdles, two years after the New Zealand product launch Frucor successfully entered the Australian market with a similar strategy to that which had by now proved so successful in New Zealand. The expansion into Australia was also facilitated by the Closer Economic Relations (CER) Trade Agreement between the two countries.

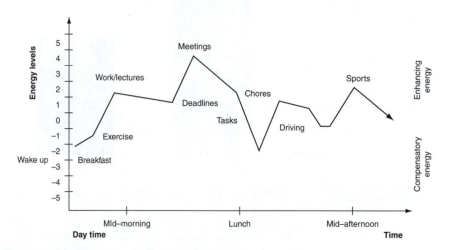

Figure 7.2 Energy need throughout the day
Source: Frucor, V Presentation.

Frucor has developed *V* into a leading brand, which is now stronger than any other energy drink brand in the Australasia region. It is a very successful product of a company whose revenue is now over NZ$500 million and which has achieved a large market share in the beverage market in both New Zealand and Australia. Despite Frucor's initial inexperience with new product forecasting but thanks to the 15 new product launches annually, Frucor's forecasting proficiency and accuracy has significantly improved over the last decade.

According to Phil Webb, the Supply Chain Manager of Frucor, sales forecasting is a very important process in the company, but forecasting for a new product can be a challenge. 'Being good at forecasting comes from thoroughly understanding your organizational processes' says Mr Webb. Accordingly, Frucor has put a strong emphasis on launching new products effectively and on developing a strong distribution system. Frucor sees itself as a risk-taker, and that view is supported by its organizational adaptability and an organizational culture that acknowledges that 'mistakes are acceptable'. The complexity of forecasting for Frucor arises from a lack of or uncertainty about market information, as in the case of *V*, and also from the interdependency of various processes that contribute to the commercial success of a new product. These processes run parallel to each other, rather than sequentially. When a new product is about to be launched, Frucor's managers collect information on topics such as the potential market size, actual sales, level of distribution, types of channels and accounts where the product should be sold, advertising and promotional plans, and so on.

Introduction: from planning to sales forecasting

According to *Collins English Dictionary* (Anderson 2007), 'planning' is 'a detailed scheme, method, etc. for attaining an objective'. The process of formal planning incorporates the following aspects (Steiner 1979, pp. 35–43). It:

- focuses attention on questions that are important to the company;
- introduces a set of decision-making forces and tools to the business, which:

  - simulates the future,
  - forces the setting of objectives,
  - provides a systematic decision framework
  - links a variety of management functions;

- provides behavioural benefits by establishing communication channels and managerial training and fostering a sense of participation.

Compared with planning, which is generally holistic and is closely related to 'preparation' and 'design', the focus of forecasting is narrower and more to do with estimation, calculation and prediction. In particular, 'Forecasting is the prediction of values of a variable, based on known past values of that variable or other related variables. Forecasts also may be based on expert judgements, which in turn are based on historical data and experience.' (Makridakis et al. 1998, p. 899). Makridakis et al. (1998) discuss two types of forecasting situation. The first focuses on patterns or relationships and their (likely) continuation (e.g. monthly/quarterly/yearly sales patterns of 500 ml Heinz tomato ketchup) whereas the second focuses on the timing of changes occurring in the patterns or relationships (e.g. when a recession will occur again). In this chapter, only the first type of forecasting will be discussed, based on the examples of two iconic companies from the Australasian region, Frucor Beverages Limited and Heinz Wattie's Limited.

One particularly important area of forecasting from a business perspective is sales forecasting. Sales forecasting is a process that provides a value or volume estimate for expected future sales of a certain product or category.[2] Sales forecasting should always refer to three key elements: what is being forecast; for what geographic area; and for what time period (Ingram et al. 2006). Table 7.1 summarizes the definitions of the most commonly used terms in forecasting.

Based on the above definitions, planning and forecasting are quite similar in some respects: they both prepare the company for the future by drawing on past (history) to hand as well as future expectations, and they both apply a set of conditions and assumptions to do this. However, in order for the planning process to be successful it must rely on a thorough forecasting process, which in turn, depends on the reliability of the data that has been collected for the forecast. Forecasting should be part of the planning process as forecasting creates scenarios with regard to the future (of a product, market, etc.) while planning chooses one or a few of these scenarios and prepares a detailed scheme for the implementation of those that are plausible. Which of the forecasting scenario appear plausible for planning purposes depends heavily upon the goals and strategies of the management of the firm, as well as upon the resources and internal or external constraints of the company.

One of the main conditions for forecasting to happen as part of the planning process is the presence of a time lag between the awareness of a future event and the

Table 7.1 Commonly used terms in forecasting

Market potential The maximum achievable sales in a particular industry in a certain geographic area for a specific period. The level of sales in a particular industry in a certain geographic area over a certain period of time.

Sales potential The maximum achievable sales of a particular stock keeping unit (SKU) or product or product category or the entire firm in a certain geographic area for a specific period.

Sales forecast The expected level of sales of a particular SKU or product or product category or the entire firm in a certain geographic over a certain period of time.

Sales target A sales goal the salesperson/company is expected to reach. Sales targets should be informed by the sales forecast. The sales target is usually used as a motivational tool for various stakeholders in the company.

Operational plan A set of managerial actions that aim to achieve the sales forecast. It should be noted that from a forecast preparer's point of view underestimating the forecast is as detrimental as overestimating it as they are usually 'rewarded' on accuracy.

[2] Mentzer and Moon (2005) note that the term sales forecasting is slightly misleading as sales forecasting predicts customer demand, namely how much our customers will buy.

occurrence of that event. This time lag allows the management to pre-empt impending events (e.g. a new competitor or product entering the market) and to prepare for it by introducing certain adjustments to the firm's strategy. In practice, however, a range of controllable events (production, storage, distribution, etc.) and uncontrollable ones (competitive actions, legislative changes) occur concurrently with the planning process. Even if the firm had been aware of certain of these events in advance, their impact on the company might still have been unpredictable. Therefore, all planning processes occur as a continuous adjustment between the company's environment and its resources.

Relevance of forecasting

The importance of forecasting has increased significantly in the last couple of decades and this can be attributed to the following factors (Makridakis et al. 1998, pp. 6–7):

1. *Complexity of organizations and their environments.* Nowadays organizations operate under increased pressure from competitors, customers, employees and legislators, among others, and they also have to comply with more rigorous standards. This increased complexity requires more information regarding the present and future potential of the company to be factored into the decision-making process. The complexity introduced by an increasing number of stakeholders is intensified by the pace at which change occurs in the marketplace.
2. *Number of people involved in decision-making.* The complexity of the firm's environment is mirrored internally as well, as an increasing number of employees tend to be involved in preparing and using forecasts. The outcome of this is an increased need for companies to formalize their planning and thus make the decision-making process more transparent and accountable.
3. *Risky decisions.* In today's environment, an increasing number of companies take a significant amount of risk to compete and to survive and, hence, one wrong decision can make or break the company. Forecasting can help organizations to transform uncertainty into manageable risk and to assess further the type and nature of the risks that the decision-maker must face.
4. *Enhancement of forecasting methods.* The factors listed above have triggered a proliferation of forecasting methods. Improved forecasting tools have offered better results and forced all companies to use the forecasting process in a more skilled manner. When determining the forecasting method one needs to consider the fit between a particular decision needing to be made and the forecasting method.
5. *Amount of available data.* The widespread collection of store scanner data in conjunction with enhanced computing power has also contributed to the significance of forecasting. However, although the increase in the amount of data available to forecasters might lead one to an assumption that statistical methods would be dominant in forecasting, the company interviews in fact seem to show a balance between statistical and qualitative methods in companies.

The forecasting process

Armstrong (2001a) outlined the stages of forecasting as follows:

1. formulate problem;
2. obtain information;
3. select methods;
4. implement methods;
5. evaluate methods;
6. use forecasts.

Many well-established companies, such as Heinz Wattie's Limited (HWL) do go through these stages, although the boundaries between stages might be somewhat blurred as processes become more of a routine and the knowledge that drives them more implicit.

Figure 7.3 shows the monthly forecasting routine undertaken by HWL; it does not, however, include what happens before this process takes place. Like many other companies, HWL has an annual plan of goals for the year. These plans centre around key financial results, such as revenue, earnings before interest and taxes (EBIT) and growth.

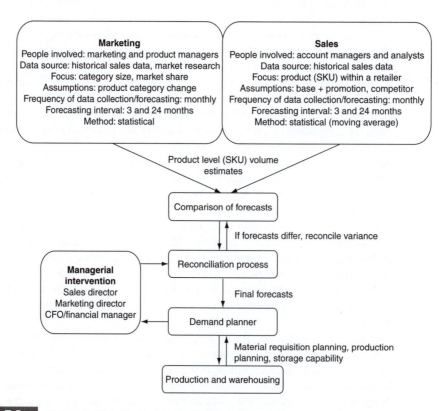

Figure 7.3 Heinz Wattie's Limited New Zealand: forecasting process

Financial goal-setting is a vital part of the company's operation, and also reassures the company's shareholders as to their anticipated return on investment. Nevertheless, the implications of this planning process should be clearly separated and distinguished from what concerns sales forecasting. While preparers of forecasts must be aware of their company's plan they should always try to forecast demand (reality) rather than slavishly following their sales targets and budget, which would make forecasting into a purely academic exercise.

The forecasting process at HWL takes a 'bottom-up' approach for all of their 1,500 stock keeping units (SKUs). The process starts with Sales Managers and analysts on one side, and Marketing and Product Managers on the other, 'building' their forecasts separately from one another. Both sides rely, in large part, on historical sales data provided by A.C. Nielsen, although marketing complements this with ad-hoc market research data. Although they both use very much the same information as an input for their forecasts, the two sides have a different focus. Marketing Managers think holistically about what the future holds for a certain product category, and aim to forecast the size of and changes within that category, as well as the share the company can achieve within it. Sales people are very much detail-oriented and forecast sales on the SKU level in respect of a particular customer (e.g. a store chain in a particular region). The main difference between the focus of the two functions is that Sales must be very conscious of its customers' (retailers, wholesalers) priorities and strategies and sales-people must constantly scan their environment for new opportunities and threats that emerge in 'their' stores.

HWL as the market leader in various product categories is in a unique position, and has a proven track record of delivering successful products that benefit the retailer. This provides the firm with advantages, such as the privilege (and the responsibility) of designing the 'shelf facing' for a category in which it is leader. In conjunction with the store and the competing manufacturers, it may decide how the shelf for a particular product category will look in a store.

To prepare these forecasts, Marketing and Sales Managers at HWL rely on different assumptions. The former builds up scenarios for market changes, whereas the latter estimates base sales (without promotions), determines the type and schedule of sales promotions and estimates their impact (promotional uplifts). Both Marketing and Sales prepare their forecasts on a monthly basis – for both the short (3 months) and long term (24 months). Sales' prime responsibility is short-term, whereas Marketing's is long-term forecasting. Both departments use statistical methods to arrive at their final volume-based estimates, which are presented in unit cases or metric tonnes at SKU level. Nevertheless, sales forecasting often produces dollar results that need to be translated into 'number of units', which will allow the (internal) forecast also to be compared with the findings of market research studies.

Since Marketing and Sales build up their forecasts by using different assumptions, it is unavoidable that there will be differences between their estimates when they are compared. If the forecasts do not agree, the difference (variance) between them must be reconciled and eliminated. The reconciliation process requires forecasters to revisit their estimates and question the assumptions behind them. This process can be done more holistically at HWL, where the company analyses every one of its products (SKU) on a monthly basis and compares its forecasts not only across Marketing and Sales, but also to the previous month's result and to the allocated budget.

Although HWL has wide experience in forecasting, some product categories such as fruits, seem to be more complex to forecast than others, and hence, forecasts between the Marketing and Sales departments differ more often than not. Differences in forecasting for fruit sales might arise from different assumptions; for instance, Sales might think that the fruit that was harvested in one season should be or could be sold before the next harvest, whereas Marketing might argue that some part of the harvest should be carried forward as it predicts a higher demand the following season. One should also realize that an assumption like this, which is primarily related to current and future (potential) demand, has a price implication. A company, in addition to simply selling a seasonal product like fruit, needs to set the right price and to schedule promotions effectively. The complexity of the fruit product category is increased by the variability of the crop – some seasons bring more or higher quality fruit than others, and this regulates the market price of this product at a macro level. Furthermore, the assumptions above have implications for the cost for production and storage. Finally, forecasting – and, in particular, Sales and Account Managers – must ensure that there is a constant flow of products into the stores, because otherwise this might affect their allocation of shelf space. One might expect that if the company sold its products in a shorter period of time than usual this would not be a problem, because the stock was there to be sold. However, running out of stock has a doubly negative impact: not only will competitor's products take over the now vacant shelf space, but it is most likely that the retailer will not buy from the company in future because it has proven unable to provide a constant flow of products. All these factors need to be considered as a whole in order to make sensible planning decisions in a product category.

In some cases, differences between forecasts might need to be reconciled by involving the Demand Planner – who at HWL is the key coordinating person between the 'front' and the 'back' of the business – or another member of the upper management (managerial intervention). Once all forecasts agree, then these are collated and aggregated by the Demand Planner, to form the total demand forecast for the company. The estimates of the Demand Planner will serve as input for the Production Manager to develop the production planning schedule and production costing. This process ensures that the company has the ability to produce the stock required and has the appropriate level of stock at any given time.

Forecasting methods and choosing between methods

This section provides only a brief review of some of the main forecasting methods, and does not claim to be comprehensive. The interested reader can refer to a variety of sources, such as Armstrong (2001a); Makridakis et al. (1998) and Lütkepohl (2005), which focus on forecasting methods in detail. Some criteria for choosing between these methods will then be discussed.

Forecasting methods (see Table 7.2) can be divided into two categories, judgemental (or qualitative or subjective) and statistical (or quantitative), and are used to predict changes and trends in the environment over the long term. Judgmental methods rely heavily on personal expertise, knowledge and foresight (Makridakis et al. 1998), whereas statistical methods require historical numerical data and an assumption that

Table 7.2		Forecasting methods
		Definition and description of the method
Qualitative, judgmental methods	Delphi approach	The Delphi method is a structured procedure consisting of multiple rounds to achieve group consensus. A researcher starts the process by inviting a panel of outside experts to participate in a discussion, where they cannot interact with each other except through the researcher. The experts are asked to comment on certain issues (usually related to uncertain future events) and their views are then evaluated and summarized by the researcher and sent back to them for further evaluation. This is an iterative process, in which each expert receives feedback as to how other experts responded (explicitly but still anonymously or through a summary) in the previous round and can revise or refine his/her views. The objective is to reduce the variance of the answers without eliminating deviant (but relevant) opinions (Makridakis et al. 1998). The process finishes when the researcher has enough information, has exhausted the topic or feels that consensus is reached. The Delphi method is advantageous if there are a number of experts available who are willing to express themselves freely without meeting each other and, thus, experiencing social pressure. It can be implemented in a shorter period of time than organizing interviews with every expert separately. A major disadvantage of the method is that the reliability of the outcome depends on the quality and variety of the experts chosen.
	Role-playing or scenario writing	This method simulates situations or describes scenarios when the most likely outcome of a situation needs to be predicted. Alternatively it can take the form of a role-play simulating, for instance, a negotiation, where parties interact with each other on a conflicting issue for which one would like to predict the potential outcome. Each alternative outcome will rely on different assumptions and the various strategies of the (multiple) stakeholders, which can lead to a realistic modelling of the scenario and its potential outcomes. Overall, the success of this technique heavily depends upon how realistic the simulation is, which is why it is only rarely used (Armstrong 2000b). It is, however, used in situations when there is no objective sales data available (e.g. in new product development).
	Expert opinions/ judgemental bootstrapping	This method involves asking between 5 and 20 experts (Ashton and Ashton 1985) for their opinion about a particular industry/market or topic, in order to generate a forecast. The experts are usually independent from each other (from different organizations) and their opinions/forecasts are weighted equally. This method can take the shape either of an unstructured meeting (of executives, experts, Sales Managers) or can be organized in a more structured manner (see Delphi approach). For a detailed comparison between the accuracy of the Delphi method versus unstructured judgement, see

Table 7.2	(Continued)	
		Definition and description of the method
		Rowe and Wright (2000). If these expert opinions are validated against the forecaster's information and translated into a set of rules, then the technique is referred to as 'judgemental bootstrapping'. Judgemental bootstrapping has been proven to be more accurate than judgemental methods in general (Armstrong 2000a).
	Market research methods	Although market research methods used in forecasting are broadly quantitative, they also use customers' subjective information (attitudes, expectations, motivation, behavioural intention) and hence these techniques are grouped with the judgemental methods. Furthermore, the term 'market research methods' covers a wide range of techniques that are used for purposes such as concept or product testing in a 'lab' (artificial environment or in the marketplace, also referred to as a test market) or conjoint analysis. Conjoint analysis is frequently used for new product/service development, which aims to find out the most attractive combination of attributes (e.g. colour), and the preferred level of those attributes (e.g. blue) that customers would be willing to buy at a certain price. Although conjoint analysis is less likely to be used in a business-to-business setting, suppliers can survey their customers (retailers) on certain issues by interviewing one or multiple informants from the customer's organization based on their roles in the decision-making process (e.g. gatekeeper, decision-maker, etc.).
Quantitative, statistical methods	Averaging methods	Averaging methods are part of what are known as 'smoothing techniques'. Smoothing means reducing (averaging) the random effects in the past (historical) observations and hence providing a 'smooth' forecast. Smoothing techniques are not considered unanimously as forecasting methods because they 'only' distinguish noise from underlying patterns and trends. Averaging methods employ moving averages that take a certain number of periods (eg. three-month moving average) and, then average values of every subsequent three-month period, which results in a smooth trendline. The weight assigned to observations is determined by the particular moving average method applied, but the observations have equal weights (33.3 per cent in the case of a three-period moving average).
	Smoothing techniques	One commonly used smoothing technique is exponential smoothing (named after the exponential function) and it is based on the principle that earlier data points are given exponentially lesser weights than recent data – weights from the past to the present constantly increase. Several variations of exponential smoothing techniques exist, such as single, double and triple, and Holt-Winter's exponential smoothing. In this technique a smoothing parameter must be determined, representing the weight assigned to the most

recent period, which accordingly also determines the weight to the observations from older periods. It is an easy to implement, and hence cost-effective method, and it is most appropriate for short-term forecasts.

Decomposition methods The quantitative methods so far discussed, enable us only to distinguish randomness from the underlying pattern in the data, but do not allow for the identification of individual components. Decomposition methods break the time series into components and predict all of them. Time series can be divided into the following components:

1. trend (T), which represents changes affecting the entire time series and shows a long-term direction;
2. cycle (C), which represents middle-range effects;
3. seasonality (S), which represents yearly, monthly or weekly repeating patterns;
4. the error term (E), which is a random component in the model.

Decomposition methods remove seasonality first, followed by the trend and finally the cycle. Forecasting with this method means extrapolating each component separately and combining them into a single forecast. By contrast with the averaging and smoothing techniques, decomposition methods require more input, more sophisticated skills and more time from the forecaster.

Regression methods Regression methods are usually referred to as causal or explanatory techniques, because one attempts to explain a causal relationship by using one or more independent variables and one dependent variable. It is also, however, referred to as time series regression, when the data is measured over time. We can distinguish between single (one dependent and one independent variable) and multiple (multiple independent variables and one dependent), and linear and non-linear regression models, where the dependent is the non-linear/linear function of the independent variable(s). The most commonly used estimation technique in regression analysis is the 'least squares' estimation. The regression equation ($Y = a + bx$) aims to fit a trendline to the observed data points by minimizing the deviation between the points and the trendline. The explanatory power of the independent variables is expressed by the measure R^2.

Econometric methods In comparison with the regression methods, econometric methods deal with more than one multiple regression equation, which are simultaneously calculated. As with regression methods, econometric models rely on theory to use the appropriate variables, understand their complex relationships and identify the best functions that describe them. Econometric models are rather complex, but do not necessarily perform better than simpler time series models (Makridakis et al. 1998). Econometric methods should be used when large changes are expected to occur in the independent (causal) variables over the forecast horizon (Armstrong and Brodie 1999).

	Definition and description of the method
Table 7.2 (Continued)	
ARMA/ARIMA models	Autoregressive Moving Average (ARMA) or (Autoregressive (AR) Integrated (ARIMA) (I) Moving Average(MA)) models are also known as Box-Jenkins models. Time series models can take AR or MA forms, or a combination of the two. In the ARMA model, the series to be forecast is expressed as a function of both previous values of the series (autoregressive terms) and previous error values from forecasting (the moving average terms) (Makridakis et al. 1998, p. 891). Therefore, these methods combine principles used in regression models (explaining variance) and smoothing techniques (averaging errors) and assume that the time series was generated by a probability process. ARMA and ARIMA models are complex and heavily rely on statistical skills.

Source: based on Armstrong 2001b; Armstrong and Brodie 1999; Makridakis et al. 1998.

past patterns will continue in the future (assumption of continuity) (Makridakis et al. 1998). There is an increasing trend for integration of the two types of methods, which can improve forecast accuracy (Armstrong and Collopy 1998).

Research shows that accuracy, timeliness (in providing forecasts), cost savings (resulting from improved decisions), flexibility and ease of interpretation have been rated as the most important factors when choosing the appropriate forecasting method by a wide range of stakeholders, such as researchers, educators, practitioners and decision-makers (Yokum and Armstrong 1995). Although the ratings were consistent across the respondents, different methods were preferred for short- and long-term forecasting. The following section provides a brief review of the most important criteria for choosing between methods, based on the work of Armstrong (2001b) and Makridakis et al. (1998).

Forecasting accuracy

Forecasting accuracy is the difference between the forecast's prediction and the actual result, and it represents success or failure for many forecasters. The accuracy of forecasting according to Kurt Allen, Financial Planning Manager at HWL is primarily determined by the robustness[3] of the forecasting process and the number of employees involved in it. The accuracy of a forecast can subsequently be measured in various ways: by using standard absolute measures, such as total error, mean error, mean absolute error, sum of squared errors, mean squared error and standard deviation of errors; or by relative measures, such as percentage error, mean percentage error or

---

[3] Robustness means that the forecasting process is reliable as a result of applying scientific principles consistently every time a forecast is made.

mean absolute percentage error (MAPE[4]). Empirical studies have provided evidence that relatively simple extrapolation methods perform as well as more complex methods in terms of forecasting accuracy (Makridakis et al 1984). HWL measures accuracy by using weighted average percentage error (WAPE[5]) based on ex-factory sales. In general, relative measures are preferred over absolute measures, as the latter do not allow comparison across forecasts. However, even when using relative measures, such as MAPE, it is hard to decide whether a MAPE of 5 per cent should be considered small or large. Therefore, rather than creating thresholds for determining what can be considered a large or small error, researchers use a so called naïve forecast, typically the most recent (previous period) information available as a base of comparison. Research shows that new product forecasting accuracy on average one year after launch is slightly above 50 per cent (Kahn 2002).

Knowledge and skills required

Skills required for forecasting depend upon the method being used in the particular company. Statistical techniques necessitate a thorough understanding of mathematics and statistics, whereas judgmental methods call for a thorough understanding of the market – in other words, business acumen. At Frucor, Stuart Sheng (Demand Planner) explains that although some more complex methods could in fact do a better job in terms of forecasting accuracy, the most important factor is that everyone should thoroughly understand the forecasting process, how the forecast estimate was arrived at and how each person's role relates to the process. The detailed mathematics behind the forecasting technique might be known only to the Demand Planner, but the qualitative insights provided by sales and marketing expertise are also critical to the accuracy of the forecast. Simplicity in forecasting ensures that it is clear to those involved how the forecast was created and there is no 'black box' between input (of data) and the outcome (forecast).

People involved in forecasting

Those potentially involved in preparing sales forecasts are Sales Analysts, Account Managers, Marketing and Product Managers and Demand Planners. HWL chooses to rely heavily on its own employees in Sales and Marketing – who are in touch with its customers and the company's market – in order to prepare forecasts. The company has only one Demand Planner, who is responsible for overseeing the forecasting process and managing the link between the 'front' (customer-facing) and the 'back' (Production and warehousing) of the business. Nevertheless, HWL recognizes that a higher number of Demand Planners would increase the level of forecasting accuracy. In contrast with

---

[4] If MAPE of zero represents a perfect fit between the actual data and the forecast, it will have no upper limit (which is a disadvantage).
[5] WAPE is a weighted MAPE and is usually used for a group of SKUs. In calculating WAPE, actual values (not forecasts) serve as the weights and thus represent the actual contribution of a particular group of SKUs.

HWL, Frucor employs more Demand Planners, who carry a level of responsibility for forecasting equal to that of its Sales and Marketing departments.

Convenience

The term 'convenience' is used here synonymously for 'inertia', which has a strong impact in business. Large, well-established companies usually stick to the method that has been in place for years and which has served them well. Convenience is driven partly by having only part-time or a small number of full-time forecasters in the company, and hence these employees cannot choose or are not concerned with choosing a different forecasting method than that already in place. According to Armstrong (2001a), forecasting methods should be chosen based on convenience only when accuracy is not vital and the market is stable.

Ease of application

Ease of application relates to how complex the method currently in use is and how much time and manual labour is involved in preparing forecasts. Most companies use spreadsheet software for forecasting, or they prepare their forecasts within the company's Enterprise Resource Planning (ERP) system, which offers certain pre-defined methods.

Market popularity

Companies often choose certain methods because they are popular among companies in general or in a particular industry. Armstrong (2001b) notes that popularity does not guarantee effectiveness, especially as it will not be clear what situations the methods are being used in.

Data patterns

Researchers must consider the type of data they have, as certain data patterns require particular methods. Some methods are more holistic than others and can be used for a range of purposes. Patterns within data consist of specific components, such as trend, seasonality and cycle. Some of these components are periodic and repeating (e.g. seasonality), while others might be non-periodic – one-off patterns that represent turning points in trends. Identifying patterns within the data also means distinguishing them from noise (random components). Single equation regression is a very versatile method for this purpose, as it can cope with various patterns as long as they can be transformed into a linear relationship. Linear and higher order smoothing, such as Holt-Winter's exponential smoothing and also ARMA models can cope with trend and seasonal patterns. Decomposition methods are the strongest for cyclical components and cyclical turning points. Multiple regression and econometric models can cope with both seasonal and cyclical patterns.

Types of time series

For short-term macro[6] forecasts, ARMA and adaptive parameter methods can be used, whereas for micro series the exponential smoothing methods are the best to use. Furthermore, the type of series used in the forecast has a significant impact on forecasting accuracy (Makridakis et al. 1984) as micro series seem to include more noise than macro series.

Time horizon

Time horizon has a strong impact on choice of the forecasting method, as in different time horizons different data patterns emerge, and the importance of these patterns also changes over time. At both Frucor and HWL there are two main time horizons: 3 months and 18–24 months. Frucor also closely monitors on a weekly basis for the first 13 weeks when introducing new products to the market. According to Makridakis et al. (1998), in the immediate term (less than 1 month) randomness is the most significant factor, in the short-term (1–3 months) it is seasonality, in the medium term (3–24 months) cyclicality and in the long term (2 years and over) the trend component appears to be dominant. Smoothing methods are the best for the immediate to short term; decomposition and ARMA methods for the short to medium term and regression for the medium to long term. Quantitative methods are the most suitable if patterns do not change. However, in the longer term it is highly unlikely that patterns will remain the same and hence with the increase in market uncertainty the use of qualitative or judgemental methods becomes more attractive.

Cost

Cost is often traded off against accuracy (quality) and ease of application. Theoretically, the overall cost of forecasting includes the cost of data and its collection, salary (and training) costs, equipment costs (e.g. software) and the methodology (start-up and ongoing costs). In practice these costs are not calculated explicitly and appear in a different form. Forecasters record time as opportunity cost, which covers the time to learn about using a particular method, the time spent on improving the method and the time to prepare the forecast.

The criteria reviewed above do not exist in isolation, but one should always consider the trade-offs between them. At one end of the spectrum there are methods that are easy to use, convenient, cost-effective and require little expertise, but the accuracy of the forecasting could be low. At the other end might be an accurate but complex forecasting system that would require a costly expert.

---

[6] Macro forecasting refers to forecasting total market demand, whereas micro forecasting refers to forecasting of the demand (market share) of individual products

Complexity in forecasting

Complexity in forecasting increases as the availability of information decreases (Bolling, 1996) and the newness of the product increases. Forecasting sales of a radically new product is very complex because information is hard to find. Table 7.3 provides examples for four scenarios according to the nature of innovation and availability of information. Starting from the upper left corner (incremental innovation and information available) and moving towards the bottom right corner of the table (radical innovation and little available data) the complexity of forecasting increases. The complexity of forecasting further increases, the longer the period one aims to forecast.

Complexity of forecasting also arises from a combination of factors, such as the following: the size of the company, the number of products (SKU) of the company and the number of departments involved in forecasting. In the next section further important issues that have a significant impact on the forecasting process are discussed.

Production and warehousing

The outcome of the forecasting process has a significant impact on the production process, production cost (structure) and the warehousing activity of the company. Overestimating demand makes the entire business suffer as it forces the company to produce more than the market will absorb, and thus higher costs result through production and warehousing. Although the company can make adjustments to the forecast and inform production of the change, the production process might not be flexible enough to accommodate the changes in the required time and, thus, the company has to absorb the fixed costs of a higher production level.

Inventory and service level

The implication of a bad forecast is that either stock is accumulated and thus cash tied up in the business through inventory, which might need to be written off (having a detrimental impact on the profit and loss statement) if it cannot be sold, or it might need to be heavily discounted in order to sell it. Alternatively, if the manufacturer runs out of stock and cannot supply the retailer with products, then the retailer will perceive the manufacturer as unreliable, and hence will have a bad perception of its so-called 'service' level. Based on the case studies presented in this chapter, companies in the FMCG

Table 7.3   Complexity of forecasting

	Available information – plentiful	Available information – little
Incremental innovation	Response to competitive actions	New packaging (e.g. microwaveable pouches)
Radical innovation	New product development in a well-established category	New product development in a new category

sector prefer to bear the consequences (higher cost) of a larger inventory rather than risk accidentally running out of stock and thus risking a poor service level. Running out of stock costs the company in terms of missed sales, because customers cannot find its products on the shelf. Furthermore, the manufacturer might lose the shelf space in the retailer's store, for the reasons explained above, as the retailer might come to prefer another company which offers a more reliable and constant supply of products. Frucor, for instance, focuses primarily on maintaining high service levels, meaning that retailers' shelves are always filled with its products. Interestingly, companies calculate the financial impact of having too much stock, mainly because it appears in the profit and loss statement, but the missed opportunity (running out of stock) is – although theoretically considered – not specifically calculated.

Sales promotion

Forecasting is also intertwined with the promotional activity of the company, as product promotions usually trigger larger sales. Promotions should be carefully planned and their impact (promotional uplift) carefully analysed and, thus, incorporated into the forecast for the product. For instance, the company might have a policy that fruit from a given year should be sold before the next harvest, or else the company accumulates stock unnecessarily. In the case of products with a short shelf life (e.g. fresh food) the product must be on the shelf before it gets too close to the expiry date or has in fact expired. Sales promotions are sometimes used as a way of selling (getting rid of) products which are soon to expire, or if the warehouse needs space for another purpose.

Forecasting skills

Forecasting comes naturally and easily to some people whereas others are more likely by nature to be subjective or biased, or can be biased because of their involvement with the product being forecast. According to some companies, Marketing Managers sometimes overestimate the likely market success of their newly developed products, which might be able to be attributed to the involvement mentioned above. Furthermore, close involvement with a new product can turn forecasts into a tool for advocacy rather than an objective assessment of the market situation. Therefore companies should monitor forecasts to ensure that employees do not misuse them in this way (Makridakis et al., 1998). Subjectivity in the forecasting process can be rectified by employing two or more people or groups to prepare independent forecasts based on different assumptions or by using two or more sources of data.

Changes in context

Forecasting methods in companies with well-established products assume the longevity of current trends. Dramatic changes in the economic environment such as a recession can reduce forecasting accuracy, significantly limiting the usefulness of certain forecasting methods.

Continuous learning

The forecasting process should serve as a tool for continuous learning for the company and its managers about themselves, their product, their competitors and ultimately the soundness of their assumptions.

Interaction between forecast preparer and user

Forecast preparers must understand the circumstances (resources, constraints) the management decision-makers work under and the goals they work towards. Forecast preparers at HWL understand the importance of their work and the implications of a bad forecast. Forecast users, on the other hand, should be able to use the forecast effectively to create production and cost plans based on the forecast. The management at HWL also ensures the full transparency of their businesses which improves the interaction between preparers and users and hence, effectiveness of the forecasting process.

Accountability

Some companies set up personal improvement plans that include the key performance indicators (KPI) an employee must achieve. The KPIs for HWL Marketing Managers are both profit and forecasting accuracy measures, whereas for Sales Managers there is less emphasis on forecasting accuracy and more emphasis on profit.

Superficially it might seem that forecasting would be a straightforward activity, but because of its cross-functional nature it has wide implications for the various departments and for the company as a whole. Successful forecasters understand every aspect of the company's operation.

> ### CASE PROBLEM REVISITED
>
> ## Forecasting in action at Frucor New Zealand
>
> The primary information source for forecasting at Frucor is the company's own ex-factory sales data, which not only shows the amount of products that are sold to retailers, but also their ordering habits. This ex-factory data is compared and contrasted with the actual (end customer) sales information provided by ACNielsen. Through its scanner panel, ACNielsen provides information about the size of the total market, changes in the market and other products launched. The primary target market for Frucor (in common with any other fast-moving consumer goods company) is their retailers, not the end customer. Frucor must prepare and present a business case to retailers to get the product accepted by them, creating buy-in and hence distribution for the

product. Companies like Frucor use their established market position and reputation to achieve channel acceptance. Nevertheless, they must prepare these business cases very carefully, as their reputation would be affected by any market failure, notwithstanding their reputation. According to Phil Webb (Supply Chain Manager at Frucor) market research (mostly in the form of customer surveys) has an important function in developing and refining the product, and monitoring the sales of the new product, but it has limited usefulness in sales forecasting. Market research is primarily used to give an indication of the market potential of the product. In addition to this information about the market and the competitors, forecasting is also supported by the intelligence gathering of the sales team and by internal or external historical data on similar products or similar markets.

The marketing department leads new product development (NPD) at Frucor, but preparing forecasts is a joint effort between marketing and sales. Frucor takes an unconstrained view in its forecasting method, which means that production and supply chain play a secondary role in relation to what the product can achieve in the market place. As Frucor does not make optimization of its supply chain its primary focus, it must absorb the additional cost for storage of unsold products. The company makes forecasts on a product level for numbers of bottles by using historical averages as reference points. They use both the bottom-up and top-down approaches. The top-down approach refers to a forecast estimate that starts at a higher and hence more aggregate level, which is then proportioned accordingly. For instance, it could mean combining the forecast for all products the company sells, and then breaking this down into forecasts for product categories and individual products. The bottom-up approach starts at a lower level (for instance individual products) and then these forecasts are aggregated or merged into product category forecasts, which are then aggregated as the company's total demand.

These approaches do not necessarily match, since using the bottom-up approach usually falls short of the top-down approach. Forecasting overall is highly dependent upon how well trained the Demand Planners of the company are, but also on their relationships and interaction with the marketing department.

Figure 7.4 shows the monthly sales forecasting process at Frucor. This process is initiated by the Demand Planner, who meets one-on-one with sales and marketing managers and reviews previous sales by account and category respectively. Meetings with sales managers focus on issues such as promotional activities and future short-term changes, whereas with marketing managers the focus is on market trends and marketing activities in the long term (4–18 months). The company's forecasts are consolidated, reviewed, and if necessary revised by a group of people from sales, marketing, demand planning and finance, before they are finalized. The final forecast will be provided to Operations, who will plan and schedule capacity and production and provide feedback to the Demand Planner if the forecast cannot be met due to operational constraints.

As Marketing leads the new product development, they prepare a forecast for different accounts, for instance grocery. Sales provides the input for the rate of sales - how quickly the product is sold in individual stores on a weekly basis, which means how quickly the products 'fly off the shelves'. This information is usually derived from sales people based on their personal experience or from the company's database. The second piece of vital information coming from Sales is the rate of distribution expressed as the number of stores which sell the company's products versus all possible stores in the market. Multiplying the rate of sales with the rate of distribution will give the company the forecast for the new product. It should be noted, however, that the distribution rate is an overall target and not all channels will be available immediately. Therefore the distribution build-up must be estimated, which requires a plan to estimate the weekly status of the distribution rate. Distribution rate might be 40 per cent in week 1, 50 per cent in week 8 and the company will then achieve the targeted 80 per cent distribution by week 13.

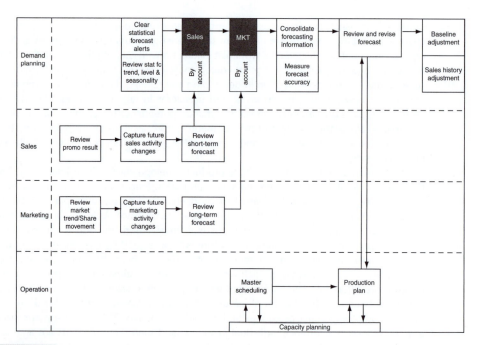

Figure 7.4   Sales forecasting process at Frucor

Once a product is launched, sales, marketing managers and the Demand Planner have a weekly meeting to compare the actual sales against the forecast. Although sales and marketing prepare a detailed and explicit forecast before the product is launched, there was formerly limited information as to how the sales forecast was derived. Similarly, while weekly data from ACNielsen fed into the forecasting system, if the actual sales were off the forecast, no one knew exactly why it had happened and where the forecast had gone wrong. For instance, an assumption could have been made that all grocery stores would adopt the product immediately, but without this information it was impossible to know why the forecast had overestimated the sales when the stores did not do so. To resolve this problem, Stuart Sheng, the Demand Planner at Frucor, initiated a major change in the forecasting process. A more formal process was adopted by the company, requiring the explicit articulation and recording of managerial (sales/marketing) assumptions in the forecasting system. Recording the assumptions based on which the forecast is built and checking whether they prove to be right or wrong, now provides a tool for instant feedback and learning for the company generally, as well as for the newly introduced product in particular.

Table 7.4 provides an overview of new product sales forecast calculations. Frucor uses this spreadsheet to calculate forecasts for one particular channel or for all channels for a period of thirteen weeks. Although this table does not show every detail of their calculations it contains the major aspects that will enable examination of their forecasting process. Every new product development forecast shows a period of thirteen weeks, the standard period for products in the FMCG market. The implication of using this period as standard is an expectation that new products should reach their full potential over a period of slightly more than three months. Assuming that the company has one thousand retailers (customer base) in a certain channel (petrol and convenience channel), with a distribution target of 100 per cent and repeat distribution of 96 per cent. The repeat distribution of 96 per cent means that 960 stores will buy again and only 4 per cent of the stores (forty stores) are expected to delist the product.

Table 7.4   New product sales forecast calculation

Customer Base	1000
Distribution Target	100%
Repeat Distribution	96%

Week	buy-in	1 - launch	2	3	...	11	12	13	Total
Distribution	5.8%	53.5%	82.3%	90.2%	...	98.3%	99.5%	100.0%	
Increase in Distribution	5.8%	47.7%	28.8%	7.9%	...	0.9%	1.3%	0.5%	
Increase in Customers	58	477	288	79	...	9	13	5	
Pipeline order (cases)	2	2	2	2	...	2	2	2	
Displays, samples					...				
Pipeline Fill	116	953	576	158	...	17	25	9	
Repeat Customers		56	513	790	...	935	944	956	
Repeat Orders	2.08	2.08	2.08	2.08	...	2.08	2.08	2.08	
Repeat Cases	–	116	1,070	1,645	...	1,949	1,966	1,991	103,529
Total Case Sales	116	1,070	1,645	1,803	...	1,966	1,991	2,000	24,011
Activity Uplift (%)					...				
Adj Total Forecast	116	1,070	1,645	1,803	...	1,966	1,991	2,000	24,011

As outlined above, distribution represents the percentage of stores which stock the product over all potential stores, which increases rapidly from week 0 (buy-in week) (5.8 per cent) to week 1 (53.5 per cent) and should achieve a target of 100 per cent by week 13. The increase in distribution in the week 1 is 47.7 per cent, which is the difference between the distribution in week 0 and week 1. Multiplying the increase in distribution with the customer base will provide the increase in the number of customers ('Incr. in Customers'), which will gradually decrease along the 13 week period. The 'pipeline order' is calculated by multiplying how many products needed to fill the allocated shelf space of a product in the store (2 cases) by the number of times the shelf space needs to be refilled for new customers (58). For instance, if the facing is two cans on the shelf, and the depth of each column is ten, then the Pipeline order is twenty units. In some cases, packaging might not exactly match the required pipeline quantity as the manufacturer might have twelve can cases, and hence one case will not be enough and two cases will be more than what is needed to fill up the shelf. The distribution calculation also needs to incorporate backup stock for the first week to ten days until the retailer's first reorder is received.

The repeat customers represent the difference between the distribution target and the repeat distribution. It is calculated by multiplying the customer base (1000) with the distribution (53.5 per cent in week 1) and with .96 (repeat distribution) to arrive at 513 customers in week 2. Since the company assumes that the retention is 96 per cent (not 100), the number of customers will be 513 rather than 535. The repeat order or rate of sale is 2.08 cases per week per customer, which represents the sales volume from repeat purchase. If we assume that there are 12 cans in a case, then a repeat order of 2.08 is calculated as the ratio of 25 cans per week per customer and 12 cans per case. By multiplying the repeat customers with repeat orders, the result is the number of repeat cases. The total case sales for the week is calculated as the sum of the pipeline fill and the repeat cases and displays and samples (if any). If there is any promotional activity, the impact (uplift) of the activity is also considered in the adjusted total forecast. An example of how changes in price affect sales will be shown in Figure 7.5. The annual sales figure is calculated based on the sales on week 13, which equals 103,529 cases (956 repeat customers*2.08 cases per week*52 weeks). This forecasting calculation can be applied to a channel, a category or the whole company.

The forecast also considers product cannibalisation: the extent to which new products will affect the sales of the company's existing products. For instance, introducing a larger bottle size of a product can reduce sales of the existing package sizes of the same product. When the product category level sales are calculated, the extent of product cannibalisation will be deducted from the sales forecast for the affected product.

Figure 7.5 shows the monthly price level and dollar sales of Coca-Cola and V at British Petrol (BP) petrol stations across New Zealand and Australia. This chart clearly shows that V achieves a high promotional uplift compared with Coca-Cola (600ml) in the petrol and convenience channel. This provides a strategic benefit for Frucor by gaining promotional slots much more easily in key accounts, and it is also beneficial for the retailer to leverage a successful brand. In New Zealand and Australia V has fifteen promotional periods (each of three to four weeks duration) in each major account every year over the different pack types, which ensures the visibility of the brand, provides incremental sales and maximizes market share.

Once a product has been in the market for some years, a seasonality coefficient can be calculated. In this example, the last two years' historical sales data are used, helping to calculate a trend line for the product and project its long-term performance into the future. Table 7.5 shows a product's two-year performance (sales quantity) by month, and its two-year total.

The Total row in Table 7.5 is the (equally) weighted sum of Years 1 and 2, which is the default option. However, depending upon the forecaster's knowledge of historical sales data, different weightings can be applied to different years. By averaging the 'Total' from January (138,000) to December (143,000) of the two years, the 12 month average of two-year sales is 80,000 units. Dividing the monthly 'Total' (138,000 for January) by the 12-month average calculated before

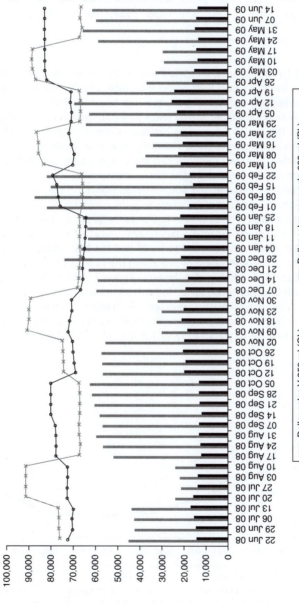

Figure 7.5 Promotional uplifts in BP petrol stations (June 2008–June 2009)

Source: ACNielsen scanner data.

Table 7.5	Two-year historical data (units)											
	JAN	**FEB**	**MAR**	**APR**	**MAY**	**JUN**	**JUL**	**AUG**	**SEP**	**OCT**	**NOV**	**DEC**
Year 1	72,000	63,000	48,000	37,000	26,000	22,000	29,000	23,000	34,000	38,000	34,000	77,000
Year 2	66,000	50,000	51,000	35,000	26,000	21,000	24,000	23,000	28,000	32,000	35,000	66,000
Total	138,000	113,000	99,000	72,000	52,000	43,000	53,000	46,000	62,000	70,000	69,000	143,000
Calculated Seasonality	1.73	1.41	1.24	0.90	0.65	0.54	0.66	0.58	0.78	0.88	0.86	1.79

(80,000) we get 1.73 for January, which is the calculated seasonality. When this value is above 1 it represents months when sales level is above average, whereas if it is below 1 then sales level is below average in those months. Therefore, it can be concluded that the product analysed is a summer product, as December-March (New Zealand summer) seasonality values are above average, whereas the rest of the months perform below average. It should be also noted that seasonality ratios can be calculated by using the base sales (without promotions) or with the promotions included. The two methods can show significantly different results, but the base sales method is to be preferred, as it is less easy to manipulate.

By using spreadsheet software, the sales values in Figure 7.3 for Years 1, 2 and Total can be plotted by using the months (January-December) – by transforming them to numbers, 1–12 - as the independent variable (y) and the sales figures as the dependent variable (x). This is displayed for individual years (blue and red interweaving lines) and also the total sales (green interweaving line) in Figure 7.6. Afterwards, one has to try to find the best fitting trendline (also displayed, more stable lines) to the observation by regressing the periods (Independent) on Year 1, Year 2 or the Total (dependent), which is also shown in Figure 7.6. From the variety of different types of trendlines, such as exponential, linear, logarithmic, power, polynomial and moving average, and so on a 3rd-order polynomial was selected, which fitted the data very well.

The regression equations coefficients and their variance explained (R2) for Years 1, 2, Total and the seasonal trendline are displayed in Table 7.6. We calculated these coefficients for Years 1, 2,

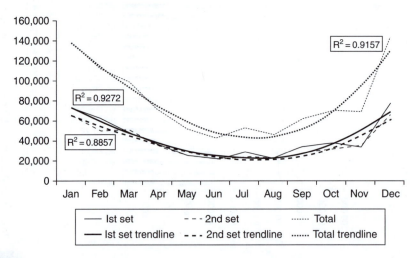

Figure 7.6	Actual sales and trendline for Year 1, 2 and Total

Table 7.6 Regression Equation Coefficients

	x^3	x^2	X	Intercept	R^2(%)
Year 1	70.58	195.42	−14010	86616	88.57
Year 2	84.82	−305.14	−9667.4	74444	92.72
Total	155.40	−109.72	−23678	161061	91.57
Seasonal trendline	.002	−.001	−.296	2.01	91.46

Total and the seasonal coefficient, but in fact one of them would have been sufficient, and in the following, only the seasonal trendline coefficients will be used. We should note that the seasonal trendline coefficients were calculated from the "calculated seasonality" values (Table 7.5). The closeness of the fit of the trendline to the data is shown by their high R2 values (Table 7.6) and also by the closeness of the trendline to the actual observations (Figure 7.6). This means that the trendline explains the actual sales very well and provides a reliable base for forecasting future trends. However, Armstrong (2001) warns that R2 should not be considered as the only measure of forecasting accuracy.

Now, having these coefficients one can create forecasts for the next 12 months. By using the Seasonal Trendline Coefficients (last row of Table 4), smoothed 'Trendline Adjusted Seasonality' can be calculated by writing out the following equation: $0.002x3 − .001x2 − .296x + 2.01 = Y$ (forecast value). Since x stands for the independent variable (1-12) one can calculate the 'Trendline Adjusted Seasonality' for January (forecast value) by substituting 1 (representing January) for x, and the equation will look as follows: $0.002*13 − .001*12 − .296*1 + 2.01 = 1.72$. The trendlines adjusted for seasonality are displayed in Table 7.7 and they can be similarly calculated for each month. 1.72 is the trendline adjusted seasonality coefficient for January (predicted value). We should note that observed ratio for January was 1.73 (see Table 7.5), which is very close to the predicted figure (Table 7.7), and similarly with all of the other coefficients.

By using these trendline adjusted seasonal coefficients (Table 7.7) it is possible to estimate the sales for the next 12 months by multiplying the average of all monthly sales values in Year 1 and 2 in Table 3 (which equals 40,000) with the respective month's trendline adjusted seasonal coefficient. For January (Period 1, Table 7.7) this equals 68,714 units (see Table 7.8).

Table 7.7 Trendline adjusted seasonality coefficients

Period	1	2	3	4	5	6	7	8	9	10	11	12
Total	1.7179	1.4314	1.1654	0.9317	0.7419	0.6076	0.5405	0.5523	0.6545	0.8589	1.1771	1.6207

Table 7.8 Estimated forecast for next 12 months

Period	1	2	3	4	5	6	7	8	9	10	11	12
Total	68,716	57,256	46,616	37,268	29,676	24,304	21,620	22,092	26,180	34,356	47,084	64,828

Summary

This chapter has highlighted some of the most important aspects of sales forecasting by using information from two iconic companies from the Australasia region to provide insights and managerial guidelines. The topic was introduced by placing significant emphasis on the process and challenges of new product forecasting. As has been shown, forecasting is an interdepartmental and non-linear process. It is interdepartmental as it cuts across departments and directly or indirectly involves almost all of the company's employees. It is non-linear, as the tasks in forecasting do not happen in a logical order but, rather, simultaneously, which creates uncertainty in the forecasting process that needs to be carefully managed. The management of this uncertainty requires a thorough understanding of the dynamics of environmental and organizational processes, and formalizing and standardizing them in a way that leaves flexibility for adaptation.

Key points

1. Forecasting means preparing for the future by handling internal and external complexity and uncertainty. Therefore, companies which are good at it should have a better chance to excel in the marketplace.
2. The potential for new products should be evaluated carefully by using various (subjective as well as objective) sources and methods. Do not be either overly conservative or overly optimistic.
3. Measure and reward forecasting accuracy.
4. Thoroughly understand your organizational processes. Create a process view of the firm.
5. Use multiple sources and people for forecasting.
6. Do not forget that the missed opportunity is as bad for the company as stock piled up in the warehouse.
7. Good company image can help get the product on the shelf. Do not forget that the same company image is hit hard if you get something wrong.
8. The outcome of the forecasting process depends heavily on input, and hence the most reliable possible information should be used. Do not forget the maxim 'garbage in, garbage out'.
9. Forecasting means being thorough, paying attention to detail and involving people with market expertise. Do not forget that 'the devil is in the detail'.
10. Companies should be good at keeping a watchful eye on their environments and understanding their market and their customers. Have you got good listening skills?
11. Forecasting should be an objective process, not a tool for advocacy. Be realistic.
12. Forecasting requires team players who pay attention to each other's activities and also a flexible organization culture. Create a channel between forecast preparers and users.
13. Spend time in the office on polishing your forecasting skills, but make sure you spend at least as much time with your customers. Be book *and* street smart.

Running a sales forecasting audit in your company

Table 7.9 is intended to provide companies with a guide to evaluate their degree of success in sales forecasting by making them aware of what they are good at and by highlighting areas that need attention. This audit might not be universally applicable to every company in every business, but sufficient aspects of forecasting are covered to represent an objective, informative and accountable process that every company should employ. Furthermore, this audit cannot take account of the qualities and characteristics of the forecasting personnel, which are at least as important as the organizational processes. The more statements answered with a 'yes', the higher the score achieved. Statements answered with 'no' should be considered as areas for improvement.

Table 7.9   Forecasting excellence audit

In our company, forecasting is 100 per cent bottom-up (or rather more bottom-up than top-down)	Yes	No
In our company, forecasting is undertaken concurrently for both the short and long term	Yes	No
In our company, forecasting drives planning and goals	Yes	No
In our company, forecasting uses an adequate internal system that captures the input from various departments	Yes	No
In our company, forecasting pays special attention to our largest as well as to our fastest-growing accounts	Yes	No
In our company, forecasting is based on a combination of objective and subjective (expert) data	Yes	No
In our company, forecasting uses a mixture of qualitative and quantitative techniques	Yes	No
In our company, forecasting uses sources to capture historical information	Yes	No
In our company, forecasting uses sources to capture potential future trends	Yes	No
In our company, forecasting uses sources that represent a good trade-off between information quality and acquisition costs (of the data)	Yes	No
In our company, forecasting accuracy is measured and managed	Yes	No
In our company, forecasting accuracy forms part of the forecaster's performance criteria	Yes	No
In our company, assumptions for forecasts are recorded, tracked and validated	Yes	No
In our company, forecasts are created by various departments	Yes	No
In our company, forecasts are cross-validated (by another department or by using a different source)	Yes	No
In our company, forecast preparers and users have regular meetings	Yes	No
In our company, forecasters spend most of their time with internal customers (departmental managers) and external customers (trade partners)	Yes	No

References

Anderson, S. (ed.) (2007) *Collins English Dictionary*, 9th edition. Glasgow: HarperCollins.

Armstrong, J.S. (2000a). 'Judgmental Bootstrapping: Inferring Experts' Rules for Forecasting', in Armstrong, J.S. (ed.), *Principles of Forecasting: Handbook for Researchers and Practitioners*. Norwell, MA: Kluwer Academic Publishers.

Armstrong, J.S. (2000b). 'Role Playing: a Method to Forecast Decisions', in Armstrong, J.S. (ed.), *Principles of Forecasting: Handbook for Researchers and Practitioners*. Norwell MA: Kluwer Academic Publishers.

Armstrong, J.S. (2001a). *Principles of Forecasting. A Handbook for Researchers and Practitioners*. Norwell, MA: Kluwer Academic Publishers.

Armstrong, J.S. (2001b) 'Selecting Methods', in Armstrong, J.S. (ed.), *Principles of Forecasting: A Handbook for Researchers and Practitioners*. Norwell, MA: Kluwer Academic Publishers.

Armstrong, J.S., and Brodie, R.J. (1999) 'Forecasting for Marketing', in Hooley, G.J. and Hussey, M.K. (eds), *Quantitative Methods in Marketing*. London: Thomson Business Press.

Armstrong, J.S. and Collopy, F. (1998) 'Integration of Statistical Methods and Judgement for Time Series Forecasting: Principles from Empirical Research', in Wright, G. and. Goodwin, P. (eds), *Forecasting with Judgement*. Chichester: John Wiley.

Ashton, A.H. and Ashton, R.H. (1985) 'Aggregating Subjective Forecasts: Some Empirical Results', *Management Science*, 31 (12): 1499–508.

Bolling, G.F. (1996) *The Art of Forecasting*. Brookfield, VT: Gower Publishing.

Ingram, T.N., LaForge, R.W., Avila, R.A., Schwepker, C.E. and Williams, M.R. (2006) *Sales Management: Analysis and Decision Making*.Mason, OH: Thomson.

Kahn, K.B. (2002) 'An Exploratory Investigation of New Product Forecasting Practices', *Journal of Product Innovation Management*, 19 (2): 133–43.

Lütkepohl, H. (2005) *New Introduction to Multiple Time Series Analysis*. Berlin: Springer.

Makridakis, S. et al. (1984) *The Forecasting Accuracy of Major Time Series Methods*. New York: John Wiley.

Makridakis, S., Wheelwright, C. S. and McGee, E.V. (1998) *Forecasting Methods and Applications*. New York: John Wiley.

Mentzer, J.T. and Moon, M.A. (2005) *Sales Forecasting Management: A Demand Management Approach*. Thousand Oaks, CA: Sage Publications.

Rowe, G. and Wright, G. (2000) 'The Delphi Technique as a Forecasting Tool', in Armstrong, J.S. (ed.), *Principles of Forecasting: Handbook for Researchers and Practitioners*. Norwell, MA: Kluwer Academic Publishers.

Steiner, G.A. (1979) *Strategic Planning*. New York: Free Press.

Yokum, T. and Armstrong, J. S. (1995) 'Beyond Accuracy: Comparison of Criteria Used to Select Forecasting Methods', *International Journal of Forecasting*, 11 (4): 591–7.

Further reading

Dalrymple, D.J. (1987) 'Sales Forecasting Practices', *International Journal of Forecasting*, 3 (1), 379–91.

Davis, D.F. and Mentzer, J.T. (2007) 'Organizational Factors in Sales Forecasting Management', *International Journal of Forecasting*, 23 (3): 475–95.

Franses, P.H. and Legerstee, R. (2010) 'Do Experts' Adjustments on Model-based SKU-level Forecasts Improve Forecast Quality?', *Journal of Forecasting*, 29 (3): 331–40.

McCarthy, T.M., Davis, D.F., Golicic, S.L. and Mentzer, J.T. (2006) 'The Evolution of Sales Forecasting Management: a 20-year Longitudinal Study of Forecasting Practices', *Journal of Forecasting*, 25 (5): 303–24.

Moon, M.A., Mentzer, J.T. and Smith, C.D. (2003) 'Conducting a Sales Forecasting Audit', *International Journal of Forecasting*, 19 (1): 5–25.

Smith, C.D. and Mentzer, J.T. (2010) 'Forecasting Task-Technology Fit: The Influence of Individuals, Systems and Procedures on Forecast Performance', *International Journal of Forecasting*, 26 (1): 144–61.

Winklehofer, H. and Diamantopoulos A. (2003) 'A Model of Export Sales Forecasting Behavior and Performance: Development and Testing', *International Journal of Forecasting*, 19 (2): 271–85.

8

Sales force organization and territory design

Piotr Kwiatek

Contents

Learning objectives

After reading this chapter, you should be able to:

- Understand the basic concepts of sales force organization and territory design.
- Identify the advantages and disadvantages of different forms of sales force organization.
- Estimate the number of salespeople appropriate for a sales department.

Chapter outline

In this chapter we concentrate on two important organizational issues in sales management, namely how the sales department should be designed and how salespeople should be deployed. First, we present the theoretical background and then discuss some implications of decisions on sales force organization. The issues presented in this chapter are illustrated by means of two case studies of companies operating in Poland. The first of these, operating in the window and hardware market, is a foreign company, whereas the other one, operating in the office supplies market, is a company with 100 per cent Polish capital.

Two case history vignettes

Fittings Master

Fittings Master manufactures wood and plastic joinery fittings (multi-point lock fittings, double door bolts, window and door hardware). It was established after the Second World War in Germany and has evolved from a small, family-run enterprise to an international company with its branch offices in several countries in Europe as well as in Asia. The company started its business activities in Poland in the mid-1990s, gaining a 20 per cent share in the market in 2009.

The Polish window and door joinery market has been divided among five companies from Western Europe (including Fittings Master), which together hold 97 per cent of the market share. The remaining 3 per cent is held by a Polish manufacturer. Fittings Master's business operations cover the entire territory of Poland, which has been divided into three geographical sales areas.

Office Service

Office Service is a distributor of office supplies ranging from pens and copy paper to office equipment and furniture. Initially, the company functioned as a network of shops located in Poznań;[1] subsequently, with growth in sales, it replaced shop sales with direct sales through a network of sales representatives. Now, with over 15 years of experience, it is well established in the market. The company focuses its business activities on selected regions in Poland. It operates in the territory of 3 voivodeships[2] and has 23 Sales Representatives.

The office supplies sector in Poland is highly fragmented, the following entities operating within it:

- small companies with several employees providing office supplies in a given city;
- medium-sized regional companies, also offering office equipment and its servicing;
- large companies operating throughout the entire country: the French Lyreco, the American Corporate Express;
- the Biuro Plus purchasing group, which brings together small regional companies from the whole of Poland.

The largest share in the market is held by Lyreco (c. 11–13 per cent share).

Introduction: the impact of sales force organization

Both academics and managers pay ever growing attention to the impact of sales force organization and sales territory design as two significant factors affecting a company's sales results (Weitz et al. 1986; Babakus et al. 1996). Decisions made in these two

---

[1] The fifth largest city in terms of population in Poland.
[2] Poland is divided into 16 administrative regions called voivodeships. For further information see: http://en.wikipedia.org/wiki/Voivodeships_of_Poland.

areas result in opportunities for creating growth in sales on the one hand, and, on the other hand, may cause substantial differences in the company's operating costs. Hence, such decisions are of fundamental importance with regard to a company's financial results. Achieving a suitable balance in sales force organization and sales territory design requires taking into account the impact of various factors and, in practice, often requires a long period for adapting the introduced solutions to the specific conditions of the market in which a company operates.

Since markets evolve (clients come and go, their needs change, new competitors appear), the sales force structure must also evolve. In this chapter we will discuss the factors affecting sales force organization and also the issue of how a company's development and its changing environment impact upon decisions concerning changes in sales management.

(Optimal) design of sales force organization

Sales force organization can be defined as a structural and competence-based arrangement of employees engaged in the sales process. In other words, sales force organization covers elements such as:

- the organization and hierarchy of the sales team;
- the scope of functions carried out by the sales staff;
- the number of sales personnel.

Therefore, from the point of view of a person managing sales activities, the following needs determining: how many sales personnel should be employed, what functions they should perform and within what type of organizational structure they should operate. In practice, the determination of these elements is connected with the necessity of solving several dilemmas. In this chapter we will deal with the issues that are most important and most frequently reported by managers. These include determining whether the sales force should be internal or external (outsourced) and the base on which the sales force should be created (geographical division, product range, customer segment, selling function). Sizing the sales force, in turn, will be covered in Chapter 9.

Taking into account two factors affecting sales force organization – namely, the stage in the company's development and the market type – should facilitate finding answers to these questions and so we will now discuss the impact of these on sales force organization.

Stage of a company's development

Often, during the first stage of a company's development, the size of the sales force, being directly related to its capital resources, is small. This applies to both newly established companies and companies that have decided to introduce direct sales when entering a new market. At the same time, the role played by the sales force is crucial, as winning clients consists in establishing relationships, which can subsequently be deepened. As a company grows, so does the number of sales force personnel, and the role of salespeople changes as well, for instance from a more entrepreneurial, exploratory sales role at the start-up phase to a more standardized selling process during maturity (Zoltners et al. 2006). Maturation of a company is typically linked with a drop in the growth rate of winning new clients, and, at the same time, increasing revenues coming from sales to already won clients. That is the reason why, among other things, companies that want to make additional profit may decide to change their sales model to an external channel (i.e. through external entities) or internet channel and create separate sales positions for their largest customers. This is because growth in profit margin is possible by way of improvement in operational effectiveness, or, in other words, through an increase in return on investment.

Such solutions were introduced by Office Service in response to the situation in the market. Customers were invited to use an e-commerce platform that facilitates sales service for the company; Office Service linked up with the retail franchise chain of the biggest mobile operator on the Polish market in order to win new accounts; and it has recently formed a key account management team to enable it to work better with with its biggest accounts.

The experiences of Fittings Master are also similar to the model of the sales structure development presented above. The establishment of a branch office in Poland and employment of a Sales Manager initiated the creation of the structure that is currently in place. It should be noted, however, that the regional division of sales areas of Fittings Master was created in the eighth year of the company's business activities in Poland. Only the achievement of a pre-determined level of sales has provided sufficient prospects for developing sales, employing more salespeople and introducing the territorial division.

Type of market

The type of market, both in terms of the sector's characteristics and the competitive structure, affects decisions related to sales force organization. For example, diversification in the medicinal products market may cause a company to create separate positions for personnel working with medical doctors (medical sales representatives) and pharmacies (pharmaceutical sales representatives).

Let us consider the example of Office Service and the office supplies market. Buying office supplies is usually a routine task, i.e. it is what we call *straight* or *modified rebuy*. The key characteristics of routine buying are that the purchase cycle is rather short and clients purchase from a set of competing suppliers.[3] Customer involvement in the category is usually low, which in turn lowers switching costs. Such conditions necessitate frequently visiting clients (or phoning them) because they will buy from the first available company. However, clients may react unfavourably to the contact initiated by the suppliers as they may be perceived as an inconvenience (see Rangaswamy, Sinha and Zoltners, 1990). Yet it is vital to note that stability of personnel

---

[3] See Rangaswamy et al. (1990) for applications in the pharmaceutical market.

is of considerable importance in this market, since the sales representative–buyer relationships are crucial.

Types of sales force organization

As mentioned above, sales forces can be organized in four distinct ways, namely by geographical boundaries, product range, type of customers and functions performed. Below we characterize these four types of organization and then Table 8.1 summarizes their strong and weak points.

Geography-based organization

Geographic assignment means that salespeople are deployed in geographical regions and tasked to offer all clients located within a given area the entire range of the company's products. This solution is relatively simple for the organization, and is therefore often used.

Product-based organization

Organization based on product range is more common for companies which offer a wide range of products in different product categories. In this case, it might be beneficial for a company to structure its sales force according to the categories on offer. If there is considerable variety in the product mix, making salespeople responsible for specific categories means they will have better knowledge of them and thus be able to serve customers better.

For example, Office Service could form two distinct sales teams, one responsible for office hardware and the other for small-scale office accessories such as pens and paper, envelopes etc. However, the size of the product section and category differentiation are not always sufficient basis for sales force organization. In this case, the offer containing almost 5,000 product indices is not technically complicated, while 70 per cent of the concluded transactions relate to a basic assortment making up just $c.$ 10–15 per cent of the products on offer. Therefore, at Office Service each of the Sales Representatives offers the whole product range.

Customer-based organization

A customer-centric organization is one based on customer type. It is, in essence, more market driven than the two earlier ones. However, we should note that the 'by-customer' split is in fact often 'by-industry'. The difference is that in the former each customer is serviced by his/her manager, i.e. a company sells to multiple 'segments of one'. In the latter what we have is a reflection of 'by-industry' market segmentation, which allows salespeople to gain in-depth knowledge of industry idiosynchrasies and needs. In some cases, especially if the number of clients in the market is relatively small and customers differ, it would be better to employ the 'by-customer' approach. This for example is the case with advertising agencies, which assign Account Managers to serve clients and coordinate work for them inside the agency. Chapter 3 presents a more detailed exploration of such Key Account Management strategies.

If customers are similar in terms of their needs and preferences and/or the market is well populated, the 'by-industry' split can be a better option for a selling organization. Otherwise, a company would have to invest a considerable amount of money only to obtain marginal (if any) benefits from closer cooperation with its clients.

Some companies decide to introduce a mixed approach, that is, Sales Representatives for the general market and Key Account Manager positions within the sales department for large accounts. Separating sales teams by the size of account may be beneficial if customers differ in their buying process.

Elavon Global Acquiring Solutions in Poland sells its payment card services to shops and small chains by Sales Representatives while selling to large national or international accounts with a Key Account Manager. The level of service provided by the company (and customer costs, accordingly) do differ but what is even more important is the demand for elasticity from the large accounts. Elavon must answer quickly to the needs and preferences of key accounts and therefore employs a Key Account Manager who coordinates all internal activities performed for the customers.

Function-based organization

A company may align its sales force organization to the different functions performed for customers. Usually, there is a split between the selling function (i.e. bringing in new accounts) and the service function (i.e. servicing current customers). In fact, many companies apply this solution. Sales managers may also decide to distinguish an in-house, telesales force and a field sales force on functional grounds. An example of this is given in the next section.

Combined methods

The methods presented above of sales force organization are ideal types. In practice, the growing complexity of sales processes and market changes mean companies often have to seek out less simple solutions. This may be by considering a joint product-market approach, for example. In the case of Office Service, this could mean the creation of a separate group of sales representatives responsible for sales of office product sets to companies belonging to the SOHO segment (Small Office – Home Office).

| Table 8.1 | | | Advantages and disadvantages of the different types of sales force organization |

Type	Usually applied if	Pros	Cons
Geography	The company is at an early stage of growth.	Relatively easy to organize and manage. Less cost consuming (in controlling sales). Good market knowledge of sales personnel (they service every account in a territory).	May result in sub-optimal division of resources across accounts in a region. The company may miss out on opportunities if salespeople take the same selling approach to all their customers in their region.
Product range	The company offers a wide range of different product categories.	Salespeople have good knowledge of products within their categories. Allows for better control of product mix and profit and loss management.	Different salespeople may visit the same client (so it demands higher level of control and sales management). This usually results in higher costs. May trigger internal conflicts between Product Managers (if they compete for the same client).
Customer/Industry	The company offers complicated products within a rather narrow category.	Good knowledge of customers or industry needs. Potentially higher probability of navigating client companies and meeting key decision-makers.	May be costly to run and difficult to manage in dynamic markets.
Function	The company needs to build up market share. The attrition rate is a problem. The company sells ongoing services.	Facilitates better focus of the employees on their tasks. Easier assessment of activities than in a multi-tasking environment.	Problems in the transfer from one salesperson to another[4] because close relationships can develop between customers and the selling company's representative.

Source: Author.

---

[4] Consider the case of Office Service. As mentiond earlier, initiating and fostering relationships with customers is crucial in this market. As a consequence, customer representatives are often reluctant to communicate with different people from the selling company.

The 'by market' split can be implemented through creating special positions to cater for major customers (i.e. Key Account Managers) or differentiating sales by channel (direct or by an intermediary) and/or by industry type. The industry type was introduced, for example, by Wavin Metalplast Buk (WMB), the Polish part of the Dutch Wavin Group. In the early 1990s, Wavin concentrated its marketing and sales activities in Poland on two markets, installation and construction ('Wavin for home' division) and infrastructure ('Wavin perfect systems') – it recently rebranded itself as Wavin in all global markets.[5]

As noted by Donaldson (1994), this 'by market' solution can be applied in some industries such as food or household goods (because of the power of major sellers/brands on the market). However, we would also extend it to more professional markets as represented in our case studies.

In the case of Fittings Master, the solution is that the Regional Director plays the role of the Key Account Manager, and directly caters for the largest clients within the region. The remaining clients are indirectly serviced by trade companies (intermediaries). The sales activities are evenly split between these two channels. Such a solution is applied by Fittings Master in all of its markets, with the exception of countries where the company has not built its own warehouse. In that case, sales activities are mostly performed through wholesale agents. Apart from managing the Sales department, the Sales Director is responsible for pricing and ongoing relationships with major accounts. Technical Consultants are responsible for solving technical issues and giving technical training to customers. They also gather information from the market that can later be used to formulate offers for customers and they can sell to customers at standard prices.[6]

Table 8.2	Sales channels at Office Service			
	Electronic platform	**Sales representatives**	**Call centre**	**Key Account Manager**
Customer segment	All segments.	New accounts. Tenders for new customers.	Current accounts.	Large/multi-branch accounts. Tenders for new customers.
Functions performed	Provides a low cost selling option.	Winning new accounts. Transferring current accounts to e-platform.	Handling incoming calls for supplies. Setting up appointments for sales representatives.	Prapares tender proposals. Negotiote terms and conditions for contracts

---

[5] The current divisions are Building & Installation for above-the-ground appliances and Civil & Infrastructure for below ground solutions. This is an example of 'by product' range/customer split. Source: www.wavin.com.

[6] At Fittings Master, Technical Consultants do not have sales targets.

In the case of Office Service, part of its sales is performed through the electronic plat-form, another part through its Sales Representatives and the remaining part through a call centre. Customers being tendered for and corporate clients (understood as multi-branch companies) are serviced separately. Office Service has also introduced a Key Account Management team (see Table 8.2). Following the geographical expansion of its business activities, Office Service decided to employ an external sales forces. This is discussed later in the chapter (see p. 217).

Delivering office supplies demands strong logistical skills and a well-established system for pro-curement of the inventory. When it comes to sales, the process should be efficient as the profit margin for the selling company is rather low (the typical gross profit margin tops up close to 50 per cent but this drops to 10 per cent or less net profit). Thus, using an esales platform can greatly reduce selling costs. However, it may be more difficult to create additional sales by win-ning more customer share, although this is an important part of the income stream for large accounts.

Functions within Sales

As mentioned earlier, one of the dilemmas to be resolved when designing sales force organization is determination of the scope of functions performed by the employees of the Sales department. Here, we deal with the strategic assumptions related to this question; it should, however, be mentioned that the detailed division of functions is dependent on the number of employees in the Sales department, a question that will be dealt with in Chapter 9.

At the strategic level, when organizing the Sales department managers need to decide whether the sales force should execute the whole sales process including man-agement of existing clients or whether this function should be separated. In the latter case, this may be by having personnel specialist team to search for new clients and conclude the first transaction and then using a separate department and personnel to manage the subsequent orders. As noted in the introduction to the Office Service case, the company started its business in traditional, brick and mortar shops, and then, to allow room for growth, the management decided to change the business model from selling to customers walking in 'from the street' to operating in the field with own Sales Representatives. At Office Service the Account Manager is primarily responsible for gathering information on competitors' activities, assessing customer potential and nurturing relationships, while Sales Representatives are responsible for new business development. The latter also target cross- and (less often) up-selling to current cus-tomers and are responsible for encouraging current customers to buy office supplies from the Office Service web page, though as this lowers sales costs for Office Service, it may pose some risk for the business.

This solution is also used by the Polish telecoms company Netia, for example, which has implemented the division of its sales personnel into *hunter* and *farmer* categories. The hunter is responsible for winning clients (this also constitutes the basis for his/her remuneration), whereas the farmer's task is to maintain and develop relationships with existing clients (see Zoltners et al. 2006).

Naturally, the division of functions within the Sales area should directly result from the strategy adopted and the operating model. Separation of the functions, as with Netia, works better when companies provide their services on a subscription model (e.g. television or internet services) and when the market is relatively large. This arises from the fact that when competing for market share the company focus is on winning new clients, while from a business point of view, a substantial amount of the profit margin may come from the existing clients buying additional products. In sales of television and internet services, for example, the development of the relationship may be linked to selling additional TV channel packages and faster access to the internet to existing clients.

Measures of sales organization effectiveness

Managerial efforts connected with designing sales force organization should always have an impact on the company's financial results. Other parameters, which may not directly and in the short term affect the financial results, are also crucial. The results of the effectiveness of sales force organization are analysed through the prism of several key parameters such as the absolute sales volume and sales dynamics, profitability (the profit margin) and the level of customer satisfaction.

Determining the size of the sales force

The Sales Manager needs to determine the appropriate size of his/her sales force, but this is not an easy task, since there are many factors to consider. In general, we can distinguish three methods that can be applied to decide this issue: determination by workload; based on sales potential; and as the result of incremental analysis. More advanced techniques for adjusting sales force size are dealt with in Chapter 9.

Own or outsourced sales force

One of the most important strategic decisions on the part of the Sales Manager is whether to hire external sales forces (so-called manufacturer's representatives) or develop an in-house team (so-called direct sales). What we mean here by an external sales force is a specialized company whose business it is to manage sales personnel to reach targets set up by the customer who bought the service (or, in other words, hired it).[7] In some industries it is a common practice while there are others where one

---

[7] Therefore we do not treat self-employed sales agents as an external sales force, though the phenomenon is very popular in Poland because it substantially lowers personnel costs.

should not outsource the sales function.[8] The possibilities (available options) vary by industry and may be country specific.[9]

Usually external sales forces are employed in the following conditions:

- The need for fast growth of business: it takes less time to reach the market with sales personnel that have already been trained rather than recruit and train one's own sales force.
- Lack of funds to cover the market: there is usually no upfront investment if an external sales force is hired compared with considerable investment in establishing one's own sales force. Because provision of an external selling operation is a business service, the company is paid on the results achieved.
- Where sales can be expanded by means of small and/or distinct customers and selling to them with one's own sales force is unprofitable.

Whatever the reason for considering outsourcing sales, the decision should always be based on profit and loss analysis.

Table 8.3 Breakeven calculation for making the decision on employing own's own or an external sales force

annual sales target (D)	€1,500,000.00
own sales force	
No. of people	10
compensation	€144,000.00
expenses	€60,000.00
administration	€12,000.00
Total cost (A)	€216,000.00
external sales force	
commission (B)	10 per cent
Total cost (C)	€150,000.00
break even	
€2,160,000.00	

Source: Author.

From this calculation we see that a company should employ an external sales force only if the productivity of its own sales force is less than €2,160,000.00. The breakeven (BE) is calculated as follows:

$$BE = A/C$$

Using Table 8.3 a reader may calculate BE for other scenarios. For example with the equation:

$$BE = A/D$$

---

[8] For more in-depth analysis, the reader may want to consult Anderson and Trinkle (2005).
[9] For example, in FMCG industries manufacturers may pay for some of their distributors' staff, who are dedicated to selling a particular range of manufacturers' goods to retail outlets, though they formally remain the distributor's employees.

We can also calculate the maximum commission that should be paid to the sales ser-vice company (i.e. 14.4 per cent). However, this simple illustration does not incorporate all factors to be considered. For example, for direct sales a company deals mostly with a fixed cost, that is, even when there are no sales the company still needs to cover the cost of having its own sales force. Manufacturers' reps, on the other hand, are a variable cost relative to the sales level achieved.[10]

There are many factors a Sales Manager should consider before opting to outsource sales, for example, if the service will be performed exclusively or the outsourcing com-pany will have the right to sell other products. Exclusivity has its price and should be incorporated into profit (more sales) and loss (higher cost) considerations.

Recently Office Service has developed an external sales force pilot programme by forming a partnership with a chain selling mobile services (Apis). In fact it is outsourcing one of the selling functions, namely winning new customers. There is a system in place that awards Apis staff for every purchase order made by its customers. This solution could normally bring about potential problems (e.g. with profit-sharing) but that is not the case here because the owner of Office Service is the co-owner of Apis.

Fittings Master do not use and does not plan to employ external sales forces. This is due to the fact that the potential market can be dealt with by the company's own resources. At the beginning the company decided to develop its own sales team for two reasons: the cost of hiring specialized personnel and the availability of an appro-priate sales unit in the sales outsource market and, more importantly, the nature of the sales relationships in the doors and windows fittings market. Well-established and long-lasting relationships with customers are, according to the management team, Fittings Master's key success factor.

Territory design

At the beginning of this chapter we emphasized the role of sales territory design in sales management as an important factor in sales effectiveness. Adjusting sales terri-tories is usually worthwhile, as some authors estimate that good sales alignment can boost sales by 2–7 per cent (Zoltners and Sinha 2005). Putting it in simple words, sales territory design is about deploying the sales force to separate sales regions. In fact, it has a broader meaning and some authors define sales territory design as the result of managerial decisions in assigning customers, products, visit and/or call frequency as well as geographical coverage to each sales person (Piercy et al. 2004; Baldauf and Cravens 1999).

There are only a few situations in which systematic sales territory design is of less importance: first, if the market is not numerous in terms of potential customers; sec-ondly, if a company starts its operations on a small scale; and, thirdly, as proposed by some authors, defining sales territories may be unnecessary if the company employs multi-level marketing or 'selling-to-friends'(Donaldson 1994) strategy.

---

[10] For more discussion and examples see Ross et al. (2005).

When designing sales territories, as we show below in the example of Fittings Master, the numbers of customers, market potential and physical access to accounts are all of fundamental importance. Some advice on how to measure the appropriateness of territory design is also given.

CASE PROBLEM REVISITED

Fittings Master

In the case of Fittings Masters the basis for defining regions was the number of potential clients located in the given areas (the size of the population, and thus customers, and therefore market potential). The second factor was ease of access to the clients (the road network and density distribution of the clients). If travelling can consume up to 20–30 per cent of sales personnel time, it should be well reflected in the territory design. This is why for Fittings Master, as for many companies operating in Poland, the Silesia region is the smallest territory (measured in square kilometres). The Silesian conurbation, which constitutes part of the South Sales Region, is highest in terms of population density ($c.$ 1,500 people/km^2) and the second most populated region of Poland. At the beginning there were no assigned regions due to the small number of employed salespeople and an insignificant number of clients. With time and the company's development, employment was increased, which resulted in a division of Poland into three distinct regions.

Sales territory design (STD) is the responsibility of the Sales Managers and should be subject to regular evaluation – remember that Zoltners and Sinha (2005) estimated that good sales alignment can boost sales by 2–7 per cent. Measurement of satisfaction (usually of Sales Managers, less often of salespeople) with existing sales territory design is the method most often used in the research of STD. Proper STD should match the market potential (the territory potential is a better predictor of territory sales than any characteristic related to the salesperson) to the work (and costs) needed to access accounts. A salesperson in a territory with too much work cannot cover all the customers and prospects effectively.

Master Fittings' Sales personnel are well satisfied with their sales territory design. The current design is based on the following assumptions:

- equal market potential of all territories;
- travel time of less than five hours between two points in the territory;
- territories that match the sales territories of a major distributor.

STD affects the results achieved by the Sales Representatives. An inappropriately chosen territory or a sub-optimal allocation of the sales force will affect the activities of the Sales Representatives and the results they achieve.

Baldauf and Cravens (1999) show that an appropriately selected sales territory is a significant and strong determinant of the effectiveness of the sales force. Piercy et al. (2004) also point to territory design as a strong predictor of performance and effectiveness.

STD is not static. As new accounts come to the market and others relocate or close their business, a selling company should respond by modifying its sales territories accordingly. Also, mergers and company acquisitions trigger the need for sales territory realignment, which can be more complicated than setting up sales territory from scratch. One of the additional issues emerging in realignment of sales territories is customer disruption, that is, a change in the salesperson servicing the account.

Summary

This chapter covered two important elements of sales management, namely sales force organization and sales territory design, and highlighted key dilemmas with which Sales Managers are confronted. It has shown that while sales organizations often evolve organically both in structure and size, there are a number of important considerations in order to find the optimal match between environmental conditions, customer requirements and the firm's resources. We took the example of two Polish companies to illustrate some of these considerations in more detail.

The science of sales management gives us a strong theoretical background to understand these practical problems. Nevertheless, there are still open questions and important issues that need answering. The editors of a special issue of the *Journal of Personal Selling and Sales Management* (Mantrala et al. 2008) on sales force productivity point to the following issues (among a few others):

- Should a company deploy its own sales force or outsource the selling function for a new product launch?
- When and how should a company deploy product, customer or functional sales specialists?
- When should team selling be utilized?
- How should sales teams be formed and compensated?

These and other questions are left open for debate among practitioners and academics.

Key points

1. Sales force organization should match the company's industry and its stage of growth. Too complicated an organization may hamper sales growth for start-ups, whereas single channel selling can limit sales in mature markets. The easiest form of territory design to organize and manage is a geographical one, i.e. where sales personnel are assigned to set territories. Usually this is done by using postcodes or other relevant geographic data. However, if market segments differ in the selling effort required, it is better to reflect this in the sales structure.

2. A properly designed sales territory will increase sales because it allows for good coverage of customers (current and prospect). On the other hand, poor territory design will undermine sales personnel morale and, in effect, will contribute to problems in sales management (e.g. by boosting turnover of sales force personnel). Nevertheless, sales structures of companies evolve and change according to market situation, business strategy, etc. and thus STD should be subject to periodic evaluation.

3. Key criteria to evaluate STD are market potential and coverage, travel distance and physical access to accounts.

Running an information audit for sales force design

Table 8.4 should help sales managers to evaluate their sales force organization and territory design.

It is advisable to have more 'yes' than 'no' answers. However the table should help you identify if you have enough information for certain activities. For example:

- If the answer for 1 and 2 is positive, you can employ a market potential approach in your sales force planning.
- If the answer for 2 and 3 is positive, you can verify STD by means of market potential coverage; if there is a 'yes' for number 5, you can calculate sales force allocation using a proxy to profitability.
- If the answer to 4 and 6 is positive, you can verify if there is a need for division within the sales team based on functions performed.
- Information related to answers to questions 7 and 8 will help you detect possible problems with the sales force organization, e.g. if both are above market average it may mean that the sales team is not properly aligned to customer preferences.

Table 8.5 enables you to assess your sales force organization. To benefit from it, try to find benchmarks for your market or major competitor.

Table 8.4   Useful information for evaluating sales force organization and territory design

Do you know or have information on:	Yes	No
1. Market potential (value/volume)		
2. Single account potential		
3. Single account contact and address details		
4. Single account contact details, including identifying the roles of different people at your customer		
5. Resource investment needed (effort needed to service) for single accounts		
6. Interpurchase time of your customers		
7. Defection rate of your customers compared to market average		
8. Sales force turnover compared to market average		

Table 8.5   Simple metrics for sales force organization and territory design

Metric	Your company	Benchmark	Meaning
Percentage of working time spent on travelling			Depends heavily on company's growth stage (may be high at the beginning) and industry (e.g. high for selling complex solutions). Consider jointly with the next point.

Table 8.5	(Continued)
Percentage of working time devoted to selling	Usually falls into 30–40 per cent range. If less, then the territory is too large; if more, then you should think about expanding sales territories.
Number of salespeople calling on one account	Should be no more than the number of categories offered. Consider jointly with the next point.
Number of salespeople calling on one account divided by the number of separate procurement agents or teams for the account	Usually should be 1 (which means you have one salesperson for one buying person/team).
Number of products handled by each salesperson	Depends on the industry specifics. For low involvement products (consider Office Supply) can be measured in thousands. For complex products can fall to one or two.
Number of accounts handled by each salesperson	Helps with territory design evaluation. Consider with the interpurchase time of you customers*
Percentage market potential divided by percentage of accounts on the market	Gives an estimate of function allocation**

* To give the reader a short example:

If the interpurchase time is, say, two weeks, your salesperson services 100 customers and within your sales team 30 per cent of working time is devoted to selling, then we have:

$$100 \text{ customers}/10 \text{ working days} = 10 \text{ customers a day (8 hours)}$$

And time for selling to a customer is:

$$(30 \text{ per cent} \times 8 \text{ hours})/10 \text{ customers} = 14.4 \text{ minutes}$$

which may be not enough to sell more complex products or services or to introduce a new offer.

** To give a short example to illustrate the metric:

Let's say your sales team has covered 80 per cent of market potential and is selling to 20 per cent of customers. Then what we have is:

$$80 \text{ per cent}/20 \text{ per cent} = 4$$

which means you have 'big shots' and may want to consider changing the organization of the sales force so as to nurture the relationships with the clients. Also a new sales channel (usually low cost) may be introduced to gain additional market share (again, consider the case of Office Supply).

References

Anderson, E. and Trinkle B. (2005) *Outsourcing the Sales Function: The Real Costs of Field Sales*. Mason, OH: Thomson/South-Western Educational Publishers.

Babakus, E., Cravens, D., Grant, K., Ingram, T. and LaForge, R. (1996) 'Investigating the Relationships between Sales Management Control, Sales Territory Design, Salesperson Performance, and Sales Organization Effectiveness', *International Journal of Research in Marketing*, 13 (4): 345–63.

Baldauf, A., Cravens, D. (1999) 'Improving the Effectiveness of Field Sales Organizations: A European Perspective', *Industrial Marketing Management*, 28 (1): 63–72.

Donaldson, B. (1994) *Sales Management: Theory and Practice*, Basingstoke: Macmillan.

Mantrala, M., Albers, S., Gopalakrishna, S. and Kissan, J. (2008) 'Introduction: Special Issue on Enhancing Sales Force Productivity', *Journal of Personal Selling and Sales Management*, 28 (2): 109–113.

Piercy, N., Low, G., Cravens, D. (2004) 'Examining the Effectiveness of Sales Management Control Practices in Developing Countries', *Journal of World Business*, 39 (3): 255–67.

Rangaswamy, A., Sinha, P. and Zoltners, A. (1990) 'An Integrated Model-Based Approach for Sales Force Structuring', *Marketing Science*, 9 (4): 279–98.

Ross, W., Dalsace, F. Jr and Anderson, E. (2005) 'Should you Set Up your own Sales Force or Should you Outsource It? Pitfalls in the Standard Analysis', *Business Horizons*, 28 (1): 23–36.

Weitz, B., Sujan, H. and Sujan, M. (1986) 'Personal Selling and Sales Management: A Relationship Marketing Perspective', *Journal of Marketing*, 50 (4): 174–81.

Zoltners, A., Sinha, P. and Lorimer, S. (2006) 'Match your Sales Force Structure to Your Business Life Cycle', *Harvard Business Review*, (7/8): 81–89.

Zoltners, A. and Sinha, P. (2005) 'Sales Territory Design: Thirty Years of Modelling and Implementation', *Marketing Science*, 24 (3): 313–31.

Further reading

Grant, K., Cravens, D.W., Low, G.S. and Moncrief, W.C. (2001) 'The Role of Satisfaction with Territory Design on the Motivation, Attitudes, and Work Outcomes of Salespeople', *Journal of the Academy of Marketing Science*, 29 (2): 165–78.

Rapp, A. (2009) 'Outsourcing the Sales Process: Hiring a Mercenary Sales Force', *Industrial Marketing Management*, 38 (4): 411–18.

Weiss, A.M., Anderson, E. and MacInnis, D.J. (1999) 'Reputation Management as a Motivation for Sales Structure Decisions', *Journal of Marketing*, 63 (4): 74–89.

Wilson, H. and Daniel, E. (2007) 'The Multi-channel Challenge: A Dynamic Capability Approach', *Industrial Marketing Management*, 36 (1): 10–20.

9

Sizing the sales force

René Y. Darmon

Contents

Learning objectives

After reading this chapter, you should be able to:

- Recognize the managerial and economic importance of keeping the right sales force size.

- Understand the difficulties of assessing the right sales force size.

- Describe the most commonly used approaches and methods of sales force sizing currently used.

- List the main advantages and limitations of those approaches.

- Understand the rationale and the advantages and limitations of the newly proposed approach.

Chapter outline

This chapter underlines the importance for a sales organization of keeping a sales force of the right size. Unfortunately, finding the optimal (or close to optimal) size is fraught with difficulties. In fact, sales force sizing and sales effort allocation methods vary from simplistic rules of thumb to extremely sophisticated analytical procedures. The former methods are easy to understand and implement, but typically they are inaccurate and probably invalid. The latter procedures may provide more accurate and valid results, but they are more difficult to explain to management and require data collection and analysis that are often quite elaborate. In this chapter, a method of optimal estimation of total sales effort level and time allocation that combines the advantages of both approaches is proposed. For each customer segment, this method requires for the optimal call effort allocation to take into account the – so far often neglected but relevant – balance between the number of calls per account during a planning period and the length of sales calls.

CASE PROBLEM

The Electrical Supplies Company

The Electrical Supplies Company (ESC) is a medium-sized company that sells electrical equipment to all kinds of businesses.[1] The firm's client (and potential client) base was estimated at over 7,000 accounts. At the time this study was initiated, the company used a direct sales force of 61 salespeople who called on manufacturing companies nationwide.

In order to monitor and control salespeople's activities, the different Sales Managers who were in charge of the sales force over the last several years had provided salespeople with sales call guidelines. Their method consisted of splitting the total national market into three segments and providing salespeople with call norms for each segment. These norms were adjusted from year to year according to management's experience and sales results. Thus, salespeople were instructed to call on key accounts twice a month, medium-sized accounts once every two months and small accounts no more than once a year. In other words, on an annual basis, key accounts were supposed to receive 24 calls, medium-sized accounts 6 calls, and small accounts only 1 call. Although these norms were not strictly enforced, they were part of the salespeople's evaluation process, and salespeople generally tried to meet these objectives. The call norm setting procedure is straightforward and had been used satisfactorily for at least the last 20 years.

A problem arose, however, when salespeople started to feel strongly that they did not have enough time to cover their territories properly, and consequently strictly to abide to the recommended call norms. In addition, many salespeople complained that in order to keep to the prescribed call norms, they were under intense pressure unduly to shorten the length of many calls. They argued that in many instances they would be more efficient if they could spend more time with certain customers while reducing the number of calls to them required.

Introduction: the typical sales force sizing problem

A Simple managerial analysis

In order to tackle the problem, the ESC Sales Manager reviewed the call norm setting procedure and asked his assistant to conduct a thorough analysis of the sales call reports that salespeople were required to email every week about their calling activities. This meant assessing the total sales force workload for covering the whole market, given the call requirements. By dividing this total workload by the average workload that a salesperson could normally handle, it was possible to estimate roughly the appropriate sales force size for adequate market coverage. In practice, the method involved the following steps:

1. *Step 1: Classification of all the accounts.* All prospect and customer accounts were classified into three customer segments believed to be homogeneous in terms of the selling effort they required.
2. *Step 2: Estimation of the required contact time.* From salespeople's call reports, for each segment the average call frequency and their average duration were estimated.

---

[1] The name of the company has been replaced in order to maintain its privacy.

3. *Step 3: Calculation of the total required time.* The total yearly workload required from the whole sales force for total market coverage was derived from these estimates.
4. *Step 4: Salesperson's annual available contact time.* The annual workload that a salesperson can handle, as well as the proportion of the time he/she must spend on face-to-face contact with clients were then estimated.
5. *Step 5: Necessary number of* salespeople. Dividing the total workload that is necessary to properly cover the whole market by the contact time available to an average salesperson provided a rough estimate of the sales force size necessary for adequately covering the market.

The analysis carried out by the ESC's Assistant Sales Manager is provided in Table 9.1. First, it shows that, at least at the aggregate level, the sales force roughly followed the prescribed call frequency guidelines (22.3 instead of 24 calls on key accounts, 5.8 calls instead of 6 for medium-sized accounts, and 1.4 instead of 1 for small accounts). Secondly, the analysis indicated that the firm was short of 12 or 13 salespeople for adequate market coverage. Note that had the sales force strictly enforced the guidelines, this procedure implies that 71 salespeople would still be needed to enable the market to be adequately covered.

Interpretation of the results

This analysis strongly reinforced sales management's suspicion that the sales force was understaffed. As a result, the Sales Manager sent a report to the firm's Marketing Manager and General Management requesting at least ten additional salespeople. The Marketing Manager, however, questioned the relevance of the call norms and suggested that these norms could be revised so as to make it possible for salespeople to meet them. His recommendation was to reallocate salespeople's efforts among the various accounts and sales calls. This could solve at least part of the problem regarding shortage of selling time and enabling the team to focus their selling effort appropriately. But it was also necessary to assess whether increasing (or decreasing) the number of calls and/or the typical length of calls in each segment would result in increased (or decreased) net profit for the company. Obviously, the reallocation would result in less contact time for all or some of the various customers in each segment. Unfortunately, this analysis method provided no indication of the impact on profit of increasing or decreasing the selling effort in each market segment.

The problem faced by ESC involved the consideration of both the total sales effort size and the allocation of this selling effort among market segments and accounts, as well as over time. A consultant was hired in order to help management rationally address this issue, which divided salespeople as well as the management team. The consultant was given the task of proposing a relatively simple and reasonably accurate procedure that could be easily understood by management and was easy to implement and then of making recommendations for call norms (frequency and average length of time) for every market segment and, consequently, the required sales force size.

Table 9.1 Example of the workload approach to sales force sizing
N = 7,040 accounts and potential accounts

Step 1 Classification of all the accounts		Step 2 Estimation of the contact time		Step 3 Calculation of the total required time
Account categories	Number of accounts in each category (1)	Number of calls/year (2)	Typical call length (3)	Required time per year (hours) (4) = (1) × (2) × (3)
1. Key accounts	335	22.3	2.5	18,676
2. Medium-sized accounts	1,492	5.8	2.2	19,038
3. Small accounts	5,213	1.4	1.8	13,137
TOTAL	7,040			50,851

Step 4
Salesperson's annual available contact time

Annual working time available to a salesperson: 45 weeks × 35 hours = 1,575 hours
Percentage of working time spent in direct contact with clients: 44 per cent
Contact time with clients per year and per salesperson: 1,575 × 0.44 = 693 hours

Step 5
Necessary number of salespeople

Number of salespeople required for covering the whole market:
50,851 / 693 = 73.38, i.e, 73 or 74 salespeople

The following sections first review the accumulated knowledge resulting from past research studies and the methods that are typically used for determining sales force sizes and effort allocations and, second, outline a method especially devised to solve the ESC problem, present the implementation results and sketch the advantages and limitations of the proposed method.

A conceptual approach to sales force sizing

Sales force sizing: a neglected source of opportunity gains

As the ESC case suggests, sales force sizing and the related issue of sales effort market allocation are important practical problems. Although they have received their fair share of attention from sales management researchers, sales force sizing remains one of the most important sources of missed profit opportunities for a large majority of sales forces. One of the main reasons for this is that the cost of personal selling is quite substantial, especially in industrial settings. Keeping too many salespeople is inefficient because of unwarranted high selling costs. Alternatively, too few salespeople result in potentially high levels of lost opportunities. The Syntex Laboratories case study (Lodish et al. 1988) that is briefly reviewed in the following section is a case in point. In practice, in spite of the profit amounts at stake, few sales managers are confident that their sales force is properly dimensioned and deployed.

The main difficulty managers experience is in assessing the additional revenue that adding one (or several) salesperson(s) to the sales force would bring and/or by how much the sales revenue would be reduced if one (or several) salesperson(s) were removed from the sales force. The problem is even more acute because determining the right amount of selling effort cannot be done independently from the way in which this effort is structured and allocated among accounts, sales activities, sales territories and over time.

Not unlike the ESC case, it is probably safe to assert that a great majority of sales forces are understaffed. One of the most obvious reasons for this is that managers tend to behave as cautiously as possible and, no doubt, it is less risky for them to be under- than overstaffed: Hiring too many salespeople increases highly visible direct costs. This might have adverse effects on a manager's personal career and may involve serious human resources management problems. In contrast, having too few sales personnel implies a failure to take advantage of possible (but hidden) opportunity gains. This is far less visible and easier to deal with than direct costs. Consequently, only Sales Managers who are bold enough to take advantage of part or all of these opportunity gains are likely to be more efficient and successful than more risk-averse managers.

A systematic approach to sales force sizing

Figure 9.1 proposes a general framework that highlights the main determinants and consequences of sales force sizing.

Figure 9.1 The main determinants and consequences of sales force size

The main determinants of sales force size

Five main factors tend to determine a sales force size, namely:

1. the firm's orientation concerning its selling objectives horizon;
2. the selling task (or workload) to be accomplished in order to fulfill sales objectives;
3. the sales force staffing activities of the firm;
4. the sales force structure and organization;
5. the sales force turnover rate.

The firm's selling orientation

A study of 50 sales forces has clearly shown that firms that pursue short-term objectives tend significantly to underestimate their required sales force size compared with firms pursuing long-term objectives (Zoltners et al. 2001, p. 79). Although the prevalent tendency is to adopt a customer orientation and build long-lasting relationships with key clients, Sales Managers often remain under pressure to achieve short-term results. This may reinforce the suspicion that, in practice, many sales forces may be even more understaffed nowadays, if the gap between short-term and long-term requirements has kept increasing.

The sales force's workload

The mission that is assigned to a sales force has a direct effect on the sales staff needed. The content of the mission implies a certain workload for the sales force. For instance, the selling mission may be defined as requiring salespeople to provide constant services to customers. Alternatively, the mission may be limited to providing potential customers with product information. In these two cases, the different mission statements certainly require different workloads from the sales force. As shown above, the total selling workload must be linked to the sales force's size.

Sales force staffing activities

The selected sales force objectives and workload typically trigger a series of managerial activities in order to bring the sales force to the required size level. These activities include (among others) recruiting (or, occasionally, firing) salespeople, training, coaching and supervising new recruits. The efficiency and competence with which these activities are carried out affect the actual sales force size.

Sales force structure and organization

The structure and organization of a sales force are closely linked to the sales force size. For instance, if every salesperson is responsible for selling only one product line, this requires several independent sales forces to cover the market with all the firm's offerings. If every salesperson is asked to sell all the product lines, different time allocations, travelling times, etc. are warranted, most likely resulting in different sales force sizes (see Chapter 8, Sales force organization and territory design, for more information).

The sales force turnover rate

The sales force size is also directly affected by the sales personnel turnover rate. Turnover includes all salespeople who quit the sales force for such reasons as voluntary leave, dismissals for inadequate performance, promotions within or outside of the sales force and uncontrollable causes such as retirement, illness or death. Departing salespeople must be replaced and this generates additional recruiting and training activities.

Note that sales performance affects sales force turnover. It is generally recognized that higher sales producers are more likely to resign than medium performers (because they are often offered more attractive job offers elsewhere) and that the same is true for very low producers (because they are fired or discouraged from pursuing a career in sales). In other words, turnover has a U-shaped relationship to performance and generates costly activities.

Because of turnover, sales forces reach their target size only occasionally (Darmon 2004). This is another reason why sales forces tend to be systematically understaffed. A simple example can illustrate this fact: at some point in time, a sales force may well have reached its objective size of, say, 100 salespeople. If the turnover rate is 16 per cent per year, then after three months, the sales force would have lost four salespeople, bringing its size down to only 96 salespeople. In the meantime, the firm would have started recruiting and training four new salespeople. Assuming that this process takes six months, eight new salespeople would have left because turnover continues to affect the sales force. Consequently, when the four newly hired salespeople are ready to be assigned to territories, the sales force would include only 92 salespeople $(100 - 4 + 4 - 8)$.

One could argue that this is certainly a very conservative hiring policy and one that generates high opportunity costs. In fact, it would be more efficient for management to anticipate turnover and recruit more salespeople than needed in order to make sure that a sufficient number of salespeople are ready to be assigned to a territory as soon as one becomes vacant. In this case, after the first three months the firm could hire twelve salespeople because it can anticipate that before the new salespeople are ready, eight more defections would have occurred. Thus, after nine months, the firm would reach its target size of 100 salespeople ($100 - 4 - 8 + 12$). This policy, however, involves direct costs of excess personnel for eight new recruits during the six months when they are recruited and trained while no territory is yet vacant. An intermediary policy is also a possibility. As discussed above, however, managers, who typically prefer incurring opportunity costs rather than direct costs, are less likely to use the latter strategy. As a result, sales forces are more likely to be systematically under- than overstaffed. In any case, this suggests that the sales force sizing problem cannot be satisfactorily addressed when turnover is disregarded.

The main consequence of sales force size

As Figure 9.1 shows, the size of a sales force determines the total level of selling effort that is deployed in the market, while the associated concepts of sales force structure and organization more directly affect the various types of sales effort allocation (spatial, temporal or among various selling activities). The market response to the deployed selling effort results in sales performance and revenues that, hopefully, match the selling objectives that have been set initially. There is no doubt that establishing the link between sales force size and sales (and profit) performance is essential for deriving the optimal sales force size. This link is called the market response to selling effort. This response is also affected by such personal variables as salespeople's aptitudes and competencies, organizational variables such as the firm's offerings and pricing policies and environmental factors such as the competitive environment.

Past research and practices

In this section, the main approaches to sales force sizing that have been followed in practice are reviewed, along with the main research methods and results on which these methods rely.

Practical methods often used for sales force sizing

The conceptual framework of Figure 9.1 highlights the extent to which various methods used in practice account for the different aspects of the sales force sizing problem. Some methods are used because they are very simple to apply, but often lack theoretical soundness. Others are built around the determinants of sales force size – and often ignore the consequences. These methods focus on the selling workload that needs to be carried out in order to meet sales objectives. Others account for the performance consequences but often overlook some important determinants. These methods focus on the market responses to selling effort and try to optimize the required selling effort (i.e. the sales force size). These three types of approach are briefly reviewed in the following paragraphs.

Some simple to implement methods

Because of the difficulties of properly sizing the sales force, managers frequently use their gut feelings or rely on crude decision rules to make sales force sizing and allocation decisions. Linking the sales force size to last year's sales volume or using industry guidelines are among the most frequently used methods because they are simple to understand and apply. Unfortunately, they generally lack theoretical grounds.

The workload approach to sales force sizing

This procedure (also called the breakdown approach) is often described (Zoltners et al. 2001). It is exemplified by the procedure used by the ESC's Assistant Manager and is summarized in Table 9.1. As Figure 9.2 shows, the analyst must specify the relevant allocation criteria (in the ESC case, market segments), determine the selling effort required by each segment and aggregate over segments in order to devise the proper sales force size.

The main advantage of this method is that it is easy to understand and apply. It has, however, four major drawbacks. First, it is difficult to find adequate estimates at the second stage of the procedure. These estimates require some knowledge of a typical client's responses to various call policies in each segment, in order to decide which one is 'optimal'. Second, the method ignores the call allocation problem. For instance, as was pointed out by many of the ESC salespeople, there is often a marked difference between the outcome of making a large number of short calls to an account versus making fewer but longer calls. As will be seen below, this limitation is also shared with the market responses to selling effort methods. Third, the procedure fails to account for the sales force turnover problem. Finally, it does not account either for the revenue or the cost and profit aspects of the problem, which should be of prime importance in the sales force sizing decision. This is why more elaborate methods are sometimes preferred.

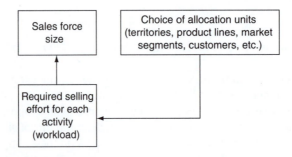

Figure 9.2   The workload approach to sales force sizing

The market response to selling effort approach to sales force sizing

The basic principle

Other sales force sizing methods rely on assessment of the responses of various allocation units to selling effort (these methods are also called the incremental approach). These are theoretically more satisfactory, but they tend to be more complex and difficult to explain to management and to implement. For instance, some firms use procedures that rely on elaborate analytical methods and/or statistical techniques (see, for instance, Horsky and Nelson 1996). These methods rely on the economic principle that markets are typically less and less responsive to additional selling effort as new salespeople are added to the sales force. If one can estimate the sales revenues that one additional salesperson can yield, the rule is straightforward: keep increasing the sales force as long as an additional salesperson yields more gross profit than his/her cost to the firm; and conversely. The typical procedure is outlined in Figure 9.3.

For each considered allocation unit, the effect of some inputs (such as sales potential or selling effort) on the unit's sales must be assessed. A certain selling effort results in sales and gross profits. Subtracting the corresponding selling costs yields the net profit. An optimization technique finds the selling effort levels that produce maximum profits. Aggregating the optimal selling effort across units produces an estimate of the optimal sales force size. Clearly, this approach to sales force sizing is more elaborate and encompassing than the preceding one.

Applying this principle requires reasonably accurate estimates of the sales and profits that an additional salesperson (or an additional unit of sales effort) can bring, at any sales force size level. Because of the difficulty of determining the market responses from objective techniques, the responses are often estimated. The various methods that have been proposed in the literature can be differentiated according to the type and level of sales effort allocations being considered. Some methods consider essentially broad types of selling effort allocations (e.g. among product lines or market segments) and require that the responses to selling effort be estimated at such macro levels.

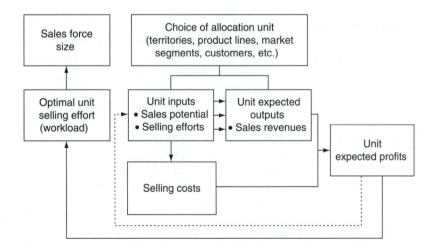

Figure 9.3   The unit sensitivities approach to sales force sizing

When, however, the problem requires more detailed sales effort allocations (e.g. among accounts or sales territories), responses need to be estimated at more micro levels.

The reliance on managerial judgements

Most sales force sizing applications based on market responses to selling effort rely, at least to some extent, on the use of subjective managerial judgements (Beswick and Cravens 1977; Lodish 1975; Lodish et al. 1988; Zoltners and Sinha 1980, 1983; Rangaswamy et al. 1990; Skiera and Albers 1998) because of the difficulties involved and the lack of sufficient and accurate hard data needed for employing econometric estimation techniques. This practice was introduced by John Little (1970) and is known as the decision calculus approach. Its rationale is that managers develop experience over time and, consequently, some useful knowledge of the responses of the units they control to selling effort. As a result, through proper questioning, managers can provide judgements about the most likely market responses to selling effort that may be as good as (and sometimes even better than) more 'scientific' estimation methods. For example, Lodish et al. (1988) report a study at Syntex Laboratories in which managers at different hierarchical levels judgementally estimated the sales responses to selling effort for various product lines and market segments. Then the sales force time resource (mentions of a product or details) were optimally allocated to products and market segments through optimization techniques. The time resource (i.e. the sales force size) was gradually increased until the net profit started declining. This procedure led to a sales force size increase from 433 to 700 salespeople that resulted in an annual sales volume increase of about $25 million. Horsky and Nelson (1996) and Misra et al. (2004) provide other examples using similar approaches.

In fact, the relationship between selling effort and sales for large units are not easy for management to estimate. It requires careful consideration, management experience and training and expert analyses. This is especially the case when managers must make judgements about the sales responses of macro level units (e.g. responses at the level of an additional salesperson).

Macro level effort allocations

Some examples   Semlow (1959) proposed the first method of this type. A simplified example of the method is provided in Table 9.2. It involves estimating territory sales revenue responses to territory sales potentials for each territory. One might expect a direct relationship between potential and sales, with marginally decreasing returns. For example, a sales territory that accounts for 25 per cent of the total market potential might yield sales of €90,000 per time period. Another territory that accounts for 5 per cent of the total market potential might produce only €24,400 if assigned to the same salesperson. In the former case, the sales per 1 per cent of potential are equal to €3,600, while they are of €4,880 in the latter case.

Given the above estimates, it is relatively easy to assess the profitability of any sales force size, taking into account the sales and revenues that could be generated, as well as all the associated costs. In the example of the former territory, four salespeople, each with a territory accounting for 25 per cent of the total potential (i.e. 25% × 4 = 100%), would be required to cover the whole market. Each salesperson would sell an average of €90,000, for total sales equal to €360,000. In contrast, in the latter case, 20

| | **Table 9.2** | Examples of sales force size determination according to the market responses to salespeople's efforts method |

	Case 1	Case 2 (optimal)	Case 3	....	Case n
Number of salespeople required	20	6	4	...	2
Average sales per territory (000 €)	24.4	68.9	90	...	100
Total sales (000 €)	488	413.4	360	...	200
Gross margin (30% of sales)	146.4	124.0	108	...	60
Cost of the needed salespeople (5,000 €)	100	30	20	...	10
Net profit (000 €)	46.4	94.0*	88	...	50

* The 6-salesperson solution maximizes net profits.

salespeople would be needed, each one having a territory with average sales potential representing 5 per cent of the total market potential. In this case, the firm could expect sales to total €488,000 (€24,400 × 20) per period. The remaining calculations are straightforward and given in Table 9.2. As a result, it is possible to assess the sales force size appropriate to gain the highest profits.

Although Semlow's relationship specification was spurious (Weinberg and Lucas 1977), the basic principle stands, and is valid as long as the above mentioned relationship between sales potential and sales does exist, is sufficiently strong and can be estimated empirically. In the same vein, Lucas et al. (1975) determined that territory potential and workload are linked to territory sales, and used similar sales response estimates for determining the optimal sales force size.

Unfortunately, in spite of their relative simplicity, these methods raise two important issues. First, the estimation procedure requires that sales territories display a large variance in terms of sales potential, which is at odds with the method outcome, which is supposed to yield equal potential territories. Secondly, they assume a well defined positive relationship between potential and sales, which, as discussed below, may not always be the case.

Territory sales potential as a measure of inputs The last two methods assume that territory sales should increase as territory sales potential increases. Theoretical and empirical studies have suggested that a higher territory sales potential may sometimes imply decreased territory actual sales. Although this might seem counter-intuitive at first glance, all other things being equal, it is possible for identical salespeople to achieve lower sales in territories with larger sales potential. Under classical economic theory (which assumes perfect and free information), this may not be the case. In practice, however, above a certain territory size, a salesperson may not have enough time to collect and process perfect information. As territory size (and potential) increases, the salesperson in charge is likely to have relatively less and less territory information and consequently less and less time to cultivate the territory. Consequently, the salesperson is likely to select the set of accounts to be cultivated *to the best of his/her knowledge*, which, by definition, must be less profitable than the optimal set with perfect information. As a result, although territory sales potential increases, the territory market share decreases and, consequently, sales decrease. In other words, such a salesperson moves to lower and lower sales response curves as the territory size (and potential) increases. This is why the relationship between sales per territory and territory potential may, under certain circumstances, be negative and display lower sales results as the territory size increases. Although this relationship has not been frequently investigated, it has already been observed empirically (see, for instance, Sengupta 1996 and, to an extent, Semlow 1959). Taking into account the shape of this relationship, however, can be used for deriving the optimal sales force size (Darmon 2002): note that this is one of the very few studies relying on the necessary time allocation between information acquisition and selling activity that any salesperson must perform in a territory of a given size.

Micro level effort allocation

Several other applications also use the concept of allocation selling unit responses to selling effort at a desegregated level (customer, territory) in order to estimate the optimal sales force effort level, and, consequently, through aggregation, the optimal sales force size. It seems that managers are more effective at exercising such judgements at micro levels (responses of one account to additional calls). In this case, however, the effort allocation and aggregation procedures are more complex and elaborate, and these methods often lose in simplicity. For instance, Beswick and Cravens (1977) devised a general sales force management model in which sales response functions are modelled as power functions, which can be used to estimate the optimal number of salespeople for a territory. Other examples are Lodish (1975), Rangaswamy et al. (1990) and Zoltners and Sinha (1980).

To sum up, although scientifically more rigorous than workload approach applications, many allocation unit sales response approach methods incur the risk of not being fully understood by analytically untrained managers. Consequently, management often lacks the confidence to use and implement the recommendations of such decision support systems.

Requirements for a new procedure

This analysis highlights the need for decision aids that are appropriate for various types of organization. Many small- and medium-sized organizations may lack the resources for implementing highly sophisticated methods and often require procedures that are simple enough to be understood and accepted by managers and, at the same time, rigorous enough to provide, if not strictly optimal, at least close to optimal solutions.

Based on these conclusions, the following requirements have been specified in order to address the ESC's problem. The method should:

- be easily understandable, and combine the simplicity of the workload approach (with which the firm has already had experience) with the rigor of the market response to sales effort approach;
- take into account the most desirable characteristics of sales response which have been shown to have strong impact on sales force size, such as carryover effects (Sinha and Zoltners 2001);

- take into account the effect of one of the most relevant time allocation issues in this context, i.e. the balance in allocation of a salesperson's time between number of calls and length of calls. Although Sinha and Zoltners (2001) have shown the importance of effort allocation and its potential impact on sales force size, no published study so far has been found to consider the effect of this important type of effort allocation on sales force size;
- overcome the simplistic assumptions of the workload method by introducing the use of a very limited number of estimated micro-level sales response functions to salesperson effort;
- derive estimates from a parsimonious set of managerial judgements as well as from hard accounting and sales call data.

Proposed solution

A newly devised procedure has been implemented for solving the ESP's problem. First, it is presented, and then the rationale for the method is discussed, followed by an assessment of the extent to which the method can be applied to other similar situations.

The optimal segmental call policy

In order to apply a new approach, some data had to be collected from accounting and managerial sources. The accounting department provided all the cost figures, notably:

1. Marg: the gross margin rates on sales (decimal form);
2. CTCOST: the cost (€) of one hour of contact time with a customer, including the associated cost of non-calling time;
3. TRCOST: the average direct travel cost (€) to an account, including travel costs, but excluding the cost of the travelling time of the salesperson.

Following an analysis of sales call reports on a representative sample of accounts from every segment, sales management provided the following data:

4. NACCOUNTS: the number of accounts;
5. NCALLS: the current average number of calls made to accounts in each segment;
6. LENGTH: the typical length (hours) of a call;
7. AVSALES: the average sales (€) from such accounts;
8. Contact: the percentage (decimal form) of contact time.

In addition, for each segment, managers were requested to provide five judgemental estimates:

9. MAXCALL: the maximum call frequency;
10. MAXLENGTH: the maximum length (hours) of a call that could be made before starting to obtain negative responses from the client;

11. MinLENGTH: the minimum time (hours) that a salesperson should spend on one call to a client;
12. NOCALLSALES: the sales level (€) that would be reached at the end of the call planning period (one year) under a no-call policy;
13. MAXCALLSALES: the expected sales level (€) that would be achieved under a maximum call policy (for validation purposes).

As shown in the following section, these estimates (Table 9.3) are sufficient for providing estimates of the optimal call policies in every segment (Table 9.4).

Table 9.3 shows that optimal call policies imply substantially higher call frequencies and call lengths than under current practice, in all segments, especially in medium-sized accounts and key accounts. The total number of hours devoted to a typical account should be increased from about 56 to 159 hours (+185 per cent) for key accounts, from 13 to 57 hours (+366 per cent) for medium-sized accounts and from 2 to almost 4 hours (+88%) for small accounts. In addition, the total optimal workload to be carried by the whole sales force would require a sales force increase from the current 61 salespeople to about 228, almost four times as many salespeople as at present. In this case, sales would almost double and the profits would increase by about 69 per cent (Table 9.5).

Table 9.3 Application data and parameter estimates

Data	All accounts	Key accounts	Medium-sized accounts	Small accounts
Accounting Data				
1. Gross margin rates on sales (decimal)		0.12	0.15	0.20
2. Cost of one hour of contact time with a client (€)	85.00			
3. Average travelling cost to an account, excluding the cost of the salesperson's time (€)	35.00			
Sales Call Data				
4. Number of accounts		335	1,492	5,213
5. Current average number of calls		22.3	5.8	1.4
6. Current typical call length (hours)		2.5	2.2	1.8
7. Current average sales (000 €)		300	50	8
8. Percentage of contact time	44%			
Managerial Estimates				
9. Maximum call frequency		48	18	12
10. Maximum call length (hours)		4	4	2
11. Minimum call length (hours)		1	0.5	0.5
12. Sales level with no calls (000 €)		5	2	0.5
13. Sales level with maximum call policy (000 €)		550	150	32

| Table 9.4 | Optimal and implemented solutions |

Data	Key accounts	Medium-sized accounts	Small accounts
Optimal Call Policy			
Optimal number of calls	43.00 (+93%)	15.64 (+170%)	2.11 (+51%)
Optimal length of calls (hours)	3.70 (+48%)	3.62 (+65%)	1.87 (+25%)
Optimal time spent on accounts (hours)	159 (+185%)	56.62 (+366%)	3.95 (+88%)
Total time per segment (hours)	53,265	84,477	20,591
Optimal sales volume per account (€)	524,293 (+75%)	124,862 (+150%)	12,993 (+62%)
Gross profit on sales per account (€)	62,915	18,729	2,599
Selling cost per account (€)	15,020	5,360	410
Optimal profit per account (€)	47,895	13,369	2,189
Implemented Call Policy			
Implemented number of calls	23.9 (+7%)	4.89 (−16%)	1.78 (+27%)
Implemented length of calls (hours)	2.5 (0%)	2.2 (0%)	1.8 (0%)
Implemented time spent on accounts (hours)	59.75 (+7%)	10.76 (−16%)	3.20 (+27%)
Total time per segment (hours)	20,016	16,054	16,682
Expected sales volume per account (€)	315,638 (+16%)	43,482 (−13%)	10,955 (+37%)
Gross profit on sales per account (€)	37,877	6,522	2,191
Selling cost per account (€)	5,915	1,086	334
Expected profit per account (€)	31,962	5,436	1,857

The rationale for the procedure

The rationale for the procedure that has been applied to the ESC relies on some basic theoretically and empirically validated propositions. Sales responses to various call policies can be expected to increase with the number of calls, but with decreasing marginal returns, at any given call length level (Figure 9.4a). In addition, in practice, the number of calls to a typical segment account will always vary between no calls and a maximum number of calls: managers know that the number of calls cannot go over a maximum number without starting to obtain decreasing responses from the account. Under a no-call policy, sales over the selected planning horizon are known to reach a certain amount because of the carryover effect of sales calls from previous periods. Such carryover effects have been shown to be often substantial (Sinha and Zoltners 2001). The NOCALLSALES point in Figure 9.4 reflects the carryover effect from previous periods.

In the same way, sales responses to various call length policies can be expected to increase with the length of calls, but with decreasing marginal returns with increase in

Table 9.5 Optimal sales force size and results					
	Current Situation	**Optimal Solution**		**Implemented Solution**	
		Value	**% increase**	**Value**	**% increase**
Sales Force Size					
Estimate of the total annual workload for covering the market (hours)	50,851	158,333	+211	52,744	+4
Actual number of hours available for covering the market	42,334				+25
Average annual contact time available to a salesperson (hours)	694	694		694	
Sales force size	61*	228	+273	76	+25
Financial Results					
Total annual sales ($000)	216,804	429,760	+98	370,075	+71
Total annual gross margin ($000)	31,591	62,584	+98	46,590	+47
Total annual selling cost ($000)	3,600	15,166	+321	7,355	+104
Total annual net profit ($000)	27,991	47,418	+69	39,255	+40

* against 73 or 74 salespeople actually needed according to an application of the workload approach.

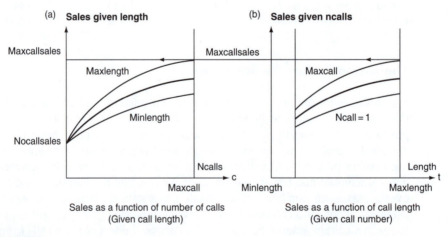

Figure 9.4 Sales responses as functions of the number and length of calls

the number of calls (Figure 9.4b). In addition, managers know that the typical call length for each representative segment account will always vary between two 'reasonable limits', the shortest possible call length that is reasonable to make and a maximum length, just before starting to upset a client.

The sales responses to selling efforts have been represented (Figure 9.4) by quadratic functions of the number of calls and typical length of calls, plus a specific interaction term between these two factors. Sales are specified to vary according to the number of calls (NCALLS) and the typical call length (LENGTH) as follows:

$$\text{SALES} = \text{NOCALLSALES} + B(\text{LENGTH})(\text{NCALLS}) - C(\text{LENGTH})(\text{NCALLS})^2$$
$$- A(\text{NCALLS})(\text{LENGTH})^2 \tag{1}$$

A, B and C are positive coefficients. For each segment, management needs to determine the call policy (NCALLS*, LENGTH*) that maximizes profits. Simple optimization techniques lead to the following solutions (see the Appendix for more details):

$$\text{NCALLS*} = (2D - E)/3C \,(\text{Marg}) \quad \text{and} \tag{2}$$
$$\text{LENGTH*} = (D + E)/6A \,(\text{Marg}) \tag{3}$$

With:

$$A = (\text{AVSALES} - \text{NOCALLSALES})/\{(\text{NCALLS})(\text{LENGTH}) - [3\text{MAXLENGTH}-$$
$$(\text{MAXLENTH})(\text{NCALLS})/\text{MAXCALL}] - \text{LENGTH}\} \tag{4}$$
$$B = 3A(\text{MAXLENGTH}) \tag{5}$$
$$C = A(\text{MAXLENGTH})/(\text{MAXCALL}) \tag{6}$$
$$D = B(\text{Marg}) - \text{TRCOST} \tag{7}$$
$$E = \text{Square root of } [D^2 + 12A(\text{Marg})(\text{CTCOST})] \tag{8}$$

As a result, estimating the optimal total contact time [(NCALLS*) (LENGTH*)] that must be spent on a typical account of a given segment is straightforward.

Note that although managerial judgements about MAXCALLSALES are not necessary for estimating the different parameters, they can be used as validation checks in order to ensure that the various estimates (from the other judgements) are consistent with this value. These estimates have been used in equation (1) in order to assess the maximum sales results that can be expected under a maximum call policy (MAXCALL, MAXLENGTH). These estimates were compared with direct managerial judgements. The two sets of values were judged close enough to accept the parameter estimates as valid.

Optimal sales force size

Now that an optimal call policy can be established for every typical account in each segment, applying the workload approach is straightforward: the total optimal workload that is necessary for covering the whole territory can be estimated by summing up the total calling time required by every segment. The optimal sales force size (N*) can be estimated by dividing the total optimal workload by the typical contact time workload that can be reasonably expected from a salesperson ((TIME) (Contact)). In this context, a salesperson's available contact time is defined as a salesperson's total working time less the time required for the accomplishment of all non-selling activities that cannot be directly attributed to specific accounts (such as training, learning about new products, etc.).

The implemented solution

The recommendation to management was not to make such a drastic change of its sales force size, at least in the short run. Other considerations needed to be taken into account alongside the analysis. For instance, could the firm supply such a large demand increase without altering its production capacity? If not, was the investment required to meet this increased demand warranted by the additional revenue? Management would need to address such questions before increasing its sales force size substantially. These results, however, clearly pointed at the direction in which the ESC should move. It clearly highlights the opportunity to increase profit through proper sales force size increases.

Following this analysis, management decided to increase the sales force from 61 to 80 salespeople. In practice, the firm was able to recruit only 76 salespeople the first year. Because the implemented solution was still pretty far from the estimated optimal solution, the question arose as to what optimal call norm should be applied to each customer segment. The problem needed to be reformulated as determining the call policies that maximize profits (equation 1 aggregated over segments) under a total sales force size constraint (N = 76). In addition, management decided not to provide salespeople with new directives concerning the length of calls, but rather concentrate on implementing a new norm for the average number of calls to be given to accounts in each segment. The solution to this problem (see details in the Appendix) is given in the two right-hand columns of Table 9.4. It shows that the number of calls to key accounts was to be increased only slightly (from 22.3 to 23.9), slightly decreased for medium-sized accounts (from 5.8 to 4.9), and increased for small accounts (from 1.4 to 1.8). Under this (deliberate) sub-optimal decision, sales could be expected to increase by 71 per cent and net profits by 40 per cent. One year later, sales and profit increases were very much in line with what the model had forecast for such a sales force increase.

Generalization to other similar situations

The optimal sales force sizing method that has been applied to the ESC case can be applied to firms that share similar characteristics, especially when:

1. The market is made up of a certain number of actual and potential accounts that can be classified into several segments that are sufficiently homogeneous in terms of their responses to salespeople's time and effort. The proposed procedure has been

designed for situations in which firms have a relatively large number of accounts and potential customers that can be grouped into a few customer response categories (or segments). It is up to management to judge how many segments should be considered, through application of a parsimony principle: management should stop dividing the market into more segments when it is felt that the increased precision that will result from the additional split does not warrant the cost (in terms of managerial time and decreased judgement validity) of the additional number of parameters to be estimated.

2. Some interaction between the number of calls and the typical call time is expected. In other words, the same time spent on a client may yield somewhat different results if it is spent as a few lengthy calls or as numerous short calls.

3. A suitable call policy is considered to consist of a certain number of calls to each account in a segment (possibly none), each call being of the same duration. Although this is an oversimplification, this should not significantly distort the final results. In practice, it will always be impossible to follow a strict policy about the number and length of calls to be given to different accounts, and any attempt to predict in advance which call pattern will be actually followed for every account is doomed to failure. The most useful practical rules that can be devised are call norms for each type of account. This is why the procedure may not provide strictly optimal call patterns, but call norms that are close to optimal.

4. Every call to an account is assumed to require a trip to that account, and the cost of a trip to a given account is constant. Some customer contacts are sometimes made through the phone or by email, but such calls have a limited objective (such as providing some missing information, inquiring about a decision or making an appointment). Generally, they do not replace the need for a face-to-face call. As a result, such contacts may be considered as one part of a face-to-face call, and their length should be included in the time length of face-to-face calls.

Advantages and limitations

The proposed procedure for estimating the proper sales force size has a number of advantages as well as some limits.

Advantages

The method outlined in this chapter has at least four advantages.

1. It combines the simplicity of the workload method and the elegance of the response function approach to sales effort sizing and allocation. It is very simple to apply and explain to management. Non-analytical staff can use it. It requires only hard data typically available to Sales Managers and a very few judgemental estimates from management. The combination of hard and judgemental data is known to provide the best results for estimating sales force decision models (Zoltners et al. 2001). In fact, the procedure also has the advantage of requiring the involvement of managers at every stage: for finding an adequate segmentation basis, for estimating and validating parameter values and for validating the results.

2. The model provides very valuable a guideline to salespeople for an adequate call policy for accounts in every segment of the market. The guideline specifies not only the number of calls per period of time, but also of the desired length of calls. In a pharmaceutical detailing situation, this could be the optimal number of mentions of a product that should be made during a typical sales call.

3. The proposed method is flexible and can be applied in more restrictive cases. For instance, for those companies that view their territories (and consequently their sales force size) as given, the problem is simpler than the general case addressed in this chapter. In many situations firms try to increase or decrease selling effort by adjusting sales force size increases or decreases and keeping the current territory design, as much as is feasible. Although this has the advantage of not disrupting the current territory configuration, this practice does not generally lead to the optimal allocation of the selling effort in the national market. Zoltners et al. (2004) suggest that their experience with a very large number of sales forces points to territory design as a major source of potential profit for many firms. In any case, such companies may apply the proposed procedure at the level of each territory. Note that in this case, when sales territories are heterogeneous, call norms are likely to vary for each territory. This may not always be an appealing feature.

4. The proposed procedure provides guidelines for designing optimally sized sales territories. As found by Sinha and Zoltners (2001), 55 per cent of territories (across a large number of situations) are too large or too small. In the present study, the optimal territory size implied by this procedure is a territory made up of an average of 1 to 2 key accounts, 6 to 7 medium-sized accounts and about 23 small accounts. Obviously, other considerations (such as salesperson competence and tenure, geographical spread of the accounts, etc.) must also be included in territory design decisions. Nevertheless, such guidelines should prove to be useful when realigning sales territories.

Limitations

The procedure also has a number of limitations that point to possible avenues for further development:

1. For several above mentioned reasons, the derived solution is not strictly speaking 'optimal'. Some simplifying assumptions have been made in order to keep the procedure as simple as possible. For instance, all accounts within one segment receive the same treatment. As can be expected, there is always variance within a segment. Increasing the number of segments can reduce this variance. Increasing the number of segments, however, involves increasing the number of judgements that managers must make (five per segment) and may have an adverse effect on the quality and validity of the various parameter estimates. As a result, management should always consider the trade-off between splitting the customer base into more and more homogeneous segments versus the burden of increasing the number of required managerial estimates and more lengthy data manipulation. More research is needed in order to provide management with guidelines for selecting the best trade-off.

2. Uncertainties affecting sales responses to selling effort are not taken into account. This has been omitted on the grounds that sales force sizing is a decision that should remain stable over a certain planning horizon and should not take into account short-term random environmental variations. This question, however, remains to be formally investigated.
3. As with all published methods, this one does not take into account the sales force turnover factor.

In spite of these possible refinements, the benefits of which remain to be demonstrated, the procedure outlined above has been demonstrated to be easy to implement and to provide actionable results.

Summary

To summarize, sales force sizing is certainly one of the most important neglected sources of potential increase in sales force performance. Practical methods for determining sales force size range from rule of thumb to methods that are based on the workload determinant and highly sophisticated methods that estimate the market response to selling effort. The former simple methods are not satisfactory because they often lack theoretical grounds. The latter methods are generally theoretically sound, but they are frequently too complex and analytically involved to be fully understood and implemented by management. Most market response to effort sales force sizing methods rely on a mixture of hard objective data and managerial judgements to provides the most accurate results. Such managerial judgements are likely to be more reliable when they refer to micro units (account, sales territory, etc.) rather than macro units (product line, market segments, etc.). In this chapter, a simpler procedure that attempts to capitalize on the simplicity of the workload approach and the rigor of the market response to selling effort approach has been used to address a sales force sizing problem. This simple procedure is summarized in Table 9.6.

Table 9.6 Outline of the proposed optimal sales force sizing procedure

Step 1
With the help of knowledgeable managers, segment the customer base into a set of homogeneous segments (in terms of size and/or responses to salespeople's selling effort). For each segment, estimate from call reports:

- The average number of calls actually made during a calling period
- The typical length of such calls, in hours
- The average sales volume expected during a calling period, in euros
- The gross margin rate on those accounts, in decimal form
- The travelling cost to an account and cost of a time unit of contact time for each segment, in euros
- The average number of customer contact hours available to a salesperson during a call period

Table 9.6	(Continued)

Step 2

For each segment, secure five judgemental estimates from management:

- The maximum call frequency
- The maximum call length, in hours
- The minimum call length, in hours
- The sales level expected from a typical segment account, under a no call policy, in dollars
- The expected sales level under a maximum call policy, in euros

Step 3

For each segment, estimate five parameters from the above data and validate them with extra managerial judgements, using the formulae (4–8)

Estimate the optimal call policies (NCALL*, LENGTH*), by means of simple formulae (2–3). The product (NCALL*)(LENGTH*) is the time required for servicing a client in a given segment.

Step 4

Follow the same procedures as in Steps 4 and 5 of the workload approach (Table 9.1).

Key points

1. Many sales forces are systematically understaffed. Several things contribute to this situation:

   a) Sales Managers often emphasize short-term rather than long-term objectives, which generally translates into sales force understaffing.
   b) Instead of risking overstaffing their sales forces, which results in highly visible direct costs, managers often prefer not to bring the sales force to its optimal level, which would give them the advantage of opportunity gains. This at best results in questionable improved performance.
   c) Managers must deal with significant turnover rates but, for the same reasons as above, tend to be very conservative in their recruiting policies.

2. Five factors determine sales force size:

   a) the firm's orientation concerning its selling objective horizon;
   b) the workload required to fulfill sales objectives;
   c) the sales force staffing activities of the firm;
   d) the sales force structure and organization;
   e) the sales force turnover rate.

   Sales force size has a major impact upon sales performance.

3. While there are many methods for estimating sales force size, the method presented is designed around a number of basic principles such as requiring data typically available to Sales Managers and relying on few managerial judgement estimates, as well as involving management input at every stage.

Appendix: optimal call norms at the account category level

A firm's sales and profits can be expressed as:

$$SALES = NOCALLSALES + B(LENGTH)(NCALLS) - C(LENGTH)(NCALLS)^2$$
$$- A(NCALLS)(LENGTH)^2$$
$$PROFIT = (Marg)(SALES) - (CTCOST)(NCALLS)$$
$$- (CTCOST)(NCALLS)(LENGTH) \tag{A.1}$$

Because a maximum call/maximum length policy should yield the maximum response from a client, and from the very definitions of MAXCALL and MAXLENGTH, the partial derivatives of the sales function (1) with respect to MAXCALL and MAXLENGTH should be equal to zero, which leads to:

$$B = 3A \ (MAXLENGTH) \quad \text{and} \quad C = A \ (MAXLENGTH)/(MAXCALL) \tag{A.2}$$

Replacing B and C by their values as a function of A (equation A.2), in the sales equation (1), and recognizing that one point of this function is known (AVSALES, NCALLS, LENGTH) yields an estimate for A:

$$A = (AVSALES - NOCALLSALES)/\{(NCALLS)(LENGTH) - [3MAXLENGTH -$$
$$(MAXLENTH)(NCALLS)/MAXCALL] - LENGTH\} \tag{A.3}$$

This value of A can be used for estimating the B and C values.

The conditions for maximizing profits are found by equating the partial derivatives of the profit function (2) with respect to the optimal NCALL* and LENGTH* values to zero and solving for these two values. This leads to the following estimates:

$$NCALLS^* = (2D - E)/3C(Marg) \quad \text{and} \tag{A.4}$$
$$LENGTH^* = (D + E)/6A(Marg) \tag{A.5}$$

where $D = B \ (Marg) - TRCOST$ and $E = $ Square root of $[D^2 + 12 \ A \ (Marg) \ (CTCOST)]$. As a result, estimating the optimal total contact time [(NCALLS*) (LENGTH*)] that must be spent on a typical account of a given segment is straightforward.

When the sales force size is given, the optimal call policy (NCALLS*, LENGTH*) is the solution of this profit maximization problem under constraints: Maximize total profits are subject to (1) the sales force size and (2) the optimal call number and length in any segment falling within the possible range. This problem is solved through standard optimization procedures by applying the Kuhn-Tucker conditions.

References

Beswick, C.A. and Cravens, D.W. (1977) 'A Multi-Stage Decision Model for Sales Force Management', *Journal of Marketing Research*, 14 (2), 135–44.

Darmon, René Y. (2002) 'Salespeople's Management of Customer Information: Impact on Optimal Territory and Sales Force Sizes', *European Journal of Operational Research*, 137 (1): 162–76.

Darmon, René Y. (2004) 'Controlling Sales Force Turnover Costs through Optimal Recruiting and Training Policies', *European Journal of Operational Research*, 154 (1): 291–303.

Horsky, D. and Nelson, P. (1996) 'Evaluation of Salesforce Size and Productivity through Efficient Frontier Benchmarking', *Management Science*, 15 (4): 301–20.

Little, John D.C. (1970) 'Models and Managers: The Concept of a Decision Calculus', *Management Science*, 16 (8): B466–85.

Lodish, L.M. (1975) 'Sales Territory Alignment to Maximize Profits', *Journal of Marketing Research*, 12 (1): 30–6.

Lodish, L.M., Curtis, E., Ness, M. and Simpson, M.K. (1988) 'Sales Force Sizing and Development Using a Decision Calculus Model at Syntex Laboratories', *Interfaces*, 18 (1): 5–20.

Lucas, H.C., Weinberg, C.B. and Clowes, K. (1975) 'Sales Response as a Function of Territory Potential and Sales Representative Workload', *Journal of Marketing Research*, 12 (3): 298–305.

Misra, S., Pinker, E.J. and Shumsky, R.A. (2004) 'Salesforce Design with Experience-based Learning', *IIE Transactions*, 36 (10): 941–56.

Rangaswamy, A., Sinha, P. and Zoltners, A.A. (1990) 'An Integrated Model-based Approach for Sales Force Structuring', *Marketing Science*, 9 (4): 279–98.

Semlow, W.J. (1959) 'How Many Salesmen Do You Need?' *Harvard Business Review*, 37 (5/6): 126–32.

Sengupta, S. (1996) 'Study: Too Many Sales Accounts Spoil the Profits', *Marketing News*, 29 July: 15.

Sinha, P. and Zoltners, A.A. (2001) 'Sales-force Decision Models: Insight from 25 Years of Implementation', *Interfaces*, 31 (3): Part 2, S8–44.

Skiera, B. and S. Albers (1998) 'COSTA: Contribution Optimizing Sales Territory Alignment', *Marketing Science*, 17 (3): 196–213.

Wienberg, C.B. and Lucas, H. C. (1977) 'Letter to the Editor', *Journal of Marketing*, 41 (2): 147.

Zoltners, A.A. and Sinha, P. (1980) 'Integer Programming Models for Sales Resource Allocation', *Management Science*, 26 (3): 242–60.

Zoltners, A. A. and Sinha, P. (1983) 'Sales Territory Alignment: A Review and Model', *Management Science*, 29 (11), 1237–1256.

Zoltners, A.A., Sinha, P. and Lorimer, S.E. (2004) *Sales Force Design for Strategic Advantage*. New York: Palgrave Macmillan.

Zoltners, A.A., Sinha, P. and Zoltners, G.A. (2001) *The Complete Guide to Accelerating Sales Force Performance*, Chapter 3. New York: American Management Association.

Further reading

Ahearne, M. and Rapp, A. (2010) 'The Role of Technology at the Interface between Salespeople and Consumers', *Journal of Personal Selling and Sales Management*, 30 (2): 111–20.

Ferrell, L., Gonzalez-Padron, T. L. and Ferrell, O.C. (2010) 'An Assessment of the Use of Technology in the Direct Selling Industry', *Journal of Personal Selling and Sales Management*, 30 (2): 157–66.

Onyemah, V., Swain, S. D. and Hanna, R. (2010) 'A Social Learning Perspective on Sales Technology Usage: Preliminary Evidence from an Emerging Economy,' *Journal of Personal Selling and Sales Management*, 30 (2): 131–142.

Zoltners, A.A. and Lorimer, S.E. (2000) 'Sales Territory Alignment: An Overlooked Productivity Tool', *Journal of Personal Selling and Sales Management*, 20 (3): 139–50.

10

International selling

John Wilkinson

Contents

Learning objectives

After reading this chapter, you should be able to:

- Explain the complexity of international selling and sales management.
- Identify the challenges facing the international sales force.
- Explain how sales leadership needs to be adapted within international operations.
- Explain how globalization affects Key Account Management.

Chapter outline

This chapter will introduce readers to the different challenges and considerations encountered when faced with the issue of internationalizing one's selling efforts. The chapter is structured as follows. After illustrating the issues that this chapter will examine through the case history of an Australian company, and following a brief introduction, we will familiarize readers with a model of the international selling process. This process will then guide us through the different issues under consideration when thinking about internationalizing the sales effort. Next we will shed light on the different options of foreign market entry and discuss their advantages and disadvantages. Following this, managerial and leadership considerations are highlighted, with specific emphasis on cultural and ethical questions. A second case study concludes the chapter.

Selling alumina and aluminium to the world

Alcoa of Australia was formed in 1961 as a joint venture between the Aluminum Company of America (now Alcoa Inc.) and Western Mining Corporation (later renamed WMC Ltd and then demerged; renamed as Alumina Ltd, it now holds a 40 per cent stake in Alcoa of Australia). This joint venture followed the discovery of bauxite in the Darling mountain range in Western Australia. Alcoa of Australia now operates the world's largest integrated bauxite mining, alumina refining and aluminium smelting and rolling system. Its major facilities are in Western Australia, Victoria and New South Wales.

Alumina, obtained by refining bauxite in Western Australia, is used within the firm's smelters at Geelong and Portland in Victoria (which produce the metal aluminium) or is exported for use within smelters owned and operated overseas by other companies (including firms associated with the parent organization, Alcoa Inc.). Aluminium is used within the firm's semi-fabrication operations in Geelong, Victoria and Sydney, New South Wales, sold to other firms within Australia or exported to firms in various foreign markets. Most alumina and aluminium output is exported. The firm is therefore a large exporter, with about A\$5 billion in exports per year, equivalent to roughly 2 per cent of Australia's total exports.

Export selling operations during the 1970s and 1980s provide useful illustrations of large-scale export selling approaches within a business-to-business context. Then, as now, Alcoa of Australia exported much more alumina than aluminium. There were relatively few alumina customers, but individual customers (operating major smelters of their own) purchased very large volumes annually. A small export marketing and sales division within the firm's head office in Melbourne, Victoria was therefore established to undertake the firm's alumina export selling activities. The senior manager within this division reported directly to the firm's Marketing Director (who, in turn, reported directly to the firm's CEO).

In effect, the group operated as Key Account Managers, travelling to meet customers and prospects in different parts of the world to undertake negotiations or maintain business relationships. The CEO and other senior managers also participated in negotiations and customer relationship development activities at appropriate times.

This approach enabled the firm to maintain a high level of control over its selling efforts, important given the large size of individual alumina customers (all being multi-million dollar accounts). It also enabled effective external and internal communication and coordination, ensuring high levels of both operating efficiency and customer service. Employment of Key Account Managers and appropriate involvement of senior company management enabled direct access to decision-makers and other senior executives within customer organizations.

Aluminium exports were made to a much larger number of industrial customers, primarily within Asia. Individual accounts were much smaller than alumina accounts, few if any reaching the million dollar per year level . The firm therefore entered these export markets by appointing agents in them and employing an export salesperson in its Melbourne head office to liaise with the agents. This salesperson made regular sales trips to Asia, and was provided with export sales administration support within the Melbourne office.

By the early 1980s, following a major expansion of smelting operations in Geelong, aluminium exports had become a higher priority. By then the firm's export markets were clearly both essential and sustainable. Therefore, a sales office was opened in Hong Kong, focusing on aluminium exports throughout the Asia region. A senior Marketing Manager from head office in Melbourne was appointed as Sales Manager in Hong Kong, alongside the existing export salesperson. The firm provided generous financial packages to enable the families of both executives to move with them to Hong Kong, taking account of the high accommodation, education and leisure-related costs there. A small sales administration team, comprising local employees, was also established, reporting to the Sales Manager.

However, the firm continued to utilize agents in all aluminium markets, without any significant changes to existing channel arrangements relating to aluminium exports. The only difference was the close proximity of the firm's Key Account Management executives to its foreign markets. Importantly, that proximity provided tangible, visible evidence of the firm's increased commitment to its export customers – agents and end-users alike.

The firm also was able to respond more quickly to opportunities or problems by having its senior export sales executives based within Asia itself. It also had greater access to senior executives from its intermediaries and was able to arrange more joint sales calls with salespeople from them, ensuring more effective coordination of end-user account strategies and tactics – and providing more opportunities to motivate agents to focus on the Alcoa brand of aluminium.

The retention of agents enabled the firm to continue to provide extensive sales representation without having to commit to even higher levels of resourcing. Importantly, its use of local sales agents provided the firm with channel partners who had high levels of market knowledge and a sound understanding of local business culture.[1]

Introduction: the importance and complexity of international selling

From the journals: the changing global marketplace

> The accelerating pace of change spurred by advances in technology, communications, media, increased travel and interaction across national boundaries, is creating new economic, political and social realities. The growth of the internet is rapidly recasting existing business models and helping to shrink geographic distances, and so dramatically changing the structure of markets. Firms also face increasing intensity of competition from diverse sources and different parts of the world. As more and more firms enter global markets, competitive pressures mount and new sources of competition emerge from small and medium-sized companies, as well as firms from the newly industrialized and emerging market countries. The task of managing international operations is becoming increasingly complex. Management has to direct, coordinate and control operations on a much broader and diverse geographic scale and often also broader in scope. While technological advances aid in this task, management has to master new tools and develop the skills required to handle global operations.
>
> (Douglas 2000, p. 381)[2]

International marketing has become increasingly important and complex over the last 30 to 40 years due to increasing globalization, resulting from changes such as those

---

[1] Adapted from http://www.alcoa.com/australia/en/info_page/australia_overview.asp, retrieved on 1 August 2009; and personal experience of the author with Alcoa of Australia during 1979–84.
[2] Reproduced with permission.

identified in the extract quoted above. Those changes have also had a major influence on the role of personal selling within an international context. There are risks and uncertainties facing firms moving beyond their domestic borders into foreign markets (Calantone and Knight 2000) and the complexity, risks and turbulent change (Marshall et al. 1998) within international markets require those involved in international selling to plan and manage their activities thoroughly.

Not surprisingly, researchers and other writers have suggested that management of international selling operations is a challenging task. Specific issues with potential difficulties include differences in culture, language and negotiation styles, and the international political setting, which in turn affect the development of trust and buyer-seller relationships (Lewin and Johnston 1997). Ethnic differences are likely to result in differences in business and buyer behaviour in different geographic markets (Rossiter and Chan 1998). Substantial variations in business ethics between different countries are likely to mean challenges for international salespeople (Wood 1995). At the organizational level, senior management must consider issues such as the structure of the international salesforce and the relative advantages of centralized versus local control (Marshall et al. 1998).

The international selling process

For the purpose of this discussion, a general model of the business-to-business selling process is illustrated in Figure 10.1. The selling process comprises three phases. First, 'identification of new business opportunities' involves prospecting (including sourcing of referrals from satisfied customers), initial contact with prospects and the qualifying of those prospects, assessment of the needs of qualified prospects and identification of solutions for those needs. This phase includes analysis of reasons for failure to obtain any business from a prospect or for the loss of an existing customer. It also includes assessment of further opportunities with existing customers (prior to identification of solutions for those additional needs). Second, 'persuasion' involves presentation of the company's offerings in an appropriate manner, participation in negotiations and closing the sale if at all possible. Third, 'relationship management' involves ensuring that the firm meets or exceeds customer expectations in the delivery of its product and customer service, follow-up and relationship building, evaluation and control of company supply performance and updating of customer information to facilitate subsequent account management activities. It includes analysis of the reasons for failure to obtain additional business from an existing customer.

Many steps within the selling process are likely to be challenging for export salespeople entering foreign markets, especially if those markets are very different from their home markets. Several steps are likely to be challenging for salespeople based in foreign markets, whether those salespeople are recruited locally or within the firm's home country. Some steps are likely to be challenging for salespeople within global firms that have extensive operations in various markets throughout the world (rather than just sales offices in 'foreign' markets).

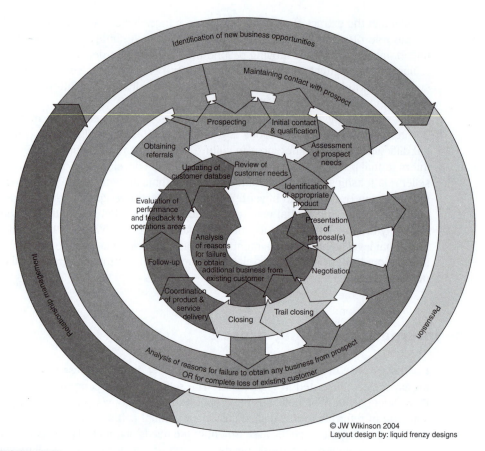

© JW Wikinson 2004
Layout design by: liquid frenzy designs

Figure 10.1 Framework of the business-to-business selling process
Source: Wilkinson (2004).

Identification of new business opportunities, especially prospecting and related steps, are likely to be more arduous for salespeople having to travel from their home country to foreign markets, especially if those markets are distant. For complex industrial products, technical experts often participate in the identification of customer needs and appropriate product offerings, perhaps through joint sales calls. Such participation is expensive and difficult to arrange within foreign markets.

In the second phase of the selling process, account executives operating in their *home* countries are often assisted by Sales Managers during presentations of sales proposals to major customers or prospects and during subsequent negotiations and attempts to close those sales. Similarly, technical experts often assist in major presentations involving complex products or applications. Again, such participation is expensive and difficult to arrange within *foreign* markets. Finally, coordination, follow-up and other relationship management activities are often more difficult for international salespeople to undertake, either because they are based in foreign markets at a distance from the home operations of their firms, or because they are based in the home country and have infrequent contact with their customers.

Foreign market entry

The 'market entry mode' is the approach used by a firm to access or reach customers when entering a foreign market – which could take up to four or five years to complete (Ekeledo and Sivakumar 2004). There are various foreign market entry options, some of which are briefly discussed below.

Foreign market entry options

Indirect exporting involves the use of an intermediary sales organization based in the firm's home country (such as an export agent) to sell its products within the foreign market. Such an approach requires little resource involvement by the firm since there is no need to develop an export department or international salesforce. However, the approach provides almost no control over export activities.

Direct exporting involves the use of the firm's own salesforce, rather than an intermediary based in its home country. The firm could employ export salespeople, based within the home office, who would travel regularly to the foreign market, either as their sole responsibility or in addition to domestic sales responsibilities. Alternatively, it could locate its salespeople in the foreign market, and would need to decide between local recruitment (in the foreign market) or the transfer of salespeople from its home country to the foreign market.

With direct exporting, the firm can sell directly to end-users or use local intermediaries (based in the foreign market) to reach end-users. (This option is equivalent to the use of a two-level distribution channel within the firm's home market.) In the latter approach, the firm needs to recruit intermediaries in the foreign market capable of providing adequate market coverage and willing to focus on the firm's products. This requires identification of the operational needs of the intermediary, provision of appropriate support to address those needs and continuing efforts to develop and maintain effective relationships with the intermediary (Lewin and Johnston 1997). Typically, an Account Manager will visit the foreign intermediary reasonably regularly and, possibly, make joint sales calls to major accounts with salespeople from the intermediary. Such visits would assist in relationship development, and provide the Account Manager with improved knowledge of the foreign market and competitive conditions as well as of the intermediary's performance.

Direct exporting provides the firm with greater control over its selling efforts than indirect exporting and enables the development of closer relationships with customers. Conversely, it increases resourcing requirements, risk and exit costs (should the firm later decide to withdraw from the particular foreign market). For this reason, firms that select direct exporting as an entry mode often initially use export salespeople based in the home country. Later, if exports to that market reach reasonably high levels and appear to be sustainable, the appointment of salespeople based within the foreign market is considered.

Licensing and franchising involves the firm allowing another firm to produce and market its goods or services, using its brand name, patents, business model, processes and technology in return for royalty payments and other fees. This form of market entry requires lower levels of resource commitment than direct investment but also provides lower levels of control. Success in the foreign market requires commitment from the local partner. There also is a potential risk of the firm's brand image being tarnished through inappropriate actions by the licensee or franchisee.

Equity joint venture involves the firm establishing a new entity in the foreign market in partnership with another organization (often a local firm). These partnerships provide the firm with greater control within the foreign market than normally available through licensing and franchising. The involvement of a local partner usually overcomes barriers in some countries regarding the establishment of wholly-owned subsidiaries by foreign firms. The local partner usually also has good knowledge of the local market. Selling within the foreign market would normally be undertaken by a salesforce within the joint venture organization.

Establishment of a *wholly-owned subsidiary* in the foreign market involves the highest levels of investment and risk. However, it also provides the firm with complete control over business and marketing decisions relating to the foreign market. Selling within the foreign market is usually undertaken by a salesforce within the subsidiary organization.

The structure of an international salesforce is clearly influenced by the market entry modes selected in different foreign markets. Some entry modes require no change to sales operations, others require the use of international salespeople, while still others require salespeople working within a local subsidiary organization.

Of course, the initial structure might change in response to later changes made by the firm regarding its foreign operations. For example, a firm might enter a foreign market through direct exporting, initially using international salespeople based in the home country. However, once that market becomes established and appears to be sustainable, the firm might set up a wholly-owned subsidiary in that market, with local marketing and production autonomy. With that change, the previous international salespeople will probably be replaced by salespeople recruited by the new subsidiary, reporting to local management.

The appropriate market entry option depends on a range of internal and external factors, including the following (Cateora and Graham 2007; Root 1994):

Internal factors

- product characteristics;
- company resources and other commitments;
- company expertise in international marketing.

External factors

Home market factors
- government and institutional export infrastructure;
- legal and political factors, including those relating to international business.

Foreign market factors
- economic factors, including availability, quality and cost of labour and other resources;
- legal and political factors, including those relating to international business;
- socio-cultural factors;

- institutional channel infrastructure and availability of partners;
- market size, structure and buyer behaviour characteristics;
- the level and nature of competition, including imports.

Foreign market entry decision-making

There are important sales management issues to consider when first entering a foreign market. Should the firm engage intermediaries or resellers to reach potential customers in those markets, or use its own salesforce? If the latter option is selected, should company salespeople be based within the foreign market or travel periodically from the home office to that market? If salespeople are based within the foreign market, should they be recruited locally or transferred from the home office?

Similar questions arise with respect to Sales Managers, as well as potential issues regarding cross-cultural aspects of salesperson recruitment and sales management.

Of course, some of these will depend on corporate level decisions regarding such issues as which foreign markets to enter, which market entry mode to adopt in each market and what marketing mix to offer in each market. A framework for the foreign market entry decision-making process is illustrated in Figure 10.2. The process includes, *inter alia*, decision-making about identification and selection of the most appropriate foreign markets to enter and the most appropriate market entry mode for each selected market.

A firm planning to enter a foreign market could use salespeople to assist in market evaluation and market entry planning. Information gathering could occur in stages, with several visits being made to obtain information, establish relationships, plan a product launch and so forth. Initial visits could focus on confirming secondary research data. Subsequent visits could 'flesh out' information gathered during the initial visit, so that an informed decision is possible on how to enter the market. Once that decision is made, the focus could shift to the selection of channel partners – agents, distributors or joint venture partners. Further visits could start the process of relationship-building between the firm and its customers, distributors and other partners.

One means of gaining an initial overview of a foreign market is to participate in trade shows or government-sponsored business missions to a country. Trade shows assist firms in identifying prospects and gathering competitor information (Kalaignanam et al. 2008). Business missions are organized by government departments and involve a group of business people, possibly from a particular industry, visiting a country in the company of a government minister or other senior government representative.

Different entry modes provide different levels of control, but also have different levels of associated risk, as illustrated in Figure 10.3. Entry mode decision-making therefore includes an evaluation of the degree of control and the level of risk related to each option (Tihanyi et al. 2005). Market entry modes involving only personal selling and other forms of marketing, such as exporting, franchising and licensing, have the lowest levels of risk since these entry modes require the lowest levels of resource commitment. Franchising and licensing also provide means of avoiding import barriers in foreign markets, without the need to undertake direct investment.

On the other hand, market entry through joint ventures and wholly-owned subsidiaries require greater levels of investment and associated risk. Joint ventures provide

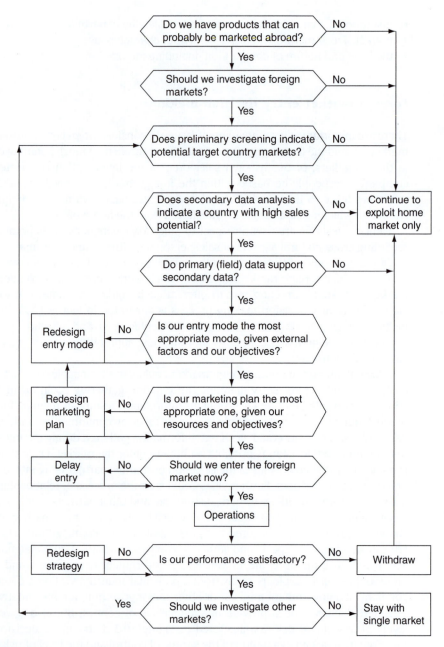

Figure 10.2   Framework for the foreign market entry decision-making process
Source: Root (1994, p. 42); reproduced with permission.

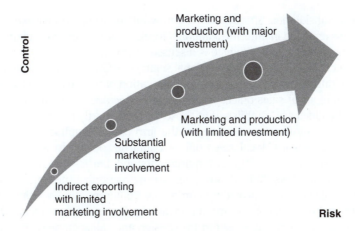

Figure 10.3 Control and risk associated with market entry mode
Source: Adapted from Mühlbacher et al. (2006, p. 415); reproduced with permission.

greater control than exporting, franchising and licensing options, and risk is somewhat reduced if a local partner with good market knowledge is involved. Market entry
via the establishment of a wholly-owned subsidiary provides the highest level of control, but also requires the highest level of investment and has the highest level of
associated risk.

Organizing and managing the international selling effort

The firm must decide whether to use its own salesforce or intermediaries, or a combination of these two options. (Note that the assignment of salespeople to foreign markets
does not necessarily remove the need for intermediaries, as illustrated by Alcoa of
Australia.) Different channel arrangements may be appropriate for different categories
of customer, as with such differences in the home market. Factors relevant to the home
market – such as selling costs, market coverage and knowledge, and control – also
apply within foreign markets, as well as issues discussed above regarding foreign market entry. Factors regarding costs, market coverage and knowledge typically favour the
use of intermediaries, especially if the foreign market is culturally and geographically
distant to the firm's home market. Conversely, control of selling operations is more
difficult when moving from home to foreign markets and using intermediaries.

The firm also needs to decide whether to base its international salesforce in its home
office, in regional sales offices or in sales offices in specific markets (possibly within
each country). Different arrangements could be adopted by the same firm in different product markets, as with Alcoa of Australia. Arrangements will probably evolve
over time, initial indirect exporting through foreign intermediaries, for instance, eventually being replaced by direct exporting through the firm's own salesforce (Lewin and
Johnston 1997). Of course, if the firm has established subsidiary operations in various countries around the world, it will usually have local sales organizations within

those subsidiaries. Strictly, such a firm would no longer undertake *international* selling, unless engaged in entering *additional* foreign markets or undertaking a Global Account Management strategy (which is discussed below).

Decisions regarding international selling operations are also influenced by corporate decisions regarding issues such as the location of production and logistics facilities. For example, local sales offices are likely to be located within foreign markets if production facilities are established in those markets, partly to enable effective and efficient internal coordination. Similarly, if the firm places emphasis on customer service for strategic reasons, local sales offices could be located in foreign markets to ensure responsiveness to customer requirements and, perhaps, to demonstrate commitment to those markets. Indeed, some firms now recognize the importance of the international salesforce in providing competitive differentiation within commodity markets (Cravens et al. 2006). In turn, the location of sales offices affects sales leadership and management control, sales territory design and salesperson recruitment, selection and training.

Other corporate issues are also likely to influence the design of international selling operations. In particular, various researchers and other writers have argued that multinational firms cannot continue to compete effectively as a group of autonomous subsidiaries since international competition increasingly requires firms to integrate their worldwide operations (Trautmann et al. 2009). Firms operating in various markets around the world through subsidiary organizations need to integrate at least their Key Account Management operations so as to enable effective coordination of sales activities as global accounts (as discussed below).

The globalization of business has another impact on firms operating in various countries. It has been argued that firms require a *global* view of likely future competitive and market developments. This will require them to undertake effective 'market sensing' on a global basis (Cravens et al. 2006). Clearly, a firm's worldwide salesforce will have a major role in obtaining information about major customers, markets and competitors on a global basis. However, this will require global coordination of relevant information-gathering activities of the salesforce.

The internet has also had an impact on international selling. In particular, it has assisted in the development of inter-company networks across the world, aimed at achieving greater effectiveness and efficiency in the delivery of products (especially services) and customer service. A typical international airline alliance provides an illustration of such networks, involving separate airline sales organizations cooperating to ensure successful customer interactions on a global basis (Cravens et al. 2006).

Sales leadership issues

Recruitment and selection of *Sales Managers* depend upon the form of international selling and, therefore, the required attributes of the international Sales Managers. For example, local candidates may be sought if the sales office is to be located in the foreign market, while candidates from the home country might be more appropriate if export salespeople are to be based in the home office. Induction, continuing management training and mentoring of Sales Managers will be affected by the recruitment and selection approach. These factors should be considered carefully, since prior research indicates that Sales Managers often have major gaps in their management training (Anderson et al. 1997; Shepherd and Ridnour 1995; Wilkinson 2005). Recruitment, selection and induction of *salespeople* also depend upon the form of international selling adopted by the firm.

Since international salespeople often make customer visits on their own, they should have expert knowledge of their products and should be able to use established contacts to develop new prospects and customers, plan sales activities, deliver effective sales presentations, develop effective relationships with customers and adapt their selling approaches from one customer to another. Additional expertise is necessary for those international salespeople (and their Sales Managers) whose firms are broadening their involvement in foreign markets. The diversity of markets resulting from such an expansion strategy requires international salespeople (including Sales Managers) to be flexible and able to adapt their selling activities to the different needs of customers in a widening range of foreign markets. Export Sales Managers in those firms need to consider the costs and risks involved in simultaneously pursuing prospective sales opportunities in many different markets. They also need to ensure that their salespeople place emphasis on identifying and understanding the range of customer needs in those diverse markets (Katsikea et al. 2005).

The activities of Sales Managers – comprising direction, facilitation, training, delegation, motivation, advice and guidance – need to take account of a range of issues, some depending upon the form of international selling. For example, if export salespeople, based in the home office but travelling regularly to foreign markets, are recruited from the home country, Sales Managers will need to ensure that they receive adequate training regarding cross-cultural factors. Sales Managers will also need to provide them with appropriate advice and guidance regarding cross-cultural issues. Of course, this implies that managers have the appropriate background or training themselves! Again, research suggests that there are gaps in the leadership support provided by many Sales Managers (Wilkinson 2009), and senior sales management within firms involved in international sales operations need to pay heed to this.

Organizational support for the salesforce is likely to be difficult to plan and implement if salespeople operate in markets far removed from functional areas that deliver this support. If travelling to foreign markets on their own, salespeople are isolated from other salespeople during the trips. Therefore, they cannot readily obtain support from their sales colleagues during their travels. Similarly, while away from the home office, it is difficult to explain complex customer- or sales-related issues to sales support staff or to staff in other functional areas of the firm.

If export salespeople normally travel on their own to foreign markets, the provision of leadership support is rather constrained during those visits. Provision of advice, guidance and short-term motivation are difficult when salespeople usually undertake sales visits on their own. It is even more difficult in such situations for Sales Managers to monitor salespeople's behavioural performance and, therefore, to analyse the reasons for their achievements or lack of success. Behaviour-based control (see Chapter 14), also becomes challenging in such situations.

It can also be difficult to remain fully informed of all external environmental factors, including sales territory factors, the competitive environment, customer buying behaviour and economic factors, when responsible for several foreign markets. So Sales Managers might provide inadequate advice and guidance relating to the impact of such factors, especially if their salesforce covers many foreign markets. This could be serious given the major external environmental differences between some countries. For example, there is a 'well-established network of buyer–supplier relationships' within the Japanese industrial market (Ellis et al. 2001). If not understood by sales management and explained to export salespeople from the firm's home office, the salespeople are unlikely to operate effectively within that market.

Occasionally, sales offices are established within foreign markets and staffed by local salespeople and support staff, but managed by Sales Managers transferred from the home office – perhaps due to concerns about the ability of locally recruited Sales Managers fully to understand the firm's sales strategies. Initially, these newly appointed Sales Managers are likely to lack adequate understanding of local culture to adopt the most appropriate leadership style or to command high levels of respect from their staff. Therefore, their ability to provide effective sales leadership is likely to be hampered until, through experience and training, they develop sufficient understanding of local issues.

Some specific sales leadership issues are discussed further in the following sections.

Recruitment and training

If the firm decides to employ its own international salespeople, it needs to consider the following recruitment and training options in addition to those described in Chapters 11 and 12:

- *Assignment of existing salespeople to the foreign market, still based in the home office but travelling periodically to the foreign market.* These salespeople might lack experience in international selling and, therefore, might need training in international issues. If these international salespeople continue to report to Sales Managers for whom the home market remains the major priority, then management of these salespeople can be challenging. (This might occur when there are only a few international salespeople, for whom a dedicated international Sales Manager cannot be justified.) In this situation, regular joint sales visits to foreign markets by Sales Managers often cannot be arranged because of time constraints. In any case, such Sales Managers often lack international experience themselves. Consequently, little or no coaching is provided regarding international selling activities.
- *Assignment and relocation of existing salespeople to the foreign market.* Depending on the scale of operation, this option could be associated with the appointment and relocation of a Sales Manager to the foreign market. Again, the salespeople and Sales Manager might have no experience in international selling and, therefore, might need substantial training in international issues. Due to the investment requirement, this option is more appropriate during foreign market development than at market entry.
- *Recruitment of salespeople from within the foreign market (to be based in that market).* Depending on the scale of operation, this option could be associated with the recruitment of a local Sales Manager for the foreign market, or the appointment and relocation of a Sales Manager from the home office. Locally recruited salespeople (and Sales Managers) will probably have good market knowledge but might lack

industry, company and product knowledge. Some company-specific training will be required, including a focus on the firm's marketing and selling strategies. A locally recruited Sales Manager will probably have a good understanding of management styles appropriate in that culture. Conversely, a Sales Manager relocated from the home office might have no experience in international selling and, therefore, might need substantial training in international issues, including management practices appropriate to the foreign culture. Again, due to the investment requirement, this option is more appropriate during foreign market development than at market entry.

If the firm adopts a Global Account Management strategy after its international operations are well established in various countries, then it will have to recruit senior sales executives to lead the global strategy or promote from within its worldwide sales organization to fill the roles. In either case, some form of training will probably be required – company-specific training, including a focus on the firm's marketing and selling strategies, for an external appointee, and Global Account Management training for an internal appointee. (See p. 268 for a detailed discussion of Global Account Management.)

Compensation and motivation

As discussed in Chapter 16, financial compensation is a major motivational factor for many salespeople. However, its effectiveness might vary throughout an international salesforce due to differences in compensation arrangements across countries (Rajagopal 2008).

Different people have different interests, needs and wants and, therefore, react differently to the same approaches to compensation and motivation. Broad differences in reward needs are likely to exist between some countries. Preferences regarding the nature and type of compensation programme (equal or equitable; fixed or variable; high or low incentive levels) are influenced by culture. In particular, there is evidence of a preference in some countries for more fixed (and, therefore, more certain) compensation arrangements than in other countries (Rouziès et al. 1999). For example, executives with an Anglo-Saxon background are more likely to prefer incentive-based compensation programmes than those with a Germanic background (Segalla et al. 2006). Not surprisingly, the proportion of total compensation paid in the form of a fixed salary varies widely across countries (Rouziès et al. 1999). Accordingly, it has been suggested that firms operating in different countries should adapt their compensation and motivation policies after identifying employees' needs and wants within each country (Lowe et al., 2002). Compensation policies of firms operating in various countries also need to take account of differences – sometimes very large – between national norms in compensation arrangements in different countries (Bloom et al. 2000). However, there is a countervailing argument, based on the experience of some multinational firms, that *similar* sales compensation programmes across a global firm might be more effective than *diverse* national programmes (Cravens et al. 2006).

If international salespeople need to travel frequently from their home country to one or more foreign markets, or are required to relocate to a foreign market, the inconvenience associated with such arrangements may require to be offset with additional compensation, especially if the salespeople have family commitments. Of course, relocations often involve a promotion (such as a senior salesperson being promoted to a sales management position in a foreign market). Relocations often require additional company expenditure if the needs of a sales executive's family are to be properly met (as illustrated in the Alcoa case).

In firms that are attempting to broaden or expand their involvement in foreign markets, international salespeople might devote a large proportion of their time to prospecting within a range of foreign markets. Given the nature of prospecting, especially in foreign markets, there is a high level of uncertainty associated with these efforts. Consequently, there may be long lead times before substantial sales volumes are achieved within those foreign markets. Compensation arrangements need to take account of this by having a high fixed salary component. In addition, international salespeople are often required to undertake non-selling activities to support foreign market expansion strategies, such as the collection of market and other information related to target markets. Again, such demands on the time of international salespeople suggest the use of mainly fixed compensation arrangements. Conversely, if firms aim to increase their international sales revenues by maximizing their market share within foreign markets in which they already operate, without entering other foreign markets, they should probably motivate their salesforce through incentive-based compensation arrangements so as to fully exploit market opportunities (Katsikea et al. 2005).

Monitoring and control

As already mentioned, there is often a major time-lag between selling effort and the achievement of sales results when firms attempt to expand their involvement in foreign markets. In such situations, it is therefore ineffective to monitor and control just through sales *results* (such as sales revenues achieved in foreign sales territories). Instead, it becomes necessary to undertake behaviour-based monitoring and control to ensure that appropriate activities are being undertaken effectively. This, in turn, requires Sales Managers to undertake reasonably regular joint sales visits to foreign markets with their international salespeople. Conversely, if a firm is aiming to increase market share within established foreign markets, with which its international salespeople are familiar, improved sales results are likely to be more directly related to increased selling effort. In such situations, it is more appropriate to use outcome-based performance monitoring and control.

Not surprisingly, research results confirm that firms following foreign market expansion strategies tend to utilize behaviour-based monitoring and control more often than outcome-based monitoring and control, while the reverse situation tends to be true for firms focusing on established foreign markets (Katsikea et al. 2005).

Account management

There is evidence that larger multinational firms are undertaking 'global sourcing', that is, 'the integration and coordination of procurement requirements across worldwide business units' (Gelderman and Semeijn 2006). Global Account Management has emerged in response to that situation.

Global sourcing

Global purchasing strategy comprises two components: the degree of centralization and the degree of standardization of purchasing. With respect to the second component, product standardization relates to the degree to which characteristics of a product being purchased are standardized throughout the firm. These characteristics include product specifications, quality standards and required after-sales service levels. Different levels of standardization might be appropriate in different buying situations or for different product categories. Product standardization also might depend on the marketing strategy of the company (Quintens et al., 2006).

Therefore, a firm aiming to sell to a global company that has adopted a global sourcing strategy needs to place greater emphasis on engagement with members of the buying centre within all functional areas of the customer organization (even including the marketing department). Global Account Management in such situations also requires use of *cross-functional* selling teams and, if relevant, effective coordination across its own global operations. In addition, the complexity and cross-functional nature of global sourcing means that international salespeople now also need a sound understanding of supply chain management (Dzever et al. 2001).

International sales management also needs to recognize that large firms undertaking global sourcing often have purchasing strategies consistent with the portfolio framework illustrated in Figure 10.4. The type of product being purchased (comprising high or low profit impact, and high or low risk for the customer organization) is likely to influence purchasing decisions and negotiations. Clearly, international salespeople should take account of such influences.

Even without a comprehensive global sourcing approach, firms with operations in several locations, whether in one or more countries, might arrange discussions between purchasing staff from those various locations to evaluate and select suppliers. The aim of such discussions would be to improve purchasing decision-making and supply terms (Woodside and Ferris-Costa 2008). Therefore, Key Account Management would need to ensure effective coordination of selling activities across all locations for each customer organization adopting such practices.

Whether or not adopting a global sourcing approach, those involved in purchasing (within purchasing departments and other functional areas) are likely to have greater concern about supply risks when dealing with foreign suppliers. These risks relate to

Profit impact	Risk Low	High
High	*Leverage items* exploit purchasing power	*Strategic items* form partnerships
Low	*Non-critical items* ensure efficient processing	*Bottleneck items* assure supply

Figure 10.4 The Kraljic purchasing portfolio framework
Source: Gelderman and Semeijn (2006, p. 211); reproduced with permission.

factors such as possible fluctuations in currency exchange rates, mistakes resulting from misunderstandings due to cultural differences and political instability within the supplier's country (Kotabe and Murray 2004). International salespeople need to be able to demonstrate high levels of supply reliability in such situations. They also need to be able to adapt to different business cultures so that they meet the social needs of potential buyers. In other words, international salespeople need to be able to 'connect with' buyers from different cultures in an effective manner.

Global Account Management

Chapter 3 has shown that there has been a trend during the past four decades towards Key Account Management in business-to-business selling generally. With respect to international selling, there has been an associated trend towards Global Account Management, which appears likely to continue.

Global Account Management has been defined as 'a collaborative process between a multinational customer and a multinational supplier by which the worldwide buying–selling activities are centrally coordinated between the two organizations' (Hui Shi et al. 2004). In effect, the role of a Global Account Manager (or global account sales team, perhaps) involves the coordination of the worldwide activities of the firm to ensure the needs of a particular global customer are met or exceeded (Sheth and Sharma 2008). Improved coordination of the supply relationship between global organizations should increase the effectiveness and efficiency of the supply operations and, therefore, improve the competitiveness of both firms.

Global Account Management is potentially complex. This complexity results from factors such as the scale of global operations requiring coordination and potential cultural differences between associate or subsidiary organizations in different regions of the world. Global Account Management is appropriate only if the customer organization:

- has global operations, although not necessarily in all countries;
- undertakes some form of global purchasing activities;
- values coordinated and consistent global supply arrangements;
- has strategic importance to the sales organization.

It requires involvement of senior company management, a high level of expertise in the area of supply chain management and an appropriate combination of global integration and local responsiveness (Wilson and Weilbaker 2004). In addition, development of consistent global sales management practices usually requires management intervention at the local level to modify existing practices (Cravens et al. 2006).

Research has suggested that there are three organizational structures that can be established when implementing a Global Account Management programme (Yip and Bink 2007). In the first option, the local sales organization within each market (or country, perhaps) retains substantial power. Global Account Management is introduced as an additional layer to the firm's sales organization (typically, within the firm's international head office), to coordinate local or national sales activities for each global customer and to ensure that local sales arrangements are consistent with global agreements. This option is appropriate when relationships at the local level are most important and the potential benefits from standardization are relatively minor.

In the second option, responsibility for a global customer is still shared between the Global Account Management group and local operations. However, the Global Account Management group has primary responsibility for the account and the Global Account Manager may enforce global agreements on local sales offices. Account executives at the local or national level often have a secondary reporting relationship to the Global Account Manager. This approach often involves the establishment of an informal global team to identify global opportunities and to coordinate the communication, relationship development and other aspects of account management. Team membership usually includes some local account executives and representatives of other functional areas (such as Manufacturing or Research and Development), as well as the Global Account Manager. Local employees devote only some of their time to involvement in such global teams. Of course, the greater depth of global coordination and planning adds to the account management costs.

In the third option, the firm establishes a separate department or division to manage global accounts, usually comprising all local account executives, customer support and technical support staff involved with global customers and prospects as well as the Global Account Management group at the international head office. The global division has the authority to access necessary company resources at the local level. This approach enables a completely coordinated approach to Global Account Management and, therefore, can result in very high levels of customer service. However, it requires major organizational restructuring for the firm and has the highest levels of complexity (for both the firm and its global customers) and account management costs. Not surprisingly, only a few firms have adopted this approach.

Special issues affecting international selling and sales management

Differences in culture

People in countries that are geographically close (such as Austria, Germany and Switzerland) or that have had substantial colonial ties (such as Australia, South Africa and the United Kingdom) and have a common language and religious heritage are likely to have similar values towards work. Thus, one can group countries with geographic (or territorial), language and religious proximity and expect similarities within each group with respect to work-related attitudes and values (Ronen and Shenkar 1985).

Differences in culture have implications for sales management. For example, in cultures with high levels of uncertainty avoidance, executives are likely to focus on risk reduction. In such cultures, variable pay arrangements (linked to performance) are likely to be less popular than in cultures with low levels of uncertainty avoidance (Segalla et al. 2006). International Sales Managers and salespeople thus need to be aware that their customers in different countries might have very different levels of risk avoidance. A person's social attributes and predispositions, such as the perception of trust, are influenced by their culture. For example, within the United States, trust is derived from written contracts, whereas honour is the basis of trust within Japanese culture. The individualism and competitive nature of North Americans perhaps explains the higher propensity of US executives to take risks and to display lower levels of cooperative behaviour; while Confucian principles explain the tendency of Chinese and Japanese executives to avoid risks, and the importance of 'saving face' explains the more conciliatory or cooperative behaviour of Chinese executives (Mintu-Wimsatt and Gassenheimer 1996). International salespeople must therefore take account of cultural differences between themselves and their customers, especially during initial meetings with prospects, presentation of proposals, negotiation, closing a sale and when asking customers to evaluate supply performance.

Ethical complexities

Chapter 6 describes how business behaviour is influenced by ethical standards, in addition to laws and regulations. Business ethics are influenced by religious, cultural, social, economic and institutional factors. Not surprisingly, therefore, significant differences have been found between firms in different countries with respect to their policies regarding business ethics (Scholtens and Dam 2007).

There are also differences between countries as a whole on various measures of ethical behaviour. For example:

> The level of corruption in India, as measured by the Corruption Perception Index (CPI), is higher than that in the United States. India's score on the CPI in 2005 was 2.9, whereas that of the United States was 7.1. The United States, in turn, is not as free from corruption as Singapore, which scored 9.4, or Finland, which scored 9.6.
>
> (Statman 2007)

It has been argued by 'ethical relativists' that morality is based on behavioural norms within a particular society at a given time and, therefore, that there are no universal moral standards applicable to all people at the same time. Such a view can justify different ethical standards being applied in different countries by the same firm, reflecting the diversity of cultures across those countries. It also suggests a need for change over time within a particular country as behavioural norms and related factors change in its society (Carrigan et al. 2005).

Export salespeople, especially those frequently travelling on their own to foreign markets, often have to work in isolation and, with little or no supervision while away from their home country, cope with cultural and language differences while working under pressure to meet sales quotas or targets. Responding to ethical issues that might arise while working with foreign customers becomes complicated by the differences in ethical norms in different cultures, so that salespeople become unable to refer to just their own ethical standards (Wood 1995). The potential problem is even greater for salespeople visiting several foreign markets with very different cultural norms and legal systems.

Globalization versus localization

Within international marketing, there are two strategic options with respect to entering and serving foreign markets: globalization and localization. Globalization involves a firm adopting the same marketing strategy in all markets (countries), as if the world constituted just one large market. It has been argued that this approach offers cost savings to the firm and enables improved marketing effectiveness through organizational learning – the firm transferring effective marketing strategies from one market to others (Wills et al. 1991). Conversely, localization involves developing a separate marketing strategy for each country (Ramarapu et al. 1999). While globalization has many supporters, critics argue that standardized products are often over-designed for some countries while being under-designed for others; that existing company–country networks risk being undermined by standardization practices; that standardization policies reduce the entrepreneurial character of marketing organizations; and that the development of global strategies does not necessarily lower costs (Wills et al. 1991).

An appropriate global strategy probably involves standardizing some components of marketing strategy when markets are somewhat similar with respect to their economies, socio-cultural factors, market characteristics (including preferences and level of sophistication), available channel partners and competitive pressures (Ramarapu et al. 1999).

With respect to international selling, the firm should probably consider starting with a common selling strategy in all foreign markets, but be prepared to alter components of the strategy in response to environmental factors in each market. Importantly, the firm should aim to transfer effective sales management and personal selling practices across all similar markets, perhaps adapting those practices in slightly different ones. As with globalization, generally there are likely to be groups of markets (or regions) in which there are sufficient environmental similarities to justify similar selling strategies. Salespeople operating within each region would benefit from some level of coordination and the sharing of information about the success of different approaches. Of course, if the firm adopts a Global Account Management policy, account management practices for each relevant customer will need to be coordinated (standardized) globally.

CASE PROBLEM

Sophisticated products for global niche markets

Codan Ltd designs, manufactures and markets a diverse range of high-value-added electronic products for government, business, aid and humanitarian, and sophisticated consumer markets. Founded in Adelaide, South Australia in 1959 and listed as a public company on the Australian Stock Exchange in 2003, Codan has grown to become an international leader in its niche markets. The firm's exports now comprise 80 per cent of its annual sales of A$150 million (roughly €100 million) and its products are sold in 150 countries.

Codan offers elaborately transformed, high-level intellectual property products targeted at low to medium volume niche global markets. Products include high frequency (HF) radio, satellite radio sub-systems and metal detectors. The first two categories are illustrated in Figure 10.5. The firm's HF radio and satellite communications customers include military and

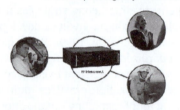

Communication Products – High Frequency (HF) Radio

- Products and systems for remote area long distance radio communications
- Used for:
  - › rapid network deployment
  - › communications without the need for transmission infrastructure
  - › back-up emergency communications

- End user organisations:
  - → aid and humanitarian (UN and NGOs)
  - → law enforcement, protection, security and military
  - → other government departments
  - › commercial e.g. mining and resources exploration, forestry, long distance transport

Communication Products - Satellite Communications RF Subsystem (Satcom)

- RF Subsystem portion of satellite communications earth stations
- Used in networks for telecommunications over satellite; for public infrastructure and private networks for government and business
- Fixed station and transportable "rapid deploy" networks
- Sold to organisations that integrate the Codan product into earth stations
- Codan specialises in C and Ku frequency bands; most commonly used bands today

Figure 10.5   Codan's major communication product categories
Source: http://www.codan.com.au/Portals/0/investorpubs/2009%20Year-end
%20investor%20presentation.pdf (accessed 14 September 2009); reproduced
with permission.

security organizations, multinational firms, the United Nations and other international aid agencies, telecommunications carriers and 'system integrators'. Its metal detectors are marketed to consumer markets and, as mine detectors, to international aid agencies and the military. The company has an excellent reputation for performance, quality and reliability. It also aims to provide outstanding customer service and support through a global network of agents, dealers and distributors. It employs roughly 400 staff worldwide, with sales offices in Australia, the United States, the United Kingdom, China and India.

Selected company highlights are as follows. In 1961, the firm launched its first HF radio transceiver, designed to meet the needs of the School-of-the-Air network operating in the Australian outback. In 1973, it commenced exports of its HF radio equipment, initially to Papua New Guinea and the United States. In 1975, it won its first Australian Export Award for outstanding export achievement. (It also won awards for Export Excellence from the Australian Electronics

Industry Association in both 1997 and 2000, and several Australian and international awards since 1997 for best practice, design and innovation.) During 1978–9, Codan acquired the New Zealand firm Electronics Project Ltd to supply HF communication equipment in that country.

In 1980, the United Nations made a significant purchase of Codan HF radio equipment for its relief efforts in Uganda. This helped to establish Codan as a leading global supplier of HF communication equipment to humanitarian organizations. In 1981, Codan produced satellite RF sub-systems to support the launch of Australia's first domestic satellite system. In 1989, it completed a satellite sub-system for the Pacific Area Cooperative Telecommunications network in conjunction with Sattel Technologies of the United States. In 2003, Codan equipment was installed in 32 Afghanistan provinces to restore telephone, facsimile, email and radio communications. In 2005, the firm opened offices in China and India. In 2009, it established a Military and Security Division in the United States to provide HF radio equipment for worldwide defence and government organizations. In 2009, it acquired Locus Microwave, a United States company focused on the design, manufacture and supply of microwave radio products for satellite communications, especially for military and government purposes.

Today, Codan has several salespeople based in Adelaide who travel to various foreign markets in Asia. It also has sales offices in several foreign markets. The office in the United Kingdom has responsibility for Europe, Africa and the Middle East, while that in the United States has responsibility for North and South America. Offices in China and India report to the head office in Adelaide. In all markets, Codan's salespeople maintain contact with agents, dealers, distributors, system integrators, end-users and other stakeholders who influence purchase decisions. Senior management assists in customer relationship management activities, such as attending company functions for its major resellers in key markets.

Competitors within the military and security markets include divisions of several multi-billion dollar global corporations, mainly with head offices in Europe or the United States. While Codan focuses on communications products for border patrols, counter-terrorism, narcotics teams and non-front-line combat units, many of its larger competitors also focus on communications products for front-line combat units.[3]

Summary

International marketing has become increasingly important and complex over the last 30 to 40 years and, therefore, management of international selling operations is a challenging task. Many steps within the selling process are likely to be challenging for export salespeople entering foreign markets, especially if those markets are very different from their home markets. This chapter has presented some of the challenges and issues involved when internationalizing the sales effort. Overall, it has shown that while some management and organizational practices can be exported into new markets, others have to be adapted to new cultural and ethical requirements.

[3] Based on information from: http://www.codan.com.au/Portals/0/publications/codan_booklet.pdf; http://www.codan.com.au/Portals/0/investorpubs/2009%20Year-end%20investor%20presentation.pdf; http://www.codan.com.au/Portals/0/investorpubs/50th_Anniversary_Press Release.pdf; http://www.codan.com.au/Corporate/AboutCodan/History/tabid/81/Default.aspx; http://www.codan.com.au/Portals/0/investorpubs/Code-of-Conduct.pdf (accessed 14 September 2009).

Key points

1. There are various foreign market entry options, the appropriate option depending on a range of internal and external factors. Different entry modes provide different levels of control, but also have different levels of associated risk. In any case, the firm must decide whether to utilize its own salesforce or intermediaries, or a combination of the two; the assignment of salespeople to foreign markets not necessarily removing the need for intermediaries. Different channel arrangements may be appropriate for different categories of customer, as with such differences in the home market. The firm also needs to decide whether to base its international salesforce in its home office, in regional sales offices or in sales offices in specific markets (possibly within each country).

2. Recruitment and selection of Sales Managers and salespeople partly depends upon the form of international selling and this, therefore, influences what attributes international sales executives will require. Activities of Sales Managers need to take account of a range of issues, including the form of international selling. Compensation arrangements need to take into account variation in cultural preferences regarding the nature and type of compensation programme. Both behaviour- and outcome-based forms of monitoring and control are required, although the emphasis depends on whether the firm is aiming to broaden or consolidate its range of foreign markets.

3. Partly due to global sourcing by some multinational firms, there has been a trend towards Global Account Management. Effective Global Account Management requires the involvement of senior company management, a high level of expertise in the area of supply chain management and an appropriate combination of global integration and local responsiveness.

4. International salespeople need to take account of possible cultural differences between themselves and customers in foreign markets, and between customers in different markets, including differences in levels of risk avoidance.

5. Responding to ethical issues that might arise while working with foreign customers becomes complicated by differences in ethical norms in different cultures, so that salespeople become unable to refer to just their own ethical standards. The problem is even greater for salespeople visiting several foreign markets with very different cultural norms and legal systems.

6. Finally, there are two strategic options with respect to entering and serving foreign markets: globalization and localization. An appropriate international selling strategy probably involves standardizing some elements of selling strategy across markets with similar environmental characteristics.

References

Anderson, R.E, Mehta, R. and Strong, J. (1997) 'An Empirical Investigation of Sales Management Training Programs for Sales Managers', *Journal of Personal Selling and Sales Management*, 17 (3): 53–66.

Bloom, M., Milkovich, G.T. and Mitra, A, (2000) *Toward a Model of International Compensation and Rewards: Learning from how Managers Respond to Variations in Local*

Host Contexts (CAHRS Working Paper No. 00-14). Ithaca, New York: Center for Advanced Human Resource Studies, Cornell University.

Calantone, R. and Knight, G. (2000) 'The Critical Role of Product Quality in the International Performance of Industrial Firms', *Industrial Marketing Management*, 29 (6): 493–506.

Carrigan, M., Marinova, S. and Szmigin, I. (2005): 'Ethics and International Marketing: Research Background and Challenges', *International Marketing Review*, 22 (5): 481–93.

Cateora, P.R. and Graham, J.L. (2007) *International Marketing*, 13th edition. Boston, MA: McGraw-Hill.

Cravens, D.W, Piercy, N.F. and Low, G.S. (2006) 'Globalization of the Sales Organization: Management Control and its Consequences', *Organizational Dynamics*, 35 (3): 291–303.

Douglas, S.P. (2000) 'Global Marketing Strategy in the 21st Century: The Challenges', *Japan and the World Economy*, 12 (4): 381–4.

Dzever, S., Merdji, M.and Saives, A.-L. (2001) 'Purchase Decision-making and Buyer-seller Relationship Development in the French Food Processing Industry', *Supply Chain Management*, 6 (5): 216–29.

Ekeledo, I. and Sivakumar, K. (2004) 'International Market Entry Mode Strategies of Manufacturing Firms and Service Firms: A Resource-based Perspective', *International Marketing Review*, 21 (1): 68–101.

Ellis, J.H.M., Williams, D.R. and Roscorla, F.B. (2001) 'Managing Japan-Europe Industrial Buyer-supplier Relationships: A Conceptual and Empirical Study of the Japanese Market for High-technology Marine Equipment', *Journal of the Asia Pacific Economy*, 6 (2): 232–43.

Gelderman, C.J. and Semeijn, J. (2006) 'Managing the Global Supply Base through Purchasing Portfolio Management', *Journal of Purchasing and Supply Management*, 12 (4): 209–17.

Hui Shi, L., Zou, S. and Cavusgil, S.T. (2004) 'A Conceptual Framework of Global Account Management Capabilities and Firm Performance', *International Business Review*, 13 (5): 539–53.

Kalaignanam, K., Kushwaha, T. and Varadarajan, P. (2008) 'Marketing Operations Efficiency and the Internet: An Organizing Framework', *Journal of Business Research*, 61 (4): 300–8.

Katsikea, E.S, Theodosiou, M., Morgan, R.E. and Papavassiliou, N. (2005) 'Export Market Expansion Strategies of Direct-selling Small and Medium-sized Firms: Implications for Export Sales Management Activities', *Journal of International Marketing*, 13 (2): 57–92.

Kotabe, M. and Murray, J.Y. (2004) 'Global Procurement of Service Activities by Service Firms', *International Marketing Review*, 21 (6): 615–33.

Lewin, J.E. and Johnston, W.J. (1997) 'International Salesforce Management: A Relationship Perspective', *Journal of Business and Industrial Marketing*, 12 (3/4): 236–52.

Lowe, K.B., Milliman, J., De Cieri, H. and Dowling, P.J. (2002) 'International Compensation Practices: A Ten-country Comparative Analysis', *Human Resource Management*, 41 (1): 45–66.

Marshall, G.W., Brouthers, L.E. and Lamb, C.W. Jr (1998) 'A Typology of Political Economies and Strategies in International Selling', *Industrial Marketing Management*, 27 (1): 11–19.

Mintu-Wimsatt, A. and Gassenheimer, J.B. (1996) 'Negotiation Differences between Two Diverse Cultures: An Industrial Seller's Perspective', *European Journal of Marketing*, 30 (4): 20–39.

Mühlbacher, H., Leihs, H. and Dahringer, L. (2006) *International Marketing: A Global Perspective*, 3rd edition. London: Thomson Learning.

Quintens, L., Pauwels, P. and Matthyssens, P. (2006) 'Global Purchasing Strategy: Conceptualization and Measurement', *Industrial Marketing Management*, 35 (7): 881–91.

Rajagopal (2008) 'Organisational Buying and Sales Administration in the Retail Sector', *Journal of Retail and Leisure Property*, 17 (1): 3–20.

Ramarapu, S., Timmerman, J.E. and Ramarapu, N. (1999) 'Choosing between Globalization and Localization as a Strategic Thrust for your International Marketing Effort', *Journal of Marketing Theory and Practice*, 17 (2): 97–105.

Ronen, S. and Shenkar, O. (1985) 'Clustering Countries on Attitudinal Dimensions: A Review and Synthesis', *Academy of Management Review*, 10 (3): 435–54.

Root, F.R. (1994) *Entry Strategies for International Markets*, 3rd edition. New York: Lexington Books.

Rossiter, J.R. and Chan, A.M. (1998) 'Ethnicity in Business and Consumer Behavior', *Journal of Business Research*, 42 (2): 127–34.

Rouziès, D., Segalla, M. and Besson, M. (1999) *The Impact of Cultural Dimensions on Sales Force Compensation*. Jouy en Josas, France: HEC Business School.

Scholtens, B. and Dam, L. (2007) 'Cultural Values and International Differences in Business Ethics', *Journal of Business Ethics*, 75 (3): 273–84.

Segalla, M., Rouziès, D., Besson, M. and Weitz, B.A. (2006) 'A Cross-national Investigation of Incentive Sales Compensation ', *International Journal of Research in Marketing*, 23 (4): 419–33.

Shepherd, C.D. and Ridnour, R.E. (1995) 'The Training of Sales Managers: An Exploratory Study of Sales Management Training Practices', *Journal of Personal Selling and Sales Management*, 15 (1): 69–74.

Sheth, J.N. and Sharma, A. (2008) 'The Impact of the Product to Service Shift in Industrial Markets and the Evolution of the Sales Organization', *Industrial Marketing Management*, 37 (3): 260–9.

Statman, M. (2007) 'Local Ethics in a Global World', *Financial Analysts Journal*, 63 (3): 32–41.

Tihanyi, L., Griffith, D.A. and Russell, C.J. (2005) 'The Effect of Cultural Distance on Entry Mode Choice, International Diversification, and MNE Performance: a Meta-analysis', *Journal of International Business Studies*, 36 (3): 270–83.

Trautmann, G., Bals, L. and Hartmann, E. (2009) 'Global Sourcing in Integrated Network Structures: The Case of Hybrid Purchasing Organizations', *Journal of International Management*, 15 (2): 194–208.

Wilkinson, J.W. (2004). *Toward an Enhanced Framework of the Business-to-business Selling Process*. Wellington, New Zealand: Australia and New Zealand Academy of Marketing Conference.

Wilkinson, J.W. (2005). *Consequences of Limited Sales Management Training*. Canberra, Australia: Australian and New Zealand Academy of Management Conference, University of Canberra.

Wilkinson, J.W. (2009): 'Levels of Sales Leadership Support: An Exploratory Study', *Journal of Selling and Major Account Management*, 8 (4): 8–22.

Wills, J., Samli, A.C. and Jacobs, L. (1991) 'Developing Global Products and Marketing Strategies: A Construct and a Research Agenda', *Journal of the Academy of Marketing Science*, 19 (1): 1–10.

Wilson, K. and Weilbaker, D. (2004) 'Global Account Management: A Literature Based Conceptual Model', *Mid-American Journal of Business*, 19 (1): 13–21.

Wood, G. (1995) 'Ethics at the Purchasing/sales Interface: An International Perspective', *International Marketing Review*, 12 (4): 7–19.

Woodside, A.G. and Ferris-Costa, K.R. (2008) 'Business-to-business Marketing, Organizational Buying Behaviour, Interfirm Relationships and Network Behaviour', in Baker, M.J. and Hart, S., *The Marketing Book*. Oxford: Elsevier/Butterworth-Heinemann.

Yip, G.S. and Bink, A.J.M. (2007) 'Managing Global Accounts', *Harvard Business Review*, 85 (9): 102–111.

Further reading

Andersson, S. and Servais, P. (2010) 'Combining Industrial Buyer and Seller Strategies for International Supply and Marketing Management', *European Business Review*, 22 (1): 64–81.

Blomstermo, A., Sharma, D. and Sallis, J. (2006) 'Choice of Foreign Market Entry Mode in Service Firms', *International Marketing Review*, 23 (2): 211–29.

Brashaer, A.T. (2009) 'International Salesforce Management', in Kotabe, M. and Helsen, K. (eds), *The Sage Handbook of International Marketing*: 429–48. Thousand Oaks, CA: Sage.

Jansson, H. (2007) *International Business Marketing in Emerging Country Markets: the Third Wave of Internationalisation of the Firm*. Cheltenham: Edward Elgar.

Part three

Implementation of the sales programme: creating and developing competencies

11

Sales force recruitment and selection*

Christophe Fournier and Juliet F. Poujol

Contents

* The authors would like to thank the Institut des Sciences de l'Entreprise et du Management for its financial support on this project. We would also like to thanks K. Wakefield from Baylor University and Geraldine Mantione Valero (PhD, Université Montpellier 1) from the Florian Mantione Institute.

Learning objectives

After reading this chapter, you should be able to:

- Recognize the critical importance of recruitment and selection in sales force management today.

- Understand the critical steps in the recruitment process of salespeople.

- Know the main tools and methods of recruitment and the key success factors.

- Identify key challenges in sales force recruitment and selection.

- Apply a systematic recruitment process.

Chapter outline

This chapter deals with a critical issue in sales force management: the recruitment, selection and retention of good salespeople. With a view to helping sales executives manage the recruitment process (from the job analysis to the integration of the candidate), this chapter is structured as follows. First, a real problem is presented to focus readers' attention on the recruitment of salespeople. Second, the relevant literature on recruitment is reviewed. The critical steps of the recruitment process are described and different tools and methods of recruitment presented. Third, the real case presented in the first part is discussed. Finally, a number of key points are offered, such as a guide to the overall process for recruiting salespeople, together with a series of 'golden' rules of recruitment for sales executives.

CASE PROBLEM[1]

In early 2009, a retail company wishes to extend its sales network in the south of France. To do this, the Sales Manager quickly has to recruit two Area Sales Managers from the local region. As a first step, a French Sales and Marketing Managers' group is contacted to find out about sales recruitment practices in France. One of the members of the group advises him to use a specialist recruitment agency and recommends the Florian Mantione Institut (FMI). Based in Montpellier, this company has several other offices in Europe.

The Sales Manager prepares to contact FMI, but various problems and questions come to mind. Indeed, the culture of this foreign company is very distinct, and its organizational system is based on a number of fairly strict procedures. Moreover, the company meets various certification standards showing that it adheres to very demanding quality objectives. The Sales Manager thus wants to be sure that the Area Sales Managers recruited will be able to quickly adapt to the company's organizational system and will fully respect the procedures. In addition, during this stage of breaking into the French market, customer follow-up is a strategic aim, with a view to allowing the company to know its French customers better and to anticipate their needs. In fact, the Area Sales Manager's mission will involve finding out information about the customers and making use of it. The Sales Manager thus needs to make sure that the future Area Sales Managersare capable of carrying out this research work. In his opinion, having thorough familiarity with information and communication technologies is important for success in this job. In particular, the successful Area Sales Manager must also effectively manage communication processes with the company headquarters.

As a result, the following questions are raised with FMI by the Sales Manager;

Questions

1. The Sales Manager wants to be really sure of the added value that will come from working in cooperation with the recruitment agency.
2. He wants to know about the various stages of recruitment and is concerned how to complete these successfully. How will FMI help him go from one stage to the next?
3. In general, given the company growth objectives on French territory, he would like to know what overall recommendations can be formulated for future recruitment of sales people?

Introduction: recruitment problems and issues

The sales force is central to any sales and marketing strategy and is the company's public face to its customers. While it is obvious that a salesperson's mission is vital, all the more so when the economic situation is difficult, it is far from easy to select and recruit good salespeople. Indeed, educational level is not enough to evaluate objectively a

---

[1] This case is completely fictional and has been devised for pedagogical purposes. Any similarity to a real situation is entirely coincidental.

candidate's qualities, personal qualities are difficult to assess by the recruiter, and experience is not always a satisfactory criterion. Consequently, the recruitment of new salespeople is a major issue for companies.

The employment market in sales personnel has been extremely tight for several years now. It is therefore important to attract good salespeople, to set up rapid selection procedures so as to decide quickly on the recruitment of quality candidates and then to ensure their loyalty to minimize 'dysfunctional' turnover. This shortage in the Sales human resources market can be explained by supply and demand. In regard to the latter, strong demand is occurring due to various factors. First, there is a highly unbalanced age pyramid in many companies, which means they will need to recruit on a large scale in the coming years simply to renew their sales forces. Second, since the turn of the century, the trend towards relational marketing that advocates the individualization of the customer has led to the creation of a large number of call centers. Most of these have recruited salespeople on a large scale. Finally, as Labourdette (1992) points out, the sales force becomes more critical under certain conditions, such as an intense market. As competition increases the sales force emerges as one of the primary instruments for defending market share.

On the supply side, individuals who might consider a sales career have a rather negative image of it, both in Europe and America (Barth and Biardeaux 2002; Swenson et al. 1993; Lee et al. 2007). Thus, strong demand coupled with an inadequate supply results in a tight market. Recruiting a salesperson is very costly. This cost includes the various tasks that have to be carried out during the three stages of recruitment, namely preparation for the recruitment (job description, writing ads, etc.), the recruitment itself (establishing communication, sorting and studying resumes and conducting interviews) and finally, after recruitment, integrating and training the newly hired salesperson into the organization. While some of these costs are variable and are linked in particular to the number of applications generated or interviews conducted,

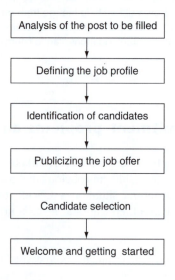

Figure 11.1 The recruitment process

others are fixed (writing recruitment ads, placing them in the press) and should be carefully considered. Since the costs involved in recruiting are far from negligible for companies, it is important on the one hand to avoid making mistakes when recruiting and on the other to minimize turnover in sales force, especially when it is 'dysfunctional turnover' (involving successful salespeople).

While there are many reasons why salespeople may leave their companies (Tanner et al. 2009), there is a strong link between staff turnover and recruitment. High turnover in the company will entail ongoing and very costly recruitment. Moreover, recruitment mistakes are liable to lead either to a rapid turnover of personnel or, on the contrary, to a lack of 'desirable' turnover (when the person recruited is not suitable but nevertheless remains in the company).

Figure 11.1 presents an overall view of the recruitment process to guide managers in fulfilling this role. According to this process, Recruitment Managers should follow six successive steps to optimize the recruitment and selection of salespeople. In what follows, we discuss these various stages of the recruitment process one by one.

Analysis of the post to be filled

The selling profession is extremely heterogenous. It is therefore important to define clearly what the company expects and wants. Indeed, simply reading job offers in sales in the press, whether regional or international, reveals the wide variety of job titles applying to salespeople. This diversity of job titles reflects a multiplicity of situations, that is, of the tasks and activities assigned to salespeople. Moncrief et al. (2006) emphasize the variety of tasks carried out, which they group into 11 main categories, namely: relationship selling, promotional activities and sales service, entertaining, prospecting for new accounts, computer use, travel, training and recruiting, delivery, product support, educational activities, office and channel support. The proliferation of terminology justifies the many attempts undertaken to try to obtain a clearer view of the world of selling and its jobs (Fournier 2001). Almost all sales typologies aim at determining the different categories of salespeople according to whether they perform – and how frequently – or do not perform certain tasks. Darmon (1993a; 1998) offers a taxonomy based on the core of the salesperson's profession, namely the relationship with the prospect/customer. The typology takes into account three criteria: the amount of information that needs to be processed in the job; the complexity of the information processing required to carry out the job successfully; and the greater or lesser extent of the salesperson's time management.

Defining the job profile

A job profile can be used directly for writing the job offer that will then be advertised. According to Mathews and Redman (2001) in a study carried out in the UK, six pieces of information are crucial for writing a job offer in the sales sector and therefore for establishing the job profile. These are as follows: location, salary, closing date, experience, qualifications and job title.

This list is indicative and not necessarily exhaustive. What is important, however, is to provide the various pieces of information needed for potential applicants to have a clear view of the job being offered. The information required might fall under the following headings, either separately or grouped together:

- the company, its customers and its environment: business sector, type of product/services produced, the company's market position, target objectives, size of the company, etc.;
- the job title;
- the position offered: indication of the roles and missions associated with the job;
- the possible relationships to be maintained and developed in the rest of the company;
- working conditions: office-based or travelling work, likely transfers within the country or abroad, etc.;
- possible development for people successfully occupying this position (evolution and career development within the company);
- salary and other benefits offered;
- qualities sought.

As we shall see below, writing the job profile is fundamental for the final stage of recruitment when integrating new recruits into the company. As Menguc et al. (2007) recommend, given that realism is a key factor for the later integration of candidates, it is essential to provide maximum information as close as possible to reality in order to give candidates a clear view of the job and to minimize the risk of disappointment once they take up the post.

From job profile to candidate profile

Moving on from the job profile to a candidate profile necessitates specifying the main qualities (whether they be in terms of competencies, personality traits, abilities, etc.) that are being looked for as a priority in the candidate for the job. The qualities sought vary according to the company, manager or recruitment consultancy. Selection criteria were classified by Churchill et al. (1997) into different categories: demographic and physical characteristics, experience and background, current status and lifestyle, abilities, personality and skills. These criteria can be classified into the main groups: competencies, personality (aptitudes and knowledge, personality traits) and personal variables. However, as Dalrymple et al. (2001) point out, choosing these recruitment criteria is far from straightforward, since:

- the conventional variables such as the salesperson's aptitude for selling, personal characteristics or competencies are not very good determinants of performance; and
- personal variables such as marital status or family history are among the best indicators of sales performance, but it is generally illegal to ask questions on such matters.

We should also add that recruitment criteria evolve with changes in the Sales function and this leads us on to a central issue in sales management: on what basis should salespersons be selected? Depending on the job context, the salesperson should be capable of adapting to:

1. The type of selling involved: a high frequency of contact with unknown prospects does not call for the same qualities as working with a known clientele;
2. Human relations: working as part of a team, for example, requires greater flexibility and cooperation than working independently;
3. Working conditions in the field: tolerating stress and organizing the work oneself require different profiles depending on the type of leadership practised by the team leader.

A salesperson's competencies are often assessed using intelligence tests on the basis of cognitive abilities (flexibility, logical thinking, visual and associative memory), verbal abilities (understanding and use of words), fluency of speaking and mathematical ability (understanding and handling of figures). The personality traits viewed as important for salespeople have evolved. At the end of the 1960s, the salient personality traits for a salesperson were empathy, sensitivity and creativity, but also a sense of planning and self-discipline. In the 1980s, Ford et al. (1988) identified six key characteristics: responsibility (emotional stability, follow-up of plans, etc.), dominance (leadership, the desire for power, etc.), sociability (enjoyment of human contact, attention, etc.), self-confidence (coping with criticism or setbacks, etc.), creativity and flexibility (openness, tolerance, etc.), the wish for success (competitive spirit, etc.) and, lastly, the desire for external power and reward. More recent studies have looked at key factors for relational performance: interpersonal relations and listening (Humphreys and Williams 1996; Ramsey and Sohi 1997) and extra-role behaviours (Netermeyer, 1997). Marshall et al. (2003) highlight the competencies needed for managing customer relationships, the foremost among them being listening, follow-up skills and adaptability. For Mayer and Greenberg (2006), the key personality traits of the successful salesperson are empathy and 'ego drive'.

In short, it is difficult to say what makes a good salesperson because of the many variables involved, but we can specify the meta-qualities needed, as shown in Table 11.1:

Table 11.1 The salesperson's meta-qualities

Personality	Enthusiasm, emotional stability, self-confidence
Intellectual qualities	Open-mindedness, flexibility, ability to analyse and synthesize
Moral qualities	Reliability, sense of responsibility, ethics
Communication	Listening, ability to present arguments, empathy
Organization	Methodical, ability to delegate and to be accountable
Actions	Ambition, dynamism, creativity
Physical qualities	Physical and mental stamina

The question of personal variables brings us back to the notion of diversity. The findings of a study on salespeople's missions and the evolution of sales forces brought out the importance, given the diversity of customers, of having diverse salesperson profiles (Tanner et al. 2008). The successful salesperson resembles his/her customers and understands them. Human diversity has many aspects: gender, ethnicity, physical and social categories, religion, and so on. Litvin (1997) distinguishes the primary discriminatory dimensions (age, ethnicity, gender, etc.) from those that are invisible (education, family situation, parental status, religion and work experience).

Identification of candidates

The third stage of the recruitment process involves choosing, among the different possible sources of recruitment, those that will in principle be most suitable for recruiting the candidate or candidates. It is advisable to distinguish two sources of candidates: internal (from within the company) and external (from outside the company). The choice of sources depends on a number of factors, including the company's resources and the time available to fill the post.

Internal recruitment

If the Human Resources Manager recruits an itinerant salesperson from among internal candidates, he/she can select sedentary sales personnel who are already familiar with the products and the types of customers, or employees in other technical or administrative departments who aspire to a different life, more rapid promotion or more contact with others. Recruiting internally will speed up both the recruitment campaign and, especially, the post-recruitment stage, since the candidates will already be fully familiar with the company, its culture, its operation and its products. It is, moreover, a powerful human resources management tool, since it allows career development or even promotions to be offered, and enhances salespeople's loyalty to the company. In addition, Darmon (1993b) points out that internal candidates are a source of long-term benefit for the company.

External recruitment

The alternative for the company is to recruit someone who is currently working outside the company. The main question then is knowing how to find the candidates. Two possibilities are available. The company can either examine spontaneous applications or can generate applications by issuing job advertisements. We shall look in more detail at these two possibilities.

Spontaneous applications

Such applications concern candidates who are looking for a job and spontaneously offer their services to companies. Under such circumstances, recruitment does not involve the cost of placing a job offer. All that needs to be done is to draw upon applications that have been received and kept – and to examine them when a position is available to see whether any applications are of interest. As well as the financial advantage, spontaneous applications come in principle from motivated applicants who genuinely want to work in the company.

Although spontaneous applications are not a recent phenomenon, the rapid growth of communication technologies and especially the internet has led in recent years to a massive increase in this type of application. Thus a considerable number of corporate websites provide a special section for potential applicants to submit their CVs. CV libraries (for example Monster, Keljob, etc.) that list people seeking jobs are an effective way of finding candidates, with the possibility of combining several search criteria. While e-recruitment enables a large number of CVs to be consulted quickly, it should nevertheless be noted that the quality of these kind of applications is not always up to the mark.

Generating applications

The other way of proceeding is to generate or encourage applications from potentially interested individuals who wish to change jobs or find one. Several ways of organizing recruitment are then possible. Although the company itself can implement the recruitment, this can also be entrusted to specialist recruitment organizations (either private firms or public agencies), as well as schools and universities, and even headhunters.

Many companies use public or private organizations specializing in recruitment to select their salespeople. National employment agencies (such as *Pôle Emploi* in France) are public bodies whose services are free of charge and are often useful for recruitment. In addition, the services of private recruitment agencies are in increasing demand as companies do not hesitate to delegate all or part of the recruitment process to experts in human resources. These agencies are specialized or segmented by business sector or function (banking, insurance, industry and sales or marketing functions). They are able either to take charge of the entire recruitment process or only certain stages that require particular competencies or are very time-demanding.

Universities, schools and colleges are also a valuable source of job candidates for companies. Publicizing job offers in such institutions enables companies to make direct contact with candidates and to offer them career opportunities quickly. The main advantage of this recruitment method is in bringing new blood, perspectives and skills into the company. On the other hand, such recruits need longer to integrate into the company, get to know its products and customers, and so on. An intermediate method involves developing training courses in professional subjects such as sales. Students who take a training course in the context of their education can thereby be familiarized with the professional world and with a particular company. At the end of the course, both the student and the company are in a position to know if they want to work together. On the students' side, this is a key factor for the success of their integration, since they get a good idea of the actual job conditions. The alumni networks and associations directly linked to these educational institutions are also excellent means of publicizing job openings.

Web-based social networks, ranging from platforms for professional interaction (Viadeo, LinkedIn, etc.) to personal social networking sites (Facebook, MySpace, etc.) can also be used for recruitment. These sites, where candidates can present their profiles and their networks, are growing rapidly. The LinkedIn network is currently used by more than 35 million professionals worldwide and more than 150 business sectors in 120 countries. Virtual worlds such as Second Life are also sources of potential candidates for recruitment, especially in sales. As of 2009, more than 15 million people meet, interact and literally live another life on Second Life. Many companies already have their own virtual space which is often linked to their website.

Publicizing the offer

Once it has been decided which method will be used for recruitment, it is a matter of designing and writing the job offer and disseminating it.

Designing the job offer

As in the world of advertising and direct marketing, more important than the number of applicants is their quality. Thus, it is essential to pay attention both to the content of the offer and its presentation.

In regard to content, the job offer will draw on what is specified in the description of the position. As already noted, a good description of the company – what it does, its constraints, its business environment – enables the applicant to obtain an idea of it that is as close as possible to reality. This helps ensure their rapid integration and success in the company. Providing a very clear description of the position and the company in the job advertisement is a key success factor for the subsequent integration of those recruited. Finally, of course, it is important to comply with legal criteria in formulating a job offer and in particular to respect the principles of non-discrimination in disseminating a job offer. A number of recommendations for writing a job offer posted on the internet are given in Table 11.2.

Table 11.2   Some recommendations for writing an internet job offer

'The job description should make people want to apply for it', emphasizes Dominique Balland, of Balland Consultants, an agency specializing in the recruitment of sales personnel. In his opinion, a salesperson is attracted not only by the remuneration, but also by the diversity of the job, the quality of teamwork, the autonomy of the role and the recognition that working for the company will confer.

Sell the job
A job announcement is 'an advertisement, the company must sell itself', Dominique Balland explains. To attract the best candidates, you should think of the job offer as a sales pitch, and all the more so for positions in sales. Define the criteria that are most likely to attract the candidates you are targeting and highlight from the outset [...].

A clear job ad
The internet does not facilitate reading. Net surfers often go from one ad to the next, skimming over them rapidly. An online job offer should therefore go straight to the key points [...].
A description of tasks and responsibilities, the profile sought (maximum four selection criteria), the location of the workplace, any travelling expected and hierarchical responsibility are the essential ones. Do not forget the procedure for application. An indication of salary, both basic and bonus-related, as well as the benefits provided, will be appreciated by salespeople looking for transparency.

Be visible on the Web

[...] To stand out from the many ads abounding on the web, it is best to choose words that have an impact. For the candidate will find your ad by using keywords: 'sales job Paris', 'salesperson large computer account', etc. Therefore choose clear and current terms for the heading of your ad [...].

Take advantage of interactivity

'The internet can help you in your task, so take advantage of it', says Grégoire Lepoutre, Sales Manager at Goto Software. For example, include a link to your company's website if this adds value. For the method of application, email is clearly best. If the ad is placed on the internet, it is because the candidates are net users. Since salespeople are often hard to find, avoid making them complete complicated online forms that may put off many potential applicants.

Source: Guinot (2008) www.focusco.fr.

Disseminating the job offer

The next stage is bringing the job offer to people's attention by using a good communication mix, with a view to generating the maximum number of useful applications.

The recruiter has a number of options for disseminating the offer. Depending on the recruitment method adopted, the job offer may be directly disseminated by the body responsible for the recruitment or, alternatively, publicized by means of a media campaign. The main objective here is to make contact with the right people rather than a large number of people, since many of the latter will not match the criteria sought.

Companies have at their disposal conventional media outlets such as the press. This includes, as well as daily national and regional newspapers, other publications including news magazines, specialist trade press and free newspapers. For certain types of recruitment profiles, the international press should be used as well. Other conventional ways of matching job supply to human resources demand include job forums and the 'job trains' that go from town to town and are an original way of bringing job-seekers and recruiters together.

The internet constitutes a prime medium for publicizing job offers, whether for companies recruiting internally or for recruitment agencies. Such agencies have their own websites or outsource this part of the process to companies that manage dedicated recruitment websites. Thus the sites previously referred to are not limited simply to collecting candidates' CVs, but also serve as a means of publicizing job offers. Some companies make use of WAP protocols, a mobile extension to the internet, to enable people to access their sites from their mobile phones, with alerts given according to their profiles, with a view to being as close as possible to interested parties and have very high response rate in recruitment.

Candidate selection

A salesperson's success depends on a large number of factors that cannot all be fully assessed during the recruitment process. The recruitment tools that we shall now present, however, aim to predict the candidate's performance and thus identify the best profiles. We begin with the major stages of the selection of the salesperson, and then go on to look at the selection tools traditionally used by companies: briefing sessions, recruitment interviews, recruitment tests and putting applicants in simulated real-life situations.

After defining the job, specifying the competencies expected and collecting the applications, comes the candidate selection process itself. This process consists of two main stages: pre-selection and then the final decision. An initial selection is made on the basis of the letter accompanying the candidate's application and the CV, or the application form provided by the company or recruitment agency.

The CV and application form are good ways of quickly assessing a candidate's background and experience. The application form has the additional advantage of providing further candidate information as determined by the company (hobbies, analysis of past experience, etc.). This implies that the human resources management department thinks through the information and topics to be included in the form. The standardization of this document has the further advantages of facilitating comparison of the candidates and saving time in the initial selection process.

At this stage it is standard procedure for the recruiter to contact the candidate's previous employer(s) to check that the information provided in the CV or application form is accurate.

European companies are also increasingly asking for recommendations and references as is done in the United States – for example, a reference from a former manager who is in a position to provide information on the candidate's personality and behaviour within the company.

The content and form of the letter or CV enable a first impression of the candidate to be obtained. Analysis of these documents can be facilitated using a grid corresponding to the characteristics of the post. The more complete the grid, the more the candidate is likely to be suited to the job. This stage is important since it allows the selection process itself to be optimized.

Recruitment interviews

Recruitment begins with an initial contact between the company and the applicant. This first encounter determines how the relationship will develop. For example, the initial phone conversation is crucial, and gives a first impression of the candidate to the person responsible for the recruitment. There are different kinds of interviews (see Table 11.3), with collective and individual interviews often being used to screen candidates.

Collective briefing session and collective interview

Prior to the individual interviews, an initial briefing session is often used when a large number of candidates have been chosen in the pre-selection process. This meeting involves the reciprocal exchange of information, and the recruitment team will use the occasion to provide further information on the job mission. In addition, it is an

Table 11.3	The different types of recruitment interviews		
	Principle	**Strong points**
Individual interview	One candidate facing one or more interviewers	Allows the interviewer(s) to get to know the candidate
Successive interviews	One candidate facing one or more interviewers successively	Enhances the reliability of the recruitment process
Collective interview	Several candidates facing one or more interviewers discuss a predefined topic or are placed in a real-life situation	Reveals how candidates respond in an interactive situation
Simulated situation	One or more candidates are placed in an imaginary situation or participate in role-playing games	Assesses the candidate's competencies and behaviours in situation

opportunity to evaluate candidates in a human relations context that approximates to real working conditions.

Many companies also use collective interviews to judge the candidate's reactions when faced with a selection committee and how he/she reacts in a competitive situation with other candidates. The advantage for the selection committee comes from placing the future salesperson in front of a group, similar to when a Key Account Manager faces a buying committee. The aim is to examine the way in which candidates intervene, the relevance of their questions and comments, their degree of understanding and their leadership qualities. It should be noted that collective interviews are difficult to handle and require the presence of a neutral observer with training in psychology, an expert meeting regulator and leader and an expert to interpret people's interactions (which may be recorded on video).

Following this initial screening, the recruiting team has a range of tools for optimizing the selection of the salesperson: questionnaires, psychological tests and role-playing games (individual and collective). The various techniques are often used in conjunction with one another. For example, a recruitment agency may begin by carrying out tests, then move on to a collective interview, follow this with an individual interview and conclude with a simulated real-life situation.

Individual recruitment interview

The hiring interview is the most frequently used technique for selecting salespeople and is a key episode in the sales recruitment process. Although almost all companies use this selection procedure, there are many methods for conducting them successfully (Darmon 1993a). These differ both in terms of the number and nature of the participants and in terms of the content or format. Interviews may be individual, collective or led by several assessors simultaneously. The meetings may take place at different points within the selection sequence and the duration and content can vary. For example, the future salesperson may be asked to participate in a role-playing game during the interview.

The interview is very important in sales force management since it enables the recruiter to evaluate the candidate's key competencies. The interviewer can, for example, observe the salesperson's behaviour in talking about him/herself and adapting to situations or solving problems. It is also a good way of assessing the applicant's personal presence. However, Darmon (2003) points out that the personal interview is the least valid and reliable means of predicting a salesperson's future performance. Consequently, he recommends minimizing the weight given to interviews in the recruitment decision. For example, applying psychotechnical tests or using case studies are further techniques that enable the quality of recruitment to be improved. To enhance the reliability of the assessment made during an interview, some companies favour a recruitment system based on several interviews. The first interview generally comprises seven successive stages (Figure 11.2).

During the discussion stage with the applicant, the recruiter often uses questions focused on action, such as: 'Why do you want to work with our company?', 'What ideas are you able to bring to the job?' The answers to these questions enable the candidate's motivation to be assessed as well as his/her preparation for the interview (knowledge of the company and its market). This resembles the visit preparation that is fundamental to any sales approach. It also enables the interviewer to assess the capacity of the potential salesperson to assess the customer situation and to be customer-oriented, a key factor in successful selling (Moncrief and Marshall 2005). The recruiter should therefore pay attention to the candidate's awareness of the customer's situation, not only that of the product (Zeyl and Dayan 2000).

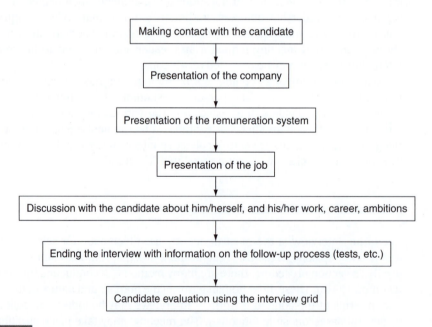

Figure 11.2 The seven stages of the individual recruitment interview
Source: adapted from Zeyl and Dayan (2000).

Table 11.4	Two styles of interview	
Style	**Principle**	**Objective**
Stressful	The recruiter adopts an aggressive approach and puts the candidate under stress	To test the candidate's reaction in a stress situation
'Psychological'	The recruiter wins the candidate's trust and encourages him/her to confide in them	To find out about the candidate's personality and his/her capacity not to lose sight of his/her objective

Of the various styles of interview, we refer here to two main variants: stress interviews and trust interviews, the principles of which are shown in Table 11.4.

These two interview techniques have different objectives aimed at testing the main abilities that need to be deployed in selling. For example, the psychological interview is intended to check whether or not candidates lose sight of their goal. This is an important point, for while the salesperson should feel empathy towards the customer, he/she should nevertheless not forget about making the sale. The two techniques are often used alternately during the same interview. The aim here is to see how candidates react to and cope with varied situations.

Another characteristic that merits attention is being able to cope with travel. Going on sales trips for a salesperson is tiring both physically and psychologically. It is advisable to find out if the candidate is aware of this and understands what this aspect of a sales job is like. Similarly, attention should be paid to how candidates speak about their setbacks. They should be capable of analysing the reasons for failure and questioning themselves, for example by acknowledging that their sales approach was inadequate. This shows that they are able to learn from their mistakes and can bounce back. Candidates should present an image and have a way of expressing themselves that closely matches the company, its products and its type of clientele. Finally, they should also fit in with the company culturally and socially.

Candidate assessment is made mostly by means of an interview grid listing the main points to be addressed in the course of the interview. These may include, for example, how candidates are dressed, how they express themselves or behave, their strength of conviction, ambition, their adaptability and their ethical attitudes. Points can be given to each of these criteria, allowing an average score for each candidate to be obtained at the end. This form of assessment aims to identify candidates' strengths and weaknesses and thus to enable comparison between them.

The evaluation grid should not be confused with the questionnaire that can also be used during the interview to measure what a candidate knows. With questionnaires it is possible to find out what potential salespeople know about the company, its products and its market. Questions may be closed or open. An example of the latter would be: 'What are the different kinds of marketing and what are their respective advantages?' The questionnaire provides a basis for comparison among the various candidates and therefore contributes to fairness. One of the conditions for its use is impartially giving all candidates the same time in which to complete it. Interview grids and questionnaires should be adapted to the needs of the company. This means thinking in advance about the assessment criteria, which are established when designing the job specification sheet. Because interviews are often considered insufficient for getting to know candidates properly, recruitment specialists frequently use a series of tests which can then serve as a basis for discussion during the interview.

Recruitment tests

Standardized recruitment tests are a way of detecting and measuring abilities or what is known about a topic and of exploring a candidate's personality. They allow recruiters to obtain technical, intellectual and psychological information about candidates (Zeyl and Dayan 2000). Their purpose is to predict a candidate's success or failure, and to compare candidates in this respect. Such tests are standardized and validated for their area of application, and some are now in digital form to facilitate processing. In France, for instance, about 4 per cent of recruiters submit their candidates to personality tests (www.cadresonline.com), and placing candidates in simulated professional situations and giving them technical tests are also increasingly used. Intelligence tests or knowledge tests, based on logic, expression or general culture, are least frequently used, but are always included in a complete series of tests.

There are three main families of tests: aptitude tests, personality tests, and placing candidates in simulated professional situations.

Aptitude tests

Also known as intelligence tests or logic tests, these measure the capacity successfully to carry out exercises of one kind or another. They are based mainly on problems involving logic (for example, series of geometric figures, numbers or dominoes). Others measure specific abilities such as verbal comprehension or reasoning. For example, sales aptitude tests aim to measure innate or acquired talents in sociability or persuasion, as well as a sensitivity for human relationships and tact (Anderson et al. 1988).

Personality tests

These try to detect the presence in individuals of supposedly relatively stable personality traits such as extroversion, seriousness, empathy, etc. Among these tests, the most well known are the MBTI (Myers-Briggs Typological Inventory; Myers 1962) and PAPI (Personality and Preference Inventory, created by the PA Consulting Group) (www.cadresonline.com; Duhamel et al. 2009). They are based on successively presented pairs of statements or propositions. Respondents are asked to choose the statement which comes closest to (or is the least distant from) what they believe themselves to be. For example, PAPI-I is a questionnaire of 90 pairs of statements such as: 'I tend to let myself be influenced by others, I tend not to respect authority.' The tool delivers a written account which covers attitudes to other people, work and the hierarchy, reactions in tense situations and the most favourable professional environment.

More specifically concerned with the recruitment of salespeople, the SPI (Salespeople's Personality Inventory) is intended to reveal candidates' general disposition for selling: Are they able to present an argument? Are they inclined to show empathy? How sociable are they? This test measures personality traits considered to be linked to success in selling, including comprehension, adaptability, self-control, sociability, tolerance of frustration, combativeness and self-confidence. The FFM (Five Factor Model; Digman 1990) or Big Five is widely used for selecting salespeople (Rothstein and Goffin 2006). This test assesses five basic personality characteristics looked for in sales-people: extroversion, openness to new experience, agreeableness, conscientiousness and emotional stability.

Scientific studies demonstrate the reliability of personality tests for predicting sales-people's future performance. Nevertheless, these tests are not infallible since they are based on the hypothesis that if the respondent is in agreement with a statement this implies that he/she is like that. Yet the candidates' desire to obtain the job can lead to them to say what they believe a good salesperson is expected to say. These exercises may in fact favour conformity rather than creativity. Original or creative people tend to censor themselves and to give answers that they consider to be the norm. One way of reducing this declarative bias is to present statements in pairs or groups of four, all of which have the same level of social desirability. The GPI (Gordon Personal Inventory), for example, uses this forced choice technique.

Apart from the problem of falsification in responding to tests, Mayer and Greenberg (2006) point out that these tests also compartmentalize the dimensions of the indi-vidual's personality. They thus mask the effects of synergy between the different personality traits making up a person. For example, someone who has strong empathy and a low ego-drive will not be able to make use of his/her empathy in a persuasive way. If the salesperson does not feel the need to conquer, understanding the customer is of no use in selling.

Simulating real-life situations

Simulating a real-life situation is another well-established practice in sales recruit-ment. This involves asking candidates to act 'as if' they were in a professional situation similar to that they might encounter as a future salesperson. This technique is often practised in face-to-face interviews. The interviewer may ask the candidate to improvize selling a simple object (e.g. a pen) or what he/she currently sells (for candidates already in a job). The candidate's capacity for improvization can thereby be assessed, and in the second case their seriousness in preparing for work and in approaching customers and prospects. Scenarios can be more fully elaborated by using case studies in which people's reactions can be tested when they are faced with a technical or relational problem.

Another approach is when the candidate is given a report on the sales position of a company which is experiencing a situation similar to that in which the salesperson will be. He/she will then be asked to come up with a diagnosis and to suggest a practical solution. The case study may be implemented on an individual or group basis. The aim here is to evaluate the candidate's comprehension and analytic ability and their aptitude for working in a team.

Companies often make use of the services of a specialist agency or assessment cen-tre for this type of test. In collective case studies, candidates are invited to work in teams under the watchful eye of representatives from the company or the recruitment agency, who observe their behaviour, role and development within the group. The content of the exercise offered to the candidates depends on their profiles: beginner salespeople are often faced with a case closely related to selling and their day-to-day situations; more experienced candidates will be given problems that are more remote from selling. Among the topics frequently used are responding to an invitation to tender or write a business plan.

Role-playing games are also widely used for testing future salespeople, often in conjunction with interviews. Here the roles are distributed among the participants. After a basic situation has been outlined, the candidates are asked to improvize playing the roles they have been given. The head of the sales force and other managers are present during the role-playing game and then discuss the participants' behaviour (which is often filmed). This simulation is strongly recommended for sales, since it allows salespeople to be placed in front of a buying committee, a buyer-engineer or an intermediary.

In this exercise, not only is how the candidates present an argument taken into account, but also body language, such as an evasive look, a forced smile, a foot tapping the floor or other non-verbal signs which may indicate that the candidate is ill at ease, and that the customer would also notice.

Welcome and getting started

The integration of newly hired salespeople is a key stage for the success of recruitment. The use of specific procedures such as mentorship are ways of increasing the chances of success in this 'transplant that is recruitment' (Martory 2005). Dubinsky et al. (1986) offer a salesperson socialization model derived from Feldman's (1976) model, which comprises three stages: anticipatory socialization, the accommodation stage and the role definition stage. Although the whole socialization process is necessary, in view of the topic of this book we shall focus on the first stage of this process, namely anticipatory socialization. Indeed, Dubinsky et al. (1986) conclude that 'realism' has a large impact on the salesperson's satisfaction, leading to key recommendations for the recruitment of salespeople. Realism means that candidates, and therefore the recruit, should have a reasonably clear and precise view of what life will be like in the company. The same principle applies to 'congruence', which the authors define as the match between the expectations and abilities of the person recruited on the one hand and the expectations of the company on the other. Thus congruence between the salesperson's profile and the inherent requirement of the job is essential. In view of this, Dubinsky et al. clearly show that in the socialization process it is typically more important to ask the question of 'Who are we recruiting?' rather than having to find out 'What do we do?' once the person is recruited. In other words, the socialization process should be taken into account from the start of the recruitment stage.

In the second stage of the process described by Dubinsky et al., the 'accommodation stage', the new recruit finds out what the company is like in reality and becomes a genuine part of it. This stage also occurs in the model developed by Menguc et al. (2007), who refer to social integration, or the process that results in newly recruited personnel absorbing the organizational culture and forming relationship with other members of the organization. Having an established integration process for newly hired personnel is important in helping them quickly become part of the company. Sponsorship and mentorship of new recruits by more senior salespeople is another way of facilitating this process.

CASE PROBLEM REVISITED

We shall now answer point by point the questions raised at the outset.

1. What is the added value to be obtained from using a recruitment agency?

The recruitment agency will take responsibility for various aspects of the recruitment process, which can be very demanding, especially in terms of time. This will proportionally lighten the load on the company's hiring personnel, who can then concern themselves with other key tasks (e.g. the job description). The company can also sub-contract to the consulting agency other stages of the process, such as the initial sifting and analysis of the many applications received. Furthermore, the agency has extensive experience that it will make available to its clients.

2. How will the recuritment agency help the Sales Manager through the various stages of the recruitment process?

The recruitment agency FMI (Florian Mantione Institut) follows the recruitment process as described in Figure 11.1 (see p. 284) and contributes its expertise and advice throughout. We shall now detail what FMI will provide at each stage.

Stage 1: How does FMI analyse the job to be filled?

First of all, FMI carries out an audit of the client company. Ideally it will visit the company and find out about its business, its way of operating and something of its culture. FMI will also suggest meeting the management and those who are directly concerned with recruitment. These meetings on the company's premises are very useful for properly preparing the candidate identification and selection stage.

The main aim here is fully to understand the mission, the job to be filled and the expectations of the company in regard to the candidate, both formally and informally. The audit is therefore fundamental for the success of the process as a whole. Having as clear a view as possible of the job and being able to communicate this to the candidate helps ensure good recruitment and successful integration of future recruits into the company.

Stage 2: How does FMI define the job profile?

The job description is essential. It is formulated after the initial contact with the company. An organizational audit is carried out, and senior managers are asked about the job profile and the competencies sought, as well as the advantages of the job for the candidate and any problems he/she will need to overcome. The aim is to become familiar with the overall context of the job and to determine the ideal candidate profile. The information collected is summarized in three sections:

- information on the employer;
- job mission;
- candidate profile.

Stage 3: How does FMI identify the candidates?

Since 2002 the agency has had a website and high performance IT tools. The website allows recruitment missions to be tracked online on a day-to-day basis – ensuring speed and reactivity – and the agency has been building a CV library and how has more than 85,000 CVs on which it can draw according to clients' requirements. These tools help FMI optimize its business and enables it to evaluate each of its operations. Through the website, it possesses statistics on the number of people who have read a job ad, the applications received and the history of correspondence with candidates who have already applied. On average, for every 1,000 job descriptions read, 100 CVs are received and a dozen of these are acted upon. This means that the opportunity for potential salespersons to see a detailed job profile are high and enables there to be a self-selection process on the part of candidates. Many applications are received in the first three days following publication of the advertisement. It is thus possible to reply very quickly to all applicants, thereby reducing the overall recruitment process time. Companies appreciate this since the position will be filled more rapidly.

Stage 4: How does FMI publicize the job offer?

The agency has a range of tools. Notices appear on the FMI website and on the main online job search engines. FMI has subscribed to an internet package comprising a number of job offer sites such as Monster and KelJob. The use of a press ad is not excluded, although less frequent. While the ways of disseminating a job offer have evolved, the content of the advertisement is little changed (see Figure 11.3). It summarizes the various components of the job profile: the company (which sometimes remains anonymous) and its business sector, the job mission, the candidate profile (educational level, competencies, experience, etc.), remuneration and further information (type of contract, working hours, starting date, etc.)

Candidates who read a job offer on an online job offer site such as Monster and who want to find out more can click on the ad. They then come to the detailed description of the position on the agency's website and can apply directly online. The application arrives in the mailbox of the consultant responsible for the mission. This makes for efficiency and quick response and greatly helps the company and the quality of its recruitment process.

Stage 5: How does FMI help in the selection of candidates?

There are two stages: pre-selection of candidates, followed by the final choice. For the pre-selection stage, FMI asks candidates to include a short accompanying letter with their applications along with standard CVs. This enables candidates to be more easily compared. The accompanying letter is very useful since it shows how candidates express themselves and whether there are any spelling mistakes (which can be an issue if the job involves written communication). A phone interview can then be arranged. Once the candidates have been short-listed, they are contacted and informed about the next stage of the process. They are sent an invitation to attend an interview with a reminder of the job specification and an application dossier to complete.

For the selection stage proper, various tools, chosen from the range available, are suggested to the company. These may include interviews, psychotechnical tests, self-assessment tests and graphology.

Our client
Job title
Job mission
Candidate profile
Remuneration
Further information

Figure 11.3 Typical job ad layout

The selection process usually begins with an individual interview with the applicant. Interviews are highly structured, with the application dossier and the job specification serving as a framework. Candidates first introduce themselves with reference to career, education and experience. Interviews then turn to the position to be filled (the company, the job context, the job itself and its various missions). The applicant's suitability for the position and his/her motivation are then discussed at length. The job specification serves as an interview guideline and also ensures that all applications are treated in the same way in order to facilitate comparison between applicants.

The interview is a key stage in the selection process. It is also the occasion for candidates to show what they are capable of doing. It is a means of getting to know candidates better and of finding out about their personality as it emerges in the course of the interview.

Stage 6: Welcome and getting started

An integration assessment is made after a month, in a meeting attended by the consultant, the new recruit and his/her immediate superior. The latter two each complete a questionnaire (with about 20 questions to ascertain the feelings of both parties), with the distinctive feature that the new recruit is asked to predict what his/her superior will say. The recruit is also asked to respond to what the manager has said. Comparison of their opinions helps to identify possible problems and to resolve them as quickly as possible. Thus FMI manages the whole recruitment process, which does not stop when the job is filled. The agency will later make sure that the right candidate for the job was selected and that there was no recruitment mistake.

These are thus the solutions and proposals that FMI can bring to the company for recruiting its future sales managers.

3. What are the main recommendations the agency would make for recruitment of sales personnel?

Through its founder and chairman F. Mantione, FMI specifies ten main rules to consider during recruitment. These are listed in Table 11.5 under the main recruitment stages.

Table 11.5   FMI's ten recommendations

Recruitment stage	FMI's recommendations
Analysis of the post to be filled	**1. Identify the real need** If a salesperson leaves the company, do not rush to replace him/her. Perhaps you need to resolve an organizational problem before even starting the recruitment process. Do not confuse an expressed need with a real need. **2. Remain in recruitment mode on a permanent basis** As in a game of chess or driving a car, you must always look several moves ahead. In leading a sales team, you should be permanently considering recruitment and activating its networks.
Creating the job profile	**3. Do not recruit a 'clone'** The company is not an organization with the parts simply juxtaposed. It is a system in which the parts interact and are never in complete equilibrium. Everything moves, including jobs and procedures. Define the job profile to match the new system. It is appropriate, in a team, to

Recruitment stage	FMI's recommendations

Table 11.5 (Continued)

have different, and complementary, profiles. In addition to competences, recruit potential.

Identification of candidates and Communicating the job offer

4. Do not be subjected to recruitment, anticipate it
You should permanently keep your networks going so that potential candidates are available to you. Hold onto unsolicited applications, recruit trainees as and when appropriate, give lectures in schools of business, keep a candidates file, keep a file on training schools and colleges, identify the best salespeople working for your suppliers, headhunt as appropriate, put up a notice on your stand at trade fairs saying you are interested in all candidates and set up a recruitment section in standby mode on your website.

Selection of candidates

5. Assess your candidates objectively but based on your feelings
The golden rule is to recruit the person you would like to work with. The trick is to separate the formal assessment and making the final choice. So arrange for the initial interviews and tests to be done by a colleague or an external recruitment agency and hold yourself in reserve for meeting the short-list. In this way you will be choosing among good quality candidates on the basis of your own subjective feelings.

6. Do not fantasize about the salesperson coming from the competition
Stop thinking that a candidate must be immediately operational. Recruiting a salesperson from a competitor testifies only to good sense and know-how. Yet having the right person is much more important: his/her personality, motivation, interpersonal skills and capacity to learn and adapt.

Welcome and integration

7. Help your new colleague to succeed
The achievements of our salespeople depend on us; one only has the salespersons one deserves. What help do you give them to enable them to achieve success in direct marketing, telesales, at your stand at a trade fair and through training?

8. Help the new salesperson become integrated
Salespeople are like any other colleagues. They need to be liked, to feel that people are interested in them, that they matter... Internally, they must be quickly integrated, trained, introduced to everyone. How things work must be explained. They need to be helped to familiarize themselves with the company culture and encouraged to express themselves and ask questions. Externally, they must be introduced to customers, prospects, suppliers and so on.

9. Choose a sponsor for your new salesperson
A good idea for facilitating a salesperson's integration is for him/her to have a sponsor. The sponsor should be from another department and not have any direct link with the salesperson, but will explain how everything works. The sponsor will serve as a point of reference, a partner, a decompression valve...

10. Arrange for integration appraisals

You do not have to decide whether or not to keep a new salesperson on the day before the end of the trial period. It is better to have an idea of the likely decision in advance from formal integration assessments whose dates are fixed at the time the new salesperson joins the company. Three people should participate in these appraisals: the salesperson, the Sales Manager and someone from human resources or an external consultant. Often these assessments enable situations to be resolved that might otherwise become acrimonious. And do not forget to emphasize objectives and performance criteria.

Source: FMI documents.

The first challenge that the recruiter faces is to analyse the post to be filled, which calls for auditing the job. Only then can the job profile be established and the candidates identified, selected and integrated. In conclusion, recruitment and selection needs method and real expertise.

Summary

This chapter was intended to help managers diagnose problems in the recruitment and selection process. It should help them to identify the main tools and methods used and to self-evaluate their practices. By guiding the reader through the steps involved in recruitment and employee selection in the sales environment, executives can identify specific issues that need to be urgently addressed to improve the effectiveness of the recruitment and selection process (diversity, etc.).

Key points

Recruitment managers should bear in mind the following:

1. There is no miracle recipe for the recruitment process. Each Human Resource Manager needs to find a strategy of recruitment and solution that fits the firm's resources and needs.
2. A firm that decides to outsource recruitment to a recruitment agency has to work with it, and the recruitment agency must have the maximum information about the firm in order to do a good job.
3. The Sales Manager can have a dramatic effect on the success of the recruitment process, especially in the last stage of integrating the candidate.

References

Anderson, R.E., Hair, F. and Bush, A.J. (1988) *Professional Sales Management*. New York: McGraw Hill.

Barth, I. and Biardeaux, S. (2002) *Les représentation des métiers de la vente chez les étudiants: confrontation d'une revue de la littérature d'une étude exploratoire* Lille: Congres de l'Association Française de Marketing.

Churchill, G.A. Jr, Ford, N.M. and Walker, O.C. (1997) *Sales Force Management*, 5th edition Irwin: Homewood.

Dalrymple, D.J, Cron, W.L. and DeCarlo, T.E. (2001) *Sales Management*, 7th edition. New York: Wiley.

Darmon, R.Y. (1993a) *Management des Ressources Humaines de la Force de Vente*. Paris: Economica.

Darmon R.Y. (1993b) 'Where do the Best Sales Force Producers Come From?' *Journal of Personal Selling and Sales Management*, 13 (3): 17–29.

Darmon, R.Y. (1998) 'A Conceptual Scheme and Procedure for Classifying Sales Positions', *Journal of Personal Selling and Sales Management*, 18 (3), 31–46.

Darmon R.Y. (2003) *Pilotage dynamique de la force de vente, Village Mondial*. Paris: Pearson Education.

Digman, J.M. (1990) 'Personality Structure: Emergence of a Five Factor Model', *Annual Review of Psychology*, 41 (1): 417–40.

Dubinsky, A.J., Howell, R.D., Ingram, T.N., Bellenger, D.N. (1986) 'Salesforce Socialization', *Journal of Marketing*, 50 (4): 192–207.

Duhamel, S., Roi, P. and Roudaut, G. (2009) *Le grand livre des tests de recrutement*, 2nd edition. Paris: Studyrama.

Feldman, D.C. (1976) 'A Contingency Theory of Socialization', *Administrative Science Quarterly*, 21 (3), 433–50.

Ford, N.M., Walker, O.C., Churchill, G.A. Jr and Hartley, S.W. (1988) 'Selecting Successful Salespeople: A Meta-Analysis of Biographical and Psychological Selection Criteria', in Houston, M.J. (ed.), *Review of Marketing 1987*. Chicago: American Marketing Association.

Fournier, C. (2001) *Gestion de la Force de Vente*, CD-Rom. Paris: Encyclopédie Universaelis.

Guinot, S. (2008) 'Rédiger une offre d'emploi en ligne pour un poste commercial', www.focusco.fr.

Humphreys, M.A. and Williams, M.R. (1996) 'Exploring the Relative Effects of Salesperson Interpersonal Process Attributes and Technical Product Attributes on Customer Satisfaction, *Journal of Personal Selling and Sales Management*, 16 (3): 47–57.

Labourdette, A. (1992) *Théorie des Organisations*. Paris: Presse Universitaire de France.

Lee, N., Sandfield, A., Dhaliwal, B. (2007) An empirical study of salesperson stereotypes amongst UK students and their implications for recruitment, *Journal of Marketing Management*, 23 (7/8): 723–744.

Litvin, D.R. (1997) 'The Discourse of Diversity: from Biology to Management', *Organization*, 4 (2): 187–209.

Marshall, G.W., Goebel, D.J. and Moncrief, W.C. (2003) 'Hiring for Success at the Buyer-seller Interface', *Journal of Business Research*, 56 (4): 247–56.

Martory, B. (2005) *Gestion des ressources humaines: pilotage social et performances*, 6th edition. Paris: Dunod.

Mathews, B.P. and Redman, T. (2001) 'Recruiting the Wrong Salespeople: Are the Job Ads to Blame?', *Industrial Marketing Management,* 30 (7): 541–50.

Mayer, D. and Greenberg, H.M. (2006) 'What Makes a Good Salesman?', *Harvard Business Review*, 84 (7/8): 164–71.

Menguc, B., Sang-Lin, H. and Seigyoung, A. (2007) 'A Test of a Model of New Salespeople Socialization and Adjustment in a Collectivist Culture', *Journal of Personal Selling and Sales Management*, 27 (2): 149–67.

Moncrief, W.C. and Marshall, G.W. (2005) 'The Evolution of the Seven Steps of Selling', *Industrial Marketing Management*, 34 (1): 13–22.

Moncrief, W.C., Marshall, G.W. and Lassk, F.G. (2006) 'A Contemporary Taxonomy of Sales Positions', *Journal of Personal Selling and Sales Management*, 26 (1): 55–65.

Myers, I.B. (1962) *The Myers-Briggs Type Indicator*. Palo Alto: Consulting Psychologist Press.

Netemeyer, R.G. and Boles, J.S. (1997) 'An Investigation into the Antecedents of Organizational Citizenship Behaviours in a Personal Selling Context, *Journal of Marketing*, 61 (3): 85–98.

Ramsey, R.P. and Sohi, R.S. (1997) 'Listening to your Customers: The Impact of Perceived Salesperson Listening Behavior on Relationship Outcomes', *Journal of the Academy of Marketing Science*, 25 (2): 127–35.

Rothstein, M.G. and Goffin, R.D. (2006) 'The Use of Personality Measures in Personnel Selection: What Does Current Research Support?', *Human Ressource Management Review*, 16 (2): 155–80.

Swenson, M.J., Swinyard, W.R., Langrehr, F.W. and Smith, S.M. (1993) 'The Appeal of a Personal Selling as a Career: A Decade Later', *Journal of Personal Selling and Sales Management*, 13 (1): 51–65.

Tanner, J.F. Jr, Fournier, C., Wise, A., Hollet, S. and Poujol, J.F. (2008) 'Executives' Perspectives of the Changing Role of the Sales Profession: Understanding their Vision of the Future, *Journal of Business and Industrial Marketing*, 23 (3): 193–202.

Tanner, J.F., Honeycutt, E.D. and Erffmeyer, R.C. (2009) *Sales Management*. Upper Saddle River, NJ: Prentice Hall.

Zeyl, A. and Dayan, A. (2000) *Force de Vente*. Paris: Editions d'Organisation.

Further reading

Adler, S. (1994) 'Personality Tests for Sales Force Selection: Worth a Fresh Look', *Review of Business*, 16 (1): 27–32.

Cron, W.L., Marshall, G.W., Singh, J., Spiro, R.L. and Sujan, H. (2005) 'Salesperson Selection, Training, and Development: Trends, Implications, and Research Opportunities, *Journal of Personal Selling and Sales Management*, 25 (2): 124–36.

Gatewood, R.D., Feild, H.S. and Barrick, M.R. (2008) *Human Resource Selection*, 6th edition. Mason, OH: Thomson.

Howell, R.D., Ingram, T.N. and Bellenger, D.N. (1986) 'Salesforce Socialization', *Journal of Marketing*, 50 (4): 192–207.

Nick, L, Sandfield, A. and Dhaliwal, B. (2007) 'An Empirical Study of Salesperson Stereotypes amongst UK Students and their Implications for Recruitment', *Journal of Marketing Management*, 23 (7/8): 723–44.

Raymond, M.A., Carlson, L. and Hopkins, C. (2006) 'Do Perceptions of Hiring Criteria Differ for Sales Managers and Sales Representatives? Implications for Marketing Education', *Journal of Marketing Education*, 28 (1): 43–55.

Renaud, S. (1988) *Sociologie de l'organisation de l'entreprise*. Paris: Dalloz.

Schwepker, C.H. and Good, D. (2007) 'Sales Management's Influence on Employment and Training in Developing an Ethical Sales Force', *Journal of Personal Selling and Sales Management*, 27 (4): 325–39.

Vinchur, A.J., Shippmann, J.S., Switzer, F.S. and Roth, P.L. (1998) 'A Meta-analytic Review of Predictors of Job Performance for Salespeople', *Journal of Applied Psychology*, 83 (4): 586–597.

12
Sales force training*

George J. Avlonitis

Contents

* Note: The author is indebted to Lamprini Piha, PhD, candidate of Athens University of Economics and Business, for assistance in the writing of this chapter.

Learning objectives

After reading this chapter, you should be able to:

- Recognize the crucial impact of training on sales force success today.
- Identify the critical issues in planning, implementing and evaluating sales force training.
- Apply a systematic process for successfully managing sales force training.
- Assess the effectiveness of a sales force training programme.

Chapter outline

This chapter looks at one of the most critical factors that affect sales force effectiveness, namely sales force training. Aiming at providing sales executives with a framework for successfully planning, implementing and evaluating sales training programmes, the chapter's structure is as follows. First, a real case history is presented in order to introduce readers to the challenges most companies face regarding the training of their sales forces. Secondly, attention is given to the typical three stages of sales training: *Sales Training Planning*, *Sales Training Implementation* and *Sales Training Evaluation*. Then, the case presented at the beginning of the chapter is discussed in detail. The chapter concludes with a summary and several important key points, such as an integrated framework for sales force training, the 'golden' rules to be followed and a sales training audit.

Pharma S.A

In 2006, Pharma S.A.,[1] a large Greek pharmaceutical company, was facing serious problems with its sales force productivity. After thorough customer and company-based research, it was shown that one of the main reasons for this was the ineffectiveness of its sales training programme. In December 2006, the Strategic Planning and Training Manager was replaced by John Petrou, former Strategic Planning Assistant Manager with many years of experience in sales. Pharma's top management believed that John had the necessary knowledge and competence to manage sales force training successfully and improve sales force productivity. A year later, John had to prepare himself for an important meeting with the board of directors, to whom he had been called to present in detail the new training programme implemented in the company. John was really anxious about whether his decisions regarding the training process and the sales force results would satisfy the board. After all, apart from proving he deserved the promotion, this meeting was also an opportunity for John to show the impact that sales training had on the company's sales force effectiveness and thus request further human and financial resources for the continuous improvement of sales force training. Would the board of directors be satisfied with his training management so far?

Introduction: why is sales force training important for sales force success?

Increased levels of competition, rapidly changing technology and a renewed focus on customer relationships are but few of the reasons why Sales Managers increasingly seek sales force training and development activities to achieve increased sales force productivity. Today, more than ever, salespeople must have a working knowledge ranging across various topics in order to meet increasing customer expectations (e.g. changes in market dynamics, business enabling technologies and business ethics). Firms are utilizing training programmes to achieve and maintain a high level of salesperson competence.

Dubinsky and Staples (1982) conceptualized sales training as providing the salesperson with requisite knowledge (e.g. product knowledge, market and competitor information, company policies and procedures) and selling skills. Sales training refers to a deliberate and formalized accumulation of information, concepts and skills that are designed to foster competence and enhance the performance of salespeople (Wilson et al. 2002).

Sales training offers a means for realizing changes within the sales force required for sales success. Through training, the sales force can be stimulated to increase communication inside and outside the organization and reduce inter- and intra-departmental misunderstandings, learn new skills, be introduced to contemporary ideas, perspectives and ways of behaving, and finally enhance its productivity.

---

[1] To preserve the anonymity of the company studied we will refer to it as 'Pharma S.A'.

It is not accidental that some of the top European business schools, such as the London Business School, INSEAD, HEC and ESADE, offer executive sales training programmes, in order to help sales executives to develop strategies, implement sales force change and maximize sales productivity, growth and profits. Those programmes last on average five days, are expensive and in some cases are developed in conjunction with American business schools (e.g. LBS-Kellogg School of Management, INSEAD-Wharton).

First stage: sales training planning

Sales training needs

The first stage of the sales force training programme involves the determination of the firm's sales training needs. According to Attia et al. (2005), two main actions should be taken in order to determine successfully those needs:

- An assessment at the firm and sales force levels to determine whether the capabilities of the sales force meet the strategic objectives of the organization and to identify any changes needed in training.
  This seems logical. Indeed, when the firm's objectives alter (e.g. new markets, new products or even marketing mix differentiations) or major changes take place in the market or in the competition, it is considered indispensable to re-examine and replan the training programme of salespeople. Such an approach ensures that sales training programmes are designed to meet organizational needs within existing support systems and organizational culture. After all, to be most effective, sales training should be aligned with organizational change initiatives and be understood within a strategic context.
- An assessment at the salesperson level in order to ascertain who, among the sales force, should be targeted for training intervention.
  Observation is a useful tool that facilitates this specific assessment, especially when it concerns the ascertainment of salespeople's weaknesses. A survey of the salespeople is also needed, in order to let them express their opinion, not only about their needs for training but also about the knowledge and skills that a good salesperson should have.

For best results, during the determination of sales training needs the above actions should be combined with research and the gathering of additional relevant information from:

- *Customers.* Data collected even from a small number of customers may provide important information concerning training needs (e.g. from questions such as 'What do you expect from a salesperson in this sector?', 'What disappoints you most in the behaviour of a salesperson?', 'Which firm in this sector possesses the best salespeople? In what way exactly are they best?')
- *Company archives.* Useful information can be drawn from firm archives concerning sales, number of customers, new customers, lost customers, size of orders, number of daily visits, etc.

When the above information is examined in combination with a salesperson's personal characteristics, experience, geographic area served and specialization, useful conclusions can be drawn about who should be trained and in what specific topics.

Research by Erffmeyer et al. (1991) showed that the most important sources of information regarding the determination of training needs are management judgment, interviews with salespeople, performance measures such as sales volume, customer service, customer complaints and organizational/sales goals. The least important source seems to be competitors' sales training programmes.

Sales training objectives

Objectives are statements of what will be accomplished through sales training (Attia et al. 2008). Given the increasing strategic importance of sales in organizations today, aligning training objectives with organizational goals is critically important. Organizational objectives are becoming more customer-centric and are embracing customer-related management or the goal of enhancing competitive position in the marketplace by developing strong, long-term relationships with customers (Rackham 2000).

As a result, Sales Managers must evaluate the abilities of the sales force and determine if it possesses the capabilities required to fulfill its role in achieving these organizational objectives. If not, managers must assess which skills, knowledge and attitudes can be acquired through the implementation of appropriate training programmes and provide accurate feedback to top management. After all, firms that are able to provide more strategically aligned sales training efforts are more likely to attain goals that lead to competitive advantage for the firm (Attia et al. 2005). In this vein, specific training objectives are necessary to guide training efforts (Johnston and Marshall 2008).

The main goal of every training programme is to increase sales volume or productivity. Most Sales Managers believe that salespeople with deep knowledge of the products and the markets, combined with sales skills, are much more efficient than their untrained colleagues.

Through sales force training, most firms not only aim to increase sales volume, but also to attain several other objectives, whose fulfillment usually leads to a variety of positive results. Honeycutt et al.(1993) developed a list of common sales training objectives by soliciting key objectives from Sales Managers, sales trainers and salespeople. Six organizational sales training objectives were identified: increasing sales volume, decreasing turnover rate of salespeople, improving customer relationships, decreasing selling costs, improving control of the sales force and improving time management. These and other objectives are presented in Table 12.1.

Training cost and duration

Training programmes are usually *expensive*, as they demand large investments in various forms of training, qualified trainers and logistics.

Considering all professional and managerial groups, salespeople receive the highest average number of training hours from their employers. In other words, companies

Table 12.1   Sales training objectives

Sales training objectives
• Improvement in salespeople's knowledge regarding:
o The products
o The firm's philosophy and culture
o The competition's characteristics
o Selling techniques
o The customers' characteristics
• Improvement in managing customer relationships
• Sales increase of a specific product or from a certain customer segment
• Increase in salespeople's self-confidence and job satisfaction
• Use of sales force as source of market information[2]
• Faster adaptation of salespeople to the demands of their job
• Decrease in sales costs
• Better time management
• Decrease in absenteeism and turnover rate of salespeople

have to invest a lot in order to make their sales forces capable of selling effectively. Particularly, in technical markets (e.g. computers, chemicals, etc.) the costs associated with the development of a single salesperson can exceed US$100,000 (Johnston and Marshall 2008). Many executives are aware that nowadays the amount spent on sales training outranks that spent on middle and upper management training.

The amount of money spent on training tends to depend on the following factors:

- the industry sector within which the company operates;
- the size of the sales force;
- the type of salespeople (trade, technical or missionary);
- the complexity of the salesperson's job (business trips, activities, etc.);
- the turnover rate;
- the firm's strategic goals and the way those goals are translated into training objectives.

The ideal budget for training has to be based on an assessment of training needs and must be large enough to guarantee their coverage. Most often the problem is not the amount of money spent on training, but the fact that the available budget is not used efficiently.

The same importance must be assigned to the *duration* of a training programme. In other words, careful consideration should be given to the length of time that a company can tolerate keeping its salespeople out of action.

Periodically, studies are conducted regarding the training cost and duration according to the category in which the sales force belongs (consumer goods, industrial

---

[2] Sales personnel are the primary contact point for the customer, are directly responsible for implementing the firm's strategies and are in an excellent position to learn about changing customers' preferences and needs (Chonko et al. 2003).

products or services). The vast majority of these studies indicate that companies selling industrial products need to spend more time and money on sales training than companies in the other two categories. Other studies show that as the size of the company increases, a proportional increase in annual sales training hours also takes place.

Second stage: sales training implementation

After the determination of training needs, training objectives and training budget, the shaping and implementation of the training programme should take place. During this second stage of sales force training, decisions should be made about the following issues.

Sales training topics

In order to choose the topics that a specific training programme should cover, Sales Managers must take into consideration the scope of the firm (products, services, markets) and the knowledge and experience level of the salespeople who are to be trained.

Various sources of information can be used to determine the appropriate content of sales training programmes. Erffmeyer et al. (1991) found that the opinions of upper management and the training department are considered the most important determinants of training programme content. Performance measures such as sales volume and customer service, job descriptions and job specifications and interviews with salespeople can also be useful sources of information for this purpose.

According to the pertinent literature (e.g. Pelham and Kravitz 2008), a typical sales training programme usually covers the following topics.

Product knowledge

The training of salespeople in almost every aspect of the product (or service) is considered indispensable. Especially in the case of manufacturing firms, salespeople must be aware of the production process and the various product uses. Salespeople, either new or experienced, should also be well informed about the strengths and weaknesses of all competitive products, in order to communicate a unique selling proposition. Moreover, due to rapid changes in many product categories, continuous training is absolutely vital.

Market and industry knowledge

All salespeople, especially entry-level ones, should be intimately acquainted with who their customers are, where they are located, what products they are interested in, their buying habits and motives as well as their financial status and credibility. In addition, it is important for salespeople to know the industry structure, and especially everything related to the company's competitors and market shares, as well as the marketing policies which characterize their market.

Company knowledge

Training, especially of entry-level salespeople, should include topics addressing the company philosophy and its policies. These might include the firm's history, its competitive position in the industry, its compensation system and its relationship with shareholders, competitors and the public at large.

Salespeople must also be aware of all company policies that affect the efficiency of their work. Such policies might relate to issues such as pricing, discounts, guarantees, credit, order-taking and the company's code of ethics.

Sales techniques

Salespeople, particularly those who have no experience in sales, should also be trained in sales techniques in order to learn 'how' to sell. These techniques usually cover all stages of the selling process (prospecting, preparation, approach, presentation, handling of objections, closing a sale, after-sale service).

Other important topics

Changes in the business environment have compelled companies to include in their training programmes topics such as management and marketing principles and even how to use a personal computer when meeting customers.

Several studies have shown that the most important topic for sales training is considered to be product knowledge followed by sales techniques. A study by Chonko et al. (1993) showed that the five most important training topics (in descending order of importance) are considered to be selling techniques, product knowledge, negotiation skills, sales aids and technical training.

Each firm can opt for all or any combination of the above in order to provide its salespeople with the necessary knowledge and skills. Through a successful training programme, salespeople can develop valuable selling skills such as negotiation and communication capabilities, self-management efficiency and presentation competence.

Sales training methods

Ideally, the salesperson enters into the relationship with the customer with a set of selling skills, knowledge about the company and its products and a range of alternatives to offer the customer. These are learned or reinforced during the sales training programme by using a number of training methodologies (Lupton et al. 1999).

The selection of the most suitable method for each sales training programme is a basic issue for the successful training of salespeople. There is no one training method that can be applied with complete success in every case. In order to select the right training method, the following factors should be taken into consideration:

- expected results from the training programme;
- number of trainees;
- experience of the trainer;
- training level of salespeople;

- former experience of salespeople and their learning ability;
- availability of training material;
- cost per trainee for each alternative method.

In any case, the selection of the most appropriate method should ideally be based upon the 'experiential learning model' (Kolb 1976; 1984). Kolb conceived learning as a four-stage cycle, maintaining that four processes must be gone through for learning to occur, as shown in Figure 12.1.

Based on the experiential learning theory, the selected training method should create the necessary conditions to allow the trainees to: involve themselves fully, without any bias, in new experiences (Concrete Experience); reflect on and observe these experiences from many perspectives (Reflective Observation); create concepts that integrate their observations into logically sound theories (Abstract Conceptualization); and use these theories to make decisions and solve problems (Active Experimentation).

The American Society for Training and Development (ASTD) separates the major sales training methodologies into self-study and workshop categories. The *self-study methodologies* are further classified as reading, pre-workshop assignments and programmed instruction. The major *workshop methodologies* consist of lectures, discussion, on-the-job training (OJT), case study and role-play.

Self-study methodologies

Budd (1987) defines self-study as 'any programme of study using a self-instructional approach without direct supervision and usually working at their own pace'. The self-study methodologies have unique characteristics such as cost-effectiveness and the ability for the learner to study at their own pace.

Historically, the training industry and managers have viewed self-study instructional methods as being limited in effectiveness. However, this view seems to be changing, at least among training professionals, who have now begun to attribute some usefulness to these teaching methods. Perhaps this change is a result of the perceived value of combining self-study methods with other training methodologies so as to give the training programme more balance.

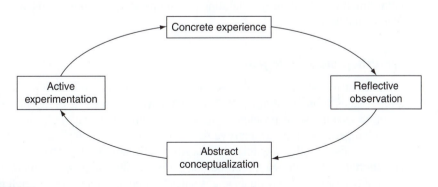

Figure 12.1   The experiential learning model
Source: Kolb (1976, 1984).

There are many advantages with the self-study methodology. Those identified in the literature primarily include flexibility in location of learning and scheduling, consistency in format and delivery, effectiveness, cost-efficiency over time, compatibility with adult learning principles and focus on the learner. The disadvantages include high development time for materials, greater difficulty in updating or revising materials, lack of interaction with peers and instructors and extensive planning requirements.

The different methods of self-study each have their own characteristics:

- *Reading* assignments from customized handouts or books. Formal training programmes have relied on this reading format more than on any other self-study tool (Chonko et al. 1993).
- *Pre-workshop assignments* take place before a sales training presentation and may include reading or the review of specific information on accounts and sales performance.
- *Programmed instruction* is based on step-by-step learning and includes direct learning through readings, audiovisual tapes and computer software. The ASTD presents the programmed instruction method as an effective tool for teaching product knowledge-based information, with the ability for the learner to set their own pace of instruction.

Self-study methodologies can nowadays be supported by several types of computer technology. E-learning is an increasingly common form of instructional delivery in business arenas such as sales force training. It has many names, including distance learning, distributed learning, online education and web learning. It covers the use of audio, video and computer videoconferencing technologies as delivery modes. Eyitayu (2005) defined e-learning as a suitable blend of knowledge and technology for progressing wide, dynamic learning–teaching development. Some of the advantages include a decrease in expenses, efficient learning and enhanced flexibility (Halawi et al. 2009).

It is worth stating that newer trainee-centered discovery learning approaches, following the Kolb cycle described earlier and utilizing IT, are also seen more frequently nowadays. As an example, several social web networking tools such as Vox, Ning and Facebook, provide the facility for salespeople to 'meet' with colleagues, exchange experiences, discuss the challenges they face and even take advice and solve problems regarding their job, thereby facilitating and simplifying peer mentoring and other forms of informal training.

Workshop methodologies

In contrast to self-study methodologies, workshop tools use information exchange among sales trainees. Reith (1987) defines a workshop as 'a group of persons with a common interest or problem, often professional or vocational, who meet for an extended period of time to improve their individual proficiency, ability or understanding by means of study, research or discussion'. Although on-the-job training (OJT) is not considered a true workshop methodology, it is equally viable where there are interactions of two or more individuals (e.g. a sales trainee and sales manager). It is therefore included in the workshop methodologies.

Ideally, the workshop methodologies can serve to enhance the success of sales training. They are outlined below:

- The traditional *lecture* requires the learner to listen in a passive manner. Although the trainer can create a positive climate for interaction, the learner is predominantly the recipient of information. This method is appropriate for disseminating lots of information to many learners at relatively small expense.
- *Discussion* is 'a purposeful conversation and deliberation about a topic of mutual interest among participants under the guidance of a trained participant called a leader'. (Reith 1987).
- *On-the-job training* is one of the quickest ways to integrate a new recruit into the sales environment. This method exposes the trainee to real sales activities through fieldwork.
- The *case study* method is a tool by which learners develop problem-solving skills and decision-making faculties outside their immediate business context. This methodology presents real-life situations that include a problem or problems that the learner is requested to resolve.
- One form of case study, *role-playing*, allows learners to act or react to different scenarios reflecting different selling behaviours and allows the learners to exchange ideas through feedback. This methodology is also often referred to as simulation.
- Finally, there are many variations of sales training workshop methodologies. For example, *presentations* are a useful method to communicate information especially about new products and sales techniques.

In addition, computer-based systems have been developed to support training programmes (e.g. business games, expert systems). These can offer new salespeople a base of experiences and techniques that have been used in the past successfully.

Research by Avlonitis et al. (1986) has shown that for different types of salespeople (trade, technical and missionary) different training methods are used:

- For trade salespeople, the methods that are used most often are 'on-the-job training' and 'discussion'.
- For technical salespeople, 'presentations' and 'lectures' are mostly used.
- For missionary salespeople, self-study methods and presentations are usually preferred.

Who should do the training?

The selection of the trainers depends on the firm's size, the products that the firm sells and the place where the training takes place. The types of trainers most usually involved are:

- *Specialized training staff*, whose specialization concerns the preparation of training material and generally the preparation of the training programme. Apart from their teaching ability, the staff are usually familiar with the use of audiovisual training methods and with appropriate training techniques. The disadvantages of this category of trainers include lack of experience regarding real situations, as those are formed in the market, and the large fixed costs that the companies incur because the training staff are included on the company's payroll and require permanent compensation.

- *Firm's sales executives.* Their participation in the training process offers additional 'weight' to the training programme as they have great experience in sales. They can be either top sales executives or middle-ranking Sales Managers (e.g. of a regional area). They know in depth the selling process and what the trainee needs in order to be efficient in sales. Moreover, through training their salespeople, they can easily communicate the objectives and the policies they want to be followed. As a consequence, less supervision is needed later. Major disadvantage might be that these sales executives may not have the necessary communication abilities for training and that their time is a costly commodity.

- *Special trainers from outside the firm.* These trainers may be responsible for the whole training programme or they may just organize it and leave the teaching to others. Small firms, which do not have the necessary funds to employ permanent staff responsible only for training, may use this category of trainers. The advantages identified in this category of trainers include the creativity, knowledge and enthusiasm they can bring to a training programme. The main disadvantage is considered to be a possible lack of familiarity with the selling process followed in the specific industry, as well as with the clients and the competitors of the company.

Studies have shown that firms of any size use sales executives, while specialized trainers either from outside or inside the firm are usually met in large firms. Chonko et al. (1993) showed that top sales executives are the most commonly used sales trainers, followed by middle-level Sales Managers, company trainers and outside sales trainers.

Where should the training take place?

The main question to be answered here is whether the training is to be centralized (taking place in the firm's central offices) or decentralized (in branch offices). The two locations are dealt with below.

Centralized training

Training takes place in the firm's central offices. The main advantage of this is that it enables more efficient learning, as it may include:

- specialized trainers;
- high quality material and new technology (audiovisual apparatus, simulation tools, etc.);
- contact with upper management and sales executives, something that has a positive influence on the trainees' psychology and gives them the possibility of learning from experienced and capable members of the firm;
- more consistency and professionalism.

On the other hand, centralized training is more costly, which may affect the duration of the programme.

Decentralized training

With this alternative, the whole training process moves towards the salesperson's work location. Seminars take place near the area where the salesperson lives and works.

The main advantages of this are:

* continuous supervision and coaching by the local (area) Sales Manager;
* knowledge acquisition relating to the circumstances that exist in the specific area;
* salespeople utilize their time better and travel costs are avoided.

The disadvantages include the fact that the local (area) Sales Manager does not usually have the necessary time to teach trainees due to a heavy workload and the fact that the content of the training programme varies from area to area.

Research by Avlonitis et al. (1986) indicated a relationship between the decision about who should do the training and where it should take place and the type of salespeople trained. Centralized training and specialized training staff are mainly used for missionary salespersons. In the case of trade salespersons, either centralized training in combination with outside special trainers or decentralized training combined with internal sales experts are used.

When should the training take place?

It is important to schedule training well in advance. Sales training must be scheduled at least 30 days in advance and changes at short notice should be avoided. Planning ahead not only helps minimize scheduling conflicts, but it also provides the opportunity for training preparation and promotion of the training event. Attendees are typically more receptive and inclined to participate when they have been given sufficient time to plan and prepare for the training (Krishnamoorthy et al. 2005).

In any case, sales training should take place before a salesperson goes out into the market to sell. This is logical, especially for technical salespeople who must know the company's products in depth in order to be able to sell them to experienced and technically educated buyers. Ideally, the training should be held close in time to when the selling skills are needed. When a vast amount of information is given to a salesperson who does not immediately use it, this knowledge may gradually fade.

Who should be trained?

There are two primary assessments for sales executives to make when selecting which salespeople will benefit most from training:

* First, he/she needs to identify salespersons who are deficient in desired competencies. This requires a process for measuring a salesperson's knowledge, skills, behaviours and personality traits (i.e. competencies) against predefined criteria.

- Second, he/she has to assess whether or not a salesperson is able to benefit from training at this particular time.

Those salespeople with deficiencies and/or those at an appropriate stage of readiness are the obvious candidates for receiving training.

Ideally, the assessment of a salesperson's capabilities and deficiencies is conducted on an individual basis, one salesperson at a time. However, this becomes increasingly problematic as the size of a sales force grows and Sales Managers become responsible for developing larger numbers of salespeople. Similarly, the autonomy of salespeople and the lack of significant direct contact with management make it difficult to assess salespeople's needs. As a result, Sales Managers may rely upon measures of performance (e.g. sales and customer satisfaction indices) and readily available knowledge of relevant characteristics to help them decide who should receive training. In effect, a segmentation approach is utilized. Segmentation of salespeople for training is conducted by employing criteria such as geographic location, market and customer characteristics, individual characteristics or some combination of these.

It is, however, important to remember that assessing salespeople's competencies and deficiencies is expensive. One Fortune 100 firm determined some years ago that a quality competency assessment costs about $1,000 per professional employee (Ennis 1998). In addition, Sales Managers must determine how assessment may affect morale. Since sales training potentially affects the future performance of those selected, sales executives must consider both the legal and ethical implications of their decisions.

Third stage: sales training evaluation

Without effective training, salespeople will never reach their full potential. Even though companies' investment in sales training programmes are particularly high, the evaluation of those programmes does not always take place. As indicated by Johnston and Marshall (2008), too often management fails to understand the importance of sales training since only costs are evaluated and not the potential revenue generated from effective training. However, sales training evaluation constitutes a crucial part of the training process and should not be absent from any sales training programme.

In a thorough evaluation:

- the effectiveness of trainers is assessed;
- the training investment is justified through cost-benefit analysis;
- the structure and content of the training programme is reviewed in order to identify areas for improvement;
- the relative benefits of the training programme for the individual trainees is determined;
- the training programme's advantages are reinforced and trainees' morale is increased.

As we have already mentioned, one of the key aspects for the design of any high quality training programme is the consideration of the needs of the trainees. However, without a proper framework for sales training evaluation, such programmes cannot, often by their very nature, adjust to those needs (Lupton et al. 1999).

Kirkpatrick (1987) defined four steps to measure the effectiveness of training programmes, as presented in Table 12.2. For each step additional information is provided in order to give specific guidelines for successful sales training evaluation.

More recent research has built on the original model by identifying more detailed sub-categories (Alliger et al. 1997) or by adding additional stages (Burrow and Berardinelli 2003; Phillips, 1998). The two most recent sales training evaluation frameworks are extensions of the Kirkpatrick model. Lupton et al. (1999) adopted

Table 12.2 Four steps to measure training effectiveness

Evaluation Level	1. Reaction	2. Learning	3. Behaviour	4. Results
Definition	*How the trainees felt about the learning experience.*	*The increase in knowledge – before and after.*	*The extent of applied learning when back on the job.*	*The effect on business by the trainee.*
Questions that must be asked	Did the trainees like and enjoy the training? Was it useful? Did they like the venue, the style, etc? What proposals for improvement do they have?	What principles, facts, and techniques were learned? What attitudes were changed? Did the trainees learn what was intended to be taught?	Are the trainees using the knowledge acquired during training? Was there noticeable and measurable change in the activity and performance of the trainees when back in their jobs?	Is the firm, the unit or the department in a better place now, after the training? What are the tangible results of the training for the firm?
Measurements	Feedback forms based on subjective personal reaction to the training experience. Verbal reaction noted and analysed. Post-training surveys or questionnaires. Verbal or written reports given by delegates to their managers back at their jobs.	Typically, assessments or tests before and after the training. Hard copy, electronic, online or interview-style assessments are all possible.	Observation and interviews over time are required to assess change, relevance of change, and sustainability of change. Assessments (e.g. evaluations by supervisors, colleagues, customers and subordinates; critical cases), need to be designed to reduce subjective judgment of the observer or interviewer.	Typical measures would be business or organizational key performance indicators, (such as sales volumes, values, percentages, timescales) and other quantifiable aspects of organizational performance (e.g. number of complaints; staff turnover, attrition, failures, achievement of standards and accreditations, growth, retention).

Kirkpatrick's framework for their five-stage model of sales training evaluation. They add 'trainer/trainee incompetence, poor employment, screening influences and other contextual influences (such as customer satisfaction)' as a fifth category. Likewise, Honeycutt et al. (2001) integrate economic utility theory and recommend evaluating the economic return of sales training as a fifth assessment level.

Organizations investing resources in sales training want to see that training expenditures actually assist them to reach their objectives. In fact, companies use a wide variety of training evaluation procedures, ranging from self-administered reports completed by the trainees and informal debriefing sessions to more elaborate calculations of whether sales revenue has been enhanced. The information and feedback emanating from these evaluation procedures are central to successful implementation of strategic organizational initiatives (Moore and Seidner 1998). However, having the right information at the correct time and using it wisely are key challenges faced by firms.

CASE PROBLEM REVISITED

Sales force training at Pharma S.A.

As stated at the beginning of the chapter, in order to understand sales force training in action better, we examine a case study from the pharmaceutical sector.

Company background

Pharma S.A., a Greek pharmaceutical company, has a long history going back many decades. During its early years, Pharma's scope was the distribution of pharmaceutical products and it did so for several years for large international pharmaceutical companies. Since 1971 the company has followed a course of rapid development and it has gained recognition, establishing strategic partnerships with leading international pharmaceutical companies.

In its sector, Pharma is a worthy exponent of Greek industrial and commercial creativity. With unique production capabilities and a workforce of more than 1,000 people, it covers the entire spectrum of manufactured pharmaceuticals and continuously upgrades the range of services offered to the market. Its financial strength, as shown by its annual balance sheets, places Pharma among the most reliable and efficient companies in Greece.

Importance of training

John Petrou, the new Strategic Planning and Training Manager in Pharma S.A. mentioned at the beginning of this chapter, began his presentation to the board by focusing on the critical importance that sales training has for the company. According to John, sales training for Pharma is extremely important for the following two reasons:

- This industry is very competitive since a large number of pharmaceutical companies exist and not one of them has more than 10 per cent market share. For example, in the antihypertensive category of medicines, there exist about 800 different brands in Greece. Therefore, salespeople must be capable of differentiating their company's products from those of their competitors and communicate the right messages. To succeed in this role, training is absolutely vital in order to survive and achieve a competitive advantage.

- The customers in this industry are very specialized and of a high educational level. Customers are doctors (80 per cent), pharmacists or executives in the health sector, such as hospital managers. Salespeople need to be adequately trained in order to know how to deal successfully with customers according to their specializations and educational level. This is the reason why, lately, medical doctors and pharmacists are entering the sales force in the pharmaceutical industry. However, this fact increases the necessity of high-level training, since well educated salespeople have high expectations from training and want to be trained on how to relate to their customers successfully.

Sales training objectives

John continued his presentation to the board by explaining the objectives set for Pharma's new sales training programmes. Through its sales training the company now aims to:

- Offer its salespeople the necessary *basic knowledge about the product category* that they handle. This means that every salesperson, by the end of the training programme, will have obtained basic knowledge of anatomy, pharmacology and the specific products they will be responsible for promoting and selling. Since salespeople will have to communicate with specialized customers on health, they must understand the basics in order to be able to communicate their message successfully (e.g. where the main human organs are, the different forms of medicine dispensed – tablets, injections, etc.) and on each customer visit, they must know all the technical and scientific facts regarding the specific diseases and the medicines to treat them.
- Give its sales force deep *knowledge of sales techniques*. It is important that salespeople acquire the necessary theoretical and practical understanding of 'how' to sell. This is crucial for a pharmaceutical firm, taking into consideration the particularities of missionary selling. In this case, the selling process is so indirect that a salesperson must be more than expert in sales techniques in order to succeed and influence the final product sale. John introduced training programmes at different grades to cater for the different needs of newcomers and more experienced salespersons.
- Give its salespeople access to the necessary customer information so that can get to *know their customers well* (preferences, habits, particularities, etc.).
- *Develop the whole sales force* through a human resource management programme. According to this programme, which is continuous for all the company's employees, salespeople's deficiencies as well as their strong points are determined and they are then helped to improve their weaknesses and take advantage of their strengths. For example, if a salesperson is found to have poor leadership ability, he/she attends a leadership-training programme. Correspondingly, if a salesperson confronts difficulties in using his/her time to full advantage, he/she attends a time management training programme.
- Offer its salespeople *deep knowledge about the whole company philosophy* (e.g. management and marketing policies) that employees should be aware of.

John also stressed that, as in every firm, the final goal of the sales training programme is *sales volume increase*, through the creation of competent and successful salespeople.

Sales training topics and duration of training

John described the duration of training for an entry-level salesperson and the training topics as shown in Table 12.3:

Table 12.3 Training topics and duration of training at Pharma

Time	Training topics
1st week	Company history, Vision, Mission, etc. (2 days) Anatomy, Pharmacology, Clinical studies (5 days)
2nd–4th weeks	Product categories, Specific brands of the categories (1 week for each category)
5th week	Sales techniques Managerial issues ('how the company works') Other company products (basic information) Use of PC software
6th week	Practice in the market accompanied by experienced colleagues (attending visits to hospitals and doctors' offices)
1 day	Exams
1 day	Handover of duty and tasks (if exams were successful)
7th–8th weeks	Practice in the market accompanied by the supervisor

After the completion of these 8 weeks of training for an entry-level rep, a month of tight supervision by the salesperson's supervisor follows.

As far as the 'older' salespeople are concerned, under the spectrum of continuing professional development, two training programmes take place:

- A training week per year that usually consists of one or more seminars outside the company and probably abroad. These seminars usually involve dynamic salespeople and may be on a variety of topics.
- Meetings, which usually last one to three days inside the company, three or four times a year, where salespeople are informed about new developments in the company or in the industry (new products, new strategies, market data, etc.). In the case of a new product, four or five days before its launch salespeople will receive training on it.

Cost of training

In order to convince the board of the necessity for stronger support for sales training in terms of human and financial recourses, John underlined that the training cost for a pharmaceutical company is a necessity, especially when the firm seeks to meet successfully the intense competition in the industry. In particular, as John pointed out, the training costs consist of:

- The time of all internal trainers and trainees. The hours spent on training are valuable since they are not 'invested' in sales.
- The payment of external trainers (e.g. doctors, trainers specializing in sales).
- The development of the training programme by the mother-company.
- The adaptation of imported training programmes to the company's specific circumstances.
- The purchase of specific training programmes.
- The cost of organizing the training (e.g. 'classrooms', catering, accommodation and air tickets – when a seminar takes place abroad, room decoration, concept creation, videotaping, handouts, presentations, etc.)
- The development of case studies and simulations.
- The evaluation process (exams, evaluation forms, etc.)

John recognized that the company spends a large amount of money every year in order to achieve a high level of training. However, he added that Pharma should consider this important expense for training an 'investment'.

Sales training methods

Almost all training methods are used in the new training programme of Pharma (reading assignments, programmed instructions, lectures, case studies, simulations, on-the-job training).

John noted that, recently, pharmaceutical companies are trying to use new training models that are oriented towards more personalized training and provide:

- less contact time of a trainer with the trainees;
- more modern training technologies using multimedia (e.g. e-learning);
- smaller groups of trainees.

Who is the trainer?

John had also prepared a table (see Table 12.4) in order to explain to the board that the type of trainer used by Pharma depends on the training topic each time.

Table 12.4   Type of trainers at Pharma

Trainers	Training Topic
Physicians of Pharma	Anatomy
Scientists of Pharma	Pharmacology
External specialist doctors	Other medical issues
External trainers specialing in sales	Sales techniques
Experienced trainers	'Trainers' session' (Training of possible trainers)
Product Managers	Product characteristics
Marketing and Sales Managers	Case studies and simulations
Training Manager	Managerial issues ('How the company works')
General Manager and other managers	Company history and philosophy

Where does the training take place?

As John described, the main training takes place in rooms especially designed and adequately equipped for training, inside or outside the company. Sometimes the training may take place in hotel seminar rooms, in order to offer the trainees a different environment. Some training seminars are held abroad, in towns chosen by the mother-company. Finally, training also takes place 'at home', where trainees study the training material.

Sales training evaluation

Towards the end of the meeting, John was asked by a member of the board whether an evaluation system for sales training existed. John was well prepared for this question. As he explained to the board member, at the end of every training section trainees are subjected to tests in order to evaluate their reaction and learning at each particular section. Moreover, a final evaluation of the trainees takes place when the training programme is completed. Only the trainees who succeed in this final exam are allowed to continue as missionary salespeople of the company. At the same time, trainees evaluate the trainers as well as their training conditions (classrooms, training materials, hotels, etc.), a fact that really helps the management to upgrade the level of sales training offered.

However, he added that the evaluation process does not end with the completion of the training programme. The evaluation constitutes a continuous process that takes place in different forms throughout the whole year, in order to monitor the behaviour and the resulting achievements of the trainees.

Finally, John mentioned that the new sales training process of Pharma had received ISO certification and, as a consequence, it was possible for Pharma to measure the training process at all levels (reaction, learning, behaviour, results), detect possible causes of problems and take all necessary actions to improve the training programme.

Pharma's training vision

The board of directors was very satisfied with John's results and urged him to continue the good work even more intensively. The CEO of Pharma stressed that 'training becomes a necessity for every firm, as the environment gets more and more competitive'. In this vein he added that 'increasing complexity in the market is radically changing the skills and strategies that determine sales and marketing success'. Therefore, turning to John, he noted that 'meeting the demands of today's new dynamics calls for innovative approaches based on in-depth knowledge and practical experience of proven and leading-edge techniques. In order to reach these new levels of achievement, pharmaceutical sales and marketing personnel must learn, adopt and implement improved ways of working.'

John responded that he aimed to continue to improve the sales training programme in order to achieve Pharma's final goals: *satisfied customers* and *satisfied employees*. The meeting ended with John stating, 'Training at Pharma is an investment and a continuous effort to offer the best possible education to people who will have to survive and win in the difficult "arena" of sales. Salespeople must feel sure of their ability and possibility to sell.'

Summary

In this chapter we have tried to present the process of sales force training through a combination of a review of the existing literature on the subject and business

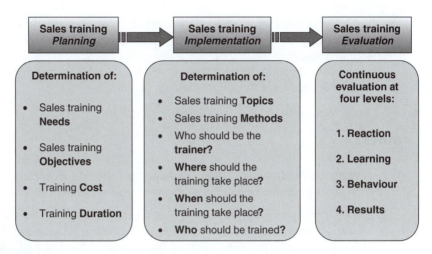

Figure 12.2   Sales force training summary framework

practice. The chapter was completed with the presentation of a real case example from business. This case study refers to a Greek pharmaceutical company and it showed how missionary sales force training is realized in practice. A summary framework for the sales force training process analysed in this chapter is shown in Figure 12.2.

Sales force training begins with *Planning*. This stage consists of:

1. the determination of sales training needs, which can be specified by considering the capabilities of the sales force, the changes that need to occur, the opinions of customers and all relevent information that the firm possesses;
2. the determination of sales training objectives, which need to be aligned with the organization's goals;
3. the determination of training cost and duration, both very important factors that also need to be specified.

The second stage of sales force training is *Implementation*, during which a firm must decide:

1. which topics the sales training programme should cover (product knowledge, sales techniques, industry knowledge, etc.);
2. which training methods will be used (self-study methodologies, workshop methodologies or a combination of both);
3. which types of trainers will undertake the training of the salespeople (specialized training staff, the firm's sales executives, special trainers from outside the firm);
4. whether the training will take place in the firm's central offices, in branch offices or outside the company;
5. whether the training will take place before or after a salesperson goes out into the market to sell;
6. which of the sales people will be selected for training.

The third stage of sales force training, the *Evaluation*, is a process through which the effectiveness of a training programme is assessed, by measuring the reaction, learning, behaviour and results of the trainees.

A careful consideration of every stage is needed in order to maximize the benefits acquired by the sales force though the training process.

Key points

1. According to Alan Dubinsky (1996), management should follow three main guidelines in order to get the best out of sales training. Management should:

   a) *Design a quality training programme*. It is crucial to determine the training needs of each trainee and then carefully design a training programme that satisfies those needs. Who provides much of the training, what types of sales training are emphasized and what level of resources is available to use in the training programme are less important than the quality of the training programme.

   b) *Give trainees their independence*. Sales Managers should offer sales personnel relative freedom shortly after the completion of the training programme. This independence will afford the salespeople the opportunity to practise what they have learned in the training programme without unnecessary instruction from the Sales Manager. As such, the returns from the training programme may be enhanced. In essence, Sales Managers should offer guidance and support to the trainees as required. Undue supervision should be avoided as it may impede the impact of the training programme.

   c) *Maintain competitive viability*. Companies in industries that are characterized by rapid product obsolescence (e.g. high-tech) should pay careful attention to the design and implementation of their training programmes. Sound training should assist their sales personnel in removing outdated products and learning about soon-to-be-released (or recently released) products.

2. Sales organizations should ensure that:

   a) training interventions are aligned with the strategic focus of the firm;

   b) reasons for training failures are accurately identified;

   c) continuous improvements in their training efforts are faciliated;

   d) the investment value of training programmes is determined.

3. All the above argue for carefully designing and implementing sales training programmes that meet the training needs of the sales force and can assist the company in achieving its objectives. For firms that take a more strategic view of training there is evidence that sales force development is effective and can provide a source of competitive advantage.

4. However, we should take into consideration that Avlonitis and Panagopoulos (2007) found an absence of association between sales training and changes in salespeople's attitudes and outcomes. This means that merely providing sales training programmes is neither a sufficient nor an adequate condition for gaining performance improvements. Consequently, Sales Managers should be very cautious when they simply assume that more training is always better. Rather, they should

strive to evaluate the quality and the effectiveness of training programmes on the basis of both qualitative and quantitative criteria.

Running a sales training audit in your company

Based on the analysis that took place in this chapter, Table 12.5 provides a Sales Training Audit that sales executives can follow in order to ensure the successful and effective training of their sales forces.

Table 12.5   Sales training audit

Sales Training Audit	YES	NO
1 Is the content and process of our firm's sales training programme in accordance with the firm's sales training needs?		
2 Are our sales training objectives clear and aligned with the organizational goals?		
3 Is it possible for our firm to 'afford' the cost and duration of our sales training programme?		
4 Do the training topics selected reflect the firm's scope and the trainees' level of knowledge and experience?		
5 Are the sales training methods chosen consistent with the number of trainees, their experience level and the capabilities of our firm?		
6 Does the selection of the trainers correspond to the firm's size, scope and market opportunities?		
7 Are the salespeople selected for training the most appropriate and ready to benefit from training at this specific time?		
8 Is the whole training programme evaluated continuously at all levels (reaction, learning, behaviour and results)?		
9 Apart from the trainees, are the trainers and the training conditions (training materials, classrooms, etc.) also evaluated?		
10 Have all the necessary actions been taken in order to resolve problems detected through the evaluation process and improve the training programme?		

References

Alliger, G.M., Tannenbaum, S.I., Bennett Jr, W., Traver, H. and Shotland, A. (1997) 'A Meta-Analysis of the Relations Among Training Criteria,' *Personnel Psychology*, 50 (Summer): 341–58.

Attia, A.M., Honeycutt Jr, E.D. and Jantan, A.M. (2008) 'Global Sales Training: In Search of Antecedent, Mediating, and Consequence Variables', *Industrial Marketing* Management, 37 (2): 181–90.

Attia, A.M., Honeycutt Jr, E.D. and Leach, M.P. (2005) 'A Three Stage Model For Assessing And Improving Sales Force Training And Development', *Journal of Personal Selling and Sales Management*, 25 (3): 253–68.

Avlonitis, G.J., Boyle, K.A. and Kouremenos, A. (1986) 'Matching Salesmen to the Selling Job', *Industrial Marketing Management*, 15 (1): 45–54.

Avlonitis, G.J. and Panagopoulos, N.G (2007) 'Exploring the Influence of Sales Management Practices on the Industrial Salesperson: A Multi-source Hierarchical Linear Modeling Approach', *Journal of Business Research*, 60 (7): 765–75.

Budd, M.L. (1987) 'Self-Instruction', in Craig, R.L. (ed.), *Training and Development Handbook: A Guide to Human Resource Development, 3rd edition.* New York: McGraw Hill.

Burrow, J. and Berardinelli, P. (2003) 'Systematic Performance Improvement – Refining the Space Between Learning and Results', *Journal of Workplace Learning*, 15 (1): 6–13.

Chonko, L., Dubinsky, A.J., Jones, E. and Roberts, J.A. (2003) 'Organizational and Individual Learning in the Sales Force: An Agenda for Sales Research,' *Journal of Business Research*, 56 (12): 935–46.

Chonko, L., Tanner, J. and Weeks, W. (1993) 'Sales Training: Status and Needs', *Journal of Personal Selling and Sales Management*, 13 (4): 81–6.

Dubinsky, A.J. (1996) 'Some Assumptions about the Effectiveness of Sales Training', *Journal of Personal Selling and Sales Management*, 16 (3): 67–76.

Dubinsky, A.J. and Staples, W.A. (1982) ?Sales Training: Salespeople's Preparedness and Managerial Implications', *Journal of Personal Selling and Sales Management*, 2 (1): 24–31.

Ennis, S. (1998) 'Assessing Employee Competencies', in Brown, S.M. and Seidner, C.J. (eds), *Evaluating Corporate Training: Models and Issues*, 183–208, Boston: Kluwer Academic.

Erffmeyer, R., Russ K.R. and Hair Jr, J.F. (1991) 'Needs Assessment and Evaluation in Sales-Training Programs', *Journal of Personal Selling and Sales Management*, 11 (1): 18–30.

Eyitayo, O. (2005) 'Experimenting e-learning with a Large Class', *International Journal of Education and Development Using Information and Communication Technology*, 1 (3): 160–72.

Halawi L.A., McCarthy, R.V. and Pires, S. (2009) 'An Evaluation of e-Learning on the Basis of Bloom's Taxonomy', *Journal of Education for Business*, July/August: 374–80.

Honeycutt, E.D., Howe, V. and Ingram, T.N. (1993) 'Shortcomings of Sales Training Programs', *Industrial Marketing Management*, 22 (May): 117–23.

Honeycutt, E.D., Karande, K., Attia, A. and Maurer, S.D. (2001) 'A Utility-Based Framework for Evaluating the Financial Impact of Sales Force Training Programs', *Journal of Personal Selling and Sales Management*, 21 (3): 229–38.

Johnston, M.W. and Marshall, G.W. (2008) *Churchill/Ford/Walker's Sales Force Management.* New York: McGraw Hill/Irwin.

Krishnamoorthy, A., Misra, S. and Prasad, A. (2005) 'Scheduling Sales Force Training: Theory and Evidence', *International Journal of Research in Marketing*, 22 (4): 427–40.

Kirkpatrick, D.L. (1987) 'Evaluation', in Robert, L. (ed.), *Training and Development Handbook.* New York: McGraw Hill Inc..

Kolb, D.A. (1976) 'Management and the Learning Process', *California Management Review*, 18 (3): 21–31.

Kolb, D.A. (1984) *Experiential Learning: Experience as the Source of Learning and Development.* New Jersey: Prentice-Hall.

Lupton, R.A., Weiss, J.E. and Peterson, R.P.(1999) 'Sales Training Evaluation Model (STEM): A Conceptual Framework', *Industrial Marketing Management*, 28 (January): 73–86.

Moore, C.A. and Seidner, C.J. (1998) 'Organizational Strategy and Training Evaluation', in Brown, S.M. and Seidner, C.J. (eds), *Evaluating Corporate Training: Models and Issues*, 19–40. Boston: Kluwer Academic.

Pelham, A.M. and Kravitz, P. (2008) 'An Exploratory Study of the Influence of Sales Training Content and Salesperson Evaluation on Salesperson Adaptive Selling, Customer Orientation, Listening, and Consulting Behaviors', *Journal of Strategic Marketing*, 16 (5): 413–35.

Phillips, J.J. (1998) 'Level Four and Beyond: An ROI Model', in Brown, S.M. and Seidner, C.J. (eds), *Evaluating Corporate Training: Models and Issues*, 113–40. Boston: Kluwer Academic.

Rackham, N. (2000) 'Face-to-Face Selling Is More Important than Ever,' *Sales and Marketing Management*, 152 (3): 34–8.

Reith, J.L. (1987) 'Meetings, Conferences, Workshops, and Seminars', in Craig, R.L. (ed.), *Training and Development Handbook: A Guide to Human Resource Development*, 3rd edition, 398–413. New York: McGraw Hill.

Wilson P.H., Strutton, D. and Farris, M.T. (2002) 'Investigating the Perceptual Aspect of Sales Training', *Journal of Personal Selling and Sales Management*, 22 (2): 77–86.

Further reading

Attia, A.M., Honeycutt, E.D. and Attia, M.M. (2002) 'The Difficulties of Evaluating Sales Training', *Industrial Marketing Management*, 31 (3): 253–59.

Avlonitis, G.J. and Boyle, K.A. (1989) 'Linkages between Sales Management Tools and Practices: Some Evidence from British Companies', *Journal of the Academy of Marketing Science*, 17 (2): 133–41.

Honeycutt, E.D., Ford, J.B. and Tanner, J.F. (1994) 'Who Trains Salespeople: The Role of Sales Trainers and Sales Managers', *Industrial Marketing Management*, 23 (1): 65–70.

Honeycutt, E.D. and Stevenson, T.H. (1989) 'Evaluating Sales Training Programs', *Industrial Marketing Management*, 18 (3): 65–70.

Kirkpatrick, D.L. (1959) 'Techniques for Evaluating Training Programs', *Journal of the American Society for Training and Development*, 13 (11): pp. 3–9.

Kirkpatrick, D.L. (1996) 'Great Ideas Revisited', *Training and Development*, 50 (January): 55–7.

Leach, M.P. and Liu, A.H. (2003) 'Investigating Interrelationships among Sales Training Evaluation Methods', *Journal of Personal Selling and Sales Management*, 23 (4): 325–37.

Pelham, A.M. (2009) 'The Impact of Industry and Training Influences on Sales Force Consulting Time and Consulting Effectiveness', *Journal of Business and Industrial Marketing*, 24 (8): 575–84.

Part four

Implementation of the sales programme: directing efforts

13

Team leadership and coaching

Paolo Guenzi

Contents

Learning objectives

After reading this chapter, you should be able to:

• Recognize the critical importance today of team leadership and coaching in sales.

• Distinguish team leadership from team coaching.

• Understand how team leaders can affect team processes and team performance.

• Understand how to apply to a sales team context the lessons learnt from team sports.

Chapter outline

Sales Managers usually lead teams of salespeople, and the sport metaphor is often used to provide guidelines and suggestions on how to lead performance-oriented teams. With the aim of enabling sales executives to obtain useful insights from coaches of professional sports teams, this chapter is structured as follows. First, a real-world problem is presented to stimulate readers' attention in the topic. Second, similarities and differences between sales teams and sport teams are discussed. Third, the relevant literature on leadership, team leadership and team coaching is reviewed. Fourth, special attention is devoted to the role of motivation in team leadership. Then, research analysing coaching in professional sports teams is presented. Finally, several key points are offered, such as a number of 'golden' rules for sales executives together with an overall model of team leadership and a team climate audit.

CASE PROBLEM

Iveco

With sales exceeding €9 billion, 31,000 employees and approximately 800 dealers all over the world, Iveco (Industrial Vehicles Corporation) is one of the world's largest manufacturers in the Commercial Vehicles (CV) business. Iveco is part of the Fiat group. It has 49 manufacturing plants and 15 research and development centres in 19 countries on the five continents, and operates in over 100 countries through joint ventures, licensees and participating investments.

The company designs, builds and sells a comprehensive range of light, medium and heavy commercial vehicles. It complements its product range with an array of after-sales, financial and used vehicle services. In Europe Iveco is market leader in the medium CV segment and second in light and heavy CV, where it operates with the Daily and Stralis brands respectively. The CV market is characterized by increasing regulation, stronger competition and the increasing focus of customers on return on investment.

Iveco's strategic vision is built around improving transport productivity by optimizing the total cost of ownership of vehicles. In fact, in the transport market margins are becoming progressively lower and transport operators that do not have critical mass are facing big difficulties. As a consequence, the market is increasingly characterized by concentration: key players operate through big fleets, and centralization of purchasing is accelerating. Hence the contractual power of customers has increased rapidly. Moreover, since most big customers operate internationally, their tenders cover many countries. This implies a greater need for cross-national coordination. Additionally, services requests are becoming more and more detailed and demanding.

Consistent with this trend, Iveco set up an International Key Account (IKA) department. This unit focuses mainly on two goals:

1. to manage the business directly with international customers at a corporate level, supported by local marketing personnel worldwide;
2. to develop coordinated control of sales processes and standards with national key accounts in each local market.

The IKA team identified 62 international key accounts which were split into nine segments according to their industry or mission. Examples of customers in the food and beverage sector are Coca-Cola, Pepsi, BoFrost, Nestlé, Procter & Gamble and Unilever. In the mail and parcel business, key accounts are companies such as Deutsche Post, UPS, TNT and FedEx. Key customers in the rental industry include, among others, Europcar and Hertz. Panalpina, Schenker and Nippon Express are some of the key accounts in the logistics market.

The typical buying process of International Key Accounts is based on tenders. Iveco's International Key Account team coordinates the information coming from the markets related to the tender and liaises with the central vehicle and Customer Service business units and Iveco Finance to solve specific problems and meet a client's requirements: e.g. countries with no local financing structure, no opportunity to purchase buy-back vehicles, the requirement for one unique price to cover every country or for special extensions to contracts.

The IKA team consists of 12 people working in Iveco headquarters in Turin, plus 50 people in the local markets. From an organizational standpoint, the ACE (Account Executives) Team includes all Key Account Managers (KAMs) and all Iveco personnel who work together on all matters concerning a Global Key Account customer (Finance, Customer Service, Used Vehicles, Quotation, Technical and Marketing Solutions, etc). In short, IKA processes typically involve people from several different departments and markets (see Figure 13.1).

In general, the International Key Account Manager is considered the process owner. In this role he/she is usually supported at headquarters by a group of colleagues (the ACE Support Team), in cooperation with their respective counterparts in the local markets, on specific aspects of the

Process owner: International KA Manager

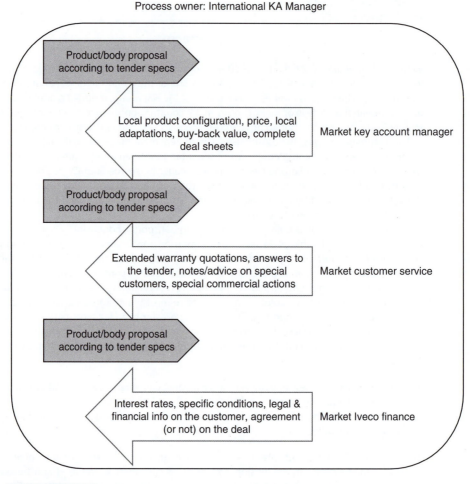

Figure 13.1 Key internal interactions in International Key Account Management at Iveco

sales process (tender specifications, customer service and financial conditions). Goals, resources and activities have to be coordinated, integrated and synchronized across different business units, departments and countries in the organization.

The Director of the IKA department thought that creating team spirit among all those involved was necessary for KAM processes to be implemented successfully. He looked at the world of sports for inspiration: what ideas, examples, best practices could be taken from that context and applied to his situation?

Introduction: what is team leadership? Why is it relevant for Sales Managers?

Sales organizations are increasing their use of sales teams, but team selling is an under-researched area where little empirical testing has been done. Companies need to

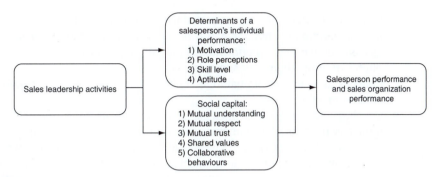

Figure 13.2 Sales leadership framework
Source: adapted from Ingram et al. (2005).

understand better how sales teams function and how interpersonal relationships influence their effectiveness. In this perspective, the role of sales teams leaders deserves special attention. According to Ingram et al. (2005), sales leaders influence the performance of teams reporting to them in two ways (see Figure 13.2). First, they affect the drivers of individual salespeople's performance by increasing motivation, clarifying roles and expectations, developing subordinates' skills and competencies and stimulating learning and risk-taking. Second, they increase the team's social capital by stimulating mutual understanding, respect and trust among team members, as well as by promoting shared values and by fostering collaborative behaviour.

Sales teams have many characteristics in common with sports teams. In fact, just like sports players:

1. Salespeople have a direct, visible and often measurable impact on an organization's performance.
2. Salespeople must typically possess innate abilities, in addition to being strongly motivated, to deliver a good performance.
3. Salespeople are highly focused on short-term goals (weekly sales are analogous to single games) in addition to yearly results (which in the sport field could be winning the championship, participating to play-offs, etc.).
4. Salespeople usually compete with each other (for example to win contests) but, at the same time, are increasingly asked to cooperate with colleagues, for example to win some customers through team selling or to maximize the overall performance of a territory. As pointed out by Ingram et al. (2005), teamwork is often required in the selling context: salespeople operate in formal and informal teams with people belonging to different functions, business units and geographical areas. In fact the traditional 'lone wolf' stereotype of the salesperson has almost entirely been replaced by the ability to be a team player and to interact with colleagues from different departments in order to be successful with customers.
5. Salespeople directly compete with opponents and can both win or lose (orders, accounts, tenders, etc.); wins and losses typically have a strong impact on the team climate.
6. Salespeople are often perceived as a separate entity from the rest of the organization.

7. Salespeople often have strong bargaining power within their organization. If they are star performers, they can hardly be replaced, in case they move to competitors; as a consequence, star performers in the sales force, just as in professional sports, often earn more than their supervisors or coaches.
8. Coaches and supervisors gain credibility if they have had a successful career as athletes or salespeople.
9. Coaches and supervisors must be able to motivate team members with non-monetary rewards (which in many cases they do not manage at all);
10. Coaches and supervisors usually have limited influence on the team's goals, which are usually set at a higher hierarchical level (be it by the team's owner or the company's CEO or headquarters); rather, both have to choose how to reach the goals by selecting the most appropriate course of action.
11. Coaches and supervisors have to manage interpersonal relationships both with each individual team member and with the team as a whole; this implies managing communications, incentives, rewards, etc. at the individual and team levels simultaneously.
12. Supervisors such as Field Sales Managers typically directly supervise subordinates and spend time with them in the field, providing support, feedback, coaching, etc.

Although relevant differences may exist between sports teams and sales teams, there are also many important similarities. This is especially true when sales teams' members possess complementary skills, are committed to a common purpose and share performance goals for which they hold themselves mutually accountable.

By interviewing coaches of professional sport teams, we aim to provide Sales Managers with some useful lessons to enable them to manage their sales teams better.

Sports teams as a metaphor for the world of business

The sports context is often used as a powerful analogy for analysing and understanding leadership. Sales Managers often look to sport for inspirational examples and useful models of teamwork. However, doubts exist about taking the principles and best practices of coaching in the sport field and applying them to managerial leadership. In one of the very few studies on the topic, Kellett (1999, p. 159) concluded 'It was clear that the coaches did not find leadership to be a representative descriptor of what they do', and suggested that 'It may simply [be] that coaching is not an appropriate analog for leadership' (p. 166). Kellett's final observation was that 'Either professional coaching does not rest on leadership, or our views of leadership need substantial revision' (p. 150). Hence, Sales Managers need to be aware of the liability of drawing on sports references because, when used inappropriately, sports comparisons can lead managers and their employees astray (Katz 2001).

In fact, there are some key differences between the worlds of sports and business: in sports, the boundaries and rules of the game are clearly delineated, games are brief and self-contained, outcomes of choices and actions are generally clear, feedback is relatively immediate and much of the coaching occurs during practice sessions. In team sports games alternate with practice, and these are clearly distinct modes of team functioning, characterized by the performance mode and learning mode respectively. Conversely, in the business context the boundaries and rules of the game are difficult to define, 'games' are lengthy and opponents may change in the middle of the action, the relationship between decisions and outcomes are often difficult to gauge and not immediate and much of the coaching does not occur during practice sessions. Based on these considerations, Peterson and Little (2005, p. 180) concluded that 'Certain principles drawn from sports coaching are useful in managerial coaching, but the necessary skills and models are fundamentally different'. Therefore, using the sports setting as a reference and a meaningful analogy for sales organizations requires identifying the typical features of sports teams and applying them to corporate contexts that possess similar characteristics.

In fact, when generalizing from the sports team to the sales team one must consider the extent to which the team in either setting is characterized by similarity of tasks, structure, time horizons, etc. For example, virtual sales teams should not be compared to sports teams, because, unlike the former, the latter typically spend time and perform activities together in a context characterized by physical proximity and interaction, which obviously affects communication patterns and relationships development. Analogously, self-managing teams cannot be compared to sports teams, which can rather be used in the analysis of hierarchical teams with a defined leadership role (i.e. the head coach).

Similarly, one should consider the team's tasks. In fact, many teams in the field of business focus on decision-making, creativity, planning, etc., while sports teams are a special type of performance team, i.e. those producing the primary outcomes of the organization. In performance teams, members have a relevant, direct, and visible impact on the organization's results and must possess innate abilities (in addition to motivation) to be successful. Sales teams typically are performance teams, and this is one of the main reasons why the sport metaphor is so attractive to Sales Managers. Furthermore, sports teams are characterized by the co-existence of competition and cooperation among team members: athletes are often concerned with their own statistics and visibility and this may be detrimental to the cooperation needed to achieve the team's success. This feature of the sport context can usually be applied to sales teams too, making comparisons meaningful.

Importantly, sports differ in terms of the degree of athletes' interdependence and the number of athletes to be managed and supervised. Hence, analogy should only be made between a sales team and a specific sport context sharing similar features. For example, baseball is a good metaphor when interdependence among salespeople is very low, and the sales team's performance is basically the sum of the performance of individual salespeople. On the contrary, when interdependence is high, basketball is a much better analogy (Keidel 1984).

What is a team? What is team performance?

While all teams are groups, not all groups are teams. In fact, according to Ingram et al. (2005, p. 189),

Groups become teams through disciplined action by:

1. *Shaping a common purpose*
2. *Agreeing on performance goals*
3. *Defining a common working approach*
4. *Developing high levels of complementary skills, and*
5. *Holding themselves mutually accountable for results.*

Hence, organizational work teams are groups that have clearly defined membership and a shared responsibility to accomplish tasks characterized by some level of interdependence.

Importantly, teams vary in terms of the degree of interdependence. For example, in most sales organizations salespeople act individually and 'team' performance is simply the sum of their individual performances. Conversely, in the case of team selling and Key Account Management, team members strongly depend upon one another to perform their tasks and accomplish their goals: in such situations team performance (e.g. winning or keeping a key account) is the result of the combined and coordinated effort of interdependent individuals. However, it is worth underlining the fact that even when task interdependence is low, team spirit and team cohesion can be important in improving performance: salespeople may share information about customers and competitors, share best practices, learn from their peers, be motivated by the feeling of being part of a meaningful social network, be willing to emulate their colleagues, and so on. Hence, even in sales organizations where task interdependence is low, Sales Managers should try to exploit the potential benefits of creating *esprit de corps*.

Similarly, in the sport context, some disciplines (e.g. football or basketball) are characterized by a high level of task interdependence among team members, who clearly bear collective responsibility for the team outcomes. On the contrary, other sports have no interdependence at all but can still strongly forge team spirit (e.g. downhill skiing).

In addition to team learning, Moon and Gupta (1997) propose two dimensions to sales team outcomes:

1. Functional outcomes (e.g. achievement of sales goals, customer responsiveness).
2. Psychosocial outcomes: of particular importance are the perceived effectiveness of the team (i.e. the perception that intra-team relationships are worthwhile, equitable, productive and satisfying, which result in feelings of affiliation and a sense of belonging) and the level of conflict, i.e. an assessment of team processes and the ability to resolve disputes. Team conflict can be defined as tension between team members due to real or perceived differences deriving from incongruent goals and values in the task, difficulties in managing process interdependence and members' interaction.

Functional and psychosocial outcomes typically reinforce each other, and psychosocial outcomes are important for the attainment of team functional outcomes especially when there is a high degree of work interdependence, that is when task completion requires a high level of interaction among team members.

Team climate captures multiple facets of the psychosocial outcomes of teams. It can be interpreted as a combination of both the level and the variance of team members' quality perceptions about vertical (i.e. leader-subordinate) and lateral (i.e. member to member) personal relationships in the team. Importantly, leadership style is a key variable in shaping team climate.

When examining interpersonal relationships in groups, an important concept is accountability, i.e. the feeling of responsibility, obligation and the need to justify one's actions to others or to oneself. Whereas specific accountability is the perceived need to perform specific behaviours (in the light of economic/contractual exchange), generalized accountability is interpreted as the perceived need to perform a broad range of behaviours (in the context of social exchange). Furthermore, when the source of accountability is external, behaviours are performed because of an obligation towards others (because it is expected by others that one should do so), whereas when the source is internal behaviours are performed because of an obligation to oneself. The existence of strong psychosocial relationships among team members can foster generalized and external accountability which, in combination with specific and internal accountability, may strongly contribute to team success.

What is leadership?

Researchers and practitioners have suggested different interpretations of leadership. According to the Globe Project, which is probably the most comprehensive international research project on the topic, leadership can be defined as 'The ability of an individual to influence, motivate or enable others to contribute toward the effectiveness and success of the organization of which they are members' (House et al. 2002, p. 5). Generally speaking, it is important for leaders to influence behaviours that have an impact on the performance of individuals and groups in the organization. These behaviours can be divided into two broad categories:

• *Task behaviours*, aimed at accomplishing the core functions of an organization;
• *Contextual behaviours* which support task behaviours and shape the psychosocial environment of the organization.

More specifically, leadership has to do with the personal influence of some people on the cognitive, affective and behavioural responses of other people. In fact, what followers do is typically affected by what they know, think and want, as well as by how they feel. How can Sales Managers impact upon their subordinates' responses in order to accomplish the goals of their organization?

Team leaders have to influence both individual members and the team as a whole. The co-existence of these two goals is extremely challenging in most situations. For example, it is generally suggested that team leaders should provide the team with group norms, shared values and common beliefs so as create a team spirit. However, at the same time, each member of the group may need individual attention and communication, because 'people who feel heard and understood are easier to motivate and influence' (Kets De Vries 2005, p. 68).

Leaders may use different approaches with different sub-groups of subordinates within a broader group. For example, since the career stage of an individual salesperson influences his/her motivators (see Chapter 15 on motivation), subordinates at different stages typically have different preferences in terms of the most appropriate leadership style. As a consequence, some leadership behaviours may be group or sub-group based (e.g. creating a vision at meetings), while others may be dyad based (e.g. praise administered face to face with a single subordinate). This complicates the job of a team leader a great deal and makes most theories on leadership largely incomplete.

Broadly speaking, effective team performance derives from the leader's ability to manage interdependence, that is, the ability successfully to integrate, coordinate and synchronize individual contributions in team processes.

Researchers have developed different interpretations of how leadership influences team responses. In the following, the most important perspectives on leadership are briefly discussed.

Leadership as power

A first perspective suggests that leadership is a consequence of *a person's power*. This perspective is often criticized by those who observe that in most organizations many powerful people may not be considered as leaders and that, at the same time, other people having weak or no formal power in the hierarchy are considered to be leaders. In fact, power is not necessarily related to one's position in the organizational hierarchy, since five bases of social power can be identified:

1. Publicly dependent types of power (i.e. those where some surveillance is needed to influence subordinates):

    a) Coercive power, where the leader can administer punishment if subordinates do not behave as desired;
    b) Reward power, where the leader can provide something of value in exchange for performing the desired behaviour.

2. Privately dependent types of power (i.e. those where no surveillance is needed to influence subordinates):

    a) Expert power, where the subordinate perceives the leader as having superior knowledge, skill or ability in relation to some task;
    b) Referent power, where the subordinate identifies with the leader and conforms in order to emulate him/her;
    c) Legitimate power, where the subordinate perceives that the leader has the right to prescribe his/her behaviour.

The lesson here is that Sales Managers can and should foster their leadership, no matter what their position (and hence, their power) in the organization's hierarchy.

Leadership as a set of personality traits and characteristics of individuals

A second perspective posits that leadership is a personality trait which 'comes from within' and denotes a person's ability to influence others. The most relevant implication of this interpretation is that leaders must possess an adequate profile of personal characteristics, typically in terms of age, gender, physical aspect and *personality traits*. The main problem with this perspective is that researchers have developed many models of personality traits contributing to leadership and there is no general model universally accepted as the 'ideal' one. Efforts to identify the prototypical profile of a successful leader have generally failed: studies on the topic suggest different inventories and found inconsistent results.

Leadership as a set of behaviours

A third perspective suggests that leadership consists of *things that leaders do*. According to this interpretation, leadership can essentially be interpreted as the set of behaviours performed by an individual. Again, the main problem with this approach is the number and variety of behaviours that can be taken into account. One of the most frequently cited taxonomies of leadership behaviours was developed by Fleishman et al. (1991), who suggested the following list of leader behaviours dimensions:

1. Information search and structuring:
   a) acquiring information;
   b) organizing and evaluating information;
   c) feedback and control.
2. Information use in problem solving:
   a) identifying needs and requirements;
   b) planning and coordinating;
   c) communicating information.
3. Managing personnel resources:
   a) obtaining and allocating personnel resources;
   b) developing personnel resources;
   c) motivating personnel resources;
   d) utilizing and monitoring personnel resources.
4. Managing material resources:
   a) obtaining and allocating material resources;
   b) maintaining material resources;
   c) utilizing, coordinating and monitoring material resources.

The recent meta-analysis by Burke et al. (2006) combines findings from 50 different studies and is probably the most comprehensive empirical study on team leadership. The authors argue that the huge set of team leadership behaviours investigated in the literature can be divided into two broad categories:

1. *Task-focused leadership behaviours*, dealing with task accomplishment, which can be grouped into three typologies:

   a) Transactional leadership behaviours, that is, providing praise and rewards, withholding punishment from team members who comply with role expectations.

These behaviours typically include using contingent rewards, active management by exception and passive management by exception.

b) Initiating structure, that is, minimizing subordinates' role conflict and ambiguity through directive behaviours such as organization of group activity, assignment of tasks, specification of the way work is to be conducted and creation of channels of communication, or through autocratic behaviours, which implies making decisions without consulting team members.

c) Boundary spanning, which consists of increasing the resources and expanding the information available to the team through politically-oriented behaviours such as collaborating with others outside the team and negotiating resources for the team.

2. *Person-focused leadership behaviours*, facilitating followers' development and interaction, which can be grouped into four typologies:

a) Transformational leadership behaviours, that is, creating meaningful and creative exchanges, developing a vision, taking calculated risk, moving team members' motivational state towards higher-level states such as self-actualization. This is typically accomplished through individualized consideration and intellectual stimulation.

b) Consideration, that is, developing close social relationships and group cohesion (i.e. shared cognition, affect and behaviours), especially by means of two-way open communication, mutual respect and trust and focusing on team members' needs.

c) Empowerment, which implies developing team members' self-management skills through coaching and participative, facilitative and consultative leadership style behaviours.

d) Motivation, that is, the ability to stimulate team members' efforts, especially in times of difficulty, through encouragement, support, reward and recognition of behaviour and performance.

Results of the meta-analysis suggest the following:

1. Overall, person-focused behaviours have a stronger impact than task-focused behaviours on all team outcomes.
2. The impact of leadership behaviours on team performance is stronger when task interdependence is higher.
3. While some leadership behaviours contribute equally to different team performance outcomes, others are differentially related to different outcomes; for example, person-focused behaviours have a stronger impact on team learning than on team productivity and perceived team effectiveness.
4. In general, the impact of leadership behaviours is stronger for subjective, perceived team effectiveness than for objective team productivity.
5. Boundary spanning and empowerment seem to have the strongest impact on team performance.

Leadership as a set of functions

A fourth perspective focuses on leadership *functions*. According to the functional perspective, leaders are responsible for ensuring that all functions critical to the organization's task are accomplished. Once again, many models have been developed. A particularly interesting model of team leadership functions is shown in Figure 13.3.

Taking a process perspective, Figure 13.4 shows the model developed by Zaccaro et al. (2001). This model emphasizes that team leadership functions affect team members' responses by influencing *cognitive, motivational, affective and coordination processes*.

The model identifies three team cognitive processes:

1. *Collective information processing*: team members should share information and opinions in order to understand team problems, set objectives and define solution alternatives, reaching consensus on the course of action and then implementing actions and monitoring the consequences.
2. Team members should develop *shared mental models* of team strategies, roles, required behaviours and team members' interaction tactics needed to take collective action successfully (i.e. knowledge and understanding of what should be done, by whom, how, when and why). Such shared mental models should be characterized by similarity and accuracy.

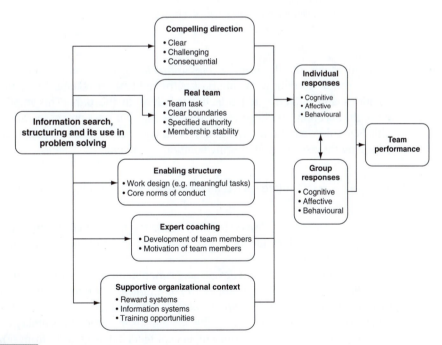

Figure 13.3   A model of team leadership functions
Source: adapted from Burke et al. (2006).

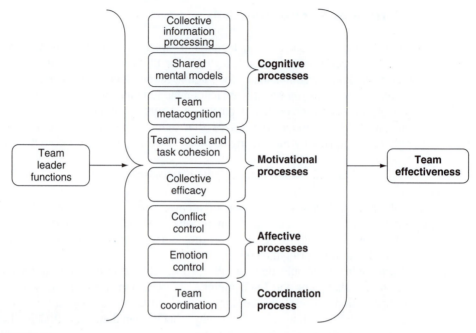

Figure 13.4 A model of the impact of team leadership functions on team processes and performance
Source: adapted from Zaccaro et al. (2001).

3. Team members should develop *collective metacognition*, i.e. individual and collective reflection upon how members constructed team problems, evaluated possible solutions and implemented selected solutions in the past. This implies *learning* through reflection on cause-effect relationships for past processes and outcomes. This is manifested in team members' behaviours such as discussing teamworking, critiquing themselves and offering solutions to others.

Team leaders can stimulate such team cognitive processes by:

1. *Adopting a participative leadership style*, encouraging and coaching team members to engage in problem identification, diagnosis, solution generation and solution selection activities.
2. *Sense-making*, which implies developing a mental model of problems and solutions; and *sense-giving*, that is, the ability to communicate to team members a model of expected behaviours and role requirements (i.e. the response to team problems).
3. *Providing feedback*: successful feedback stems from the leader's ability and willingness to provide and accept criticism, accept feedback and ideas from others, focus on task-focused feedback instead of person-oriented feedback, provide specific and constructive suggestions, stimulate active participation during meetings and include teamwork issues in meeting discussions.

The model also highlights two fundamental team motivational processes:

1. *Group cohesion*, that is, individual team members' attraction to the group. Group cohesion includes both social cohesion (number and intensity of friendship relationships among team members) and task-based cohesion (i.e. members work together and are committed to the group because individual goal attainment is inevitably bound to collective achievement).
2. *Collective efficacy*, that is, individual and collective belief and confidence that together members can be successful. In fact, self-confidence in the team's capabilities motivates working hard, persistance in the face of obstacles and acceptance of and success in difficult tasks.

Motivational processes can be stimulated by four leadership processes:

1. *Adopting a transformational leadership style*, which implies performing activities such as inspiring and empowering, and fusing and aligning individual goals and motivational states with the team's mission and purpose.
2. *Modelling behaviours* that lead to successful performance.
3. Implementing *persuasion* and social influence processes to raise the team's perceptions of self-efficacy.
4. In a broader sense, all team leader behaviours can increase perceived self-efficacy *indirectly* by building a history of success.

As for team members' affective processes, it is essential to control conflict and (mainly negative) emotions by reducing stress, promoting emotion-control norms and stimulating cognitive conflict.

Finally, coordination processes are mainly affected by the way the team is created and organized, as well as by how tasks and strategies are designed and their progress critically monitored to identify essential improvement areas.

Leadership as a combination of characteristics and behaviours: leadership styles

A fifth perspective suggests that both personal characteristics (e.g. personality traits) and specific behaviours give rise to different *leadership styles*. The huge literature on leadership styles identifies many potential combinations of characteristics and behaviours and academics and practitioners have developed many different models of leadership styles. In the field of sales management, researchers have mainly focused on the debate on transactional and transformational leadership.

Leaders adopting a *transactional* style administer rewards and punishments contingent upon performance (Bass 1985). This is basically a 'give and take' approach to leadership. Research generally shows that contingent rewards and positive supervisory feedback positively affect subordinates' attitudes, role perceptions and performance while, conversely, non-contingent punishments and arbitrary behaviours have dysfunctional consequences. On the other hand, leaders adopting a *transformational* style articulate a vision, provide an appropriate model, foster acceptance of group goals, set high performance expectations and provide individual support and intellectual stimulation. Transformational leaders emphasize higher motivational development and encourage subordinates' motivation through creating for them an inspiring vision of the future.

Findings of empirical research generally suggest that, compared to the transactional style, transformational leadership has a stronger positive impact on subordinates' attitudes, role perceptions, performance and organizational citizenship behaviours.

Importantly, these two leadership styles do not represent a dichotomy and should not be seen as polar opposites. In fact, evidence suggests that transformational leadership has an augmentation effect on transactional leadership. As a consequence, the positive impact on performance strongly increases when leaders successfully combine the two approaches.

The situational leadership perspective

Most of the research on leadership style adopts a situational perspective by attempting to identify what leadership styles work best under specific circumstances. An example of this perspective (see Table 13.1) is represented by the six leadership styles suggested by Goleman (2000).

Many researchers have tried to develop prescriptive models based on a contingency approach to leadership. In this perspective, different leadership characteristics and behaviours are prescribed, given different situations that a leader might face, so the leader's adaptability is the key.

Table 13.1 Leadership styles

Style	Leader's modus operandi	When?
Coercive/ commanding	Demands immediate compliance	When the leader is in charge of managing a crisis or a turnaround
Visionary	Mobilizes people towards a vision	When followers in the company need a clear direction
Affiliative	Creates harmony and emotional bonds	When the leader's most important task is to motivate people in difficulties
Democratic	Forges concensus through participation	When it is possible to get useful inputs from valuable employees
Pacesetting	Sets high standards of performance	When most of the followers are motivated and competent
Coaching	Develops people for the future	When the focus of the leader is on long-term growth of the followers

Source: adapted from Goleman (2000).

According to Fiedler (1967), the effectiveness of the leaders and whether they are able to affect the behaviour of their followers is influenced by three main categories of factors:

1. the quality of the relationship between the leader and his/her followers;
2. whether the leader is able to structure and communicate the tasks to be performed;
3. the leader's positional power, i.e. his/her freedom to assign tasks and to reward and praise.

In a broader sense, the situational leadership perspective suggests that the most appropriate leadership style depends on the followers' characteristics, on the personality traits, attitudes and predispositions of the leader and, more importantly, on a number of relevant situational characteristics of the situation, such as characteristics of the leader's organization (e.g. its culture), time pressure, characteristics of the task, characteristics of the group (e.g. size, cohesion, history, etc.) and the leader's authority and power in decision-making. For example, according to the situational leadership perspective, managers should match their leadership style to the desired leadership behaviours of subordinates, which in turn are typically affected by their maturity, competence and motivation (Butler and Reese, 1991).

What is team coaching?

Team coaching can be defined as 'direct interaction with a team intended to help members make coordinated and task-appropriate use of their collective resources in accomplishing the team's work' (Hackman and Wageman 2005, p. 269).

Following Hackman and Wageman (2005), we contend that in analysing the drivers of team performance, three team coaching functions can be identified:

1. *Collective effort* expended in carrying out task work necessitates team *motivation.* This requires *motivational coaching* aimed at minimizing free riding and building shared commitment.
2. *Appropriateness* to the task *of the performance strategies* the group uses in its work (i.e. choices made about how to carry out the work, e.g. sports tactics) implies use of *consultative coaching* aimed at inventing adequate ways of proceeding with the work.
3. *Knowledge and skills* of team members can be developed through *educational coaching.*

Although these three functions are interdependent, we focus here mainly on the first function (i.e. motivational coaching) for the following reasons.

First, consultative coaching in sport substantially differs from the same function in companies. In fact, in most cases functional leaders (e.g. Sales Managers) can choose only how to implement a given strategy. In other words, functional leaders in companies usually have less freedom, compared with coaches of professional teams, in choosing the most appropriate course of action in terms of strategy definition. Rather, they usually only select ways of proceeding in terms of strategy implementation.

Second, educational coaching in sports differs substantially from educational coaching in business in terms of frequency, closeness of supervision and overall time spent in training, among others.

In short, comparisons between sports and the world of business are much more meaningful for motivational coaching than for consultative and educational coaching.

A fundamental aspect of motivational coaching in teams is perceived equity. In fact, team leaders' non-contingent punishments and arbitrary behaviours have dysfunctional consequences on team members. Hence, team leaders should communicate clear expectations, observe performance carefully, consider all relevant information when appraising performance, provide regular performance feedback and develop self-improvement plans for their subordinates. In addition to this, to optimize the perceived equity of the evaluation process, coaches should build a warm relationship with team members. Perceived equity is especially important in performance appraisal processes. Team leaders should be aware that team members usually evaluate their performance appraisal based on four types of justice perceptions:

- system procedural justice, i.e. perceptions about the fairness of the appraisal procedures adopted by the organization as a whole;
- rater procedural justice, i.e. perceptions about the fairness of the application of appraisal procedures adopted by the rater;
- interactional justice, i.e. perceptions about the fairness of the interpersonal communication during the appraisal process;
- distributive justice, i.e. the perceived equity of the performance rating (input-output perspective).

To sum up, perceptions of unequal treatment may lead to perceptions of unfairness that will decrease subordinates' motivation. Hence, the key challenge for team leaders is to treat subordinates as individuals while, at the same time, treating them equitably. Subordinates need to be made aware that fairness is not necessarily equal treatment, but this is not easy to accomplish.

What is the role of motivation in team leadership?

Team leaders can enhance their followers' motivation through many behaviours, such as making subordinates' jobs more interesting, providing subordinates with a sense of being part of something larger, creating a positive work environment, celebrating accomplishments, profiling opportunities, describing the future to subordinates, setting an example for subordinates and identifying the strengths and weaknesses of subordinates (Kouzes and Posner 1987).

Communication processes are a key component of team leaders' functions. Hence, they must develop adequate skills and capabilities for managing such processes properly. For example, Lowe (1995) suggests that team coaches should listen actively, ask questions, provide feedback and make suggestions when communicating with team members.

Motivational Language Theory (MLT) (Sullivan 1988) specifically and explicitly addresses motivational communication processes. Motivational communication is an important component of leadership communication and supervisor-subordinate communication. In fact, its goal is to energize, direct or sustain the behaviour of others.

According to MLT, motivational communication can be categorized as three types of speech actions:

1. *Uncertainty reduction* actions that mainly increase employee knowledge.
2. *Meaning-making* actions, which lead employees to feel their place in the organization is meaningful and to make choices consistent with the organization's goals.
3. *Affirming/bonding* actions that develop interpersonal relationships and reaffirm the employee's sense of self-worth.

Importantly, these three kinds of actions are not mutually exclusive or easily separable. Since messages are almost always multifunctional, leaders should emphasize the motivational communication acts that best fit with their communication goals.

Uncertainty reduction communication actions can increase team members' motivation in many ways. In fact (see Chapter 15 on motivation):

- in goal-setting theory (Locke and Latham 1990) motivation stems from information that reduces process and goal uncertainty;
- in self-efficacy theory (Bandura 1982) people are motivated by information that reduces uncertainty regarding their abilities. Such information may stem from past performance of the team, vicarious experience (i.e. observation and comparison of own team capabilities with those of successful teams), verbal persuasion (i.e. encouragement, positive appraisal, structuring situations that promote success) and empowerment (i.e. stimulating self-improvement and self-confidence);
- in expectancy theory (Vroom 1964) information that reduces reward uncertainty is motivating;
- in equity theory (Adams 1965) people are motivated by information that reduces uncertainty about fairness.

The implication for sales team leaders is that they should focus on communication that reduces goal, process and reward uncertainty, increases team members' self-confidence and maximizes perceived fairness. However, team leaders should also try to motivate team members by increasing the perceived meaningfulness of their tasks, goals and roles as well as by stimulating interpersonal bonding, friendship and social cohesion with and among team members.

In practice, motivational communication may take the following forms (Zorn and Ruccio 1998):

1. Modelling success, for example by sharing personal stories, demonstrating hard work and pointing to the future.
2. Providing individual attention, for example by solving problems of team members and by encouraging them personally.
3. Exuding energy/having fun, which can be accomplished by conveying a positive attitude, creating opportunities to have social fun and providing constant friendship.
4. Empowering and giving responsibility.
5. Breaking down overall goals into weekly and daily goals.

Insights from professional sports coaches for team leadership

The following observations are based on interviews with 31 professional coaches of sports characterized by different forms of interrelated team membership and therefore representative of different organizational models (Keidel 1984): football, volleyball, basketball and athletics. Each of them is, or was, the coach either of major league professional sports clubs or national teams. The age, the experience both as a coach and as an athlete and the background of the respondents varied. These face-to-face interviews focused on team leadership and team coaching. They were primarily aimed at answering the following questions:

- What are the main functions performed by professional sports coaches in order to positively influence team performance?
- What specific behaviours are adopted to influence team performance, in particular through their impact on motivation?

Figure 13.5 summarizes in a model the findings of the interviews and the key concepts drawn from team leadership and coaching literature. While recognizing that team performance is affected by educational, consultative and motivational coaching, here

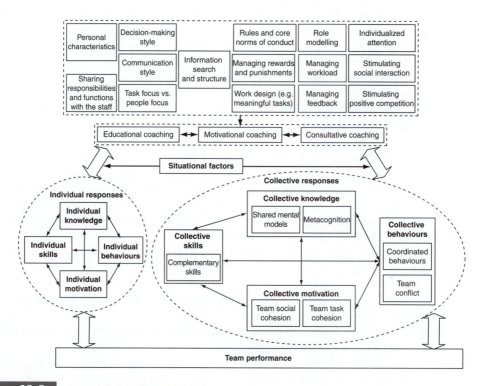

Figure 13.5   A model of team coaching

we mainly focused our attention on the team leader-related dimensions of motivational coaching.

In summary, the framework stresses the variables a team leader and his/her staff may use to influence team response and therefore team performance, especially by enhancing, both directly and indirectly, the motivation of the team as a whole as well as its individual members.

Such variables are a combination of some of the coach's *personal characteristics*, *focus*, *decision-making and communication style* (which we discuss in more detail below) and the ability and will to perform a set of *functions* (together with the staff):

1. *To acquire information* in a planned, active and permanent way, through both the observation and analysis of signs and a constant and sincere willingness to maintain a dialogue and to listen and exchange views, as this enables better decisions to be made and impacts upon all the other variables.
2. *To define and communicate precise rules* and behavioural norms so as to clarify role expectations and curtail uncertainty about being treated equally. The involvement of team members in defining rules and subsequent rewards and punishment in the event of their observance or non-observance may make this work more significant, as it increases responsibility, self-esteem and appreciation. The team leader should pay special attention to choices concerning the object of the rules and who is to carry them out, as well as how they are defined and applied. In this respect, perceived equity and accountability are fundamental concepts.
3. *To manage rewards and punishments*, which can influence motivation in many ways, in line with the model of transactional leadership.
4. *To provide educational coaching* so as to improve team players' ability to perform their tasks and to enhance their perception that the team, as well as they themselves, has developed and will continue to develop the skills and competencies necessary to achieve performance targets, while also reducing uncertainty about both individual and collective abilities.
5. *To design tasks in a challenging and stimulating way*, in order to reduce the risk of negative psychological reactions such as job stress, emotional exhaustion, and burnout.
6. *To manage the workload according to the results achieved*, in order to maximize the level of psychic and physical energy of team members.
7. *To provide some feedback to the team* (both positive and negative), so as to reduce uncertainty and increase the perception of both personal and collective self-efficacy.
8. *To give individual attention*, so as to stimulate social bonding and to fortify the quality of the interpersonal relationship between coach and team members.
9. *To provide role models*, so as to reduce uncertainty and facilitate social learning.
10. *To stimulate positive competition among team members*, in order to support social learning and make conflict within the team explicit and rationally addressable.
11. *To stimulate socialization among team members*, in order to improve the quality of the relationship among them.

In the following sections, we discuss in more detail the other variables in the model.

Personal characteristics

Successful team leaders should possess particular personal characteristics. Coaches often mentioned their own personal *credibility* as the main factor in managing a team successfully, especially as far as winning the team's *trust* was concerned. Such credibility arises from several characteristics (such as, for instance, the fact that the coach has been a great athlete himself), among which technical competence is absolutely essential. More generally, credibility stems from the coach's own way of being, working and relating to team members. It is therefore the combination of *what* they do and *how* they do it.

A recurrent theme was that, to motivate his own athletes, a coach should be motivated himself. Generally speaking, *passion* and enthusiasm are often said to be the essential traits of a good coach. Also the importance of personality profile often came out in the interviews: in particular, *spontaneity* and the ability to 'be yourself', to act naturally, showing your own faults and qualities. Whatever the combination of personal traits, many coaches underlined the need for *consistency* between their own 'style' and ideas, as far as tactics and group management are concerned, and the club's culture, goals and strategies.

Sharing responsibilities and functions with the staff

Successful team leaders create and manage a well-organized and coordinated staff of specialists to share the responsibilities and functions needed to shape and influence the tasks and contextual behaviours of team members. In fact, the functions performed by the coach are typically shared with a technical staff (assistant coach, athletic trainers, etc.). Because of the shortage of resources (notably time and specific competence) coaches just cannot handle a constant, personalized relationship with each player and therefore the other staff members share such responsibility with them. Due to the number of athletes and the specialized tasks involved, it takes a technically skilled group of people to lead a team; such a group is made up of a coach, an assistant coach, athletic and goalkeeper trainers, doctors, masseurs, physiotherapists and someone in charge of storage and equipment. They all have to be coordinated but they are free to operate within their own competence and sphere of duties.

Those who collaborate with the coach are an essential support, not only because of their own technical competence, but for their contribution to the management of the relationship between coach and team. In fact, staff members often play the fundamental role of a 'cushion' for tensions, as well as being confidants and counsellors for the coach. In view of this, the importance of all members of the technical staff having common goals, trusting each other and being consistent in their communication with athletes was particularly stressed. The role of *assistant coach* is especially important to this end, as he often acts as a confidant for players, who usually feel quite comfortable talking openly with him and complaining, especially if he has been a team mate previously.

In short, motivation of both individual players and the entire team depends on a series of functions, activities and behaviours which are the responsibility not only of the coach, but of his whole staff as well.

Decision-making style

One element which significantly characterizes and differentiates coaches is the way they approach decision-making processes. In keeping with literature about leadership, there is a sharp distinction between coaches with a directive (autocratic, coercive) style and others with a participatory style, who think that imposing things is detrimental, since personal involvement should be encouraged instead. Both styles may have a positive effect on motivation, however, though from completely different viewpoints. In fact, where the directive style can motivate people through its function of reducing uncertainty, the participatory style can contribute to motivation by both enhancing the meaning of the job and stimulating a more satisfactory, personal relationship between athlete and coach. Successful team leaders should match their decision-making style to the specific situation they have to deal with. Whichever style they choose, all models of situational leadership can be applied.

Task-focus and people-focus

Another important aspect which reflects the typical categories to be found in studies on leadership relates to the main focus of a coach's attention, interest and energy. Task-focused coaches think that the success of the team primarily depends on the players' ability to perform their tasks in the best possible way. This basically means dedicating attention to the development of their skills and, therefore, investing resources in educational coaching.

Other coaches, on the contrary, mainly focus on creating a good atmosphere and psychosocial context for the tasks to be performed, and then dedicating special attention to the relationship with and among athletes, and the establishment of long-lasting emotional bonds among players. Coaches who are mainly people-focused believe that the team's success depends on single players' will to place themselves at the group's disposal and on their motivation to work with others. This implies, in relative terms, that more attention be paid to motivational coaching.

In principle, all coaches say that it is important to be able to manage both functions. Yet, in most cases it is possible to perceive, for each coach, whether they are prominently oriented one way or the other. Coaches who are mainly *task-focused* feel that their main role is to teach players how to perform their own tasks the best they can, so as to achieve team goals. This means a great emphasis on the function of educational coaching, namely the development of the skills and competence of athletes, their personal growth and learning. Furthermore, educational coaching has an important impact on the motivation of both individuals and the team, as it enhances players' security and self-confidence, thus making them less prone to a sense of failure.

Coaches who are mainly *people-focused*, instead interpret their role as someone helping people to become united in pursuit of a common goal and to feed and fuel the team's social capital by optimizing individual relationships, stimulating team cohesion and facilitating emotional bonds, because they are convinced that the atmosphere, team spirit and quality of interpersonal relationships are the main elements for a team's success.

Communication style

The processes of communication with the team are the core of coaching. As far as motivation is concerned, communication often plays an essential role, mainly because it reduces uncertainties. Several respondents stressed that coaches must pass on certainty, not doubts, in order to enhance self-esteem: if you reduce insecurity about the skills of both single players and the team as a whole, you stimulate self-confidence, motivating each athlete and the team alike.

Some coaches said that *synthesis* and *simplicity* are two essential traits of effective communication with the team. Another aspect of reducing ambiguity and uncertainty to a minimum that was frequently mentioned was *clarity* and transparency of communication. Here again the reduction of insecurity about expected goals, strategies, roles and behaviours may have a positive and motivating effect on the team.

Even though some of the respondents do not feel they should give explanations for their choices, unless in special cases or under specific circumstances, for most coaches it is advisable to give the *reasons for your own decisions*, explaining them to players, so as to facilitate their acceptance. The impact of this coaching attitude on the team's motivation arises from both the reduction of uncertainty and the creation of a strong interpersonal relationship between coach and player.

Many coaches have pointed out how difficult it can be to find the right moment to communicate with the team. Such choice of the best *time* often takes into account the impact what they are going to say may have on the spirit and the motivation of both the group and single players. For example, one coach declared:

> On Sunday morning I only speak to the team for some ten minutes, briefly summarizing what we have done throughout the week on the blackboard. Then I say nothing else to the players. To repeat again and again the instructions given would mean to pass on insecurity and lack of confidence.

It is especially recommended to avoid moments characterized by high emotion as this risks jeopardizing the ability to resolve *conflicts* and issues in a rational and constructive way as it may damage the atmosphere within the team:

> I try to avoid talking to the team after the game, unless under special circumstances. This is because a coach is still too involved emotionally and players are still under pressure. [...] we have to be able to pick when we intervene, choosing the right time and the right way.

As for communication, coaches who favour a participatory and democratic leadership style are convinced that it is necessary to stimulate everyone to make a contribution to discussion, and to ask even the shiest player for advice and suggestions. A coach must be a great collector of information and must be able and willing to listen to others, as well as have the humility to accept advice and suggestions. In this respect, many coaches have stressed the importance of dialogue, *listening* and exchange of views. Willingness to both listen and talk play an important, motivating function, as they suggest and often imply personal consideration, care and involvement. As meaningfully stated by a coach, 'individual motivation has to be searched for day by day, through dialogue and personal care'. Listening to athletes is therefore another way to make them feel important, esteemed, and appreciated, as well as to give them personal care and to improve the quality of the relationship between leader and team members.

The model also shows that motivation (both of the individual and the group) interacts with individual and collective knowledge, abilities and behaviours, while also influencing team performance.

The model also suggests that, when choosing the best ways to affect team processes and performance, team leaders should consider a number of situational variables. Particularly relevant are team dimension, the basic traits of team members (especially the level of their competence and motivation), the nature of tasks assigned, the degree of interdependence required to perform tasks, the leader's power to decide and the frequency and duration of personal interaction among team members, as well as between leaders and followers. First and foremost, managers who wish to apply concepts, models and behaviours employed in sport to their own team should choose examples and make comparisons with teams and sports that are most similar to their own business sector as far as the above mentioned characteristics are concerned.

CASE PROBLEM REVISITED

What can Iveco managers learn from sports teams?

After an in-depth analysis of some of the best practices in sports team coaching, the Director of the IKA department at Iveco learnt some lessons on how to motivate a team and how to structure a team and its work (Katz 2001). As to motivation, he learned three main lessons.

First, contrary to his initial assumption that high performance teams are exclusively cooperative, he understood that he had to promote an optimal mix of cooperation and constructive competition among team members. In fact, he realized that attempting to eliminate competition means that the team misses the opportunity for members to push one another to perform at their best by striving to outdo one another and to maintain the drive to keep improving. Hence, he thought he should imitate coaches of winning teams by carefully shaping how, when and for what teammates compete.

A second lesson he learned from sports was to orchestrate some early wins. In fact, the success of their first efforts can strongly affect the path a team will follow in the future by setting a self-fuelling upward curve in motion. The manager thought that he should split the team's larger tasks and goals into a sequence of smaller tasks. The first ones should be easy to reach and short-term, concrete and unambiguous, so that team members could experience clear and immediate success. In addition to this, the manager thought that he should emphasize this success both internally and externally, to increase self-esteem and appreciation.

A third lesson was that he had to break out of losing streaks by reversing downward spirals so as to avoid team members' negative feelings undermining the team's self-confidence and enthusiasm and colouring future performance so that their doom-mongering became self-fulfilling. To do this, the manager realized that he had to shape the way in which team members apportion blame when they encounter setbacks. It is important to avoid team mates attributing problems to causes that are stable and uncontrollable. Hence, the manager should guide the team through an assessment of all potential causes for a setback and focus team members' attention only on those factors that they can influence.

The Director of the IKA department at Iveco also learned from sport coaches some lessons on how to structure the team and its work to improve team performance. A first idea was to carve out some time and space for practice, so that team members had opportunities to learn, experiment with new methods to accomplish tasks and innovate. To do this, he realized he should promote 'intelligent failure' by providing an environment where controlled conditions allow the team to observe the impact of changes and draw causal inferences. He thought he should not only tolerate mistakes, but stimulate them instead. Similarly, evaluation apprehension should be completely avoided.

A second lesson was the idea of calling half-time, i.e. to establish temporal mid-points where team members could be stimulated to question and revise task strategies, methods, etc. This implies looking back, examining what has been accomplished and what has not, reflecting on the reasons why something went right or wrong and projecting what will be accomplished in the future if the team continues to work in the current manner or if it modifies strategies, resources allocation and behaviours, and so on.

Another lesson learned from successful sports teams was the need to try to keep team membership stable because team mates have to know each other to clarify roles, share experience, learn how to work together and combine their efforts effectively and efficiently.

The last lesson was to study the game video, i.e. formally and regularly to make a ritual of debriefing on failures and, even more important, successes. In fact, teams are typically reluctant to analyse successes critically and to find mistakes they have made in these situations, which could make them truly productive in terms of learning.

Summary

In the world of selling, companies increasingly adopt sales teams. Since sales teams and sports teams share many similarities, Sales Managers can look to professional sports teams as a source of inspiration to learn how to manage their teams better.

Team leaders play an important role in influencing a team's performance. This impact depends on their ability to perform a set of functions, which in turn is affected by both their personality traits and behaviours.

When trying to learn from sports team, leaders of sales teams must consider the extent to which the teams in either setting are characterized by similarities of tasks, structure, time horizons, etc. Choosing the appropriate analogous team and avoiding the pitfalls of misleading generalizations is a key success factor in enhancing team management.

Key points

1. Team leaders have different leadership styles, and their effectiveness and efficiency is strongly affected by contextual variables and situational factors: there is no single best way to lead a team. The fit between the context/situation and the leader's style is a key success factor, together with the leader's ability to understand the context and adapt his/her style to the situation at hand.
2. Leaders can foster team performance by improving a number of team processes: this implies an in-depth understanding of team members' cognitive, affective and behavioural processes.

3. Among the functions of team leaders, team coaching is particularly relevant. Team coaching involves motivational, consultative and educational coaching, which jointly affect the individual and collective responses of team members by influencing their knowledge, skills, motivation and behaviours.
4. While consultative and educational coaching in sport are radically different compared to the business field, most concepts and practices of motivational coaching can be transferred from sport to business.
5. Communication processes are the most important component of motivational coaching.

Running a team climate audit in your company

The following audit is intended to help Sales Managers diagnose problems in team management.

Leader recognition	Do members acknowledge that the team leader and his/her staff possess the personal characteristics and competencies (knowledge, skills, motivation, etc.) needed to perform the job successfully?
Purpose	Do members share a sense of why the team exists and are they invested in accomplishing the mission?
Priorities	Do members know what needs to be done next, by whom, and by when to achieve team goals?
Roles	Do members know their roles in getting tasks done and when to allow a more skilful member to do a certain task?
Information	Do members provide the team leader and his/her staff with an adequate quantity and quality of information to support decision-making processes?
Decisions	Are authority and decision-making lines clearly understood?
Conflict management	Is conflict dealt with openly and considered important to decision-making and personal growth?
Individualized attention	Do members feel their unique personalities are appreciated and well utilized?
Norms	Are group norms set for working together and are they seen as standards for everyone in the group?
Role models	Do members have clear models to emulate?
Meaningful job	Do members perceive their role in the team (as well as the related tasks) as meaningful?
Perceived equity	Do members perceive themselves as treated equally, especially with regard to provision of opportunities, workload and performance appraisal processes?

Social relationships	Do members know, respect and like each other? Do they have enough opportunities to develop social interaction?
Communication effectiveness	Do members find communication processes (e.g. team meetings) efficient and productive and look forward to this time together?
Feedback	Do members clearly know when the team has met with success/failure and why?
Training	Are opportunities for updating skills provided and taken advantage of by team members?

References

Adams, J.S. (1965) 'Inequity in Social Exchange', in L. Berkowitz (ed.), *Advances in Experimental Social Psychology*, Vol. 2: 267–300. New York: Academic Press.

Bandura, A. (1982) 'Self-efficacy Mechanism in Human Agency', *American Psychologist*, 37 (2): 122–47.

Bass, B.M. (1985) *Leadership and Performance Beyond Expectations*. New York: Free Press.

Burke, C.S., Stagl, K.C., Klein, C., Goodwin, G.F., Salas, E. and Halpin, S.M. (2006) 'What Type of Leadership Behaviors are Functional in Teams? A Meta-analysis', *Leadership Quarterly*, 17 (3): 288–307.

Fiedler, F.E. (1967) *Theory of Leadership Effectiveness*. New York: McGraw Hill.

Fleishman, E.A., Mumford, M.D., Zaccaro, S.J., Levin, K.Y., Korotkin, A.L. and Hein, M.B. (1991) 'Taxonomic Efforts in the Description of Leader Behavior: A Synthesis and Functional Interpretation', *Leadership Quarterly*, 2 (4): 245–87.

Goleman, D. (2000) 'Leadership that Gets Results', *Harvard Business Review*, 78 (2): 78–90.

Hackman, J.R. and Wageman, R. (2005), A Theory of Team Coaching', *Academy of Management Review*, 30 (2): 269–87.

House, R.J., Javidan, M., Hanges, P. and Dorfman, P. (2002) 'Understanding Cultures and Implicit Leadership Theories across the Globe: An Introduction to Project GLOBE', *Journal of World Business*, 37 (1): 3–10.

Ingram, T.N., LaForge, R.W., Locander, W.B., MacKenzie, S. and Podsakoff, P.M. (2005) 'New Directions in Sales Leadership Research', *Journal of Personal Selling and Sales Management*, 25 (2): 137–54.

Katz, N., (2001) 'Sport Teams as a Model for Workplace Teams: Lessons and Liabilities', *Academy of Management Executive*, 15 (3): 56–67.

Keidel, R.W. (1984) 'Baseball, Football and Basketball: Models for Business', *Organizational Dynamics*, 12 (3): 5–18.

Kellett, P. (1999) 'Organisational Leadership: Lessons from Professional Coaches', *Sport Management Review*, 2 (2): 150–71.

Kets De Vries, M.F.R. (2005) 'Leadership Group Coaching in Action: The Zen of Creating High Performance Teams', *Academy of Management Executive*, 19 (1): 61–76

Kouzes, J.M. and Posner, B.Z. (1987) *The Leadership Challenge*. San Francisco: Jossey Bass.

Locke, E.A. and Latham, G.P. (1990) A Theory of Goal Setting and Task Performance'. Englewood Cliffs: Prentice-Hall.

Lowe (1995) *Coaching and Counseling Skills*, McGraw-Hill, New York.

Moon, M.A. and Gupta, S.F. (1997). 'Examining the Formation of Selling Centers: A Conceptual Framework', *Journal of Personal Selling and Sales Management*, 17 (2): 31–41.

Peterson, D.B. and Little, B. (2005) 'Invited Reaction: Development and Initial Validation of an Instrument Measuring Managerial Coaching Skills', *Human Resource Development Quarterly*, 16 (2): 179–85.

Sullivan, J.J. (1988) 'Three Roles of Language in Motivation Theory', *Academy of Management Review*, 13 (1): 104–15.

Vroom, V.H. (1964) *Work and Motivation*. New York; Wiley.

Zaccaro, S.J., Rittman, A.L. and Marks, M.A. (2001) 'Team Leadership', *Leadership Quarterly*, 12 (4): 451–83.

Zorn, T.E. Jr and Ruccio, S.E. (1998) 'The Use of Communication to Motivate College Sales Teams', *Journal of Business Communication*, 35 (4); 468–99.

Further reading

Adair, J. (2006) *Effective Leadership*. London: Chartered Institute of Personnel and Development.

Butler, J.K. Jr and Reese, R.M. (1991) 'Leadership Style and Sales Performance: A Test of the Situational Leadership Model', *Journal of Personal Selling and Sales Management* 11 (3): 37–46.

Chelladurai, P. and Saleh, S. (1980) 'Dimensions of Leader Behavior in Sports: Development of a Leadership Style', *Journal of Sport Psychology*, 2: 34–45.

Day, D.V., Gronn, P. and Salas, E. (2004) 'Leadership Capacity in Teams', *Leadership Quarterly*, 15 (6): 857–80.

Day, D.V., Gronn, P. and Salas, E. (2006) 'Leadership in Team-based Organizations: On the Threshold of a New Era', *Leadership Quarterly*, 17 (3): 211–16.

Greenleaf, R.K. (1977) *Servant Leadership: a Journey into the Nature of Legitimate Power and Greatness*. New York: Paulist Press.

Hackman, J.R. (2002) *Leading Teams: Setting the Stage for Great Performances*. Boston: HBS Press.

Mathieu, J.E., Maynard, M.T., Rapp, T. and Gilson, L. (2008) Team Effectiveness 1997–2007: A Review of Recent Advancements and a Glimpse into the Future', *Journal of Management*, 34 (3): 410–76.

Yukl, G. (1998) *Leadership in Organizations*. Englewood Cliffs, NJ: Prentice Hall.

14

Sales force control systems

Vincent Onyemah

Contents

Learning objectives

After reading this chapter, you should be able to:

- Recognize if your organization has a sales force control philosophy.

- Know what type(s) of sales force control system suits your organization.

- Understand how control systems drive salespeople's attitude, behaviour, and performance.

- Understand how inconsistencies among the constitutive elements of control systems harm salespeople.

- Evaluate the level of inconsistencies among the constitutive elements of your sales force control system.

- Observe important significant differences across six countries (France, Hungary, Ireland, Italy, Spain and the United Kingdom) and four industries (fast-moving consumer goods, industrial goods, information systems and technology, and pharmaceutical) with respect to the control systems and the level of inconsistencies experienced by salespeople working in these countries and industries.

Chapter outline

In this chapter a framework for understanding the evaluation and control of salespeople is presented and discussed. A number of circumstances dictate the suitability of any given sales force control system. However, each system has inherent advantages and disadvantages. The typical constitutive elements which reflect sales force control philosophies are also examined. Achieving consistency among these elements requires maintaining a balance of emphases across them. Given that inconsistencies among control system elements harm salespeople, a diagnostic tool for routinely assessing the level of inconsistencies is demonstrated. The chapter closes with a description of the results of a survey of sales force control practices and inconsistencies in six European countries (France, Hungary, Ireland, Italy, Spain and the United Kingdom) and four industries (fast-moving consumer goods, industrial goods, information systems and technology, and pharmaceutical).

Sales force evaluation

One of the objectives of sales force evaluation is to help salespeople excel in their selling assignments. The following are common sales force performance indicators:

- Total sales volume, and increase over last year
- Degree of quota attainment
- Selling expenses, and decrease compared with last year
- Expense-to-sales ratio, and improvement over last year
- Profitability of sales, and increase over last year
- New accounts generated
- Customer retention
- Improvement in the performance of administrative duties
- Improvement in service provided to customers
- Adherence to company policies

In order to assist salespeople in the pursuit of the goals defined by these indicators, many organizations utilize some form of sales force control system.

Introduction: what is a sales force control system?

A sales force control system is a set of practices used by an organization for monitoring, supervising, directing, evaluating and compensating salespeople with the intention of influencing their performance. These practices should in principle form a set of logically connected elements or dimensions that offer salespeople programmatic guidelines for how to fulfill their sales roles. They constitute formal (i.e. management-initiated and written) controls as opposed to informal (i.e. worker-initiated and unwritten) controls, for example, professional and cultural control mechanisms respectively. To date most studies have focused on formal controls.

Sales force control systems are related to a number of other aspects of sales organizations. For example, since sales force control systems offer salespeople guidelines, they often reflect the nature of leadership envisaged by top management (see Chapter 13). Also, in order for salespeople to follow the guidelines, rewards (salary and incentive schemes) and motivational tools in general need to be designed accordingly (see Chapters 15 and 16). Furthermore, the design and implementation of any sales force control system have to be sensitive to the sales force's size and organization (see Chapter 8) because of the need to balance the cost of gathering information with the benefits derivable from close monitoring. Finally, given the personality and motivational differences of individuals, it is often the case that some people perform better under a 'suitable' control system than under control systems that do not match their orientation. Thus control systems also have implications for sales force recruitment and selection (see Chapter 11).

Examination of one of the most popular sales force control system frameworks

There are eight basic constitutive elements or dimensions of most sales force control systems. These are:

1. Focus of performance criteria
2. Number of performance criteria
3. Extent of management intervention
4. Frequency of contact with management
5. Degree of task monitoring
6. Amount of coaching offered
7. Transparency of evaluation criteria
8. The relative proportions of fixed and variable compensation

These elements combine to affect the way salespeople feel and think about their roles, perform their jobs, evaluate and make trade-offs and decide on what performance indicators to focus on. When putting in place a sales force control system, management chooses the degree of emphasis to place on each of the eight elements. This is particularly important because the emphasis on any of these elements reflects an underlying control philosophy.

The sales force literature (e.g. Anderson and Oliver 1987) has identified two opposing prototypical control philosophies – outcome-based control philosophy (OC) and behaviour-based control philosophy (BC). OC and BC define a continuum of control philosophies. While OC and BC represent pure philosophies, the continuum they define contains control system combinations best described as hybrid control philosophies (HC).

In its purest form, OC focuses primarily on managing output (i.e. the outcome of an effort) whereas BC focuses on managing input (i.e. the behaviour and/or effort that are expected to yield a desired outcome). Thus OC tends directly to reward or punish results while BC tends directly to reward or sanction behaviours. OC is a system in which the attainment of results is largely the responsibility of the salesperson, who is free to select his/her methods for achieving them. Under an OC, the salesperson is like an entrepreneur, bearing considerable risks, operating with great autonomy and accountable for outcomes, i.e. results such as sales volume. In contrast, BC places the principal responsibility for results on the firm's management. Sales management obliges salespeople to conform to a given set of rules (e.g. presentation technique, call patterns, etc.) in the belief that results will follow.

Sales force control philosophy as reflected by its constitutive elements

Table 14.1 summarizes how each of the eight constitutive elements can reflect different control philosophies on the OC-BC continuum depending on the emphasis placed on any element at a given time.

| Table 14.1 | Control philosophies and constitutive elements |

	◄──────── Continuum ────────►	
	Outcome-based Control (OC)	**Behaviour-based Control (BC)**
1. Focus of performance criteria. Does management value how sales results are achieved (the effort expended) or simply the results themselves (the outcomes)?	Managers pay particular attention to bottom-line results.	Managers pay particular attention to the methods used to achieve outcomes.
2. Number of performance criteria. Does management judge salespeople using only two or three factors, or does it look at a dozen or more metrics?	Management evaluates a salesperson's performance according to a few observable metrics, primarily market-related, such as sales volume.	Management evaluates a salesperson's performance subjectively, using many criteria.
3. Degree of management intervention. Who makes the final decision on important issues related to sales assignments, the salesperson or the manager?	Managers typically offer relatively little supervision. Salespeople make final decisions.	Managers give relatively heavy supervision and make final decisions.
4. Frequency of contact. Are interactions between salespeople and management easy to enact?	Managers and salespeople have little to no contact.	Managers and salespeople are frequently and extensively in contact.
5. Degree of management monitoring. Does management show serious interest in salespeople's call and activity reports, or are these just a bureaucratic requirement?	Management rarely monitors its sales staff.	Management constantly monitors its sales staff.
6. Amount of coaching offered. Does management suggest ways that salespeople can improve their selling skills and abilities?	Managers offer little to no coaching.	Managers offer frequent, heavy coaching.
7. Transparency of evaluation criteria. How objective, clear, and precise are evaluations at the company?	Evaluation criteria are very transparent.	Evaluation criteria are opaque.
8. Compensation scheme. Is the pay check based largely on variable compensation triggered by outcomes? Or does it have a large salary component with a performance bonus driven by management's judgements?	A salesperson's compensation is mostly variable, keyed to results.	A salesperson's compensation is mostly fixed, keyed to salary or management's evaluations.
	◄──────── **Continuum** ────────►	

Source: adapted from Anderson and Onyemah (2006).

Imagine a firm X with an OC. Strong emphasis is placed on sales outcome. Due to the complexity and cost of gathering information, the firm bases performance appraisal on a few easily observable results (e.g. sales volume) rather than on a broad set of measurable inputs. Consequently firm X uses light monitoring and employs few managers. Salespeople spend more time in the field and have little contact with management. Coaching by management is not intense since this would interfere with the entrepreneur-like salesperson's development of his or her own method of effective selling. The small number of criteria and the objectivity of sales results make evaluation and performance appraisal more transparent and understandable. The incentive component of total compensation is often high and tied to sales results.

In contrast to firm X, firm Y operates a BC. The firm believes it knows the most effective selling method and discourages salespeople from innovation. Paramount in firm Y is input into selling operation (e.g. presentation techniques, sales call patterns, etc.). Constant monitoring and enforcement require an army of managers. In addition, frequent contact with management is encouraged. Salespeople receive intense coaching and direction. The subjective nature of behavioural evaluation places most power in the hands of managers. The proportion of salary in compensation is often high.

Advantages and disadvantages of outcome- and behaviour-based control systems

Table 14.2 outlines, comparatively, the feelings, thoughts, and behaviour of salespeople under pure OC and BC.

When should a firm lean towards outcome-based control systems?

A firm needs more outcome control when it wants an extremely motivated sales force focused on tangible, short-term results. OC is also desirable when the firm is willing to permit salespeople to be very independent and make considerable money (often more than their managers). It is also advisable when the salesperson's skills and efforts are the greatest determinant of sales, for example in the following circumstances:

- when customers need a significant amount of information (new problem, new solutions);
- when the presentation is capable of framing the customer's thinking;
- when the sale is open (i.e. many influences intervene) as against pre-sold (e.g. heavily advertized and/or promoted products and services);
- when the customer cares a great deal about the salesperson (hence, open to switch to whatever the salesperson recommends);
- when management knows that many different behaviours can be effective;
- when management does not know which behaviours work and which ones are ineffective;
- when a firm has good measures of output (i.e. the measures are accurate, timely and individualized);
- when a firm cannot afford to support an expensive sales organization (e.g. a start-up).

| Table 14.2 | How salespeople feel, think and behave under OC and BC |

Outcome control philosophy (OC)	Behaviour control philosophy (BC)
Salespeople focus on targets and obtain 'tangible' results now.	Salespeople are less focused on 'tangible' results now.
Salespeople tend to be excellent at individual selling.	Salespeople tend to be excellent at team selling.
Salespeople possess a strong sense of personal motivation and accountability.	Salespeople possess a somewhat weaker sense of personal motivation and accountability.
Salespeople may take the customer's side at the expense of management's viewpoint.	Salespeople are more likely to see management's viewpoint when balancing customer and company demands.
Salespeople tend to have independence of mind (will freely disagree with their managers).	Salespeople are relatively cooperative with management.
Salespeople are less affectively committed to the organization. Turnover is more frequent.	Salespeople exhibit stronger affective commitment to the organization. Turnover is less frequent.
Salespeople are very interested in tangible, visible rewards such as money, trips and recognition.	Salespeople are interested, but less so, in tangible, visible rewards such as money, trips and recognition.
Salespeople are somewhat interested in non-tangible, invisible 'self-rewards' such as feeling a sense of achievement, personal growth, satisfaction and enjoying offering a good service.	Salespeople are very interested in non-tangible, invisible, 'self-rewards', such as feeling a sense of achievement, personal growth, satisfaction and enjoying offering a good service.

When should a firm lean towards behaviour-based control systems?

BC is more appropriate when salespeople may not figure out and do what is required of them if they are paid by results. Examples of such situations include:

- when salespeople are inexperienced;
- when a firm is particularly concerned about how salespeople present its name or brand;
- when the sales task is complex;
- when the product or service to be sold is dangerous when applied incorrectly;
- when a firm wants to present a consistent image and deliver a consistent service experience;
- when a firm wants its salespeople to set high non-sales priorities, e.g. undertake administrative activities and/or participate in new product development;
- when a firm requires a very loyal sales force, especially when turnover is particularly expensive and job knowledge, relationships and experience are highly valuable;
- when there is a need to instill long-term orientation in salespeople;
- when a firm is not impatient for results now;

- when the overhead of an expensive sales organization is affordable;
- when team selling is involved;
- when knowledge of the behaviour required or discouraged is clearly known;
- when it is impossible to track performance by measure of results.

The reality

There is no one control system that gives excellent results in all circumstances. Rather, each firm should use a system that fits its own particular circumstances. Pure OC and BC systems are rare extremes. Most companies function somewhere in the middle of the OC-BC continuum, seeking a balance between controlling the results achieved by salespeople and how those results are achieved (Oliver and Anderson 1995). Critical, however, is the firm's ability to maintain consistency among the control system elements at any point on the OC-BC continuum (Anderson and Onyemah 2006).

The drawbacks associated with OC and BC compel firms to seek hybrid control philosophies (HC) by steering a middle ground, somewhere on the continuum and away from the ends of OC and BC. While this approach has intuitive appeal, achieving the right balance is daunting. Striking a balance between customer empowerment (critical in pure OC) and manager empowerment (indispensable in pure BC) requires a careful mix in the emphases placed on the eight constitutive elements. When adequate attention is not given to this, the entire sales force control system philosophy becomes exposed to inconsistencies. Inconsistencies occur when emphases on the constitutive elements do not follow logically from one to the other to form a coherent ensemble. In much the same way that a firm's overall human resource practices must be consistent in order to economize on administrative cost, aid on-the-job learning and attract an homogenous workforce, the elements of a sales force control system should consistently convey the firm's expectations to each salesperson. For example, it is expected that a firm that bases its performance appraisal on conforming to company goals should minimize pay differentials and give less emphasis to incentive compensation schemes (i.e. BC). On the other hand, a firm that bases its performance appraisal on measurable outputs should emphasize incentive compensation schemes (i.e. OC). In each of these archetypical firms, the two control system elements (i.e. focus of performance criteria and compensation) are consistent with each other. When the constitutive elements of a sales force control system lack internal consistency, the consequences are often negative, e.g. high role ambiguity and conflict, job dissatisfaction, high turnover of sales staff, weak affective organizational commitment and low performance (Onyemah and Anderson 2009).

How inconsistencies among control system elements damage salespeople's performance

Just as inconsistent human resource policies give mixed signals to employees generally (Baron and Kreps 1999), inconsistent control system elements create frustration and demotivation among members of the sales force and interfere with their performance.

Perhaps one of the most vivid examples of potential control system inconsistency is between the two elements: *focus of performance criteria* and *compensation scheme*. If the focus of performance criteria is output (i.e. sales volume), salespeople will expect their reward to be commensurate with the output achieved. This can be assured only if the compensation scheme emphasizes incentives (i.e. the proportion of salary in compensation should be low). The drive for sales suffers if compensation is not sensitive enough to sales volume, the focus of the performance criteria. Thus inconsistency between the focus of performance criteria and the compensation scheme will hurt sales performance.

Consider another pair of elements: the *degree of monitoring* and *amount of coaching offered*. Provision of intense coaching is consistent with increased monitoring to observe the effectiveness of the coaching offered. The desire to justify the time devoted to coaching should accentuate the intensity of monitoring. Furthermore, the design of the contents of coaching (e.g. skills set to be imparted) could also benefit from observations made during monitoring. A disconnect between the skills set being imparted and the skills set needed to improve sales volume is more likely when the amount of coaching is not matched by the degree of monitoring. This can be confusing and frustrating for salespeople and the frustration that comes from spending valuable time on the acquisition of 'useless' and/or 'irrelevant' skills could lead to demotivation, with negative consequence for sales performance.

Consider yet another pairing: the *focus of performance criteria* and the *amount of coaching offered*. If the focus of performance criteria is output (i.e. sales volume), salespeople should devote more time to customers. Will the simultaneous provision of intense coaching boost sales volume? It will in a BC-dominated environment but not in an OC environment: with the latter, once salespeople realize that the focus of performance criteria is sales volume, they will guard their selling time and will most likely devote less time to non-selling or administrative activities such as receiving coaching from Sales Managers. They might rebel if the Sales Managers insist upon giving them coaching. For these salespeople, 'time spent with Sales Managers is time lost with customers and foregone sales opportunities'. So if the drive to spend more time with customers conflicts with the time requested for intense coaching, the resulting tension and frustration might lead to demotivation and hence lower sales. This will not be the case if the focus of performance criteria is input because provision is already made for coaching time to ensure that salespeople understand the various inputs that are expected of them during the sales process. A counter-argument to the foregoing is that coaching could make the salesperson better (more efficient). The essence here is the idea that a sales volume-focused firm attracts salespeople who feel that they can do better if left alone and coaching will not add much value.

Finally, consider this pair: *number of performance criteria* and *transparency of evaluation criteria*. Our premise is that phenomena that are directly observable (e.g. sales volume) are easier to measure than those that are not (e.g. commitment to a company's policies). In the latter case, there is usually a tendency to seek and combine different manifestations of the phenomena for the purpose of measurement. Consequently, phenomena that are not directly observable tend to require more measures or criteria. Furthermore, these measures or criteria tend to be evaluated subjectively. Thus, use of fewer performance criteria tends to be associated with higher transparency while multiple performance criteria tend to be associated with lower transparency. For example in OC systems, the performance measure might be restricted to total sales volume, a simple, highly transparent criterion. What happens when few performance criteria are matched with low transparency? For example, when sales performance is measured by total sales volume but team selling obfuscates the contribution of individual sales force members. This inconsistency can be frustrating. The knowledge that only one criterion (e.g. total sales volume) counts, coupled with uncertainty about the assignment of sales, might lead to demotivation and hence withdrawal of effort.

Collectively, therefore, inconsistencies among the eight constitutive elements undermine sales performance. This happens not only because of the frustration and demotivation just discussed but also as a result of the confusion engendered. This confusion leads salespeople to misdirect their efforts, which in turn makes it difficult to achieve the critical effort level required to achieve sales targets.

Salespeople frequently live in a world characterized by trade-offs (Fudge and Lodish 1977). Sales force control systems should clearly communicate corporate philosophy about these. To this purpose, each of the elements must be consistent with each other, otherwise the resulting confusions and distractions will undermine salespeople's ability to perform well.

The confusion and frustration generated by inconsistent elements destabilize salespeople – a salesperson, in an attempt to cover every base, might decide to play it safe and respond to every signal that emanates from the control system elements. He/she might then end up satisficing on different incompatible strategies, e.g. trying to make as many calls as possible (in response to result-oriented performance criteria) while at the same time trying to write a large number of call reports (in response to intense monitoring). This might result in his/her making too few calls (below critical call frequency per prospect) and producing too few poorly written reports and neither he/she nor his/her boss would be satisfied with either. Further, when salespeople invest their efforts about equally in all directions in an attempt to cover every base, they dissipate energy faster and may not have enough strength left to make the next, maybe critical, call.

In addition to their destabilizing effect, inconsistent elements impair on-the-job learning. Learning theories suggests that messages are more salient and recalled more favourably when the multiple stimuli being transmitted are consistent and reinforce the same theme, as in effective advertizing campaigns and brand-building strategies (Baron and Kreps 1999). In the same vein, salespeople who experience consistent control elements will progress through their learning curve faster because the learning cues from the eight elements reinforce a common philosophy. To the extent that this learning translates into useful selling skills, sales performance should improve. In summary therefore, the effectiveness of control systems in ensuring salespeople achieve superior sales performance is undermined when control system elements are inconsistent with each other.

Graphical examples of inconsistent control system elements

Anderson and Onyemah (2006) describe three archetypical forms of control system inconsistency: 'ever-present manager', 'sublime neglect', and 'black hole'. Figure 14.1 graphically depicts these forms.

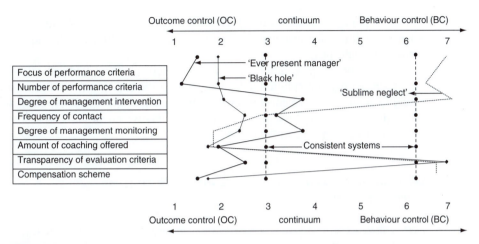

| Focus of performance criteria |
| Number of performance criteria |
| Degree of management intervention |
| Frequency of contact |
| Degree of management monitoring |
| Amount of coaching offered |
| Transparency of evaluation criteria |
| Compensation scheme |

Figure 14.1 Examples of consistent and inconsistent sales force control systems
Source: adapted from Anderson and Onyemah (2006).

The 'ever-present manager' problem is exemplified by a company that generally uses an OC system (i.e. managers are supposed to focus on a handful of important results when evaluating salespeople's performance and calibrate compensation accordingly) but nonetheless has interventionist managers (BC philosophy) who insist on frequent contact with salespeople and monitor their activities intensively. These are managers who although working within an OC system cannot let go or let the salesperson develop his or her own method of effective selling. The problem is exacerbated because often such managers do not coach the staff as much as a genuine BC system calls for. In such a setting, salespeople will tend to resist management's interference and will try to focus on their own method for achieving the best sales results. Meanwhile, managers will try to correct salespeople's 'excessive' focus on generating what they believe to be 'unprofitable' orders, will complain that salespeople are uncooperative and will strive to refocus salespeople's attention on whatever the managers think they should be doing. As a result, tension, confusion and frustration reign. Based on this description, plotting each element on the OC-BC continuum yields the bold, solid, zigzag pattern in Figure 14.1.

A 'sublime neglect' form of inconsistency is characterized by a BC system that does not provide salespeople with the coaching they need. Salespeople are often not aware of what management expects and how they 'should behave', and yet are not given the freedom to pursue their own methods. Sales Managers in this setting tend to have selling responsibilities in addition to their administrative assignments. In this situation, salespeople will be confused, lonely and distrustful of the company. Also, they will be deprived of the necessary selling skills. The corresponding plotting connecting the positions of the elements on the OC-BC continuum yields the dotted zigzag pattern in Figure 14.1.

A 'black hole' form of inconsistency arises in a fundamentally OC system with opaque evaluation methods. Salespeople feel that their organization is focused exclusively on results but how those results translate into individual performance evaluation and corresponding compensation is unclear. Here, salespeople will be distrustful and frustrated with their evaluations. The corresponding plotting yields the thin zigzag pattern in Figure 14.1.

While the three zigzag patterns in Figure 14.1 depict inconsistent control system elements, any straight line plotted (i.e. each point for the eight elements lies on a vertical straight line) represents a control system whose elements are perfectly consistent with each other regardless of where on the continuum between OC and BC it lies (e.g. the two vertical dashed lines in Figure 14.1).

Who survives better under inconsistent control system elements?

Age, selling experience and organizational tenure diminish the tendency for inconsistent control systems elements to lead to negative job-related outcomes such as under-performance, role stress and less affective organizational commitment. The sales force literature (e.g. Cron and Slocum 1986; Dubinsky et al. 1986) underscores career stage and organizational tenure as important factors that influence the link between salespeople's job-related outcomes and organizational factors such as control system elements. A salesperson's prolonged exposure to a company's control system should give him or her better understanding of what it takes to succeed in the company. Over time, incumbents build expertise that contributes to their ability to obtain results, regardless of the circumstances. Long-tenured salespeople will have developed an ability to discriminate among inconsistent control elements and will no longer find it necessary to react to every cue. Essentially, they learn which elements they can ignore and which they should focus on, creating a working level of consistency for themselves within an inconsistent system.

In the same vein, more experienced salespeople tend to have a better understanding of the relationship between efforts and results and hence often do a better job of optimizing the allocation of their time and effort among competing demands. It is important to note that the relevant experience here relates to the sales profession itself and not just experience within a particular organization. Experience in dealing with objections and reconciling parties are transferable skills. Thus, general selling experience should be an additional resource on which salespeople can draw when faced with inconsistent control system elements.

Likewise with age, individuals learn useful survival techniques. Longer professional exposure (regardless of the type of position occupied before moving into sales) may provide older salespeople with experience-based solutions when faced with complicated choices in a work environment. Thus the combined effect of age, general selling experience and organizational tenure should provide salespeople with coping mechanisms when faced with the confusion, frustration and demotivation occasioned by inconsistent elements.

Overhauling entire systems to achieve consistency is generally too arduous and costly because the sales force control systems in most firms date back many years and are in great part institutionalized. Younger, newer and/or less experienced salespeople should therfore be made the target of remedial efforts such as socialization practices involving senior salespeople.

The situation in six European countries

Between 2002 and 2006, a survey of sales force control systems was conducted in six European countries: France, Hungary, Ireland, Italy, Spain, and the United Kingdom. The survey was conducted in the official language of each country. A total of 867 salespeople from 18 organizations and 4 industries (pharmaceutical, fast-moving consumer goods, industrial goods, and information systems and technology) participated in the survey.

In the questionnaire-based survey, salespeople expressed their opinions on a series of questions that formed the measures for the eight control system elements.

Measures

The level of control system elements as perceived by salespeople

The goal here was to capture salespeople's perceptions of the control system elements they experience. Some companies might have a corporate-wide control philosophy or guideline. However, in practice, Sales Managers often modify the philosophy to reflect the heterogeneous circumstances of their subordinates. Hence, empirical measures of sales force control system philosophies often measure the constitutive elements *as perceived by the individual salesperson* because the best informants regarding implemented sales force control systems are the salespeople themselves.

The items, wording and structure of the questionnaire is contained in the Appendix. Except for the compensation scheme (i.e. the proportion of salary in total compensation), each element was measured with multiple items. Since each item was anchored on a 1 to 7 scale, the proportion of salary in compensation was transformed into a 1 to 7 scale.

Finally, the scores for the eight elements were averaged to form an index of salesperson 'degree of behaviour control system' (versus 'outcome control system' represented by lower scores). For example, a mean score of 7 reflects a pure behaviour control (BC) system while a mean score of 1 reflects a pure outcome control (OC) system. Mean scores that fall between 1 and 7 reflect hybrid control systems.

Construction of an inconsistency index based on the level of control system elements perceived by salespeople

The pattern of scores on the eight control elements depicts a profile: either a zigzag profile, (reflecting inconsistencies, as in Figure 14.1) or a vertical straight line (indicating that the perceived elements share exactly the same degree of behaviour- or outcome-based control). Understandably, some zigzags will be more pronounced than others, depending on the level of inconsistency. In other words, the higher the level of inconsistency, the more pronounced the zigzag.

A summary statistic to capture the extent of zigzag (i.e. the level of inconsistencies among the control system elements) is the standard deviation of the scores in the eight control system elements. This can be calculated for each salesperson. Specifically, a standard deviation of zero will reflect a state of consistent or perfectly co-aligned elements (i.e. a vertical straight line that connects the plots of scores for the eight elements) while higher standard deviations will reflect an increasing level of inconsistency or absence of co-alignment (i.e. increasing level of zigzagging). For example, a salesperson who scores 2 for every element will obtain a standard deviation of 0, whereas a salesperson who scores 2, 3, 6, 1, 3, 1, 3 and 6 for the eight elements, respectively, will obtain a standard deviation of 1.959 (Onyemah and Anderson 2009). The elements perceived by the first salesperson are consistent with each other while those of the second salesperson are inconsistent.

Summary of survey results

Country-level and sector-level summaries are provided in the following order:

1. Distribution of respondents;
2. Demographics (i.e. selling experience, organizational tenure and age) of respondents;
3. Average scores of each control system element;
4. Index of the 'degree of behaviour control system' (versus 'outcome control system' represented by lower scores);
5. Index of the level of inconsistencies among the control system elements.

Of the 867 salespeople who responded to the survey, 14 per cent were based in France, 12 percent in Hungary, 8 per cent in Ireland, 14 per cent in Italy, 44 per cent in Spain and 8 per cent in the United Kingdom (Figure 14.2).

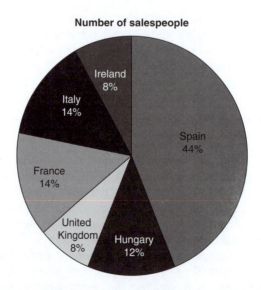

Number of salespeople

Figure 14.2 Distribution of salespeople across countries

Number of salespeople

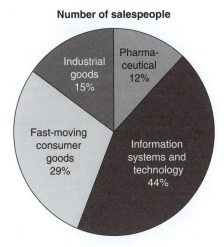

Figure 14.3   Distribution of salespeople across industries

The industries represented were fast-moving consumer goods (29 per cent), information systems and technology (44 per cent), industrial goods (15 per cent) and pharmaceutical (12 per cent). Figure 14.3 depicts the distribution of respondents across the four industries.

The sample averages for age, selling experience and organizational tenure were 38.5 years, 11.5 years and 8.5 years respectively (Figure 14.4).

Salespeople from fast-moving consumer goods and industrial goods industries were older (43 and 40 years respectively) than their counterparts in pharmaceutical and information systems and technology industries (33 and 36 years respectively)

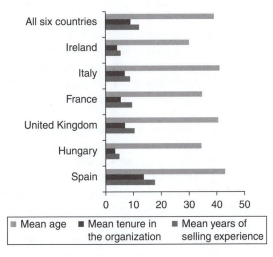

Figure 14.4   Country comparison of salespeople's demographics

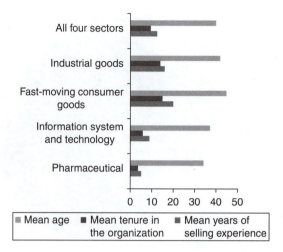

All four sectors

Industrial goods

Fast-moving consumer goods

Information system and technology

Pharmaceutical

0 10 20 30 40 50

■ Mean age   ■ Mean tenure in   ■ Mean years of
                  the organization   selling experience

Figure 14.5   Industry comparison of salespeople's demographics

(Figure 14.5). The average years of selling experience and organizational tenure depicted a similar pattern to that for age.

Results for control system elements: country comparison (Figure 14.6)

Mean of focus of performance criteria: Salespeople in Hungary and the UK experienced the greatest pressure to produce results (i.e. they felt the output of their efforts was more important than their input). Salespeople in France and Spain reported that more emphasis was generally placed on their effort and comportment rather than on the outcomes these yielded. In the remaining two countries (i.e. Ireland and Italy), there seemed to be a balance between the demands for input and output.

Mean of number of performance criteria: Salespeople in Hungary, France and Spain were expected to do well on many performance indicators. Those in Ireland and Italy faced slightly fewer performance indicators. Salespeople in the UK experienced the least number of performance indicators. Overall, the number of performance indicators reported in each of the six countries was greater than the mid-point of 3.5 on the OC-BC continuum.

Mean of extent of management intervention: Salespeople in Ireland, Hungary and France experienced the least autonomy, while those in Italy appeared to have more job autonomy, followed closely by salespeople in the UK.

Mean of frequency of contact with management: The country averages for the frequency of contact with management suggest that salespeople in all the six countries fell in the second half of the OC-BC continuum. This was especially true for salespeople in the UK, Ireland and Italy.

Mean of degree of task monitoring: Salespeople in Hungary reported the highest level of monitoring by management. They were followed by those in Spain, Ireland and France. In Italy salespeople were subjected to the least monitoring.

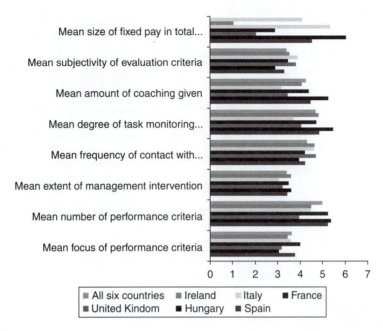

Country comparison of sales force control system elements

Mean of amount of coaching offered: Salespeople in Hungary received the highest amount of coaching, and it was considerably higher than that experienced by salespeople in Spain, France and Ireland (in that order). Salespeople in Italy and the UK received relatively little coaching, a situation that placed them in the first half of the OC-BC continuum. Their counterparts in Hungary, Spain, France and Ireland occupied the second half of the continuum.

Mean of subjectivity of evaluation criteria: Salespeople in Italy and the UK experienced more subjective evaluation criteria than salespeople in Ireland and France. While salespeople in these four countries, based on the level of subjectivity faced during performance evaluation, occupied the second half of the OC-BC continuum, those in Hungary and Spain occupied the first half of the OC-BC continuum.

Mean of size of fixed pay in total compensation: This element produced the largest variations in perceptions. Whereas sales force compensation in Hungary and Italy tended to be largely fixed, that in Ireland and the UK tended to be largely variable. In Spain, the fixed portion of total compensation was also high, though not as high as that for Hungary and Italy.

Results for control system elements: industry comparison (Figure 14.7)

Mean of focus of performance criteria: Pharmaceutical salespeople felt that the outcomes of their actions were more important to management than the actions themselves (i.e. input). In contrast, industrial goods salespeople reported that inputs to the selling process were emphasized more than outputs (i.e. results). The relative importance of

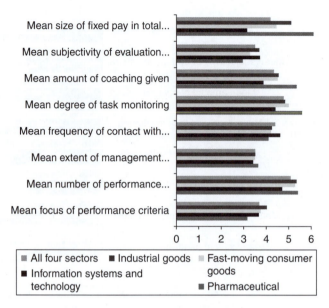

Mean size of fixed pay in total...
Mean subjectivity of evaluation...
Mean amount of coaching given
Mean degree of task monitoring
Mean frequency of contact with...
Mean extent of management...
Mean number of performance...
Mean focus of performance criteria

■ All four sectors ■ Industrial goods ▪ Fast-moving consumer goods
■ Information systems and technology ■ Pharmaceutical

Figure 14.7 Industry comparison of sales force control system elements

inputs and outputs appeared to be balanced for salespeople in fast-moving consumer goods and information systems and technology.

Mean of number of performance criteria: The number of performance criteria reported were many for all industries represented, thus clearly placing them in the second half of the OC-BC continuum.

Mean of extent of management intervention: There was no significant difference in the level of management intervention across the four industries. There also appeared to be a balance in this element along the OC-BC continuum (i.e. the results placed salespeople in all industries at the middle of the continuum).

Mean of frequency of contact with management: Information systems and technology salespeople reported the highest frequency of contact with management staff. They were followed by salespeople carrying industrial and fast-moving consumer goods. Pharmaceutical salespeople had the least opportunities to interact with management staff.

Mean of degree of task monitoring: While pharmaceutical salespeople were the most monitored, information systems and technology salespeople appeared to be the least monitored. Between these two extremes were salespeople in industrial and fast-moving consumer goods sectors.

Mean of amount of coaching offered: the pattern of results here was quite similar to the one reported for degree of task monitoring: the intensity of coaching was greatest for pharmaceutical salespeople. Information systems and technology salespeople experienced the least amount of coaching. Again, salespeople in industrial and fast-moving consumer goods received a moderate intensity level of coaching.

Mean of subjectivity of evaluation criteria: Salespeople in information systems and technology and industrial goods sectors reported the highest level of subjectivity in evaluation criteria, followed by fast-moving consumer goods salespeople. Pharmaceutical salespeople appeared to experience less subjectivity with respect to their performance evaluation criteria.

Mean of size of fixed pay in total compensation: While the fixed portion of the total compensation for information systems and technology salespeople was generally low (in the first half of the OC-BC continuum), that for salespeople in other sectors, especially pharmaceutical, was on average high (in the second half of the OC-BC continuum).

Results for the index of control system (country comparison, Figure 14.8)

Given the OC-BC continuum, this index gives the degree of behaviour-based control system (BC), as opposed to the degree of outcome-based control system (OC) represented by lower values.

In none of the countries did the salespeople experience either pure OC (1) or pure BC (7). As expected, the average salesperson in every country faced a hybrid control system. Salespeople in Hungary experienced the highest degree of BC (4.41), followed by salespeople in Spain (4.18). Salespeople in the UK and Ireland faced lesser degrees of BC (3.50 and 3.66 respectively). In fact, salespeople in the UK, given their mid-point position on the OC-BC continuum, demonstrated perfectly the notion of a hybrid sales force control system. Salespeople in France and Italy occupied the second half of the OC-BC continuum with indices of 4.01 and 3.94 respectively.

Results for the index of control system (industry comparison, Figure 14.9)

There were significant differences across industries with respect to the degree of control system faced by salespeople. Pharmaceutical salespeople experienced the highest degree of BC (4.43) while information systems and technology salespeople experienced the lowest degree of BC (3.83). Industrial goods salespeople were the second most

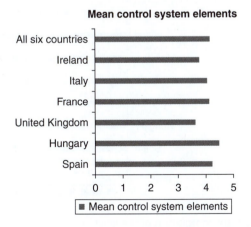

Figure 14.8   Country comparison of the position of salespeople on the OC-BC continuum

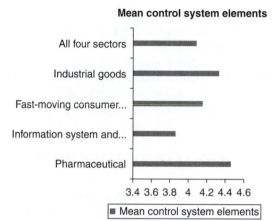

Figure 14.9 Industry comparison of the position of salespeople on the OC-BC continuum

exposed to BC (4.30), followed by salespeople in the fast-moving consumer goods industry (4.12).

Results for the index of inconsistencies (country comparison, Figure 14.10)

Salespeople in Ireland and Hungary were the most exposed to control system inconsistencies with levels of 1.73 and 1.68 respectively. Next were salespeople in Spain (1.52), the UK (1.51) and France (1.49). Salespeople in Italy were the least exposed to inconsistencies (1.36).

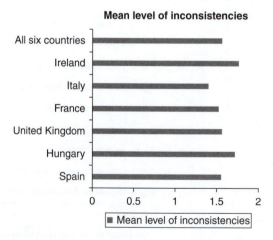

Figure 14.10 Country comparison of the level of inconsistencies among control system elements

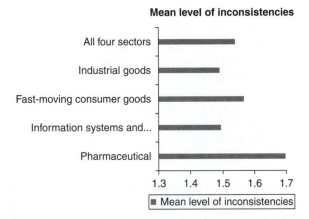

Figure 14.11 Industry comparison of the level of inconsistencies among control system elements

Results for the index of inconsistencies (industry comparison, Figure 14.11)

Pharmaceutical salespeople were by far the most exposed to control system inconsistencies (1.69). Those in fast-moving consumer goods experienced the second highest level of inconsistencies (1.56). The least exposed to inconsistencies were salespeople in industrial goods and information systems and technology sectors. The level of inconsistencies faced by salespeople from these two sectors was 1.48.

Summary

Collectively, the evidence given above suggests that the quest for the 'right' sales force control system should be matched by a genuine concern for design consistency. When control system elements are consistent with each other, they become mutually reinforcing; every element defines the same level of outcome or behaviour control, such that the message sent by a given element is reinforced by that sent by other elements. The resulting synergies translate into more efficient dispensation of duties by employees.

The European data presented in this chapter confirmed the prevalence of hybrid control systems. These are indeed more appealing than pure outcome- or behaviour-based control systems, and can effectively and efficiently address a wider array of control problems. However, when the combinations are poorly implemented (i.e. when the constitutive elements do not reflect the same degree of outcome- or behaviour-based control), dysfunctional outcomes such as inferior sales performance might result. Also, decisions on the emphasis to be placed on each of the constitutive elements of a control system should be made collectively rather than in isolation.

The methods and framework elaborated here can be used by management for audit and diagnostic purposes. For example, if a Sales Manager wants to know whether or not the control system elements perceived by his or her salespeople have internal consistency, the manager can submit the questions in the Appendix to his/her team. Using the resultant data, the manager can plot the responses of each salesperson to reveal the extent of zigzagging. Sales Managers can also use the results for benchmarking and designing remedial actions.

In practice, the overhaul of an existing control system to achieve consistency can be costly and lengthy due to competing interests and organizational inertia. As a short-term measure, given that older, more experienced and longer-tenured salespeople are the most resilient to control system inconsistencies, it is advisable for younger, newer and/or less experienced salespeople to be made the focus of immediate corrective actions.

Agreeing on a sales force control philosophy does not suffice. It is important to ensure that, during implementation, the constitutive elements of the chosen control system, whether it be pure or hybrid, have internal consistency so that they reinforce each other to form a coherent whole that makes the work environment conducive for salespeople's success.

Key points

There is empirical evidence that:

1. The control systems faced by salespeople can be distributed on a continuum.
2. The vast majority of salespeople are faced with hybrid control systems (systems that combine emphases on both outcome and behaviour control philosophies).
3. The difficulty associated with achieving a balance between these two hypothetically opposing philosophies makes hybrid control systems prone to internal inconsistencies.
4. Inconsistencies among the elements of sales force control systems exist.
5. The level of sales force control system inconsistencies is quantifiable.
6. These inconsistencies increase role stress, reduce satisfaction and undermine salespeople's performance.
7. Although control system inconsistencies are harmful to salespeople and their organizations, their destructive capacities are reduced as salespeople grow older, spend time in the same job and/or organization and acquire selling experience.
8. Differences exist across countries and sectors with respect to the foregoing.

Questionnaire for auditing the consistency of sales force control systems in an organization

Guide questions to establish scores for each control system element

Focus of performance criteria
1. I think that what really matters most to management are the results I achieve, rather than how I achieve them (R*).

2. I think management does not care a great deal about my input into the job, instead it focuses on my output (R*).
3. In my opinion, management puts a lot of emphasis on the outcome of my effort, but puts little weight on the effort itself (R*).
4. Only my tangible results matter to my management (R*).
5. No matter how well I behave and how well I struggle to achieve results, at the end of the day my promotion and career progress depend mostly on my bottom line (R*).

Anchor: 1 (completely disagree) to 7 (completely agree).

Number of Performance Criteria
1. When management rates my performance, it takes many things into consideration.
2. I think management considers only a handful of things when determining my performance evaluation (R*).
3. To get a favourable performance evaluation I only need to pay attention to a few factors (R*).
4. In my opinion, there are just a couple of requirements I need to meet to get a good performance evaluation (R*).

Anchor: 1 (completely disagree) to 7 (completely agree).

Degree of management intervention
1. Management grants me a great deal of autonomy (R*).
2. Management allows me to do almost as I please (R*).
3. I make the final decision on practically everything that has to do with my selling assignment (R*).
4. Management allows me freedom to organize my work (R*).

Anchor: 1 (completely disagree) to 7 (completely agree).

Frequency of contact with management
1. I do not get day-to-day contact with management (R*).
2. I have many opportunities to interact with management.
3. I am isolated from management (R*).
4. Management does not spend time with me (R*).

Anchor: 1 (completely disagree) to 7 (completely agree).

Degree of management monitoring
1. Management tracks my activities.
2. Management keeps a close watch on how I spend my time.
3. Management takes my call and activity reports seriously.
4. Management carries out a detailed examination of my call and activity reports.
5. Management keeps informed of my activities.
6. Management checks to see if I am following its instructions.

Anchor: 1 (completely disagree) to 7 (completely agree).

Amount of coaching offered

1. I receive a lot of coaching from my boss or those I report to.
2. Management provides a lot of on-the-job suggestions and tips on ways it thinks I can improve my selling skills and abilities.
3. There are senior salespeople designated by management who offer me a lot of coaching.
4. Management makes sure I know how to carry out my assigned tasks.
5. Management gives me training intended to improve my productivity.

Anchor: 1 (completely disagree) to 7 (completely agree).

Transparency of evaluation criteria

How would you describe the criteria management seems to use in evaluating your performance?

1. Not at all clear ... Very clear (R*).
2. Very imprecise ... Very precise (R*).
3. Very vague ... Not at all vague (R*).
4. Subjective ... Objective (R*).
5. Very partial ... Highly impartial (R*).

R* Reverse to score the direction of behaviour control.

Compensation scheme

Proportion of salary in compensation.

References

Anderson, E. and Oliver, R. (1987) 'Perspectives on Behaviour-Based Versus Outcome-Based Sales Force Control Systems', *Journal of Marketing*, 51 (4): 76–88.

Anderson, E. and Onyemah, V. (2006) 'How Right Should the Customer Be?', *Harvard Business Review*, 84 (7/8): 58–67.

Baron, N.J. and Kreps, D.M. (1999) 'Consistent Human Resource Practices', *California Management Review*, 41 (3): 29–53.

Cron, W.L. and Slocum, J.W. (1986) 'The Influence of Career Stages on Salespeople's Job Attitudes, Work Perceptions, and Performance', *Journal of Marketing Research*, 23 (2): 119–29.

Dubinsky, A.J., Howell, R.D., Ingram, T.N.and Bellenger, D.N. (1986) 'Sales Force Socialization', *Journal of Marketing*, 50 (4): 192–207.

Fudge, W.K. and Lodish, L.M. (1977) 'Evaluation of the Effectiveness of a Model Based Salesman's Planning System by Field Experimentation', *Interfaces*, 8 (1): 97–106.

Oliver, R.L and Anderson, E. (1995) 'Behaviour- and Outcome-based Sales Control Systems: Evidence and Consequences of Pure-form and Hybrid Governance', *Journal of Personal Selling and Sales Management*, 15 (4): 1–15.

Onyemah, V. and Anderson, E. (2009) 'Inconsistencies among the Constitutive Elements of a Sales Force Control System: Test of a Configuration Theory-based Performance Prediction', *Journal of Personal Selling and Sales Management*, 29 (1): 9–24.

Further reading

Baldauf, A., Cravens, D.W. and Piercy, N.F. (2005) 'Sales Management Control Research-synthesis and an Agenda for Future Research', *Journal of Personal Selling and Sales Management*, 25 (1): 7–26.

Cravens, D.W, Ingram, T.N., LaForge, R.W. and Young, C.E. (1993) 'Behaviour-based and Outcome-based Salesforce Control Systems', *Journal of Marketing*, 57 (4): 47–59.

Cravens, D.W., Lassk, F.G., Low, G.S., Marshall, G.W. and Moncrief, W.C. (2004) 'Formal and Informal Management Control Combinations in Sales Organizations: the Impact on Salesperson Consequences', *Journal of Business Research*, 57 (3): 241–8.

Joshi, A.W. and Randall, S. (2001) 'The Indirect Effects of Organizational Controls on Salesperson Performance and Customer Orientation', *Journal of Business Research*, 54 (1): 1–9.

15
Sales force motivation

Antonis C. Simintiras

Contents

Learning objectives

After reading this chapter, you should be able to:

- Recognize the nature, role and importance of sales force motivation.

- Have a critical understanding of the relationship between motivation, job satisfaction and performance.

- Appreciate the diversity of explanations offered by different theories of motivation.

- Have a comprehensive understanding of the impact of the fulfilment of job-related expectations on motivation.

- Critically assess the impact of rewards and recognition programmes on motivation.

- Develop the ability to evaluate salespeople's motivation.

Chapter outline

One of the most fundamental questions that Sales Managers are constantly faced with is 'What causes good and bad performance?'. The answer to this and similar questions (e.g. 'How can Sales Managers get the most out of their salespeople?') rests upon an understanding of the concept of motivation. This chapter revolves around this issue and it is structured as follows. First, a real-world problem is presented to introduce the complexity of motivation in sales organizations and to serve as an illustration of the need to identify motivational determinants. Second, motivation is defined, the relationships between motivation, performance and job satisfaction are delineated, the main theories of motivation are reviewed and an integrated approach to motivation is offered. Third, various types of motivational incentives are discussed, methods for evaluating salespeople's motivation are presented and the usefulness of a sales motivation audit is explained. Finally, some key points are presented that could serve as implementation examples for motivating salespeople.

EPAL Ltd[1]

The company and its products

EPAL is Europe's leading supplier of residential doors, windows and window-shutters . The EPAL brand stands for high quality, high value systems solutions from one source. All EPAL systems offer thermal insulation and have physical properties that mean they do not require maintenance after installation. Besides being maintenance-free, the systems have the advantages of unique insulation, security, longevity and aesthetics. The company constantly innovates and has registered several patents during the last 15 years.

EPAL is a fairly new but very dynamic company. It was established on 17 May 1992 in Thessaloniki, Greece as a manufacturer of aluminium-based doors, windows and window-shutters. Employing 12 people initially, the company increased its staff to 25 in 1993, one year later. Today, the company employs 90 people and is in the process of building another manufacturing site in the same location to meet the increasing demand for its products not only from Greece but also from overseas. The success of the company is attributed to its philosophy of offering high quality products at a reasonable price.

EPAL offers a wide range of windows, external doors, internal doors, banisters and mechanical doors. Its products have many advantages over those of its competitors in the European market. The products' competitive positioning is based on the following:

1. All products (windows and doors) are equipped with thermal insulation frames and a mechanism called 'perimetric locking' that offers superb insulation capability and added security.
2. Windows, doors and banisters are maintenance-free. Once they are installed, they maintain their properties for many years (they have a lifetime guarantee).
3. Window and door fitting is not performed in the traditional way but using a special EPAL-developed support technique. The company offers same-day fitting, and all installations are performed by the company's specialized fitting teams.
4. In addition to offering a unique range of aesthetically designed windows and doors, the company also produces bespoke products to customer specifications.
5. EPAL provides excellent service.

Motivating the EPAL sales team

EPAL, with sales exceeding €6 million in 2006, relies heavily on a dynamic and highly motivated sales force and an active network of agents to meet and satisfy customer demand. Currently, the company employs ten salespeople and the sales team is headed by Aristotle Risperis,[2] a Sales Manager who has been with the company since it was established. He is in charge of planning, organizing, implementing, directing and evaluating the sales effort both in Greece and in foreign markets. He applies the same motivation approach to both his sales force and his agents.

Aristotle, who is in his early fifties, was a successful salesperson for many years prior to becoming Sales Manager at EPAL. Based on his experience and creative thinking, he seems to have

---

[1] For more information about the company visit its web site at www.epal.gr.
[2] The name of the Sales Manager has been disguised.

discovered a way of effectively motivating his salespeople and, with a motivational approach that works, he is now convinced that he has the secret that most other Sales Managers lack. His approach to motivation is fairly simple and straightforward. Based on the notion that the success of his salespeople is the only success worth experiencing as a Sales Manager, Aristotle motivates his salespeople and agents in the way explained below.

In an ideal world, Aristotle explains, salespeople aim to seek employment in companies that will provide the means for fulfilling their expectations, while companies seek to employ salespeople who will achieve the company's objectives. Conventional wisdom states that salespeople's job-related expectations need to be fulfilled if they are to be motivated, but fulfilment is the end-state and, as such, it is not able to generate motivation. What causes motivation is the anticipated fulfilment. For as long as a salesperson thinks that his/her expectations will be fulfilled then he/she will be motivated. More to the point, when fulfilment of their expectations is anticipated, salespeople experience high levels of job satisfaction.

What is important to know, he continues, is that when salespeople think that their work is going to comply with or facilitate the conditions for the fulfilment of their job-related expectations (regardless of what these job-related expectations might be) they become satisfied. When this happens, the two most crucial conditions for motivation, according to Aristotle, are met. Specifically, salespeople find a very good reason for motivating themselves (anticipated fulfilment) and develop an affective positive attitude (feelings of job satisfaction based on the anticipated fulfilment). This is the mechanism for releasing instigating forces, hence the cause of motivation.

If a company is unable to fulfil salespeople's job-related expectations then the conditions for motivating them are not met and their efforts in the workplace will not be maximized. The critical issue, he argues, is correctly to identify the job-related expectations of the salespeople and then genuinely to try hard to fulfil them or to facilitate conditions for their fulfilment. However, salespeople develop new job-related expectations and modify old ones as time goes by and the task of a Sales Manager is to adjust the conditions for their fulfilment in order for salespeople to believe in the anticipated fulfilment and experience job satisfaction, which in turn causes motivation and high performance levels.

In practice

The salespeople meet every week at the company's office in Thessaloniki and discuss various issues including, among others, calls and sales made, new customers identified and/or approached, routing plans, customer queries, sales lost to the competition and the performance of sales quotas for each salesperson and for the entire team. In addition, Aristotle meets each individual salesperson separately once a month for approximately one hour to discuss their job-related expectations and appropriate ways for fulfilling them. In this session, the Sales Manager listens to their personal objectives and concerns. This is what he calls a counselling session for both himself and the salesperson. It is in these sessions that he wins the hearts and minds of his salespeople, a prerequisite for maximizing their motivational levels.

Introduction: what is motivation?

Motivation addresses the question as to why individuals behave as they do. For example, it is easy to assume that some salespeople work longer hours than others, make greater efforts to secure sales and are more attentive to customers, and when they are asked what motivates them, the likely answer is that they like working hard and being loyal to the company, enjoy winning customers and take pleasure in keeping customers satisfied. This set of statements certainly covers almost all of what motivation is about. A simple explanation of such behaviours is that these salespeople work hard to maximize their financial rewards. By suggesting a motive, a reason or purpose for behaviour (e.g. making money), we can find unity beneath the apparent diversity of behaviours. Motivation, in general, could be described as an intervening variable which is not observed directly but helps to account for relationships between various stimuli and responses. As an intervening variable, motivation helps to explain why different stimuli could lead to the same response, and why the same stimulus could produce different responses.

Motivation and its determinants

Motivation at work is the amount of effort the salesperson decides to expend on his/her job. Put in a different way, motivation is the inner force that causes action and guides behaviour (see Chapter 17 on salespeople's self-management). When motivation is seen and considered as an inner 'force', it implies that it can be expressed in terms of *intensity* of thoughts and feelings leading to expending effort which *persists* over time and has a *direction*. Clearly, when the intensity is high and persists over a long period of time, it results in a high level of activity or motivation. In a sales context, this means that highly motivated salespeople work very hard because they want to do as well as they can in their jobs. Alternatively, when the intensity is low and persists only for a short period of time, the motivation level is sub-optimal. From a managerial perspective, motivating salespeople is one of the most difficult of tasks for Sales Managers.

When attempting to influence the motivation level of salespeople a number of issues must be considered. First, salespeople are removed from direct observation and supervision. They spend a significant amount of their time meeting customers outside the company and therefore it is difficult for Sales Managers to know how motivated they are. Second, salespeople's efforts do not have a linear relationship to their performance. For example, salespeople may try very hard in the job but economic conditions or other environmental factors may prevent them achieving the targets set by their company. Third, salespeople occupy a boundary role position, which means that they always need to find the right balance that will allow them to keep both the company and the customers satisfied. This is a potential source of conflict and tension between the company and the salesperson and, if not addressed, may lead to low levels of motivation (see Chapter 17 for a discussion of such role conflicts).

How much effort a salesperson is prepared to expend in his/her job is determined by many factors. For instance, some salespeople may be motivated by money, but others could be motivated by their ambition for success, loyalty to the company and quest for power. Still others are motivated by comparing themselves with other salespeople and their desire to match their efforts, or even by the value that they attach to the anticipated recognition in the workplace. Attributes such as authority, competitiveness, assertiveness, independence, competence and self-determination are also capable of motivating salespeople. The list goes on, but the points to be made here are that, first, the motivational effort varies over time for the same salesperson; second, the determinants of motivation differ among individual salespeople; and third, motivational determinants may cause different motivational levels at different times.

The relationship between motivation and performance

Understanding the relationship between motivation and performance is of utmost importance; the reason being that salespeople are the revenue producers for any company, and their motivation and subsequent performance determine how successful a business will be. It is always true that, all else being equal, highly motivated salespeople perform better than less motivated salespeople. However, what is important to realize is that in certain circumstances the high performance of salespeople may not always be the result of high motivation. For instance, when the market conditions are very fertile for sales, salespeople can easily meet the sales targets without necessarily having to expend the maximum levels of effort. In such a case, the actual performance of the sales force is less than its potential and the effect is a weakening, in the long term, of the overall market position of the company, allowing competitors to grow faster than they otherwise would have been able to do.

In difficult economic and market conditions, even maximum levels of effort on the part of salespeople may not lead to high performance levels. When high motivational levels are not followed by correspondingly high performance levels, it is rather difficult to keep salespeople motivated. However, when salespeople achieve low performance levels despite their high levels of effort, Sales Managers should evaluate the results of their salespeople's efforts using multiple criteria. Such criteria could be related to behavioural measures of performance such as, for example, the number of sales calls per salesperson, the number of visits to prospective customers, the number of company reports completed on time and the sales meetings attended (see Chapter 14 on sales force control systems and Chapter 18 on sales force evaluation). In this way, the performance of salespeople will be judged more holistically and possible errors in the assessment of salespeople's motivation and performance levels will be avoided. An accurate evaluation of the motivation level of a salesperson can itself become a motivational determinant.

In conclusion, high motivation usually (but not always) leads to high performance levels, and high performance levels achieved are often (but not always) the result of high motivation. The relationship between motivation and performance needs to be understood in the context of the overall environment, market and organization.

The relationship between motivation and job satisfaction

Job satisfaction (dissatisfaction), or a salesperson's positive (negative) attitude towards work and the job itself, is inextricably linked with motivation. A sales job may or may not meet the personal needs and expectations of a salesperson. However, individuals have different personal needs they seek to satisfy and different job-related expectations that they attempt to fulfil, although some aspects of the work setting appear to appeal to almost everyone. Researchers have found that job satisfaction is influenced by numerous factors, such as quality of work-life, whether the job is challenging, and the degree of autonomy and authority the employee has.

Several companies worldwide have experimented with participative decision-making (PDM), which gives employees a voice in making decisions, which in turn boosts their morale, lowers rates of staff turnover and absenteeism and increases job satisfaction. However, while research findings provide evidence that PDM increases job satisfaction, this does not always lead to increases in motivation and productivity.

The critical question therefore is: what is the relationship, if any, between job satisfaction and motivation? Using common sense, it could be easily argued that a happy and satisfied salesperson is a productive salesperson. Inversely, an unhappy and dissatisfied salesperson is not likely to be a productive one as far as realising his/her full potential is concerned, even if the performance levels achieved at the workplace are relatively high. In addition, job dissatisfaction is negatively related to the quality of work-life. The way that satisfaction contributes to increases in motivation and performance should be examined in the light of the motivation process. Salespeople experience satisfaction and/or dissatisfaction at the workplace as a result of the anticipated fulfilment or non-fulfilment of their job-related expectations. It is the satisfaction or dissatisfaction which results from what is anticipated that is causally related to performance (this is discussed below, see p. 401).

The main theories of motivation

The need for a deeper understanding of human behaviour in relation to motivation has provoked researchers' interest in systematically examining this phenomenon and developing theories capable of explaining the motivation process and its determinants. The theories of motivation, which have been developed over many years, can be grouped into three distinct categories. Namely *content* theories (or theories that attempt to identify the determinants of motivation and answer the question 'What motivates salespeople?'), *process* theories (or theories that try to explain the process of determining the amount of effort to be expended and answer the question 'How do salespeople decide what action to take?') and *reinforcement* theories (or theories based on what can be observed in terms of responses triggered by various stimuli and the consequences of those responses, in a continuing cycle). In the following paragraphs the most widely known theories of motivation are presented and discussed.

The main *content* theories of motivation are Hierarchy of Needs, ERG and Two-factor. These theories are mainly concerned with factors that arouse and initiate motivational behaviour. In particular, the Hierarchy of Needs theory (Maslow 1954) relies on the principle that the needs of an individual are the primary mechanism of motivation, and its conceptual framework is based on three fundamental assumptions.

First, that individuals have needs and their needs influence their behaviour; second, needs are arranged in an order of importance (from basic to most complex); and third, individuals advance to a higher level of needs when the lower level needs are at least minimally satisfied. The need categories identified by this theory in hierarchical order (from the most basic to the most advanced) are:

1. physiological;
2. safety;
3. social;
4. self-esteem;
5. self-actualization.

It is interesting to note that according to the Hierarchy of Needs theory, the effectiveness of money as a motivator declines as one progresses to higher order needs.

ERG theory (Alderfer 1972) identifies three main categories of needs in a hierarchical order. From the basic to more advanced needs these are: Existence (E), Relatedness (R), and Growth (G). The assumptions underlying ERG theory are:

1. the lower the level of satisfaction in a need the more it will be desired;
2. the higher the satisfaction in lower level needs, the greater the desire for satisfying higher level needs;
3. the lower the satisfaction in higher level needs, the greater the desire for satisfying lower level needs.

ERG theory introduces a motivational mechanism based on satisfaction-progression on the one hand and frustration-regression on the other hand. From a managerial point of view, when Existence (E) and Relatedness (R) needs are gratified, both drop out as motivational forces and individuals seek to satisfy their Growth (G) needs.

The Two-factor theory (Herzberg 1966) identifies two categories of needs, psychological and animal, and distinguishes between two sets of factors: satisfiers or motivators and dissatisfiers or hygiene factors. More specifically, the theory states that when the psychological needs are fulfilled satisfaction results but when they are frustrated no satisfaction results. When animal needs are frustrated they result in dissatisfaction and when they are fulfilled no satisfaction results. Satisfiers/motivators are capable of causing motivation (answer the question, 'Why work harder?'), whereas dissatisfiers/hygiene factors refer to the necessary preconditions for successful motivation (answer the question, 'Why work here?'). Consequently, Sales Managers must make certain that 'animal needs' (or hygiene factors) are met, so that there is no underlying job dissatisfaction, prior to fulfilling salespeople's psychological needs.

Without underestimating the value and impact of the content theories of motivation, it has been argued that they fail to address the issue of the choice of the behaviour that will lead to the satisfaction of a need. This choice aspect of motivational behaviour has been attempted by the process theories of motivation. The most widely known *process* theories of motivation are the Equity theory, the Expectancy theory, and the Intrinsic-Extrinsic theory. These theories provide a process explanation of how and why employees choose to adopt a particular behaviour or how and why individuals choose their actions.

The Equity theory (Adams 1963) postulates that the choice of how much effort is to be expended at the workplace is the result of comparison between one individual's input effort and output and another individual's input effort and output. Input/output ratios are used by individuals to determine relative equity at the workplace; if the two ratios are not in balance, the individual is motivated to reduce the inequity. Inequity creates tension in the individual proportional to the magnitude of the discrepancy in terms of subjective perceptions or objective reality. The individual who is perceived to be inequitably treated can change his/her inputs, outcomes, person of reference (i.e. with whom they are comparing themselves) or even leave the situation. Sales Managers should always remember that some salespeople are more sensitive than others to perceptions of inequality (Greenberg 1989).

The Expectancy theory (Vroom 1964) suggests that motivation is a function of a person's anticipation that a particular behaviour will lead to outcomes that he/she values. Motivation according to Expectancy theory is a function of the expectancy (or belief in the likelihood that a certain amount of effort will lead to successful performance), instrumentality (the direct relationship between an act and a given outcome, that is that one leads directly to the other) and valence (the strength of preference that is associated with each of the possible outcomes of the act). The expectancy theory of motivation suggests a multiplicative relationship of its components. Consequently, Sales Managers will have to indicate paths offering the greatest probability of success and design a reward system that will be valued by their salespeople.

The Intrinsic-Extrinsic theory (Deci 1980) is based on an individual's desire for competence and self-determination. Specifically, intrinsic motivation suggests that giving an individual a sense of self-determination in their various work choices and encouraging their sense of competence through positive feedback can facilitate motivation, on the assumption that competence presupposes self-determination. Extrinsic rewards are concerned with control and feedback. When the control aspect is important, intrinsic motivation decreases, whereas when the feedback aspect is important, positive intrinsic motivation increases. It is important to remember that performance results in two kinds of rewards: intrinsic rewards, which are intangible, such as a feeling of accomplishment and achievement, and extrinsic rewards, which are tangible outcomes such as pay.

The *reinforcement* approaches to motivation (Skinner 1953) rely on the consequence of past actions influencing future actions in a pattern of cyclical learning. The behaviour will or will not be repeated if it is, or is not, reinforced. More specifically, the theories state that there is a stimulus that triggers a response. When the consequence of that response is rewarding, the response is likely to be repeated. When the consequence of a response is not rewarding, the response will not be repeated. Operant conditioning, which is one of the reinforcement approaches, focuses on the objective measurable behaviour of individuals rather than their inner states, the contingencies of reinforcement (i.e. the stimulus-behavioural response-consequence relationships in learning and maintaining motivated behaviour), the reinforcement schedule or time interval between response and consequence and the perceived size of the reinforcer. In essence, the above approaches postulate that if in the past an action has been reinforced, then the individual is changed in such a way that the same action is more likely to occur thereafter.

The theories of motivation described in this section provide insights concerning the motivational process and its determinants. In the next section a model of motivation will be presented which explains how to increase the motivation of salespeople (see Figure 15.1). This model draws heavily on the process theories of motivation and introduces additional theoretical perspectives.

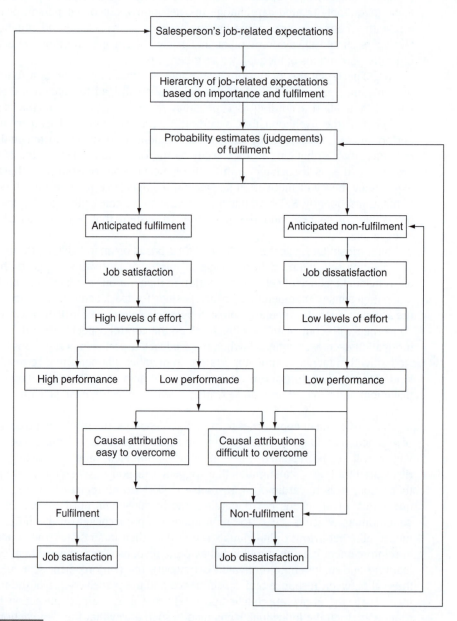

Figure 15.1   The motivation process based on the fulfilment of job-related expections

How does fulfilment of job-related expectations motivate salespeople?

The fulfilment process model of motivation relies on the concept of expectations and their fulfilment. Expectations, in general, are being formed and changed in response to various influences (e.g. personality, past experience, present circumstances, etc). Job-related expectations are cognitive perceptions of future-oriented, targeted, valuable and desirable work-related outcomes, events or occurrences that are associated with prospective attainment. Subjective perceptions of the probability of anticipated outcomes (e.g. fulfilment or non-fulfilment) are also attached to job-related expectations. As such job-related expectations are future-oriented affective states, these condition the behaviour to be employed. Both salespeople and organizations have expectations (i.e. targeted desirable outcomes) arising from each other and both make judgements concerning the fulfilment of their expectations. However, their job-related expectations may or may not be fulfilled.

The fulfilment of salespeople's and companies' expectations will satisfy both sides. As far as salespeople's job-related expectations are concerned, these are: hierarchically structured; prioritized in terms of preference in their fulfilment; and assessed on the likelihood of them being fulfilled or non-fulfilled. The assessment refers to the judgement of how confident the salesperson is in effectively executing his/her job and whether his/her expectations will be fulfilled. The outcome of this judgement can either be positive (e.g. fulfilment to be anticipated) or negative (fulfilment not anticipated). When fulfilment is anticipated, the salesperson experiences job satisfaction and the process of fulfilment is initiated. This process leads to high levels of motivation because it provides a direction (i.e. the purpose of fulfilling his/her expectations), an intensity (i.e. the fulfilment of his/her expectation is of value to the salesperson) and persistence (i.e. the salesperson persistently tries to reach the desired outcome which is the fulfilment of expectations). When the resulting performance levels are high, the salesperson again experiences job satisfaction and anticipates fulfilment of his/her expectations. When the expectations are fulfilled, the virtuous circle is initiated and is repeated, keeping salespeople highly motivated at the workplace.

Despite high motivational levels, there are instances where the performance levels of a salesperson are low. In this case, she/he does not expect fulfilment of his/her expectations and tries to attribute the low performance levels to some causes. If the causes are attributed to internal, unstable factors (e.g. misunderstanding of what had to be done, wrong tactics, etc), the salesperson starts again the process of fulfilment and maintains high levels of effort. However, if low performance levels are attributed to external, stable factors (e.g. job difficulty) or internal, stable factors (e.g. lack of ability), then the salesperson finds it difficult to reach the performance levels required for the fulfilment of his/her expectations. Attributions of low performance to external or internal stable factors will lead to low performance levels and subsequent low performance.

When fulfilment of job-related expectations is not anticipated, the salesperson finds no reason to be motivated and experiences job dissatisfaction. This brings the salesperson into a vicious circle and she/he eventually quits his/her job. It is therefore necessary for Sales Managers to identify the job-related expectations of their salespeople and to try to facilitate conditions for their fulfilment. Anticipated fulfilment leads to job satisfaction, which results in high levels of effort. High levels of effort lead to high performance levels and to the fulfilment of expectations, and this, in turn, perpetuates job satisfaction. Performance, therefore, is dependent upon the importance and desirability of fulfilling job-related expectations and the accuracy of the salesperson's judgements regarding their anticipated fulfilment or non-fulfilment.

Perhaps an important remark should be made at this point. This concerns the relationship between performance and job satisfaction. The model makes the a priori assumption that job satisfaction or dissatisfaction is initially a function of the anticipated fulfilment or non-fulfilment of job-related expectations respectively. Job satisfaction experienced following assessed performance levels is the result of the fulfilment of the salesperson's job-related expectations. Job satisfaction due to anticipated fulfilment causes high motivational levels, whereas job satisfaction due to fulfilment of expectations reinforces the strength of the belief that effort expended at the workplace leads to valuable outcomes.

In the introductory case, Aristotle Risperis, the Sales Manager of EPAL, considered that the identification and fulfilment of his/her salespeople's job-related expectations were more important and powerful in influencing their behaviour than manipulating commonly used reward systems indiscriminately simply because they are perceived to have motivational potential. He therefore decided to hold separate sessions every month with each salesperson employed in order to identify their job-related expectations and establish conditions facilitating their fulfilment. According to him, this approach is very effective for motivating his salespeople.

The fulfilment process model of motivation offers a way to:

1. maximize job satisfaction both during anticipation and after fulfilment;
2. identify motivational determinants of salespeople (e.g. identify their job-related expectations);
3. take actions that enable high motivation and performance levels (e.g. facilitate conditions for the fulfilment of salespeople's expectations).

Sales Managers' proactive response in diagnosing salespeople's job-related expectations and genuine efforts to facilitate the fulfilment of their job-related expectations also enhance the relationship between managers and their salespeople.

Table 15.1 provides information on the categories in which job-related expectations fall, and offers examples of ways in which Sales Managers can establish conditions for their fulfilment. Although the 'implementation examples' are classified under a particular motivator, such actions may have much wider implications and are often capable of fulfilling job-related expectations that fall into different categories.

Motivation is individual, time and situation specific, and the Sales Manager's job is to create the appropriate conditions in which salespeople will maximize their efforts all the time. Consider the following alternatives:

Table 15.1   Motivating factors and appropriate managerial actions

Motivator	What they mean	Implementation example
Monetary compensation	Salespeople want to earn a good living for themselves and their family. The opportunity to increase their earnings can move them to higher levels of motivation and performance.	Bonuses, tiered commission structures, sales contests with valuable prizes, profit-sharing.
Social Acceptance	Many salespeople are motivated from a desire to be appreciated and accepted by their peers.	Create sales teams to solve problems.
Status	Many salespeople are ego-driven, thriving on competition and savouring their peers' admiration.	Exclusive benefits for top performers – special education or other development opportunities
Recognition	Salespeople enjoy praise for their efforts and achievements. They need to know their work is worthwhile and creates value.	Recognize salespeople's successes in sales meetings, name a salesperson of the month, take time to just say 'well done'.
Challenges	Most salespeople want the opportunity to succeed, but some – often the most successful – thrive on stimulation and need to take ownership of their careers.	Career counselling, continuing education and expanding their responsibilities as a trainer, Sales Manager, or mentor for new salespeople
Belief in the company and its leadership	Salespeople want to know they have a capable manager they can look up to and rely on.	Make yourself available to salespeople when they need you, treat salespeople with respect, communicate and let them know you care about them.
Involvement	Salespeople like to feel involved in the company's planning and decision-making process.	Hold staff meetings in which you solicit ideas to make the company more profitable, conduct regular worker surveys.
Fairness	A perception that a manager plays favourites or does not ensure that work is equitably distributed is a disincentive.	Develop and stick to the company's policies and monitor paid employees to see if anyone seems overburdened and needs help
Fulfilment	Motivated salespeople are those who do not feel frustrated. It is the manager's job to remove any obstacles.	Survey staff about needed administrative support and keep all equipment in good repair and supplies in stock.
Enthusiasm	Nothing saps morale more than negativity.	Do not keep chronic complainers in the office, plan regular events to celebrate the company and its success.

Source: 'Ten Motivators' (*Realtor Magazine* online, 2007).

Why is motivating salespeople different?

The sales job, in a broad sense, can be compared to that of athletes who hold world records and maintain rigorous training schedules throughout their athletic careers in an attempt to reach higher and higher goals – like them, salespeople are expected to work long hours, travel out of town and be away from home, and often do much more than what is contractually required from them to reach their goals and satisfy others' expectations (for salespeople, this for instance involves continuously searching for new customers, satisfying customers' needs, meeting ambitious sales quotas and socializing with customers during out of office hours). Salespeople who enjoy expending considerable effort strive for excellence and take pride in achieving high performance levels and are motivated to master tasks and experience intense job satisfaction from doing so.

Unlike jobs that are very structured and easy to supervise, which gives employees very little say in deciding what to do and how to do it, sales jobs offer personal challenges, autonomy and many rewards. As such, the sales job provides satisfaction, feelings of excitement and rewards that are often potentially large. The characteristics of the sales job require that Sales Managers:

• encourage salespeople to aim for difficult goals;
• offer salespeople praise and other financial and non-financial rewards for success;
• help salespeople to find more ways to succeed;
• prompt salespeople to move to even more difficult challenges.

Encouraging salespeople to achieve difficult goals is one way to increase their performance and satisfaction. Furthermore, the goals that are most effective in maintaining work motivation ought to have the following characteristics. First, they must be personally meaningful; second, goals need to be specific and concrete; and, third, goals can only be effective when management supports goal-setting by salespeople, offers special rewards for reaching goals and provides constant encouragement.

Salespeople, unlike other types of employees, need to be motivated to enhance their ability to understand their own emotions and the emotions of those with whom they interact. This ability is known as *emotional intelligence* and has the following four aspects (see also Chapter 17):

1. Salespeople must recognize and understand their own feelings and emotions as they experience them.
2. Salespeople should be able to control their emotions in order to avoid acting impulsively.
3. Salespeople must be able to recognize customers' emotions (known as empathy).
4. Salespeople should use emotions to interact effectively with customers.

As will be discussed in detail in Chapter 17, emotional intelligence is fundamental in the application of adaptive selling approaches.

Although the nature of the sales job itself can be a motivating factor in its own right, other environmental stimuli such as incentives can also be used to motivate salespeople. The type of incentives and the value a salesperson places on them at a given time are important determinants of motivated behaviour. For example, if recognition in the form of 'best salesperson of the year' is of value to a salesperson, then he/she will be motivated and engage in the appropriate behaviour in order to achieve this award. Given the motivational potential of incentives, the following section provides a brief analysis of some basic incentive and recognition programmes used in sales settings.

The impact of rewards and recognition programmes on motivation

Salespeople's job-related expectations range widely and their formation is influenced by organizational factors and/or factors that are not related to the organization (e.g. personality, family, friends, etc). An expectation influenced by factors not relating to the organization, for instance, is when a salesperson wishes to attend university to pursue an MBA for career enhancement and progression and expects to receive funding and time off work from the company in order to fulfil his/her expectation. Other expectations may be formed at the workplace. For example, recognition programmes aim to give salespeople more challenging tasks in recognition of their achieving specific sales objectives or non-financial rewards for outstanding performance. Given that independent thinking and creativity, the ability to cope with a wide range of behaviours during sales negotiations and competitor-oriented strategic and tactical skills and competencies are required by salespeople, such programmes may provide salespeople with job-expectations that they will strive to fulfil.

Sales contests and competitions are short-term incentive programmes, providing salespeople with an opportunity to compete in the workplace for prizes in cash, merchandize or travel. Incentives help the company achieve specific short-term sales objectives (see Chapter 16 on sales force compensation). These need to be carefully designed in order to be effective in terms of motivating salespeople. More specifically, successful sales contests and competitions will have to:

- be clearly defined in terms of their objectives;
- provide an exciting and attractive theme for salespeople;
- offer equal probabilities of winning;
- be linked to attractive rewards;
- be promoted and managed properly.

When these conditions are met, and the winning of a contest becomes a desired expectation of salespeople, then sales contests and competitions can prove effective motivators. Nonetheless, poorly designed and managed sales contests and competitions will not motivate salespeople and can cause problems such as influencing salespeople to engage in inappropriate and, at times, unethical sales tactics in order to meet sales targets and win the contest.

Recognition programmes are aimed at rewarding salespeople's outstanding performance. Recognition programmes are often linked to non-financial rewards such as promotion and praise. For example, many companies award titles such as 'best salesperson of the year' for 'highest sales volume', 'biggest percentage increase in sales' and 'largest sales per account' to salespeople who deliver an outstanding performance. Recognition programmes offer an excellent opportunity for influencing the job-related expectations of salespeople since they are mainly aimed at satisfying the higher order needs, and provide salespeople with emotionally-based justification for their high levels of effort and performance. As with the sales contest, recognition programmes need to:

- be strictly performance-based and well planned;
- offer equal opportunity for all salespeople to win;
- be adequately publicized.

The above are important ingredients of a successful recognition programme.

Sales Managers can motivate their salespeople by helping them identify specific behaviours that will lead to the fulfilment of their expectations while benefiting the organization as a whole. Individual incentive programmes in which salespeople can earn extra pay and recognition programmes in which 'salespeople of the month' are singled out to receive gifts or trophies may increase salespeople's extrinsic motivation. Salespeople are extrinsically motivated when they are engaged in activities aimed at obtaining money, recognition and other rewards. However, when salespeople are motivated by tasks that they find interesting, enjoyable and challenging, they are said to be intrinsically motivated. Often Sales Managers try to instil in their salespeople a feeling of intrinsic motivation, but longstanding research findings indicate that tangible rewards undermine intrinsic motivation (Deci and Ryan 1980). The question therefore arises, if rewards undermine intrinsic motivation, how do successful Sales Managers make effective use of incentives? To put it differently, can rewards be used to enhance intrinsic motivation?

Rewards may serve two different functions. The first function is the 'controlling' function of rewards; that is, when rewards are perceived as controlling a person's behaviour. For instance, when people are paid for engaging in an enjoyable activity they often come to lose their intrinsic interest in that activity. The second function is the 'informational' function of rewards; that is, rewards have informational value when they provide positive feedback about a salesperson's competence or the quality of their performance. Rewards controlling in type/design adversely affect intrinsic motivation, whereas informational rewards have a positive effect on motivation. Sales Managers should therefore develop incentive programmes that emphasize the informational function of rewards.

Methods for evaluating salespeople's motivation

Salespeople's motivation cannot be easily measured. Methods and measures for assessing motivation of salespeople are seldom used and when some methods are used they do not relate to the theoretical construct of motivation. In a sales context, the manifestations of motivation are behaviour- and performance-based indicators, which may or may not be accurate measures of motivation as in the case where a productive salesperson may not necessarily be a highly motivated salesperson (see Chapter 14 on sales force control systems and Chapter 18 on sales force evaluation). A reliable method for evaluating the motivation of a salesperson is motivational interviewing.[3] Motivational interviewing is a direct method of communication between Sales Manager and salesperson for the purpose of measuring effort and productivity. The method is based on accurate understanding (empathy) and genuineness (congruence) so as to reach a mutually agreed motivation rating. Sustainable, effort can be measured in terms of commitment and dedication towards work and the job itself. Based on the above measures, salespeople fall into one of the following four motivational categories (Bragg 2007):

1. 'Want to' attitude-driven salespeople, who are the most highly motivated;
2. 'Have to' attitude-driven salespeople, whose motivation is sub-optimal;
3. 'Ought to' attitude-driven salespeople, whose motivation is sub-optimal;
4. 'Don't care' attitude-driven salespeople, who are the least motivated.

More specifically, 'want to' attitude-driven salespeople are very committed and come to work with more positive attitudes, are more willing to expend additional effort when it is needed and are more willing to take on additional responsibilities. In contrast, 'have to' attitude-driven salespeople are trapped employees and stay at work for reasons other than liking the job they are in (e.g. they cannot find another job, they are close to retirement, they have health problems, etc.). 'Ought to' attitude-driven salespeople stay in the job because they feel obliged to their employer (e.g. returning a favour to an employer for giving them a job when they needed it, or because 'this is the right thing to do' according to their value system). 'Don't care' attitude-driven salespeople are disconnected or uncommitted employees who are actively looking for other employment (Bragg 2007).

The interviewing method for evaluating the motivational levels of each individual salesperson is based on questions and answers covering all aspects of overt behaviour. For example:

- *Sales process.* Which of the following motivational categories (i.e. want to, have to, ought to, don't care) describes best your effort towards: prospecting, qualifying, approaching, making a presentation, handling objections, closing and following up.
- *Selling style.* Which of the following motivational categories (i.e. want to, have to, ought to, don't care) describes best your efforts towards: creating solutions for your customers, developing long and lasting relationships with customers, convincing customers and closing sales, etc.
- *Sales performance.* Which of the following motivational categories (i.e. want to, have to, ought to, don't care) describes best your efforts towards: opening new accounts, maximizing business with existing accounts, minimizing complaints, keeping your customers satisfied, etc.
- *Activity management.* Which of the following motivational categories (i.e. want to, have to, ought to, don't care) describes best your efforts towards: sales meetings,

---

[3] A grouping of techniques was provided by West and Uhlenberg (1970). These techniques are: 1. production measures, 2. self-reporting instruments, 3. observer ratings, 4. projective tests, and 5. objective tests. Motivational interviewing is made up of observer (e.g. Sales Manager) ratings blended with production measures.

training programmes, report writing, routing, entertaining customers, training new salespeople, etc.

A Sales Manager's efforts to assess motivation holistically are rarely effective. Assessment of motivation will have to be derived from the identification, categorization and quantification of overt behaviours on concrete assessment criteria as in those described above. More refined and precise data, however, can be obtained through the use of motivational interviewing.

Summary

In the ever increasing competitive landscape, sales organizations must effectively utilize the human capital they employ. The issue of motivating salespeople remains one of the most important tasks of Sales Managers as it has a direct impact on organizational performance. In this chapter, various theories and perspectives on sales force motivation are provided along with a discussion of the process of designing, implementing and evaluating a motivational programme. In general, highly motivated salespeople achieve high performance levels, high performance levels lead to job satisfaction, and satisfied salespeople are highly motivated. This is a virtuous circle that every Sales Manager should strive to manage successfully. The materials in this chapter provide the necessary background that Sales Managers need to accurately diagnose the motivational requirements of their sales force and devise effective motivational programmes.

Key points

1. Motivation is an inner force expressed in terms of the dimensions of intensity, persistence and direction. All dimensions are equally important in maximizing the motivation level of salespeople.
2. When motivation, job satisfaction and performance levels are high, they form a virtuous circle and salespeople in such a motivational virtuous circle tend to be happy, committed and loyal employees.
3. The theories of motivation (i.e. content, process and reinforcement) provide a range of complementary perspectives and contribute to a better understanding of the complex nature of motivation.
4. The 'fulfillment of job-related expectations of salespeople' model provides an explanation of the causal links between motivation, job satisfaction and performance – the ingredients for establishing a motivational 'virtuous circle'.
5. There are many ways to motivate salespeople, but the nature of the sales job should be taken into consideration when designing and implementing motivational programmes.
6. Motivational interviewing allows Sales Managers to measure intense striving based on concrete assessment criteria such as sales process, selling style, activity management and sales performance.

7. A sales motivation audit is an indispensable tool in the hands of Sales Managers for assessing whether the sales organization is achieving its motivational objectives with the available resources.

Running a sales motivation audit

The sales motivation audit is an objective, structured, systematic and periodic examination of the sales motivation system and procedures of a sales organization to assess whether it is effectively achieving its motivational objectives with the available resources. Sales motivation audits are usually performed by Sales Managers as opposed to external auditors. To conduct a sales motivation audit, the scope of the audit needs to be determined and a reliable methodology must be used. It is important to note however, that a sales motivation audit:

- is not synonymous with performance measurement;
- only shows if the route or approach chosen was the most effective, and is not to be used to decide whether the motivational objectives are met;
- indicates whether particular approaches need to be intensified, adjusted, or dropped.

Sales motivation audits collate activities that salespeople are already doing, recognize them for actions already taken and provide ongoing opportunities for them to take further steps and become more involved in their work. The audit includes certain steps for strengthening motivation over time and should be used continually, aiming to identify the most relevant motivators. When appropriate changes, as a result of the sales motivation audit, are introduced, then these changes are expected to improve staff morale, motivation and retention levels significantly. Using the audit ensures that the investment in salespeople is continuously monitored and assessed. A sales motivation audit should include a set of questions[4] such as:

- Do we have all the information that is needed to develop a motivational programme?
- What obstacles, if any, constrain salespeople's motivational efforts?
- What motivates our salespeople?
- Are our salespeople motivated by financial rewards, status, praise and acknowledgment, competition, job security, public recognition, fear, perfectionism and/or results?
- Do our salespeople feel empowered?
- Do our salespeople feel they have job descriptions that give them autonomy and authority and allow them to find their own solutions, or are they given a list of tasks to perform and simply told what to do?

---

[4] This list of questions is for illustration purposes only and it is by no means exhaustive. Questions can be added or deleted depending on the needs of the company.

- Are there any recent changes in the company that might have affected the motivation of our salespeople?
- What are the patterns of motivation in our company?
- Who is most motivated and why? Are there any lessons to be learnt?
- Are salespeople's goals and the company's goals aligned?
- How do our salespeople feel about the company?
- How involved are our salespeople in company development?
- Are there regular opportunities for our salespeople to give feedback?
- Is the company's internal image consistent with its external one?
- How far do we consider our salespeople's motivation when making important business and strategy decisions?
- How far do our reward and recognition systems encourage salespeople's motivation?
- Is work organized in a way that will motivate salespeople?
- How does leadership style in our organization affect our salespeople's motivation?

To perform a sales motivation audit the auditor is required to perform the following tasks. First, he/she needs to identify the most relevant questions to be asked and ensure that the questions will be well within the capabilities of both the auditor and those who will be completing the audit. Second, he/she must decide how the responses will be taken (e.g. interviews) and suggest courses of action arising from the responses. Third, he/she needs to prioritize the courses of action according to urgency, cost and likely impact, implement them and closely monitor their implementation (Wilson 1982).

References

Adams, J.S. (1963) 'Towards an Understanding of Inequity', *Journal of Abnormal and Social Psychology*, (5): 422–36.

Alderfer, P.C. (1972) *Existence, Relatedness and Growth*. New York: Free Press.

Bragg, T. (2007) 'Motivating Salespeople: How You Can Improve Employer/Employee Commitment', *Progressive Distributor*, http://www.mrotoday.com/progressive/online%20exclusives/MotivatingSalespeople.htm.

Deci, E.L. (1980) *The Psychology of Self-Determination*. Lexington, MA: D.C. Heath.

Deci, E.L. and Ryan, R.M. (1980) 'The Empirical Exploration of Intrinsic Motivational Processes'. in Berkowitz, L. (ed.), *Advances in Experimental Social Psychology*, Vol. 13: 39–80. New York: Academic Press.

Greenberg, G. (1989) 'Cognitive Re-evaluation of Outcomes in response to Underpayment Inequity', *Academy of Management Journal*, 32 (1): 174–84.

Herzberg, F. (1966) *Work and the Nature of Man*. Cleveland, OH: World.

Maslow, H.A. (1954) *Motivation and Personality*. New York: Holt Rinehart and Winston.

Realtor Magazine online (2007) www.realtor.com, http://www.realtor.org/rmotoolkits.nsf/pages/brokerlead03b.

Skinner, F.B. (1953) *Science and Human Behaviour*. New York: Macmillan.

Vroom, V. (1964) *Work and Motivation*. New York: John Wiley & Sons.

West, S. and Uhlenberg, D. (1970) 'Measuring Motivation', *Theory into Practice*, 9 (1): 47–55.

Wilson, A. (1982) *Marketing Audit Check Lists: A Guide to Effective Marketing Resource Realisation*. London: McGraw Hill.

Further reading

Bernstein, D.A., Clarke-Stewart, A., Roy, E.J., Srull, T.K. and Wickens, C.D. (1994) *Psychology*, 3rd edition. Boston: Houghton Mifflin Company.

Brehm, S.S. and Kassin, S.M. (1990) *Social Psychology*. Boston: Houghton Mifflin Company.

Brown, S.P., Evans, K.R., Mantrala, M.K. and Challagalla, G. (2005) 'Adapting Motivation, Control, and Compensation Research to a New Environment', *Journal of Personal Selling and Sales Management*, 25 (2): 156–67.

Dubinsky, A.J. and Skinner, S.J. (2002) 'Going the Extra Mile: Antecedents of Salespeople's Discretionary Effort', *Industrial Marketing Management*, 31 (7): 589–98.

Jaramillo, F. and Mulki, J.P. (2008) 'Sales Effort: The Intertwined Roles of the Leader, Customers, and the Salesperson', *Journal of Personal Selling and Sales Management*, 28 (1): 37–51.

Jaramillo, F., Locander, W.B., Spector, P.E. and Harris, E.G. (2007) 'Getting the Job Done: The Moderating Role of Initiative on the Relationship between Intrinsic Motivation and Adaptive Selling', *Journal of Personal Selling and Sales Management*, 27 (1): 59–74.

Leach, M.P., Liu, A.H. and Johnston W.J. (2005) 'The Role of Self-regulation Training in Developing the Motivation Capabilities of Salespeople', *Journal of Personal Selling and Sales Management*, 25 (3): 269–81.

Low, G.S., Cravens, D.W., Grant, K. and Moncrief, W.C. (2001) 'Antecedents and Consequences of Salesperson Burnout', *European Journal of Marketing*, 35 (5/6), 587–611.

Miao, F.C. and Evans K.R. (2007) 'The Impact of Salesperson Motivation on Role Perceptions and Job Performance: A Cognitive and Affective Perspective', *Journal of Personal Selling and Sales Management*, 27 (1): 89–101.

16
Sales force compensation

Dominique Rouziès

Contents

Learning objectives

After reading this chapter, you should be able to:

- Understand the importance of sales force compensation decisions.
- Identify the pros and cons of salary and combination plans.
- Design compensation plans for team selling.
- Develop compensation plans for international environments.

Chapter outline

Compensating salespeople is a fundamental concern of Sales Managers. A good compensation plan attracts the best salespeople and motivates them to work along the lines defined by management. However, designing a good plan is a difficult exercise as illustrated by the case study presented in the first part of this chapter. It focuses on the challenges of restructuring a firm's sales compensation after a merger. The second part of the chapter sheds more light on the importance of this issue for the success of sales organizations. In particular, the third and fourth parts of this chapter provide guidelines for structuring compensation plans. The fifth part of the chapter examines the challenges involved when compensating new sales roles. Solutions for the case study are then examined. Finally, the last part of this chapter reviews the key points.

A compensation challenge at SigmaKalon[1]

SigmaKalon is an international company specializing in the decorative paints market, for both the Building and Consumer Sectors. This market represents around €1.4 billion in factory prices. SigmaKalon was formed from the 1999 merger of the Petrofina and Total petroleum products groups. In 2003, SigmaKalon was the industry leader in the French market with a turnover of more than €450 million, a workforce of 2,700 and a total market share in paints of around 20 per cent. However, despite this industry leadership, SigmaKalon's revenue growth started slowing down. In order to stem this slide in sales, Alain Martel was named Sales Director for the Building Sector and given the task of significantly improving the profitability of SigmaKalon's commercial operations. At the time, SigmaKalon marketed its building products mostly via two integrated, but competing, channels: Direct Peintures Seigneurie (or DPS, offering the Seigneurie brand) and Comptoirs Peintures Gauthier (or CPG, offering the Peintures Gauthier brand). The combined market share for trade professionals was 49 per cent. The DPS channel had sales of around €100 million with 70 branches and 430 salespeople. The CPG channel generated sales of around €90 million, with some 70 sales points and nearly 400 salespeople. Since the SigmaKalon Executive Committee was considering a merger of the DPS and CPG channels (selling both Seigneurie and Peintures Gauthier brands) Alain Martel needed to develop a single compensation system for the combined sales force and measures to manage the different selling cultures.

Introduction: why is sales force compensation a critical issue for firms?

As the battles for markets have intensified over the last decade, marketing budgets have come under scrutiny. Because in many corporations, sales force compensation represents the dominant sales expense, the design of effective compensation plans is an issue of substantial corporate importance. In addition to salary, commissions and bonuses that are discussed below, firms offer benefits (e.g. company car, pension plan, etc.) that vary widely across companies and countries (mostly for tax reasons). Few researchers have studied this compensation component and it is therefore difficult to provide guidelines for the best type of benefits. The rule of thumb, however, is for firms to match competitive offers with attractive benefits.

Salespeople play a determinant role in building long-term relationships with customers because they represent critical means of promotion for most business-to-business (B2B) firms. As a result, they can strongly influence a firm's performance. However, as many sales jobs involve frequent situations of rejection, salespeople need to be constantly encouraged. These factors highlight the importance of salespeople's motivation for the success of organizations. The model shown in Figure 16.1 provides a framework that can help managers understand the mechanisms involved in the compensation issue. This framework is composed of three basic elements: the

[1] This case history was written by Anne Macquin, Honorary Professor, and Dominique Rouziès, Professor, HEC-Paris, in collaboration with Loïc Derrien, Marketing Director, Decorative Paints, PPG Architectural Coatings EMEA.

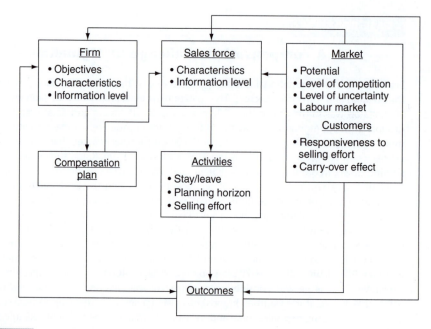

Figure 16.1   Sales force compensation framework

company, the sales force and the market. As sales forces are usually heterogeneous, the sales force sub-model includes dimensions that may differ across salespeople (e.g. attitude towards risk, time horizon). The model illustrates the relationships between each element: the company's decision process, the salesperson's decision process and the customer's decision process.

The company's decision process

Before even deciding on compensation plans, firms have to make a choice between using internal salespeople (generally paid with a salary and other compensation elements) or independent agents (generally paid on commission) (see Chapter 8 on sales force organization).

The compensation plan structure should be tailored to the firm's strategy. Digital Equipment Corporation (DEC) and Data General (DG) provide good examples of the link existing between strategy and sales force compensation. While DEC followed a differentiation strategy and paid its sales representatives a straight salary, DG adopted a low-cost strategy and offered incentive compensation. When firms set compensation plans, they use the information they have about sales territory sales response functions, the labour market and the salesperson's characteristics. Because salespeople typically operate in the field, their knowledge of the selling environment is generally superior to that of managers. However, managers do learn about salespeople's skills in a long-term relationship. Firms also need to have information about how salespeople react to financial incentives (i.e. their utility functions) in order to anticipate which selling activity they will choose. But companies themselves are likely to differ with respect to their attitudes towards risk and to make decisions regarding sales force compensation accordingly.

The salesperson's decision process

The second mechanism shown in Figure 16.1 is the salespeople's decision process, involving three major selling decisions. First, salespeople use a time horizon to plan their activities. Some are more short-term oriented than others, depending on their personal constraints (e.g. house mortgages, new cars, vacations). Second, they will decide either to stay or leave the company depending on the level of the utility they think they will derive. Finally, if they choose to stay, they will decide on the level and allocation of their selling effort. These decisions depend heavily on the perceived utility of short- and long term revenues and the salespeople's attitude towards risk (in cases where the compensation plan includes a variable component). In order to make the decisions described above, salespeople combine their estimation of the sales response functions with their understanding of the company's remuneration scheme and their assessment of their own characteristics (i.e. ability and utility functions) and of the labour market. Of course, this estimation is refined by information provided by the outcomes (i.e. pay and satisfaction levels) previously achieved. Needless to say, the level of information available to salespeople is critical for these estimations. When the market is volatile or when salespeople start in a new territory, salespeople will probably not have complete information. Similarly, when salespeople do not understand their compensation scheme they cannot estimate their future income. Consequently the plan will fail to create the necessary motivation to be successful.

The customer's decision process

The third mechanism depicted in Figure 16.1 deals with the market's response. A number of market characteristics influence this, market potential and the levels of competition and uncertainty among others. Additionally, salespeople's choice of effort allocation (i.e. to selling or non-selling activities, the various types of prospects/customers and over the short or long term) generates purchasing decisions and income, as well as job satisfaction. These elements trigger customer responses which create outcomes for the salesperson and firm (i.e. satisfaction, remuneration, sales revenue, selling costs and financial results).

Problems in designing compensation plans

Interestingly, B2B sales jobs have characteristics that complicate the design of compensation plans. First, B2B salespeople often know more about their territories, customers and competitors than management, making it difficult for the latter to specify the best way to succeed. Since management has less information than salespeople about customers and competitors, performance evaluation becomes a difficult exercise. It comes as no surprise then that 79 per cent of sales leaders participating in the 2008 Deloitte and Oracle survey used sales revenue as a metric for variable pay to motivate, monitor and direct salespeople.

Second, a compensation plan signals values to the job market. It is a way for companies to attract and retain talent. To fill challenging selling jobs, companies usually offer higher pay. Similarly, to compete for the best salespeople, firms offer attractive, above average remuneration. However, such decisions must take into account organizational career paths. Thus, some firms create human resource policies which push salespeople into managerial positions. Such career paths meet with resistance from the salespeople if their current compensation levels are much higher than those of Sales Managers. Initially lower salaries for Sales Managers can be somewhat offset if the career opportunities are particularly attractive in the long run. In any case, when the turnover rate of high performers increases, firms need to reassess their compensation plans. Hence a compensation plan influences the profile of salespeople who fit into the organization.

Third, myriad compensation schemes exist in practice, providing evidence of the inherent complexity of sales compensation decisions. Those decisions encompass not only the level of compensation but also its structure (i.e. the ratio of incentive to fixed compensation). In fact, compensation plans often become increasingly complex because firms keep adding incentives to support certain decisions or specific conditions. For example, they may want to push new offerings, identify new opportunities that need to be exploited, or, alternatively, want to correct some weaknesses in their current compensation scheme. However, they may end up with more problems than solutions either because too many aspects of performance are tied to financial rewards or because salespeople are unable to estimate confidently their future compensation level. Consequently, these plans are ineffective in motivating salespeople. Indeed, salespeople may not understand what is expected from them (e.g. too many objectives or conflicting sales priorities). They may also be unable to understand the relationship between their sales efforts and resulting compensation. It comes as no surprise then that only 41 per cent of sales leaders are 'satisfied' or 'very satisfied' with their sales compensation programme (Deloitte and Oracle 2008). Fortunately, sales leaders are making the simplification of sales compensation plans their top priority (Deloitte and Oracle 2008). In Europe, most compensation plans fall into one of the following categories: either straight salary plans or combination plans. Each has its own specific strengths and weaknesses and these are discussed in the next section.

Why do managers choose a salary plan?

In Europe, about 30 per cent of compensation schemes feature no real incentive component (i.e. less than 5 per cent variable pay) (Rouziès et al. 2009). In comparison, Zoltners et al. (2006) estimate the figure to be about 15 per cent in the United States. Under straight salary plans, salespeople receive pay at a fixed rate, although salaries may be adjusted in the long run to reflect productivity. Indeed, most sales leaders (77 per cent) conduct a compensation plan review at least annually (Deloitte and Oracle 2008).

There are a number of factors to take into account when choosing to implement a straight salary plan, as indicated in Table 16.1. In particular, there are four important considerations: the salesperson's job satisfaction, management control, motivation and business strategy.

| Table 16.1 | Guidelines for choosing salary plans |

	PROS	**CONS**
JOB SATISFACTION	Security of a regular and stable income Less sales force turnover	Income levels tend to be lower than commission plans
CONTROL	Higher level of loyalty. Better control over salespeople for non-selling tasks. Useful if there is a problem in measurement of sales impact Better administrative control over compensation. Easier to induce salespeople to work consistently with company strategy.	Subjectivity of job evaluation.
MOTIVATION	Elimination of factors beyond the control of salespeople influencing remuneration. Easier recruitment during economic downturns.	May breed complacency. Difficult to motivate high performers when salary plans create the possibility of salary compression where the new trainee may earn almost as much as the experienced salesperson. Sales leaders risk mutiny if they set wide salary gaps between high and low performers. Profile of salespeople recruited may not be top performers.
BUSINESS STRATEGY	Relatively fixed selling costs. More freedom in switching territories, reassigning salespeople, entering new territories or selling new product lines. Realization of greater profit when business is good.	Burden for the firm during economic downturns. Risk associated with uncertain selling environments is bared by the company.

Source: adapted from Rouziès (1992).

Job satisfaction

The income regularity and stability of salary plans are likely to have a positive impact on salespeople's job satisfaction, thereby reducing the turnover rate. For a number of managers, high turnover rates represent a potential threat for the company since customers lose their familiar and first source of product information. However, salary plans may not bring as much satisfaction to salespeople as incentive plans because salary plans tend to deliver overall lower levels of remuneration compared with plans featuring incentives. This can be generally explained by the increased risk firms face in guaranteeing a certain level of remuneration regardless of the sales actually made.

Control

Straight salary plans are deemed appropriate when it is difficult to assess salespeople's impact on sales results. Indeed, when Sales Managers do not know enough about salespeople's efficacy, they evaluate their behaviours. The downside of such a measurement problem is the resulting subjective performance evaluation. However, straight salary plans are easy to control since they do not vary. In addition, they provide better control over salesperson activity and behaviour since the salesperson has little justification for charting a separate sales strategy. It is therefore generally easier to induce salespeople to accomplish non-selling tasks or to follow a given selling process under a salary plan than under an incentive scheme (see Chapter 14 for further details of sales control systems).

Motivation

Salary plans allow managers to reward salespeople when factors beyond their control impact upon their results (e.g. new competitors or an economic downturn). Indeed, when business is difficult, it is easier to recruit salespeople with salary plans than with pay based on merit. However, when business is good, the profile of salespeople recruited under salary plans may not be the top performers. Hence, since salespeople are paid even if their efforts and results are poor, salary plans can breed complacency. Moreover, salary compression may exist in the sales organization because managers generally tend to avoid wide fixed salary gaps between high and low performers to discourage anti-group behaviour.

Business strategy

When a new strategy requires different allocation of selling effort across territories, product lines or customers, salary plans provide a high degree of flexibility for communicating and guiding such changes. More precisely, when prospecting new territories, selling new product lines or contacting new customers (e.g. when selling environments have high levels of uncertainty), a salary plan is a necessary but risky investment for a firm. Nevertheless, salary plans can result in greater profits under favourable economic conditions because the selling costs are lower than under merit plans.

Why do managers choose a combination plan?

Combination plans involve, in addition to fixed salary, some type of incentive pay (e.g. commissions or bonuses) linked to given levels of sales performance usually measured with three or fewer measures (Deloitte and Oracle 2008). Commission is often tied to sales volume and paid for each sale. Bonuses, on the other hand, are discrete payments made after certain performance levels are achieved. They are more often 'one-shot' payments rather than the more or less continuous commissions linked to sales. The interesting point is that unless salespeople reach the next level of performance, they do not receive their bonus, thus making bonuses very effective motivators of sales personnel. Combination plans are very common, accounting for about 75 per cent of all the plans used in Europe and the United States to compensate people selling industrial products (Heide 1999; Rouziès et al. 2009).

Because salespeople tend to select firms that fit their selling profiles, firms using compensation plans featuring a high level of commission payments are likely to attract high performers who are results-oriented and opportunistic. On the other hand, firms using compensation plans featuring high levels of fixed salary and bonuses are likely to attract more loyal salespeople (Zoltners et al. 2006, pp. 236–7).

Across the board, the message seems to be clear: since salespeople apparently are motivated principally by money, merit pay should be used to achieve high performance. Therefore, in the development of a compensation plan, a critical issue is the emphasis placed on salary versus incentive compensation. Table 16.2 presents a number of factors influencing the structure of combination plans, as explained below.

Table 16.2 Guidelines for establishing the structure of combination plans

HIGH RATIO OF INCENTIVE TO TOTAL COMPENSATION	PROS	CONS
JOB DIMENSIONS	Salesperson's impact on sales is important. Sales effort productivity is high. Sales job is programmable. Performance criteria are measurable.	Salespeople are primarily taking orders, checking inventory, providing customer service or indirectly generating sales. Team selling. Sales cycle is long. Selling process is complex. Salespeople have little experience. Performance criteria cannot be measured.
BUSINESS STRATEGY	Firm's advertising, sales promotion and/or public relations investments are low. Offering's competitive advantage is not significant. Firm is unknown. Strategic objective is to increase sales volume. Firm's financial position is weak. Firm's emphasis is on selling new products.	Firm's advertising, sales promotion and/or public relations investments are high. Offering's competitive advantage is significant. Strategic objective is to emphasize long-term customer relationships.
SELLING ENVIRONMENT	Not risky.	Risky.

Source: adapted from Rouziès (1992).

Job dimensions

When the salesperson's skills, motivation and efforts are critical to generate sales, a higher amount of incentive is advisable to ensure that salespeople are rewarded for their work. Conversely, salespeople taking orders, checking inventory or servicing accounts do not contribute directly to results. Therefore, lower amounts of incentive pay are recommended. Similarly, when it is difficult to evaluate the individual impact of a salesperson because of the selling method used (e.g. team selling), decreased amounts of incentive compensation are recommended. Also, when sales cycles are long and complex, lower levels of incentive compensation are suggested in order to keep salespeople motivated throughout the selling process. The same reasons apply to inexperienced salespeople, for whom lower levels of incentive compensation are also recommended. Finally, it is important to note that performance must be measurable and measured before incentives can effectively motivate salespeople.

Business strategy

When advertisements, sales promotions, a product's competitive advantage or a firm's reputation are important drivers of sales, it is generally better to decrease the level of incentive compensation because the direct impact of salespeople is less important. Also, when companies want to emphasize long-term relationships with their customers, less incentive pay encourages salespeople to pursue this long-term goal. Finally, when a firm's financial position is weak, higher levels of incentives are recommended to keep fixed costs as low as possible.

Environment

Combination plans should feature a lower proportion of incentive to total pay when environmental uncertainty is high so that companies, not salespeople, bear the sales risk. Although many of the above arguments drawn from the sales management literature appear uncontroversial, the fact is that some rules have not been empirically tested. Thus, inconsistencies sometimes appear. For example, John and Weitz (1989) note that the recommended use of more salary for complex selling tasks (in technical sales for example) contradicts the prescription to increase the level of incentive pay when the salesperson's skills (technical skills, for example) are determinant in making sales. Likewise, the rule stating that when a salesperson's primary objective is selling new accounts (these probably requiring more negotiating skills) he/she should receive higher levels of incentive compensation contradicts recommendations for more salary when the impact of the salespeople on the sales outcome is determinant because of their skills. Finally, the prevailing wisdom that firms without good reputations need to offer higher levels of incentive compensation to attract talent contradicts another common notion that high incentives lead to lower salesperson loyalty. Such inconsistencies call for a more rigorous examination of the sales force compensation issue.

Designing sales force compensation plans for new sales roles

B2B salespeople are increasingly responsible for managing long-term partnership relationships with key customers. As a result they are embedded in both their firm's and customers' organizations because they need to know both their customers' businesses and their firm's resources in order to develop offerings tailored to their customers' needs (Bradford et al. 2010). In addition, the selling environment is increasingly international. Brown et al. (2005) note that much of the research into compensation plans does not take into account these new developments.

International environment

The 2008 Deloitte and Oracle survey found that more than half sales leaders (52 per cent) are managing sales representatives in several countries. Among other decisions, managers make choices concerning the relative weight of fixed or variable compensation and the allocation rules (equally or equitably) for distributing financial rewards to sales team members. As mentioned in Chapter 10, research found that managers with a Germanic background are less likely than Anglo-Saxon ones to favour incentive compensation. Researchers have also investigated the allocation rules of financial rewards. Some firms, such as Dun and Bradstreet, split all sales commission equally between the salespeople in each team (Churchill et al. 2000, p. 114), while others such as FedEx opt for individual bonus and commission tied to salespeople's individual performance (Cohen et al. 2004). Segalla et al. (2006) found British, German, French and Italian managers more reticent in applying the equity rule (i.e. allocation of financial rewards by individual performance) than their Spanish counterparts.

In another research study involving over 14,000 selling jobs in five B2B industry sectors in five European countries, Rouziès et al. (2009) highlight the impact of tax regimes on compensation decisions. In particular, they showed that *net* pay motivates employees by supporting their lifestyle and that companies need to raise the ratio of incentive to fixed pay in high tax regimes in order to increase income differentials between high and low performers because highly progressive tax systems can significantly narrow after-tax income.

Team selling

In keeping with Zoltners and Sinha (2001), the previous discussion provides evidence for the complexity of compensation decisions. It is unsurprising that team selling compensation is an even more difficult situation. In fact, only 36 per cent of sales leaders believe their compensation plan effectively drives team selling 'well' or 'very well', even though team selling is a common sales practice. Over two-thirds (69 per cent) of sales are done on a team basis, necessitating splitting the team's achievements and rewards (Deloitte and Oracle 2008). As explained above, incentives can be shared equally or tied to individual performance. But sharing the credit for good performance can be divided however management or team members decide. In order to avoid free-riding though, team goals should be set with good knowledge of the team members. Hence, corporate goals are likely to be less effective than regional goals. Moreover, team-based incentive schemes are likely to work better when team members depend on each other's work. Of course, team-based incentive plans require team performance to be measurable.

A compensation plan for the new SigmaKalon sales organization[2]

Company and market background

As indicated earlier, SigmaKalon is a company specializing in decorative, marine, anti-corrosive and industrial paints that came into being as a result of the merger of the Petrofina and Total groups in 1999, which combined their paint branches (Sigma Coatings for Petrofina and Kalon for Total). In 2003, the company was bought by Bain Capital. SigmaKalon currently employs 10,000 people, producing a turnover of €1.7 billion from sales across its various European markets. Three-quarters of this turnover comes from decorative products (exterior walls, interior masonry, wood, varnishes, wood stains, lacquers and decorative paints). The remaining quarter is divided among anti-corrosive and marine paints (15 per cent) and industrial and sheet metal paints (10 per cent).

The decorative paint market represents around €2.1 billion in terms of distributor prices and €1.4 billion in factory prices. SigmaKalon's sales are split between the professional Building Sector market (80 per cent) and the Consumer market (20 per cent). At the time Bain Capital bought SigmaKalon, sales were starting to decline and so, as mentioned, Alain Martel, Sales Director for the Building Sector, was tasked with turning the sales division's performance round.

The Building Sector

The Building Sector market segment covers paints designed for professional painters on building sites, in construction (a developing market) and in the renovation of buildings (slight growth expected); the relative portions for new building and renovation are around 30 per cent and 70 per cent respectively. The Building Sector segment as a whole sells a total of 295,000 tonnes (i.e. 34 per cent of the paint market). The largest portion (70 per cent) of paint sales for building is in the residential sector: new housing (individual and collective), maintenance and renovation of existing homes. The rest involves public, industrial and commercial buildings. The Building Sector market consists of around 45,000 painting and decorating companies: 1,000 with more than 20 employees (28 on average), 22,000 with between 1 and 20 employees (3 on average) and 22,000 sole traders. Broadly speaking, small businesses (a rapidly expanding segment) focus on the individual private housing market, whereas companies with a staff of over 20 people service the public and non-residential Building Sector.

---

[2] This section was written by Anne Macquin, Honorary Professor, and Dominique Rouziès, Professor, HEC-Paris, in collaboration with Jean-Marie Griendl, CEO, Gaëtan Bartra, Channel Manager, Thierry Millet, Human Resources Manager and Communication and Pascal Tisseyre, Finance and Administration, Director Southern Europe, PPG Architectural Coatings EMEA. This case presents a simplified version of the decorative paint market in France for pedagogical purposes.

Paint manufacturers sell their products to painters and decorators in the Building Sector principally through wholesalers and their own distribution channels. They also develop direct relationships with large companies (sometimes relying on their own integrated channel) and get their products written into the building specifications of architects and developers.

Distribution of decoration products

Paint is generally sold with other decoration products such as wallpapers and floor coverings. The distribution of decoration products in France represents a market of between €5.2 and 5.3 billion before tax (trade and consumer markets combined). This is achieved via consumer (DIY super-stores, superstores specializing in floor coverings, etc.) and trade channels, which, respectively, account for 59 and 41 per cent of sales. The trade channel includes wholesalers that are either multi-specialists or specialists (flooring, paint or wallpaper). The former are clearly in the majority (80 per cent of the turnover). Wholesalers mainly target professional decorators (painters), who represent around 70 per cent of their sales. Their second major group of customers comprises private individuals who want professional quality. The latter group has the advantage that they pay a higher price and in cash. However, they are looked down upon by trade professionals who do not like buying their materials alongside private individuals. To conclude, the most marked developments involving the distribution of decoration products over the last four years have been:

- channel concentration, essentially driven by paint manufacturers;
- independent wholesaler mergers to compete with integrated channels
- growing importance of specialists;
- increasing power of multi-specialists with an emphasis on paint in their product range;
- balance between trade and consumer channels;
- emergence of new types of distribution channels providing a consistent product range (one-stop shopping) and 'calibrated' services (commitment to availability, lead times, waste recovery etc.);
- price war among major players in the market.

The SigmaKalon brands

In 2003, SigmaKalon had a large portfolio of brands whose volume market share is decreasing. Two of its main brands (Seigneurie and Peintures Gauthier) had dedicated (integrated) distribution channels in the building market.

Seigneurie was the leading brand (11 per cent volume market share with the highest brand awareness) for paint professionals in France. It was positioned to meet the needs of painters working on large sites. It was also the brand of choice for major accounts but specifications from architects and developers had tended to decrease. It benefitted from a very strong high-tech image and offering a wide range of products for interior masonry and exterior walls. It was distributed via direct sales and an integrated channel, Direct Peintures Seigneurie (DPS, through its own shops with little or no self-service and customers served by sales assistants). Peintures Gauthier (7 per cent volume market share) offered a full range of paints. It was a non-specialist high performance, high quality brand which benefitted from a user-friendly image. Its reputation was closely linked to that of its own distribution channel, Comptoir Peintures Gauthier (or CPG), which also offered tools and decoration products. Its level of brand awareness in was among the highest the market, although not as well known as Seigneurie. It was positioned as a value product for professional painters working on private or small sites. Architects and developers tended to specify it less.

SigmaKalon's integrated distribution system in the Building Sector

Between them, as mentioned earlier, SigmaKalon's two integrated channels, DPS and CPG, covered 49 per cent of sales to paint professionals. Before the company buy-outs and mergers which created SigmaKalon, the two channels were direct competitors. In spite of the change in ownership, in 2003 they were still in face-to-face competition With similar turnover (€100 million and €90 million respectively), DPS had just over 70 branches, while CPG, had some 70 points of sale spread all over France. At CPG outlets customers could find not only paints, but also decoration products either sold under the manufacturer's brand name or as a retail brand. In this channel, SigmaKalon had established a service policy: technical support in the form of recommendations made by technical sales staff, colour advice via the presence of technicians specialized in colorimetry at points of sale, and on-site support help for new products. This distribution channel emphasized being close to the customer and providing customer satisfaction.

The different orientations of the DPS and CPG channels were reflected in the breakdown of their turnover by product and by type of customer. Whereas DPS mainly sold paint (80 per cent of its turnover), CPG relieds less on paint (48 per cent of its turnover) than its three major competitors (Akzo, Lafarge and Zolpan). Consequently, there were more professional painters on DPS's customer base (85 per cent of its turnover) than those of its competitors (from 70 per cent to 78 per cent of their turnover). Moreover, DPS had more large accounts (50 per cent more) than CPG, whereas CPG focused more on small accounts (50 per cent more) than DPS.

SygmaKalon's sales force in the Building Sector

In 2003, 430 people held a sales job at DPS,while CPG had 400 employees. Most of these (40 per cent and 44 per cent of DPS and CPG respectively) were retail salespeople (i.e. work in stores), salespeople in charge of calling on customers (25 per cent and 24 per cent) or Account Managers (12 per cent and 3 per cent).

The cultures of the two sales forces were very different. DPS salespeople saw themselves above all as sellers of paint, while CPG sales staff saw themselves as sellers of decoration products. This was partly because of the way the brands developed: Seigneurie started with major accounts then moved to small paint firms, Peintures Gauthier did the opposite. Alain Martel comments on this difference in culture:

> In terms of culture, the CPG sales force has a real distributor mentality and thinks in terms of distribution margins.[3] They are extremely attached to their corporate image and to the Peintures Gauthier brand. They are focused on all the needs of painters [i.e. paints and other trade products]. They sometimes go too far in their efforts to provide customer satisfaction [sourcing tailor-made products]. On the other hand, their DPS counterparts consider themselves as sellers of paint. They capitalize on the technical image of their paints and the elaborate language that goes with it. Indeed, they have a larger technical range of paint to offer. They are very proud of their brand, which they personify in the eyes of their customers. They are its main ambassadors. They have a major account culture to begin with and think like manufacturers rather than distributors. This means that they work contract by contract and establish their prices according to the margin based on the manufacturing cost. They balk at selling decoration products other than paint, insofar as they make a margin of around 30 per cent compared to 65 per cent for paint,[4] as these are sourced externally.

[3] Price invoiced to the customer – purchase price of the goods by the agency.
[4] Margin based on manufacturing cost.

Sales force compensation

The compensation of CPG and DPS salespeople reflected the differences described above.

Salespeople

The average remuneration of CPG salespeople was €32,465, with 85 per cent fixed salary and 15 per cent variable. For DPS salespeople, the figures were €42,595, 88 per cent and 12 per cent respectively. For both channels, the mechanisms for allocating financial incentives were quite similar, except that DPS salespeople's financial incentives were based on 'non-paint' turnover (created to motivate Seigneurie sales staff to broaden the product range they offer) and the region's operating profit. The calculation of those financial incentives, paid on reaching 100 per cent of the target, constituted the major difference between the two systems: identical bonuses for each salesperson at DPS, whereas the amount depended on the salesperson's fixed salary at CPG, leading to a wide variation in the financial incentives for them.

Account Managers

The average remuneration was €44,800 for CPG and €65,000 for DPS, with both channels having similar compensation structures (i.e. 85 per cent fixed and 15 per cent variable). See Tables 16.3, 16.4 and 16.5 for details.

Table 16.3 Financial incentives allocation systems for salespeople and Account Managers

	Salespeople		Account Managers	
	CPG	**DPS**	**CPG**	**DPS**
Bonuses at 100% of targets	% of fixed salary	€6,900	€9,147	€13,800
Nature of the targets	Paint turnover Overall margin		Paint turnover Area results	
Threshold for triggering, % of the targets	90%		95%	
% of the associated bonus	50% of bonus		50% of bonus	
Ceiling in % of the targets	120%		110%	
% of the associated bonus	150% of bonus		150% of bonus	
Other criteria		Non-paint + regional operating profit		Non-paint + Key Performance Indicator
Maximum associated bonus (other criteria)		€3,450		€6,900
Maximum expected earnings	% of fixed salary	€13,800	€13,721	€27,600
Average observed amounts	€4,900	€5,200	€6,720	€10,000

Table 16.4 Distribution frequency of financial incentives at 100 per cent of targets for CPG salespeople and Account Managers

Financial Incentives at 100% of the targets €/year	Distribution Frequency		
	Salespeople	Account Managers	TOTAL
< 4,560	3	0	3
4,560	8	0	8
5,490	32	2	34
6,400	11	0	11
7,320	32	4	36
> 7,320	10	6	16
TOTAL	96	12	108

Table 16.5 Distribution frequency of financial incentives at 100 per cent of targets for DPS salespeople and Account Managers

Financial Incentives at 100% of the targets/year	Distribution Frequency	
	Salespeople	Account Managers
€6,900	108	
€13,800		52

Merger of DPS and CPG

SigmaKalon Executive Committee decided to integrate DPS and CPG sales channels on 1 January 2005. This merger allowed management to use marketing, commercial and administrative synergies. The new entity was named after both channels: Le Comptoir Seigneurie Gauthier. It claimed to offer 'everything for the painter' and became the largest distributor of paint in France, with 50 per cent more points of sales than its nearest competitor. New stores were bought to cover most geographical areas, while others were closed. Store design was reviewed in order to better convey the new positioning. Management decided to focus on the painter and cover all of his/her needs (i.e. points of sale closeness, wider range of paint/non-paint offerings, customized solutions, more services, easier and faster ordering procedures, technical assistance, etc.). The Seigneurie and Peintures Gauthier brands would be sold in the same points of sale. Consequently, they were repositioned through targeted marketing campaigns: more up-scale, leader and innovator identity for Seigneurie, and a more middle-of-the-road, challenger position for Peintures Gauthier. The market segmentation was also reviewed and the offerings were better targeted at those segments.

Issues related to the integration of DPS and CPG sales forces

The sales force integration put an end to a situation where some customers were called on by both DPS and CPG salespeople. In that situation, instead of working against competitors, DPS and CPG sales forces had been competing against each other.

Because of the existing cultural differences between the two sales forces, the integration of the sales forces had to be carefully and rapidly implemented. First, a number of meetings and a communication campaign informed sales personnel of the merger and its consequences. The most critical issue was to convince sales staff of the new organization's advantages and of the situation's urgency. To help in the process, the most widely respected salespeople from each channel were involved closely in the integration process through the creation of a project committee. They helped design sales territories and customer portfolios. Second, new sales roles were quickly specified in order to reassure sales personnel. To that end, customer and sales allocations were reviewed in order to optimize salespeople's efficiency. As a result, each salesperson ended up with a new portfolio of product offerings (including the previous competitor's brand) and customers. Needless to say, switching customers was not an easy task as some salespeople felt a degree of ownership over their customers. Moreover, extensive training was provided in order to ensure all salespeople mastered the entire range of offerings. At the same time, a new sales management team was nominated and a new sales force automation system was implemented. This new tool allowed management to improve selling effort allocation thanks to an improved centralized information system. Call frequency norms were imposed for each segment of customers.

Comptoir Seigneurie Gauthier Sales Force Compensation

As management felt it was essential not to privilege one sales force over the other, compensation gaps had to be reduced. As shown in Tables 16.2 and 16.3, before the sales force integration, CPG salespeople's yearly incentive compensation varied widely because their financial incentives were based on fixed salary: for one group of salespeople around €5,500 and for another group, around €7,320 at 100 per cent of the target. Their DPS counterparts got a fixed yearly bonus of €6,900 at 100 per cent of the target. In order to reduce discrepancies, management decided to award the same DPS bonus for ex-CPG senior salespeople (i.e., €6,900) at 100 per cent of the target. The other ex CPG salespeople, depending on whether they were categorized as junior or experienced salespeople, got a bonus of €4,500 and €5,500 respectively at 100 per cent of the target. The maximum bonus awarded for senior salespeople in the new system is identical to what ex-*DPS* salespeople used to receive, that is, €13,800. For junior and experienced salespeople, the bonus is €9,000 and €1,1000 respectively. Finally, in order to ensure salespeople direct their efforts toward SigmaKalon core business (i.e., paint) and profitability, the targets set up for those incentives involve the paint sales turnover (40 per cent of the target) and the global margin (60 per cent of the target). In summary, the system of incentives based on fixed salaries for CPG salespeople was suppressed and replaced with a version of the DPS compensation plan featuring categories of salespeople. Those categories (i.e., junior, experienced, senior) rely on sales turnover, selling experience or number of customers. Moreover the fixed salary of ex-CPG salespeople was progressively increased (about 2 per cent a year) in order to reach that of ex-DPS salespeople while the fixed salary of the latter was frozen. For Account Managers, the new compensation system was identical to that of senior salespeople described above.

Such a standardized compensation system presents several advantages. First, it is a simplified system of earlier versions of compensation schemes designed for groups of salespeople and account managers from different cultures. Recall that compensation plan clarity is a requirement since salespeople need to understand and anticipate the outcomes of their activities. Second, it provides the best possible distribution of maximum earning expectations. Management believed it was important to maintain those expectations as much as possible in order to encourage sales success. Third, at 100 per cent of the target, its cost is globally identical to that of 2004 because the exceptional bonuses of ex-DPS salespeople were reduced while the fixed salary of ex-CPG salespeople was increased. Fourth, the creation of three categories of salespeople based on objective measures provides a rationale to justify differences in bonus allocation for ex-CPG salespeople. That step was critical for reducing potential conflicts between the two sales forces. Finally, perks (i.e., 13th month salary, holiday bonus) previously allocated to DPS salespeople were extended to the ex-CPG sales force in order to lower the remuneration gaps. Management expects remuneration gaps between ex-CPG and ex-DPS sales staff to disappear completely when some of the most well paid personnel will retire.

Case Conclusion

The firm's executives correctly anticipated a number of reactions by the sales staff. First, because the sales staff now worked under a new hierarchy, new customers, new offerings, a new control system, and a new compensation system, management expected an increase in staff turnover. Indeed, about 15 per cent of the sales force quit after the integration. Second, the transition period resulted for a short period of time in ordering difficulties, logistics problems, delays, and new pricing policies for the "less" visible customers, (i.e. the small paint firms) essentially because salespeople first focused on their most important customers. Therefore, financial turnover first decreased by about 20 per cent in 2005. Over the following two years though, it started to increase sharply again. Third, to make sure both sales forces would work with one another, training sessions and portfolio allocations mixed both groups. Finally and most importantly, management made sure the new compensation system (1) would be perceived as fair by both sales forces and (2) would equally promote offerings (through the paint targets) from both *Peintures Gauthier* and *Seigneurie* and (3) would improve the company's profitability (through the global margin targets).

Summary

Sales force compensation is a critical issue for most sales organizations. Compensation has a strong impact on both costs and revenues and is a key driver of salespeople's effectiveness and efficiency. It affects the responses and efforts of salespeople and is related to many other decisions such as sales force structure (e.g. choice of direct or independent sales force) and motivational processes. Most companies frequently redesign their sales force compensation plans to find the best fit with internal and external conditions.

Key points

While there are a number of sales force compensation plan structures and levels, there are some general principles for designing efficient sales force compensation plans:

1. Plans should be linked to a firm's strategic objectives.
2. Plans should be clear so that salespeople can anticipate their income.
3. Plans should be fair and motivating. Pay disparities resulting from management's decisions are not well accepted, whereas pay disparities resulting from customers' decisions are motivating (when selling effort has a strong impact on customers' decisions).

4. Plans should be adaptable to accommodate new conditions.
5. Plans should provide attractive rewards. In particular, the amount of risk, level of income and horizon of incentive payments must match the desired salesperson's profile.

Running a compensation audit in your company

As discussed earlier in this chapter, sales force compensation plans may present a number of flaws, with symptoms including those featured in the following table.

	Yes	No
Is your sales force compensation plan attractive compared with those of your competitors?		
Are your salespeople able to estimate the pay they will receive?		
Do your best performers earn significantly more than your worse performers?		
Do your worst performers leave your company?		
Do your best performers stay with your company?		
Are your salespeople focusing their selling efforts on strategic offerings?		
Are your salespeople focusing their selling efforts on strategic customers?		

Managers using successful compensation plans answer 'yes' to each question.

References

Bradford, K., Brown, S., Ganesan, S., Hunter, G., Onyemah, V., Palmatier, R., Rouziès, D., Spiro, R., Sujan, H. and Weitz, B.A. (2010) 'The Embedded Salesforce: Connecting Buying and Selling Organizations', *Marketing Letters*, 21 (3): 239–253.

Brown, S.P., Evans, K.R., Mantrala, M. and Challagalla, G. (2005) 'Adapting Motivation, Control and Compensation Research to a New Environment', *Journal of Personal Selling and Sales Management*, 25 (2): 156–67.

Churchill, G.A. Jr, Ford, N.M., Walker, O.C. Jr, Johnston, M.W. and Tanner, J.F. Jr (2000) *Sales Force Management*, 6th edition. Boston, MA: McGraw-Hill and Irwin.

Cohen, A., Gilbert, J. and Ligos, M. (2004) 'Extreme Makeovers', *Sales and Marketing Management*, 156 (5): 36–43.

Deloitte and Oracle (2008) 'Strategic Sales Compensation Survey', http://www.deloitte.com/dtt/article/0,1002,sid%253D26551%2526cid%253D211796,00.htm (accessed 10 July 2010).

Heide, C.P. (1999) *Dartnell's 30th Sales Force Compensation Survey: 1998–1999*. Chicago: Dartnell Corporation.

John, G. and Weitz, B. (1989), 'Salesforce Compensation: An Empirical Investigation of Factors Related to Use of Salary Versus Incentive Compensation', *Journal of Marketing Research*, 26 (1): 1–14.

Rouziès, D. (1992) 'The Effects of a Salesperson's Utilities on Optimal Sales Force Compensation Structures' (Ph. Dissertation, Faculty of Management, McGill University).

Rouziès, D., Coughlan, A.T., Anderson, E. and Iacobucci, D. (2009) 'Determinants of Pay Levels and Structures in Sales Organizations', *Journal of Marketing*, 73 (6): 92–104.

Segalla, M., Rouziès, D., Besson, M. and Weitz, B.A. (2006) 'A Cross-national Investigation of Incentive Sales Compensation', *International Journal of Research in Marketing*, 23 (4): 419–33.

Zoltners, A. and Sinha, P. (2001) 'Sales-force Decision Models: Insights from 25 Years of Implementation', *Interfaces*, 31 (3): S8–S44.

Zoltners, A.A., Sinha, P. and Lorimer, S.E. (2006) *How To Design and Implement Plans That Work: The Complete Guide to Sales Force Incentive Compensation*. New York: AMACOM.

Further reading

Albers, S., Krafft, M. and Bielert, W. (1998) 'Global Sales Force Management: Comparing German and U.S. Practices', in Bouer, G.J., Baunchalk, M.S., Ingram, T.N. and Laforge, R.W. (eds), *Emerging Trends in Sales Thought and Practice:*193–211. Westport, CN: Quorum Books.

Davenport, R.J. (2001) 'Designing Reward Systems for Today's Sales Professionals', in Fay, C.H., Thompson, M.A. and Knight, D. (eds), *The Executive Handbook of Compensation*: 214-237, New York: Free Press.

Joseph, K. and Kalwani, M.U. (1998) 'The Role of Bonus Pay in Salesforce Compensation Plans', *Industrial Marketing Management*, 27 (2): 147–59.

Misra, S., Coughlan, A.T. and Narasimhan, C. (2005) 'Salesforce Compensation: An Analytical and Empirical Examination of the Agency Theoretic Approach', *Quantitative Marketing and Economics*, 3 (1): 5–39.

Werner, S. and Ward, S.G. (2004) 'Recent Compensation Research: An Eclectic Review', *Human Resource Management Review*, 14 (2): 201–27.

Part five
Salespeople's responses

17

Salespeople's self-management: knowledge, emotions and behaviours

Susi Geiger

Contents

Learning objectives

After reading this chapter, you should be able to:

- Describe the different personal and psychological attributes that a salesperson needs for sales success.

- Acknowledge the role of positive and negative emotions on salespeople's motivation and well-being.

- Appreciate the extent to which salespeople are prone to role conflict, role ambiguity and role overload.

- Discuss stress management and coping mechanisms that can be taught to salespeople.

- Discuss the role of management and management systems in channelling salespeople's attitudes, behaviours and feelings.

Chapter outline

This chapter considers the emotional, cognitive and behavioural elements of the sales profession at an individual basis and discusses, through the introduction of academic concepts, how knowledge of the various issues attached to these elements of the sales existence can help sales organizations foster individual well-being and collective success. Overall, the chapter shows that many costs that sales organizations incur, such as high turnover or customer churn, can be reduced through a mindful approach to managing sales personnel. The chapter proceeds as follows: after the introduction of a fictitious mini-case history, we discuss a model of salespeople's emotions, attitudes and behaviours; subsequent sections then break this model down into its component parts. The final parts of this chapter provide guidelines to sales management and salespeople on how to develop coping and mindfulness strategies for sales success and well-being.

CASE PROBLEM

Introduction[1]

Ben Smyth's mobile phone rang just as he was about to pull his car into the car-park of Kyona Ltd's Dublin headquarters. He had been eagerly awaiting this particular phone call – he knew that one of his five key accounts would award a three-year exclusive supply contract worth several million euros today. For the past three months, Ben had been liaising closely with his main contact in the client company, Patricia O'Dwyer, in order to place Kyona in the best position to win the contract for the second time running. Ben had been working for Kyona, a privately-owned distributor of speciality industrial chemicals supplies and services, for over three years, first in a technical support role and then as a Key Account Manager and sales executive. With a BSc in chemistry and a Masters in management, Ben was not only highly familiar with the products and services he sold to his industrial clients but also well aware of the financial impact his actions had on the survival of the company. As a medium-sized Irish company, Kyona found it increasingly difficult to compete with the large multinational chemical manufacturers who often had their own worldwide distribution and service systems in place. Kyona's main selling points were highly personalized service, high levels of technical knowledge and speed and flexibility of product delivery. Accordingly, the sales team was trained to be customer- and relationship-focused in its client interactions and to position Kyona as a specialized premium vendor. Since 2008, however, the global recessionary environment had made many clients increasingly cost-focused, which had often swung purchasing decisions in favour of the lowest-priced bidder – whose prices Kyona could rarely match. Ben knew that several of his fellow seven sales executives had lost high-profile accounts to competitors in the past six months; given the significant volume of the current deal he also knew that he simply *had* to win this upcoming contract, for his own and for his company's sake.

Ben's heart skipped a beat as he answered the phone. From the display, he saw that it was indeed Patricia on the other line. 'Ben Smyth at your service, Patricia,' he attempted to sound light-hearted. 'Hi Ben, how is it going?' Patricia's voice sounded grave. 'Better, if you told me that Kyona's won the tender!' answered Ben. By now he had started to sweat and his hands were shaking. 'Well, that's why I am ringing you myself, Ben. You know that I really like you as a person and that I like working with Kyona as a company. I am really sorry, Ben, but this time round the board has decided to go with another vendor for the next three-year chemicals contract.' Ben felt as if someone had hit him in the stomach. 'Thanks for ringing Patricia. I'll be in touch again' was all he managed to respond; in reality, he felt like crying and screaming at the same time. This could simply not be true.

Introduction: the sales existence at the 'coal face'

Today's sales environment is without a doubt a challenging one. Sales organizations and selling personnel alike have to cope with highly uncertain and complex selling contexts, with heated competition in slow-growth and no-growth markets and with customers who have adopted highly professional and value-focused approaches to their purchasing function. Sales departments are also coming under pressure from

---

[1] This case is fictional and has been devised for pedagogical purposes only. Any similarity to a real situation is entirely coincidental.

growing internal productivity demands, where cost-cutting is typically accompanied by sales quotas that seem unattainable to many sales executives. More so than ever, the world of selling is a highly charged and stressful work environment, often providing a veritable emotional and psychological rollercoaster for the individuals who work within it.

While salespeople's duties and responsibilities vary dramatically depending on their industry, employment position, career stage and other factors, there are a few commonalities that most sales jobs share. Salespeople typically lead a professional existence that is in equal parts self-reliant, performance-oriented and people-centred. Many people in sales jobs enjoy the relative autonomy that the profession offers and take pride in the fact that much of their success is directly related to the effort and skill they put into their selling tasks. They often also enjoy the daily contact with a wide variety of customers and peers. Accordingly, salespeople have often been described as tenacious, self-motivating and materialistic, but also as empathic and good at communication. Above all, salespeople have often been described as wanting to succeed – a desire that fuels their actions but that can also lead to emotional problems if the anticipated success fails to materialize. While many sales organizations have formal and informal mechanisms to share successes among the sales force – such as presidents' clubs, award ceremonies, 'salesperson of the month' lists, etc. – salespeople are often required to deal with the lows that their jobs entail on their own. Indeed, in some sales organizations it is near taboo to talk about sales failures or to linger too much on the negative aspects of the job. Yet, research has shown repeatedly that there is a close connection between salespeople's perceptions, attitudes, emotions and behaviours, and that once this feedback loop slides into negative territory it can quickly become a vicious circle that can lead to slumps in performance, salesperson turnover or even burnout. This chapter aims to draw a picture of sales job demands 'on the ground' and how managers and the sales staff themselves can maintain a successful, performance-oriented and healthy environment for all sales employees.

An attitude-behaviour framework of selling

In what follows, we explore how salespeople cope with the daily demands of their profession both cognitively and emotionally, what effect successes and failures may have on salespeople's well-being, motivation and performance, and how management systems can be put in place to help sales personnel manage job demands. As would be expected, there are many elements impacting on salespeople's attitudes, behaviours and emotional balance. While it is impossible to cover all of these elements, this chapter will raise a few vital issues concerning salesperson self-management in these areas.

Theoretically, we can develop this book's overall conceptual model of the sales management process from Chapter 1 to show the interaction between some of these elements, as shown in Figure 17.1. Figure 17.1 draws heavily on psychological research on attitudes, emotions and behaviour (see, for instance, Fishbein and Ajzen 1975). Attitude research posits that how people behave is related to both a cognitive component and an emotional component. This adds important depth to predominantly

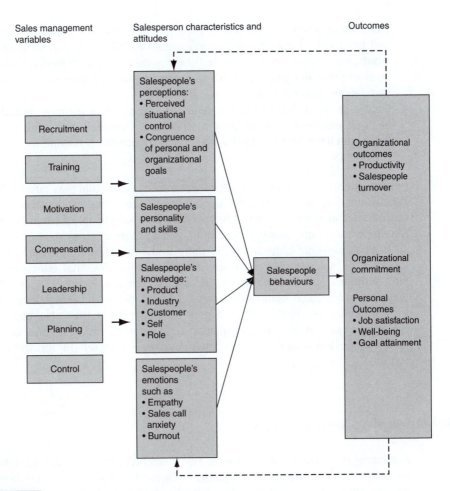

Figure 17.1 An attitude-behaviour framework of selling
Source: Author.

cognitive motivational theories such as the expectancy model or the goal theories presented in Chapter 15, showing how emotions fuel salesperson motivation and influence behaviours. Recent developments in attitude theory also show that how motivated people are to engage in certain behaviours depends on their perceived level of control they exert over their tasks, which outcomes they expect to reach with the behaviour and the extent to which these outcomes are aligned with their personal goals. These psychological theories teach us a few simple lessons that we will explore further in the rest of this chapter:

1. In understanding how and why salespeople engage in certain behaviours, sales management has to consider salespeople's emotions as well as their perceptions, knowledge and beliefs.
2. Personal goals and stakes are important driving forces for salespeople that can explain many of their actions if Sales Managers understand how salespeople perceive the personal impact of a selling situation.

3. The level of control a salesperson perceives herself to have over her environment and tasks will play a role in her motivation to behave in certain ways. In other words, a salesperson who feels that she has the power to influence a situation will be more motivated to do so than a salesperson who feels powerless in changing her own fate or that of a particular selling process.
4. Successes and failures not only influence salespeople's learning, but also impact on their emotions and on their motivation to succeed next time round. Thus, there is an important feedback loop between perceptions, cognitions, emotions and behaviours.

In subsequent sections, we will consider some key issues that may affect sales professionals and managers, as illustrated in Figure 17.1, and that explain how perceptions, cognitions and emotions work together to shape salespeople's behaviours and performance outcomes. Many of the managerial issues discussed in other chapters, such as salespeople recruitment, training and motivational systems, will have an influence on salespeople's attitudes and behaviours. The final effects of salespeople's attitudes and characteristics, as can be seen in Figure 17.1, working their way into sales force behaviours, can be found at an individual level in relation to job satisfaction, well-being and goal attainment, but they also become apparent at an organizational level in relation to individuals' organizational commitment, performance levels and turnover intentions (see Chapter 18 for these outcome factors).

Salespeople's perceptions

According to research into attitudes, two perceptual factors seem to influence the attitude-behaviour relationship depicted in Figure 17.1 more than any others, namely the perceived level of control a salesperson has over her actions and the personal goals or stakes that drive the individual.

Perceived level of situational control

In general, people exert effort when they perceive that they are able to make things happen by doing so, when they can exert some control over their environment. In sales, a salesperson's level of effort will therefore chiefly depend on the extent to which she perceives that more effort will actually lead to a better outcome. To use the sports metaphor drawn in Chapter 13, if an athlete believes that she can win an important race by training an additional two hours a day, and if she has the opportunity to do this, she is very likely to put in the extra effort to make it happen. If a salesperson believes that she can win an important account if given 5 per cent pricing latitude by her manager, this is going to motivate her to make it happen because she feels more in charge of her own destiny and of the outcome of her actions.

Congruence between personal and firm goals

In situations where people are asked to exert effort, they automatically evaluate their personal stake in doing so. If a salesperson values materialistic things and a particular sale could make or break her yearly bonus, she will be highly motivated to work hard to achieve that sale, and she will also maintain a high level of involvement in a particular selling process. If a salesperson is highly competitive, a competition run in the sales team may motivate her to work overtime. Likewise, if a Sales Manager asks a salesperson to do relationship maintenance on her accounts but the salesperson fails to perceive a direct link from doing so to her personal goals because such activities are not rewarded or recognized in the organization, she will put little effort and care into that behaviour.

We will see in the subsequent chapters that a salesperson's perceived level of control and perception of congruence between her personal and the firm's goals influence both the emotions that she experiences and the cognitions and behaviours she engages in.

Salespeople's skills

It is widely believed that sales success is based on a sound management approach at an organizational level and a combination of personality traits and selling skills at the individual salesperson level. While personality traits such as confidence, competitiveness, tact, openness and extroversion are innate qualities that sales recruiters may need to screen for during the recruitment process (see Chapter 11), selling skills are acquired capabilities that sales training can instil and foster in the sales force. Chapter 12 on sale force training has laid out in detail how such nurturing of selling skills may be accomplished in practice. For the purpose of this chapter, it is worth emphasizing once more just how broad a skills base a modern salesperson needs to possess in order to be effective. Traditionally, persuasion skills, professionalism and what is commonly known as 'people skills' have been regarded as central attributes of successful sales executives. With the increasing centrality of customer orientation in many industries, relational skills such as listening skills, conflict handling and communication skills have been added to the skills mix. And even more recently, researchers have highlighted the importance of salespeople's technology skills for sales success (Reday et al. 2009). Sales Managers need to realize that the need for such a wide skills base is an indication that the sales job places significant personal, cognitive and emotional demands on the individual.

Salespeople's knowledge

Sales organizations operate in an increasingly turbulent environment where market contexts and client relationships are constantly changing. In this environment, organizations as well as individuals have to be willing to engage in continuous learning if they want to remain successful. While learning ultimately needs to occur at an institutional level, sales organizations can only learn through the accumulated experiences of their individual members. Individual salesperson learning is of particular importance in industries where deep product knowledge and/or long-term relationship building with clients are important for success. In such environments, it is vital for a firm to have salespeople who are both able and willing to learn and to disseminate their knowledge within the sales organization. For this to happen, sales management and IT systems have to encourage knowledge dissemination and, in turn, make sure that salespeople are equipped with intelligence emanating from other sources in the company, such as Marketing, Product Development or Logistics. If such give and take between the sales force and other company departments can be routinized, environmental change can be successfully negotiated. This section will briefly discuss the five crucial components of salespeople's knowledge:

- product knowledge;
- market knowledge;
- customer knowledge;
- self-knowledge;
- role knowledge.

All five of these knowledge components are not only important for individual sales success, but that they are also stepping-stones in organizational learning and environmental adaptation.

Product knowledge

A deep level of continuously updated product knowledge is often considered the basic requirement for successful salespeople. In many technical industries, salespeople and Account Managers are often recruited from technical positions or on the basis of their technical education. In addition, as Chapter 12 indicated, much sales training is aimed at briefing the sales force on new product technologies or developments. While companies seem to be aware of the importance of equipping salespeople with a good level of product knowledge, they may focus less on garnering product feedback from the market through salespeople. Strong feedback loops between Sales and other departments responsible for product development, manufacturing and marketing are thus necessary in order to ensure that salespeople possess the requisite level of product knowledge when selling complex solutions to prospects and customers, and to make sure that salespeople feed their own knowledge of customer-required product specifications, modifications and performance back to those in charge of product formulation.

Market knowledge

It is almost a truism to say that the deepest knowledge of competitors and of industry dynamics is found in those who are on the road the most. One only has to picture the many potential meeting places of salespeople working for firms in the same market – customer premises, hotel lobbies, industry events – to understand why this is such an obvious statement. A firm's salespeople are often the first to hear about new competitive products, new pricing policies or mergers and acquisitions between firms in the industry. Surprisingly, many firms fail to capture salespeople's market knowledge systematically and to feed it back into the organization. As with the other types of knowledge discussed in this chapter, there has to be a systematic give and take between the Marketing and Sales interface; Marketing has to ensure that salespeople are empowered with market research information, but, in turn, it also has to be willing to gather market intelligence from salespeople.

Customer knowledge

A deep understanding of customer needs and well-developed customer knowledge is essential for successful selling, especially in relational and customer-oriented selling modes. In the Customer Relationship Management strategies explored in Chapter 5, much emphasis is put on 'extracting' salespeople's customer knowledge and making it accessible to anyone in the organization who may come into contact with the customer. While doubts have been voiced as to whether some salespeople may feed back biased and self-serving information about their clients, generally speaking what salespeople know about their customers needs to be considered as an important organizational asset.

Weitz et al. (1986) discussed how salespeople can learn to work smarter instead of working harder, and they also showed that those salespeople with the most detailed customer knowledge are also those who are most likely to practise adaptive selling (which we will explore in more detail in the section below). In recent years, sales researchers have shown that it is not necessarily what salespeople know about the customer that makes them successful, but rather their willingness to learn and update their customer knowledge that affects sales success (see, for instance, Turley and Geiger 2006). For example, in a social situation such as the sales encounter, even very intricate knowledge of sales techniques can be ineffective if the salesperson's knowledge structures are not 'flexible' enough to accommodate instant changes during the process of the sales interaction. So, the truly successful sales professional may not be the one with the most technical knowledge, but the one who possesses the greatest capacity to learn and react quickly to new information during customer interactions.

Self-knowledge

Sales Scenario

Imagine the difference between two salespeople who have just lost out on an important sale to a new customer. One of the salespeople says to herself, 'I will never make a sale again, I am useless at this job and sooner or later I will be found out and fired', whereas the second tells herself, 'It is a pity that this account was lost, but I am confident of my product and my selling abilities and I will learn the lessons from this loss and approach the next sale differently'. Chances are that the two salespeople will approach the next sales call in a different mind-frame: salesperson one will most likely be so preoccupied with 'not wanting to fail again' that she may miss out on vital customer cues and perhaps will lose another sale, while salesperson two will tune herself into the customer much more carefully. They will also probably filter incoming information differently; human beings tend to process information that confirms existing knowledge or schemata much more easily than information that conflicts with it. If their Sales Manager approaches our two salespeople by saying, 'Hard luck about this account, I am sure it wasn't your fault, maybe the competitor offer was simply cheaper', salesperson one will interpret this as 'My manager feels sorry for me, he won't hold on to me for long', while salesperson two may say 'He's probably right, but I can still try harder next time; in any case, my manager's on my side'.

This scenario suggests that how salespeople process information from the environment depends partly on the self-image or self-knowledge they possess. Lee Godden, author of *ZenWise Selling* (2004), asserts that a salesperson's self-knowledge is the basis of their knowledge and understanding of their customers. He exhorts salespeople to ask themselves the following questions: Who am I? What are my values? and How can I bring these values into my daily work? Godden claims that if salespeople know the answers to these questions and consistently act in accordance with their values and their self-image, they will lead a more successful and happier professional existence. While this may sound somewhat esoteric to hands-on salespeople and managers, research has indicated that the best salespeople display a deep knowledge of themselves, their strengths, weaknesses and skills. Such self-knowledge in turn allows these salespeople to understand their customers and co-workers better, leading to more success in their jobs. In contrast, Verbeke and Bagozzi (2000) noticed that negative emotions such as sales call anxiety often coincided with a salesperson's unrealistically negative evaluation of herself and excessive ruminations about past mistakes. The lesson from these and other researchers is that the better a salesperson understands who she is and the more realistic her self-schema is ('Who am I and what are my strengths and weaknesses?', 'What role do I play when I walk into a customer's premises?', 'What values do I bring to this call?'), the more she can make realistic evaluations of her own and other people's actions and the more she will able to learn from mistakes and focus on the future rather than the past.

Role knowledge

Sales personnel are prototypical boundary-spanners, mediating directly and personally between buying and selling organizations (Geiger and Finch 2009). Sales personnel often need to perform the role of being in two organizations at once, which requires a good level of role knowledge and sound management systems to alleviate potential role stresses emanating from such boundary-spanning. Without thorough role knowledge, role stresses can stem from three sources:

1. *Role conflict* occurs when a salesperson feels incompatible expectations from two sources weighing upon her. For instance, a sales rep may deal with a long-standing client, who expects the salesperson to act in that client's best interest, but her boss expects her to up-sell that customer to a new package even though the client may

not need it in the short term. In general, the closer salespeople get to their customers, the more they will be drawn to see their customers' perspectives and the harder they will find it to act against the interests of these customers, even if their own organizations request them to do so. It is almost as if the salesperson, as a boundary-spanner, has started to stand on the customer's rather than her own organization's side. This is important to know for management; while, generally speaking, customer-oriented and relational salespeople will display greater job satisfaction, in those cases where these behaviours lead to chronic role conflict, both their job satisfaction and organizational commitment are likely to be low. In this case, management will need to ensure two things: first, that salespeople are well embedded and socialized in their home organization, and, second, that they encourage salespeople to voice potential conflicts of interest that they perceive between what their manager asks them to do and what they see as in their customers' best interest.

2. *Role ambiguity* occurs when the salesperson lacks information on how to perform her role adequately or is uncertain about what is expected from her. This stress factor occurs perhaps more frequently in sales than in other professions, due to the relative job autonomy many sales executives enjoy. While job autonomy is often perceived as positive by the salesperson and is an often necessary part of a job that happens predominantly outside direct supervision, if there is too little definition and structure to their job this can be perceived as frustrating and unpleasant. Role ambiguity can be perceived by salespeople who are unclear about any pertinent element of their job, such as the scope of the job and the tasks associated with it, their superiors' expectations, which criteria will be used to evaluate their performance, which behaviours are expected for promotion and so on. Generally speaking, it seems that the more ambiguity a salesperson perceives regarding her job, the greater the likelihood of negative consequences such as job tension, turnover and low performance. A clear job description, good performance measures and a transparent behaviour-based control system can help provide greater role clarity to the salesperson. Moreover, clear and unambiguous lines of communication and written policies and procedures, including for instance such issues as ethical conduct and handling customer rejection, can help provide salespeople with a more tangible picture of what is expected of them. Finally, internal and external social support, as described below, can be a valuable coping mechanism for salespeople dealing with moderate levels of role ambiguity.

3. *Role overload* occurs when the job demands are persistently perceived as greater than that the salesperson can handle, given her skills base and motivational level. As discussed in the chapter on motivation (Chapter 15), psychologists contend that the relationship between job demands and job performance corresponds to an inverted U-shape. This means that if job demands are too low, job performance will suffer; on the other hand, if job demands and stresses are too high, performance will suffer as well. Organizational realities in many companies, such as staff shortages or internal productivity demands, may lead many salespeople to feel that their skills and resources are continuously strained. It is likely that with the recent changes in the selling environment, overload conditions are now more acute than ever before. Management needs to be aware not only of the signs of role overload, but also of the levels of demand and pressure passed onto the sales force, in order to avoid

potential burnout. Singh (1998) highlights that a job that involves a lot of variety and good management feedback can go some way to buffer role overload, but ultimately and over extended periods of time managers need to scale salespeople's jobs to a realistic level if they want to maintain employee motivation and performance at healthy levels.

Salespeople's emotions

In recent years, emotional intelligence has been widely discussed in management and academic circles as one of the key ingredients for success. In a profession that mixes high levels of interpersonal interaction with a highly pressurized job environment, salespeople's ability to perceive, interpret and manage their own and others' emotions effectively will play a central role in their individual well-being and in the success they will enjoy in their job. Because emotions betray the personal stake a salesperson has in an action, they are an important antecedent for the amount of planning and effort a person will put into their job; they can also be used by management to understand and increase employee motivation (Brown et al. 1997). While we cannot consider all possible emotions that may impact upon salespeople on a daily basis – joy, pride, excitement, delight, anger, guilt, embarrassment and jealousy form only part of the possible range of emotions felt by salespeople – we will examine three emotional factors that are shown to have a significant relationship to salespeople's performance: empathy, sales call anxiety and burnout.

Empathy

When asked for the secret of a great sales executive, one highly successful hardware Sales Manager responded to the author of this chapter: 'One of the major attributes of a good salesperson is that they create tremendous empathy with the customer. They have this thing in that they are almost on the customer's side against the company in some ways. And it's very hard to describe, and when you are recruiting salespeople it's probably the most difficult job you can do, because it's not easy to spot the good ones, there are no common characteristics and salespeople don't come in a particular size or fit. But the one thing that they do have – and you only find out later if the new recruit has this – is this empathy with the customer. Almost as if they are able to sort of come along and put an arm around the customer's shoulder and share his problems in some way.'

Judging from this account, empathy is a core emotive aptitude for salespeople, especially when they are operating in a relational or customer-oriented selling mode. In the psychology literature, empathy is defined as the ability to understand deeply the world of another person and to communicate this understanding to her. It is seen as a learned emotion, so even people who are not born with this quality can learn to be empathic. Empathic sales professionals will actively listen to their clients and act on the knowledge gained in their interactions with them. Interestingly, prior research on the effect of empathy on sales success has yielded mixed findings, even suggesting that high levels of empathy could be counter-productive to performance. McBane (1995) for instance observed that 'emotional contagion' from the customer to the salesperson had a negative effect on selling success because salespeople took their customers' problems too much to heart. Such a negative effect could be caused by the fact that empathic sales professionals may find themselves with a conflict of loyalty between their own organization and their client's. Thus, while it is advisable for Sales Managers to keep an eye out for highly empathic individuals and assign relational accounts to them, they should also be aware of the downsides of salespeople getting too deeply involved with their clients' problems – ranging from an inability to 'talk tough' with the client to feelings of rejection if and when the relationship dissolves.

Sales call anxiety

Every salesperson knows the tingling feeling of nervous anticipation before going into an important sales call or before calling on a new contact. While the average sales professional is most likely used to that feeling and some individuals may even rely on it to spur them on to better performance, sometimes the feeling of anticipation can turn into a debilitating emotional burden. When this happens, a salesperson may be suffering from sales call anxiety, an emotional condition akin to social anxiety. As mentioned earlier, selling is a highly goal-directed activity; a salesperson usually has clear objectives in view when making a sales call. This means that a salesperson can also anticipate her reactions to either reaching this goal or failing to reach it. Unfortunately, selling offers as many opportunities for frustration as it does to reach one's goals . While some sales professionals are able to shake disappointments off just like the proverbial duck shakes water off its back, others seem to choose the profession partly because of a need to be liked and approved of by other people. If such salespeople experience an accumulation of negative events and failure to reach their goals, they may develop a propensity for remembering the hurtful negative experiences rather than the positive ones. Often, this has a negative influence on a person's self-knowledge and self-evaluation generally. As a result, the fear of failure, personal rejection or disappointment becomes bigger and bigger over time, often to a point where the salesperson becomes dysfunctional and may, indeed, develop physical symptoms such as shortness of breath or sweating, or engage in self-protective behaviours such as avoiding threatening situations in the future.

Thankfully, sales call anxiety seems to be both situation-specific and curable. For one salesperson it may appear only before cold calls; for another, it may be related to asking a client for a commitment. Because of this specificity to particular situations, managers may be able to identify the causes of the anxiety. In order to help the salesperson develop appropriate coping mechanisms, a Sales Manager's first task is to make the salesperson recognize that their performance suffers from their anxiety, and to identify what triggers this anxiety. Next, once the individual in question is aware of the cues and symptoms of her sales call anxiety, the Sales Manager and executive together need to develop coping mechanisms. Verbeke and Bagozzi (2000) suggest the following strategies to help individuals cope with sales call anxiety:

- *Constructive self-analysis.* The salesperson learns to interrupt negative self-evaluations by asking herself questions that allow her to step back from the immediate emotional reaction, such as 'What makes you think that this customer doesn't like you?'.

• *Lessen the need for approval-seeking.* If managers realize that some of their sales-people have an excessive need to be liked, they need to help them have a better appreciation of their self-worth independent of other people's opinions (or else not recruit individuals who are obsessive in their need for approval). Incidentally, while a moderate need for being liked seems quite widespread among sales professionals, those who overemphasize the importance of other people's opinions may not be very well equipped for the job in the long run.

• *Learn counteracting strategies* to avoiding the threatening situation; for instance, the saleperson commits to engage in a certain number of the anxiety-inducing sales calls or develops scripts for dealing with difficult situations.

• *Professional treatment.* If sales call anxiety becomes overwhelming for an individual and is displayed across many different selling situations, the Sales Manager may need to encourage the individual to seek professional help or use self-help books to overcome their condition.

Note that helping the salesperson avoid the anxiety-inducing situation by, for example, taking her off cold calls is not a good coping strategy – it will most likely only worsen the condition further!

Burnout

Marketing and sales have been identified repeatedly as professions that are highly susceptible to burnout because jobs in these areas typically involve a strong interpersonal component and high levels of role stresses. Psychologists have defined burnout as a state of emotional exhaustion, leading to reduced performance, motivation and self-esteem. Burnout is said to be a psychological condition attained as an outcome of perceived cognitive stress, with significant behavioural consequences. Burnout is often a consequence of an accumulation of factors, including the presence of several sources of role stresses (conflict, ambiguity or overload). What is worrying for Sales Managers is not only that burnout can be a significant organizational strain in terms of employee turnover, absenteeism and reduced productivity, but that burnout is also likely to lead to what researchers call 'depersonalization', namely the likelihood that boundary-spanners will detach themselves emotionally from the people they are expected to serve – the customers. To make matters worse, researchers have also pointed out that in order for employees to experience burnout, they have to have been 'on fire' at some stage, meaning that often the most ambitious and enthusiastic sales reps are those most likely to experience the condition. Table 17.1, adapted from Singh et al.'s (1994) measurement scales, may help Sales Managers and employees to evaluate their current level of 'burnout proneness'. It is a diagnostic, not a clinical tool; while there is no benchmark as to what score may be considered particularly high, filling out this short survey periodically may help salespeople and their managers diagnose changes in perceived emotional pressures on particular individuals and develop early detection strategies to alleviate them.

| Table 17.1 | Self-test: are you or your salespeople in danger of experiencing burnout? |

Please answer the following questions by ticking the most appropriate box:	Is very unlike me	Is somewhat unlike me	Is somewhat like me	Is very much like me
Working with customers is really a strain for me.				
I feel I am working too hard for my customers.				
I feel a lack of personal concern for my customers.				
Working directly with my boss puts too much stress on me.				
I feel emotionally drained by the pressure my boss puts on me.				
I feel frustrated because of working directly with co-workers.				
I feel I work too hard trying to satisfy co-workers.				
I feel dismayed by the actions of top management.				
I feel burned out from trying to meet top management's expectations.				
I feel alienated from top management.				

Source: adapted from Singh et al. (1994), p. 568.

Salespeople's behaviours

This section will explore what salespeople can be observed to do in their daily work, and how these behaviours in turn impact upon and are impacted by the other elements of the model presented in Figure 17.1. A recent study of what salespeople do revealed a staggering 105 different activities routinely engaged in (Moncrief et al. 2006)! These behaviours can be categorized into the indicative customer- and non-customer-facing dimensions shown in Figure 17.2.

It needs to be pointed out that some estimates have indicated that the average business-to-business salesperson may spend as little as 20 per cent of their working time engaging in customer-facing activities. Salespeople often deeply resent this perceived waste of their 'productive time'. For management, two messages can be taken from the fragile balance depicted in Figure 17.2 – first, that the balance should ideally be tipped towards customer-facing behaviours; and, second, that activities such as travel, training or office work can be made much more efficient by a well-thought out management control system and good back-office support.

In the remainder of this section, we will discuss in more detail how the main customer-facing sales activities, namely selling and relationship-building and maintenance, can be made more effective. Judging from an extensive body of literature

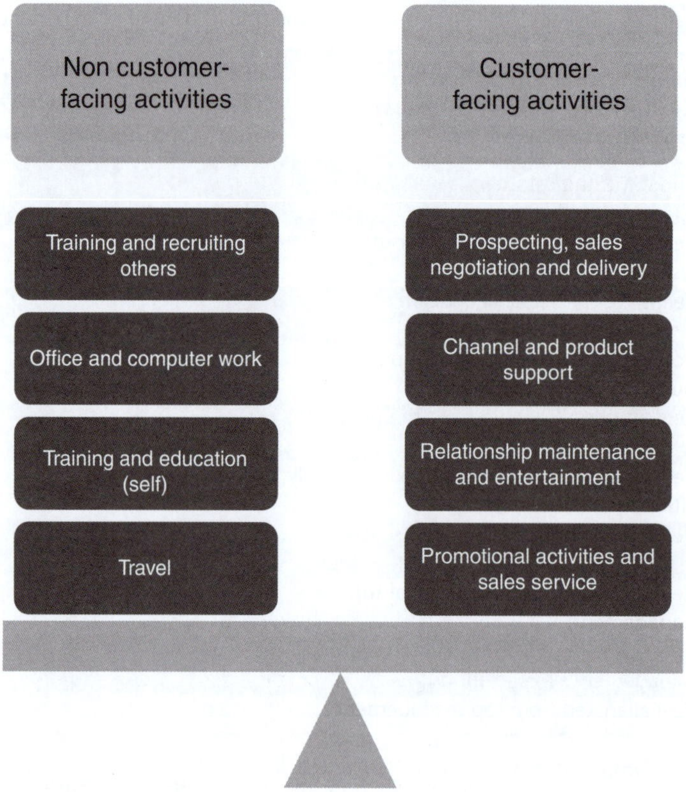

Figure 17.2 Dimensions of sales activities
Source: author, adapted from Moncrief et al. (2006).

in these areas, much can be learned about how to engage in these activities by thinking through the following three questions:

1. How can our salespeople be more adaptive in their customer interactions?
2. What is the most appropriate balance between customer- and selling-oriented behaviours for our selling context?
3. How does relationship-building happen, and how can salespeople contribute to relationship development at each stage?

We will now discuss each of these three questions, drawing on existing research evidence, in turn.

Adaptive selling behaviours

In line with our previous discussion of the knowledge structure within a sales organization, it seems that some salespeople are more adept than others at altering their behaviour in different selling situations or from customer to customer. Simply put, some salespeople seem to use the same approach no matter which customer they find themselves in front of, while others seem able to adapt their body language, manner of speaking or sales presentation in response to situational requirements. More precisely, those salespeople with an interest in learning are also the most likely to practice adaptive selling (Weitz et al.1986), which underlines the need for Sales Managers to evaluate the cognitive flexibility of potential employees during the recruitment process. Sales Managers should also know that training can help salespeople recognize the need to adapt their selling behaviours and teach them what clues to look for when deciding on a situation-specific approach. Rather than telling them simply to dump their 'canned' presentations and 'be adaptive', however, it is advisable that training demonstrates how and in what aspects of their behaviours salespeople may find it worthwhile to be adaptive. Figure 17.3 points to four areas where salespeople can fruitfully adapt their behaviours to client or contextual clues – information provision, solution provision, communication approach and sales process. It is easy to see how such adaptation can be particularly important in international selling contexts or in environments with very diverse customer bases.

Training for adaptive selling can also be used to change salespeople's attributions or perceptions of the causes of failures in their current selling approaches. If they can be convinced that a change in their selling style may influence future sales outcomes positively, they are more likely to attempt to practise adaptive selling in future sales calls. This sales management investment in training and recruitment seems to be worth the effort: a recent meta-analysis of research into adaptive selling behaviours (Franke and Park 2006) clearly demonstrated that salespeople who practise adaptive selling not only enjoy their jobs more than those who deliver the same presentation again and again, they are also the better performers.

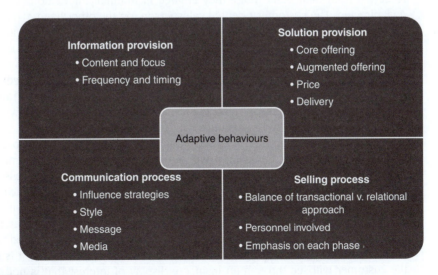

Figure 17.3   Facets of adaptive selling
Source: adapted from Eckert (2006).

Customer- versus selling-oriented behaviours

At the risk of simplification, how salespeople approach their customers can be categorized into transactional behaviours that follow the traditional prospecting schema with a strong focus on closing the sale, and customer-oriented behaviours that focus on servicing the client and increasing customer satisfaction.

In transactional selling, the salesperson's task is to present the product or service in such a light that her own belief in it spills over to the customer. In this situation, assertiveness and self-confidence are key characteristics for salespeople and they also need to have a strong belief in being able to be in control of the situation and its potential outcome. Customer-oriented behaviours, on the other hand, depart from the stereotype of the 'pushy' salesperson who is only interested in closing the sale. Rather than just selling a product, the customer-oriented salesperson positions herself as a reliable service partner, and her overriding goal is to achieve customer satisfaction. Examples of this type of behaviour would be helping customers to achieve their goals, assessing customer needs and low-pressure selling. From a skills perspective, while communication is important in both selling modes, in transactional selling, salespeople need to focus their communication skills on delivering a convincing argument; in customer-oriented selling, they need to practise listening behaviours in order to pick up on the subtle feedback that signals customer needs and opportunities to develop the customer relationship. Customer-oriented sellers also need to be able to practise adaptive selling and to be empathic.

The two selling approaches harbour different potential psychological and performance challenges for salespeople. Salespeople who engage in transactional behaviours may have to contend with frequent rejection, but may also be rewarded by the 'thrill' of the chase and successfully hunting down new customers. At the same time, there are few non-economic gains the transactional salesperson can or wants to derive from their behaviours; they engage in minimal interactions that are non-goal directed. The customer-oriented salesperson, on the other hand, typically adopts a long-term perspective, often foregoing immediate economic gains for both long-term gains and non-economic rewards such as satisfaction and social benefits derived from their behaviours. To put it simply, if a (customer-oriented) salesperson invests a great deal of effort in getting to know and understand a customer and her needs, then any rejection on the part of the client also implies personal rejection. If a (transactional) salesperson faces too frequent rejections, her fundamental belief in her own skills may be at risk, and she may start avoiding such situations in the future.

Indeed, questions have been raised about whether salespeople who simply display customer-oriented behaviours without believing in customer-orientation as a modus operandi or actually liking to deal with customers can be successful in generating customer satisfaction (Stock and Hoyer 2005), which would indicate that the three elements – behaviours, knowledge and emotions – have to be aligned for a customer-oriented selling 'mode' to be effective. Stock and Hoyer's research cautions managers against compelling salespeople to engage in customer-oriented behaviours without fostering customer-oriented beliefs and emotions in them, as it is likely that the customer will see through an insincere display of interest that is not backed up by an underlying customer-oriented mindset. Managers are thus encouraged to filter

Table 17.2   Customer orientation versus selling orientation

	Customer-oriented selling	**Sales-oriented selling**
Perspective	Long-term	Short-term
Object	Latent customer preferences	Articulated customer preferences
Means	Listening to customers; dialogue	Convincing customers; monologue (sales presentation)
Success derived from (possible key performance indicators)	Customer satisfaction; intrinsic rewards	Sales volume; margin; extrinsic recognition
Indicative behaviours	Discussing customers' needs, helping customers achieve their goals; building on the quality of the customer relationship	Presentation and demonstration of product or service; negotiation; closing

Source: author.

potential employees not only for those candidates who display the right behaviours, but also for those who genuinely like dealing with customers.

In terms of performance, it should be mentioned that research has been surprisingly ambiguous in relating either customer or sales orientation to job performance. Contrary to many expectations, sales orientation does not seem to impact job performance negatively – the 'pushy' salesperson does not seem to frighten customers away. Likewise, while many studies have indicated that customer-oriented salespeople are stronger performers, recently researchers have demonstrated that these effects may only be visible in the long term (Jaramillo and Grisaffe 2009).

Table 17.2 compares customer- and sales-oriented behaviours for a range of relevant dimensions. This table may help managers analyse which behaviours (or indeed which balance of behaviours) is appropriate in the different selling contexts faced by their sales forces. Such an analysis will also help managers assign the right people to the different facets of the sales job and give them an indication of examples of key performance indicators for each type of behaviour.

Relationship-building behaviours

In their seminal paper on buyer-seller relationships, Dwyer et al.(1987) liken the development of buyer-seller relationships to a marriage, with a courtship phase including awareness and exploration, followed by an expansion and a commitment phase, which in most cases will eventually be succeeded by a dissolution phase. Attempting to follow such a relationship trajectory, illustrated in Figure 17.4, salespeople have to engage in very different behaviours depending on the stage the buyer-seller relationship is going through (which again reinforces the importance of adapting one's selling approach to the given situation). In the courtship phase, for instance, the seller's main tasks are to appear as an attractive relationship partner to his counterpart, which, according to Dwyer et al., requires a certain amount of 'posturing' activities.

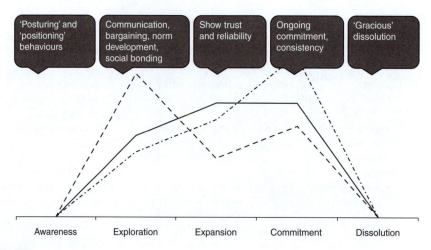

| 'Posturing' and 'positioning' behaviours | Communication, bargaining, norm development, social bonding | Show trust and reliability | Ongoing commitment, consistency | 'Gracious' dissolution |

Awareness   Exploration   Expansion   Commitment   Dissolution

Figure 17.4 Hypothetical relationship trajectories and selling behaviours
Source: author, adapted from Dwyer et al. (1987).

Once the possibility of a relationship is being considered in earnest by both partners, the seller has to engage in significant amounts of communication and bargaining, which may include revealing some important information of one's own agenda in exchange for receiving information about the buyer's needs, and the demonstration of effort to engage in the relationship. Such 'exploratory' behaviours are followed by the establishment of mutually acceptable patterns of behaviour and standards of conduct – the seller for instance has to establish a clear call pattern, open lines of communication and set common goals. In the expansion phase of the relationship, both parties need to prove to the other that they can successfully fulfill their relational commitment; demonstrations of both reliability and trustworthiness are required from a salesperson during this phase. Reliability can be demonstrated, for instance, by timely delivery of products and services and cost control; trustworthiness can be instilled by what Doyle and Roth (1992) call the five 'trust builders' – candour/truth; predictability of actions; competence displays; intent and responsiveness; and likability.

In the commitment phase, sellers have to demonstrate to their buyers that they are consistent in their behaviour over the longer term. They also need to engage in actions that signal their willingness for relational continuity – frequent after-sales visits, courtesy calls or customer education newsletters are examples of behaviours that sellers engage in to maintain and nurture their seller-buyer relationships. Finally, while astute conflict management and acknowledgement of any problems in the relationship may prolong the engagement, if and when it comes to the dissolution phase, sellers need to devise strategies for disengagement that enable both parties to emerge with the least amount of damage possible from the 'break-up'. If the dissolution is passed off with a minimum amount of harm for both parties, it may even leave the door open for future re-engagements. Managers need to note however that termination of such relationships almost always acts as a significant source of psychological, emotional and physical stress.

Managing salespeople in the long run: coping mechanisms and self-help strategies

Managing salespeople's reactions to successes and failures

According to some learning theories, human beings learn as a direct response to rewards and punishments experienced in the past. Unfortunately, this learning is not always accurate in its inference of cause-effect relationships, as attribution theory teaches us. The basic idea behind this theory is that the attributions for successes and failures that an individual makes will influence his or her expectations of future success and failure and therefore subsequent behaviour. For instance, an unsuccessful sales call may be attributed to an external cause and therefore appear outside the control of the salesperson, in which case she is likely to avoid similar situations in the future, or it may be attributed to the salesperson's own mistakes, in which case the cause may appear controllable and lead her to work smarter in the future. Dixon et al. (2001) demonstrate that in sales the main causes for sales call success or failure are often seen to be effort, ability, task, strategy or luck (or lack thereof). While perceived internal causes for failure such as lack of effort or ability often lead to increased effort or the seeking of assistance, and therefore to positive behavioural intentions, external attributions such as 'the job was too difficult' or 'the client was impossible to deal with' can lead to salespeople avoiding a similar situation in the future. Interestingly, salespeople appear to be much less inclined to attribute their failures to external forces than other professional groups that have been studied, which may be an indication of the self-motivating and self-reliant nature of many sales personnel. Where however a salesperson sees an external cause for her failure, management needs to help the salesperson unravel the situation and assess objectively which factors may have contributed to the lack of success in that particular instance, and how those causes can be remedied should a similar situation arise again. Such managerial intervention is especially important for less experienced salespeople who are both more likely to experience failure and who may be less adept at correctly identifying the causes of their failures. Dixon et al. (2001) recommend that managers conduct debriefs with salespeople after unsuccessful sales calls to find out what they see as the causes for this outcome and what future actions they intend to take with regard to this or similar situations. Managers can then either reinforce correct attributions and ensuing plans of action or offer assistance in identifying the correct causes for lack of success and the appropriate actions to take in the future. Such a process can also enable salespeople to deepen their self-knowledge and lessen the negative emotional response to failure. The well-being audit at the end of this chapter gives Sales Managers a check-list to enable them to assess whether salespeople have developed adequate response mechanisms to deal with their successes and failures.

It is imperative for Sales Managers to be aware of the potential negative effects of successive failures for salespeople in combination with other stressors. While disappointment can never be completely avoided, in order to alleviate additional stressors and reduce the possibility for burnout, managers should also:

- manage role knowledge and the role expectations of their employees;
- communicate a clear and realistic set of performance indicators;

- boost salespeople's belief in their self-efficacy, that is the belief that they can master the situations they are exposed to with the internal and external resources they have at their disposal;
- prevent feelings of powerlessness by offering training in time management and personal effectiveness;
- provide social outlets for negative *and* positive emotional experiences through team meetings or other community of practice tools as detailed below.

Self-management for well-being and success

Self-management can be defined as the efforts of an individual to exert control over certain aspects of her decision-making and behaviour. It is a set of behavioural and cognitive strategies that assists individuals in structuring their environment (at work or elsewhere), establishing self-motivation and increasing performance. It is worth pointing out that while every professional practises self-management, not everyone is effective at doing so and some individuals may engage in dysfunctional self-management. Fortunately, because self-management is learned, individuals can enhance their performance through self-management training. For sales executives, one of the first steps of effective self-management is to develop a set of sound cognitive and emotional responses to everyday successes and failures.

Thought self-leadership is a strategy explained by Godwin et al. (1999) as a way of improving one's goal attainment, which can be applied by sales executives and managers in order to improve their self-knowledge. According to the authors, thought self-leadership strategies include self-management of:

- one's beliefs and assumptions, particularly self-deprecating and destructive beliefs;
- self-dialogue, or what we tell ourselves;
- mental imagery.

When practising thought self-leadership, a salesperson needs to examine, first, where potential negative beliefs and assumptions come from and to understand that black-and-white thinking can never represent an objective evaluation of her performance. She then has to stop negative self-dialogue and turn it into constructive self-talk. Finally, positive mental imagery, as used by many successful sportspeople, can be utilized to visualize the salesperson closing the sale or being in the presence of a satisfied customer.

Another important learning methodology for salespeople is to develop *stress management* responses. Stress will be present when there is a disjunction between the pressures that are put on an individual (the 'stressors') and the individual's ability to cope with them. While in a sales environment external pressures cannot always be reduced in the short term, salespeople can learn appropriate responses to short-time stress. Sometimes, they may even be able to re-appraise stress as something challenging and positive, rather than debilitating. Stress management strategies that may be developed include: ·

- *'Time off'*: while many salespeople and Sales Managers feel they need to be on call virtually 24 hours a day, it is important to be able to switch off from the job demands at some stage. If an employee works from home, switching off the business telephone line after official work hours or applying an 'email curfew' are good strategies to keep personal and work life separate. Taking regular holidays also improves our ability to cope with stress.

- *Maintaining a healthy lifestyle*: relaxation techniques, exercise, regular spa visits and healthy food may not be miracle tools that solve all of the problems a salesperson may have, but it will give her a better basis from which to deal with the stresses of the job.

- *Keeping a stress-free environment*: most humans feel stressed when they feel out of control of a situation. Keeping on top of paper work, practising time management and maintaining an uncluttered office environment will all help a salesperson to feel a little more in control of her working day and can be incorporated into sales training.

- *Maintaining perspective*: it is easy to lose perspective of the enjoyable aspects of the job when the going gets tough. While one does not have to practice blind optimism, it is healthy to try to put recent failures into perspective with the positive sides of the sales career, such as the latitude of freedom enjoyed or the range of interesting people one can meet.

- *Finding solutions to problems*: while a tendency to 'flight' rather than 'fight' may be a natural response to stressful situations, problems seldom go away if ignored. If a customer seems intent on making one's life a misery, it may be time to call for assistance or coaching from a peer or from a manager the salesperson trusts. If a sales quota seems unattainable, it may help to understand why it has been set so high, and to see if it can be renegotiated. Again, facing problems will help salespeople to feel more in control of their own destinies.

Communities of practice as a means for salespeople to self-manage

We have seen throughout this chapter that salespeople do not always have an easy job. Rejection and disappointment are part of their daily existence, pressure is usually high and, to top it all, salespeople are often physically, socially and psychologically disconnected from back-office functions. As practitioners know all too well, the sales existence can be a very lonely one. In the typical sales dyad, the sales professional faces the task of developing client relationships in an environment devoid of immediate external feedback. Even though the Sales Manager generally provides a certain amount of professional and moral back-up, sales executives may be afraid to share all their experiences – bad and good – with their immediate superior. Therefore, for many sales representatives, their sales team provides a valuable support network. Similarly to the sports teams analogy drawn upon in Chapter 13, for salespeople the sales team represents quite literally a 'home base' where other individuals understand one's experiences and frustrations, and where they can share them openly and honestly.

Many sales teams make a point of meeting up regularly even if the individual sales executives are geographically dispersed. During such meetings they can discuss their activities and client dealings, vent their anger over 'unreasonable' customers and share anecdotes about competitors' activities. Facing their clients on their own throughout most of their working days, it appears that individuals almost intuitively resort to their peers for moral and professional support, thereby establishing what Geiger and Turley (2005) describe as a 'community of practice' in sales. Simply put, many sales executives create a 'family' for themselves among their colleagues and thus obtain a psychological support structure and a vital coping mechanism, offering each other moral support and nurturing. From management's perspective, it is important to realize that such forums are more than just a way of letting off steam or a potential breeding ground for team unrest; they are, above all, a useful vehicle for the transfer of selling skills and tactics and for sharing the 'tacit' customer knowledge that is so hard to elicit through technological means. These communities can thus represent a central ingredient not only for the long-term well-being of the salesperson, but also for organizational learning and peer leadership. While Sales Managers may refrain from actively participating in these informal forums, they should make sure that employees have the time and whereabouts to meet regularly with their peers. Facilitating informal meetings is especially important in sales teams that are geographically dispersed. Managers need to keep in mind that if salespeople do not have access to their own colleagues, they may turn to other support structures – family, friends, competitor salespeople or even customers – for moral support, which may loosen their organizational affiliation and even be counter-productive in some instances.

CASE PROBLEM REVISITED

Case conclusion

After answering Patricia's phone call, Ben sat still for a while. He knew that the loss of this tender was devastating not only for his own sales quota, but also that it would be a real blow to the company. Fortunately, after the first high-profile account losses, Kyona's Marketing and Sales Director Paul Quigley had foreseen what consequences this might have for the individual account managers. While the money was not there to pay for expensive stress management training, Paul had called all of his reps in for a chat. He had explained that the economic situation might generate difficulties for the firm as well as for individuals, but that under his watch nobody would be left to deal with them on their own. As far as he was concerned, he would not tolerate a culture of blame or shame. He had exhorted his reps to engage in peer reviews of individual successes and failures – while Paul jokingly called these 'group therapy sessions', his long experience in the selling field had taught him just how important such peer support could be. Thinking about Paul's pep talk, Ben picked up the phone again, this time dialling Paul's number. 'Paul, I think I need a chat'. He knew his boss would be less than happy about the news, but he also knew that he would do his best to help Ben over this disappointment and do better next time. After all, in sales, there's always a 'next time'!

Summary

In order to achieve sustained individual and organizational performance it is important for managers to consider the realities of salespeople's existence 'at the coal face' in detail. This reality is often characterized by a high performance, high pressure environment that makes significant demands upon salespeople's emotional, cognitive and behavioural resources. This chapter has outlined a number of issues that may help

Sales Managers and salespeople alike to analyse behavioural patterns and change behavioural responses for the better by considering the close interaction between salespeople's knowledge, emotions and behaviours. In other words, if Sales Managers want to foster a positive work attitude that leads to positive organizational outcomes such as high performance, loyalty to the firm and citizenship behaviours, they should make sure salespeople have a constructive outlet for all those emotions that are part of the sales existence, and that salespeople's thoughts and behaviours are aligned. They should also make sure their employees understand the basic notions of self-management for well-being. Most importantly, they should consider how a community spirit may be fostered within the sales force, which can go a long way towards nurturing the positive aspects *and* perhaps counterbalance some of the more negative components of the sales existence 'at the coal face'.

Key points

1. While many motivational theories only consider cognitive elements, salespeople's emotions will strongly influence their performance levels and goal attainment. Three emotional management issues of importance are empathy, sales call anxiety and burnout.
2. Salespeople's customer knowledge and beliefs about their customers will have an important influence on how they behave towards them.
3. A good level of self-knowledge is a necessary basis for other knowledge. Salespeople may choose to practice thought self-leadership to deepen their self-knowledge and channel it constructively.
4. Role knowledge can influence the extent to which salespeople are prone to role stresses. Salespeople need to be clear about what is expected from them; to be able to voice any conflicts they perceive in their roles; and, over the long term, to be sheltered from chronic role overload.
5. Sales orientation and customer orientation require different behaviours from a salesperson; these behaviours need to be in line with a sales- or customer-oriented mindset and attitude and the personal and professional goals that a salesperson is trying to attain.
6. In building customer relationships, salespeople need to adopt different behaviours at different stages of the relationship trajectory. They will also need to tap into different psychological resources. The longer a relationship lasts, the greater the potential for emotional distress when it dissolves.
7. Salespeople and Sales Managers alike have to work together to create a healthy work environment. This includes self-management strategies, but also the establishment of peer support groups (or 'communities of practice') and an education in stress management techniques.
8. Sales management needs to create a culture that is supportive both of the successes and of the failures of sales executives. An overly competitive 'blame and shame' culture is not conducive to salespeople's well-being.

A well-being audit for Sales Managers and personnel

Managers may use this check-list as a 'health check' to assess areas where individual and organizational performance may suffer because salespeople's beliefs, emotions and behaviours are unaligned. They may also use this checklist as a tool to align their management systems with their sales staff's day-to-day reality of selling.

- *Job analysis*

  Are sales staff's responsibilities unambiguous?

  Is there any conflict between what salespeople feel is expected from them by their superior and what their customers want or need?

  Are salespeople overwhelmed by their jobs or their quotas?

- *Behavioural analysis*

  Are goals, behaviours and mindsets aligned? If salespeople are asked to be customer-oriented, do management allow them the space to get to know their customers, and reward such behaviour?

  Are salespeople displaying behaviours that are in line with the developmental phase of the client relationship?

  Do salespeople know how and what parts of their interactions they can adapt to individual customer requirements?

  Do salespeople have appropriate behavioural responses after failures?

- *Cognitive analysis*

  Are there feedback mechanisms for salespeople's product and market knowledge to other parts of the company, and vice versa?

  Are salespeople recognized for feeding customer, product and market information back?

  Are salespeople aware of their customer knowledge?

  Do they use this knowledge to improve their relationships with customers?

  Are they aware of their own strengths and weaknesses?

  Do they have an adequate perception of their role and responsibilities?

- *Emotional analysis*

  Do salespeople have the opportunity to talk about both successes and failures?

  Is there a culture in the sales force that is supportive to the individual?

  Do managers perceive their role as developmental rather than punitive?

  Are there mechanisms for the sales force to get together informally?

- *Well-being analysis*

  Are salespeople encouraged to practise well-being techniques?

  Are there discounts offered to employees for gym memberships?

  Could there be a regular seminar series or self-help instructions for stress management, time management, healthy eating or relaxation techniques?

References

Brown, S.P., Cron, W.L. and Slocum, J.W. Jr (1997) 'Effects of Goal-Directed Emotions on Salesperson Volitions, Behavior, and Performance: A Longitudinal Study', *Journal of Marketing*, 61 (1): 39–50.

Dixon, A.L., Spiro, R.L. and Jamil, M. (2001) 'Successful and Unsuccessful Sales Calls: Measuring Salesperson Attributions and Behavioral Intentions', *Journal of Marketing*, 65 (3): 64–78.

Doyle, S.X. and Roth, G.T. (1992) 'Selling and Sales Management in Action: The Use of Insight and Coaching to Improve Relationship Selling', *Journal of Personal Selling and Sales Management*, 12 (1): 59–64.

Dwyer, F.R., Schurr, P.H. and Oh, S. (1987) 'Developing Buyer-Seller Relationships', *Journal of Marketing*, 51 (2): 11–27.

Eckert, J.A. (2006) 'Adaptive Selling Behavior: Adding Depth and Specificity to the Range of Adaptive Outcomes', *Mid-American Journal of Business*, 21 (1): 31–9.

Fishbein, M. and Ajzen, I. (1975) *Belief, Attitude,Iintention, and Behavior: An introduction to Theory and Research*. Reading, MA: Addison-Wesley.

Franke, G.R. and Park, J.-E. (2006) 'Salesperson Adaptive Selling Behavior and Customer Orientation: A Meta-Analysis', *Journal of Marketing Research*, 43 (4): 693–702.

Geiger S. and Finch, J. (2009) 'Industrial Sales People as Market Actors', *Industrial Marketing Management*, 38 (6): 608–17.

Geiger, S. and Turley, D. (2005) 'Personal Selling as a Knowledge-based Activity: Communities of Practice in the Sales Force', *Irish Journal of Management*, 26 (1): 61–70.

Godden, L. (2004) *ZenWise Selling – Mindful Methods to Improve Your Sales…and Your Self*. Signal Hill, CA: Telsius Publishing.

Godwin, J.L., Neck, C.P. and Houghton, J.D. (1999) 'The Impact of Thought Self-Leadership on Individual Goal performance: A Cognitive Perspective', *Journal of Management Development*, 18 (2): 153–69.

Jaramillo, F. and Grisaffe, D.B. (2009) 'Does Customer Orientation Impact Objective Sales Performance? Insights from a Longitudinal Model in Direct Selling', *Journal of Personal Selling and Sales Management*, 29 (2): 167–78.

McBane, D.A. (1995) 'Empathy and the Salesperson: A Multidimensional Perspective', *Psychology and Marketing*, 12 (4): 349–70.

Moncrief, W.C., Marshall, G.W. and Lassk, F.G. (2006) 'A Contemporary Taxonomy of Sales Positions', *Journal of Personal Selling and Sales Management*, 26 (1): 55–65.

Reday, P.A., Marshall, R. and Parasuraman, A. (2009) 'An Interdisciplinary Approach to Assessing the Characteristics and Sales Potential of Modern Salespeople', *Industrial Marketing Management*, 38 (7): 838–44.

Singh, J. (1998) 'Striking a Balance in Boundary-spanning Positions: An Investigation of Some Unconventional Influences of Role Stressors and Job Characteristics on Job Outcomes of Salespeople', *Journal of Marketing*, 62 (3): 69–86.

Singh, J., Goolsby, J.R. and Rhoads, G.K. (1994) 'Behavioral and Psychological Consequences of Boundary-spanning Burnout for Customer Service Representatives', *Journal of Marketing Research*, 31 (4): 558–69.

Stock, R.M. and Hoyer, W. (2005) 'An Attitude-Behavior Model of Salespeople's Customer Orientation', *Journal of the Academy of Marketing Science*, 33 (4): 536–52.

Turley, D. and Geiger, S. (2006) 'Exploring Salesperson Learning in the Client Relationship Nexus', *European Journal of Marketing*, 40 (5/6): 662–81.

Verbeke, W. and Bagozzi, R.P. (2000) 'Sales Call Anxiety: Exploring What It Means When Fear Rules a Sales Encounter', *Journal of Marketing*, 64 (3): 88–101.

Weitz, B.A., Sujan, H. and Sujan, M. (1986) 'Knowledge, Motivation, and Adaptive Behavior: A Framework for Improving Selling Effectiveness', *Journal of Marketing*, 50 (4): 174–91.

Further reading

Artis, A.B. and Harris, E.G. (2007) 'Self-directed Learning and Sales Force Performance: An Integrated Framework', *Journal of Personal Selling and Sales Management*, 27 (1): 9–24.

Ashkanasy, N.M. and Daus, C.S. (2002) 'Emotion in the Workplace: The New Challenge for Managers', *The Academy of Management Executive*, 16 (1): 76-86.

Babakus, E., Cravens, D.W., Johnston, M. and Moncrief, W.C. (1999) 'The Role of Emotional Exhaustion in Sales Force Attitude and Behavior Relationships', *Journal of the Academy of Marketing Science*, 27 (1): 58–70.

Cooper, R.K. and Sawaf, A. (1998) *Executive EQ: Emotional Intelligence in Leadership and Organizations*. New York: Perigee.

Part six
Evaluation of the sales force

18
Sales organization performance and evaluation

Paolo Guenzi and Susi Geiger

Contents

Learning objectives

After reading this chapter, you should be able to:

• Integrate the points made in the previous chapters into the sales management process model presented in the Introduction.

• Understand the multitude of factors that influence sales performance.

• Discuss the advantages and disadvantages of traditional models of performance analysis in sales that centre on financial contributions.

• Design a balanced score-card for your sales organization.

Chapter outline

Sales performance is largely the result of a sales organization's ability consistently to manage a number of interdependent decisions, especially the ones shown in the model adopted in this book (see Figure I.1 in the Introduction). We introduce this chapter by first looking at a real-world example of how sales force evaluation should be used to help salespeople improve their performance and hence increase overall sales organization success. Second, the multifaceted nature of sales performance is discussed. Third, the need for a more comprehensive approach to the understanding and management of sales success is emphasized. From this perspective, special attention is given to the notion of developing a balanced score-card approach to sales performance evaluation. Finally, several key points are offered.

Evaluating sales performance at Bearzot Italy[1]

Adriano Pirlo, Industry Division Manager at Bearzot Italy, was analysing the performance of his sales force. He wanted to understand how best to assess performance in order to provide each member of his sales force with specific feedback and implement individualized coaching for them. Furthermore, he wanted to identify potential organizational improvements in terms of both the efficiency and the effectiveness of his salespeople. He was convinced that the best way to increase efficiency was to optimize the allocation of sales force time and that achieving maximum effectiveness lay in the proper allocation of sales force skills to the right customers and prospects. Pirlo had collected much data to work on. He had to find the best method to use it.

The company

With sales above $6 billion per year, Bearzot is the global leader in the specialty chemicals sector. The company has more than 20,000 employees worldwide and serves customers in more than 160 countries across North America, Europe, Australasia, Latin America, the Middle East and Africa, delivering comprehensive programmes and services to customers in many different industries. With more than 14,000 sales and service experts, Bearzot employs the industry's largest and best-trained direct sales and service force, which advises and assists customers in meeting their operational needs.

Sales management at Bearzot

The Industry Division of Bearzot provides programmes that address customer needs in the areas of production safety and security, operational efficiency and end-user customer satisfaction. Its comprehensive approach includes plant-wide solutions, a broad range of chemical treatments, feeding systems, equipment and services. The sales force is a typical business-to-business one made up of highly qualified individuals who are able to identify and address customers' process problems by delivering value-adding solutions through chemicals, equipment and services that improve and, at the same time, make customers' production processes safer, cost-effective and more reliable.

Every customer has different industrial needs and several solutions can be provided at different points of the production process. It is possible that Bearzot and its competitors may sell different solutions to the same customer for different parts of the production process, depending on the ability of the different companies' salespeople and solutions to meet the customer's specific requirements and the value they expect.

In such a complex business, the sales cycle for gaining new accounts is normally quite long (6 to 12 months). Effective execution and management of the whole sales process is critical in order to achieve consistent and repeatable sales success in this business sector.

The typical sales cycle in this industry involves four steps, each of which can last some months (see Figure 18.1). First, in the relating phase, the salesperson will gain the customer's trust. Next, in the discovering phase, the salesperson will come to understand and agree with the customer the nature of their technical problem or need. Then, in the promoting phase, Bearzot's solution is proposed and, finally, in the support phase, the salesperson puts in place the solution and monitors it to ensure the desired results are obtained and that the purchase is repeated.

---

[1] The name of the company has been disguised to preserve anonymity.

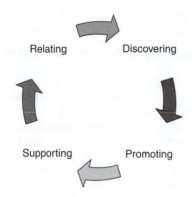

Figure 18.1 The typical sales process at Bearzot

The rate of success in gaining new business depends on market conditions, the sales situation, the salesperson's experience and their individual performance. On average, only 15 per cent of the potential chemical solutions, also known as applications, identified for qualified prospects are turned into new business. The average value of each application in the industry is €8,000 per annum and each customer may have several applications needs in the production process and therefore different sales potential.

Pirlo believed that the sales performance of each salesperson in such a business environment was typically the consequence of three main drivers: technical competence, sales skills and planning ability. Just as in any other company, the salespeople at Bearzot pursue two main goals:

1. to maximize revenue from existing customers;
2. systematically to identify and manage new prospects.

To accomplish these, the sales person has to execute both service calls (mainly aimed at fostering customer satisfaction and consequently repurchasing behaviours from existing customers) and sales calls (mainly to ensure organic sales growth).

Sales management goals in this business focus on driving the efficiency of the sales force by controlling the number of service calls to maintain the existing business and driving the efficacy

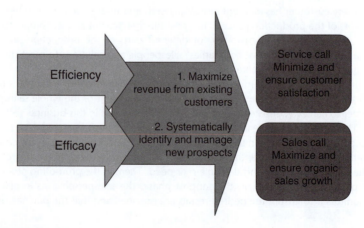

Figure 18.2 Efficiency and efficacy goals for the sales force at Bearzot

of the sales force by maximizing sales calls to gain new business from the competition (see Figure 18.2).

Bearzot is a very sales-focused company and every salesperson in the Division knows that ensuring sales growth of 10 per cent over the prior year is one of the requirements for being considered a Top Performer and rising up the ladder in the company. In designing the reporting systems, Pirlo had adopted a number of tools to help salespeople reach their individual targets and, at the same time, enable Field Management to monitor their activities and achieve the necessary efficiency and effectiveness in the sales force. He believed that by identifying the most important behaviours that lead to sales results, his Field Sales Managers could make better business decisions and provide effective coaching for salespeople.

Introduction: evaluating sales success

This book has introduced readers to a variety of issues that are pertinent to sales organizations in the twenty-first century, from 'how to change an organization without interrupting it too much' to 'what makes a healthy work environment for salespeople', and introducing many managerial processes and models along the way. Throughout the chapters, one question has reappeared continually, namely 'What makes a sales organization successful?'. While we do not claim to have a definitive answer to this holy grail of sales management issues, in this final chapter we will bring together the opinions of various authors in this book and prior research on sales force performance issues in an attempt to answer this question and draw some conclusions.

Figure I.1 in the Introduction is the overall theoretical and procedural model that has guided us through this book. Collectively, the authors of the chapters have shown that sales success needs to be based on a strategically sound foundation: an organization that keeps adapting to changing external and internal circumstances, an organization where individual departments pull in the same direction, where management systems and salespeople's responsibilities and latitudes are designed with a strategic perspective and with a view to maximizing customer value, and an organization where ethical decision-making is paid more than lip service. Once this foundation has been laid, a sales organization then needs to decide on the structure that best fits its specific selling environment. Structural decisions need to be made on how many salespeople to employ, how to organize the sales force at home and abroad and how to allocate the sales effort. After that, processes need to be put into place for adequate leadership regimes, the recruitment and training of salespeople, the best possible motivation and compensation systems and planning and control systems that monitor the ongoing performance of both the processes and the people involved. Finally, it is vital to consider the circumstances of the people at the coal face, their skills, motivations, perceptions, knowledge and feelings, and how these elements influence and are in turn influenced by their behaviours.

If a sales organization adopts the procedural model suggested in this book, it thus needs to engage in a considerable amount of planning, strategy-setting and reflecting upon its own performance, something which is often anathema in a highly pressurized world where structures frequently grow organically, processes are adopted on an ad hoc basis and often in a reactive manner and salespeople are left to figure out the best way forward on the job. The question therefore arises as to whether the managerial time and effort that needs to be spent on building up a sales force strategically is worth it – in other words, will the firm's performance and non-performance related outcomes be any better?

The general goal of sales force performance evaluation is to identify the reasons behind a salesperson's success or failure. This understanding is the precondition for designing and implementing corrective plans when needed and for crafting appropriate coaching interventions.

Evaluating sales force performance is certainly a critical process, since it affects reward allocation and hence the motivation of salespeople. Additionally, evaluation is often the starting point for making a number of important sales management decisions, such as career promotions, the choice of recruitment criteria and the identification of training needs. However, companies commonly do not devote enough resources to evaluation processes, as demonstrated by evidence that in Fortune 500 companies performance appraisal is performed in 73 per cent of cases less than twice per year, in 50 per cent of cases informally and only in 28.2 per cent of cases with a direct link with reward systems.:

Sales force performance evaluation can be based on a number of indicators. These can be divided into the main categories shown in Table 18.1.

Table 18.1   Sales performance evaluation criteria

Sales performance evaluation criteria	Examples
1) SALES OUTPUTS	
1a) Sales	Volume or value of sales, in general and/or by product/customer/channel, sales growth, new account sales, sales versus market potential, etc.
1b) Market share	Volume or value of market share, market share growth.
1c) Customers	New accounts, lost accounts, customer retention rate, etc.
1d) Profitability	Gross margin, net profit, profit as a percentage of sales, return on investment, return on sales investment etc.
1e) Orders	Number of orders, average order size.
2) SALES INPUTS	
2a) Calls	Number of calls, number of calls per customer, number of calls by customer type.
2b) Sales costs	Selling expenses, selling expenses as a percentage of revenue, average cost per call.
2c) Behavioural measures	Number of reports turned in, number of sales meetings attended, number of presentations made to customers.
2d) Time allocation	Selling versus non-selling time, time spent to plan calls.
3) QUALITATIVE MEASURES	
3a) Competencies and skills	Product knowledge, market knowledge, selling skills, communication skills, entrepreneurial spirit, creativity, time management skills, planning skills, teamwork.

Below we will discuss how sales organizations can design and use a sales-specific balanced score-card to evaluate performance. In fact, the key drivers of sales success can be better understood by combining a strategic view of the firm with an operational perspective and metrics of sales force performance. In addition, just as the central idea behind a balanced score-card approach is to draw together external and internal perspectives on a firm's success, it is also advisable to draw on different sources when appraising individual salespeople's performance. A so-called '360 degree' approach is often advocated in human resource research; this seeks to gather feedback on an employee not only from his direct superiors, but also from reporting employees, peers and, crucially for salespeople, customers. While there have been indications that such comprehensive review systems may decrease feedback effectiveness, they can be powerful tools in assessing performance from a broad perspective when designed carefully (DeNisi and Kluger 2000).

Whatever the performance criteria adopted, it is useful to emphasize five critical success factors needed to build and run successful evaluation systems:

1. *Comparability.* When evaluating salespeople, Sales Managers should try to maximize perceived fairness in the evaluation system and process. For example, in addition to considering sales outcomes, the effort needed to reach those results should ideally be taken into account. In fact, two salespeople in the same company may reach similar results, but in markedly different conditions. For example, the number and type of customers per territory (workload approach) and the geographical dispersion of customers may be very different for the two salespeople under consideration. The same may be true for the market potential in their territories. When comparing the outcomes of different salespeople, these factors should always be kept in mind. For example, sales revenue and sales growth per se are not very meaningful: their absolute value should be interpreted compared with territory potential and overall sales growth per territory (i.e. a relative measure of performance should be used).
2. *Completeness.* Using incomplete or partial measures of performance can be misleading. The number and quality of performance indicators used should allow Sales Managers to have a clear picture of their sales force's performance. In terms of the number of metrics to be used, most managers think that there should be between 3 and 5.
3. *Clarity.* From goal-setting to the provision of feedback, the evaluation system should be easy to understand and communicate to salespeople. This means that ideally the evaluation system should combine parsimony and ease of calculation with completeness.
4. *Consistency* between the evaluation criteria used and the ultimate aim of evaluation goals. For example, evaluation criteria adopted for administering short-term incentives should not be the same ones used to make decisions on career progress.
5. *Credibility* of the decision-maker.

Elements of sales organization success

Financial performance is just one, albeit the most visible and central, success criterion a sales firm may consider. Other markers of success that also contribute to the long-term viability of the firm are, for example, staff turnover and the organizational commitment of the sales force. At an individual level, managers may also regard job satisfaction, employee well-being and citizenship as indicators of success. We will now consider these elements in turn.

What influences sales performance?

In one of the most cited sales articles of all time, Churchill et al. (1985) summarized 116 research papers in a meta-analysis to find out 'The Determinants of Salesperson Performance'. Their search yielded a staggering 1,653 reported relationships between potential determinants and sales performance, which signals just how many different factors may have an impact on a firm's and an individual's sales performance! For the sake of clarity, Churchill et al. categorized this large number of potential influence factors into the following six categories:

- aptitude;
- skill levels;
- motivation;
- role perceptions;
- personal variables (e.g. appearance, education);
- organizational and environmental variables.

Although it may be questioned whether a replication of their classic study would utilize the same six factors – the sixth factor of 'organizational and environmental variables' in particular seems rather broad from a contemporary perspective – their findings provide interesting pointers in our quest to determine what makes a sales organization successful. The most dominant of their findings was that none of the six factors under study were able to explain a large variance in sales performance on its own. Clearly, this means that all of the issues discussed in this book *together* make a difference in how a sales force performs. For instance, engaging in a meticulous recruitment process utilizing personality or aptitude tests is important – but employing people with the right personalities and aptitudes needs to go hand in hand with an organizational structure that supports and nurtures these individuals. Incidentally, this contention is reinforced by the finding that those factors that can be influenced by well-thought out and job-specific human resource management – role perceptions, skills levels and motivation – had a stronger impact on performance than 'enduring' personality or aptitude factors. So it seems that salespeople are more made than born, after all!

In the light of these findings, and in keeping with many researchers and experts, we argue that salespeople's job satisfaction is an important proxy of the quality of sales management decisions and processes. In fact, job satisfaction (or dissatisfaction) is clearly affected by, for example, the quantity and quality of training received from the company, the employee's personal relationship with his/her leader/coach/supervisor, workload (i.e. by decisions on sales force size), compensation and rewards and job design (which in turn is influenced, for example, by the roles and responsibilities given to Marketing as opposed to Sales, price delegation, the adoption of KAM programmes, and so on). At the same time, many empirical studies suggest that salespeople's job satisfaction is a strong predictor of their performance in the market.

Therefore, and in a broader sense, we highlight that, in addition to the more traditional measures of market or financial performance, world class sales organizations should devote special attention to salespeople-related measures of performance. This means considering variables such as organizational commitment, turnover of personnel and organizational citizenship behaviours.

Measuring sales performance

One possible response to the Churchill et al. (1985) study could be that Sales Managers might say, 'well, if no one factor has a large impact on performance on its own, then we may just as well leave everything up to chance'. In recent recessionary times in particular, many sales organizations have realized that this is not the way forward, however. It seems that across many industries and countries, firms have become more scientific in their approach to predicting, measuring and evaluating performance. Traditionally most companies evaluated sales performance through often rather basic performance data such as revenue, volume or profit. Some companies also utilized ratio measures such as net profit margins, deducting direct selling costs from gross profits, return on capital investment (ROI) or return on assets managed (ROAM) figures. Lukes and Stanley (2004) suggested going one step further and calculating the return on sales investment (ROSI), which can include more intangible variables such as the conversion rate for a new customer or time invested per unit sale per product. Robust Customer Relationship Management (CRM) systems such as those discussed in Chapter 5 should provide the Sales Manager with the data necessary to make such more detailed performance analyses.

In the example shown in Table 18.2, for €1 spent selling into customer segment B, the firm gets a return on investment of €1.60. In contrast, €1 spent selling to customer segment A will yields a return of just over €3. This top-line financial analysis should lead the Sales Director in question into making a deeper analysis of the causes of this difference in ROSI. Could it be the sales teams' different skills or motivational levels, or is segment B simply a 'tougher' market? Upon closer inspection, the Sales Manager may find that customer segment B consists of mainly small customers who receive many visits from sales staff and who place lots of small orders with telesales reps. In this instance, the Sales Manager should in future make a concerted effort to decrease sales investment into this customer segment so as to bring it to a more sustainable level.

Many sales organizations use measures such as ROSI to calculate and evaluate sales performance. The advantage of these financial performance measures is that data on sales volume, revenue or gross profit margins are often readily available in the organization. Moreover, if such data are used to evaluate the sales force's overall performance, there is a continuity from individual level performance evaluation to the group or department level evaluation, as many salespeople continue to be evaluated mainly on financial performance figures (see Chapter 14 for a critical discussion of outcome-based control systems). Additionally, if ratio or return on investment models are used, the relationship between certain assets and performance or activities and

| **Table 18.2** | A simple customer profitability and return on sales investment calculation |

Sales investment	Customer segment A	Customer segment B
Sales Manager's time (allocated as per activity reports or timesheets)	200,000	200,000
Sales Representatives' time	600,000	950,000
Internal telesales reps' time	450,000	550,000
Support personnel's time	150,000	200,000
Overheads	350,000	350,000
Other sales-related expenses (e.g. travel)	100,000	250,000
Overall attributable sales investment	**1,850,000**	**2,500,000**
Revenue	**30,000,000**	**25,500,000**
Cost of goods sold	22,000,000	19,000,000
Gross margin	8,000,000	6,500,000
Net Profit (Loss)	**6,150,000**	**4,000,000**
Return on Sales Investment (net profit/sales investment)	**332.4%**	**160%**

performance can become visible. For instance, loss-making customers, products or territories can be identified and measures taken to remedy the problems underlying these losses. Such evaluations may even drive decisions on sales force structure change in terms, for example, of sales force size (see Chapter 9) and sales force organization (see Chapter 8).

A sales-specific balanced score-card

While detailed ROSI figures can help Sales Managers pinpoint where resources are well deployed and where changes are needed, critics of such purely financial measures have pointed out that they cannot determine the reason for weak (or indeed strong) performance, and because of their historical nature they are not very useful for predicting future performance, especially in turbulent market environments. In the past decade, many accountancy and management researchers and practitioners have therefore advocated the use of a balanced score-card (BSC) approach, and this can also be a useful performance tool in a sales context. First described by Robert Kaplan and David Norton at the Harvard Business School in 1992, the BSC approach is based on the premise that exclusive reliance on financial measures in a management system often drives behaviour that sacrifices long-term value creation for short-term success. The BSC approach advocates a broader picture of company success than just financial performance, one that is line with a firm's strategy and vision and that promotes a long-term perspective that takes into account various stakeholders.

A sales-specific BSC could for instance take into account the following factors; in the list, 'lagged' measures are those that indicate historical performance and 'leading' measures are those that are informative of future performance:

- Financial performance measures (lagged measures):

  - activity cost analysis by selling task;
  - net profit margin per product (revenue minus sales cost per unit sold);
  - market share per customer segment;
  - customer profitability (revenue minus sales cost per customer).

- Customer value measures (lagged and leading measures):

  - customer attrition rates;
  - customer lifetime value;
  - customer satisfaction;
  - relationship strength.

- Employee value measures (leading measures):

  - tender success rate;
  - employee satisfaction;
  - staff turnover;
  - organizational commitment;
  - training effectiveness,

- Ethical value measures (leading measures):

  - citizenship behaviours;
  - compliance with ethical codes of conduct.

- Internal process measures (leading measures):

  - communication efficiency inside sales force;
  - communication efficiency between Marketing and Sales;
  - communication efficiency between Sales and Operations.

Companies may add to this list any number of other criteria that are of importance in their specific environment and industry. The critical point in devising a balanced score-card is that the measures have to be in line with the corporate or business unit strategy, robust over time and objectively measurable and actionable (i.e. drive salespeople's behaviours). Most researchers suggest that a BSC with no more than 20 to 25 measures is most efficient. In selecting their specific measures, managers should keep in mind that the old business idiom 'what gets measured gets done' has been proved again and again; they are therefore advised to think carefully about the measures they include in their particular BSC. For the same reason, a sales organization's BSC also needs to be closely aligned with both its motivation, compensation and incentive systems and its control system.

In the sample list above, three measures merit further discussion because many research studies have shown them to be central indicators of management success in sales, namely staff turnover, organizational commitment and citizenship behaviours. Logic dictates that staff turnover is negatively related to organizational commitment, which in turn can positively affect citizenship behaviours. Because they are so central to sales force success and so often overlooked in sales force evaluation systems, we will now discuss these three variables in turn.

Staff turnover – a critical financial and human resource performance factor

Chapter 9 on sales force sizing emphasized just how costly a high rate of sales force turnover can be. Indeed, as far back as ten years ago, it was estimated that the cost of turnover could push the overall cost of selling from an average of 3 per cent of sales to as much as 14 per cent of sales (Wilkening and Company 1998), and more recently figures quoted indicate that for a firm with 100 sales employees, a 40 per cent yearly turnover rate could cost up to US$12 million per annum (Hrehocik 2007). While Sales Managers need to distinguish between functional turnover, which may result in a net benefit for the firm, and dysfunctional turnover, resulting in a net loss (Darmon 2004), it is clear that turnover is an issue many Sales Managers are concerned about.

Research has shown that there is a clear relationship between performance and turnover, and that it is a two-way relationship. On the one hand, as pointed out in Chapter 9, Sales Managers can anticipate that the highest and the lowest performing salespeople are those most likely to quit the company. Thus, individual sales performance will have an impact on the firm's turnover rate. On the other hand, because of the costs associated with turnover and associated recruitment and training, high turnover will negatively affect both the total cost of selling and the total return on sales investment. Moreover, there may be a vicious circle, in that the more disruption is caused by turnover in a sales force (e.g. from incumbent salespeople having to service parts of unoccupied territories), the greater in turn the propensity to leave may be. To make matters worse, excessive salesperson turnover can also have a negative effect on customer satisfaction and retention, a firm's industry reputation, opportunity costs in uncovered territories and low morale among existing employees. Thus, a successful sales organization will not only keep an eye on overall performance levels, but must also attempt to keep dysfunctional turnover to a minimum.

What do managers need to do to lower turnover to a 'healthy' level? Researchers and industry commentators (e.g. Boe 2009) agree that there are a number of factors that can directly and substantially affect a company's retention rates. Some of these are:

- *Adequate leadership.* Boe (2009, p. 20) argues that 'salespeople don't quit companies, they leave managers'. This means that not only is the quality of the employee-manager relationship fundamental in a salesperson's decision to leave, but it also indicates that sales organizations have to be careful to promote only those individuals to management ranks who demonstrate proven leadership qualities (see Chapter 13).
- *Sound recruitment practices.* While this factor may not guarantee that top performers can be retained, a careful recruitment process such as the one described in Chapter 11 can minimize the need to dismiss inadequate salespeople.
- *Training and development.* While (especially highly performing) salespeople may be reluctant to spend time away from their customers and prospects, training has been

shown repeatedly to increase job satisfaction and lower their propensity to leave in the long run (see Chapter 12).

- *Growth opportunities.* High performers in particular may not be terribly interested in staying in the same job for long if it stops presenting new challenges to them. Managers therefore need to plan career trajectories for these employees.
- *Motivation and rewards.* Chapters 15 and 16 highlighted just how much impact recognition and rewards have on employee motivation. In turn, these are also powerful tools in preventing good performers from seeking recognition elsewhere.

To summarize, turnover impacts upon the success of a sales force not only through short-term cost, but also through opportunity costs that may only become visible in the longer term. Therefore, successful sales organizations utilize the process tools described in this book with a view to keeping their employees satisfied and on board.

Organizational commitment

Maybe less visible than turnover but just as important for Sales Managers to consider is the level of commitment that employees have to their company. Organizational commitment can be defined as the degree to which an employee both identifies with and is involved in an organization. Unsurprisingly, there is a direct relationship between job satisfaction, organizational commitment and turnover, which means that satisfied salespeople are more likely to be committed to an organization, and committed salespeople are in turn less likely to leave the company (Rutherford et al. 2009). Moreover, organizational commitment is also a powerful predictor for sales performance (Jaramillo et al. 2005). This emphasizes once more the advantage of a balanced score-card approach in comparison with using purely financial data to evaluate sales success; while past performance acts as a lagged performance indicator, organizational commitment can help a Sales Manager predict future performance.

Similar to job satisfaction, organizational commitment seems to have a strong emotional component. Chapter 17 suggested that salespeople who feel burned out are likely to become less engaged with their jobs; the more emotionally exhausted a salesperson feels, the less likely he/she is to feel passionate about the company for which he/she works. Sales Managers should therefore take care to encourage their employees to engage in the practices for well-being given in Chapter 17, and they should also be careful not to overwork their employees in order to keep long-term performance high.

Organizational citizenship

A relatively new area of research in sales has begun to demonstrate the importance of organizational citizenship behaviours – and, conversely, the cost of so-called anti-citizenship behaviours. Organizational citizenship behaviours are defined as 'behaviours on the part of a (sales) person that are believed to promote directly the effective functioning of an organization' (MacKenzie et al. 1998). They are sometimes also called extra-role behaviours, because they represent a range of actions by the employee that go over and above what is expected from him through his job description. Such behaviours can for instance be helping colleagues with a work-related issue or helping to resolve interpersonal conflict; voluntary actions that show that the salesperson is concerned about the life of the company, such as attending non-compulsory meetings or participating in committees; or a willingness to put up with non-ideal circumstances without complaining. Such extra-role behaviours are an important and not to be neglected aspect of a salesperson's performance and significantly assist the effective running of a sales organization, thus boosting overall organizational performance. As may be expected, there is a strong link between job satisfaction/organizational commitment and organizational citizenship. Those salespeople who are happiest in their jobs and therefore likely to be more committed to the organization are also those who will be willing to 'go the extra mile' for the company without receiving a direct payback for such actions. Note that this 'extra mile' is often also walked to the advantage of the salesperson's customers!

However, there is also a somewhat darker side to this phenomenon; namely anti-citizenship behaviours. Jelinek and Ahearne (2006) have highlighted the dangers and potential costs of such employee misbehaviours as flagrantly refusing to abide by sales rules, holding up team work, avoiding work, showing open hostility toward colleagues or managers and even airing the organization's 'dirty laundry' in public. As boundary-spanners, salespeople may have somewhat greater latitude in their actions and are therefore perhaps more likely to engage in these negative behaviours. In addition, the frequently very competitive and maybe even 'warlike' culture in some sales organizations may inadvertently foster winning 'at all cost'. Many of these anti-citizenship behaviours impact negatively on organizational effectiveness and performance, but they are difficult to police or manage through control systems. If the behaviours are not overtly unethical, managers may find themselves at a loss as to how to sanction them; yet if they are not sanctioned, they may present a precedent for other sales employees.

Given the above, when considering the question of 'what makes a sales organization successful', Sales Managers should urgently contemplate how they can foster organizational citizenship behaviours and prevent anti-citizenship ones from taking hold in their sales forces. Researchers have pointed to the following factors:

- *Justice versus injustice*: It is imperative that salespeople feel that rewards (and punishments) are fairly distributed not only among the sales force, but also between, for instance, Sales and Marketing. Jelinek and Ahearne (2006, p. 460) quote one respondent as saying, 'When sales are up, my company credits the product and rewards the people in Marketing who did the research that went into the product's development. When sales are down they blame salespeople like me for not being able to sell the stuff.' Sales and Marketing Managers should take care to heed the suggestions given in Chapter 2 for encouraging good relationships and equitable treatment between these two departments.
- *Group cohesiveness versus intra-group competitiveness*: While salespeople are often naturally competitive and work in cultures that promote such competitiveness, this can also lead to salespeople setting themselves unrealistic goals and attempting to achieve them by deviating from written or unwritten codes of conduct. This may be exacerbated when salespeople don't have a lot of face-to-face contact with their colleagues and their manager. Managers should thus make sure that there is a certain level of group cohesiveness by encouraging, for instance, the community

of practice approach described in Chapter 17. From a broader perspective, team leadership should be managed carefully in sales organizations (see chapter 13).

- *Role clarity versus job stress:* Clearly, it is more likely that stressed out and emotionally exhausted salespeople will engage in anti-citizenship behaviours than happy, secure salespeople. Once again, managers are called on not only to provide their sales force with a maximum level of role knowledge (see Chapter 17), but also to encourage them partaking in the previously mentioned well-being programmes. This may be especially important in difficult markets or recessionary economies where people feel that they simply have to 'cut corners' in order to achieve an acceptable level of performance.

- *Setting standards*: As discussed in Chapter 6, clear and enforced ethical guidelines are probably more important in the sales arena than in any other business field. Managers have to lead by example and engage in organizational citizenship themselves if they want their employees to do so; they also have to be seen to explicitly state the desirability of such behaviour. As Chapter 10 has indicated, enforcement of ethical standards may be particularly complex in geographically dispersed sales forces that may include different cultural settings and backgrounds. Again, this is an area that can be included in a balanced score-card performance appraisal, at corporate, departmental and individual levels.

CASE PROBLEM REVISITED

Sales reporting tools at Bearzot

The reporting system in the company is designed to deliver monthly outcome-based and activity-based data which can be aggregated to provide management with valuable and actionable indicators. These indicators are then used to make sound business decisions in order to deliver on a consistent basis both efficiency and effectiveness in sales force deployment.

The Service Plan (Figure 18.3) is used for the purpose of managing the time to service existing customers. This tool helps the salesperson to plan in advance, for a given period, the number of visits and the hours per visit for every single account. At the end of the period (e.g. a quarter), actual data are compared to the plan.

Territory manger   *The service plan*

Account	CUSTOMER			Call/Yr	JAN				FEB				MAR		
	Existing sales	CPDs Equipm	Sales potential	Hrs/call	Plan/Actual				Plan/Actual				Plan/Actual		
					WK 1	WK 2	WK 3	WK 4	WK 1	WK 2	WK 3	WK 4	WK 1	WK 2	WK 3
Total calls				0	0	0	0	0	0	0	0	0	0	0	0
Total hours				0	0	0	0	0	0	0	0	0	0	0	0

Figure 18.3   The Service Plan tool

Note: CPDs are compounds, Equipm is equipment

Name	Territory Manager				
Week Number	XX				
PLANNING SCHEDULE					
	CUSTOMER	Address	Service	Sales	Purpose
M					
T					
W					

Figure 18.4 The Planning Schedule

Similarly, in *the Planning Schedule* each salesperson specifies the weekly plan of calls to his/her customers. In this case, for each account, the nature of the call (sales or service) and the specific objective of the call have to be formally reported (see Figure 18.4).

Another tool is the *Call Report*: here the salesperson has to fill in information about the calls made in the period (Figure 18.5) for both service and sales calls. In this report, the salesperson also reports the hours spent and the activities per day and per customer (service) and prospect (sales). As described, sales of new applications can happen both at existing and new customers. Therefore selling hours are split into three different categories: Conversion Selling (hours spent on competitors' customers; CS); Expansion Selling (hours spent on current Bearzot customers that are partially served by competitors; ES); and Retention Selling (hours spent on Bearzot customers

Name / title	Territory manager
Week number	XX

Number of working days	5	The call report

Date	New accounts	Sales			Time service	Time travel	Time admin.	Name, location of company	Name of contacts	PS	Competition	Value	Customer expectations and actions required
		CS	ES	RS									
	Compounds												
	Equipment												
	Compounds												
	Equipment												
	Compounds												
	Equipment												
	Compounds												
	Equipment												
	Compounds												
	Equipment												
	Compounds												
	Equipment												
	Compounds												
	Equipment												
	Compounds												
	Equipment												
	Compounds												
	Equipment												
	Compounds												
	Equipment												
	Compounds												
	Equipment												
	Compounds												
	Equipment												
	Compounds												
	Equipment												
	Compounds												
	Equipment												
	Compounds												
	Equipment												
Total	Compounds												
Total	Equipment												

PS - Prospect status 1-Potential prospect, 2-Qualified prospect, 3-Interested prospect, 4-Hot prospect, 5-New account

Number of Sales Calls	
Number of Sales Calls (Repeat NA)	
Number of Sales Calls (Equip&Serv)	
Number of Sales Calls (**CS**)	
Number of Sales Calls (**ES**)	
Number of Sales Calls (**RS**)	
Number of Service Calls	
Number of Service Calls (Compounds)	
Number of Service Calls (Equipo)	
Number of Service Calls (Total)	
Number of working days	

Number of sales hours	
Number of sales hours (repeat NA)	
Number of sales hours (one off NA)	
Number of sales hours (**CS**)	
Number of sales hours (**ES**)	
Number of sales hours (**RS**)	
Number of service hours	
Number of service hours (compounds)	
Number of service hours (equipment&service)	
Number of service hours (total)	
Number of admin. hours	
Number of time travel hours	

Figure 18.5 The Call Report

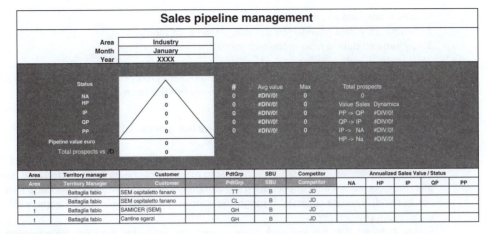

Figure 18.6 The pipeline management tool

for up-selling, responding to competitors' actions, etc.; RS). In this form the salesperson also reports the hours spent on service, travel and administration per customer/prospect.

The generation of new business is of the utmost importance for delivering good results and, given the length of the sales cycle, management of the new sales pipeline is critical. This funnel management is done by a reporting document on the sales pipeline (Figure 18.6). This tool reports, for a given period, for each individual salesperson, the number and value of customers at five different stages in the sales funnel:

1. potential prospects (PP);
2. qualified prospects (QP);
3. interested prospects (i.e. ones showing interest in Bearzot products and services) (IP);
4. hot prospects (i.e. those considering a proposal made by Bearzot) (HP);
5. new accounts (i.e. those which have placed an order) (NA).

The tool also reports other customer information, such as their business segment in the industry, the specific applications targeted in the production process, competitors currently serving the prospects and so forth.

All these pieces of information can be sorted by different criteria. For example, an analysis combining area plus segment plus competitor provides the Sales Manager with information on what is in the pipeline in a specific area, in a specific segment, and against a selected competitor.

All this data, on a monthly basis, is handed in by salespeople, and then it is aggregated into a divisional pipeline for the benefit of Sales Management. As well as management of prospecting activity and forecasting new business generation, this funnelling technique provides the manager with valuable information on each salesperson's performance and abilities.

The productivity report

This monthly report provides sales management with valuable pieces of information.

In essence, its purpose is to link sales results to salespeople's behaviours by aggregating and interpreting multiple data. Three different kinds of data are used in the report:

1. actual sales and planned sales;
2. productivity data provided by the salesperson each month;
3. aggregated data, a ratio of the two above.

The productivity report provides sales management with plenty of data regarding the productivity of individuals, groups of individuals and the whole sales force.

Finding meaningful KPIs for the sales force at Bearzot

At Bearzot, the long and complex sales cycle made it important to be able to forecast well in advance the sales force's performance in order to make the necessary business decisions, knowing that these decisions would impact upon the company's results in the medium to long term. With this in mind, the data collected through the various reporting tools could be aggregated into useful productivity reports.

Pirlo believed that the key performance indicators (KPIs) for the sales force needed to be designed to provide him with quantitative data that would allow him to assess its efficiency and efficacy. He felt strongly that the KPIs should consist of homogeneous, unbiased and comparable data, since sales force members would be compared with each other using the benchmarks of these indicators. If well designed, the KPIs could also provide a starting point for individual coaching interventions aimed at improving performance.

Pirlo wanted to design productivity reports and meaningful KPIs using the following data collected by the tools described above:

1. number of sales calls made;
2. number of service calls made;
3. sales goals;
4. actual sales;
5. working days/hours available in the month/year per salesperson, excluding holidays;
6. total hours in front of customers;
7. number of sales hours;
8. number of service hours;
9. total attrition: variation between sales in current year versus sales in the previous year for the customer base (i.e. excluding new/lost accounts in the current year) for the same period of time;
10. sales increase of current year versus sales in the previous year including the carryover effect of new accounts, for the same period of time;
11. number of proposals;
12. total value of proposals;
13. number of orders;
14. total value of orders;
15. number of new accounts;
16. value of new accounts;
17. number of lost accounts;
18. value of lost accounts.

Summary

This final chapter of the book has drawn many aspects of the previous chapters together in attempting an answer to the question 'What makes a successful sales organization?'.

Sales force evaluation is a critical process. If well managed, it helps Sales Managers understand the causes of successful and unsuccessful salespeople and hence make the best decisions to improve performance, especially through coaching interventions and feedback management.

As mentioned, there are many ways of improving organizational effectiveness in sales and ensuring a company's long-term survival. Of course, internal and external stakeholders and environmental factors will influence the degree to which any Sales Manager will be able to 'get the best' out of their sales force. As editors, we hope that this book has given sales students and practitioners both food for thought and an impetus for continuous improvement.

Key points

While there are many more aspects to an effective sales force than those mentioned here, some pointers to sales force effectiveness are listed below:

1. There has to be a consistent flow from strategy and culture to organizational structure to sales processes and individual attitudes and behaviours. The most successful companies worldwide are those where this cohesion is ensured. This also means that all the strategic considerations and processes presented throughout this book *in concert* contribute to making an organization successful.
2. Sales organizations need to consider performance as a broader construct than just based on historical financial data. The balanced score-card approach, introduced in this chapter, demonstrates to managers what such a broader definition of performance may resemble.
3. For many sales organizations, personnel turnover is a significant and costly issue. Managers are encouraged to use the processes presented at various points in this book – recruitment, training, motivation, compensation and others – to keep turnover to an acceptable level.
4. Extant research has shown that organizational commitment is a clearer indicator for future success than job satisfaction. A balanced score-card programme should thus consider including this construct as part of an organizational performance review.
5. Recently, the potential impact of both organizational citizenship and anti-citizenship behaviours on organizational effectiveness has come into focus. Sales forces seem particularly prone to the latter because of their boundary-spanning existence and low level of contact with the company's home base. Managers should be aware of this issue and strive to create an ethical, fair and pleasant work environment.

References

Boe, J. (2009). 'Retention is a Problem That Won't Go Away', *The American Salesman*, 54 (3): 19–22.

Churchill, G.A., Ford, N.M., Hartley, S.W. and Walker, O.C. Jr (1985) 'The Determinants of Salesperson Performance: A Meta-Analysis', *Journal of Marketing Research*, 22 (2): 103–18.

Darmon, R.Y. (2004) 'Controlling Sales Force Turnover Costs through Optimal Recruiting and Training Policies', *European Journal of Operational Research*, 154 (1): 291–303.

DeNisi, A. and Kluger, A.V. (2000) 'Feedback effectiveness. Can 360-degree Appraisals be Improved?', *Academy of Management Executives*, 14 (1): 129–39.

Hrehocik, M. (2007) 'The Best Sales Force', *Sales and Marketing Management*, 159 (8): 23–7.

Jaramillo, F., Mulki, J.P. and Marshall, G.W. (2005) 'A Meta-analysis of the Relationship between Organizational Commitment and Salesperson Job Performance: 25 years of Research', *Journal of Business Research*, 58 (6): 705–14.

Jelinek, R. and Ahearne, M. (2006) 'The ABC's of ACB: Unveiling a Clear and Present Danger in the Sales Force', *Industrial Marketing Management*, 35 (4): 457–67.

Kaplan, R.S. and Norton, D.P. (1992) 'The Balanced Scorecard: Measures that Drive Performance',*Harvard Business Review*, 70 (1): 71–9.

Lukes, T. and Stanley, J. (2004) 'Bringing Science to Sales', *Marketing Management*, 13 (5): 36–41.

MacKenzie, S.B., Podsakoff, P.M. and Ahearne, M. (1998) 'Some Possible Antecedents and Consequences of In-role and Extra-role Salesperson Performance', *Journal of Marketing*, 62 (3): 87–98.

Rutherford, B., Boles, J., Hamwi, G.A., Madupalli, R. and Rutherford, L. (2009) 'The Role of the Seven Dimensions of Job Satisfaction in Salespersons' Attitudes and Behaviours', *Journal of Business Research*, 62 (11): 1146–51.

Wilkening and Company (1998). *Sales Force Turnover: The Hidden Costs of Selling*. Park Ridge, Illinois: White Paper.

Further reading

Ahearne, M., MacKenzie, S.B., Podsakoff, P.M., Mathieu, J.E. and Lam, S. K. (2010) 'The Role of Consensus in Sales Team Performance', *Journal of Marketing Research*, 47 (June): 458–69.

Baldauf, A. and Cravens, D. (1999) 'Improving the Effectiveness of Field Sales Organizations: A European Perspective', *Industrial Marketing Management*, 28 (1): 63–72.

Hunter, G.L. (2004) 'Information Overload: Guidance for Identifying when Information Becomes Detrimental to Sales Force Performance', *Journal of Personal Selling and Sales Management*, 24 (2): 91–100.

Johnson, D.S. and Bharadwaj, S. (2005) 'Digitization of Selling Activity and Sales Force Performance: An Empirical Investigation'. *Journal of the Academy of Marketing Science*, 33 (1): 3–18.

Pettijohn, C., Pettijohn, L.S., Taylor, A.J. and Keillor, B.D. (2001) 'Are Performance Appraisals a Bureaucratic Exercise or Can they be Used to Enhance Sales-force Satisfaction and Commitment?', *Psychology and Marketing*, 18 (4): 337–64.

Index

Page numbers in *italics* refer to Figures and Tables.

485

palgrave
macmillan

Sales Management draws on an international team of academics to confront contemporary issues in sales management, such as ethics, change management, strategy, motivation and control. It gives students the opportunity for analysis and reflection to encourage a deeper understanding of these issues, but also adopts a solution-oriented approach, outlining potential and actual resolutions to problems.

Key features:

- Unique focus on European and international sales management
- Global case studies to illustrate the applicability of all theory to real-world scenarios
- Companion website featuring answers to case study questions, PowerPoint slides and other essential resources

Sales Management is ideal for advanced undergraduates and postgraduate students.

Paolo Guenzi is Associate Professor in the Department of Marketing, Università Commerciale Luigi Bocconi, Milan, Italy. He has previously been a Visiting Scholar at the University of Auckland and the University of Michigan.

Susi Geiger is Senior Lecturer at University College Dublin Business School. She has previously been a Visiting Scholar at the University of Auckland and worked with a range of industrial and consumer companies such as Siemens, Disney and Diageo.

'The contributions presented in *Sales Management* are individually interesting and original, making an outstanding contribution to moving the field forward. I have no hesitation in recommending this book to marketing and sales executives and scholars worldwide.'
– **Professor Nigel F. Piercy**, *Professor of Marketing & Strategy and Associate Dean, Warwick Business School, The University of Warwick, UK*

'The scarcity of sound research-based books on sales management is alarming. Guenzi and Geiger have put together a wide-ranging book based on a detailed model of sales management. The case studies and models ensure the book will be of interest to sales academics as well as practitioners.'
– **Professor Lynette Ryals**, *Professor of Strategic Sales and Account Management, Cranfield School of Management, UK*

'*Sales Management*, with its numerous cases and latest research findings, greatly contributes to improving sales education, whilst also acting as an important guidebook for sales managers in their daily business.'
– **Professor Christian Homburg**, *Professor of Marketing, University of Mannheim, Germany*

Companion website:
www.palgrave.com/business/guenzi

ISBN 978-0-230-24595-2

9 780230 245952

Printed in China

www.palgrave.com